# Bandits in Republican China

# BANDITS
## in Republican China

## PHIL BILLINGSLEY

1988
STANFORD UNIVERSITY PRESS
Stanford, California

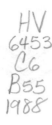
Stanford University Press
Stanford, California
© 1988 by the Board of Trustees of the
Leland Stanford Junior University

CIP data appear at the end of the book

For Gonchan and Nonchan,
Whose share in the making of this book was greater
than they know.

And for T. H.,
Whose anger and affection played an equal part.

# Acknowledgments

THIS BOOK first saw the light of day as a Ph.D. dissertation from the University of Leeds in the summer of 1974. A number of people provided valuable assistance in the compilation of that dissertation, and it is a pleasure to acknowledge those debts here. For passing on his unflagging enthusiasm in the face of what many assured me was an "unresearchable" subject, my first thanks go to my supervisor Bill Jenner. Owen Lattimore, who oversaw the research for the first few months, was a constant source of firsthand information drawn from his own inimitable experiences along the Inner Asian Frontiers of China. Christopher Howe, as director of the Contemporary China Institute where I was employed as Research Fellow from 1972 to 1973, read sections of the draft for me, and the fruits of his criticism remain today. The late Ryōtai Kaneko of the Tōyō Bunko in Tokyo opened the doors of his private office to me long after those of the general reading room were slammed, and is warmly remembered not only for his help but also for his firm and self-less friendship. Lucien Bianco and Jonathan Unger also contributed valuable constructive criticism of the completed dissertation, which helped launch it onto the road to publication. Finally, I owe a debt of appreciation to Mr. Leslie Lyall and the staff of the China Inland Mission in London for readily opening their offices and files to me in the winter of 1970. Sincere thanks are also due to Charles Curwen, David Goodman, John Hall, Winston Hsieh, John Lust, Peter Nolan, Nozawa Yutaka, Ogata Yoichi, Shimada Kenji, Tim Spengler, Ronald Suleski, Shu T. Tanaka, Anthony Whitehorn, and Eugene Wu, all of whom helped, perhaps more than they realize, at various stages of the work.

After a hiatus of more than four years I began revising the dissertation for publication in 1979. As the text grew in length and complexity a number of people were once again kind enough to read it for me. Ralph Thaxton and Elizabeth Perry, who undertook to read the first draft, gave me important advice on reorganizing what was threatening to grow into an unwieldy mass of detail. Joseph Esherick, who agreed to read the second draft despite his own very tight schedule, provided painstaking criticism of both the substantial contents and the text itself, allowing me not only to iron out the analytical flaws which studded the manuscript, but also to reduce its enormous volume. As reader for Stanford University Press, he repeated the task with equal care. The debt that the present text owes to his detailed reading on those two occasions is immeasurable.

Over the years since 1979 numerous other people have offered helpful advice and criticism or provided me with copies of their own work, and I am glad to be able to acknowledge their kindness here: Robert Antony, Parris Chang, Roger Des Forges, Ed Friedman, Linda Grove, Talbott Huey, Ed Krebs, Jonathan Lipman, Shimamoto Nobuko, Bob Somers, Gary Tiedemann, Marjorie Topley, and Odoric Wou. The staffs of the following libraries also furnished me with valuable assistance: the Imperial War Museum, London; the Public Records Office, London; the University of Hong Kong; Osaka City University; Osaka Women's University; the Tōyō Bunko, Tokyo.

P. B.

# Contents

*Four pages of illustrations follow page 192*

# Preface

*Unscrupulous, defiant, stern as the fates, but true in covenant and brave in conflict, these men and women are not of the smiling, temperate, human sort; they are terrible: beings of the cave and the mountain den. Their implacable demand ... for a justice which the law is too feeble and too corrupt to give underlines the cruelties and oppressions of an age when right is defenseless and authority takes the side of the wrong-doer.*

—G. T. Candlin, Chinese Fiction *(Chicago, 1898),*
*quoted in Ruhlmann 1960: 169.*

"BANDITS": few people could claim to be totally unmoved by at least one of the variety of images the word evokes. Whether a symbol of romantic protest or the object of self-righteous anger, bandits and their basic stance of living off the proceeds of others have produced strong preconceived notions. Indeed, systematic analysis of banditry and the conditions that produced and nourished it was almost non-existent until recently.

In 1969 the English social historian Eric Hobsbawm published a seminal work entitled *Bandits*, an extended treatment of the subject of one chapter of his earlier *Primitive Rebels* (1959). Despite its modest length, the second book was the cue for a spate of scholarly research on the topic of banditry. The pioneering nature of Hobsbawm's work not only gave it a kind of mythical quality but also ensured that it would become the target of scrutiny and elaboration from various quarters. During the years since its appearance, scholars have examined the phenomenon of banditry in every continent of the globe.[1]

Despite the title of his 1969 book, Hobsbawm made it clear on the first page that he would be dealing with only one variety of bandits, namely, "those who are *not* regarded as simple criminals by public opinion ... [but] as heroes, as champions, avengers, fighters for justice, perhaps even leaders of liberation, and in any case as men to be admired, helped and supported."[2] This "social banditry," as Hobsbawm called it, could be found "wherever societies are based on agriculture (including pastoral economies) and consist largely of peasants and landless labourers ruled, oppressed and exploited by someone else—lords, towns, governments, lawyers, or even banks."[3]

The defining characteristic of "social banditry," as spelled out by Hobsbawm, was its strong connections to the peasantry. Operating within the peasant community that had given them birth, social bandits in their words and actions reflected the morality of that community; and as long as they did so (such as by choosing victims from among those defined by the community as its enemies) support was usually forthcoming. The relationship was a mutual one: the social bandit remained in the local community because its support—a conspiracy of silence concerning the gang's whereabouts, a network of informers supplying knowledge of the enemy—would be lacking elsewhere; the community in turn maintained its support because the bandit offered at least limited protection, and symbolized its unspoken resentment toward the officially sanctioned order.

The fact that the deeds leading the social bandit into outlawry did not contravene local values is significant, implying an ideological conflict between the local community and the wider community—the state. The social bandit was the armed representative of the former against the efforts of the latter to impose its own values by the use of military force. The social bandit's choice of victims from among the enemies of the poor—the rich and privileged—rather than from the oppressed community itself was an active expression of that conflict of values.

On the other hand, as Hobsbawm unequivocally stressed, social banditry contained certain built-in limitations that made it less than revolutionary: "As individuals, they are not so much political or social rebels, let alone revolutionaries, as peasants who refuse to submit.... *En masse*, they are little more than symptoms of crisis and tension in their society.... Banditry itself is therefore not a programme for peasant society but a form of self-help to escape it in particular circumstances."[4]

Bandits, that is, were primarily interested in their own survival, and this fact provided the point of departure for Anton Blok's fundamental critique of Hobsbawm's views. By paying too much attention to the peasants and to the bandits themselves, asserted Blok, Hobsbawm had failed to take into account the relationship of the peasant community to higher levels of society around it, "which included the landed gentry and the formal authorities."[5] Bandits, as one aspect of the community, were as constrained by that relationship as anyone: "Given the specific conditions of outlawry, bandits have to rely very strongly on other people.... Of all categories, the peasants are weakest.... It may hence be argued that unless bandits find political protection, their reign will be short." [6]

The revolutionary limitations of the social bandit were attributed by Blok not to modest ambition or a lack of appropriate organization and propaganda, but to the fact that "their first loyalty is *not* to the peasants." [7] Bandits with political ties tended to "prevent and suppress" autonomous peasant activity, either by putting down that activity through terror, or by "carving out avenues of upward mobility" and thereby lessening class tensions. [8] By suggesting an alternative route to wealth, power, and happiness, banditry ultimately impedes revolutionary potential. [9] In short, according to Blok, banditry is "essentially conservative," expressing no more than "man's pursuit of honour and power." [10]

Blok illustrated his argument with examples drawn from his research on the Sicilian Mafia, primarily Salvatore Giuliano, "who shot down peaceful Communist demonstrators upon orders of high-ranking politicians," and Liggio, whose activities were "primarily aimed at the demobilization of the peasants who had just begun to organize themselves in order to attain agrarian reform." [11] Other bandits who had come to terms with their overlords were given special charge of public security, an avenue to "respectability" that was institutionalized in the Mafia.

Despite the apparent disparity between Blok's and Hobsbawm's positions, detailed case studies such as those of Singelmann and Lewin on northeastern Brazil have generally shown both their arguments to be true. Bandits, that is, were "social" in the sense that anyone with ties to other people is social, yet, their social ties extended not only to the powerless peasants but also to the powerful overlords. For bandits who proclaimed themselves champions of the poor knew only too well that long-term survival meant forging some relationship with the elite. The book that follows is an attempt, focusing on the Chinese case, to understand better the nature of that paradoxical situation.

Twentieth-century Chinese banditry, by the sheer number of its practitioners, made itself impossible to ignore. By placing not only banditry itself but also the individuals who filled its ranks in the context of a system of unequally distributed power and privilege, the present study uses a perspective that is rarely taken into adequate account in studies of China's rural unrest. Instead of approaching the "bandit problem" in relation to other issues such as peasant mobilization, warlord control, or the organization of mercenary armies, this book focuses upon the bandits themselves, emphasizing the close relationship between sociopolitical environment and consciousness. Usually portrayed as the desperate, frenzied reaction of men with a paranoid grudge against society, banditry was on the contrary often a rational course of action taken in response to particular natural or social conditions and as a means of satisfying certain deeply felt needs. In the process of the discussion some bandits will appear in a darker light than others; but this does not deny them the right to serious consideration by historians, and the significance of their behavior will be closely examined. Among other things, this will involve jettisoning the standard manipulationist vocabulary that saw bandits as living in "lairs," referred to areas with strong bandit traditions as "brigand-infested," and envisaged bandits as "skulking" rather than walking, "scuttling" rather than marching.

Bandits, in the end, were people caught up in a grim situation and reacting to it as appropriately as they could. The massive increase in banditry in the years following the 1911 Revolution underlined as well as anything else could the harshness of peasants' lives during those years. Amid a general atmosphere of violence and insecurity encompassing all China and every level of society, bandits looked out for themselves just as anyone else did. The literature on China, however, has treated them only from the perspective of those whose bitter enemies they were. Terms such as "outrages," "looting," "atrocities," and so on expressed the values of the propertied classes and totally masked the bandits' own perceptions of what they were doing. Consequently, though innumerable observers tossed the time-worn bandit clichés around, and some even experienced bandits at first hand by becoming their ransom "tickets," few considered them worthy of study in their own right. As one eminent authority has already pointed out, bandits have usually meant more to the security policeman than to the social historian.[12]

Evidence for the present study has been drawn from all over China, but principally from the northern half of the country, with the main focus on the peripheral areas of south and west Henan, Anhui, Shandong, Jiangsu, and Shaanxi. Despite regional variations, the common properties uniting bandit attitudes and activities everywhere is remarkable. It is the author's hope, therefore, that this book will provide a basis for generalizations about Chinese bandits as a whole.

Chapter 1 begins by outlining the nature of banditry and its twentieth-century manifestations. The word "bandits" became a key motif of early twentieth-century China, but the difficulties of gaining a clear view of what was meant by the term are enormous. The authorities manipulated the word to discredit their political enemies, and there was a widespread tendency to confuse banditry with other forms of association such as secret societies. Just how wide a range of activities the word "bandit" could encompass is indicated by the careers of the three major chiefs introduced to round off the chapter: Bai Lang, who led a powerful army of peasant rebels; Lao Yangren, who masterminded the "soldier-bandit" strategy and led tens of thousands of his followers on rampages across north China; and Fan Zhongxiu, the "bandit-militarist" who spent twenty years alternating between outlawry, the army, and the revolution.

Chapter 2 looks at the physical conditions conducive to banditry: political and geographical remoteness from provincial or county core areas; the frequency of natural disasters such as floods or drought; and inhospitable terrain such as mountains and forests, where banditry often seemed a more profitable occupation than farming. Areas with these conditions often saw the creation of actual "bandit villages"; but even where banditry was not chronic, certain times of year, when the resources to sustain life became scarce, saw outbreaks of it. The common denominator in all this was poverty; the insecurity it created provided the backdrop to banditry throughout the ages and all across China. The advent of "warlordism" and the incessant fighting between rival local militarists debased the conditions of life in the countryside still further, with the result that bandits became more numerous than ever. A province-by-province review reveals starkly the close relationship between banditry and warlordism.

Chapter 3 provides a detailed case study of Henan province, defining and explaining both the physical and the social characteristics of those counties traditionally known as "bandit regions," and drawing out the connection between poverty and banditry by employing the distinction between developed and degenerating areas. It then traces the evolution of twentieth-century banditry from the rebellion of Bai Lang in 1912–14 through the rise of the "soldier-bandits" of the 1920's to the all-out "banditization" of the province in the 1930's. By the latter period, joining a bandit gang had come to be regarded as almost the only available form of "life insurance."

The motives that drove men and women into bandit gangs were many and complex, and Chapter 4 seeks to account for them. For most people, banditry was a last resort, and their decision to take the final plunge was based on primal considerations—imminent death from starvation or the inability for various reasons to show their faces in the village. For the majority of bandits it was a temporary activity, resorted to when conditions demanded it and abandoned when farming became viable once more. For the rest it became a permanent way of life that not only satisfied the whims of self-indulgence or sadism but also offered a solution to more profound issues resulting from a particular individual's personality or life-situation.

Chapters 5 and 6 examine bandit gangs from the inside. The ways they came together, the kinds of leadership structure they evolved, the

delegation of power and responsibility within them, and the enforcement of discipline all reflected not only the insecurity of being fugitives
from the law but also their complex relationship with the "straight"
world and the pervasive influence of the traditional Chinese family. The
relationship between leaders and led was no feudal relic but a relative
balance of power that made the bandit gang not only a reasonably effective fighting machine but also a body much more responsive to its
members' needs and demands than many regular military units. The disciplinary rules major gangs evolved were designed not only to aid the
gang in its permanent confrontation with the authorities but also to
provide members with a distinct sense of identity.

For most of its participants, banditry meant a life spent on the run,
and the emotional state of most rank-and-file bandits reflected the harshness of their lives. At the same time, Chapter 6 shows that banditry offered young men a chance to satisfy some of the basic needs permanently
frustrated by the humdrum life in a poor village: the impulse to appear
brave and self-confident in the eyes of others, and the need to vent aggressive energy. Although a clear distinction can be made between chiefs
and followers, most bandits' behavior suggests that they were seeking
the recognition denied them in straight society. Bandit lives were short,
however, and the resentment they felt at being forced into such a precarious life, coupled with anxiety about the future, resulted in a powerful
current of violence, particularly toward women. To blur the reality of
their grim lives as well as to confirm their distinctness from the outside
world, bandit communities evolved complex alternative vocabularies
and often a repertoire of signs and gestures, which they combined with a
comprehensive pattern of speech and behavior taboos.

Chapter 7 takes up bandits' role in the local power structure. The local
elite—magistrates, military commanders, and gentry figures—had a
vested interest in reaching some sort of modus vivendi with the bandits
of their vicinity that would eliminate the need for expensive and dangerous suppression campaigns. For the bandits, too, the realities of power
meant that the safest road to realizing their dreams was to come to terms
with some political patron. By manipulating their elite connections,
bandits were sometimes able to wield considerable local influence. Yet
they could not ignore the local peasants completely. Their relationship to
them was based on a combination of love and fear, so they cannot be
thought of romantically as "liberators"; at the same time, there was a
paramount need not to alienate the local community because of the protection it could offer. The result was a special relationship based on common local affiliations without which no bandit gang could survive.

After the inauguration of the Chinese Republic in 1912, banditry
underwent a major transformation, as described and analyzed in Chapter

8. The militarization of Chinese society made bandits a potent force and opened up new avenues of advancement for ambitious chiefs. The wholesale absorption of gangs into the regular military, the degeneration of former military units into mammoth, undisciplined bandit gangs, and the manipulation of the new gangs created by the unsettled conditions to destabilize rivals all became fundamental motifs of twentieth-century Chinese politics. So numerous did bandits become that all political operators—including foreign aggressors such as the Japanese—were obliged to seek to win them over to their own side. Far from being no more than pawns in other people's chess games, bandits were in fact a vital factor in the warlord-period political equation, having reached the point where they could not be ignored.

Chapter 9 traces the involvement of bandits in the revolutionary movements from 1911 to 1949 (with a brief glance at events thereafter), showing how revolutionaries by and large inherited the manipulative attitudes of their predecessors, since they were unable to ignore bandits yet unwilling to regard them as anything more than expendable aux-iliaries. Bandits in turn reacted to them as they had reacted to earlier patrons. Behind this uneasy relationship was the fact that bandits and revolutionaries were created by and obeyed the dictates of totally differ-ent worlds. The mutual distrust was partially eliminated by the patient and thoroughgoing approach of the Communist movement, but in the end the only approach most bandits appreciated was the big stick. Only by managing to establish both political and military dominance did the Communists effectively solve their bandit problem. Even then, in areas like Henan that had a tradition of predatory self-help, banditry con-tinued to be the automatic response to insecurity long after 1949.

Chapter 10 tries to draw some conclusions from the preceding data. It stresses the need for social historians to examine the workings of bandit-ry through the bandits' own eyes, and suggests a connection between banditry and popular attitudes in the peripheral areas where it was most commonly found: a different approach to "law and order" on the part of both the local elite and the peasants; and a different perception of what was or was not "rational" behavior. Given the nature of banditry itself as defined in the preceding pages, I suggest the virtual impossibility of pure "social banditry" and stress instead the situation of bandits them-selves within a local structure of power and influence whereby they were obliged to create a viable working relationship with all concerned. Finally, I suggest that the disturbed conditions of the warlord period, creating increased poverty and insecurity throughout China instead of merely in selected areas, broke down the traditional distinction between "center" and "periphery," so that in a sense the whole country beyond the walls of the cities became the "periphery." The bandits created by

this development reacted accordingly: where they had once sought alliances with local elite figures to ensure survival, they now did the same
on a national level, creating connections with warlords and other political figures, and, ultimately, with the Communists and the Japanese.
With this development it could indeed be said, in the words of the despairing cliché so commonly heard after 1911, that China had at last
become a "bandit world."

# Bandits in Republican China

## CHAPTER ONE

# Introduction

*Whenever there is political decay, history teaches us, there will be bandit outbreaks taking advantage of it.* —*Nan Yan 1924: 4*

*Since the Republic was inaugurated, there has been no bandit-free district, nor a year without brigands.* —*Dai Xuanzhi 1973: 61*

*Bandits are a disease of China's vitals, and that disease has now begun to affect the critical region around the heart.* —*Osame 1923: 1*

BETWEEN THE TWO Chinese revolutions of 1911 and 1949, newspapers and magazines were filled with lurid reports of bandit-provoked chaos and mayhem in the rural interior. Despite the repeated passage of "anti-bandit" legislation, bandit numbers increased rather than decreased, underlining Lao Zi's famous dictum that "the more laws and ordinances there are, the more thieves and robbers there will be."[1] By 1930 the country's total bandit population was being conservatively estimated at some twenty million,[2] and local gazetteers echoed a popular refrain when they complained that "the nation has all but ceased to be a nation, and is becoming instead a bandits' world!"[3] Chaff to the mill of the domestic law and order brigade among the expatriate community, too, the "bandit problem" became a frequent theme. The accepted treaty-port view of bandits, or "*tufei*," saw only "orgies of murder, robbery, violation of women, and indulgence in opium dreams."[4] Few foreigners saw in banditry the birth pangs of profound social change. At the same time, "bandit outrages" confirmed the racist and imperialist convictions already held by contemporary advocates of the "white man's burden" and provided the pretext for constant threats of foreign intervention. Japanese and American "China watchers" concluded almost simultaneously that China itself was no more than one huge bandit gang ("400,000,000 outlaws"), so that a study of banditry might reveal nothing less than the hidden workings of the Chinese national character itself.⁵ "China," as one typical treaty-port joke put it, "can't put ban in banditry until she has put the try." ⁶

Banditry, unsung and practically unstudied, was one of the commonest peasant reactions to oppression and hardship. In China its origins went back at least to the beginnings of private property and the state, and celebrated bandits of antiquity included the semilegendary Dao Zhi ("Robber Zhi") and Zhuang Jiao ("Robber Zhuang"), both of whom flourished as more or less "noble robbers" during the Warring States period (481–221 B.C.). The former evidently became a sort of bandit "patron saint," with ornate temples dedicated to his memory in at least one of the traditional bandit regions. Even Daoist visions of Utopia evidently assumed the presence of outlaws.⁷

Behind the seemingly repetitive cycle of dynastic decline and renewal spanning some two thousand years of Chinese history lay an equally predictable pattern of popular upheaval characterized by Mao Zedong as "without parallel in world history." ⁸ The motive force for these regular upheavals was provided by peasants pushed beyond the point of no return by desperation and encouraged by the promises of salvation held out by millenarian societies like the White Lotus Sect (*Bailian jiao*). Among the first to respond were bandit gangs, and indeed many of the rebel chiefs who challenged the imperial order with varying degrees of success over the years had originally been bandit chiefs.

The rebellion of Li Zicheng at the end of the Ming dynasty (1368–1644) was a classic case and has been widely drawn upon for comparative data in the present study. Li was a former groom in the government postal service in Shaanxi. After losing his job in 1629, he first became a Ming soldier, then mutinied a year later to join one of the many bandit gangs flourishing in northwest China because of a long famine. In a short time he emerged as a leader and set about bringing the numerous bandits and ex-soldiers like himself into a unified paramilitary federation. By 1641 he was strong enough to establish a provincial base in Henan; in 1644 he proclaimed himself emperor of a new dynasty based in Shaanxi, and within three months his troops were in control of Beijing. Li's triumph was short-lived, however, for his men paid little heed to discipline and soon alienated the city's population, with the result that when the Manchus invaded from the north shortly afterward they faced little resistance. Li fled south with the remnants of his army but was quickly defeated and killed.

Just over two hundred years after Li Zicheng, North China was shaken once again by the Nian Rebellion. Like all other peasant rebellions, it came about as a result of imperial decay and grew in pace with a series of natural disasters whose effects the authorities did little to alleviate. After years of scattered local activity by bandits and secret societies, during which the word "Nian" came to be more and more widely heard, a co-ordinated rebel movement finally emerged in about 1853. Unlike the contemporary Taiping Rebellion, which developed a complex hierarchy and sought to gain acceptance as an alternative state to that of the Manchus, the Nian retained an emphasis on decentralized guerrilla activity based on fortified villages that reflected the powerful role played by former bandit chiefs and salt-smugglers. Their local popularity was enormous, since it was founded on village and clan ties; but the Nian were weakened by the persistence of intercommunity feuds resulting from that very tendency to organize along village or clan lines.

The Nian's evolution from guerilla marauding to conscious rebellion was partly prompted by the passage of the Taipings' Northern Expeditionary Force in 1853. After 1856 cooperation between the two groups became regular, and after the fall of the Taiping Heavenly Kingdom in 1864 the Nian movement swelled to unprecedented numbers with the influx of refugees. Unfortunately, the Taipings' defeat also meant that the government could turn its full attention to the suppression of the Nian. By destroying the latter's bases in the fortified villages and terrorizing the local population into submission, the government was able to force the movement onto the defensive. The years from 1864 to 1868 consequently became a period of roving banditry. The Nian were still a considerable military force, and after dividing themselves into Eastern and Western sections along Taiping lines they campaigned all over North China, even managing to surround and kill the government's top commander. The loss of their local ties and their inability to secure supplies proved crucial, however, and in the concerted campaigns of 1867–68 the government forces were finally able to encircle, divide, and destroy them.

For refusing to bend before the wind as the Confucian Analects had predicted they would before a just ruler, those who joined the rank and file of bandit gangs became implicit enemies of the state, but few of them entertained any political conception of their activities. Bandit chiefs, on the other hand, were for a variety of reasons highly sensitive to the possibility of playing a role in political change, especially during the imperial era. The doctrine of the "Mandate of Heaven" meant that a dynasty showing obvious signs of decline could be charged with having lost Heaven's "mandate to rule." The parallel concept of the "right to rebel" expounded by the ancient philosopher Mencius justified attempts to overthrow a ruler whose policies gave rise to social grievances. It also implied that a state which punished upright individuals put its own legitimacy into question. When the Heavenly Mandate was going begging, it was easy for ambitious chiefs to convince themselves that they and they alone were qualified to win it. Whereas social banditry was a worldwide phenomenon, therefore, the transition from outlawry to outright rebellion was perhaps commoner in China than anywhere else.

Ambitious chiefs' aspirations were given further impetus by the traditional glorification of outlaws in much vernacular literature and drama. The most famous example was Shi Naian's sixteenth-century novel *Shuihu zhuan*,[9] but stories of the "knights-errant" (*youxia/wuxia*) had already been popular among the ordinary people for centuries. The knights-errant were brave men (sometimes women) who traveled the country defending the weak against the strong and the poor against the rich, and who were known for their dedication to justice and individual freedom, their altruism, and their contempt for money. Their selflessness was inherited by the 108 heroes of the *Shuihu zhuan*, a novel based on the exploits of a real-life gang of outlaws who, in protest against the policies of the twelfth-century Northern Song dynasty authorities, took to the inaccessible marshes surrounding Mount Liang in modern Shandong province. To be "forced to climb Mount Liang" (*bishang Liangshan*) thereafter became the standard expression for those forced into banditry by factors beyond their control.

The story features a series of violent incidents interspersed with riotous drinking scenes and ludicrous episodes, but the main emphasis is upon the Robin Hood nature of the heroes' lives, robbing the rich to help the poor and living together in a spirit of righteous solidarity. As well as providing inspiration for generations of bandit chiefs, the story has continued to forge the dreams of young people right up to the present. Its depiction of a non-hierarchical community as an alternative to the Confucian model of human relations, however, made it anathema to the imperial authorities, and it was frequently banned,[10] a fact that only heightened its appeal to those feeling dissatisfied with the existing order.

Real-life bandit gangs were a far cry from the idealized behavior of the *Shuihu* heroes. Still, the more politically conscious chiefs sought usually to locate themselves in the heroic tradition, and the bandit gang's isolation from the everyday village routine fostered a romantic image that compensated for the less than heroic behavior bandits were sometimes obliged to resort to. Bandit gangs consequently became rallying points for militant activity in every peasant rebellion, revolting sometimes in the name of restoring the mandate to the old dynasty, sometimes in the hope of founding a new one. By adopting an imperial title or displaying superior ability, an astute chief could win the allegiance of hundreds or thousands of followers, and also attract surrounding bands to serve under a single banner. When this happened the basis was formed for a stable coalition that under the right conditions could transform marauding banditry into a mass rebellion of the peasantry. The only problem was that in order to make the full transition to imperial pretender bandit chiefs had to enlist support from members of the traditional elite, which meant that they could not rock the boat too much. At this stage the egalitarian slogans that had inspired popular support were largely forgotten, to be replaced by the familiar trappings of dynastic rule. Peasant rebellions, whether led by bandit gangs or by secret societies, thus offered little hope of any fundamental change in the nature of the Chinese polity.[11]

In its simplest form, rural banditry may be summed up as the practice of armed robbery carried out in gangs numbering from a dozen to several hundred people. It could be found wherever there existed an impoverished and oppressed peasant majority, but it flourished particularly at certain times of year and under certain practical conditions: where political control was loose, or where the natural environment made subsistence through agriculture impossible. There were, broadly speaking, two main bandit types, who differed both in their motivations for "taking the dangerous path" (*ting er zouxian*) and in their behavior.

The first type, whom we may call the "occasionals," were those who took to banditry as a temporary resort, either because they faced an alternative of death from starvation, or because they faced some short-term financial crisis. The second type, the "professional" or full-time bandits, had for reasons of their own taken to banditry as a permanent way of life, establishing themselves in a well-defended hideout beyond the reach of the law. Unlike the occasionals, who maintained one foot in village life, the professionals' life-style frequently required no more than marginal village ties. Even when there was little to be had from banditry itself, they would usually remain in their hideout, rarely carrying out attacks and often unmolested in return. A constant attraction for those struggling to make ends meet, at the same time they provided the authorities with an abiding reminder of the tenacity of "bandit power."

Put briefly, the "bandit problem" was inseparable from the existence of a set of authorities determined to maintain their control over a system heavily weighted against a poverty-stricken majority. When political corruption or bureaucratic negligence prompted desperate and strong-minded people to seek the ever-inviting mountains and marshes (the traditional bandit haunts), and when, in addition, natural or man-made disasters swelled their numbers with the starving and the hopeless, banditry was likely to become an established part of the social landscape. Within ten years of the 1911 Revolution, newspapers had begun referring to China not as *minguo*—"republic"—but as *feiguo*—"bandit nation"—a situation that the self-respecting social historian cannot leave to the attentions of the police.[12]

Attempting to focus on bandits at the subjective level is easier said than done, however. Whereas studies of banditry in other parts of the world have often benefited from information contained in the confessions of captured bandits,[13] law-enforcement officials in late imperial and Republican China inherited a tendency—bequeathed to them by two millennia of Confucian moralizing—to condemn all outlaws out of hand. Genuine confessions were usually deemed necessary only in the case of serious rebellions, and small-time recalcitrants were frequently executed without ceremony or after replying to a set of routine questions. The documents that resulted, designed chiefly to justify the execution, reveal little of the victims' real life histories, and even less of their primary motivations; indeed, they often amounted to no more than a series of violent, self-denigrating vignettes studded with gory clichés. This approach remained very much alive in the twentieth century, not only in local gazetteers, which were of course compiled by "respectable" elite figures, but even in popular journalism.

Trying to get at the bandits themselves for information, meanwhile, could be even more difficult. The rural poor as a whole were extraordinarily adept at concealing their everyday lives from outsiders, whose appearance usually spelled trouble, and no self-respecting bandit chief was likely to accept assurances that some friendly interviewer was not really a spy for the military. Moreover, bandits rarely left their own accounts of their entry into and experiences within the "greenwood," * for the simple reason that most bandits, like the majority of peasants, were illiterate. The shortness of the average bandit career (few bandits survived for more than a few years) and the difficulties of writing on the march and under the grim conditions most gangs endured also reduced the likelihood that even literate bandits would write their memoirs. On those occasions when bandits did succeed in achieving the security of official recognition, and thereby the leisure to write about their experiences, they generally proved more concerned to cover up the dubious aspects of their early careers than to publicize them; as the proverb went, "a great man does not talk about his lowly birth."[14] Ex-bandit warlords Zhang Zuolin and Zhang Zongchang, in confessing to being graduates of the "school of forestry" (*lülin daxue*; i.e., banditry), were as unusual as they were untruthful, and their "revelations" were probably designed to add luster to what had been in each case an extremely tawdry and self-seeking career.[15] The most charitable thing one can say about the lack of

---

*Just as the English expression "to go to the greenwood" romantically expressed the idea of becoming an outlaw, in Chinese, too, *lülin* ("green forest") became a popular euphemism for banditry. It originated in the name of a mountain in north Hubei from which some first century A.D. rebels launched a successful bid for power. See *Ajia rekishi jiten*, vol. 9, p. 310, and also Ch'ên 1970: 820.

analysis of bandits, then, is that it was difficult to find out much about them anyway.*

Whereas the authorities placed themselves atop a pillar of unassailable moral superiority, for many educated Chinese an irresistible aura of mystery and masculine romance surrounded the rebel or bandit image. In contrast to official accounts, which carefully edited out from rebel confessions anything that could be construed as justifying the disruptive life, "outlaw novels" from the classic *Shuihu zhuan* to Yao Xueyin's 1947 *Changye* (*Long Night*) have consistently held a strong grip on the Chinese male imagination. In dramatic performances the bandit chief was often surrounded by an aura of Robin Hood—like heroism, and the philosopher Mencius pointed out sagely that robbery, too, could be an expression of "The Way."[16] As a result, Chinese intellectuals were capable of condemning bandits but at the same time possessed an instinctive understanding of their motivations. In a word, "their persons [stood] at the gates of the emperor's palace, but their hearts were in the rivers and lakes."[†]

The ambivalent character of most bandit activities, however, made generalization difficult. Born usually of the poor, bandits were not always their most reliable allies. Though some were genuine "social bandits" who took to banditry to vent their rage against injustice and oppression, attacking the rich in order to help the poor, others undoubtedly fitted the traditional stereotype of men bent on murder, rape, and mayhem. More important, because the odds of power were weighted in favor of the rich, successful gangs were usually those that judiciously contracted some sort of arrangement with the rich and powerful. In other words, it is within the context of power relationships that banditry must be understood.

Many bandits, it is true, were the terror of the powerless rural majority—but so were the county magistrate and his underlings, the local

---

*An important source of information for the present study was the memoirs of people captured by bandits who lived to tell their tale. The foreign victims who became so common after 1920, in particular, left a large body of writing in which they described their experiences with varying degrees of perspicacity. Some of them recorded in detail conversations in which bandits talked openly about themselves—their route into banditry, their feelings about being a bandit, their hopes for the future, and so on. Though missionaries were frequently too inspired with the wrath of God against transgressors of "law and order" to pay much heed to what the bandits themselves wanted to say, others revealed a great deal about the "intimate" aspects of banditry so hard to pin down in other sources. In combination with other materials, these memoirs provide a dynamic picture of Chinese bandits as they really were (or wished to be, which is equally important).

†Wen Yiduo 1948: 22. Wen wrote this essay as a critique of a statement by H. G. Wells that "within the souls of most Chinese, a Confucian, a Daoist and a brigand struggle for mastery" (cited in Wen Yiduo 1948: 19). I have been unable to locate the original source of this statement, which Wen praises as highly accurate. "Rivers and lakes" (*jianghu*) was a popular euphemism for the Chinese underworld.

gentry and their levies, and above all the military. As armed groups they all embodied the use or threat of force. If bandits protected some people at the expense of others, so did the rest according to their own set of priorities. If bandits used violent methods to grab what power they could for themselves, it was hardly a surprising reaction in the context of the violent society of twentieth-century China. If at times they were forced to select targets from the defenseless poor instead of the well-protected rich, the responsibility lay also with those who upheld by force the system of inequality that had created the poor in the first place. If, finally, they sometimes showed little concern for the peasants who lived under their sway, this did not distinguish them so greatly from most people with power over others' destinies. In fact, under certain conditions bandits could be an improvement over the official authorities. Their problem was that the control they exercised fell outside the sphere of state-dictated legitimacy, and was therefore impermissible.

The bandit gang, however, was only one of the many varieties of militant rural combination deemed illegal by the authorities. Another was the so-called "secret society," and the two have often been confused.* The old saying that "the officials draw their power from the law, the people from the secret societies" should really be extended to include bandit gangs. Both bandit gangs and secret societies provided "meeting places for the destitute," and both formed a kind of substitute family for those whose natural relatives were dead, or scattered, or far away.[17] Though the leaders, especially of secret societies, often came from the wealthier classes, members of both were primarily the poor.

Bandit gangs are traditionally distinguished from secret societies by their lack of the latter's ritual procedures, but in practice this distinction is hard to maintain, for not only did the degree of ritual differ from society to society, but certain bandit gangs adopted their own sets of observances. On the other hand, whereas bandit gangs usually preserved a degree of secrecy in the interests of security, secret societies were not necessarily secretive: their nominally clandestine nature was often more the result of inept official intelligence-gathering than the product of a deliberate policy of concealment.[18]

Both bandit gangs and secret societies, though sharing a tendency to stress egalitarian sibling ties over traditional hierarchical organization, at the same time allowed a leader to reign as supremely as any Confucian patriarch. Discipline was strict, reflecting the fact that both acted, if

---

*The term "secret society" is itself misleading, masking the distinction between the more religious societies that predominated in North China, exemplified by the White Lotus Sect, and the more political kind found mainly in the south. To distinguish between them, the term "sect" has often been adopted to describe the former. See Overmyer 1976 and Naquin 1981.

not in opposition to, then at least in fear of the elite. Many gangs also observed the "social bandit" code usually associated with secret societies.

One area in which differences sometimes occurred was recruitment. Recruits to bandit gangs, apart from those just seeking to stave off hunger, included those who had lost their land; those who were too unruly to adjust to the village routine; and those who, thanks to some past deed, had become permanent outcasts from "straight" society. Such a blend of motivations meant that gangs frequently assumed an aggressive, predatory stance, and had little attraction for those who already possessed relative economic security, such as the middle peasants. By contrast, secret societies, though they could sometimes be aggressive, frequently remained law-abiding for centuries if left alone.[19] Recruits to the societies usually sought not so much a vehicle for retributive behavior as a source of practical mutual aid or spiritual comfort in time of crisis, something bandit gangs could not usually offer unless extremely well settled.

The clearest distinction between bandit gangs and secret societies was perhaps the following: whereas ideology and rituals were the reason for the existence of secret societies and could sustain them over long periods of time, gangs that employed rituals did so as a form of self-strengthening, not self-definition; when a gang disappeared owing to the death of its chief or to some change in local conditions (such as its recruitment into the military), its rituals probably disappeared with it. As a result, bandit gangs tended to be loose and transient compared to secret societies, and have received relatively disparaging treatment from observers.

Bandits may not have opposed the Confucian system as such, but they certainly gave it unwanted problems. In so doing they inevitably aroused the natural conservatism of both those who operated the system and those who had a vested interest in its continued operation, but the difficulties of understanding the workings of banditry are further increased by the Chinese authorities' tendency to use the term "bandit" as an abusive epithet. Since the origins of private property and the state, governments have preferred to classify disruptions of "order" as forms of larceny, usually involving "violence," or as local incidents of no political significance. In China, as throughout the rest of the world, the word "bandit" has traditionally been the most useful one for discrediting political enemies, whether of the older kind (popular rebels) or the new (Republicans and Communists). The word suggests strong-armed, recalcitrant, antisocial individuals engaged in a futile personal vendetta against all and sundry, lacking even the would-be legitimacy of heterodox ideology. Whether bandits are seen as tawdry misfits or as romantic, primitive rebels, it is the apparent futility of their position that ultimately defines them. To the framers of the law, the police, and all those with a modicum of power, this image provided the ideal means of drawing attention away from any genuine peasant grievances bandits might represent, and of defaming or belittling political adversaries. The word "banditry," that is, could be used to subsume the whole range of stealing, from a chicken to a kingdom—from petty thieving to political revolution—and the effect was to tar all those to whom the term was applied with the same brush.

Until the Qing period, official records seeking to employ this device most often used the terms *dao*, *zei*, and *kou*, but in the late eighteenth century a new term appeared, *fei*. Originally used chiefly to refer to the contemporary White Lotus Sect, *fei* became more and more common, usually in combinations like *daofei*, *feitu*, and *tufei*, as the Qing dynasty became increasingly concerned with bolstering its claim to political legitimacy. In practice there was little to distinguish among these expressions, all of which suggested a person or persons involved in mere local or small-scale disturbances, and by the twentieth century *tufei*, signifying essentially a rural desperado, had become almost universal.[20] For the authorities it was the perfect combination. On the one hand, the *tu* element explicitly denied any broad significance to the individuals or movements it was applied to (Old China Hands often translated *tufei* as "scum of the earth," since *tu* can mean "earth" as well as "local");[21] on the other, the *fei* element, by excluding the law-abiding, carried notions of sedition.*

It was this second element that furnished the Confucian state and its successors with the perfect means of condemning their enemies. Revolutionaries such as Sun Zhongshan and Huang Xing, for instance, were repeatedly referred to in government notices as "bandits" or "brigands" (*tufei*, *feitu*) throughout the period of local insurrections leading up to the Revolution of 1911,[22] and within a few years of Sun's relinquishing the Provisional Presidency to Yuan Shikai in 1912 he had become a "bandit" once more. As the old aphorism went, "one who succeeds becomes a prince; one who fails becomes a bandit."[23]

During the warlord period, a common practice was for the central authorities to label a certain militarist a bandit (*fei* or *zei*) and appoint a commander to eliminate him in the name of "bandit suppression" (*jiaofei*).[24] Individual warlords also used the term to assert their moral supe-

---

* Some of the most common "*fei*" combinations included *feijiao* ("bandit sects"); *fufei* ("turbaned bandits"); *huifei* ("secret society bandits"); *jiaofei* ("religious bandits"); *nifei* ("rebel-bandits"); *xiaofei* ("owl bandits," meaning salt smugglers); and *yanfei* ("salt-" or "opium-smuggling bandits," depending on the character used). Twentieth-century political adversaries expanded the traditional vocabulary by introducing such terms as "*Maofei*" and "*Jiangfei*" (for Mao Zedong and Jiang Jieshi [Chiang Kai-shek], respectively), *gongfei* ("Communist bandits"), and *hongfei* ("Red bandits").

riority over opponents, referring to their factional wars as "anti-bandit operations" and so on.[25] Even anti-establishment figures found *fei* and *zei* useful tools, radicals referring to the warlords and their underlings as "bandits in office" (*guanfei* or *guantufei*), and the anti–Yuan Shikai movement of 1913 calling its troops "Bandit-Extermination Armies" (*Taozei jun*).[26] And the practice did not die out with the demise of the warlords: after the establishment of Jiang Jieshi's National Government in 1928, *fei* remained the perfect label to apply to its Communist rivals.

> By some curious trick of psychology which anyone living in China, and feeding upon the carefully concocted reports of an official Press agency, might unconsciously adopt with the greatest of ease, the campaigns against the Communists had ceased to be regarded as "civil war" in the generally accepted sense. Hence the real cleverness of the label "Communist bandit" [*gongfei*]. In China, bandits, like the poor, are always with us; and bandit suppression must appear a normal operation of any effective authority, local or national.... The Communists were never bandits....[27]

The Japanese invasion of 1937 consequently found the government, the Communists, and the Japanese all using the term "bandit" indiscriminately, trying to stretch it to include all their political opponents and so present themselves as the only source of respectable political authority.[28]

For the investigator, therefore, the words "bandit" and "banditry" can be both treasure trove and trap, hiding a wealth of different grassroots activities but simultaneously classifying them according to the priorities of the establishment. The subjective nature of the terms, in other words, makes it almost impossible to understand at a glance the real nature of any rural outbreak to which they are applied. The historian who does not appreciate this risks falling into the trap of accepting the state's one-sided interpretation of events as the only version of the truth.[29] Only after examining carefully all those activities loosely classed as "banditry" and distinguishing very clearly what was really happening can we isolate and scrutinize those cases that can be acknowledged as genuine banditry. By reading between the lines of official and quasi-official reportage, the historian can draw out a rich supply of sociopolitical data of value not only to the study of popular insurrections but also to that of local politics.

The lives of three major North China chiefs, spanning the period from 1911 to 1930, symbolized the changes affecting Chinese banditry as a whole during those years. All hailed from the same corner of the traditional bandit area of southwest Henan, and all achieved considerable national fame (or, more precisely, notoriety). In this respect they were not typical bandits, who were rarely known more than a few miles from

their native villages; nonetheless, they represented three important pa-
rameters of bandit destinies under the political conditions of warlord
China, and were powerful models for other chiefs who sought to follow
in their footsteps.

The movement led by Bai Lang through five provinces of North
China—Henan, Anhui, Hubei, Shaanxi, and Gansu—from 1911 to 1914
exemplified the best of traditional banditry, which often verged on full-
scale peasant rebellion. Bai himself was a "social bandit" (insofar as that
ideal type can exist), implacably opposed to gentry power, and considered a hero by the peasants of his home district. His movement sparked
off security scares in such major cities as Beijing, Shanghai, and Wuhan,
created disorders in more than seventy North China county seats, and
almost brought about a foreign intervention. It had active support from
both Republican revolutionaries and Manchu revanchists. The nickname
"White Wolf," * symbol of the "low-class Chinaman's hero," [30] retained its talismanlike effect for years, not only on subsequent Henan
chiefs, but also on Chinese and foreign newspaper correspondents
whenever a bandit incident occurred. [31] Even in the 1960's, comic dialogues broadcast over Taibei radio still continued to remind listeners of
the "roving bandit White Wolf who had set North China politics
a-tremble." [32]

Bai Lang's legacy was inherited by one of his former followers named
Zhang Qing. Being tall and thin, with a white face and big eyes under
long lashes, [33] Zhang acquired the nickname of Lao Yangren, or "The
Old Foreigner," and it was under this name that he achieved his notoriety. He shared many of Bai Lang's social-bandit qualities, but by staking his career on gaining admission into the regular military, he adapted
the old ways to meet the demands of the new political situation of warlord China. In the process he discarded many of the characteristics normally associated with social banditry, but he continues to be regarded in
his home districts as a native son to be proud of. Second only to Bai
Lang's in notoriety, Lao Yangren's name was repeated nervously in accounts of Chinese banditry decades after his death. [34]

Fan Zhongxiu,† whose long career both predated and outlasted that
of Lao Yangren, was in many respects an archetypal representative of
this period, a man who switched from banditry to the military with

* Bai Lang was often erroneously known as the "White Wolf" after the authorities
deliberately substituted a homophonous character meaning "wolf" for his given name
Lang.
† Fan was also sometimes known as "Fan Laoer." Laoer, apart from being the title
given to certain functionaries of the Elder Brothers Society (*Gelao hui*), was a euphemism
for "banditry" in many parts of China. Although Fan Zhongxiu may have become a
member of the Elder Brothers Society while in Shaanxi, where its membership was very
large, no evidence has yet been found to support such an idea.

greater regularity and more success than most. His accommodation to the new system's demands was even more successful than Lao Yangren's was, if measured by length of time alone. Like Bai Lang, he had links with a variety of political causes from reactionary warlords to Republicans and Communists. Although known to the history books as a "militarist,"[35] he spent much of his career in the wilderness. Like Bai Lang and Lao Yangren, he is remembered in his native southwest Henan as a representative of the area's social-bandit tradition who inherited the mantle of rebellion left vacant by his two illustrious predecessors. Paradoxically, because he was neither the complete bandit nor the complete militarist, his name lacks the same degree of widespread public recognition that those of Bai Lang and Lao Yangren evoke.

This study has drawn heavily on the episode known as the "Lincheng Incident," perhaps the most notorious of all bandit "outrages" under the Republic because of the large number of white captives involved. On the morning of May 6, 1923, the foreign community in China woke to the news that a thousand bandits had attacked and derailed the luxurious "Blue Express" at Lincheng (also known as Xuecheng) on the Tianjin-Pukou Railway in southern Shandong, carrying off up to 300 passengers, including some thirty whites. One American was killed in the attack.* After escaping with their captives to the mountains, the bandits made a number of demands. These included a call for the removal of government troops from Shandong; an official pardon for all involved; reinstatement or enrollment in the army for those who wished it; and guarantees by six foreign powers that the demands would be met.[36] Over the next two months negotiations swayed back and forth until Shanghai Green Gang (*Qing bang*) boss Du Yuesheng intervened and secured the release of the captives for a ransom of $85,000 (very little of which seems to have reached the bandits themselves).† Some three thousand bandits were taken into the army, and the leaders, including supreme chief Sun Meiyao, received commissions. The upshot was a sudden rash of bandit assaults on foreigners all over China, as well as a new boom in train-wrecking.‡[37]

In the wake of Lincheng, foreign pressure forced the Chinese authorities to draw up rigorous new regulations providing for regular police patrols along the Tianjin-Pukou Railway, armed guards for every train,

---

* This was not the first bandit attack on a passenger train in North China—for precedents, see Tachibana 1923: 34; Osame 1923: 3–4. Earlier incidents had involved only Chinese victims, however, and had been quickly forgotten—if even noticed.

† The $85,000 here, and all other dollar amounts mentioned in text, refer to Chinese *yuan* rather than U.S. dollars.

‡ Eighteen months after the Lincheng Incident, Sun Meiyao's brother Meisong tried to repeat the episode by stopping a train on the Longhai Railway near Xuzhou (Jiangsu) and carrying off three foreigners and several Chinese. See *Shina jihō* 1, no. 3 (Dec. 1924): 31–32.

cessation of nighttime service, military responsibility for railway security, scouts to report on bandit activity in advance of each train, patrol trains to precede regular ones, and so on. The powers further demanded high rates of compensation as well as indemnities for medical treatment and loss of earnings. Lest "further steps" become necessary, they ominously added, sanctions were to be applied against top officials, not only those deemed responsible for the Incident itself, but all those liable for security matters in the "brigand-infested" provinces.[38] As in the case of the Boxer Indemnity twenty years before, the foreign powers were obviously determined to make "the Chinese" pay for the indignities heaped upon "the whites" at Lincheng.*

*The "Lincheng Indemnity" was not finally paid until February 1925 (*The Times* [London]: 23 Feb. 1925). For details on the powers' demands and the Chinese government's response, see "Diplomatic Notes on the Lincheng Incident"; *NCH*, 18 Aug. 1923: 440–42. The incident provided the inspiration for the 1932 Paramount film *Shanghai Express*, starring Greta Garbo.

CHAPTER TWO

# From "Bandit Kingdoms" to "Bandits' World": The Growth of Banditry Under the Republic

*The Chinese Nation (Chūka) is in fact the Chinese Calamity (Chūka);
the Republic of China (Chūka minkoku) is actually the Banditland
of China (Chūka hikoku).* —Kōkaku Sanjin 1924: 160

*In a China rampant with soldiers and bandits, the events most likely to
attract people's attention are, of course, the calamities of war and the
"bandit miasma" (feifen); the most outstanding personalities are consequently warlord leaders and bandit chiefs. But in the past three
years . . . the affair of the [1922] Zhili-Fengtian War has been far overshadowed in influence and impressiveness by both the Henan bandit
outrages and the Lincheng train holdup. And . . . to the names of warlord
leaders like General this and Marshal that should be added those of the two
bandit chiefs, Lao Yangren and Sun Meiyao.*
—DFZZ 21, no. 3 (10 Feb. 1924): 7

IN MANY PARTS of China, endemic banditry persisted over centuries,
resisting all attempts at suppression. Rather than dismissing such traditions as a sign of "unruly" local tempers, we have to consider the possibility that such resistance represented the attempts of local peasants to
survive in the face of hostile ecological conditions.

Certain physical or geopolitical environments tended to produce a
powerful strain of banditry. Areas that were chronically poor or that
suffered periodic natural disasters, for example, or whose traditional economic patterns had been disrupted, became regions of widespread unrest
when farming became impossible and all else failed. Areas situated far
from political centers, or along national, provincial, or county borders
where official jurisdiction was weak and divided, witnessed strong cur-

rents of direct action whenever survival demanded it. Finally, at particular points in the cycle of the seasons, when food became scarce and there was little agricultural work to be done, the level of outlawry rose. In sum, bandits could be created by a variety of factors, the common denominator being that grim reality made alternative survival modes impossible.

Poverty, in other words, always lurked at the back of the perennial bandit presence, and starvation gave a powerful impetus toward outlawry. A bandit captured in Sichuan, for example, told his army interrogators that the reason for his having become a bandit could be found in his stomach if they cared to cut him open. The intrigued official in charge did just that after the execution; the stomach was found to contain nothing but grass.[1] As bandit confessions frequently pointed out, "it was death that made them climb Mount Liang and become bandits."

As well as the environmental factor, official ineptitude or dishonesty played a major part. In fact, the two often went hand in hand: the temptation for ill-prepared local officials to protect their careers by ignoring a bandit problem was a permanent difficulty for the forces of law and order. Where banditry was chronic it usually involved to a certain degree even the local elite, making it still more difficult for an official to put his best intentions—if he had any—into practice. The conditions that produced banditry, that is, were the very conditions that hampered official efforts to suppress it.

In this way, necessity and opportunity had always gone hand in hand where bandits were concerned, but by the end of the second decade of the twentieth century new political and military developments were adding fresh dimensions to this traditional pattern: the decline of central control and the rise of the "warlords" following the death of President Yuan Shikai in 1916. Over the next decade most of China was reduced to the level of a battlefield. Economic security plummeted, deepening the crisis in regions already suffering and extending it to those previously able to maintain life at a subsistence level. An increase in the number of bandits under such conditions was inevitable, and many provinces or parts of provinces once free or relatively free of them now became host to "bandit kingdoms" of unheard-of proportions.

## Locales of Banditry

Any region where the necessary resources to sustain life were in short supply was likely to produce a subcurrent of banditry. Where the shortfall between resources and consumer demand was a chronic problem, banditry too became a permanent feature of the social landscape. Wide expanses of plain, liable to frequent floods and consequent famine, were an example of the kind of area where banditry could become a way of life. The North China Plain, particularly the "Huai-bei" area between the Yellow and Huai rivers, was described by one geographer as "a gigantic alluvial fan over which the course of the Yellow River has swept back and forth like the tail of a gigantic dog."[2] Basically fertile and once heavily populated, the low-lying fields of "Huai-bei" suffered from an unstable ecosystem in which floods and droughts followed hard upon one another. The easy passage afforded to armies (of both the bandit and the official kind) made this region a constant focus of banditry, rebellion, and other forms of collective militancy.[3]

One result of the plains environment was the important role played by horses. During the autumn a mounted gang could move rapidly as the ground gradually hardened after the summer rains, and as riverbeds became easily fordable once the floodwaters receded. Terms used to refer to banditry in these regions often reflected the horses' role—for example, *xiangma*, the mounted highway robbers who ran freely through much of the capital region of Zhili and Shandong from the mid-Ming period until the late nineteenth century. On and around Manchuria's trackless plains, too, the term "horse bandits" (*mazei*) came to be used indiscriminately of all outlaws regardless of whether they actually rode horses. Of those who did, it was said that they were capable of riding long distances without feeling fatigue and even of sleeping on horseback; they could also fire accurately with both hands without losing control of the reins, and needed neither saddle not stirrups.[*]

Though the economic factor was rarely absent, difficult or isolated environments—such as mountainous or forested districts, border zones, flood-prone estuaries, and newly opened territories—also provided the conditions for outlawry. Where arable land was scarce, banditry often became an essential side-occupation for tillers, too (they were known as "farmer-bandits" [*nongfei*]). Indeed, banditry could become an accepted way of life involving everyone, either as active bandits or as fences (sometimes willing, sometimes not), informants, even servants. In Xuzhou, in northwestern Jiangsu, for example, the bandit population was described as "numerous, very numerous.... There are even families where [banditry] is passed down by blood...so that one is born a bandit. The whole village knows you as such, but no one talks about it."[4] Within the bandit regions the "rule of law" was largely ignored,

---

[*]He Xiya 1925a: 16. The term *"xiangma"* came from the local practice of sending a sounding-arrow (*xiangjian*) to announce the gang's approach. The name was rarely heard after 1911, most of the practitioners having either drifted into Manchuria (where horses were equally effective) or used their riding skills to win army enrollment (*ibid.*). *Mazei* was originally a Japanese term (pronounced *bazoku*), but, during the period of Japan's involvement on the Asian mainland, it seeped steadily into the Chinese vocabulary too. See Watanabe 1964: 38.

and from the administrative standpoint such regions seem to have been largely written off, except for the occasional spasm of conscience on the part of newly appointed officials or military commanders. Troops stationed there were often former bandits recruited to save the cost of suppression campaigns; along with the local officials and the few representatives of the landed gentry who remained, they were obliged by the hostile surroundings to live and let live. Many isolated families spent their whole lives without ever encountering an official,[5] and bandits often filled the gap.

These isolated communities, highly insular, tightly knit, and virtually impenetrable to the outsider, often developed reputations as "bandit villages," places to be avoided when possible, appeased when not. To travelers everything appeared quite normal: adults tilling the fields, children helping them or playing. At the first sight of strangers, however, signals would have been passed along, and long before the travelers reached the village itself the whole community would be lying in wait. To avoid being robbed, the travelers would have to pay a high "protection fee"; but in return they were generally safe within the jurisdiction of the village. For an additional fee they might acquire an escort to the next village, where the process would begin all over again.[6] Trade routes passing through or skirting the mountains were another major source of revenue for such villages, many of which, grouped together for additional strength, developed into full-time raiding communities, descending periodically upon the more vulnerable plains villages below.*

The mountain thus had considerable symbolic significance for the Chinese underworld. In Shaanxi, where bandits serving with the army were said to have "returned from the northern hills" (*gui hui beishan*), "*beigui*" eventually became not only an alternative name for banditry itself, but also a standard way of referring to ex-bandit militarists.[7] Emphasizing their isolation from straight society in the same way that wilder mountain ranges formed a world apart from the better-policed plains, bandit hideouts as well as secret society headquarters were often designated as "mountain lodges" (*shantang*).[8]

It was border regions, however, that were the traditional sites of chronic banditry in China. Local government control being weaker there than in central areas, this kind of banditry was also inextricably connected with such non-farming occupations as smuggling, and with

---

*One group of houses high up in the hills of Guangxi province became known locally as "Chetyang," or "robbers' den," because the inhabitants, unable to grow much rice or to subsist on the proceeds from charcoal-burning and tea cultivation, had taken to obtaining their daily needs through robbery. Similarly, descendants of soldiers sent to pacify the Muli district of Yunnan generations before had settled down as professional bandits, and the two villages they founded became known as "Daozei," "Banditville." See, respectively, Fischle 1930: 61–62; and Rock 1947: II, 419–20.

the cultivation of and traffic in opium. Places where three or more provinces or counties converged were especially problematic, for officials often felt their responsibilities ended when troublemakers left areas that were clearly within their jurisdiction. Bandits could thus escape capture and punishment simply by slipping off to or across these border regions when threatened, fortified by the knowledge that when the central government ordered troops of one province into another for bandit suppression, officials on both sides often refused to pay them.[9] In this way the border zones, known since time immemorial as the "three no-control" (*san buguan*), provided safe havens for fugitives, a constant focus for bandit operations, and, not least, a painful reminder to the government of the limits to its authority. When the area was mountainous or forested or both, as was often the case, the scope for illegal activities was even further enhanced.[10] Provincial officials frequently exploited these conditions by settling "pacified" bandit soldiers as "border defense" detachments, the principal object being that they should cause trouble for officials of the neighboring province.

The major characteristic of the border zones was their insecurity, which tended to create tightly knit communities, inbred and conservative in their social relations but mobile and less subject to the "tyranny of work" than others. Threats to their freedom of movement aroused vigorous reactions, and distrust of the authorities ran deep. It was difficult to raise feeling against bandits, since there was at least a strain of banditry present in every village. Permanent centers of overt discontent, the border zones were the birthplace of many peasant insurrections, including the Taiping Rebellion, as well as the twenty or so rural soviets set up by the Communists between 1928 and 1945.[11]

Banditry also flourished along international boundaries, sometimes instigated to further the interests of one government against another, but usually a result of the pressures of colonization and the clash of populations. Along the Mongolian frontier, for example, banditry broke out on the fringes of Chinese colonization where Mongols had lost their pastures or been inadequately provided for. Mongol bandits regularly patrolled the length of the Inner Mongolian frontier, their targets usually the vulnerable Chinese communities. Chinese bandits often crossed over into Mongolia from Shaanxi and Shanxi to avoid capture, and some of them furnished recruits for the 1916 Mongolian Independence Movement.[12]

The point where China, Russia, and Korea met in the forests of southern Manchuria was another bandit zone, where a typical gang was likely to include people of all three nationalities and even the occasional Japanese.[13] Russo-Japanese rivalry for mastery over Korea added a new element from the nineteenth century on, and many gangs came to be openly manipulated by local agents of the two powers.[14] The border between China and Vietnam was another scene of persistent banditry, and gangs frequently found themselves fighting as proxies for one or the other of the two sets of authorities involved.[15]

Bandits were also closely involved in the colonization process. In Manchuria, for example, "the pioneers were often squatters, wanderers and outlaws by turns. . . . Manchurian bandits found[ed] more villages probably than any outlaws in the world, and though lawless [were] an effective advance-guard of normal settlement and exploitation."[16]

Finally, coastal regions, inland waterways, lakes, estuaries, and any area where several streams converged or split creating swamps and marshes provided traditional haunts for bandits—classed by the authorities as "pirates" (*shuikou, haidao*). Here too it was tempting and usually easier to live off the pickings from robbery than to rely on fishing or to till the probably flood-prone or saline fields.

To the majority of peasants living on the brink of disaster, climatic fluctuations were an added burden, especially in North China. Rainfall was erratic; not only did it vary from one year to the next, it sometimes fell entirely in one small area, creating the strange phenomenon of floods in one county and drought in the next. Whether floods or drought, famine was the result, and that meant flight or starvation—or, ultimately, banditry—for much of China's village population. As the old saying went, "it is better to break the law than to starve to death." Bai Lang's rebellion was a case in point.

By the end of the Qing period, rapid population growth coupled with widespread neglect of rural problems had led to the "banditization" of much of North China.[17] In March 1911 local press correspondents in southeastern Henan reported an increase in robberies as a result of the serious flooding there.[18] That summer, counties farther west were hit by a devastating hailstorm that destroyed the crops in the fields before they could be harvested. Thousands of starving peasants forced into the hills heard officials refuse to waive taxes and landlords sniff at pleas to postpone rent collection.[19] By the end of 1912, after a severe winter followed by more floods made it impossible to plant the autumn crop, banditry was commonplace all over Henan, even in the usually more peaceful region north of the Yellow River. Refugees brought by the train-load down to the double-crop area farther south, however, were greeted by yet another severe winter.[20] Amid this series of disasters Bai Lang's band grew swiftly from a raggle-taggle "blunderbuss corps" (*benpao dui*) into a major popular force numbering some three thousand.[21]

By the spring of 1913 the band had amassed still more recruits as a result of another winter famine. No rain had fallen in southwestern

Henan for six months; the roads leading southeast into Anhui were packed with refugees; and the bodies of the dead lay emaciated and festering along the way. By June there was still no appreciable rainfall, and crops were withering in the fields. For the first time since the Great Famine of 1877 people began to devour the flesh of corpses, and plague ran rampant.[22] Bandit attacks became daily occurrences. As the famine continued unabated throughout that summer, Bai Lang's several thousand followers became the area's most powerful rebel army since the Nian and Taiping rebellions some sixty years before.[23]

Even in an average-to-good year, seasonal factors strongly affected patterns of banditry, for the agrarian cycle often left periods of slack that were a natural spur to predatory activity. On the North China Plain, for example, the cereals that could be grown were mainly crop-extensive rather than labor-intensive. Whereas in South China more than 90 days of human labor per hectare were required every year to bring in a crop, in North China only 30-odd days were required. Moreover, the growing season as a whole was much shorter.[24] Agricultural work was concentrated in the autumn, between late August and October; in the early spring, from late February to March; and in the summer, from May through late June. This left considerable free time, notably the four-month winter period when almost no farm work was done, and the transitional months of April and July, immediately preceding the wheat and gaoliang harvests, respectively.

It was no coincidence that all these periods also saw remarkable increases in banditry. Whereas at other times the "tyranny of work" resulting from the agrarian cycle prevented tillers from abandoning their farming routine for long, during these slack periods enforced inactivity temporarily softened the tyranny, and for men, spending a few months in banditry was a common resort. Though boredom undoubtedly played its role in an individual's decision to "climb Mount Liang," the danger usually made economic necessity the determining factor.[25] The gang that captured a young Englishwoman in Manchuria at the end of 1932 was a good example: during the members' absence their farms were minded by their wives.[26] The most obvious candidates for this type of banditry were the landless laborers, penniless after exhausting their autumn wages, but even among the relatively impoverished owner-occupiers, who characterized much of North China, banditry became a common resort of the underemployed in order to "make the yellow meet the green"—i.e., to tide them over from one harvest to the next.

It is possible to trace the seasonal ups and downs of banditry, beginning in the spring, taking the North China Plain region as a model once again. By April most people had exhausted the previous year's stocks, and many took to banditry to avoid starvation—but only temporarily, since May was the time to get in the wheat harvest and plant the next soybean crop, and all hands were required on the farm. When these tasks were finished, the tide changed once more (the Lincheng Incident, for example, came just at this time). As midsummer neared and the "green curtain" of gaoliang began to stretch as far as the eye could see, weapons carefully buried since the previous season were unearthed and cleaned, horses were rounded up if available, and scouting parties were sent abroad to spy out suitable targets for attack. Finally, a plan of campaign was devised.

Gaoliang, a hardy sorghum popular in North China because of its resistance to flood and drought and because it provided both food and fuel, bore an intimate relation with banditry that many observers have noted: "gaoliang invites banditry; banditry invites gaoliang" was a well-known lament among the rich and powerful.[27] Gaoliang's attraction for bandits was that from late June until mid-August (in Manchuria until September) it towered some ten feet or more over the plains to constitute a vast forest of green. It was tall enough to hide even a rider on horseback, and thick enough to screen what was happening even a few paces away. Tracks hacked out between villages and towns enabled gangs to move quickly when necessary, and the dense foliage on either side provided refuge if attacked.* Hence gaoliang provided natural cover for launching surprise attacks on market towns and rich villages, and of course on errant travelers, and bandits became known for their capacity to "appear like spirits and fade like demons." When it was cut down the bandits usually faded once again, back into the peasant community whence they had come. During the final pre-harvest weeks no one ventured abroad unless escorted and well-armed.[28]

By early autumn banditry again dwindled to a minimum, its participants mostly back in the fields working, their loot divided and their weapons buried until they would be needed again. There was a busy schedule to keep during the next two or three months, for once the gaoliang harvest was in, the land had to be plowed in preparation for the wheat planting in September, and the soybean crop had to be got in at the same time. Nights were shorter, villages buzzed with activity, most people had work, and there was little danger of starvation. Banditry thus saw a lull until the end of October.

From November to February, however, there was little for the men

*So crucial was gaoliang to plains bandit strategy that the Japanese Guandong Army, when it began garrisoning Manchuria in September 1931, saw fit to burn the entire crop and place a permanent ban on cultivation for 1,000 meters on either side of the South Manchurian Railway, the region's major economic lifeline. (Kanamaru 1933: 103; Bertram 1937: 227; Böcher 1932: 74. See also Dailey 1923d: 359; Zhi Ning 1936; Johnson 1934: 208, 218; and Uchiyama 1978: 214–15)

to do. The nights were growing colder and longer. With no work to do in the fields people no longer came and went in the villages as before, and the opportunities for slipping out increased. Ironically, this was also the time when money was most required, both for the land rent and for the traditional New Year settlement of debts.[29] Either from boredom, or from inability to pay what was due, or from the thought of the rich pickings to be had from those who were able to pay, men once again saw robbery as a logical path to follow.* Banditry thus recorded another sharp increase, especially in December and January, and village dwellers of the North China Plain admonished each other "never to go out in the sixth and twelfth [lunar] months."[30] Then it was March, and time to get busy again plowing the fields to receive the new crop of gaoliang. Weapons were hidden or buried once more, and banditry dropped to another seasonal low.

## Banditry and Warlordism

This seasonal cycle of banditry had prevailed for centuries in China, but the endemic banditry of the twentieth century was a new phenomenon. In many parts of China bandits had already begun to multiply before the Republic as a result of socioeconomic decline in the late nineteenth century, but Republican China's constant repetition of wars, struggles for power, and economic chaos allowed banditry to develop into one of the primary symbols of the era.

Yuan Shikai, appointed Provisional President of the new Republic in 1912, consolidated his control over China by a series of timely military moves and political eliminations. After his sudden death in 1916, central control gave way to the unsteady rule of numerous contending militarists or "warlords" (*junfa*), who exercised control over areas of varying size, nominally on behalf of the central government. Ironically, though their political futures depended more on the strength of their military alliances than on government blessing, none of them was able to defeat all his rivals, nor was any combination among them permanently viable. The constant refrain of achieving a unified China by stabilizing the central government came second to retaining regional power.

A "warlord" who controlled his territory at the expense of the central government, which lacked the power to assert its own control, had much in common with the "bandit chief" who operated in a remote corner of the warlord's realm, again on the sufferance of the unwilling

---

*In Zhejiang province in the eighteenth century, all known thieves were rounded up and thrown in jail every year-end in order to reduce the seasonal wave of robbery. The method was self-defeating, for it forced the victims into permanent outlawry by making it impossible for them to go straight. See Fu-mei C. Chen 1975: 138–39.

TABLE 2.1

*The Spread of Warfare in China Under the Early Republic, 1912–30*

| Year | Provinces affected by war | No. of soldiers (000) | Year | Provinces affected by war | No. of soldiers (000) |
|------|---------------------------|-----------------------|------|---------------------------|-----------------------|
| 1912 | 1 | 649 | 1921 | 7 | 1,050 |
| 1913 | 6 | 572 | 1922 | 10 | 1,060 |
| 1914 | – | 457 | 1923 | 6 | 1,190 |
| 1915 | – | 520 | 1924 | 8 | 1,330 |
| 1916 | 9 | 700 | 1925 | 13 | 1,470 |
| 1917 | 5 | 690 | 1926 | 15 | 1,580 |
| 1918 | 9 | 850 | 1927 | 14 | 1,700 |
| 1919 | 2 | 914 | 1928 | 16 | 1,830 |
| 1920 | 7 | 900 | 1929 | 14 | – |
|      |   |     | 1930 | 10 | – |

SOURCES: For the provinces affected, Zhang Youyi et al. 1957: II, 609; for the numbers of soldiers, Young 1977: 164.

NOTE: The number of soldiers is an estimate.

patron. Each existed by extracting from a more or less reluctant populace the means of subsistence in the form of either taxes, military requisitions, or extortion, and to the peasants it made little difference whether the exactions were "legitimate" or not. In Chinese political practice, however, the individual in office monopolized the available stock of legitimacy and was awarded a title appropriate to his position: "general," "commander," etc. Out of office meant out of mind—one became a bandit. Amid the constant struggle for political and military influence that characterized Republican China, at the point where one level of authority lost the ability to enforce its rules there was always another ready and willing to take its place. Although the number of bandit chiefs who achieved recognition as warlords was far less than has often been assumed, the interchange between them and the minor or "petty" warlords was fairly constant.*

An obvious characteristic of warlordism was war. Between 1911 and 1928 some 140 wars among a total of more than 1,300 rival militarists made much of China the scene of constant fighting.[31] (See Table 2.1.) Significantly, the provinces where bandits were most numerous—Shandong, Henan, Sichuan, northern Anhui, northern Hubei, and Guangdong— were also those supporting a neofeudal balance of power among several contending warlords.[32]

In many provinces the fighting tended to concentrate on the railways. Control over them was jealously guarded, not only because it could de-

---

*In fact the warlords' need to retain their regional power bases could make them more vulnerable than bandit chiefs. Whereas the latter could leave their home areas when pressed and return when the heat was off, a warlord could not leave his power base without risking losing it to a rival and with it the source of his legitimacy.

cide the outcome of a conflict but also because commercial traffic provided a useful source of tax revenue. Troops who could not be moved by rail instead marched through the countryside, leaving a swath of destruction as they went. An army in transit and living off the land would take pigs and poultry, vegetables and fruit to eat, and draft animals and able-bodied men to carry their supplies. By losing livestock farms lost fertilizer, especially from pigs. To maintain the previous level of fertilization less land was sown, severely reducing the harvest. Where draft animals and men had been taken, the capacity to prepare the soil, sow seeds, irrigate the land, and weed and harvest crops was weakened. Thus output fell, the cultivated area declined, and many peasants began producing for home consumption only. The direst effects occurred where cash crops had replaced food crops.[33]

To wage war a warlord needed large numbers of troops, and the economic disruption and social dislocation that resulted from generalized war created a permanent store of that basic military ingredient. It was, in fact, a vicious circle: on the one hand, the promise of a relatively steady supply of food and clothing, the possibility of pay, and the prospect of occasional looting made the army highly attractive; on the other, such wholesale absorption of rural labor power further debased living conditions, creating still more recruits, so that the circle revolved in ever-increasing intensity.

Other features of warlordism also contributed to agricultural decline and the consequent increase in banditry, even when no war was in progress. Imposing supplementary taxes on top of regular ones, forcing peasants to plant the more profitable opium in place of food crops, and arbitrarily interrupting communications—such as by withholding railway rolling stock or motor vehicles—were all standard practices. Failure to allay the effects of famines or plagues for fear of expending precious monetary resources was also common, and was directly blamed by the American Red Cross for the great famine of 1928–29 in which millions of people died.[34]

For China, therefore, warlord rule was a self-perpetuating tragedy. It disrupted the economy, reduced many peasants to unendurable poverty and even death, brought the military to the center of the national stage, and thereby institutionalized violence as the primary means of settling problems. Violence from above provoked violence from below. While warlords maintained themselves in power by the sacrifice of hundreds of thousands of young peasants, the poor increasingly reacted by forming or joining bandit gangs or defense-oriented secret societies. The gentry, buffeted by both military exactions and bandit attacks, formed local militias to protect themselves, or else neutralized local gangs and societies by buying off or intimidating their leaders. Many such gentry figures became essential factors in warlordism, collecting taxes and suppressing troublemakers on behalf of their patrons, often by employing the services of their bandit proxies. As a result of warlordism, that is, China was militarized at all levels from the poorest village right up to the national center, each class or group using military strength to protect and promote its own interests. It was the close link between poverty and militarization that made warlordism and banditry so intimately related.

This was not the first time that banditry had reached such proportions: any period of political disorder—the last years of a dynasty or a time of invasion or internal fighting—was likely to destroy the fragile basis of peasant existence and swell the numbers who sought survival in direct action. In the past such disorder had usually been settled by the restoration of political stability. In the twentieth century, however, the decline of administrative control was complicated by an external factor: the inroads of foreign capital and China's increasing involvement in the international economy. Mass-produced foreign goods distributed at rock-bottom prices in the rural areas often threw Chinese producers out of business or made them dependent upon the fluctuations of the world market.[35] Equally important, the widespread introduction of cash crops like tobacco by landlords and warlord-landowners out for quick profits turned peasant producers in many parts of China into mere economic integers whose function was only to grow the crops that made the profits that kept the market thriving. When the glut came and prices fell, such peasants had nothing left to fall back upon for subsistence.

In this way, both decommercialization—the switch to producing for home consumption only—and commercialization—fragile reliance on cash sales—could disrupt peasant lives beyond the point of no return. Once the traditional mechanisms for preventing dissatisfaction from turning into direct action fell into disuse, banditry became for millions of people the only alternative to starvation. As usual, "it was better to become a bandit than to die of hunger."

The economic transformation of China in the twentieth century, carried out at the expense of those with least control over their own fortunes, created banditry unprecedented in both numbers and desperation, but at the same time it set in motion the changes that would promise an end to banditry: primarily, the construction of roads and railways necessary to ensure the rapid transit of cash crops to the marketing centers. This not only removed one of the most attractive sources of bandit income—slow-moving freight traffic on highways and waterways— but also made the transport of antibandit forces faster and easier. The crescendo of banditry was thus simultaneously its protracted death-wail. Certain political factors, however, operated to delay the effect of those economic changes.

As well as being the only road to survival for the starving, banditry was increasingly attractive because of the growing practice of enrolling its practitioners as warlord troops or as local peacekeepers. Improved communications may have initiated the slow process of removing some of the optimum physical conditions for banditry, but instead new martial possibilities opened up for bandits to act as servants of the state or its representatives. Banditry, instead of disappearing, was becoming an institutionalized route to power and influence.

For many peasant recruits to warlord armies, a return to the farm was unthinkable after once tasting the excitements of military life. Having seen the power of the military in action, former soldiers who found themselves back in their villages or demobilized far from home fixed their sights once more on the army. Most of them found that the quickest way to realize their ambitions was to adopt the traditional hit-and-run tactics of banditry. These were the "soldier-bandits" (*bingfei*), armies thousands or tens of thousands strong capable of rampaging their way across a province in a matter of days. As a result of this "apotheosis of brigandage,"[36] by the 1930's commentators were deploring China's plight not as a "bandit nation" but as a "soldier-bandits' nation" (*bingfei guo*).[37]

In many parts of China, soldier-banditry replaced the traditional pattern, destroying the latter's potential for local defense, and transforming once-modest bandit dreams into crude military or even political ambition. Essentially, however, soldier-banditry was an adaptation to changed sociopolitical conditions; though it appeared to differ widely from previous patterns, the social origins and basic motivations of its participants, its tactical methods, and the internal characteristics of most gangs showed it to be a development rather than a replacement of old-time banditry.

The conditions that created the soldier-bandits, meanwhile, were the same ones pushing the Chinese revolution toward its conclusion, and bandits found themselves drawn into the strategies of all contenders. Traditional banditry was the prototype of modern guerrilla warfare, yet its essential peasant character also created weaknesses: localism, short-term thinking, and fluctuating membership—the classic drawbacks of all peasant rebellions. Bandit forces could be mobilized just as easily by a strong charismatic leader using superstition to reawaken atavistic urges; by an ambitious local power-boss offering military prestige and economic security; and by revolutionaries, using ideological education in an attempt to create organizational cohesion and allow political guidance. In the long run, however, bandits remained peasants, and those who sought to use them usually found doing so harder than they had bargained for.

## A Nationwide Overview of Banditry

The difficulties of reliably estimating the extent and distribution of Republican-period banditry were stressed by the contemporary author He Xiya. Unlike soldiers, who are stationed at fixed points, bandits are always moving, and it is easier to interview a troop commander for information than a bandit chief. Bandit life-styles further hinder the investigator: operating as outlaws and peasants by turns; "returning to rectitude" (*fanzheng*) as regular troops only to desert again; scattering and regrouping to evade suppression campaigns. Thus no statistical survey of bandits has any long-term value, and even He Xiya's should be taken as no more than a rough summary. He lists some 113,500 bandits in the dozen or so provinces he was able to investigate (many were inaccessible because of insecure conditions or warlord conflicts),[38] a gross underestimate since the figure refers only to permanent gangs and ignores the seasonal influx described above. For my own rough calculations, based on a variety of contemporary sources, see Table 2.2.

The Three Eastern Provinces of Fengtian (later Liaoning), Jilin, and Heilongjiang—collectively known as "Manchuria"—boasted a comprehensive system of militant village-protection groups. Classed by the authorities as "mounted bandits" (*mazei* or *honghuzi*—literally "Red Beards"), they gave the region a troubled image that was not really accurate, at least until the end of the 1920's. Growing out of the need for "aggressive defense" against a largely hostile world, Manchurian banditry was in effect a kind of "'frontier banditry,' organically different from the banditry of social disintegration and despair which characterizes so much of China proper."[39]

Apart from the atmosphere of violence that frontier societies usually create, in Manchuria's case both the international boundaries with Russia and Korea and the area's natural characteristics—an arch of mountain ranges providing perfect refuges and a bleak climate making farming unattractive—strongly influenced the extent of both real and so-called banditry. Most peasant families had a gun, both to protect themselves from predators and to allow them to "go bandit" themselves should the need arise. Particularly in northernmost Heilongjiang, banditry was predominantly a means of survival, and it was said that "all the villagers there have the flavor of banditry," though the mixture of people grouped together in these bands made the "bandit" label almost meaningless. All in all, there were probably more than two million guns in private hands.[40]

Opium planting in the remote mountain valleys, the influx of weapons from soldiers as local warlord Zhang Zuolin began to expand his

TABLE 2.2
## Number and Size of Bandit Gangs in the 1920's, by Province

| Province | No. of gangs | Total no. of bandits | Size of largest gang | Source and date of estimate | Comments |
|---|---|---|---|---|---|
| JILIN | 24 | 7,900 | 1,000 | He Xiya 1925a (1924) | Major gangs only |
| | 17 | 4,290 | 600 | Zhu Xinfan 1930 (1924) | |
| | 37 | 21,355 | 3,500 | Nagano 1938 (1925) | Bandit-Suppression Commission survey |
| | 48 | 24,270 | – | Nagano 1938 (1925) | Represents all Manchuria |
| INNER MONGOLIA | 14 | 10,700 | 2,000 | He Xiya 1925a (1924) | |
| SHANXI | 24 | 19,500 | 2,000 | Zhu Xinfan 1930 (1924) | Certain border gangs only |
| | 30 | 24,800 | 3,000 | Nagano 1938 (1923) | Border regions only |
| SHANDONG | 47 | 18,400 | 1,000 | He Xiya 1925a (1924) | Famous gangs only |
| | 47 | 25,760 | 3,000 | Zhu Xinfan 1930 (1924) | |
| | 54 | 39,170 | 5,000 | Nagano 1938 (1924) | |
| HENAN | 52 | 51,100 | 6,000 | He Xiya 1925a (1924) | |
| | 40 | 21,850 | 3,000 | Zhu Xinfan 1930 (1924) | "One quarter of the real total" |
| | 42 | 25,280 | 3,000 | Nagano 1938 (1923–24) | |
| ANHUI | 8 | 6,500 | 3,000 | He Xiya 1925a (1924) | Northern counties only |
| | 13 | 4,310 | 1,200 | Zhu Xinfan 1930 (1924) | Northern counties only |
| | 15 | 8,060 | 5,000 | Nagano 1938 (1923–24) | |
| HUBEI | 5 | 4,500 | 2,000 | He Xiya 1925a (1924) | |
| JIANGSU | 15 | 4,080 | 800 | " | Xuzhou area only |
| HUNAN | 6 | 1,300 | 300 | " | Western counties only |
| SICHUAN | 8 | 4,300 | 1,000 | " | Small selection only |
| | 18 | 55,200 | 10,000 | Zhu Xinfan 1930 (1924) | Southern and eastern counties only |
| | 26 | 77,350 | 10,000 | Nagano 1938 (1923) | Southern and eastern counties; major gangs only |
| GUANGDONG | 6 | 2,000 | 800 | He Xiya 1925a (1924) | Excludes pirates |
| | 85 | 102,340 | 10,000 | Shibuya 1928 (1926?) | |
| | 54 | 4,343 | 400 | Nagano 1938 (1926) | Nat. Rev. Army survey |
| | – | 26,100 | 3,500 | " | Major gangs only |
| | 10 | 6,700 | 1,300 | " | Prov. Security Commission survey |

NOTE: Where only rough estimates of gang size are available, "few" and "several" hundreds or thousands have been calculated as 300 (3,000) and 500 (5,000) respectively; where a range is given, as "6,000–7,000," I have used the upper figure.

military influence, and the vacuum caused by Zhang's escalating involvement in national politics south of the Great Wall were also important factors in the development of Manchurian banditry. Of the three provinces, Fengtian, the capital region, was least affected, and Jilin the most. As elsewhere, Manchurian banditry frequently spilled over into neighboring provinces like Rehe ("a thicket of brigandage"), Chahar, and Suiyuan on the Inner Mongolian frontier.[41]

The backdrop to banditry in Shaanxi province, characterized by one famine relief official as "like a dying beggar,"[42] was extreme poverty. Known of old as a "bandit-producing region," as early as 1911 the northernmost section had become "a nest of plunderers lost in a wilderness,"[43] and under warlordism Shaanxi became the domain of men of violence of every hue from genuine peasant rebels to warlord-backed bandit armies and landlord-sponsored militias. Struggles for power among rival military factions and a protracted anti-government rebellion allowed many local bandit chiefs to set themselves up as petty warlords with the eventual expectation of official recognition. Apart from the north of the province, birthplace of many peasant rebellions in the past, and the south, famine-prone and always troubled by bandits, during the Republican period even sections of the fertile Wei River valley were host to strong and long-lived gangs. Although accurate figures are hard to come by, Shaanxi's mid-1920's bandit population undoubtedly numbered several tens of thousands. With borders facing Gansu, Ningxia, Suiyuan, Shanxi, Henan, Hubei, and Sichuan, Shaanxi was also constantly prone to incursions by outside gangs.[44]

Shaanxi's transformation into a "bandit world" significantly affected its western neighbor Gansu. Enmity between Moslems and Han nationality residents had produced sporadic banditry there for centuries, encouraged by cyclical bouts of famine. The province as a whole, however, far from the center of national politics, did not see widespread predatory behavior until it came under the control of the warlord Feng Yuxiang in 1925. Severe exactions levied to pay for Feng's military adventures, the forced planting of opium poppies, and the conscription of large numbers of reluctant young peasants amid a severe famine caused rampant starvation and led to a major Moslem revolt as well as to widespread banditry. The influx of ex-soldiers fleeing from Feng Yuxiang's battlefield defeats and of Shaanxi gangs along the old east-west opium trail completed the picture, and by 1930 Gansu's bandits featured regularly in the domestic and foreign press.[45]

Shanxi, under warlord Yan Xishan, was hailed as China's "model province," but on the provincial boundaries bandits were as numerous as anywhere in China; a conservative 1924 estimate put them at more than 25,000.[46] For thirteen years Yan conserved his position, remaining aloof from national military affairs until it was no longer possible to do so. After 1924 military exactions began to rise, triggering widespread popular mobilization both by "Red Spear" (*Hongqiang hui*) village-protection societies and by predatory bandit gangs. Incursions by gangs from Suiyuan to the north, Henan to the south, and Shaanxi to the west caused most of the trouble, particularly after the appearance of the soldier-bandits. Yan Xishan increased his own difficulties by absorbing hundreds of thousands of these soldier-bandits into the provincial army.[47]

The northern section of Zhili province, containing until 1928 the national capital of Beijing, was kept relatively free of bandits until Feng Yuxiang's coup d'état against Wu Peifu in October 1924, after which the province became steadily embroiled in the struggle for power between rival militarists. Soldiers tramping and pillaging through the countryside, together with sharp increases in military exactions, forced many people into banditry to make ends meet. Many more joined to make their fortunes, taking advantage of the growing tendency to absorb gangs into the regular army. As in Shaanxi, ex-soldiers, mostly the disbanded troops of Wu Peifu, accelerated this trend toward banditization. Southern parts of the province, much poorer than the north and constantly vulnerable to incursions from Henan and Shandong, had long been known as bandit areas, whereas northern counties bordering on Manchuria and Rehe dated their decline to Zhang Zuolin's defeat in 1920, which sent many former soldiers fleeing with their weapons into the local mountains.

The conclusive factor in the expansion of Zhili banditry was the arrival of the Nationalists' Northern Expedition in 1928, which was further compounded by a severe famine. The number of bandits in the province soon soared to five million, or almost 20 percent of the population.[48] After that, and especially after 1930 when the Nationalist regime was challenged by a coalition of northern warlords, big gangs became common even in northern counties. The removal of the capital to Nanjing eliminated the need for maximum security, and within a few years there was said to be nowhere in Zhili unaffected by bandits.[49]

The focal point of North China banditry was the lower reaches of the Yellow River—eastern Henan, southern Shandong, northern Anhui, and northwestern Jiangsu, particularly the region where the tangled boundaries of the four provinces met (see Map 1). The area's reputation for foiling even the best-prepared suppression schemes went back at least to the seventeenth century, when Li Zicheng had been able to maintain his rebel army intact by exploiting military localism. The Nian rebels also used the area's natural advantages to enable them to surround and kill the crack government general Seng-go-lin-qin in 1865.[50] In the twentieth century the authorities made constant but vain recommenda-

Map 1. Twentieth-Century China. Traditional bandit regions are shaded. Adapted from Hsi-cheng Ch'i, *Warlord Politics in China, 1916–1928*.

tions for cooperation between the four provinces.[51] Following the Lin-cheng Incident, a new "Bandit Suppression Law" designated the border zone as a "bandit-suppression zone," but missionaries on the spot still accused the newly formed Four-Province Suppression Force of collusion with the bandits.* Even for reasonably conscientious commanders, suppression was difficult; apart from the possibility of slipping into another province, bandits had for hiding-places the mountains of southern Shandong or the fens and marshes created by the constant flooding of the Huai River and its tributaries.[52] It was no accident that this area had provided refuge for the most famous of all Chinese bandits, the 108 heroes of Mount Liang commemorated in the *Shuihu zhuan*. Poor and unprofitable, with a tradition of belligerence (*daofeng*: literally, "bandit wind"), in the days of the empire the border region had been largely written off by the authorities. Aggression had become a primary means of coping with frequent floods and famines and general ecological instability.[53]

Shandong's notorious reputation was encapsulated in the old saying, "The kingdom of Lu (southern Shandong) teems with bandits" (*Luguo duodao*). Bandits remained the principal problem for those who sought to stem the tide of the 1911 Revolution in the province, and estimates of bandit numbers for the mid-1920's ranged between 20,000 and 30,000.[54] On the whole, the southern counties—the original kingdom of Lu— were most affected, their relative prosperity compared with their poverty-stricken northern Anhui neighbors making them a prime target for the latter's gangs.

The culmination of Shandong's suffering began in 1925 with the three-year rule of the ex-bandit warlord Zhang Zongchang. Zhang encouraged his bandit henchmen to set themselves up as local potentates and used them to crush all resistance, so that before long even the poor walked in fear of their lives. The passage of the Northern Expedition in 1928 and the rebellion by the northern warlord coalition in 1930 added further to Shandong's burdens. Destitute war refugees picked up the guns dropped by retreating soldiers and became bandits themselves, reinforced by large numbers of army deserters. By 1930 the province's

---

*Passed on August 30, 1923, as a direct reaction to post-Lincheng foreign pressure, the "Bandit Suppression Law" sought to solve the problem of converging provincial boundaries by instructing civil and military officials in the four provinces to cooperate on pain of severe punishment. Arms and ammunition for bandit suppression were to be supplied by the authorities of the provinces in which the bandits were currently active. If bandits appeared in one province but closer to the garrison of another, the latter was to send troops without fail *if so requested*. For details, see Nagano 1924: 261–66; *DFZZ* 20, no. 17 (10 Sept. 1923): 4–6; SD 893.00/5344 (Hankou to Beijing, 13 Dec. 1923); *NCH*, 29 Sept. 1923: 895–96; *The Times* (London), 21 Sept. 1923. Addition of the rider "if so requested" was a revealing admission that no plan for concerted bandit suppression could succeed as long as warlord rivalries continued.

bandit population was being put at more than 200,000, a tenfold increase in the space of five years.[55]

Like that of Zhili, Anhui's bandit subculture was originally limited to one half of the province, in this case the poor, "traditionally unruly" northern half. Incursions by gangs from Henan and Shandong, coupled with factional rivalries among the local military, gradually caused the boundaries of the bandit-affected area to expand to the more prosperous south. By the late 1920's, following several local conflicts and the passage of the Northern Expedition, bandits spread throughout the province; the scattered local gangs of the past were replaced by large, soldier-based gangs along the new pattern.[56]

Jiangsu's case was similar to Anhui's. Although the eastern, coastal counties were fairly peaceful apart from the traditional piracy, the north-western section of the province, which jutted deeply into Shandong and Anhui, had long been a refuge for "guest-bandits" (*kefei*) fleeing their own local authorities. Here, too, the inhabitants had a reputation for rough tempers, and the Xuzhou region, encouraged by the relative prosperity farther east, enjoyed a reputation throughout North China for its large number of resident bandits. As elsewhere, the crucial factors in the province's total "banditization" were its passage in and out of the hands of different warlords and the seemingly interminable civil conflicts of the 1920's. Like Anhui, Jiangsu saw its bandit areas gradually spread southward to absorb the already troublesome but relatively localized subculture centered on the lake-studded central and southern counties. Encouraged by the passage of the Northern Expedition and swollen by thousands of deserting warlord troops, gangs from these southern counties soon expanded sufficiently to begin raiding the outskirts of Shanghai, Nanjing, and Suzhou. By 1930 the government admitted that the province was a serious bandit irritant.[57]

Hubei province to the west was most affected by banditry in its northernmost and westernmost counties bordering on Henan and Sichuan, where gangs often several hundred to a few thousand strong used natural hideouts in the thickly wooded mountains to elude pursuit. Farther south the province was relatively trouble-free, especially around the key urban center of Hankou. Like Anhui and Jiangsu, Hubei's bandit areas gradually expanded under the impact of warlord struggles and the Northern Expedition. By the late 1920's even the Hankou region was playing host to large gangs, many of which provided local people with protection against unreliable garrisons.

Another factor in the expansion of Hubei banditry was the disruption and increasing poverty that followed in the wake of the struggles between government troops and the Communist Red Army, which was based first along the border with Hunan and Jiangxi to the south, and then, after 1929, along the border with Henan and Anhui. It was often difficult to distinguish the activities of the regular bandits from those of "Communist bandits," not only because of the official government practice of referring to them both in the same breath, but also because many of the early Communist bands were dominated by former bandits who continued to raid and kidnap even while flying the red flag of revolution.[58]

The pattern in Hunan, Hubei's southern neighbor, derived from its natural habitat: a tiny lake-studded central plain surrounded by hills. The province, especially its central corridor giving access to Hubei and thence to Beijing, experienced countless major and minor wars between southern and northern militarists after 1911, and the number of army deserters turned outlaws not only made kidnapping a daily hazard for better-off Hunanese but also gave the province's bandits a nationwide reputation for cruelty.* Though often shunned elsewhere, kidnapping of women and children was commonplace in Hunan, and the treatment of captives was generally harsh. Though the agriculturally more prosperous central plain held its own for most of the period, the western counties bordering on Sichuan and Guizhou had been notorious bandit haunts for centuries and remained so. Their densely forested mountains, populated by various local nationalities, sheltered hundreds of thousands of bandits in gangs whose origins might lie in any one of the three provinces.

Hunan's southern border with Guangxi provided another focus for banditry, gangs sometimes several tens of thousands strong operating in unison across the border, hiding in the forests and mountains when pressed. A third point of focus was Dongting Lake in the north. Combining land and water techniques, local gangs (known as *hufei* or "lake bandits") made a living by attacking the freight traffic that plied between the lakeside ports or the smaller coastal towns and villages. Finally, the passage of the Northern Expedition, spreading unrest from the always troubled borders to the more peaceful central and eastern areas, turned predatory banditry into a provincewide affair. As in Hubei, the establishment of soviets along the southern and eastern borders in 1929–30 added a fresh complicating factor.[59]

The banditization of Jiangxi and Zhejiang provinces east of Hunan and south of Anhui is sometimes blamed on the establishment of local soviets in the late 1920's, but in Jiangxi at any rate banditry increased as a result of the fighting accompanying the 1911 revolutionary movement. Because of the province's crucial proximity to the Yangzi River, bandit activities gradually grew in both mobility and violence, principally in

---

*In 1914, for instance, the alleged atrocities of Bai Lang were already being condemned by a Japanese current affairs magazine as typical of only the worst Hunan bandits. See "Kōnan dohi no kako genzai": 24.

the prosperous southwest, which was subject to raids from the forested mountains straddling the Hunan border. The disruption unleashed by the passage of the Northern Expedition and the resistance put up by local warlords completed the process, and the mountainous counties surrounding the central plain were largely taken over by powerful full-time gangs. In time these gangs formed alliances with the newly arrived Red Army, and by 1930 Red Army–bandit control extended to most of Jiangxi's border regions.

Zhejiang was less affected than most provinces, and prior to the Northern Expedition saw no more than isolated pilfering and kidnappings within a fairly restricted area: principally the northeastern corner and the southern shores of Lake Tai astride the border with Jiangsu, long the scene of widespread piracy or "lake banditry." Although the bandit areas gradually spread inward from the peripheries under the influence of the growing Communist bases and the suppression campaigns mounted against them, the absence of any significant military clashes within its boundaries spared Zhejiang serious problems.[60]

Fujian, east of Jiangxi on the coast facing Taiwan and almost entirely mountainous, was the classic "bandit province" in this part of southeastern China. Fujian society was dominated by clan networks, and banditry here often originated in clan feuds in which the losing side was forced to take to the hills. Frequent clashes between rival militarists took place in which both sides exploited the rich bandit subculture, and as time went by the bandits, without waiting to be called up, took to using ornate military titles, exacting road and river tolls, selling "protection" to foreign and Chinese lumber companies, and so on. They also became known for their close links to the military. Gangs were generally big, rarely numbering less than several hundred, and were usually well armed and organized. By the late 1920's the "bandit spirit" (daofeng) in Fujian was strong enough to permit the sacking of county seats as well as large villages. The northern border was being called no less than an enormous "bandit base," and the western border with Jiangxi, where the Red Army had made several incursions, was rapidly going the same way. Various captives noted a strain of cruelty among Fujian bandits similar to that found in Hunan, influenced perhaps by the passions aroused by violent interclan strife and the losers' desire for revenge, but also, no doubt, by the presence of so many undisciplined military units and the persistent local wars (bandits in provinces to which such fighting came later, such as Manchuria, enjoyed milder reputations).[61]

In watery environments piracy naturally became the dominant mode of predatory behavior, and it had been established along the coasts of Fujian, Zhejiang, and Guangdong since the early Qing period. Gangs of buccaneers, many of them led by women, hijacked ferries, levied tolls on fishing villages, and fought running battles with Chinese and foreign gunboats until well into the modern era.[62] The "twentieth-century pattern" was for the pirates to board a ship posing as passengers, then to take it over once on the open sea. Ransoming of the wealthier passengers rather than robbery became almost the rule. For local officials, too, there was considerable profit to be made in turning a blind eye in return for a cut in the profits. Piracy continued to flourish along the South China coast until 1937. British ships were the commonest victims, and altogether twenty Merchant Marine officers were killed. Countless Chinese were kidnapped and never heard of again.[63]

The difficulties of clearing up the maritime pirates, according to one British officer, were increased by the fact that "both merchant and fishing junks take a hand in it when their normal trade is at a low ebb.... [A] boat engaged in piracy one day may itself be a victim on the following.... Honour among the thieves of rival ports appears to be unknown." Other pirate groups allowed boatowners for a monthly fee to fly a flag that guaranteed their protection.[64]

Sichuan, despite a reputation for rebelliousness dating from the time of the Three Kingdoms (A.D. 221–65), until 1911 had been one of China's most peaceful provinces. After that, constant fighting between rival warlords combined with regular invasions from Yunnan to the south made the whole province a battlefield, so much so that in 1925 Pacification Commissioner Liu Xiang announced that "of all the 146 counties in our province of Sichuan not one is free of bandits." Amid the fighting, peasants became bandits (known locally as *bangke*, "guests of the cudgel"), bandits became soldiers (*laoer duiwu*), and soldiers became bandits again until Sichuan ranked alongside Henan, Shandong, and Fujian as one of the most heavily banditized provinces (a 1931 estimate gave a total of at least 1.5 million).[65] The entire Yangzi River valley from Chongqing to the Hubei border was allegedly controlled by bandits, many of them in frequent contact with the army and possessing modern rifles, machine guns, and even cannon. As a result, the Sichuanese were said to make no distinction between bandits and soldiers. Attacks on river steamers were common, some villages supplementing their meager farm earnings by either ambushing or levying a transit tax on the lightly defended, slow-moving craft, even after these began flying foreign flags for protection. Here, too, the gradual spread of Communist base areas encouraged and enlarged existing bandit gangs, and several alliances were established.[66]

Conditions in Yunnan, known of old as a bandit province, have been testified to by several missionaries unfortunate enough to fall into bandit hands in the 1920's.[67] Merchants were unable to transport their wares, the Salt Commissioner (a European) could not take up his post, foreigners were kidnapped everywhere, and factories had to pay extortion money to the bandits to stay open. Only the railway zones were relatively free of bandits, and travel by any other means in the mountainous province was "almost a military operation." In neighboring Guizhou, bandits were strong enough even to take over the provincial capital of Guiyang temporarily, but detailed information on this isolated and mountainous province is hard to obtain. Yunnan and Guizhou banditry was given a political hue by the activities of Miao national minority gangs.[68]

Last of all come the two southernmost provinces of Guangdong and Guangxi, bordering upon Vietnam and Hong Kong. As suggested by the commonly heard expression "the pirates of Guangdong, the bandits of Guangxi," both had time-honored reputations for producing outlaws, partly because of the international political factor, partly because of sharp social differentiation. Guangxi banditry, as in Fujian, was particularly notable for its close links with the military: well-known chiefs strutted openly through the towns, chatting about the bandit life in full view of soldiers, who regarded them as equals and made no attempt to arrest them. By the late 1920's the majority of bandits were in any case former soldiers created and then left stranded by the tides of constant interfactional fighting. Many had defected with their weapons to the mountains to live as outlaws until it seemed safe to attempt a "return to rectitude."

Guangdong banditry soared following the end of the 1911 hostilities, after many of the "people's armies" (*minjun*) raised to fight on the Republican side reverted to or were forced into banditry. The inauguration of Sun Zhongshan's Provisional Government in Guangzhou a few years later led to constant fighting with surrounding militarists, and as losing troops took to the hills bandit numbers soared again. Some of the gangs were big enough and sufficiently organized to assume regular military formations, and train holdups became a constant hazard. Rich local notables, by sponsoring a group of bandits, could set themselves up as local potentates under the gang's protection, for the constant fighting had made even the prosperous feel more secure with their bandit rulers than with the regular troops, whose atrocities were legendary.

Originally concentrated in the central region around Guangzhou, the bandit areas began to spread north, east, and west after the split between the Nationalist Party and the Communists in 1927 and the beginning of independent Communist activities. As in other provinces, however, it was initially hard to distinguish between bandit operations and those of the Communist raiders. Even in 1926 an official report estimated Guangdong's bandits at 100,000 (though He Xiya insisted there were few large gangs) and complained that official inaction had allowed parts of the province to become "altogether a bandits' world."[69]

In sum, during the second and third decades of the twentieth century the traditional modes of banditry, economically motivated and varying with the seasons, were overwhelmed by the remorseless militarization and concomitant disruption under the warlords. A look at the preceding nationwide summary reveals a number of significant patterns. First, behind the astonishing growth of banditry lay an enormous increase in the number of soldiers and in the amount and frequency of fighting. Deserting through lack of pay, disbanding after a defeat, running amok when victorious, soldiers sometimes joined gangs with their weapons, sometimes formed their own independent armies, sometimes simply made economic conditions so precarious that peasants had no choice in their turn but to become bandits. The Northern Expedition, too, despite its object of national unification, accelerated economic disruption, left a political vacuum in the areas it touched, and brought about a dramatic increase in banditry.

Second, the process of militarization broke down the traditional distinction between civil and military authority, making many officials the tame creatures of their military overlords. The task of bandit suppression, always a delicate one for the ambitious local magistrate, became all but impossible in many parts of China as the bandits themselves took on more and more of the trappings of regular military units.

Third, economic disruption, which intensified as the period went by, paradoxically created trends of both commercialization and decommercialization as peasants sought desperately to survive in the face of overpowering odds. Whichever mode local conditions dictated, the end result was often banditry, for behind both trends lay the fact that peasant fortunes had become more fragile than ever.

Last and perhaps most important, almost every province experienced banditry spreading inward from the border regions—traditionally unruly —toward the once-peaceful central areas. The tendency for gangs from poorer districts to prey upon their richer neighbors also grew to provincewide and finally nationwide proportions. In this way, China's traditional "bandit kingdoms" in many parts of the country spread and fused to create no less than a veritable "bandits' world." The insecurity that had traditionally formed the background to life in the peripheral areas flowed inward to embrace the once-protected core regions, and with it came a tendency to violent solutions—primarily banditry. The growth of banditry in Republican China, that is, not only reflected the economic impact of warlordism on everyday life, but also indicated that the political values dominant in the peripheries—basically power-broking backed by violence—had become those of the country as a whole. Banditry, always closely tied to the system of violence, thus turned from an isolated security problem to a central motif of twentieth-century China.

## CHAPTER THREE

# "Cradle of Banditry": A Case Study of Henan Province

*Top-grade people become bandit chiefs, spending money like water;*
*Second-grade people take up a gun and stick close by their side;*
*Third-grade people shoulder a rifle, fighting and killing at every turn;*
*Fourth-grade people negotiate terms for the captives, both sides using*
*    elegant phrases;*
*Fifth-grade people become the bandits' spies, bringing ruin to ordinary*
*    people;*
*Sixth-grade people take care of the loot, filled with anxiety and fear;*
*Seventh-grade people look after the captives, their eyes gone blind from*
*    worry and exhaustion.*                        —*Jing An 1930: 4*

HENAN PROVINCE, particularly its southern and western counties, was a classic example of the "bandit kingdom." Known for centuries as a hotbed of revolt, Henan was a sharp thorn in the side of would-be rulers throughout the Republican period, and even after Liberation in 1949 remained a hot-spot of banditry as well as gaining a reputation as one of the most militantly Maoist provinces. Official reports described the province as a whole as "a place that had always spawned bandits," and particularly troubled counties as "spots where bandits had always abounded." For the authorities, the fundamental cause was the "tough" and "warlike" personality of the local inhabitants, people who instead of "bending before the wind" "thought the greatest happiness to be carrying a stick."[1]

These comments applied chiefly to counties south of the Yellow River, above all to the foothills of the mountains that flanked the province's boundaries in an arc stretching from the northwest to the southeast. A trip through these regions took one at one's peril through a series of well-known bandit "lairs";[2] significantly, most of them had been focal points of rebellion in centuries past, both Li Zicheng and the Nian insurgents, for example, having drawn heavily upon them for recruits, and their example was followed by Republican revolutionaries in 1911.[3] The central and northern counties remained relatively unaffected by banditry until 1924–25, when provincewide fighting between ex-bandit militarists extended the chaos to them as well. A survey carried out soon thereafter gave Henan the highest number of bandits of any single province. From then on, the combined impact of warlord conflicts, natural disasters, and the fighting surrounding the creation of a Communist base area in 1929 made Henan come to resemble in truth the "robber province" it had always been in name.[4]

## Poverty and Banditry

Southwestern Henan provides a good illustration of the correlation between poverty and banditry. Unlike the northern and central counties, where land was relatively fertile and conditions sometimes prosperous, the southwestern counties were capable of maintaining themselves when conditions were stable but slow to recover from disruptions. The hilly land yielded little, and productive capacity was low. In contrast to the general North China pattern, tenancy rates were high, especially around the towns.[5] In Baofeng and Lushan big landlords owned almost all the land in some villages, and their tenants sang songs like the following as they worked:

> The boss just sits and talks, never lifting a finger,
> But his tenants must run their legs off on his errands.[6]

Rental arrangements were also harsh, landlords demanding on average some sixty percent of the yield. For the hungry, eating unripe crops (*chiqing*) was a luxury; rice or millet husks, tree bark, moss clinging to stones, and even goose droppings were all frequently consumed in bad years. When disaster struck it was a case of "wife gone and children scattered, bleached-white bones littering the roads," as one local proverb put it. Many families in this region gave up everything to seek work elsewhere or to beg aid from the more fortunate. Some migrated permanently; others preferred to plant the spring wheat, then take seasonal work further south before returning in time for the harvest. Still others eked a living out of non-farming sidelines.[7]

In Baofeng and Lushan the main auxiliary occupations were mining and ditch-digging. Lushan in particular was of some local importance for its coal output, the area abounding with slag heaps as a result of the iron-smelting industry.[8] Conditions in the pits were appalling: miners were beaten and given no more than a pittance for the hazardous hours spent in the flood-prone workings. That peasants entered voluntarily into this living death highlights the brutalizing poverty that surrounded them. Not surprisingly, for many the mining areas became places to steer well clear of. The importance of irrigation in the hilly terrain made ditch-digging another well-established sideline. The shortage of good arable land led to the nearby foothills being plowed up and farmed, and this required dikes, terraces, and irrigation ditches to channel water and prevent soil erosion. The building and upkeep of these works became a standard male activity during the winter slack season, and the teams of young men recruited for it were known as *tangjiang*. By the beginning of the Republican period there were estimated to be tens of thousands of *tangjiang* in Lushan alone.[9]

Another auxiliary occupation in southwest Henan was the carriage of goods. Owing to the high labor surplus, men were taken on at rates often little better than those applied to animals: the price of a meal at the end of the journey, for instance. If there was a glut in the haulage market, one's last hope might be to become a link in a chain of bodies forming a human bridge across unfordable rivers.[10] When even this last alternative fell through, the only recourse for a family was beggary or banditry. As another proverb put it: "When people are starving, the weak among them become beggars, the strong become bandits."

According to one local gang leader, few poor peasant families in southwest Henan survived without resorting to encouraging one or more of their members to take up outlawry at least once. Since the mountains were the haunt of the more or less full-time bandits, it was natural that the link between them and the poor peasantry should come through the *tangjiang*, who not only worked in the hills but were recruited in teams by a jobber (*gantou*) to whom they often felt a strong allegiance. It was an easy step from *tangjiang* team to bandit gang when work slackened, and the line between the two increasingly blurred until the Lushan dialect word for "bandit" actually became *tangjiang*, using another character for *jiang* but undoubtedly reflecting the implicit association between the ditch-diggers and the bandits who shared the mountains with them.[11]

Though the Republican period saw a general trend toward what Ralph Thaxton has called "immoral landlordism,"[12] in the southern parts of Henan relations between tenants and landlords had already reached a nadir long before. After 1917 landlords came under strong pressure from warlord rulers for more revenue to finance the latter's military adventures, and they began to impose more and more exactions on the peasants. One result was the enforced transition to cash crops such as cotton, tobacco, and opium instead of the traditional subsistence crops of millet, wheat, and gaoliang. Cash crops sold on the market bolstered warlord revenues, and landlords received rewards for forcing their

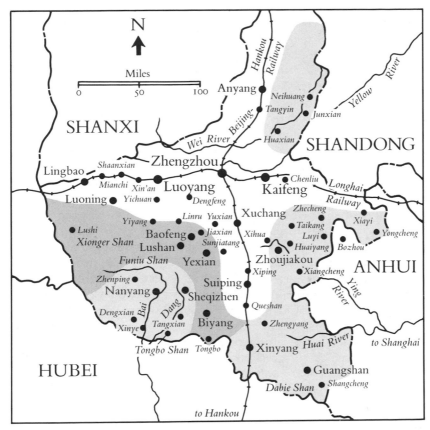

Map 2. Henan, Cradle of Banditry. Developed areas are unshaded, economically degenerating areas are shown in light gray, and traditionally underdeveloped areas are shown in dark gray. Adapted from Odoric Wou, *The Impact of Differential Economic Change on Society in Honan in the 1920's and 1930's.*

tenants to raise them. In this way the traditional relationship between landlords and their tenants, which had often saddled the former with a certain degree of Confucian obligations, was overwhelmed by the new one between landlords and the military.[13]

An interesting light is thrown upon Henan's spiral of poverty by looking at the province in terms of the concepts of "developed," "under-developed," and "degenerating" regions (see Map 2).[14] The map shows the province in the 1920's and 1930's, and what is clear at once is that the "developed" areas closely parallel the railways that bisect the prov-ince. The "degenerating" areas, by contrast, mostly follow the river systems, a result of the switch from water to rail transportation at the turn of the twentieth century. During the Qing period, waterways—

principally the Wei basin in northern Henan, the Huai basin in the east and southeast, and the Bai basin in the southwest—had been instrumental in moving agricultural products to major marketing points, and towns along them had thrived. With the building of the railways, especially the Beijing-Hankou trunk line (completed in 1906) and the east-west Longhai line (completed in 1916), these towns began to deteriorate. Like Zhoujiakou (also known as Shangshui), once the assembly point for waterborne goods bound via the Ying and Huai rivers for Shanghai, many major centers lost importance except as local markets. As they declined, so did the auxiliary markets surrounding them. Sheqizhen in southwest Henan had been the loading point for goods bound via the Dang and Bai rivers for Hankou. Caravan traffic from Mongolia and the northwest stopped here to transfer their loads to riverboats, and boats bearing goods from the south unloaded here before returning. Sheqizhen, in a word, was one of the country's wealthiest trading marts until the building of the railway lines deprived it in one stroke of all its commercial activities except local trading in sesame oil, wine, and a few other goods. By the 1920's it had become little more than a dusty market town. The existence of islands of thriving activity within such declining areas—such as Nanyang and Lushan in the Bai basin, which survived on the proceeds from silk production, Guangshan in the southeast, and Zhoujiakou, which survived because of its relative proximity to the Beijing-Hankou tracks—only accentuated the aura of economic decay in the surrounding regions. That these declining areas became important centers of banditry is not, under the circumstances, very surprising.

Parallel to and providing a buffer between the degenerating zone of southwest Henan and the developed zones was a traditionally under-developed corridor linking Luoning (known until 1912 as Yongning) and Biyang. The area was mountainous, dominated by the Xiong'er and Funiu ranges, and its inhabitants engaged mostly in subsistence farming with little salable surplus. Cultivable land was rare and production levels low. Commercial and handicraft activities were almost nil. Most trading was carried out at local markets in the mountains.

As the map shows, railway building created a T-shaped developed zone in the center of the province. The possibility of making a living from cash crops, particularly cotton and tobacco, made local farmers more market-oriented here than elsewhere, and large-scale trading evolved in towns blessed with stations. Zhengzhou, at the juncture of the two lines, was transformed in a few years from a small town into the province's most important urban zone. However, the concentration on cash crops, especially a single crop, could reduce farmers, particularly tenants, to destitution in bad years. Centrally located Xuchang was by the 1920's virtually a tobacco colony, with the majority of farmers in the area working on a contract basis for commercial firms like the British-American Tobacco Company, and the worldwide slump at the end of the decade left the area reeling.

In short, the building of the railways turned Henan into a land of light and shadows. Whereas the opening of its railway station transformed Anyang in the north into a major industrial center, Luoning in the west, though an administrative center, was a tumbledown city of twelve and a half acres whose magistrate's yamen had collapsed from lack of repairs. It was said that a rickshaw-puller in the railway center of Xinyang was likely to have a higher standard of living than a 100-*mou* landowner in the undeveloped west.* The resulting cultural conservatism was reflected in high rates of female infanticide and footbinding.

Sharp animosity was the inevitable result of such contrasts, heightening the inclinations toward violent survival strategies that the poorer districts nourished anyway. Towns and villages on the edges of the developed zones became the targets of raids from underdeveloped and degenerating zones in both the east and the west, raids that often resulted in large-scale and long-lived feuds such as that between the market town of Sunjiatang on the central plain and the mountain villages thirty miles away to the west.[15]

The pattern of distribution of bandit gangs and secret societies in Henan also reflected economic considerations, bandits being most numerous in the poorer parts of the province, societies predominating in the more stable districts. The polarization grew as economic conditions declined, and significantly it was the richer districts that first produced the Red Spear self-defense societies. Whereas in 1911 cooperation between gangs and societies had sometimes been successful, by the 1920's the west Henan bandits and the village-protection groups had become bitter enemies. In short, banditry became the stock response of the poor to poverty, taking the form of predatory attacks on those perceived as more wealthy than themselves; secret societies like the Red Spears, dominated by the more secure, prosperous classes seeking to defend the property that symbolized their power, became the vehicle for group defense against bandit raids.†

---

* The *mou* was a unit of land measurement equivalent to approximately one-sixth of an acre.

† In practice, the distinction between bandit gangs and Red Spear chapters often blurred. In the latter's heyday, for example, bandits frequently adopted their trappings and slogans to improve their gang's image. On the other hand, local Red Spear chapters often, especially after the movement passed its peak, behaved more like predatory bandits than self-defense groups, preying on other chapters in pursuance of long-standing regional feuds. Immediate self-interest usually decided where they would put their allegiance, and neighboring chapters might even find themselves fighting each other on behalf of rival warlord patrons, employed as auxiliary troops just as bandit gangs often were. For an example, see Mitani 1974.

The North China Famine of 1921–22, the climax to several years of alternating flood and drought, left millions dead and tens of millions destitute and was another tragic example of how fragile the rural economy could be.[16] Erratic weather patterns had provoked many peasant uprisings in the past, and they now triggered fresh outbreaks of banditry. Travelers in central Henan noted the almost total absence of young men among the thousands of refugees who thronged the cities. Most had become either soldiers or bandits, and trains stranded by floodwaters along the Beijing-Hankou tracks provided perfect targets for hungry and desperate outlaws.[17] During the terrible summer of 1922, a missionary captive traveling with one of these gangs commented that the dust was three or four inches thick on the roads from the lack of rain for several months.[18] One of the clearest illustrations of the acute social distress affecting north China was the rising level of migration to Manchuria. Emigration from 54 villages of west Henan's Yexian county almost tripled between 1927 and 1929, and Henan's share of total migrants rose from 1 percent to 11 percent during the same period. Few returned, for wages in the Northeast averaged three to four times those in Henan.

In addition to this largely permanent exodus, there were also patterns of regular seasonal migration from degenerating or underdeveloped areas. During the winter slack season, poor peasants left the area south of Xuchang en masse for Hubei, either to beg or to work as coolies; farmers from the remote villages of the Dabie range sought refuge downriver in Jiangxi; and in Lushan and Baofeng a minimum of 10 to 20 percent of village households left to go begging on the roads in an ordinary year. Residents of one village recalled that 90 percent of the population had had to leave at some point in their lives to seek survival elsewhere,[19] and local folk songs with such titles as "Flight from Famine" bear them out.[20]

## Henan's Bandit Kingdoms

Officials singled out four areas of Henan as "warlike" or "militant" (*yongwu*). Interestingly enough, they correspond largely to the areas just identified as either underdeveloped or degenerating. The largest of these "bandit kingdoms" consisted of counties in the underdeveloped west and southwest—Dengfeng, Songxian, Yiyang, Linru, Lushan, Baofeng, and Jiaxian—especially the "ungovernable" areas of them where their boundaries converged. Another was in the extreme east, embracing Zhecheng, Luyi, Xiayi, and Yongcheng. A third was the degenerating zone of the Wei River valley in the north consisting of Huaxian, Junxian, Neihuang, and Tangyin. Last was the degenerating zone of the Bai River basin surrounding the city of Nanyang, an area of frequent floods leaving behind great expanses of sand.[21]

Travelers approaching towns in the "bandit kingdoms" were greeted by the sight of yellowed, rotting heads suspended in cages on the walls or gates.[22] Decapitation and exposure of the head had been a common punishment for bandits and rebels since the Qing period, especially in the traditional "bandit provinces."[23] Intended as an edification for passersby and as a warning to local youngsters to forgo the "dangerous path" of outlawry, such grisly demonstrations of law and order had little effect. Known in bandit slang as "viewing the city wall" (*wang chengjuan*), the punishment befell most of the important chiefs whose careers will be referred to in subsequent pages.

As the proverb put it, however, "a rabbit does not eat the grass outside its own burrow." Bandits did not usually rob their home areas, mainly because to do so would alienate them from their own people, but also because such areas were probably too poor to be worth the trouble. They therefore looked elsewhere for targets, so that a place listed as having no resident gangs was often worse off than one with a high bandit population. Zhenping, for example, a silk-producing county in the southwest, was a frequent victim of gangs from neighboring Dengxian (a "bandit haunt") but is not mentioned in any of the gang-distribution tables we have; in similar fashion Shaanxian, a cotton town on the Longhai line in the far west of the province, constantly fell prey to attacks from Luoning. Luoning's formidable bandit population—6,700 according to He Xiya, 3 percent of the county's people and almost a third of all bandits in west Henan—was as much a result of its proximity to the visibly flourishing Longhai catchment area as of its own extreme impoverishment. As these examples suggest, the counties that recorded the highest number of bandit attacks were always those on the fringes of economic zones. Thus Yuxian, on the edge of the central tobacco zone, suffered 26 raids in thirteen years; Zhengyang, near the Beijing-Hankou tracks bordering the undeveloped south, logged 27 raids in twenty years; Huaiyang, by the eastern degenerating zone, had 22 attacks in eleven years; and Xihua, in the Ying River degenerating zone, had 26 attacks in 21 years. In the highly developed northern counties, however, with strong law-enforcement agencies or military detachments, recorded attacks were few. Anyang, for example, suffered none at all during the 22 years after 1911 (with the exception of two secret society incidents). Market towns that formed islands of relative prosperity in a sea of poverty were also places around which bandits naturally gathered: Nanyang, a thriving silk-production center, was completely surrounded by gangs hiding out in declining nearby market towns like Sheqizhen,[24] and travelers found it impossible to hire porters to carry their effects after the first hint of dusk.[25]

Wealthier towns and cities within striking range of the "bandit kingdoms" lived in constant fear of attack. Surrounded by earthen or

Map 3. West Henan's Bandit Kingdoms. The inset shows the area closely associated with both Bai Lang and Lao Yangren, and is adapted from *Bai Lang qiyi diaocha baogao*.

stone walls according to their degree of prosperity, all of them were strongly girded for defense. The gates, plastered with reward notices and adorned with cages containing the heads of recently caught unfortunates, were closed tight at dusk and opened to no one before the sun rose again; those facing the mountains were often permanently closed. Goods coming in and out were carefully inspected for illicit or dangerous objects—such as guns being smuggled inside in preparation for a co-ordinated attack from within and without (a popular bandit trick).

The provincial capital of Kaifeng, standing in the middle of the central plain, not only had the thickest walls of any city in North China (hence its long and successful resistance to siege by both Li Zicheng and the Taipings) but also employed an early-warning system of beacon mounds and shops for gathering information along all roads leading to the city. Surrounding villages put up thinner, gated earth walls for defense, and also served as inadvertent beacons themselves to alert Kaifeng's defenders to the approach of bandits, for the smoke from their burning houses could be seen a long way off.[26] Few towns could stand up to a concerted attack by a bandit army, however, and some had a long history of suffering. Taikang, a rich east Henan trade mart known before the advent of the railways as "Silver Taikang," recorded sackings by Li Zicheng in 1643; by the Nian in 1852, 1856, 1861, and 1863; by the Yellow Way Society (*Huangdao hui*) insurgents in 1911; by the Cha Tianhua band in the same year; by Lao Yangren's soldier-bandits in October 1923; by a chief named Sun in December 1924; by unspecified bands in November 1925; by Niu Shengwu's band in January and June 1926; and by unspecified bands again in March 1927, March 1928, winter 1930, and January 1932.[27]

Folk songs eloquently expressed the general air of apprehension affecting towns regularly visited by bandits, as witness the following lyric that circulated in Xin'an and nearby Mianchi:[28]

> In daylight don't dare leave the town,
> At nighttime don't dare hear a dog bark;
> At the sound of a single shot
> All folk fear the worst.

## The Western Henan "Bandit Kingdom"

It is the first of the "bandit kingdoms" described on p. 46, embracing south and west Henan, that will mainly concern us here. This part of Henan, once considered the "cradle of civilization," was by the twentieth century more commonly referred to as a "cradle of banditry."[29] (See Map 3.) The government had always found it hard to bring the area to heel, lamenting of the "bandit haunt" of Ruzhou (Linru) that "the district is secluded, the people are fierce, and swordsmanship is respected. Being lazy, the people prefer robbery to hard work. This has always been a refuge for bandits."[30] Missionaries also found the area difficult to penetrate. The Augustana Synod Mission, for example, encountered fierce tempers when in 1908 it attempted to expand its evangelizing activities to "...old Juchow [Ruzhou] on the narrow plain between the mountains, Juchow the famous centre of robber activities, the city to which the traveller should not arrive after dark and which he should not leave before daylight, according to statements current among the Chinese."[31] One suppression commander whose career spanned most of the Republican period asserted that nowhere did the situation approach the "gravity" of west Henan after 1911, even though all over China bandits were "as numerous as the hairs on an ox" (*duo ru niumao*).[32] Inns that still catered to the few travelers who risked the narrow trails through the mountains had superstitiously given up referring to food by the usual term, *fan*, for the word was homophonous with another meaning "criminal" or "rebel." Lest mention of the word bring about the prompt appearance of its feared namesake, to mollify fate alternative terms were used.[33]

In these mountains, banditry was a part of everyday life, passed down from parent to offspring: "Fathers encouraged their sons, brothers urged their younger brothers, and women incited their husbands [to become bandits]. Those who were unwilling were despised by their wives for their weakness. Those who happily complied were commended by father and brother for their spirit."[34] These communities had a morality of their own, for there was no clear distinction between "bandits" and others, and robbery in itself was not considered a crime:

Personally...I am inclined to believe that there really is no distinction as between "bandits" and "people" further than that by bandits are meant those who are at the time under arms and "on the war path" and by people the women and children and the aged who carry on small businesses in the poorly stocked markets or till the land. But that [*sic*] the people are really the fathers and mothers, and sisters and brothers of the bandits, and profit by their activity insofar as those who are active in the profession divide their gains with the folks at home.[35]

A family that produced a well-known chief could walk around with heads held high, for neighbors greeted the emergence of a new chief with the expectation that they, too, would receive protection against outside predators. Most of the "better-class brigands," it was said, were *daoke*,* which was "considered a title to be proud of."[36]

---

*The *daoke*, or "Sword-fighters" (literally "guests of the sword"), were popular carriers of the old knight-errant tradition who specialized in protection and individual

Links between bandits and villagers were strengthened by performances of the distinctive local operas. Composed by village storytellers and itinerant dramatic troupes, they portrayed the deeds of past heroes drawn both from real life and from the *Shuihu zhuan*, and glorified the retribution of the poor against the rich and privileged. Young people watching the operas often sought an opportunity to emulate the deeds on the stage, and with their batteries thus charged it was but a short step from stage heroics to the real-life kind.[37]

Within the western Henan "bandit kingdom" there were a number of distinct subsidiary areas, one of which embraced the four counties of Linru, Baofeng, Jiaxian, and Lushan. Although quite small, only thirty miles across and a little more from north to south, the area, especially the "*san buguan*" or "three no-control" section along the county boundaries, had a reputation for popular activity going back as far as Li Zicheng and spawned many of the most famous bandit leaders of Republican times: Bai Lang, Lao Yangren, Fan Zhongxiu, and Zhang Guafu. During the Republican period, bandit incidents here were said to number several score a day. The area's center was "the walled robber capital" of Daying in the lower foothills of the Funiu range, whose "battle-scarred walls" stood sentinel over the area's proud traditions. Of other settlements it was said that they "more resemble fortresses than peaceful towns, and, in effect, are such.... [L]oop-holes in the houses are not infrequent, and especially in [those]... that face open spaces or street lengths, while bullet pitted walls... and ragged ruins of houses... tell of fierce feudal strife or the vengeful retribution of some chief meeted [*sic*] out to a whole family or even village community."

On the other hand, the inhabitants of the region were "as democratic a community as exists anywhere, and are a law unto themselves except... [during] an invasion by the military.... Among themselves they have laws, customs, and even a language, such as may not be found in any other part of the country. They are ruled by their chieftains and their chieftains are not only elected but are obliged to 'accept office' if elected or run the risk of incurring great displeasure...."[38] Not surprisingly under the circumstances, the traditional refrain of "become an official and make your fortune" (*shengguan facai*) was replaced here by

acts of bravery, and who probably came closest to the ideal of the "social bandit." By the end of the Qing period, although the title remained common, most were armed with modern rifles. Their strength was such that local officials often shrank from brushing with them (*ZHMGS:* 80). With the militarization of North China after 1911 they disappeared as a separate category in the bandit tradition, but the more prominent or lucky among them, such as Yang Hucheng, Chen Shufan, and Hu Jingyi, later became noted warlords, and many others made careers for themselves lower down in the military hierarchy. For details, see "Guanzhong daoke." A similar tradition was that of the "braves" (*youyong*) of Guangxi and Guangdong, and it too produced a number of noted military figures, including Liu Yongfu and Lu Rongting (see Lin Baohang 1961).

one far more appropriate:

> If you want to be an official, become a bandit chief;
> If you want to ride in a palanquin, go looking for people to kidnap.[39]

Lest an over-utopian impression be given, it should be pointed out that an element of compulsion was evidently present even in these "bandit democracies." Young men found it difficult to evade "active service" with the nearest gang, and families were under strong pressure to do as they were told. A missionary observed that his bandit captors expected and received all kinds of services while they were in transit.[40]

Another well-known bandit subregion was found farther west in the upper foothills of the Funiu and Xiong'er ranges, taking in the counties of Songxian, Luoning, Lushi, and the whole area between the Luo and Yi rivers. The Funiu range, a granite wall rising to some nine thousand feet at its highest point south of Songxian, was a natural stronghold that had been a popular refuge since at least Ming times. The area was frequently devastated by floods that left behind sand and stones and made farming an extremely unreliable business; many communities instead lived off the lucrative opium traffic coming down from the poppy fields of Shaanxi to the markets of Hubei, or else became full-time raiders.[41]

Inheritors of the local rebellious tradition, chiefs here were often highly self-conscious, and many became local champions. Wang Tianzong, for example, the "robber King of Honan" whom "no governor . . . had ever been able to catch,"[42] supported his several hundred followers through a toll on the local rich, while the poor contributed reports on enemy troop movements.[43] Wang and his band of "country heroes" "exploited Songshan's natural advantages . . . and demonstrated their superiority by repeatedly repulsing the government's suppression campaigns." During one such campaign, General Xie Baosheng, an expert bandit-catcher recently brought in from Hebei, suddenly saw on a nearby mountaintop Wang's silhouette outlined against the sky:

> Oy! Xie Baosheng! Don't be too sure of yourself! Our paths have crossed many a time, and the only reason I've spared your life up to now is that I'm waiting to see if you've the heart to become a good official or not. If you don't believe me, just watch!

So saying, Wang sent a single bullet through the top of the general's peaked cap. Xie, it is said, ran for his life and never relaxed until he had put several miles between himself and Wang Tianzong.[44] This area was also the scene of strong popular mobilization in the cause of the 1911 Revolution as well as in the anti-warlord struggles of a decade later.[45]

The southwestern corner of the province, bordering on Hubei and enjoying easy access to both Sichuan and Shaanxi, was a third bandit subregion whose centers were the old Nian stronghold of Nanyang and neighboring Dengxian. After 1919 Nanyang "saw not a day of peace; on merely hearing its name pronounced people shook their heads and refused to go farther."[46] Prominent chiefs in this region were powerful enough to issue safe-conduct passes through the mountains and to establish their own arsenals. Even the "notorious" Sun Yuzhang, too violent to become a popular hero, managed to shine under the corrupt and bloody rule of military governor Zhang Zhenfang, and in 1913 a delegation of local representatives even requested his protection against the exactions of gentry-controlled "local self-government boards."[47]

The last of the bandit subregions was slightly to the east of the Nanyang-Dengxian one, where Hubei jutted sharply northward providing an additional means of escape when needed. Its nucleus was the celebrated Tongbo range, said to "specialise in harboring bandits." Resident gangs would plunge down from their hideouts among its 3,000-foot peaks to attack the foothill cities Tangxian, Xinye, and Biyang, and the railway towns Xinyang and Queshan. Both Tangxian and Xinye were notorious "bandit districts." Roads through the area, though providing one of the few overland links between southern Henan and northern Hubei, were virtually impassable.[48]

One of the area's favorite bandit haunts was a mountain in Biyang county named "Sow Gorge," an isolated natural fortress surrounded on four sides by sharply rising mountains and accessible only by a single narrow track. Its strategic importance was accentuated by its convenient location near the borders of six different counties and within easy striking distance of Suiping and Queshan. Gangs occupying Sow Gorge could hold off a large military force indefinitely and slip away when they liked over the narrow paths through the peaks. A popular refuge for centuries, it had also been one of the more enduring centers of Nian activity. In 1913 Bai Lang was able to ambush and defeat the army of suppression commander Zhang Xiyuan here, and a decade later Lao Yangren's soldier-bandits rested here after their pursuit by the troops of warlord Wu Peifu. Lao Yangren, to relieve the rigors of a long campaign, apparently felt secure enough to have actors captured en route put on a dramatic performance while Wu's troops circled helplessly outside. Later in 1923 the hideout was taken over by a notorious gang that had killed an Italian priest captive and consequently sparked off enough diplomatic ire to set thousands of government soldiers on their trail.[49]

Bandit power was confirmed over south and west Henan with the rebellion of Bai Lang. Officials confessed that "a certain number of towns and villages are voluntarily obeying his law . . . [and] the people are glad to be protected by the White Wolf against the regular troops who, submitting to no authority or discipline, lay waste to the country."[50] Even after Bai Lang's demise, the area remained the outlaws' domain. In 1922 bandits were able to burst into Wu Peifu's well-defended headquarters in Luoyang, warn the 4,000-man garrison against interference, kill a well-known merchant for refusing to pay them financial tribute as demanded, and even threaten to carry off Wu himself. Though surrounded by crack troops, Wu confessed himself unable to guarantee the personal safety of missionaries beyond the city's walls (or even within them, he should have added).[51]

## From Bai Lang to Lao Yangren

Following the harsh suppression of the nineteenth-century rebellions, Henan had seen a period of relative calm. Anti-Qing secret societies like the Elder Brothers Society helped keep the spirit of resistance alive, however, and after an appalling famine from 1875 to 1878 in which an estimated nine and a half million people died, unrest began to spread once more. In Lushan, traditionally militant *tangjiang* led tens of thousands of peasants to open landlords' granaries after the latter refused to provide famine relief. For the rest of the century, bandit gangs continued to dominate the local hills and mountains, extorting protection money from landlords and kidnapping the rich for ransom.[52]

Toward the end of the century unrest began to peak anew, provoked partly by further natural disasters, partly by the government's so-called New Policy, a last-ditch effort to bolster state authority by increasing the power of local gentry.[53] Even in the relatively prosperous central districts it was said that "Everything rose in price; with every day life became harder, and the number of wanderers greater. The rich all joined the ranks of the poor, and the poor all joined the bandits."[54]

After the Boxer years, lingering unrest coupled with the effect of the "reforms" and the weight of the "Boxer Indemnity" helped create or revive many of the popular groups active during the previous century. In southern Henan small-scale bandit outbreaks became bold attacks on local landlords, with a strong flavor of social banditry in the traditional cries of "kill the rich and succor the poor!"[55] Passions rose still higher when an anti-opium crusade brought in troops who uprooted the crop but provided nothing for the growers in its place. A series of riots between 1902 and 1911 was an impressive record of popular anger and provided the groundwork for the revolution to come. One body of missionaries arrived in 1905 to find the province in a state of "insurrection,"[56] and two years later Viceroy Bao Fen was noting that his subjects "not only kill government runners in revenge for quarrels, but even oppose our troops, and set up ramparts for defense."[57]

By 1911, Henan officials were complaining bitterly of the difficulties of keeping the province's "bandit districts" in line, noting dazedly that "there was almost no one who was not a bandit."[58] Gangs that once operated at night in outlying villages now launched daylight raids on towns, which consequently began to close their gates by four or five o'clock in the afternoon. Once the last resort of unemployed vagrants, banditry had become a kind of popular custom, and the victims were afraid to report it for fear of reprisals. Before long, new slogans like "rotten gentry must be killed!" and "level up the rich and the poor!" left local notables feeling insecure even behind locked doors.[59] Worst of all, spluttered Bao Fen, these bandits actually shared their income with the poor instead of merely dividing it among themselves.[60]

Given this background, it is not surprising that southwest Henan gave birth to China's last major peasant rebellion, led by Bai Lang, the so-called "White Wolf."* Born in 1873 in the village of Daliu in Baofeng county, Bai came into frequent conflict with authority during his youth, and by late 1911 headed one of the innumerable small peasant bands that so irritated local officials. Dressed at first in ragged cotton tunics and armed with makeshift weapons, Bai and his followers, their activities strongly rooted in peasant discontent, soon were strong enough to keep the local garrisons pinned down behind strong city walls "like tortoises afraid to poke their heads out of their shells."[61] The principal targets were missionary property and the institutions set up under the universally unpopular New Policy: post and telegraph offices, Western-style schools, local self-government premises, and so on. At last Bai Lang's name began to be mentioned in anxious government dispatches.[†62]

* A host of theories concerning Bai's origins sprang up during his rebellion and have been repeated in one source after another ever since: that he was a former army officer; that he was a Moslem; that he was a revolutionary student returned from Japan; even that he was himself Japanese. The theories are summarized in Lai Xinxia 1957b: 11–12, and in Shimamoto 1974: 56–58, 73–75. Lerberghe and Monestier (1915: 121–25) actually identify Bai Lang with the Shanxi revolutionary Qiu Liang, an ally of Wu Luzhen who disappeared soon after Wu's murder in November 1911. This fascinating assertion is unfortunately not corroborated by other evidence, though some theories, without mentioning Qiu Liang, have suggested that Bai had formerly served under Wu. All these hypotheses were finally laid to rest by the publication in 1960 of the results of an investigation in Bai Lang's home county of Baofeng. In November 1959 a team of eleven investigators from Kaifeng Teachers' College carried out several weeks' intensive fieldwork in Baofeng and neighboring Lushan and Linru. They interviewed two of Bai's own daughters and many of his close associates, and also held group discussions to elicit as much information as possible from local peasants. Their report (see *BLQY* and the summary in "Bai Lang qiyi diaocha jianji" 1960) has been the major source of information on Bai Lang for the present study. Among the Augustana Mission's converts was one whose next-door neighbors had included "the notorious robber chief, 'White Wolf.'" He spoke of him as a kind and good-hearted playmate" in his youth (Augustana Mission 1925: 165).

† The first official reference to Bai Lang (*ZFGB* 179 [27 Oct. 1912]), as well as various contemporary accounts (Yamazaki 1913: 18; *BLZX*: 6), give the original characters for his name, not the homonym meaning "White Wolf," underwriting the theory that the latter was deliberately substituted later by the authorities to give Bai's activities a more ferocious aura. This had been a common feature of anti-rebel propaganda in the past, too. (see Tao Juyin 1957–58: II, 38) The 1959 investigation confirmed that Bai never used the "White Wolf" title himself (*BLQY*: 81).

In the autumn of 1912 the Henan authorities commenced a policy of "incorporation and reorganization," in fact a code name for slaughter. Bai was one of the few local chiefs to resist the tempting offer of military status, and his caution was vindicated when in October no fewer than eighteen major chiefs who had accepted were massacred.[63] Almost the only peasant leader of any reputation left, Bai Lang naturally became the focus of the resistance that picked up thereafter, and his band swelled quickly to several hundred fighters.

Over the next year Bai's force, enormously popular because of its anti-establishment stand—the press charged him with carrying out a "crusade of revenge" against the gentry[64]—grew steadily into the most powerful peasant army the area had seen for more than half a century. Joined by most of the other remaining local chiefs and their followers, Bai Lang was soon the supreme leader of several thousand fighters, chiefly landless peasants, unemployed farm laborers, coal miners, and ditch-diggers, and disaffected local soldiery. December 1912 saw the first of many premature announcements of his death.[65]

This stage of Bai Lang's career also demonstrated how fraught with contradictions the career of a successful bandit chief could be. For even while enjoying massive peasant support, Bai was simultaneously obliged to pay court to forces that fundamentally threatened popular initiative: the Manchu loyalists. Whether Bai Lang himself entertained monarchist sympathies has never been determined (though as a peasant rebel from an area with a long history of attempts to "restore the Mandate of Heaven," monarchism must have had more appeal for him than any newfangled "republicanism"). Still struggling to establish himself and to protect his followers' lives amid vicious pogroms and great political uncertainty, Bai Lang was ready to accept any offer of support that brought the promise of material aid in the form of guns and cash. In this sense his subsequent transfer of loyalties to the Republicans appears less incongruous, for he was evidently doing no more than seeking to hold his own in a world whose balance was weighted against him.

The catalyst for Bai Lang's monarchist ties was the pro-Manchu "Royalist Party" (*Zongshe dang*), organized in 1912 with the aim of restoring the deposed Qing dynastic line. There were two factions, joined by their common desire to see an end to Yuan Shikai. Though the extremists insisted on nothing less than the restoration of Qing rule, the moderates were evidently willing to settle for monarchy in some form, either Han or Manchu.[66]

With Yuan's accession to the presidency, the Royalist Party set out to cause as much trouble as it could in North China. One potent source of recruits was the many unpaid or disbanded veterans of the 1911 fighting. In July 1912, for example, troops of the Sixth Henan Division, incited by party agents, rioted at Luoshan, where they were joined by the bandits of Qin Jiaohong, an early confederate of Bai Lang.[67] It also seems likely that the party's inflammatory propaganda was behind the hostile popular reaction to the government's 1913 anti-opium campaign, for according to the *North China Herald*'s reporter, villagers declared: "If this be the method of a Republic, the sooner we rise and strike for a monarchy the better."[68] Yuan Shikai took this persistent sniping extremely seriously, not least because of the involvement of several political figures including, as rumor had it, the Yangzi Valley warlord Zhang Xun.[69]

Bai Lang's links with the Royalists were clearly established during 1912. The first concrete evidence we have dates from the winter of that year when he and his followers, fleeing the anti-peasant pogroms of the gentry-led "Future-Safeguarding Society" (*Shouwang she*), moved south into the mountains of north Hubei. Hubei was a hotbed of Royalist Party activity, and from this time on Bai Lang began to "extend his teeth and fangs." By April he had joined forces with the "Seas and Lakes Society" (*Haihu hui*), a branch of the Big Sword Society on Nine-Dragon Mountain in Suixian, and was publicly supporting the deposed Manchu court.* Descending periodically from the mountains to attack houses and shops and to capture weapons from local militia groups, Bai Lang and his followers were soon strong enough to repulse two regiments of provincial troops with heavy casualties. Notices announced that "when the great Qing government returns it will kill all republican traitors without quarter." Flags carried such slogans as "Avenge the Wrong Suffered by the Great Qing Court in 1911!," proclaimed Bai the "Commander for Weeding Out Traitors of the New Nation of Great Qing," or portrayed a sleeping dragon, with the implication that the imperial throne, symbolized by the dragon, would soon awake to seek its revenge. By early 1913, Bai's forces, said to be five thousand strong and armed with modern weapons including machine guns, moved north into Henan's Tangxian and Yuxian to continue their crusade against the new morality, killing all those without queues and attacking Western-style schools.[70] (See Map 4.)

In July 1913 the Republicans launched their own "Second Revolution" and immediately began paying court to Bai Lang, by then the strongest popular leader in strategic Henan. Odd as it may seem that

---

*Yamazaki (1913: 18) presents the improbable theory that Bai Lang himself was a Manchu who had studied in Japan and once served as an army training officer. When the 1912 peace negotiations showed that the Qing court no longer possessed the capacity to repulse its enemies, Yamazaki continues, Bai resigned his commission and entered the hills to fight for the imperial cause in his own way. Because of his military skills he was soon elected chief of the local secret society groups of northern Hubei, and he used his monarchist connections to build up his followers' strength (*ibid.*).

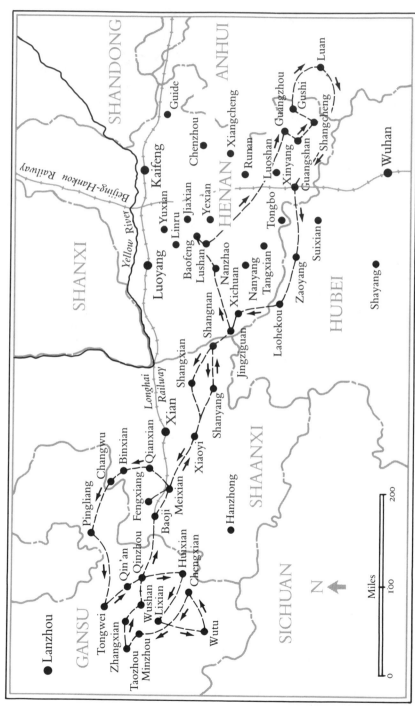

Map 4. Bai Lang's Rebellion, 1911–14.

Republicans should seek the support not only of a bandit but of one still apparently a committed monarchist, the fact was that Republicans and monarchists shared a common hatred for President Yuan Shikai. Yuan reacted to the Second Revolution by strengthening his military positions all over North China and declaring martial law in Henan, a move that also enabled him to have leaders of the Royalist Party arrested and shot. As a result, refugees of both Republican and monarchist sentiments were driven into the mountains to join Bai Lang.[71] We can only assume that a kind of tug-of-war ensued over the orientation of Bai Lang's forces. Two subsequent episodes support this assumption. First, the monarchist warlord Zhang Xun was widely reported to have "courteously" received Bai Lang's secret emissaries at his Xuzhou headquarters early in 1914.[72] Second, strong pressure was applied by certain unidentified elements while Bai Lang was in Gansu to take over a local walled city in order to proclaim either a Qing restoration or Bai's own accession to the throne.[73] The flavor of these episodes strongly suggests that they were the work of Royalist Party moderates within the band. Back in Henan, meanwhile, newspapers were referring to a small boy traveling with the band destined to be the next emperor, and local correspondents reported a sudden recrudescence of the queue allegedly intended to propitiate the "wolves" on their return from Gansu.[74]

Despite signs or rumors to the contrary, however, from the middle of 1913 it was his working alliance with Republicans that dominated Bai Lang's strategy. Refugees from anti-radical pogroms brought added cohesion and a sense of direction, and over that summer and autumn Bai Lang launched a major military campaign culminating in October in the sack of the important northern Hubei city of Zaoyang. The capture of several missionaries there, followed by the accidental killing of a French priest at Luan, Anhui, in January, put a dangerous political complexion on the movement, however.* Yuan Shikai, under intense foreign pressure to exterminate the rebels immediately, was obliged to begin planning their suppression.[75]

The first campaign was set in motion when the rebels were far from their native haunts in western Anhui, richly laden with opium and fine clothing looted from a string of county seats across southeastern Henan. The suppression forces, consisting of 100,000 soldiers from three provinces under Yuan's crack generals, and advised by a bevy of foreign military attachés, failed ignominiously as Bai led his band quietly back along

---

*The Luan episode continued to reverberate into the 1920's and 1930's. A subsequent occupation by the Big Sword Society (*Dadao hui*) in 1924 would be recalled by eyewitnesses as "Anhui's most serious bandit emergency since the White Wolf disturbances" (Xing Bei 1924: 8), and a 1935 report spoke in similar tones (Zhuo Ran 1935 [July]: 120). See also Arlington 1931: 239.

mountain paths into Henan, invisible even to the French-loaned airplanes droning overhead.*

At the urging of his Republican advisers, Bai had by this time over-come the reluctance of his subchiefs and decided to try to establish a temporary base in Sichuan.† Surging across the northern half of Hubei, the band paused en route to stage a successful attack on the prosperous river mart of Laohekou, where their sacking of foreign concerns like British-American Tobacco and Singer Sewing Machines prompted even local merchants to welcome them, but alarmed the British sufficiently enough to send HMS *Woodlark* up the Han River from Hankou in a show of "gunboat diplomacy." Despite the rich store of munitions captured in this raid, however, Sichuan proved impenetrable, and Bai and his followers began a 600-mile trek through Shaanxi and Gansu to approach the province from the northwest.[76] Pursued by no fewer than 200,000 government soldiers in Yuan Shikai's most concerted suppression effort, they reached the border in early May almost unchallenged, only to find the river crossings in full flood and guarded by hostile troops.‡

The collapse of the bold roving strategy, coupled with the difficulties of creating good rapport with the Moslem peasants, seriously affected the band's morale. They began to vent their frustration on local villages despite a strict ban on license. Bai's dream of a revolutionary base not-withstanding, they also began to hanker after home. Finally it was re-solved to return to Henan and safety before it was too late. Numerically

---

*Huang Guangkuo 1960b: 34. The force Yuan assembled was the strongest North China had seen for many years, and was backed up by an air squadron, artillery units, legal offices, medical and veterinary stations, a mobile telegraph office, and a Red Cross unit, all obviously designed to increase Yuan's prestige with the British and Russian ob-servers accompanying the force under the protection of his personal bodyguard (Xiong Bin 1980: 304; see also Huang Guangkuo 1960b: 34). The junior officers involved in the operation included Sun Chuanfang, one of a number of warlords whose reputations were made in the campaigns against Bai Lang (Cai and Xu 1980: 1099).

†Du Qunhe ed. 1980: v. The British military observer, Major D. S. Robertson, opined that the revolutionaries' real motive in sending Bai Lang off to Sichuan may have had as much to do with diverting government troops from the Yangzi Valley, where they intended to stage an uprising, as with setting up a base in the interior (FO 371/1942, Beijing to London, 30 Mar. 1914). On the other hand, Bai himself might have been en-couraged by hearing stories of the great White Lotus chief Wang Cong'er, who led her army of south Henan peasants through southern Shaanxi into Sichuan along similar paths in 1796–97 to link up with local White Lotus units. She and her force occupied the border despite suppression campaigns for more than a year (Shi Li 1975: 131–32).

‡Later guerrillas, learning from Bai Lang's experience, would make a more successful passage from Henan into Sichuan via Shaanxi. Two decades after Bai's death, the Fourth Red Army, fleeing from the shattered Eyuwan Soviet, not only followed many of the same mountain trails that Bai Lang's force had used (guided by an old former bandit who may well even have been there on that previous occasion), but also occupied the same towns and fought government troops at many of the same vital spots. See Chang Kuo-t'ao 1972: 310–14.

they were still a formidable force, and their capacity for rapid movement saw them back in southwestern Henan within a matter of weeks. Except for Shaanxi locals dropped off on the way and a few stragglers who drifted into banditry in various parts of Shaanxi and Shanxi, they were more or less in one piece. Only after their return did the disintegration truly set in. Finding the main roads heavily guarded by soldiers, and harried along the mountain paths by landlord-gentry militia,[77] the band quickly succumbed to the centrifugal effect of localism, always a limiting force on its development. By the time he slipped back into Baofeng in early August, Bai had only a hundred or so fighters remaining with him. Their last stand was a two-day-and-night battle in which thousands of government soldiers held back from attacking the hill on which the few score weary remnants of the once great rebel army were ensconced. It was the final, reluctant tribute to Bai Lang's astonishing charisma.

On the night of August 7, after food and ammunition ran out, Bai dismissed all but his closest bodyguards, hoping to slip away under cover of darkness, but he was surprised and cut down by a military patrol.* Bai's severed head was identified and sent to Kaifeng, where it was displayed in a cage on the great south gate as a warning to all who dreamed of following in the footsteps of the "White Wolf."

For the peasants of southwestern Henan, however, the memory of Bai Lang was not so easily erased. Despite vicious pogroms, his banner was being raised afresh within weeks by myriad tiny bands of poor-peasant marauders who continued to raid outlying rich residences and villages by night and hide or work by day. Many were Bai Lang remnants, including one band led by Zhang Qing, alias Lao Yangren, "The Old Foreigner." Born in 1893 into a desperately poor peasant family in Linru county under the shadow of the Funiu range, the twenty-year-old Zhang was already one of the most promising local successors to Bai Lang's heritage.[78]

The rise of Zhang Qing coincided with political changes on a national scale—the death of Yuan Shikai and the rise of warlordism—that would also take banditry itself onto a new plane. When thousands of defeated soldiers from the Zhili-Fengtian War of mid-1922 came streaming into the mountains of southwestern Henan, the stage was set for the emergence of "soldier-banditry."[79] Zhang Qing, now better known under his alias,[†] was the first representative of this new stage in banditry. By

---

* One source states (Cai and Xu 1980: 334) that an old man led the soldiers (at bayonet-point?) up the little-known path to the rebels' camp that Qing forces had used to sneak up on ensconced Taiping insurgents fifty years before.
† Accounts of Lao Yangren's raids refer to him by a variety of names, including Zhang Guowei (NCH, 11 Aug. 1923: 375) and Zhang Guoxin (Yanling xianzhi, I, "Dashiji": 27). The reason, according to his widow when interviewed in 1959, was that he liked to change his name every time the band reached a new spot (BLQY: 98). The

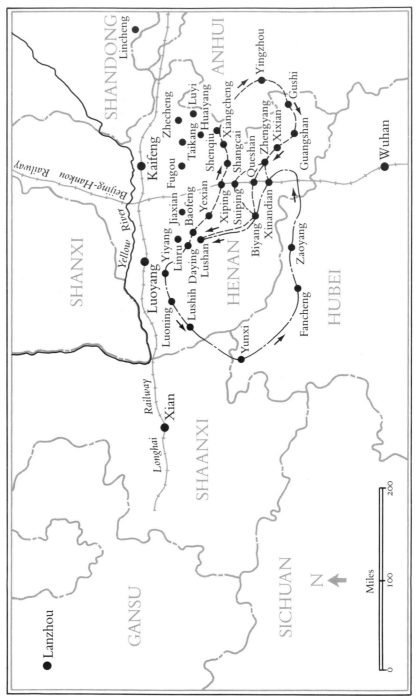

Map 5. Lao Yangren's Campaigns, 1922–23.

the summer his several thousand followers had left a string of major Henan cities in ruins. Suppression attempts failed miserably because of warlord rivalries.[80]

The soldier-bandits' principal objective was incorporation into the military, and Lao Yangren was no exception. That autumn he led his band on a two-month campaign of calculated, fast-moving destruction along a path close to that previously followed by his former commander Bai Lang. (See Map 5.) By the time they returned to their old haunts they had not only left a swath of ruin across much of Henan and western Anhui, but had also armed themselves with a dozen foreign captives as bargaining cards in their negotiations with the military. Once again foreign pressure settled the issue, and by the end of 1922 Lao Yangren was a military officer.[81]

One of the everyday hazards facing all ex-bandit officers was treachery, and in this respect too Lao Yangren was a pioneer. Only six months after the apparent realization of his dreams he was a bandit again, eluding a pincer operation by suppression troops and sweeping clear across Henan, this time to the western borders with Shaanxi and Hubei. According to eyewitnesses his forces were now 20,000 strong and more formidable than ever before as they once again sacked a chain of local towns and cities. Then in January 1924 came the sudden news that the great chief was dead, assassinated by one of his subchiefs in return for a large reward and promises of military honors. Lao Yangren's second raid had lasted just three months.[82] Those of his followers who were not absorbed by one or another local warlord scattered into the mountains and resumed banditry, awaiting the emergence of a new chief who would act as the carrier of their military ambitions. The future was rosier than they could have imagined.

---

name "Guoxin" ("Pledged to the Nation") was thus adopted to celebrate his army enrollment in 1923 (Nagano 1924: 222). Zhang Guowei ("For the Glory of the Nation"), on the other hand, was not Lao Yangren at all but one of his subchiefs, originally named Zhang Desheng, who had also decided to celebrate his new-found legitimacy. Another subchief, Li Mingsheng, took the new appellation of Li Baoguo ("To Defend the Nation") (*ibid.*).

The prefix "Lao," incidentally, is commonly attached by Henanese to close acquaintances or to those with impressive reputations, regardless of age or moral acceptability. Bai Lang, for example, was often referred to as "Lao Bai Lang," and suppression commander (later Henan military governor) Zhao Ti as "Lao Zhao," despite their very different reputations.

Zhang Qing's nickname inspired numerous tall stories. The journalist Upton Close, who claimed to have met him personally, described him as "an immense fellow with a high fur cap and entirely too much beard for a pure-blood Chinese." The bandits told him they called their chief the "Old Foreigner" because of his beard, his fluency in Japanese, and his having spent several years in Taiwan (Close 1924: 23–24). That Close probably never met Lao Yangren at all is further suggested by comments elsewhere attributing the Lincheng Incident to him (*ibid.*: 20). Just whom he did meet, however, is a mystery.

## Henan Becomes a "Bandit World"

By 1923 Henanese politics were almost totally dominated by the army. Eighty-four percent of the provincial budget for that year was consumed by military expenses, and the number of soldiers rose to un- precedented heights.[83] The level of banditry also rose accordingly: by 1924 the average Henan bandit gang—swelled by army deserters—was several thousand strong, and bands of a few hundred were considered negligible.[84] The situation was rendered even more complex by the extraordinary balance of power at the top of the province's military hierarchy, the belated effect of alliances struck between Republicans and bandits in 1911.

Many of the bandit chiefs who had played a role in the fighting of 1911 were subsequently taken on as military officers and, in combination with their former Republican advisers, over the succeeding decade became influential local figures. A typical combination was that of Han Yukun and Liu Zhenhua. Liu had risen to the military governorship of neighboring Shaanxi, and in the wake of the Second Zhili-Fengtian War of 1924 hoped to install his protégé Han in the same position in Henan. Unfortunately their ambitions were opposed by another ex-bandit militarist named Hu Jingyi, powerful because of his alliance to the great warlord Feng Yuxiang. Eventually Hu was named military governor, whereas Han received jurisdiction over only western Henan in his ca- pacity as Bandit Suppression Commander for Henan, Shaanxi, and Gansu. Not surprisingly, each of them greatly resented the other's pre- sence, and both soon set about preparations for war, swelling their forces with the vast numbers of bandits created by the suppression of Lao Yangren in January—some 80,000 of them. Any chief with eight or nine hundred followers could count on being made a regimental commander, and one with two to three hundred a battalion commander. By early 1925 the province was supporting more than 200,000 "regular" soldiers. Since payment was impossible, these troops were ordered to live off the long-suffering countryside, Han and Hu each seeking thereby to pro- voke the other into a false move.

The war that finally broke out in March 1925 was short but fierce. Thanks mainly to the defection of Zhang Zhigong, a former chief in the same band as Han Yukun, Liu and Han were routed and fled back into Shaanxi. In the aftermath of the war Liu Zhenhua was cashiered from the Shaanxi governorship, Han Yukun committed suicide, Hu Jingyi was confirmed as Henan's military governor, and the province came under the firm control of Feng Yuxiang.[85]

Marked by repeated defections and counterdefections, the affair would serve as an archetypal warlord conflict except for one significant characteristic: it ultimately amounted to a conflict between opposing forces of *bandits*, led by top commanders who were themselves *ex-bandits*, each claiming to represent legitimate authority, and each opposing the other in the name of "bandit suppression." Though the dividing line between warlord and bandit was frequently hard to define, this was probably the first time anywhere that rival forces of bandits and ex-bandits had taken over all the regional power resources and battled for legitimacy on a provincewide scale. Thus far had Henan's bandit sub-culture come.

Back in the villages, meanwhile, the level of banditry had reached unheard-of proportions and risen to unprecedented heights of brutality. In 1925, as the province became totally immersed in an "era of chaos," people looked back on the confused events of the previous year as a time of tranquillity. Military expenditure exceeded the previous year's for Zhili, Shandong, and Henan provinces *combined*.[86] Given responsibility for restoring order, the new military leaders, subordinates of Feng Yuxiang, resorted to the usual tactic of enrolling their former adversaries into their own forces, and by the summer the provincial military totaled over half a million men, mostly former bandits. People commented sardonically through folk song:

> Comes a certain army and calls up the bandits,
> Selling them bullets, selling them guns,
> Telling them they are the emperor's legions—
> Who'd believe they were all a bunch of weasels?

Those bandits who were unwilling or unable to be called up returned to the hills which many of them had left but a short time before, often claiming allegiance to the army without waiting to be officially enrolled. East of the Beijing-Hankou tracks in Zhengyang, two missionaries* sent an agitated report to the U.S. consul in Hankou describing former bandit soldiers occupying the city as "vandals of the worst kind.... Lao Yangren and his robbers were gentlemen in comparison."[87]

The confusion unleashed by this period of bandit rule completed the "banditization" of Henan. By mid-1925 a writer was conservatively estimating the number of bandits in permanently established gangs—that is, excluding those who took to banditry as a survival tactic and those tens of thousands now considered part of the military—at more than 51,000. Of these some 34,000 were active in the western mountains,

---

* Both missionaries were, in their own fashion, "bandit veterans." One, the Reverend Borg-Breen, had been held for ransom by Lao Yangren in late 1922; the other, the Reverend Holm, had been captured by Bai Lang at Zaoyang, northern Hubei, in December 1913.

11,000 in the south and east, and 6,000 in the far east and northeast bordering Anhui and Shandong.[88] Many of the plush residences dotting the plains, once host to the province's cultured elite, had either fallen into ruin or become headquarters for the innumerable bandit gangs that had come to dominate the countryside. Those occupants who had not fled or been killed remained to make the best living available from conniving with and protecting the nearest chief.[89]

Things then went from bad to worse. In 1926 the China Inland Mission's Annual General Meeting heard from a missionary with thirty years' experience in Henan how the bandit situation had deteriorated since 1911. Once, he said, bandits had attacked only the rich, and the poor were pleased because the bandits often strewed money and goods along the streets as they passed; they also protected missionaries. Nowadays, however, bandits robbed indiscriminately, taking for ransom everyone they could find.[90]

A combination of warlordism and natural calamities underlay the bandits' growing desperation. Although 1926 was yet another famine year of disastrous proportions, Henan's warlord rulers, to pay for their latest conflict, had begun to levy taxes in advance up to 1929 and in some places even to 1930. The land tax soared, the transit taxes were harshly enforced, and ad hoc military exactions outstripped everything else. The tobacco crop, worth about £15 million, was also expected to be a "dead loss," since all railway rolling stock had been sequestered and could only be used on payment of exorbitant "squeeze"; in any case, transportation was likely to be delayed for several weeks by military operations. Soon even the middle peasants were on the verge of bankruptcy, and village-defense groups like the Red Spears spread all over the province.[91]

In the autumn of that year an American traveler reported from Yong-cheng near the Anhui border: "There was not a single time or place, when I was on the major road, that I was out of the sight of refugees. They have been passing all the fall, and conditions grow worse and will continue to do so till a wheat harvest is gathered."[92]

Amid all this suffering bandits led by a north Anhui chief called "Old Chicken Wang" occupied the county seat of Xiangcheng for a month, burned down 20,000 houses, and cost the city ten million dollars in damage. The next year's attacks over a period of two months saw 3,000 dead, 30,000 homes burned, and twenty million dollars' worth of damage. In 1928 the county was again devastated after being occupied for some time by another gang. In such conditions not only did bandits lose whatever pretensions they might once have had to "social banditry"; would-be defense groups like the Red Spears too lost the wherewithal for defense and became predators.[93] It was a war of all against all.

By the late 1920's, Henan's bandits were gloomily reported ubiquitous, having spread even to the previously untroubled northern districts.[94] Many took to robbing the numerous ancient tombs dotted about the western half of the province.[95] In these "dark ages," as one local gazetteer put it, one could not go more than a few *li* outside the gates of Kaifeng without being attacked by peasants looking for guns, the province's only passport to safety since with them they might be accepted into either the army or a local bandit gang. New editions of local dictionaries, it was alleged, no longer listed the traditional proverb which held that "good iron is not made into nails; good men do not become soldiers."

As socioeconomic conditions collapsed, bandits and village-protection societies joined forces to militarize the Henan countryside almost completely, creating a situation into which outsiders entered only at their own risk.[96] By 1927 nine-tenths of the villages in seventeen once-prosperous counties south of the Yellow River were pronounced desolate, the people all having moved into the towns; the population of Suiping on the Beijing-Hankou Railway, for example, swelled to three times its original size because of the influx of refugees:

> Our family's in trouble, our home's in dire straits;
> Afraid to stay home, we fled here to the city,
> Dreading that the bandits should make off with everything.
> Our house suffers bitterly, our times are hard,
> We bought a home at $2.50 a room—
> But if the garrison mutinies, we'll be ruined forever.[97]

An eerie silence reigned in the ghost villages, for even the birds in the trees had taken wing for healthier climes. The population of Dengxian was found in a 1928 census to be half what it had been in mid-Qing times, a development blamed entirely on banditry.[98]

Conditions did not improve with the establishment of the National Government in 1928; if anything, the contrary held. The fighting of the past three years had left troop remnants scattered throughout the province and raised local tensions to an unprecedented pitch. Such was Henan's economic despoliation, moreover, that even in combination with equally ravaged Gansu and Shaanxi it could not supply its new governor, Feng Yuxiang, with all the funds and resources he needed, so that Feng began to eye neighboring Shandong, too. Ruthless taxation to supplement the provincial coffers exacerbated a new famine raging all over North China to get the "new era" off to an ignominious start.[99] Feng's campaigns against local rivals, followed by the revolt of the so-called "warlord coalition" against the government in 1929–30, were the last straws. Most of the latter fighting took place in south and west

Henan, already sorely afflicted by yet another famine that had left at least seven million destitute and sent hundreds of thousands fleeing into the cities.[100] To finance the wars, military requisitions reached a level forty times that of the land tax. Thousands of peasant conscripts were slaughtered, and crops were left to wither in the fields. Starvation became commonplace, and by 1931 the total number of bandits throughout the province was put at 100,000.[101] In 1933 a village survey lamented of the western counties that "almost everyone" was involved to some degree in banditry; not only did every household own a gun, the more fortunate even boasted machine guns, and in Linru alone there were 80,000 guns in private hands. Where bandits were most numerous the land had been allowed to grow wild and had fallen into the hands of rich (absentee) landlords,[102] resulting in more banditry. By 1937 Henan's bandits were put at 400,000 by the government's suppression commander Zhang Fang, and southern and western counties remained strongly affected throughout the Anti-Japanese Resistance War. By 1938 a Japanese journalist well-versed in bandit affairs commented that the only safe places remaining in Henan were the northern bank of the Yellow River and the immediate vicinity of Kaifeng. Those who ventured out of doors did so only if well-armed, noted local Communist organizers. Almost everyone spent the night in strong and constantly guarded local fortresses, the only security remaining.[103]

Under such conditions, bandit gangs and militant secret societies achieved a new significance. Alongside the destruction of villages and scattering of families and communities went the annihilation of the social relationships they had supported. The importance of the predatory group at such times was its capacity to persist and even thrive through its ability to employ force and other nonlegal means of subsistence. Such groups were consequently able to take over the binding functions hitherto exercised by village and family, and to play an important role when social conditions made the line between survival and extinction even thinner than usual. Under the circumstances, peasants who held up travelers for cash to buy weapons were behaving quite rationally in terms of the alternatives left open to them to ensure survival. The prospect of joining a bandit gang in the environment of 1930's Henan must surely have seemed less of a leap into the dark than at normal times.

Henan province was indicative of a trend affecting most of Republican China. Though the pace of development and degree of severity varied from province to province, the weakening of the official power structure owing to warlordism was accompanied almost everywhere by the rise of banditry. The apogee of banditry that Republican Henan symbolized saw the boundaries of the old bandit areas expand to include almost the whole province. The Royalists' and Republicans' wooing of

Bai Lang set off a trend, and before long those seeking or holding power found the bandit presence impossible to ignore. There was a dialectic process at work, for the growth of new opportunities in turn stimulated the appearance of more bandits. The result was the apotheosis of banditry itself.

## CHAPTER FOUR

# "Climbing Mount Liang": Who Became a Bandit?

*Let not the young read* Shuihu; *let not the old read* Sanguo.
—*Chinese proverb*

*Politeness and righteousness are the children of wealth and contentment; brigandage and robbery are the offspring of poverty.*
—*Chinese proverb*

"NO ONE gets into this life for the fun of it!"[1] The bandit who spoke these words put it in a nutshell. The dangers of the outlaw life relative to the prospects it offered, the "tyranny of work" which tied the majority of peasants to the soil, the responsibility of a family, and, finally, the opprobrium attached to the very expression "*tufei,*" made banditry no easy option. Those who did get into it were a minority, those whose desperation overrode such considerations. In the words of the classic aphorism, "the officials compelled the people to rebel" (*guanbi minfan*). It was a constant theme in real life as well as in fictionalized, romantic accounts of banditry like the *Shuihu zhuan,* implying that behind every bandit was the action (or inaction) of some uncaring official.

For most of its participants, banditry was a reaction to extraordinary circumstances that stretched the normal level of poverty beyond the point of endurance. It occurred first among the groups most vulnerable to economic fluctuations: those too poor to own land to fall back upon. Even then, in most places a majority preferred to wait for death than to loot to save their lives. Those who took the plunge did so because there was no alternative, and their resort to banditry was usually temporary, ending when conditions improved sufficiently to allow a return to farming.

Much more interesting than these "occasional" recruits were those whose way of life gave them the potential to become "professionals." The first candidates were the non-tillers, people whose lives were marginal to peasant society and therefore largely independent of its demands. Those who felt the need to live up to an otherwise unachievable image of heroic masculinity, or those, mainly the young, who reacted against society's humdrum demands also found banditry an attractive outlet, while people who lacked a natural family of their own often found a comforting substitute within the community of the gang. Finally, there were the people who by some act of vengeance had alienated themselves from "straight" society; those who had fallen victim to some injustice; former soldiers who craved to taste the power of the gun once more; and those for whom some personality quirk made village life impossible.

These were the traditional bandit categories. In the unsettled conditions of the Republic, social disruption and militarization made more recruits available than ever before, just as political instability increased banditry's attractiveness as a means of treading water for those whose fortunes were temporarily adrift. On the whole, it was a case of "more of the same" rather than of any qualitative change in the basic categories. People became bandits in increasing numbers because the opportunities to do otherwise had dwindled impossibly.

## The Basic Stock of Banditry

In normal times, the natural ties of extended kinship and mutual-aid traditions in a village tended to cushion the shock of social dislocation. This meant that a resort to banditry was rare where the soil could be relied upon to meet a community's needs; tillers rarely became permanent recruits to bandit gangs. Banditry tended to flourish where the land was not productive enough to sustain the local population, or where individual landholdings were so small as to leave a surplus labor force. It was this surplus that created the pool of chronically unemployed or underemployed that furnished the basic stock of banditry. "Curious[ly] enough, results of a continuous observation and inquiry coincide in this fact: That all the bandits are propertyless and they are unemployed. What they may possess is personal and comes only with the success of their reckless adventure. . . ." [2]

In many poor-peasant families there were too many sons for the tiny plot of land the family farmed, and the younger ones were forced to take up alternative pursuits. When possible they would work as part-time laborers on another family's plot; otherwise they found work guarding livestock, peddling, carrying commercial goods, and so on, or drifted into various illicit occupations like smuggling, crop-stealing, trouble-shooting, gambling, or even small-time robbery. Unstable, lacking roots in the agricultural routine, people like these were always a reservoir of potential bandits. Many were already supplementing their income by seasonal bursts of predatory activity, and when economic conditions made hunger outweigh the risks involved, or when their faces became known to the authorities, a life devoted more or less permanently to outlawry was a frequent and logical choice.

The presence of these unattached marginals was a continuous reminder to those around them of alternatives to a life spent tilling the soil. When resources sank below the minimum for assured survival, as periodically happened in most parts of China, that presence became magnetic. Under such conditions, the "village bully" came into his element.[3] In peaceful times, the aura of danger he exuded might make him the "village king," one whom the other villagers learned to leave alone. When he combined with others he drew upon a reserve of men with similar temperament but without the courage or the initiative to act individually. In bad times, the village bully might shade over into the bandit chief (although the two were by no means the same thing), and the men who gravitated to him might become his lieutenants, attracting peasants who normally preferred a more peaceful, law-abiding way of life. When local conditions declined far enough, the bandit alternative—abandoning the village for a life spent in the mountains or some similar refuge—often seemed more promising than the agricultural one, and thus a new gang was born.

The way in which village or community gangs could evolve into bandits has been noted by Eberhard. Under normal, stable conditions these landless young men would be regular farm workers, employed in the slack season to do odd jobs for their family or community such as repairing irrigation ditches or mending tools. Any crimes they committed —like stealing crops from another village, picking fights with other gangs, or individual violence—were a part of the everyday life of the village and were usually connived at by the elders. When economic conditions declined, the incipient gang's horizons began to expand. From being simply tolerated, it might actively be employed by the elders to steal from a rich landlord in another village, to beat up a tax-collector, or to rob a greedy merchant, for at times like this the community that did not learn to look after itself became a victim. In turn, other communities might mobilize for their own protection, either by requesting the help of constables, or by bringing the guilty elders to court, or by employing a gang of their own. If legal measures were taken, the usual result was that the elders went free while the original gang became scapegoats and were forced to take to the mountains to become full-time bandits.[4] When the regular turn of the seasons created large numbers of "occasionals," these permanent gangs provided both rallying points and organizational experience. Endemic banditry could thus be self-perpetuating, the passage of a gang not only attracting young men into activities previously unthinkable, but also providing the poor with a quick chance to help themselves, and even tempting the beggars to seek rich pickings in the gang's wake—if only they avoided the pursuing soldiers.* A 1927 report claimed that the massive looting of the east Henan river mart of Zhoujiakou the previous September was largely the work of local peasants allowed to help themselves in return for bringing the gang provisions.[5]

What most characterized professional bandits was their landlessness (though the chiefs were sometimes an exception). Even if they had possessed some land before joining the gang, it would have been quickly confiscated as soon as their identity was known. The social and psychological implications of this fact were profound, for possession or non-possession of land was a basic criterion of peasant society: "as long as a family owns even an inch of land they consider themselves on a par with their fellow villagers." The landless were accordingly the "out" class in much of rural China, forced to live on the outskirts of the village, and subject to various kinds of discrimination.[6] Unable to accumulate wealth, the accepted avenues of social advancement closed, people like these had nothing to lose and everything to gain from a confrontation. The decision to become a bandit, smuggler, or soldier was less agonizing than usual since there was little alternative.

South Shandong's stock of landless men had long been a favorite source of recruits for military adventures, as when the Chinese government decided to send coolie battalions to Europe in 1917 to fulfill its part in the Great War effort. Returning to find conditions unchanged and what slender ties they had once had permanently sundered, most drifted into either beggary or banditry.[7] Several of the Lincheng captives made reference to these men,[8] noting that some of them spoke English or French, or seemed to have advanced political ideas.†

In Henan, too, as noted already, non-farming occupations like ditch-digging, coal-mining, and carting were intimately tied to the tradition of banditry. Bai Lang's followers, for example, were almost all from the

---

* Hsiao Kung-chuan 1960: 706–7; Dannic 1912: 519. Beggars often maintained good relations with bandits as fellow-denizens of the underworld. A so-called "Beggars' Guild," for instance, the "Tao-fan Hui," gave free lodgings to bandits at its numerous hostels, and informed on merchants who refused to pay the guild "protection." See Stott 1927: 830–31.

† A Japanese writer (Gotō 1928: 27) has suggested that the bandits were originally inspired to carry out the holdup by films they saw in France, and sought to make trouble for the government by creating an international incident. Nagano Akira (1924: 43), however, writes that this applied only to a semi-autonomous left-wing faction within the gang represented by the ideologue Wang Jixiang, whereas the majority, represented by Sun Meiyao, were in the Liangshanpo tradition and lacked any long-range political vision.

rootless sector—vagrants, peddlers, herd-boys, wandering adventurers, strolling players. Many more were famine refugees, another fruitful source of bandit recruits when they failed to find work at the end of their wanderings.[9]

In imperial times the nationwide commercial network and the large numbers of non-farming occupations it spawned—guards, carriers, peddlers—had created vast quantities of potential recruits for bandit gangs and anti-government armies (Li Zicheng was a good example). Lacking family or village ties, linked to the regional market or even to the road itself, their rootlessness made rebellion or banditry a relatively easy decision when an economic downturn destroyed the system's cohesion.[10]

In many parts of China the racial factor also contributed to bandit traditions, usually as a result of Han Chinese expansion displacing indigenous groups and leaving them few other means of survival. Along the Inner Asian frontier, disinherited Mongols became the scourge of the encroaching Chinese communities. To the south, in Hunan, Guizhou, and Yunnan, local minorities like the Miao, the Yi, and the Tujia were forced by Han pressure to move to higher, more marginal land, where a mixture of resentment and poverty helped them to develop reputations as dangerous, predatory raiders.[11]

Frontier conditions in Manchuria also created a pool of bandit recruits. The area was originally reserved for pure-blooded Manchus, and Chinese who penetrated it in search of its natural wealth were obliged to defend both their lives and their gains against fierce repression. Even after the restrictions were lifted, pioneers failing to come to terms with local conditions were likely to be driven away and could do little but turn to banditry. The state monopoly over minerals and other valuables also automatically made outlaws of those seeking medicinal treasures such as ginseng and elk horn. The so-called "Gold Bandits" (*Jinfei*) were originally Heilongjiang gold miners who had armed themselves to fight off both government troops and roaming predators. Armed settlements such as the "Zheltuga Republic" sprang up as the miners, branded as bandits by the authorities, came to rely on their own strength to survive. The transition to genuine banditry in the form of robbing non-mining villages to swell their earnings was a fairly simple one, and was subsequently repeated by opium farmers frustrated by the corruption of the local military.

Immigration from China Proper was another factor contributing to frontier banditry. New arrivals, after working a season in the lumber camps in the mountains of Jilin and Liaoning, often gambled away their first season's pay. Unable to return home or to find work in the off-season, yet without local roots, these men had no choice but to take permanently to the now familiar mountains. Armed with unrivaled knowledge of local topography, trade routes, and hiding places, they could make a reasonable living through raiding and highway robbery. Once this step had been taken it was not easy to return to regular work. Among Manchurian bandits there were always more Chinese than Manchus or Mongols, and more China-born than Manchuria-born Chinese.[12] Japanese settlement of Manchuria in the 1930's naturally fostered banditry, too, for most of the land given to the settlers to farm had been forcibly purchased from the Chinese (or sometimes from Korean immigrants) at rock-bottom prices. Deprived of their livelihood, many peasants had no choice but to leave their families behind and live in the mountains as bandits, attacking chiefly the settlers who now occupied their old homes. Such "bandits" were natural recruits for the anti-Japanese guerrilla armies that sprang up to resist the occupation.[13]

Even where banditry was endemic, however, not everyone was equally likely to join a gang. On the whole it was young people, and predominantly young men at that, who formed the vast majority of bandit recruits. The short period before they assumed the burdens of marriage and family was the time when they were freer than they had ever been or ever would be again. With their ambition, strength, and unhampered openness to new ideas and challenges, they were a ready store of potential followers for any martial adventure.

Among the traditional armed communities, banditry seems to have been regarded as a unique chance to see the world. Young boys and occasionally girls between the ages of sixteen and twenty were even sent to do a round of duty with the local gang under the chief's personal tutelage and protection. The most promising among the "adopted youths" (*gan erzi*) were carefully groomed, and many rose to become respected fighters and even chiefs, esteemed not only for their martial experience but also for their worldly knowledge: "Some of them feel they are having an unusual opportunity for education. Banditry is a university to them. They have seen but very little outside of their own communities before.... So now they feel that, finally, the fetters have been broken and they are free.... Many mere boys are seen in the crowd. These are especially jubilant. They exclaim, 'This is quite an education! Now we get to see the world....'"[14]

Foreign captives have confirmed the preponderance of the young among their captors, from boys in their early teens down to small children. Indeed, boys in their teens made up perhaps half the personnel of the average Henan gang, the rest being mostly young men in their twenties.[15] No wonder, then, that the official wisdom abjured the young not to read the *Shuihu zhuan* lest it tempt them into rasher behavior than ever. The writer Yao Xueyin, who in his teens spent 100 days as a captive of west Henan bandits in 1924, was probably the kind of person this old adage was aimed at. Yao, a spirited youngster, took to the bandit life like a duck to water, and his captors took to him equally as he helped them burn down houses and even took part in attacks.[16]

All in all, thirty was the crucial age for banditry. Those who were not bandits but had yet to marry and settle down were reckoned to have little else before them but a life of outlawry or living by their wits; those who had been in banditry since their youth would be urged to "wash their hands" before it was too late, find a marriage partner, and care for their parents' old age. As the proverb went, "if you haven't made a success of your life by the time you're thirty, better to 'fall into the weeds'" (to "fall into the weeds" [*luocao*] was a popular euphemism for beginning banditry, just as to "wash your hands" [*xishou*] euphemized giving it up).[17] Chiefs for whom details are available all turn out to have been extremely young: Sun Meiyao (the man responsible for the Lincheng Incident) was 25, Lao Yangren was 28 or 29 at the peak of his career, two Bai Lang subchiefs were 29 and 20, and Bai's contemporary Gao Yongcheng was only 17 when he began his career. Han Yukun and Zhang Zhigong, with some years of banditry behind them, were still but 20 and 24, respectively, in 1911; in Manchuria, 25–26 was evidently the average age for chiefs.[18]

How long chiefs lasted usually depended on how they behaved. A wild one or one strong enough to threaten local security seriously could not be ignored even by the lethargic Chinese local authorities and was almost certain to be cut down in the prime of life; one who was satisfied with operating on a scale tolerable to the authorities, particularly one who set up a working relationship with them, could expect to live longer. Whereas Bai Lang lasted only three years after his decision to rebel, for example, the special conditions of the later Republican period allowed a capable chief like Fan Zhongxiu to alternate between banditry and the military for almost twenty years.* Another category of older bandits consisted of those too poor to marry, who spent their whole lives alternating between day labor and banditry. At Lincheng men like these accounted for a group of chiefs that included two in their mid-thirties, three in their forties, two in their fifties, and even two in their sixties.[19] In general, though, a high attrition rate and a hard life-style kept the average age of most bandits under thirty.

The eyewitnesses cited above also described the majority of bandits, significantly, as "boys" or "lads." For good reasons, there were very few

---

* Bai Lang was exceptional among bandit chiefs, being 39 when, despite his protests of being too old for the "dangerous path" of banditry, he was drawn into the widespread peasant disturbances in southwest Henan in 1911 (*BLQY*: 82). For another exception, see Howard 1926: 135. In connection with this point, it should not be forgotten that life expectancy in rural China was extremely short: the fifties were considered to be ripe old age, and fewer than 60 percent of people survived their tenth birthday (Davin 1979: 76).

women or girls among the bandit rank and file (though there were plenty of female chiefs). The main reason was the binding of small girls' feet, which prevented them from walking freely and prefigured the restricted existence they would lead thereafter. The active life of a bandit or rebel was clearly out of the question, except in special cases: on the North China Plain, horses allowed women greater freedom, as evinced by a number of female Nian chiefs; and in Guangxi the predominance of the Hakka minority, among whom foot-binding was rare, not only permitted the Taiping rebels to form whole regiments of women fighters, but must also have given a distinctive flavor to Guangxi banditry as a whole.[20]

Foot-binding, then, was highly successful in its intended task of keeping women at home and out of trouble. In addition, the ideology of male superiority whose outward expression it formed wrapped women in such a cocoon of obedience and timidity that banditry would have been a hard choice anyway. There was strong social prejudice against a woman leaving her home, and to be observed in the company of men was to invite malicious gossip or worse. Married women were even more housebound than young girls. Besides doing a share of the farm work, they performed subsidiary occupations as well as household chores. Moreover, whereas men's work was mostly seasonal, allowing them to turn their hands to banditry in the slack periods, women's domestic and subsidiary duties were continuous.[21]

Even without the crushing burden of life, banditry was probably far less appealing for women, for whom bravado was not culturally prescribed, than it was for men. As we shall see, the majority of women bandits, known as "female polished sticks" (*nüguanggun*),[22] made the decision to become bandits for personal reasons.

For young men, who were not subjected to such a crushing combination of physical disability, domestic work, and ideology, life presented at least the possibility of existence beyond the family, even if convention stressed filial piety. Those who could not endure the stress of kinship ties had an escape route: to leave the village and join a nearby secret society or bandit gang, thus entering a fictive kinship system whose values were closer to their own aspirations, and also acquiring the antidote to powerlessness they required to restore self-confidence.

For those able to marry, the event was the major watershed in life. An unmarried son was considered still an irresponsible child, and any scrapes he got into were usually condoned and covered over if possible by his parents. Once he married, however, his actions were not so easily excused, and the bandit option became less viable. Yet among the poor there were always those unable to afford a wife.[23] Already suffering the ignominy of being landless or almost landless in a society where prestige was measured by landholding, to be denied even the right of producing male heirs was intolerable. Such men—the "polished sticks" (*guanggun*) —usually lived with their parents until the latter died and alone thereafter. Their family ties were relatively weak, and they could even justify their becoming a bandit in terms of filial piety if they sent regular contributions for their parents' upkeep. There was always the chance, too, of acquiring a wife at gunpoint, while for those physically unable to produce their own heirs the custom for chiefs and subchiefs to adopt captured children as foster sons and daughters added still more to banditry's attractiveness.[24]

Rural practices tended to aggravate the problem. Infanticide of baby girls, for instance, resulting in a strong preponderance of men over women, meant that in places like the Huai River region some twenty percent of young men might be permanently unable to marry.[25] The implications were enormous in terms of both lost self-respect and rootlessness, and were enough to push many young men into banditry. Men with some physical disability such as a hunched back[26] may also have discovered in outlawry a salve for their injured masculine self-respect. Although they were considered liabilities as fighters and usually given mundane jobs like guarding prisoners and cleaning weapons, the fact that they were admitted to the gang at all was highly significant. Mistreatment by a step-mother following a widowed father's remarriage, a constant problem in traditional families, also provided numerous bandit recruits.

The appeal of traditional novels like the *Shuihu zhuan* was particularly powerful to young men like this, who felt themselves less than men in the village. The virile life of the armed brotherhood related by the marketplace storytellers promised the romantic element of bravado hitherto lacking in their lives.

For married men too, despite family pressures, the outlaw band had considerable attraction, and cases of poor-peasant husbands going off to become bandits while their wives held the fort alone are common enough.[27] One reason was that women of the poor peasantry, like those in poor communities anywhere, tended to be more independent-minded and critical of an unsatisfactory husband. Among the poor, despite the image of male superiority conveyed by proverbs and folklore, families dominated by the wife were not unusual.[28] Denied the chief culturally prescribed assets of patriarchal society—submissive, dependent womenfolk—and humiliated by the vision of the rich surrounded by their wives and concubines, is it any wonder that poor males should long to rediscover their lost identity in the security of the all-male brotherhood?

Alongside the quest for their stolen masculinity, many men also found the outlaw group a comforting substitute for a lost family. Such was the primary importance of the family in Chinese life—even friends and neighbors addressed each other in familial terms like "elder brother," "uncle"—that many individuals naturally came to feel dependent on their kinship bonds.[29] Though some stronger types rejected the constraints of filial ties, the lack of such ties led most people to seek alternatives elsewhere. For the poor, it was often the secret society or bandit gang that filled the bill. This applied especially among communities of people whose work took them beyond the confines of the kinship area— traveling entertainers, peddlers, transport workers, and so on—and also among poor peasants and hired hands whose natural kinship ties were either lacking or insufficient to satisfy their social and economic needs. Even Red Army commander Zhu De found, in the early days of the revolutionary movement, that the Communists were attracting the same sort of recruits as had joined the Red Gang secret society: those without a family.[30]

Secret societies and bandit gangs thus tended to increase in times when family bonds were being rapidly sundered, when people were forced to roam in search of work and security. As we saw in the case of Henan, substitute institutions like these often proved more resilient than either the family or the village, providing not only security (emotional and physical), but also a wide-ranging vehicle for acquiring forcibly the means of survival unobtainable otherwise. To emphasize the familial nature of the bond, founders were worshiped as ancestors and initiation ceremonies often involved drinking a little of each other's blood.[31] For young people in particular, the gang or society had an obvious attraction beyond the chance to display their bravado. Reports of members aged only thirteen or fourteen suggest that the lack of a guaranteed future with their natural family, compounded by family arguments resulting from such insecurity and anxiety, made the band attractive as an alternative family. One of the strongest hints that bandit gangs provided this sort of familial function is the fact that whenever possible the bodies of bandits who had been killed were carefully buried; dire punishments were meted out to any who dared desecrate their graves or who refused to return the bodies.[32]

Ex-soldiers were another vital source of bandit recruits. They too were essentially marginal and consequently free of the trammels of peasant existence. Being battle-trained as well, in the eyes of the state they were the most dangerous of all. "The more soldiers, the more bandits," went a popular saying.[33] The army had been recognized as a strong contributor to the bandit problem long before the appearance of the soldier-bandits, and in Republican China the dilemma posed by ex-soldiers became particularly acute. If army strength was increased, the men could not be paid and deserted to become bandits; if it was reduced, the discharged troops, lacking other means of livelihood, also became bandits. In imperial times the laws against vagrant soldiers had been harsh,[34] and during the twentieth century many vain attempts were made to eliminate superfluous troops. One writer even labeled the entire regular army a massive "prep school" for banditry, and by 1930 a survey of Shandong province stated emphatically that *all* bandits were soldiers of one kind or another.[35] Banditry and soldiery were often parallel modes of mobilization: whether an individual became a bandit or a soldier depended largely on local factors such as tradition and the balance of power.

According to the "Suppression of Banditry Law" of October 1912, the poor conditions in the military meant that "to station a soldier was to create a bandit." Later it was estimated that between 15 and 30 percent of all Chinese troops deserted. Lack of pay and/or provisions was the most frequent complaint, particularly as armies burgeoned after 1911.[36] Henan, for example, was a traditional recruiting ground, and the numbers of its soldiers rose steadily from some 16,000 in 1911 to more than 200,000 in 1924,[37] the lack of secondary occupations in the purely agricultural province making the army the only legal outlet for the unemployed. Owing to bad treatment and low pay, however, the army was "practically a shop for turning out bandits, and there will soon be so many of them that honest folk will be reduced to beggary."[38]

Remnant troops of a defeated army were also a potent source of bandits, especially if they retained their weapons. Having seen the persuasive power of a gun, they were hardly likely to want to settle down as farmers again. A large number of the Lincheng bandits, for instance, were ex-soldiers, the chiefs having served as officers with the former Hunan warlord Zhang Jingyao.* In 1920, after Zhang's defeat, they streamed back at the head of their men to their home area of southern Shandong to become the region's most powerful bandit presence for years. One captive estimated that ex-soldiers made up some 60 percent of the gang's numbers.[39]

Finally, disbanded troops, especially if far from home and with no means of livelihood, were natural recruits for banditry. Rather than accept the paltry severance fee they were offered, many preferred to escape to the hills with their rifles (the danger was exacerbated by the venality of many commanders, for whom discharging troops could be a source of considerable profits).[40]

Troops of the warlord Zhang Xun, for example, disbanded by the government following Zhang's abortive 1917 Manchu restoration at-

---

*Zhang Jingyao was another warlord to have made a name for himself in the campaigns against Bai Lang (Tao Juyin 1957–58: II, 45). Like many other ex-bandit militarists, he eventually went over to the Japanese (Ch'ên 1968: 596).

tempt, found themselves stranded because funds earmarked to tide them over had been pocketed by the local military commanders. As a result, most of them drifted into the mountains along the Shandong-Jiangsu border waiting for their leader's star to rise again. In combination with the former soldiers of Zhang Jingyao, who arrived soon after, they brought a new element of disciplined efficiency to the area's bandit subculture, the significance of which would become clear with the Lincheng Incident.[41]

All three categories of soldiers outlined above—deserters, the defeated, and the discharged—provided recruits for Bai Lang's rebellion. A strong current of conservative opinion at the time actually sought to write that rebellion off as no more than one of the numerous mutinies then erupting all over the country.[42] It was much more than that, as we have seen, but the presence of large numbers of soldiers in the rebel army is undeniable, and the momentum they provided as well as their role in planning strategy must have been considerable.*

Henan's troop problem dated back to the opening months of the Republic. Nervous at having so many soldiers within marching distance of Beijing, the Yuan Shikai government ordered the disbandment not only of the irregulars who had served the revolution so faithfully, but also of many regular units, particularly those known to be led by commanders with radical tendencies. These troops naturally felt resentful at being betrayed by a "revolutionary" government in whose creation they had played a major role. Fobbed off with empty honors and a few months' pay, many took to the nearest hills.[43] By May 1912 these troops, together with many more who had deserted with their weapons without waiting to be disbanded, were roaming through Henan in bands of more than 3,000, outnumbering the troops available to resist them. Two months later a new rash of mutinies and desertions was reported from all over the province. In October investigations showed that these bands had been further swollen by disbanded soldiers of the old-style Henan *Yi Jun* (Steadfast Army). Troops sent to suppress the recalcitrants, many of them their former comrades-in-arms in the recent fighting, refused to face them.[44] In May 1913, it was revealed that when the Sixth Division had been ordered south from Henan earlier that month the "entire army" had deserted.[45] More mutinies were reported throughout the ensuing months.

By November 1913 newspapers were complaining of the impossibility of distinguishing bandits from soldiers. Yet later that winter, more than a thousand overage troops were again disbanded in Henan.[46] All of these contributed to the growth of Bai Lang's rebellion, making it pos-

---

*Mutinies by disgruntled troops were a constant feature of the warlord period, and were frequently said to have been "instigated by bandits" (see Shou Kang 1923).

sible for Bai and his forces to begin attacking walled cities like Baofeng and Lushan instead of isolated towns and military outposts as before.

Apart from the firepower they brought with them, the soldiers could also appeal effectively to their former comrades within the walls not to resist.[47] During Bai's long treks east into Anhui and west to Gansu, their role was crucial in this respect: in 1914 alone, garrisons that went over to the rebels included those of Guide, Chenzhou, Nanyang, Xiangcheng, Laohekou, Jingziguan, and Fengxiang. At Fengxiang (Shaanxi) and Laohekou (Hubei), whole regiments went over; at Jingziguan in western Henan thirteen battalions followed suit—some 3,000 men if at full strength.[48] Sometimes bandit spies in the soldiers' camp seduced them with solicitations like the following:

> How poor you are! If you come over, how you will benefit!
> If you wish to drink wine, you will have a large cup;
> If you wish to eat, there is a big piece of meat;
> If you want a girl, there are numbers, here.

As a further enticement, soldiers who changed sides were offered double their current salary (Bai Lang followers were then receiving ten ounces of silver a month compared with the army salary of four ounces).[49] By February 1914 some 60 percent of Bai Lang's followers were said to be ex-soldiers, some once loyal to Shanxi governor Yan Xishan, others formerly with the Shaanxi and Henan provincial armies. Local people said that when the soldiers saw the bandits prospering they joined them; when the bandits were beaten they became soldiers again.[50]

The same kind of precarious environment that produced bandits in large numbers was also likely to engender sporadic vendettas as families or villages fought over the allocation of scarce resources. In time such feud situations could themselves develop into predatory banditry, as in one well-documented case from Jiangsu in 1928. Immigrant settlers from the poverty-stricken Huai area were resented by resident groups because of the economic threat they presented. When bandits appeared in 1927 the newcomers were immediately suspected, since they themselves rarely suffered attacks, and the angry residents burned down several of the immigrants' houses. For protection the immigrants formed a chapter of the Small Swords secret society (*Xiaodao hui*), active in their native Huai area, whereupon the residents in turn organized themselves into a branch of the locally active Big Swords (*Dadao hui*). In September 1928 some 2,000 Small Swords, aided by bandits, swept through the Big Sword villages demanding food, money, and weapons. Six villages that refused were burned to the ground, and many inhabitants were killed.[51]

As this example shows, bandits not directly concerned in a feud could also take a part in fomenting its development. Their interest in doing so was the increased opportunity for pillage or enrichment resulting from the consequent insecurity.[52] As clans grew weaker after channeling their resources into a feud, for instance, it was not unusual for bandits to be taken on as mercenary fighters. At a later stage, an entire clan might be forced to take to the hills to escape annihilation, completing the transition from feuding to banditry. In this way, clan politics, more common in South China than in the north (with the possible exception of Manchuria[53]), could also force individuals into banditry.

A common method of settling clan feuds was to accuse a person falsely of being a buying agent or intermediary for a gang, or even of being a bandit chief himself. During a serious famine in northern Fujian, for example, a wealthy but generous-minded local farmer named Su Ek proposed to other prosperous farmers that they begin selling the stored-up rice in their granaries cheaply for the duration of the famine. The others agreed readily on condition that Su Ek's bins be opened first. When Su's rice was exhausted, the poor were sent on to another wealthy farmer nearby who, according to the agreement, would sell them rice at the same price. This second farmer, however, sniffing a chance for a killing, refused to sell his rice cheaply, insisting upon the regular price. The whole agreement, in fact, had been a plot to ruin Su Ek. After a long argument, the people helped themselves to the rice they needed, leaving behind a sum of money on the terms explained to them by Su Ek. Soon after the incident this second farmer disappeared, and it later transpired that he had been in nearby Fuzhou city setting up a deal with the army for a "bandit-extermination" campaign in the famine area. The name of the bandit chief was none other than that of his rival, Su Ek; all those known to have taken part in the episode at the informer's rice bins, and those against whom he had an old score, were named as Su's followers—the more prominent among them being noted as his lieutenants. When the soldiers arrived, though Su Ek managed to escape into the forests, those left in the village suffered as people took advantage of the soldiers' presence to even old clan scores. Many innocents were shot as bandits. Finally, members of weaker clans also took to the hills and joined Su Ek, who thereafter gained a reputation as a powerful bandit chief. Guns and ammunition were purchased from illicit suppliers near the coast, and within six months these victims of circumstance had been transformed into a bandit gang hundreds strong, capable of taking on and defeating the soldiers on their own terms. Affairs like this contributed greatly to the widespread "banditization" of Fujian during the Republican period.[54]

The remote and unpoliceable hills of western and southern Henan bore a strong resemblance to western Sicily in the tradition of family feuds or vendettas (known locally as the *daye*—"retribution") that were a feature of village society there. Members of rival families frequently fought for generations as fathers on their deathbeds passed responsibility for the family's "honor" on to their sons or daughters, who, to avoid official repercussions, went off to join relations and friends in the nearest bandit gang once the vow was fulfilled. Even before they reached the gang, however, such people would have become bandits or outlaws in the eyes of the law simply by taking retribution into their own hands, though the local community took it as a matter of course. It also sometimes happened that families would sell off everything to buy guns to kill their enemies rather than resort to legal justice. As outlaws *and* destitutes, they then had no choice but to seek refuge and security in a gang.[55] As in Sicily, such feuds were never reported to the authorities, who could have done little about them anyway.*

Riots followed a similar pattern to clan feuds in the sense that, though both were essentially different from banditry, they could often force the participants to become bandits in order to avoid punishment. A good example was the series of disturbances immediately preceding the 1911 Revolution in Henan, which contributed not only to the recruitment of the peasant armies that played such a large part in the insurrection there, but also to the rapid growth of Bai Lang's rebel army soon afterward.[56] The ringleaders of the riots, once identified, were forced to take to the hills, where the abilities that had led them to the forefront of the riot stood them in equally good stead as bandit chiefs. Local gangs might even have provoked the riot in the first place for just this purpose, or in order to take advantage of the confusion to ransack the surrounding area.

A special category of bandits consisted of those coerced into joining. For most gangs these were certainly no more than a small minority of the active fighters. In parts of Henan, Yunnan, and Manchuria where gangs provided essential local security, active service with the nearest one was more or less compulsory.[57] In the case of transient gangs or those lacking such obvious local ties, the motive was less clear, for such recruits would always be a security risk as well as bad fighters. After Bai Lang occupied a town he evidently forced a number of townspeople to ac-

---

*The comparison with Sicily goes still further. In both cases there was a clear-cut division between eastern and western regions, the latter poor, mountainous, and riddled with bandit gangs, the former slightly more prosperous, less mountainous, and consequently less affected by bandits. Whereas life in the west was largely controlled by the underworld, the east was freer except in times of insurgency. Moreover, just as Allied troops could not have taken Sicily in 1944 without underworld support, west Henan bandits were essential allies for revolutionaries seeking control over the province. On Sicily, see Lewis 1967 and Maxwell 1956.

company the band when it moved on,[58] and one bandit at Lincheng claimed to have been a farmer until one night the gang raided his home, carried off his sisters, but spared his life after he agreed to join them.*

Hostile accounts have suggested that coerced bandits were forced to fight in the front line to draw the enemy's fire, those trying to escape being shot by the regulars waiting in the rear,[59] but it seems more likely that the majority of people taken on in this way were originally required as porters or servants. Bai Lang was said at one point to be seizing all single travelers and offering them the choice between joining the gang or instant execution, but a captive who escaped recalled that the first task of such victims had been to carry off the loot; those unwilling or unable to do so were shot.[60] On the other hand, it was evidently possible for conscripted porters and captives to apply for membership at a later date.[61]

Other roles people might be coerced into taking included those of doctor, blacksmith, and scribe. Bai Lang, for example, kept two men permanently on call to serve as both physician and letter-writer. Unhappily, such people, even old men and children, suffered the same fate as the other bandits if caught: a twelve-year-old boy forced to work for one of Bai Lang's subchiefs was executed by soldiers following his capture and forced confession.[62]

The state itself, meanwhile, apart from the neglect that was one of the chief contributory causes of banditry, increased bandit numbers still further by making it difficult for those already involved to give it up. Unwilling recruits were shown little leniency when captured, as we have seen. Even those who returned home voluntarily were usually arrested and executed unless they could find themselves some sort of protection by joining a landlord's militia or a magistrate's staff of runners. To the majority of bandits, therefore, as one sympathetic captive put it, "leaving seems ... exactly the same as throwing themselves into the jaws of death."[63] The Shandong soldier-bandit chief Fan Mingxin, for example, declared himself to be a victim of circumstances and a bandit against his will. On every occasion over a period of twelve years when he tried to "return to rectitude" (*fanzheng*) he had been forced back into banditry by the military's treachery in order to save his and his followers' lives.[64]

In any case, it was not easy to return to a humdrum life on the farm after having once tasted the excitement of quick proceeds and hard riding, and so the few longtime bandits who did realize their ideal of be-

* *CWR*, 2 June 1923: 3; Powell 1923b: 915. The Liangshanpo heroes also sometimes resorted to a similar sort of coercion to induce a valiant fighter to join the band, usually in order to break the strong ties of family or state (see Shih Nai-an 1963: 695). On the other hand, many bandits when caught would claim to have been coerced into the gang in the slim hope of more lenient treatment.

coming farmers again usually found themselves drawn back onto the "dangerous path." (It was the state's implicit recognition of this fact that caused it to execute all captured bandits without distinction.) Many bandits thus preferred to take up the new opportunities offered by the military, or, as with a section of the Lincheng gang, to remain bandits regardless.[65]

The last factor to be considered is lawsuits. A lawsuit could represent a major tragedy in the corrupt world of Chinse law: it could impoverish a party's family, so that no other alternative but banditry was available; or it might drive a person to banditry out of rage at injustice suffered; or it could cause a victim to flee to escape arrest. This theme, so familiar in the pages of the *Shuihu zhuan*, was still a common one in the early twentieth century. Bai Lang's family, for example, went bankrupt after selling off its land to buy him out of jail, where he had been thrown following a false accusation by a rival family. Another Henan chief, Li Yongkui, had originally been forced to take to the hills to avoid lawsuits pending against him.[66]

Though the permanent stock of marginals provided a ready store of potential chiefs for the smaller village-based gangs, in the case of larger and more complex gangs the chiefs' social origins usually set them apart from the rest. Quite a number (like Bai Lang) were from once-prosperous middle-peasant families. They had taken to banditry after their family fell upon hard times, or when they found themselves unable to get ahead in the legitimate channels of social mobility, or simply from a desire to sow their wild oats before knuckling under to family pressure, secure in the knowledge that most of their transgressions would be overlooked. Many, again like Bai Lang, fell into the category of "those who made themselves respected." People like this either formed their own gangs or rose quickly through the ranks to become chiefs, their charisma usually ensuring rapid recruitment. Others, especially in troubled times like the early twentieth century, had some military or political experience, but had found themselves in the wilderness following defeat on the battlefield or a brush with their superiors. As the Republican period showed, this enhanced role for the military made it easier for those of poor-peasant or landless/marginal origins to reach the position of major gang leader (Lao Yangren was a good example).* In the tra-

---

*In another troubled period, the years preceding the fall of the Ming dynasty, the bandit-rebel Zhang Xianzhong, known like the ex-bandit warlord Zhang Zongchang chiefly for his propensity for violence, managed to become the dynasty's second-strongest rival. It was his counterpart Li Zicheng, however, with more political acumen, who was finally to take Beijing and put an end to the Ming (Shih 1967: 380–82; Parsons 1970: 247–52).

ditional bandit areas, too, it was not uncommon for children of impoverished families to become widely respected gang leaders alongside those of more affluent origins.

As an illustration of this last point we may cite the contrasting cases of Du Qibin and Gao Yongcheng (alias Qin Jiaohong), leaders of strong local gangs in southwestern Henan in the period immediately preceding the rise of Bai Lang (in fact, it was their capture and execution in late 1912 that made Bai the principal chief in this region). Du was from a distinguished and prosperous Baofeng literati family, and had received several years of classical education. Unfortunately, he was extremely hot-tempered and turned bandit after being double-crossed by the local magistrate. His gang soon overshadowed all the other local ones, and many lesser chiefs (including Bai Lang) came under his wing when he first emerged as a chief in early 1911. After the end of the insurrection Du sought to negotiate recruitment terms with the local army commander, but the terms were rejected by his followers as unsatisfactory and Du remained a bandit.

Gao Yongcheng, on the other hand, was a typical "greenwood hero": born into a landless poor peasant family, a "hooligan" (*wulai*) since childhood, adept at shooting and strong in a fight. His nickname Qin Jiaohong ("Red Pepper Qin") came from the fact that when angered he would turn bright red. Gao was still only seventeen or eighteen when he became a bandit following the execution of two of his brothers, but he soon led 500 followers, with many more ready to take his orders when called upon.[67]

A good example of a chief driven into banditry by frustrated ambition was the Lincheng leader Sun Meiyao, who justified his actions in terms appropriate to any rebel: "This is to notify the facts [*sic*] that we have hitherto been law-abiding citizens, and that we have no desire to become robbers; but in this troubled era of unreliable government we find ourselves compelled to take risks in order to obtain redress for our grievances." One of Sun's subchiefs echoed his sentiments: "I am a very polite man. . . . All I want is our political rights in this district."[68]

The high degree of militarization that resulted from the 1911 disturbances also created a stratum of disappointed would-be leaders. After the fighting ended, many local defense groups, considered little better than bandits because they were irregulars, sought to get themselves recognized as regular military units, only to be rejected as their erstwhile Republican allies compromised with the new authorities and forgot their ties with the "country heroes."[69] Even among bandits who were regarded as popular champions, there were few who did not cherish the desire to see themselves acknowledged as something more—whether as army officers or as rebels. To be cast back into the role of mere bandits was intolerable.

Political injustice could also drive a person into crime, as those formerly holding legitimate positions found themselves out in the cold following some sudden swing of the pendulum, or became scapegoats to protect their superiors. For people like these banditry offered a means of survival as well as a breathing space to plan their revenge. Two chiefs encountered by an American captive were typical. One a former police magistrate, the other a militia captain, they burned with resentment at the treatment they had received, and both had turned to banditry to seek revenge. Another chief of the same gang was a former subordinate of Zhang Zuolin who had fallen afoul of Zhang's hot temper.[70] As the level of political complexity increased in any given area, the number of chiefs created in this way grew proportionately. A career in such circumstances, unless one was very deft, could be extremely hazardous.

Flight following a retribution killing (or "righteous homicide") was another classic category. Like the traditional hero Guan Yu of the *Romance of the Three Kingdoms*, Zhang Damazi, an early bandit associate of Zhang Zuolin, "climbed on his horse" (*shangma*) after killing a number of distant relatives in revenge for some past affront. Significantly, the retributive act was considered necessary or justifiable within the home community, though it was a crime in the eyes of the law. West Henan chief Han Yukun had been forced to leave home after killing a local tyrant who had murdered his brother. Another chief in the same gang, Guan Laojiu, had been obliged to flee after killing two bullies in revenge for the death of a friend.[71]

Also within this category fell chiefs such as Gao Yongcheng, whose primary motivation was to avenge some official atrocity. He Long, one of the few Communist generals to graduate from banditry, was popularly reputed to have murdered a local magistrate who had killed He's uncle for tax arrears. Forced into the hills, He quickly gained a kind of Robin Hood reputation for aiding the poor and never taking for himself.[72]

A number of female chiefs began their careers to avenge a husband's death. This was the case with Su Sanniang, a bandit turned Taiping rebel.* Another example comes from Yunnan in our period. In 1920 the influential bandit chief Yang Tianfu had been enrolled with his forces as a military unit, but in a subsequent political struggle Yang was executed as an associate of the ousted military governor Tang Jiyao. Yang's

---

* Su Sanniang and her fellow chief Qiu Er were among the first bandit leaders to join the Taiping rebels when the latter called for recruits in 1851. The women controlled some 2,000 followers each, and they were set to serve as outposts on either flank of the main army (Meadows 1856: 151; Curwen 1972: 69). Though Qiu Er soon left to resume banditry (she was captured and killed by imperial forces almost immediately), Su Sanniang remained until the end. Enjoying a powerful reputation for "killing the rich and helping the poor," she became the hero of many a poem extolling her exploits (Jen Yu-wen 1973: 67–68). See also Qiao Zhiqiang 1981: 537–40; Lin Paohang 1961: 542).

widow promptly led some 20,000 of his followers back to the mountains to commence a campaign of terror against the new government, under banners reading "To Avenge My Husband's Death!" She continued bandit activities for the next year, finally being called upon to lead the advance guard of Tang Jiyao's triumphal return to power.[73] Her subsequent fate is not recorded, nor is that of the widow of the Shaanxi chief Guo Jian, another woman to take to banditry to avenge her husband's murder by the authorities.[74]

Among the many female chiefs in Jilin province, one of the best known was Yizhi Hua ("Flower," nickname of a female *Shuihu* hero), who operated in the mid-1920's in the Changchun area. Formerly the "daughter of a respected family," when her husband was arrested without cause she flew into a rage and became a bandit. Women chiefs with her charisma had little difficulty in attracting followers, and she soon had a thousand at her command.* Another episode from Manchuria relates the story of a young girl who began her bandit career by setting out with pistols blazing to kill a local chief who had murdered her father. Xu Qunpu was yet another woman to find herself a bandit in this way, going on to play an important role in the popular resistance to the Japanese invasion in the 1930's.[75]

In Henan, among the famous chiefs of the Republican period was Zhang Guafu, the "notorious Widow Chang." To avenge the murder of her two sons by enemies, Zhang sold the family property to buy guns (in true western Henan style) and launched herself into banditry calling herself a "savior of the people." The wife of the north Anhui chief Xiao Qunzi (like most of the other women, her own name is not recorded) also took up arms and became a bandit after Xiao was treacherously murdered by Lao Yangren.[76]

Banditry was a hard life. Recruits mostly joined because they had to. For the "occasionals" it was a temporary resort to tide them over a crisis, and improved conditions sent most of them back to their farms. For the "professionals," a combination of economic, political, and psychological factors overrode any initial reluctance, making the hardships involved a secondary concern. Usually lacking the land required to make an "honest living," most bandits of this sort could not give up the life even if they wanted to. Humiliated as men or outraged as wives, sick of being

---

*He Xiya 1925a: 79; Nagano 1938: 287–88. Another source (Gotō 1928: 56–58) claims that Yizhi Hua was actually a former *geisha* who married a local bandit chief and changed her name to conceal her Japanese origins. After the chief fell ill, she took over command of his followers and became an acknowledged chief herself. Other Japanese women who found themselves at the head of bandit gangs will be discussed elsewhere. For details, see Watanabe 1964: 55–57, 125–33, 175–82; Tsuzuki 1976: 310–23; Watanabe 1981: 308–16.

victims or scapegoats, charged by bravado or battle-hardened, languishing for lack of family bonds or just incapable of enduring the humdrum life-style village society demanded, these "professionals" revealed through their range of motivations the real complexity of twentieth-century Chinese banditry.

## CHAPTER FIVE

# "Fierce Democracy":
# The Creation and Organization of
# a Bandit Gang

*I was beginning to learn that this band had a company organization,*
*with its officers, its bank account, and its own system of records and*
*bookkeeping.* —*Howard 1926: 98*

WITH SO MANY motives driving people of different sorts into banditry, the methods that gangs adopted to keep themselves together
naturally require examination. He Xiya depicts bandit chiefs as despots
worshiped by their followers, whose only source of exultation was the
loot from their raids.[1] Though this description contains some points of
truth, the reality was more complex, as this chapter will seek to show.

The first binding element in any gang was the fact that its members
were all fugitives from the law, seeking safety in numbers and united by
their common involvement in crime. Their immediate priority was not
to get caught, so in choosing a leader they naturally looked for someone
capable of holding the gang together in the face of superior odds. As
typified in the *Shuihu zhuan*, loyalty was inspired above all by a leader's
ability to command respect. This led in turn to a system of personal allegiances that provided the gang's second binding element. Third, since
people often joined a gang in an attempt to gain acceptance in a surro-
gate family, gang structure and values usually reflected that fact. Finally,
and possibly most importantly, there was local affiliation. When government pressure or enticement made martial valor meaningless and personal loyalties shaky, it was the local factor that usually remained to bind
together the gang's hard core. All in all, then, it took more than just
strength to become a successful chief. A combination of brain, brawn,
luck, and charisma was indispensable to make a mark on society and
maintain control over volatile followers.

There were three basic types of bandit outfit: the simple gang, often seasonal and tied to a small locality; the complex gang, larger, sometimes permanent, and wider-ranging; and the bandit army, thousands or tens of thousands strong, operating over and partially controlling a considerable geographical area, and possessing under suitable conditions the potential for rebellion. The larger a gang grew, the less cohesive it threatened to become without the addition of more formal organization. Where the small village gang relied largely on the personal relationship between leader and followers, the larger gang had to possess a certain degree of organization and discipline, plus a flexible command structure—if only to allow it to beat a decent retreat. In many complex gangs the delegation of duties and the status hierarchy were extraordinarily elaborate. Most major gangs also adopted a set of disciplinary rules that were, from the point of view of survival, entirely logical: keep secrets, help other members when in need, and so on. The methods adopted to ensure a cohesive organizational structure provide a fascinating counterweight to the standard presentation of banditry as mere haphazard pilfering studded by occasional explosions of cruelty. One aspect of He Xiya's characterization, however, holds true: leadership was strictly enforced, whatever the size of the gang. Until challenged, the leader reigned supreme—though not omnipotent—over a kind of "fierce democracy" among the rank and file. Authority, absolute in theory, varied according to the situation: strong when in camp, laxer when out on a forage.

## How Gangs Were Created

Smaller gangs, often numbering no more than a score or so, generally coalesced around a chief with charisma, meaning the ability to command the respect of the rank and file through thick and thin. The "simple gang" was the basic bandit unit, closely tied to its particular locality, which it defended to the best of its abilities against encroachment by enemies (though not to the point of endangering its own existence). It generally operated on a seasonal basis, and was a standard feature of many rural communities. Most of its members were those dissident marginals described in the last chapter; apart from a hard core whose faces were known, most came and went between the gang and the community, working in the fields when there was work to be had, returning to the gang when not.

Gangs were usually very jealous of their local sway—or at least their leaders were. The bounds of their territory, coinciding with those of the village or marketing area with which they identified, were often safeguarded by regular patrols or scouting parties, especially in Manchuria.[2] Feuds between gangs were common enough, particularly where a valuable prisoner was involved, but the commonest relationship was cool nonbelligerence.[3] If soldiers or militia tried to exploit a territorial dispute to launch an attack, rival gangs would usually join forces until they were driven off.[4]

This "unity among thieves" was always a transient, pragmatic affair. Gangs from adjacent areas maintained friendly relations and even cooperated as long as each received equal dividends. A powerful gang like that of Bai Lang, or one with some promising captives, did not usually experience much opposition from other gangs regardless of existing animosities. Even a band being pursued by troops would be allowed to cross another's territory—after making a formal application—if it could do so without endangering the hosts, and if some profit seemed likely to accrue. But where the hosts' safety could not be guaranteed, such a gang would be resisted by force or even sold to the military.[5]

There were certain conditions, however, that could bring gangs together in at least temporary alliance—pressing economic conditions, mutual danger from troops, or the rise of an outstanding new leader. Above all, in areas liable to natural calamity, this basic pattern of isolated simple gangs could change. Destitution simultaneously affecting the territory of several simple gangs made it illogical to continue independent activities, and leaders often agreed to merge their forces at least for the period of the crisis.[6]

The "complex gangs" that resulted usually operated much more widely, for the obvious reason that the foraging necessary to survival had to be extended beyond the area affected by the calamity. Where banditry was endemic, the complex gang was the standard pattern, gangs coming together or falling apart as local conditions and the whims of their leaders dictated. Some formed temporary alliances at the beginning of the busy season in late summer when the gaoliang was high, but at other times kept mostly to themselves. Even after such an alliance was formed the new gang usually operated as a combined unit only to carry out whatever big raid it was planning. A common practice was for component gangs to operate independently for a while to confuse and tire any pursuing troops, regroup at an appropriate time to carry out the raid, then split up again until the next occasion.[7]

Complex gangs were also formed in response to tactical considerations, less able leaders seeking to join forces with those of superior ability or prospects (even a marriage between two chiefs was by no means unheard of). In the wake of the train wreck at Lincheng, for example, bandits from the nearby mountains of Anhui and Jiangsu flocked to join the Shandong gang that had carried out the attack. Even after troops had cordoned off the area, bandits made constant attempts to break through. One of the original gang's chiefs told a captive that he could raise between 4,000 and 10,000 followers at a moment's notice.[8] The lure, of course, was not only the prospect of a large ransom for the foreign captives, but also the strong possibility of military enrollment in the aftermath of the affair. In Bai Lang's case, too, a neighboring chief named Sun Yuzhang chose to join him only at the height of his power in 1914. Sun was a noted chief in his own right, "for years the ravager of South Henan" (as one source put it), but because their spheres of operations were quite distinct no alliance had hitherto been discussed. Such alliances did not always work out as hoped, and Sun was reported killed in the final stages of the rebellion.[9] Had he resisted the temptation to join Bai Lang and preserved his local connections, he might well have survived for some years longer.

Mutual protection against superior odds was another frequent catalyst. At Lincheng it had been the military's harsh suppression campaigns that originally pushed angry and desperate local chiefs into a protective alliance. Once the affair had died down, damaging attacks by local Red Spears again prompted several prominent south Shandong chiefs to combine their forces.[10]

When all the above circumstances combined in sufficient degree, the result was the "bandit army," an array of several complex gangs each under its own semi-autonomous chief and subchiefs, swelled to enormous proportions by local marginals, famine refugees, and so on. Even before the phenomenon of soldier-banditry arose, bandit armies of this kind had been regular features of peasant unrest. Among the followers of Li Zicheng, for example, were many ex-soldiers and permanent outlaws who had "evolved a predatory and highly militarized ethos... quite at variance with the passive life-style of ordinary peasants."[11] In modern times, too, this type of banditry, like the roving guerrilla or *haiduk* model cited by Hobsbawm, could frequently verge upon rebellion.[12] The attitudes of the participants, particularly the leaders, were transformed by the very size of the gang, which swelled their egos and bolstered their confidence. Moreover, isolation from the peasant routine brought a sense of untrammeled liberty.

The best twentieth-century example of the bandit army before the rise of the soldier-bandits was that of Bai Lang. Bai was described by a captive as inspiring "absolute confidence."[13] His approach at the head of his few thousand regulars usually triggered widespread local mobilization, and by absorbing these minor gangs he was able to command a force several times larger. At the sack of Guangzhou in southeastern Henan, for instance, more than half the bandits accompanying him were recognized as locals.[14] More distant bands, through some sort of rural grapevine, simply acknowledged his prowess from afar, and not infrequently used his name too. By early 1914 the press was reporting "Yellow

Wolves," "Black Wolves," and bogus "White Wolves" in most of the provinces surrounding Henan and even as far south as Fujian and Guangdong[15] (though in Fujian a "wild bandit" who exploited a reputed chief's name received an automatic death sentence from the offended chief[16]). Such gangs were a potential source of recruits should Bai Lang happen to come their way. Even more interesting, leaders of more consciously political peasant insurrections as far away as Shanxi and Sichuan established formal paper alliances with Bai,* showing two directions in which his own rebellion might have expanded had things gone differently.

Local gangs which latched onto an army like Bai Lang's were often used as diversionary or rearguard forces while the main force made its escape.[17] This sort of relationship was not as one-sided as it at first seems, for the local gangs, possessing greater mobility than a bandit army, could use their familiarity with the terrain to slip away unseen. Charges in various hostile sources that Bai Lang exploited such locals to absorb the shock of attacks[18] were usually the result of grasping the wrong end of the stick. In return for the risk they did run, such local gangs stood to gain more profits from the alliance than were likely to come their way otherwise.

From the long-term political point of view, this policy of exploiting the occasional elements was self-defeating, but there was often no choice. Under constant military pressure, Bai Lang was forced to use these least reliable elements to protect his hard core, whereas under ideal conditions he might have assigned cadres to turn them into disciplined fighters, or even used them to establish the nuclei of local guerrilla bases. As it was,

---

* *STSB*, 21 June 1914: 9; Huang Guangkuo 1960a: 27. According to official reports (see *ZFGB* 755 [13 June 1914]), Gong Fukui, the leader of the Shanxi insurrection, had formerly been an officer under local warlord Yan Xishan. Like Bai Lang, he was said to have revolutionary advisers serving with him (*NCH*, 11 July 1914: 151), and his own revolutionary ties went back at least to 1907 when he was sent by the Alliance (*Tongmeng hui*) to Suiyuan as an agitator. He remained in the area for several years, and was a major figure in the 1911 insurrection in north Shanxi (*XHGMHYL* V: 197, 200–201, 203). Newspaper accounts (*STSB*, 21 June 1914: 9, 11 July 1914: 9), however, described him as a rich merchant. In July he was reported to have led his four thousand followers into Shaanxi, and since many of them had formerly been with the Shaanxi provincial army, his intention may have been to link up with Bai Lang's force as it returned home from Gansu. As luck would have it, Gong was heavily defeated and forced to retreat into Mongolia. Like Bai Lang, he gave himself the title "*Da Han jiangjun.*" Bai Lang remnants presumably trying to reach him in the autumn of 1914 were quickly mopped up by Yan Xishan (*XHGMHYL* V: 183). Along with many other 1911 revolutionaries, Gong eventually found his way into the regular military, and in 1925–26 was a brigadier-general under Feng Yuxiang (Wen Gongzhi 1930: II, 38, 177, 180, 303; *DFZZ* 22, no. 1 [10 Jan. 1925]: 111).

Gong Fukui's Sichuan counterpart was Xie Bingkui. The possibility is strong that this connection was at least partly contributory to Bai Lang's decision to attempt to find a refuge in that province.

of the 50,000 fighters who allegedly followed him at the height of his career, apparently only the first of the three great sections that made up the army, composed mainly of local recruits, did any real fighting. This kind of organization, geared to the needs of war rather than those of popular mobilization, has been cited as a principal cause of Bai Lang's eventual defeat.[19]

## The Structure of Command

Though gang alliances were a normal part of bandit strategy, the unity thereby achieved was circumscribed by the need of individual chiefs to retain their followers' loyalty. Although lesser chiefs might recognize another's superior ability, their ultimate motivation was either survival or self-advancement. Seen on paper, the formation of complex gangs seems ideal: chiefs (*toumu*) of several minor gangs, also known as "family heads" (*dangjiadi*), might decide to blend their forces of "younger brothers" (*dixiong*) and "elder brothers" (*dage*). Acknowledging one among them as "supreme leader" (*datoumu*) or "patriarch" (*dajiazi*),* they thereby agreed to submit to the latter's overall guidance, and to become his or her subchiefs or lieutenants (*xiaotoumu, erdangjia, erjiazi,* etc.); rank-and-file members remained younger and elder brothers.[20]

The use of terms like "family head" and "brother" was not coincidental. The bandit gang, at whatever level of complexity, was a power hierarchy modeled upon and sometimes even substituting for that of the traditional Chinese family. As in the natural family, the authority of the patriarchal "family head" was total, allowing the chief to hold all wealth on behalf of the gang as a whole and to delegate appropriate shares to other members. Just as in the traditional family subordinate members had no individual right to dispose of family property, so rank-and-file bandits, overseen by their subchiefs, were expected to turn their personal takings over to the gang.

What distinguished the bandit gang from the traditional family was that it provided a mode of family organization that did not conform to the vertical, filial pattern laid down by Confucian orthodoxy. The *Shuihu zhuan* provided the model; although its legendary heroes gave first priority to establishing the order of seniority among themselves,[21] authority in the gang was fraternal, not paternal, structured along elder

---

*The terminology varied according to locality. In Manchuria the terms *zonglanba* and *lanba* were commonly used to mean "supreme chief" and "chief" respectively (Watanabe 1964: 15; Kuchiki 1966). Other gangs, such as the Lincheng one, replaced the former with *zonggui*, literally meaning "general manager" (Tanaka 1934: 156; Cai and Xu 1980: 1288). For a highly readable account of Zhang Zuolin's early alliances, including vivid descriptions of the haggling over ranking, the selection of outlaw names, and the swearing of blood oaths, see Yu Ming 1965: 38–47.

brother—younger brother lines, not parent-child ones. Ties were confirmed by the taking of vows of blood brotherhood binding on all those who considered themselves "good fellows" or *haohan*. These vows, which produced great loyalty and solidarity among their takers, also created a more egalitarian atmosphere within the gang.

Yet the fictional Liangshanpo community of outlaws was an ideal case, not an authentic one. By authorial design as much as by historical precedent, the forces of authority make no serious attempts to eliminate the gang until the novel approaches its close. The kinds of relationships that pertained among the *Shuihu* brothers were most likely to be honored in the breach when survival was at stake. Though the book makes bare mention of the rank-and-file membership at Liangshanpo, they were in fact the most important attribute of any chief, and in most real-life gangs a clear pecking order was established according to the strength of each chief's following.

Though the supreme leader of the complex gang always made the major decisions concerning both internal affairs (such as distribution of income) and external affairs (such as ransom discussions),[22] the subchiefs (who often included one or more personal relatives of the chief) provided a secondary level of command. In the event of the chief's death or absence, they could take over to prevent the gang's disintegration, taking primary responsibility for their own followers while seeking to restructure the gang according to the previously established hierarchy. They had the right to participate in all decisions concerning the gang's future, and the possibility of their seceding placed limits upon the supreme leader's power.* The Lincheng gang, for example, established a kind of "committee system" consisting of six major chiefs who discussed all moves among themselves before coming to a decision. All were well-known chiefs in their own right, some originally from Jiangsu, others of local origin. Sun Meiyao and other top leaders could thus attend ransom negotiations without jeopardizing their control, or send subchiefs to negotiate on their behalf if necessary. Other reports mentioned a total of *three hundred* subchiefs, among whom twelve of the most important were responsible for discussing the prisoners' release.[23]

In part this multiple command structure reflected a gang's diverse origins. At Lincheng, as we have seen, many of the chiefs owed ultimate allegiance to former warlord patrons like Zhang Jingyao and Zhang Xun; others had previously been officers under Henan's former military governor Zhao Ti; still others were of pure bandit origin, hailing from various parts of eastern China. The frequent conferences held after the

---

* After Li Zicheng's capture of Beijing in 1644, it was observed that "Although rebel Li is the chief, there are more than twenty who hold power in balance, and everything is decided by the group as a whole." See Shih 1967: 378.

attack[24] almost certainly indicate that subsequent plans had yet to be agreed on. The most radical divergence in views was between the older and younger chiefs: the former, with long records, saw few prospects in the regular army even should the authorities agree to enroll them; the latter viewed the military as the most promising option available. Negotiations for the captives' release deadlocked until the older "professionals" were guaranteed the right to remain bandits and to retain their Chinese prisoners after their fellow-chiefs had been commissioned as officers. In the meantime, much of the Jiangsu group had evidently already slipped away with its share of the proceeds without waiting to haggle over the captives.[25]

Bai Lang's command structure also included several subchiefs (known as *gantou*, or "support heads," their component gangs being referred to as *gan*, "supports") who had been noted gang leaders before they joined him. Song Laonian and Li Hongbin were prominent examples, permitted to use Bai's name even when leading raids themselves[26] (a practice known in south Henan slang as *jiao paizi*).* Song (after he lost an eye in a clash with soldiers he was often referred to in official and press reports as Song Yiyan or "One-Eyed Song") had already been a bandit for some years before Bai Lang emerged.† His name is recorded as early as 1908, and again in the summer of 1911;[27] but it was not until two years later, when Bai's supremacy was assured, that he brought his 2,000 fighters over to his side.[28] Aged only 22 or 23, he eventually became the older Bai's adopted son (this was a frequent practice in bandit gangs). He maintained his separate identity throughout the campaign, leading raids on his own account and usually mentioned by name,[29] and at one point the entire army became known as the "Bai-Song bandits." Named the official inheritor of Bai Lang's mantle, Song eluded the government's reprisals and escaped with a thousand or so followers to northern Shaanxi, where he became a small-time militarist in the provincial army led by another ex-bandit named Chen Shufan.[30]

Li Hongbin, the army's leading tactician after Bai himself, was already commanding his own band by September 1912.[31] Known as the

---

* *BLQY*: 85; *STSB*, 14 Dec. 1913: 8. It was customary in south Henan for those who had made the decision to become a bandit to proclaim the fact publicly in a loud voice. The custom was known as "calling one's name" (*jiao paizi*), and the term was extended to include the practice of subchiefs acting in their superior's name. When Bai Lang had expressed reluctance to "enter the greenwood" in 1911, already active chiefs threatened to "call his name" anyway so as to leave him no other choice (*BLQY*: 82).

† Song Laonian's sister-in-law, recorded under the name "Mrs. Zhu," had also been a well-known bandit chief, operating alongside her husband Song Laoda. Her shooting and riding skills soon brought her the nickname "*Shuihu* Tiger Mother" after one of the female heroes of the book. Captured by soldiers in early 1914, she sang ballads reviling the authorities on her way to execution, and proclaimed her impending death as a glorious climax to her career (*STSB*, 14 Apr. 1914: 4).

rebel army's best planner and fighter, he was responsible for rearguard operations during the western expedition until his death in Gansu in mid-1914.* A captured subchief testified before his execution in 1914 that all the chiefs working under Bai Lang—among whom at least one was a woman (named Yi Laopo)—had a distinct identity that he or she *chose* to subordinate to Bai's own.[32] Defeat in battle simply meant that the gang went underground, scattering to confuse pursuing troops and regrouping later at a prearranged rendezvous.

With such a cellular structure, decisions affecting the whole gang inevitably involved lengthy and heated discussions. Bai Lang's experience again provides useful examples. In March 1914 Bai called a great conclave on the Shaanxi border to debate with his subchiefs whether to adopt mobile warfare or set up a permanent base in the familiar mountains of Henan. The site was only a few miles from that of a similar strategy meeting called by Li Zicheng in 1635, and in both cases the decision was hotly debated. In Bai Lang's case, though all the major subchiefs eventually accepted the decision for mobile warfare, many of the lesser ones did not. Activities thus continued in Henan even during the main body's absence in the west.[33] A second conclave followed in Gansu two months later after Bai's forces failed to break through into Sichuan. Royalists were pushing to declare a new dynasty; others argued against beating about on the borders of Tibet when Henan itself provided a perfectly safe sanctuary within easy reach of Beijing; still others were simply homesick, particularly after a typhoid epidemic claimed numerous lives, or were fed up with the constant hunger and the buffetings received at the hands of anti-Han militias. Many fighters as well as a number of the best subchiefs had already been lost, and Bai, though he and his revolutionary advisers favored another push toward Sichuan, finally had no choice but to begin the long journey home.[34] Back in Henan, pressed by soldiers and vigilantes on all sides, he assigned the majority of the army to his lieutenants and slipped away with those he most trusted—those from his own village (including his next-door neighbor), the gang's real hard core.[35]

The organization of complex gangs was thus cellular, component

---

* *ZFGB* 783 (11 July 1914). There were in fact two Li Hongbins, both using the same characters to write their names. The second one, known as "Little Li" to distinguish him from his older, more experienced namesake (*ZFGB* 741 [30 May 1914]), was an associate of the noted subchief Wang Chuanxin who, rather than accompany Bai's main force when it moved west into Shaanxi, had remained behind with a thousand or so others in the impregnable fortress of Sow Gorge. Li's gang continued to be active even after Bai Lang's death (*Xiping xianzhi*, "Feijie": 3b). After "washing his hands" of banditry and escaping to Wuchang to seek work, he was tempted to return to Henan by the news that rebel remnants were being recruited into the provincial army. En route he was recognized and arrested in August 1915 and made a full confession (Du Qunhe ed. 1980: 221–22).

groups pledging obedience to the overall chief while maintaining their own identities and owing ultimate allegiance to their original leaders (they also retained the right to their own captives, apparently).[36] The strengths of such a federal structure were enhanced democracy, a clearly defined chain of command, the capacity to disperse and regroup at will, and the possibility of delegating authority when necessary. The weaknesses mostly derived from the fact that loyalties were personal; the cellular pattern meant that cells had almost complete liberty to leave and—since most chiefs were basically looking after their own interests—often did. Hard realities rather than a desire for structured responsibility itself prompted chiefs' decisions to merge their forces, a fact that made them less than reliable allies.* Though paying lip service to the supreme chief, subchiefs retained jealous control over the people they had brought into the band; and should necessity so dictate, they were never loath to swing them behind another force that offered better prospects (this was less true of chiefs with a consciousness of personal mission, and also sometimes of those who had established blood-brother relations among themselves, though the latter could be a flimsy tie). Decision-making crises and revolts against the leadership were thus as common among twentieth-century bandits as they had been among the peasant rebels of history; as one writer put it, life for a chief was "as delicate as walking on eggshells."[37] In the end, as Bai Lang's experience showed, the strongest factor on which the beleaguered chief could fall back was the emotional tug of native-place sentiment, which often took precedence even over loyalty to the gang itself.

Not surprisingly, a gang's internal harmony varied according to its fluctuating fortunes. Although Zhang Zuolin, the bandit chief turned dictator of Manchuria, surrounded himself with former bandit confederates right up to his death in 1928, the wavering, even treacherous attitude of the latter when he seemed about to be toppled by a revolt of professional officers in 1925 was highly instructive.† Moreover, since the

* The problem of maintaining authority over their subchiefs had always been a thorny one for rebel leaders. Huang Chao, after expelling the Tang emperor from Luoyang in A.D. 880, faced difficulties with his generals, mostly formerly independent gang leaders who expected great rewards and high ranks in return for acknowledging Huang's supremacy. Since there were not enough spoils to be shared equally, the former emperor was able to stage a comeback by winning over the disgruntled generals (Eberhard 1965: 93–94). Li Zicheng, too, when he asked his followers to refrain from looting after their capture of Beijing, was told, "The power of being an emperor belongs to you, the power to loot belongs to us. Please say no more" (Shih 1967: 378).

† Sonoda 1927: 557; McCormack 1977: 165–67. In this sense there was little difference between the bandit gang and the average warlord army, even where the officers were not, like Zhang Zuolin's, former bandits. Both ultimately relied upon a loose alliance of chieftains bound by personal allegiances to one individual recognized as supreme; both progressively lost cohesion as the leaders sought to increase the number of their followers. As a result, alliances among both warlords and bandits were strictly short-term (see

overall chiefs always profited more than the others from whatever good fortune accrued to the gang, the subchiefs were naturally alert to the chances of putting themselves in their shoes. The authorities were equally aware of this fact, and frequently exploited it in their attempts to put down troublesome gangs.

It was an age-old axiom of antibandit strategy that the first priority was to get rid of the leader, after which the rest would take care of itself. This could be done in various ways. One of the most common was to send in a former bandit to notify the subchiefs of the rewards they might expect from betrayal. Another was to announce a graded list of bounties to entice those with a price on their heads to sell out the leader and save their own skins:

> The effect upon those whose names were on the list was profound. The whole band was stunned. The "marked hung-hutzes" went back to their huts with pale and anxious faces. They had heard their doom pronounced—the same as if they had been called by name to place their heads upon the executioner's block. This, indeed, was serious business. From now on, it was war to the death. . . .[38]

With leaders who enjoyed popular support, this was probably the only way of eliminating them short of a scorched-earth campaign costly in lives, money, and credibility.* If they were powerful it was certainly the easiest way, and naturally the credit for their "suppression" was claimed by the police and military whose direct efforts had been so ineffective.

Betrayal was a daily hazard for bandit chiefs everywhere. Evidence strongly suggests that Bai Lang's fate was, as the Corsican proverb puts it, to be "killed after death, like a bandit by the police."[39] Lao Yangren and Sun Meiyao also died in this way, murdered by former subchiefs; though the traitors received military honors as a reward, the military itself claimed credit for the "suppression."[40] Most chiefs accordingly took elaborate precautions to protect their own lives. When the Lincheng

---

Sheridan 1966: 21–22; Ch'ên 1968: 574–75; Laffey 1972: 92–93). Just as the best way to dispose of a bandit chief was to purchase the allegiance of one or more subordinates, so the easiest way to end a warlord conflict was to bribe a rival's officers. When a warlord was defeated, his men, instead of transferring their allegiance to another general, often scattered to join or form bandit gangs (Nagano 1932: 178). Similarly, bandits whose chief had been eliminated did not automatically go over to the appointed successor. "Little Li" Hongbin, for example, chose to remain in Henan because Bai Lang had executed his superior Wang Chuanxin for insubordination.

*In December 1913, military governor Zhang Zhenfang put 20,000 dollars on Bai Lang's head and 10,000 each on those of Song Laonian and Li Hongbin. Within six months Bai's bounty had risen to 50,000 dollars, half that offered for Huang Xing during the Second Revolution and equaling that offered for Huang's lieutenant Chen Qimei. One anti–Bai Lang general was also offering a choice of five hereditary titles for the three chiefs' apprehension (*STSB*, 14 Dec. 1913: 8; *NCH*, 24 July 1914: 2; *NCH*, 13 June 1914: 841).

negotiations reached a delicate stage, Sun Meiyao stayed with his captives on an isolated mountaintop rather than join the other chiefs deeper in the mountains. Others, like Zhang Zuolin, changed their sleeping quarters every night, or chose to surround themselves with bodyguards, usually from their home area.[41] Fan Zhongxiu ensured his safety by putting a close relative in charge of his personal bodyguard, whereas the Shandong chief Zhao Yongling, better known as Mama Zhao (Zhao Mama), chose a bodyguard composed entirely of women. He Long, too, after joining the Communists in 1927, surprised them by admitting that as a bandit chief he had carried a gun at all times. He slept with it under his pillow at night, and reached for it instinctively at the slightest sound. When his band was on the move he kept carefully out of sight to avoid assassination attempts. "To be a bandit," he noted, "one must be very clever, and, most important of all, one must be vigilant."[42] In the prophetic words of the Sicilian chief Salvatore Giuliano: "I can look after my enemies, but God protect me from my friends."[43]

Ideal and practice rarely meshed where bandit gangs were concerned. The contradictions inherent in maintaining horizontal ties within a vertical organization were exposed in the shape of the delicate relationship between chief and subchiefs. Under the right conditions, the cellular structure allowed a gang to function more effectively than the rule-bound regular army, but when pressure was applied from outside it led naturally to fragmentation rather than consolidation. Behind the organizational structure of the gangs lay the pride and ambition of all the individuals involved, a fact that put considerable limits on the chief's freedom of activity.

## The Conditions of Leadership

Most outside commentators on bandits have concentrated on the martial qualities required by the chiefs. He Xiya, exploiting his readership's desire for titillation, claimed that though all bandits had to be possessed of unusual fighting qualities, leaders needed at least one or two exceptional qualities, such as being able to "slither about on their stomachs like snakes," being "light and good at jumping," being "able to walk on their hands," or being able to "snap iron chains with their bare hands." Along the same lines, Nagano Akira declared that the chief had to be the best shot, the most competent commander, the most ruthless and the most fearless member of the gang.[44]

As leaders of people for whom fighting was an everyday occupation and hazard, bandit chiefs' need for such qualities is of course undeniable, but this sort of leadership was usually limited to the simple gang, and represented the "local tough" or "village bully" character discussed in the previous chapter. Strong in mind and temper, the outstanding among these toughs provided natural charismatic leadership. Such men could effectively organize the fundamental bandit activities of looting and burning, but it took other qualities if a gang was to transcend these activities and achieve for itself reasonable prospects of survival, if not official recognition. Such qualities included innate shrewdness, political or military experience, and the natural confidence that came from being accustomed to taking a leadership role. Though the characteristics of both types *could* be combined in one person, the distinction is nevertheless analytically important. Leaders like this, the "intellectual schemers" or "politician" types, became focal points of endemic banditry, for chiefs of ruder qualities usually sought to merge their forces with those of one who seemed likely to go far. The "local bully" type was often found at the level of the subchief.

Leaders of complex gangs, both as physical specimens and as emotional types, were consequently anything but what one would expect from the characterizations of He Xiya and Nagano Akira. Eyewitnesses recalled them in such terms as "not... at all impressive," "anything but physically powerful," "amiable," and "quite a decent sort."[45] Many of them were also "types in which the intellectual rather than the animal predominated," possessing "abilities that should have brought them a large measure of success in whatever work in life they might have taken up." In other words, though courage and fighting ability might have been enough at the level of the simple gang, what the superior chief needed above all was a good head, a strong will, and the capacity to think coolly under pressure. These qualities were what ultimately set the chief apart from the rest. A rhyme that circulated in southwestern Henan around the time of the 1911 Revolution thus encapsulated the qualities of the ideal bandit chief by listing the respective attributes of seven prominent local "heroes":[46]

> Righteousness itself in word and deed:
> Guan Laojiu and Lao Zhang Ping;
> Diligent pupil and respected teacher:
> Zhang Zhigong and Zhai Yunsheng;
> Alert to every trick and wile: Wang Tiancong;
> Leaping into every breach: Han Yukun;
> A demon who can kill at will: Tao Furong.

Like any other leaders, bandit chiefs had to inspire in their followers both respect and fear. They had to be sensitive enough to their followers' feelings to maintain the organization in smooth working order, but not so sensitive as to appear weak. Bai Lang, for all his image as a popular hero, usually directed the band's operations from an ornate palanquin borne by eight men. Lao Yangren and his fellow soldier-bandit chiefs

were described as "riding high-spirited horses.... They sit straight in
their saddles as if they own the whole world, and aim to make everyone
in the village feel that they are their superiors."[47] At the same time, of
Lao Yangren it was said that "men jumped when he spoke"; Bai Lang
was "a man of definite and immediate action" who did not hesitate to
execute even his own subchiefs for breaches of discipline; and Fan Mingxin "could be a holy terror when properly roused."[48] Yet though bandits would usually continue to follow a chief even after a defeat, one
who risked the gang's lives in reckless adventures would not last long.

As a rule, then, the pure "bully" type of chief described in the previous chapter was less successful than the intellectual-schemer type. In the
disturbed conditions of Republican China, such individuals, represented
by the warlord Zhang Zongchang, could sometimes come into their
own. More typical, however, was the case of his superior, Zhang Zuolin.

Zhang Zuolin, "a tiny, frail-looking, mustachioed illiterate,"[49] typified a leadership style that evidently encompassed both bandit chiefs and
warlords. In 1904, when he was still a south Manchurian bandit chief, a
Japanese army officer had been sufficiently impressed by "his mien gentle
as a woman but his speech and manner bold and direct" to intervene to
save him from a Russian firing squad. In 1907 Zhang vindicated this assessment by murdering one of his most powerful rivals along with his
entire bodyguard after inviting them all to a feast.[50] Among his contemporaries he was known as "a good man with a gun, gifted with
exceptional leadership ability, possessing both constructive courage and
diplomatic finesse; he was adept at seizing opportunities ... knew when
to fight and when to negotiate and when to concentrate on building up
his army."[51] In this combination of qualities lay the reasons for Zhang's
extraordinary later success.

Obviously, though, a bandit chief had to expect to get into a fight
sometimes: with rivals, with soldiers, and even with villagers when leading the gang on a raid. Leadership rivalries were often decided by single
combat or were fought out with the help of only a small bodyguard.[52]
In Manchuria at least, newly appointed chiefs had to carry out a kidnapping before being confirmed in their position. As well as intelligence,
forcefulness, and skill, a good chief needed luck. Living on the brink of
death as they often did, bandits believed strongly in the power of providence. Those who aspired to high position had to demonstrate first of all
the ability to survive against impossible odds, a property that would then
presumably accrue to all who followed their leadership. Chiefs who
could walk unscathed through a hail of bullets could in no time gather
followers who were prepared to accompany them to the Gates of
Hell. Conversely, those who failed to demonstrate this quality, who
seemed dogged by ill-fortune, soon found themselves with no followers
whatsoever.[53]

There were other qualities, too, including the willingness to deceive the rank and file in the name of the chief's perception of the gang's best interests. By the twentieth century, wily leaders were holding their followers together not by the magic omens and prophecies that had served traditional rebels,[54] but by rumor and "white lies."* When Bai Lang led his army into Anhui province in late 1913, for instance, the rank and file believed that they were going to join revolutionary leader Huang Xing, said to be holding government troops at Jiujiang in Jiangxi with 100,000 soldiers. Huang had the support of seven foreign nations and had married a Japanese princess. When they returned westward following the defeat of Huang's Second Revolution, it was ostensibly to support the Mongol Independence Movement then taking shape on the Chinese border. Later attempts to enter Sichuan, which lay in the opposite direction from Henan, were justified by exaggerating the ease with which a revolutionary regime could be established there.[55]

Like their counterparts in the past, twentieth-century chiefs also encouraged the spinning of a web of myths around them to add a mystical quality to their leadership. The stories about the Lincheng chief Sun Meiyao were a good example: "Once he fell off a roof, but went back to do it again to discover the reason. Again, he stubbed his toe on a rock and was so angry that he shattered it with his rifle butt, to show nothing could defy him."[56]

Though chiefs nominally possessed supreme authority within the gang, that authority could not become arbitrary, and leaders could not become aloof from their followers. One respected chief, despite his acknowledged authority, engaged in "violent quarrels which sometimes lasted for hours" and "had to swallow many nasty insinuations impugning his honor as...chief."[57] Lao Yangren was murdered when he sought to lead his starving followers across the breadth of Henan in search of military reinstatement, and Bai Lang had originally been reluctant to declare openly for the Second Revolution since his followers were "mere bandits" and might not follow him.[58] Indeed, Wang Zuo and Yuan Wencai, two chiefs who had occupied the Jinggangshan mountain base in south Jiangxi before the arrival of the first Communist Red Armies in 1929, both perished at the hands of their own followers when they attempted to lead them over to the anti-Communist side.[59]

The relationship between chief and gang is summed up most vividly

---

*In mid-1914 newspapers reported that a small boy was being kept with the band because he experienced revelations about how best to stage attacks, where valuables were hidden, and so on (*NCH*, 6 June 1914: 749). While Bai Lang may have been aware of stories of Li Zicheng's having used young boys in the vanguard to exploit some magical advantages they were thought to possess (Parsons 1970: 191), it is more likely that superstitious peasants, among whom such myths were deeply entrenched, falsely attached religious significance to someone who was probably no more than a youthful bandit or a hanger-on.

and concisely in the reflections of Kohinata Hakurō after twenty years as
a bandit chief (under the name Xiao Bailong) in Manchuria:

> I have always sought to be carried along by them like a portable shrine
> (*o-mikoshi*) in a procession, taking every effort to make myself as easily carried as
> can be. Just as the shrine-bearers carry their heavy burden cheerfully until they
> drop from exhaustion, so too must a bandit chief be borne aloft by his or her
> followers. Once aloft, however, those on top must absolutely never make petty,
> troublesome demands. Once they start complaining "I don't like this," "that's
> no good," the people beneath doing the carrying soon lose their cheerfulness.
> The essential thing ... is to have them carry you in such a way that they are
> pleased to do so.[60]

Appointment of new leaders was essentially democratic, based upon
achievement and acknowledged ability. People who demonstrated obvious leadership skills could find their way to the top in a very short time,
like the Bai Lang subchief who within four months of joining the rank
and file in February 1914 was able to discuss tactics with Bai himself.
Equally rapid was the rise of Kohinata Hakurō. He was only seventeen
when captured while traveling in Manchuria, but his ebullience so
appealed to his captors that he was eventually admitted to the gang as a
confederate. Such was his performance on his first raid that he was made
a subchief on the spot, and within two more years, after several more
demonstrations of his ability, he was appointed supreme leader.[61] As he
found, moreover, among the Manchurian gangs (as among those of
western Henan), a person elected leader could not refuse.[62]

Kohinata was not the only foreigner to be offered the position of
chief, though he seems to have been the only one who accepted (the
Japanese *rōnin*, or adventurers, who acted as the advance guard of imperialism in Manchuria throughout this period, were a different case and will
be discussed in a later chapter). One American captive was approached
secretly one night by several rank-and-file bandits who told him that,
on the basis of his being a Freemason (which they understood as making him a kind of American bandit), his height (over six feet), his
strength, his fearlessness in resisting capture, his education and skill as a
doctor, and his fluency in Chinese, he was "just the man to be their chief.
It was an elective position among them, and a number of them had
already decided to offer it to me."[63] The striking aspects of this episode
were its revelation of how easily a new gang leader could emerge, and
the evident disregard for the incumbent chief's views on the matter.

## Internal Organization of the Gang

In the interests of smooth functioning, any social organism has to
delegate duties and responsibilities. The bandit gang was no exception.

As in all status hierarchies, moreover, the most tiresome and thankless tasks tended to devolve upon those whose credit was lowest: new recruits, the disabled, and the overage. Otherwise, apart from tasks requiring special skills such as military planning, written communication with the authorities, and keeping track of the gang's finances, functions were generally shared out equally among the rank and file. As the acknowledged authority within the gang, the chief had ultimate control over its internal functioning: organizing raids, distributing arms, deciding roles, dividing income, and so on. Everyday tasks were carried out under the chief's direct or indirect supervision.

Formal, stratified organization was less important for simple gangs since close personal ties to the chief and to other members resulted in a sort of unspoken discipline. Moreover, the gang's limited activities and tasks required only minimal planning and direction. As a gang attained greater complexity, however, responsibilities increased accordingly. The following discussion thus refers principally to complex gangs and bandit armies.

Since the bandit gang was above all a fighting organization, the highest rank was given to the military tacticians, known in bandit slang as *paotou* or *menshen*—the former term said to have derived from the practice of winding (*bao*) a turban about the head (*tou*).[64] There were usually several according to the size of the gang, appointed to lead the rank and file on raids, supervise withdrawals, and take charge of all other military operations. Each was responsible for a given number of fighters. When a complex gang had been spontaneously formed (that is, not formed through an alliance of existing gangs), these were usually the chief's relatives or close confidants from pre-bandit days. In many cases, however, the tacticians were themselves chiefs, and the fighters they superintended were mostly their own followers. They were consequently regarded with great respect. Even when a person rose to the position of *paotou* without an independent following, as Kohinata Hakurō did, he or she generally enjoyed the aura of a hero. At the same time, however, the incumbents were in a position of great responsibility, for the *paotou* were liable for the safety of their commands, just as the chief was for the safety of the whole gang. Yet, even in the case of a damaging defeat, they were not automatically demoted unless seen to be clearly responsible.[65]

With the possible exception of the chiefs, most bandits, like the majority of peasants, were illiterate. Had it been possible for the gang to maintain itself entirely independent of the "straight" world surrounding it this would have caused no great problems. However, bandits were connected to that world by various strands of necessity, one of which was the need to communicate such things as ransom demands, threats, proclamations, and proposals. For this purpose every gang employed or borrowed from another gang at least one secretary, known as "white fan" (*baishan*; also *niuyi*).[66] The importance of the lifeline these secretaries provided between bandits and the authorities is indicated by the high position they enjoyed, for they often doubled as advisers. In a complex gang such as the one that carried out the Lincheng attack, there was usually one to every chief.[67] Most were scholars fallen on hard times, sometimes even men who had achieved high degrees in the old imperial examination system but who found themselves suddenly reduced to an anachronism; others included opium smokers unable to satisfy their craving except through banditry. With such men in the band it was not uncommon to see letters couched in elegant classical prose on the theme of the amount of ransom required before a captive's ears would be cut off.[68]

The biggest problem with these educated people was that they rarely possessed the stomach for a fight, and tended to give up or run away at the first opportunity. Most gangs were constantly on the lookout for educated helpers, and where willing scribes were lacking normally commandeered the services of a suitable captive, or even captured someone specifically for the task. Christian converts were frequent targets, since many had received a rudimentary education in some mission school.[69] Such unwilling secretaries would not possess the same status as the "white fan," unless, as sometimes happened, they elected later to formally join the gang. Still, the essential nature of their role usually kept them out of harm's way at least until the appearance of a rival whose calligraphy was superior. When a full-time scribe was unavailable, any educated person filled the bill: Bai Lang made do with one of the band's coerced doctors.[70]

Another position commanding respect was that of accountant, known as *zhangjia* or *shuixiang* (*shui*, or "water," was a general bandit slang term for property). Theoretically the accountant was charged with all matters pertaining to the gang's financial affairs, though in practice the chief often assumed this function:

The bandits always complained of being poor. The only one among them whom I saw with money was [the leader] Shuang Shan. He always made it plain that what money he carried belonged to the . . . bandit organization. Theirs was evidently a typical community life where one man handled whatever loose money happened to come their way. . . .[71]

Most organized gangs also required a "commissariat chief" (*liangtai*), responsible for all practical matters such as ensuring that sleeping quarters and food were prepared in the district where the gang proposed to spend the next night.[72]

Security was a constant problem for bandit gangs. To avoid being surrounded while on the move, when conditions allowed they would spread out over a wide area rather than move in a concentrated group. When mountain or forest paths forbade such a formation, they would string out in a long line. In either case, lookouts posted at each end of the line passed any important news along to the center, resulting in what one captive recalled as a "bewildering calling and answering...heard in every direction."[73]

Even when resting a gang could not relax its guard, and every bandit camp posted a number of lookouts to keep track of all who approached. Whether a specialized occupation or a rotating responsibility within the gang is not clear, but sentry duty warranted a special term in bandit slang, *xunlengzi*, *xun* meaning "to watch" and *lengzi* ("sleet") being used to refer to police or soldiers.[74]

Sentries were particularly important when occupying a village considered unfriendly, to keep informers in as well as to keep others out. Posted on surrounding mountains or hills and on the roads, the first line of sentries was unarmed and dressed unobtrusively in everyday clothes, but the inner cordon, known as *jubu* or *bashou*, consisted of armed bandits ready to defend the camp while the others escaped. Their role was often a sacrificial one, as was that of the "door-carriers" (*gangshan*), who broke down the gates and walls of villages under attack, and the "fire-carriers" (*baohuo*), who carried the torches for a night attack. The latter task, which made illuminated targets of those concerned, was one for which only the most daredevil would volunteer.[75]

Within the gang, too, most chiefs had their spies, known as *jicha*, whose duty was to report back on the thoughts and behavior of the rank and file.[76] As provision against the ever-threatening stab in the back, such precautions were only natural.

Another specific term described those bandits appointed to spend long periods of time in surrounding areas gathering information about military developments and relaying important news. These were the *ta-xian* or *zouxian*, meaning those who "walk the line." Other spies were employed solely to investigate the ransom prospects of local notables. These *chaqian* or "tally takers" would ascertain the size of a possible victim's fortune, the appearance of his house (location of the exits and entrances, possible hiding places, defensibility), and the number of people living there, and they would then take the news back to the camp. To make the attack easier, whenever possible a servant in the house was bought over. When all this information was digested and an attack pronounced feasible by the chief, the gang moved into action.[77]

Yet another specialized occupation was that of the *yashui*—"press water"—whose duty was to pose as an innocent passerby sent by the bandits to inform the prospective victim of the sum required to forestall his kidnapping—that is, to tell him the price of his "ticket" (*piao*), since captives were generally referred to as "meat tickets" (*roupiao*).[78]

Preparation was extremely important to bandit strategy. Manchurian gangs sent out scouting parties (*xunfeng*) in the spring to acquire information necessary to plan the summer campaign.[79] Attacks on towns, feasible only for bandit armies, needed particularly careful planning. Bai Lang's spies would drift in several days prior to an attack disguised as peddlers or vagrants; the information they gathered was passed secretly to the gang, which was waiting a suitable distance away. When the attack was launched, these spies operated as a fifth column, lighting fires, opening the gates, and so on.[80]

The need for "safe houses" (*jiazi lou*) arose when the bandits were operating far from their camp, to avoid the possibility of their being overtaken before they could conceal their haul and scatter. Goods could then be shipped back in small quantities, or captives moved unobtrusively one by one.[81] The poor were ready enough to play this role in the hope of sharing in the bandits' profits, and those who did were known in underworld slang as "stableboys" (*caoer*).

Other external duties included establishing and maintaining friendly relations with neighboring gangs, and contracting with mercenary arms dealers in the treaty ports. The former was particularly important when pursuit drove a gang into another's territory, and often marked the origin of gang alliances, which could then stretch over hundreds of square miles.[82]

As noted earlier, the most mundane and distasteful jobs were reserved for the very young, the old, and the disabled. Such jobs included exacting punishments, carrying weapons, and guarding prisoners.[83] New, young recruits (known as "adopted sons," *yangzi*) were especially liable for such duty. When Zhang Zuolin joined his first bandit gang in his teens he found himself to his disgust looking after the captives all the time, and soon left to find more inspiring work. Kohinata Hakurō found his first few months as a raw recruit worse than any he had known, and concluded that "the new recruit was ranked even lower than the animals."[84]

Most other bandits left in charge of the captives, known as "seedling houses" (*yangzi fang*),* shared this resentment, no doubt because looking after people constituted the precise opposite of the earth-shattering, romantic, virile life they had expected. Many captives accordingly came in for rough treatment, especially from younger bandits (older bandits, by contrast, displayed occasional kindness).[85] Guarding captives could

---

*Sources give homophonous characters for the two versions of "*yangzi*," suggesting that the two were in fact synonymous.

also be assigned as a penalty for some misdemeanor, and punishment was stiff if a captive was allowed to escape.[86]

Other routine occupations such as barber and cook (particularly the latter) were delegated to people with experience when available, and to the youngest bandits otherwise;[87] woe betide the raw recruit who failed to learn the necessary skills quickly.

Reflecting the traditional Confucian preoccupation with seniority, a special position was reserved for the aged. At Lincheng a 66-year-old former bandit, too old to fight and exercising no practical command functions, was nevertheless included among the gang's dignitaries (*shanzu*) and referred to as the "Old Gentleman" (*Lao taiye*).[88] In rare cases such men were able to retire on what they had amassed from banditry to live the lives of prosperous old gentlemen while directing gang operations from some city.[89]

In Manchuria weapons belonged entirely to the chiefs, who to preserve their supremacy generally bought them from deserters hoping to join the gang. To minimize the risk of assassination, weapons were distributed before a raid and collected again later. This was obviously possible only for gangs that maintained a permanent base or strong village contacts, or that were active for only a small part of the year. In gangs where rank-and-file bandits could own their own weapons, possession or non-possession of one became a crucial distinction. A bandit owning more than one gun would normally loan the spare one out. In some cases bandits using a borrowed gun had to obey the owner's orders, could not introduce new members, and were not entitled to share in the gang's income.[90] Many gangs, understandably, forbade new recruits to carry weapons until they had proved themselves; to be given one marked their true initiation as bandits.[91]

Since even the most powerful gang rarely possessed more than a small number of rifles, the loss of one was a major event. Bai Lang allegedly detailed five people to each rifle to catch it should its holder be killed. When bandits were taken into the army, it was on the basis of the number of guns they had rather than the number of actual bandits—another reason to look after the guns carefully.[92]

Opium was an essential source of bandit revenue, and accordingly was carefully controlled, even to the extent of having an "opium treasurer" to regulate the gang's opium income, and an "opium collector" to exact an opium "tribute" from local farmers.[93]

There were many variations on the style of distributing cash income known as "blossoming flowers" (*kaihua*) or "arranging visiting cards" (*pai pianzi*), depending on local custom as well as on the chief's personal preference. In Manchuria it was usually divided among the gang at the end of the raiding season, after expenses had been deducted. About a half or three-fifths went to the chief, who had provided the guns and other supplies such as food, and the rest was divided proportionately among the subchiefs and their followers. The average income of a Manchurian chief was over 5,000 dollars a year, a subchief earning between 300 and 500 dollars, and a rank-and-file bandit between 150 and 300 dollars. Many gangs denied new recruits a share in the spoils.[94]

This practice of sharing profits out at the end of the season prompted one observer to liken the typical bandit gang to a joint-stock company; the difference was that the shareholders were not people with money but people with guns. A rifle and its holder each constituted one share, and when the income was divided it was on the basis of the overall number of shares, not the number of bandits. Those borrowing a rifle paid that rifle's share to its owner as the "loan fee." A gang of 250 armed bandits therefore contained 500 shares, and if all the rifles were loaned out by the chief each individual received one share and the chief took the remaining 251.[95]

In the majority of cases, such as that of Lao Yangren, bandits were obliged to empty their pockets following a raid; they then received back a proportionate share of the total. Though their cash income was often small, they were amply recompensed in opium, furs, gems, and general uproariousness, and this usually satisfied them.[96] Bai Lang used the "three-seven" system, three-tenths of the total proceeds going into a pool and the remainder distributed appropriately. The punishment for deception was death.[97] To discourage defections and guard against deceit, distribution was usually carried out after the gang had returned to its camp, or even at the end of the season, and always in the presence of the chief.

The formality of the distribution procedure, whether of opium or of cash, depended on the gang's having a clearly defined sphere of operations, and also upon the character of its leader. For a gang that was constantly on the move or whose leader paid little attention to discipline, things were much more haphazard. Almost all witnesses agreed, however, that some kind of procedure was enforced. Squabbling was strictly forbidden, even when no formal distribution was carried out, and refusal to submit one's gains to common inspection warranted severe punishment.[98]

## Discipline Within the Gang

Any fighting organization requires its members to subordinate their personal interests to those of the whole, and stiff penalties for infractions like desertion, divulging secrets, insubordination, or incompetence were as typical of the average bandit gang as they are of the modern army or militarized state. The fate of a bandit who because of a weak heart had lagged behind on a forced march was instructive: "Shuang Shan calmly told him that his bandit days had better be over. The pale, gasping 'hung hutze' understood. Without a word he took his rifle, went around the bend of the river, and disappeared in the marsh grass. Presently a shot rang out. We knew that his bandit days were over, forever."[99]

Bandit discipline, as this episode indicates, was harsh. It stemmed ultimately from the leader, who exercised the power of life and death over the other bandits.[100] This strong discipline was both created and sustained by the pressures that had brought the gang together and that maintained it in continual confrontation with the authorities. Regardless of the gang's size, discipline affected both internal and external affairs. Just as in the *Shuihu zhuan* the internal discipline at Liangshanpo is set constantly against the wavering character of relationships on the official side, twentieth-century bandit gangs conformed superficially at least to the classic ideal; in their case, though, the need to observe certain rules to ensure survival probably outweighed anything else.

The accepted image of the bandit gang was frequently inaccurate. Arson, looting, and murder, though sometimes indulged in for their own sake, were often calculated strategies intended to create fear and chaos; bandits were strictly punished when they exceeded or contravened the chief's orders in this regard. Gang regulations, few but fundamental, stipulated the death penalty for a variety of offenses: as a missionary remarked of his Yunnanese captors, "life is cheap."[101] A reporter on the spot following Bai Lang's sack of Binxian, Shaanxi, in April 1914, for instance, was shown a large pool of blood said to mark the spot where Bai had personally beheaded a bandit for breaking rules he had set down. A Fujian city that fell into the hands of bandits was also placarded with the rules of occupation, which prescribed death for any bandit who insulted a woman, looted a shop, or desecrated Christian property. Kohinata Hakurō, upon appointment as chief, immediately posted his three basic regulations fixing death as the penalty for rape, for committing crimes in the home area, and for provoking strife.[102] Discipline was strictly applied, even at the top of the gang hierarchy: a south Henan chief named Wang Chuanxin was executed for refusing to follow Bai Lang to the northwest, though earlier he had been described as "one of White Wolf's . . . leaders."[103]

A gang's behavior varied according to whether it was on home ground or out on a raid. Away from home the rank and file were difficult to control, particularly the numerous camp followers who were always present.[104] At home, however, they were on a code of good behavior that they infringed at their peril:

One day . . . a great cloud of darkness comes over the chief and the entire camp. One of his men has disobeyed orders. . . . [H]ere in the robber area [of west

Henan] the chiefs are very jealous of their honor. The bandit in question has stolen a blanket in the name of the chief. When news of this reaches the chief's ears, he becomes perfectly beside himself with wrath, and orders that this particular bandit be executed immediately. Many friends of the bandit come to interview the chief about this matter... but all their efforts are of no avail.... For several days, the feeling in the camp is one of great despondency. The chief himself... lives in an atmosphere of diabolic cursing.[105]

Several essentially identical sets of behavioral regulations existed, varying from locality to locality and according to the size of the gang. As a gang approached the pattern of a formal organization in which personal ties lost their preeminence, the need for formal disciplinary rules grew. According to He Xiya, most gangs followed the "Four Covenants, Eight Regulations on Rewards, and Eight Regulations on Beheading" originally set out by the Red Gang secret society (this is consequently another area in which the distinction between bandit gangs and secret societies becomes hazy). The death penalty was prescribed for the following offenses: (1) revealing secrets; (2) failing to obey orders; (3) running away from a battle; (4) secretly communicating with the enemy; (5) leading troops to the gang's camp; (6) personally using the gang's property or finances; (7) insulting one's comrades; and (8) flirting with women. The following deeds, on the other hand, were to be rewarded: (1) loyalty to the affairs of the gang; (2) repulsing government troops; (3) fighting the greatest number of battles; (4) extending the influence of the gang; (5) gaining information about the enemy; (6) leading the largest number of followers; (7) fighting bravely in the front line; (8) pulling one's weight within the gang.[106]

The most comprehensive set of regulations attributed to a bandit chief was that proclaimed by "White Horse Zhang" (Zhang Baima), a Manchurian chief who probably devised it for his band after the fall of the "Zheltuga Republic" in the early twentieth century. There were altogether thirteen injunctions.

Zhang began by setting out clearly who could and could not be plundered. Attacks on lone travelers, women, old people, and children were to be punished, but officials, whether honest or corrupt, were legitimate targets when trespassing on the gang's territory. Whereas a corrupt official would lose all his possessions, an honest one would forfeit only half. Foreigners, however rich, were to be protected to avoid diplomatic problems. Attacks on women were punishable by death.

Zhang's stipulations on behavior within the gang were equally strict. Prospective recruits had to be presented by at least twenty members, accept the chief's authority, go through an investiture ceremony performed by the chief, and undertake an expedition as a test of their ability. Members were instructed to respect the principles of justice and not to create disorders. On pain of death, they were to protect the gang's secrets, refrain from plunder for personal gain, and perform whatever task was allotted to them. Negligence and laziness were also punishable by death. Zhang made a clear distinction between what he considered suitable and unsuitable backgrounds for members, such "parasites" as soothsayers and astrologers being strictly excluded from membership. People who attached importance to such practices were forbidden to hold positions of responsibility, or if already occupying such positions were to be put to death.

To bind the gang together as tightly as possible, Zhang stressed the importance of group ties over both individual and natural ones—for example, requiring members to carry out executions of rule-breakers, even close relatives, under penalty of death for refusal.

Finally, the income from each expedition, regardless of the amount, was to be divided into nine parts: two for the common pool; one to the person whose tip made the raid possible; four for distribution among the gang members; one as a bonus for those who had taken part in the expedition; and one for the families of those previously killed or wounded.[107]

It is clear from Zhang Baima's Thirteen Regulations that at least one bandit chief possessed high social and political awareness, as well as leadership ability, and Kohinata Hakurō's recollections leave a similar impression. In Manchuria, however, banditry was a far more complex phenomenon than was usually the case farther south. *Honghuzi* bands, for historical reasons, often acted as community-protection groups, and the trust local people placed in them naturally heightened their social consciousness. Thus it would be unwise to generalize from Zhang Baima's regulations to banditry as a whole; moreover, in reality some rules were enforced more than others. The stipulations against robbing foreigners, lone travelers, women, old people, and children clearly did not apply to kidnapping, and by the 1920's a foreigner's life had become the bandit gang's "ticket" to legitimacy and a rich reward. Bai Lang, we have noted previously, gave lone travelers the choice between joining the band and death; he also forbade implementation of the traditional west Henan vendetta code.[108] Still, the bandits who captured Kohinata Hakurō during his lone trek through Manchuria and Mongolia refused to kill him despite his demands for them to do so.[109] Clearly, Zhang Baima's regulations were no idle propaganda for them.

The stipulation on behaving "honorably" could be found in all idealized accounts of banditry, as could the justification of attacks on official property. The heroes of the *Shuihu zhuan* regarded all officials as corrupt because of their connection with a degenerate state bureaucracy, and therefore their property deserved "plunder."[110] Gang leaders similarly sought to present themselves as upholders of morality, particularly sexual morality, though in practice this principle was often ignored.

Initiation ceremonies were not characteristic of most bandit gangs, but some that had a permanent base developed fairly complex quasi-religious rituals.[111] The power of such a ceremony was undeniable, binding individuals to the group by forcing them to break normal taboos, and demonstrating the gulf between the group and the world outside. In practice, whether a formal ceremony was performed or not depended on circumstances. Out on a raid a gang would be more concerned with a recruit's practical qualities than with personal morality; possession of a rifle was usually enough to gain admission, and when a gang was hard-pressed even this was sometimes waived.[112] Applicants who seemed unlikely to keep discipline were often rejected, however, lest they escape later with a precious rifle (hence the general reluctance to issue rifles to new recruits). In a few gangs would-be recruits were immediately ordered to be executed to test their nerves.[113]

The gang's solidarity was most commonly expressed (and tested) when the authorities countered a kidnapping crisis by taking bandits' relatives hostage in return. In one case, when soldiers released only 25 of 26 bandit relatives seized to ensure a captive's freedom, negotiations were halted until the last relative was released. Captives were frequently killed in retaliation for the government's execution of bandit hostages.[114]

The stipulation against leaving the gang was at least as old as the *Shuihu zhuan,* for those who left were assumed to be contemplating divulging the gang's secrets for their own profit. In any case, it was a betrayal of trust. When a disgruntled subchief left Kohinata Hakurō's band with his followers, his elimination became Kohinata's first priority, and all other affairs were set aside until he was dead.[115]

To ensure the loyalty of younger members who might be unknown to the authorities and thus able to return to "straight" society if they wished, a black pigment was sometimes inserted under the skin near the elbow, a practice inherited from the Nian and Taiping rebels.[116] Under the circumstances, it was not surprising that when bandits found a scar on one American captive's shoulder marking his initiation into a college fraternity, they immediately took it as evidence of his membership in an American bandit gang.[117]

The practice of carrying out executions on demand was often delegated to younger bandits as a test. One Bai Lang veteran recalled that he had been ordered to carry out more than ten executions during his time with the band.[118]

Zhang Baima's stipulation against "negligence and laziness" presumably referred to those who were reluctant to fight, but among Kohinata's band "only those who want[ed] to go [took] part in the battles"; on the other hand, only those who took part regularly were given rewards.[119] The regulations against "parasitic" professions like astrology, meanwhile, seem to have been Zhang's personal innovation, for many gangs set great stock in the workings of fate and fortune.

The taboo against rape and flirting with or ill-treating women, including those held for ransom, reflected a universal ideal for outlaws, but in practice these were the most difficult rules to reconcile with reality. There were sound practical as well as moral reasons for this ban. In the classic *Cases of Lord Peng (Peng Gong An)*, a series of fictional criminal cases devised to convey moral points, it is written that "to kidnap respectable young women and grown-up girls is to court Heaven's wrath and people's hatred," and throughout the book rape and adultery are considered the most heinous of crimes.[120]

In the Chinese heroic tradition the ban on rape stemmed more from superstitious fear of the effect of the women's *yin* element than from any genuine concern for women (this will be considered in the following chapter). In the twentieth century chiefs who forbade rape were most likely thinking of their reputation; conversely, those who did not were usually as demoralized in other respects, too. For the "wild" bandit wishing to demonstrate his rage against his social "betters," however, rape could be highly satisfying.

A number of chiefs apart from Zhang Baima and Kohinata Hakurō have been noted as particularly strict on rape. Bai Lang, for example, sent back girls provided as concubines, and urged his men not to molest women but to keep them as hostages so as to get the ransom money.[121] A veteran recalled that "whenever Bai Lang was around none of us dared even look at a woman. If he caught us smiling at one he would revile us, shouting 'Filthy lechers! What are you staring at?'" Fan Mingxin enjoyed a similar reputation.[122]

In practice, however, it was difficult to restrain a gang when it was out on a raid, especially when it attracted local marauders, and most chiefs abandoned the attempt. After Bai Lang's sack of Binxian in Shaanxi and Xichuan in Henan, reporters alleged that not a single girl over the age of ten was left unviolated.[123] Even allowing for official exaggeration,* it seems clear that women were still the "last colony," the individuals whom men forced to live in perpetual fear and subjection.

Some observers have suggested that bandits, unlike soldiers, rarely committed rape,[124] but it would be more accurate to say that whereas soldiers were totally indiscriminate, bandits were careful to choose targets far from their home area. Mongol bandits, for example, went on annual long-range forages along the Inner Mongolian frontier, threatening to raze villages unless women were left for them.[125]

---

* As one critic (Ch'ên 1970: 818) has written, however, "lewdness is the deadly enemy of Confucian society which is built on the proper sexual relationships between men and women." Accusations like these were traditionally showered upon Chinese rebels and bandits as proof of their fundamental iniquity, one aspect of the stereotyped reporting which continued right up to the anti-Communist campaigns of the 1930's and the Communists' own repression of secret societies in the 1950's.

The picture we receive from eyewitness accounts shows women regarded as legitimate bandit targets. One captive saw "the women out in the fields rounded up like cattle" and heard the bandits talking about "abusing [them] unto blood." Another gang demanded a mission schoolgirl in exchange for a captive's release (to double as concubine and scribe?). Yet another gang, when it commandeered a village, commandeered the women, too, afterward discussing their performance in front of a female captive. One chief had stolen his wife from a farm, leaving behind her husband and two small children. Needless to say, the safety level for women reached a nadir with the appearance of the soldier-bandits. Given the equally rapacious behavior of the regular soldiers, too, we can agree with a contemporary observer that "when a town [had] been sacked and left behind it is safe to say that there [had] not been left behind a single young woman who may claim to be a virgin."[126]

There is not as much information as one would desire concerning female chiefs' attitude toward rape. The Manchurian chief Yizhi Hua lost some two-thirds of her thousand followers because of her ban, which carried a death sentence for men caught in the act (the two or three hundred men who remained are perhaps more worthy of attention). One nineteenth-century pirate chief, apart from introducing a code of behavior regarding the overall treatment of women prisoners, punished promiscuous intercourse by death and decreed "No person shall debauch at his pleasure captive women taken in the villages and open places and brought on board a ship; he must first request the ship's purser for permission and then go aside in the ship's hold." Unfortunately, the men often forgot the rules in the heat of victory and the tug of lust.[127]

All in all, despite charges that women were paraded naked before the whole gang so that the leader might select the best,[128] bandit chiefs seem to have been less responsible for atrocities against women than their rank and file, who were not burdened with overall responsibility. A Lao Yangren subchief is on record as having refused a request to let a young female captive go free because of what his men might do to her once she got outside.[129]

## Maintaining Secrecy

Security precautions in the Chinese underworld reached their greatest complexity in the formalized "dark language" (*heihua*) of the secret societies. Though few bandit gangs achieved this degree of rigor, bandits did have a secret language. Less complex than that of the secret societies, it was usually based on a pure form of a local dialect intelligible only to natives, with the addition of certain special words derived either from the macho nature of bandit activity or from the particular superstitions associated with the bandits' daily lives. Some have said that every bandit chief possessed a booklet containing the gang's secret words, which every member had to learn. The task took from six to eight months.[130] The practice of adopting pseudonyms or borrowing the names of past heroes also had as much to do with secrecy as with romance.[131] Finally, secret signs, though less developed than those used in traditional secret society rites, played a part in maintaining secrecy. Such practical rituals as passwords and handclasps, designed to strengthen solidarity and increase cohesion, reflected the need to exclude outsiders, but just as often stemmed from illiteracy, which prevented written communication.

Bandit argot was less standardized than that of the secret societies. Whereas the latter's was designed to allow members to move from one lodge to another and be recognized as "brothers" or "sisters," a bandit gang's operations were usually based on a relatively restricted locality, and the argot was similarly limited. The isolated border and mountain regions where banditry flourished often possessed their own distinctive dialects, which were naturally reflected in the slang used by local bandits. One Henan bandit dialect was based on that spoken in the Xuchang region of central Henan, a traditional center for bandit operations and the disposal of illicit income. It was so intermixed with slang expressions as to be virtually impossible for the uninitiated to understand: "Before our captivity, we [had] heard about a secret language among the robbers, but without realizing to what extent it [was] in use.... About half of the terms employed by the robbers are different from ordinary Chinese."[132]

Specific terms were used both to cope with the habits and superstitions that banditry inspired and to allow the secret exchange of ideas and the verification of strangers. Superstition (dealt with in the next chapter) was behind the origin of most new words, those of bad import being replaced by less offensive ones. He Xiya sees most bandit argot as originating in the special vocabulary of the Red Gang, which provided an alternative name for everything, and lists a total of 134 terms used specifically by bandits.[133] In west Henan animals all had different names from those customarily used, as did everyday objects like chopsticks, socks (*choutong*, "smelly tubes"), cigarettes (*caojuan*, "grass scroll"), and weapons: guns were "arms" (*gebo*), "rockets" (*pentong*), or "flags" (*qizi*), and bullets were "white rice" (*baimi*).* Even such mundane activities as shaving the head and walking were given specific argot equivalents. To be killed by the people was to be "eaten by the old citizens."[134]

It is difficult to find any superstitious basis or security reason for such changes; they reflect rather the importance of language in general, par-

---

*By the 1930's, north Manchurian chiefs had evidently begun to introduce Tibetan terms to increase security (Tanaka 1934: 164).

ticularly for outcast groups. A specific language helps strengthen group ties, and makes an individual feel distinct from "the rest" outside the group. In using their "dark language," bandits were reaffirming their personal identity as outlaws. In plain terms, it brought them a sense of togetherness.

Formalized dialogues designed to test strangers, though more often associated with secret societies, have also been identified among Henan bandits:

1. Q.  Where are you coming from?
   A.  I am coming from where I come.
   Q.  Where are you going to?
   A.  I am going to where I shall go.
   Q.  What do you bring with you?
   A.  I bring three pieces of incense, and 500 cash. Friends, rich may come to you and go behind. (The stranger points behind him when speaking the last few words.)
2. Q.  Where are you going?
   A.  I am going to visit the captor.
   Q.  Which captor do you want to visit?
   A.  I am going to visit so and so captor.
   Q.  Why do you want to visit the old captor?
   A.  I have a certain job to do with him. (OR I want to send him money.)

A stranger who answered these questions correctly was not robbed.[135]

Passwords were also important among larger gangs, especially at night and in the heat of battle. Before setting out on a raid the chiefs would call the gang together and announce both the schedule for the attack and the secret passwords to be used, usually involving a set challenge and response.[136]

Secret signs have been less easy to trace than speech peculiarities, but some witnesses, all from Manchuria, have recorded examples of the "bandit salute" that show a striking mutual resemblance: "The individual brought himself to an erect position, and at the same time clicked his heels together. Slapping one hand behind the other, the two hands were thrown up to a point on a line with, and about four inches in front of the right shoulder, and then with a quick movement the hands were dropped to the sides."[137] Also known as "enclosing the fist and bowing" (*baoquan jugong*), this salute was traditionally substituted for a much more stylized greeting when *honghuzi* were armed for action. By the twentieth century the old stylized form had almost died out, and even the simplified version was used mainly by chiefs, subchiefs paying only formal heed to it and ordinary bandits ignoring it altogether.[138] Although captives' descriptions differ in details, they all include the action of bringing both hands to one side so as to proclaim one's peaceful intentions, making them recognizable to armed communities and other outlaws anywhere in the world.

## Conclusion

Bandit gangs emerged and developed in reaction to a combination of factors including both external pressure—natural disasters, dangerous enemies—and internal dynamics—the ambition of a particular individual to monopolize all the local power resources, the accretion of other bands trying to grab a share of that power, and so on. This basic model of growth, repeated throughout history and wherever bandits were found, also peaked and declined in a fairly standard pattern. On the one hand the natural environment improved, making gang alliances no longer imperative for survival; on the other, the forces of suppression pressured the larger gang at its weakest point—the pragmatic ties binding chief and subchiefs in a union generally founded on mutual convenience.

Within the gang, too, centripetal forces placed clear limits on a chief's power. The utilitarian nature of the basic bandit alliance, the gang's strong local identity, and the knowledge that for most bandits outlawry was a means, not an end, made chiefs careful not to overstep their authority. Just as a supreme chief could not disregard the wishes of subchiefs, neither could the latter ignore their followers. Chiefs who tried to behave like traditional patriarchs were likely to be either stabbed in the back or sold to the authorities; at the very least they stood to lose their followers and thereby their identity as chiefs.

The relationship between bandits and their leaders thus contained a high degree of flexibility. There was certainly more room for discussion and argument than in the average Chinese family, or even in the average warlord faction, with which bandit gangs have often been compared. For the rank and file there was the possibility of eliminating an overbearing chief or of leaving the gang altogether. On the other hand, the penalties both for attacking a chief and for leaving a gang were harsh, and the chances of getting away remote. The chiefs' options were increased by their acknowledged authority, allowing the punishment of recalcitrants, or even the dispersal of the gang altogether—the latter threat being generally enough to quell resistance, since bandits depended on their leaders for everything from military tactics to food and opium supplies.[139] Power relations within a gang thus resulted more from mutual convenience than from rigid control, the ultimate fact being that all were fugitives from the law. The gang held together in the knowledge that profits as well as survival came easier to a band than to a single individual. Rights and obligations were clearly set out on both sides.

At the same time gangs also developed clearly defined rules and punishments in the interests of ensuring their object of survival. The larger a gang grew, the more vulnerable it became, and in all but the simplest outfits elaborate ways were found both to defuse the threat of annihilation and to keep a tight lid on secrets. Severe penalties for all infractions, alongside the assurance of mutual protection, made the bandit gang not only a vehicle for predatory activity but also a viable fighting machine and a source of mutual security.

CHAPTER SIX

# "Some Men Are Brothers":
# Bandit Lives and Perspectives

*The bandit's life is one of killing and burning; of rape and plunder; of shock and fright with no guarantee of another night; of quick joy and sudden misery, shadowed by death from gluttony or starvation; of running east and fleeing west with never a chance to settle; of rejecting human society and being rejected by it; of unadulterated self-interest with no concern for others; of existence in the world but no attempt at living with it; in short, a life which has quite turned its back upon the principles of human coexistence.* —He Xiya 1925a: 41–42

*Until that hour . . . I had thought of "hung hutzes" as more or less mythical beings. As I looked upon them standing or lying meekly before me, heard their complaints, and saw their scarred and diseased bodies, I comprehended with a new understanding that I was dealing with human beings not unlike those with whom I had been meeting all my life.* —Howard 1926: 88–89

IN THIS CHAPTER we will try to present a picture of bandits' everyday lives; what they did; what they looked like; what interested them; what pleased, worried, or angered them; what they thought of themselves and of their fellow humans; what they saw in the future; and what they did when harsh reality pressed in on them too closely. Since the majority of the information has been culled from captives' accounts and concerns gangs that achieved some far-reaching notoriety, however, many of the conclusions arrived at here probably apply more to gangs that existed independently of village ties, and to professional bandits rather than occasionals.

For most young would-be heroes in China, such high-sounding phrases as "restrain the strong and succor the weak" and "rob the rich to aid the poor" represented a living ideal they had to appear to acknowledge. The romantic image of bandits these slogans suggested, however, was often a far cry from the real thing. For most, banditry meant a life on the run, a means of staving off hunger—and the privations showed in the bandits' emotional makeup. Nevertheless, for chiefs as well as for the rank and file, membership in a gang satisfied a number of psychological needs: it provided a chance to see the world, an opportunity to parade one's bravado and self-esteem before others, a means of venting aggressive energy against those weaker than oneself, and a chance for the kind of conspicuous consumption that set them apart from the mass.

Official propaganda notwithstanding, bandits were as human as any peasant, and they cherished dreams of a brighter future like anyone else. In practice, however, banditry was no road to riches except possibly for the chiefs. For those in it full-time with little hope of a return to the soil, the best prospect was enrollment in the army or in a local militia or landlord mafia; others dreamed of making enough money to take it easy on their farms with a concubine or two; still others lived from day to day hoping for the break that rarely came.

Resentment at the bad luck or injustice that had forced them into their hard life, the danger that threatened to cut off their lives at any moment, and the impulse to show themselves as strong as their oppressors frequently combined in a deep strain of violence, particularly toward women, which has colored the bandit image everywhere. It was, however, violence of the avenging kind, aimed at specific objects of peasant resentment or, at worst, at anyone weaker than themselves. Meanwhile, bandits attempted to draw a veil over the implications of their behavior by inventing alternative expressions to replace those that smacked too strongly of grim reality.

## Life as a Bandit

For both chiefs and followers, the bandit life was a violent sequence of fear and joy, with a doubtful future put firmly out of mind until disaster threatened. One night, confident of having outdistanced pursuing soldiers, a gang settled down with their captive to light fires and cook a meal. "The forest rang with our laughter and banter as we passed up our bowls to be filled." Suddenly there came a shout of "Run!" Soldiers had used the opportunity of the party to sneak up and surround the gang:

Mosquito tents were torn from their stakes. Rifles, blankets and coats were snatched from the ground. The Chinese captives grabbed the things nearest to them and ran, with their guards at their heels. I was barely able to get hold of my sheep-skin coat before being shoved headlong down the hill. Several bags of millet and half of the other belongings of the band were left behind.

The only escape route was up the middle of a mountain stream against a roaring current right through the path of the oncoming soldiers. To cap it all, a heavy, cold rain had begun to fall. After several hours of wading hip-high the whole gang was exhausted: "More than one weeping bandit vowed that if he ever got out of this plight alive, he was through with banditry for the rest of his life. I declared myself to be of like mind."

A few days before there had been a similar incident. Trying to cross a stream to elude the same pursuing soldiers, the bandits were swept in their boat onto a mudbank, where they remained until morning with the rain pouring down and the river water washing around their ankles: "The physical and mental distress, combined with the seeming hopelessness and uncertainty of their position, was too great for several of the bandits, and one by one they began to cry like small children...." Yet the next morning, safely across the river and out of danger, the bandits behaved as if nothing had happened.[1]

In this way, bandits tended to live from one crisis to another, particularly when kept on the move by pursuing troops. But even among the highly organized *honghuzi*, everyday life was enough to dash the romantic dreams of young people like Kohinata Hakurō, who as a chief eventually echoed the conclusion of He Xiya: "a bandit's fate is to be alive today with no certainty about the morrow."[2]

One of the functions of bandit chiefs was to anticipate and forestall the kind of despair that would make their followers inefficient fighters and therefore liabilities. When one gang was prevented from crossing into Jilin to evade pursuing troops, many of the bandits felt their end was at hand. Their chief, however, "reproved them sharply, saying that they must not forget that they were 'hung hutzes,' and that they could expect many more disappointments like this." Sometimes this responsibility involved endangering their own lives, as in the case of a chief who, to inspire his followers during a fierce battle with soldiers, emulated the *Three Kingdoms* hero Zhuge Liang by climbing upon a wall amid a hail of bullets to sing and play unconcernedly on a Chinese lute.[3]

Though Kohinata Hakurō led a charmed life during his twenty years as a *honghuzi* chief, the numerous bullet wounds displayed by some bandits provided a telling illustration of the precariousness of their lives. In his capacity as the gang's temporary doctor, a captive found one chief to have

the scars of several bullet wounds. A year before he had been shot in the chest... and the bullet had come out of his back.... He had also been shot through the abdomen, as proved by a scar in front and one in the back.... He then showed me a big scar on his elbow. He had been shot through the joint....

He said that the joint pained him some and complained of limitation of motion.[4]

Such wounds, or "decorations" (*tiejin*), were something of a masculine status symbol, and comparing them commonly served to pass the time.

Disease and illness were also major hazards, especially syphilis, gonorrhea, trachoma, and gastric troubles resulting from excessive opium smoking. Although most larger bands had a doctor willingly or unwillingly accompanying them, there was little time and certainly no equipment for serious treatment, let alone surgery, and postoperative convalescence was out of the question except for gangs with secure hideouts. Treatment in one gang consisted of laying out the sick man facedown, then lifting him up by the flesh between the shoulders and dropping him repeatedly for fifteen minutes. After that the skin around the neck and down the spine was nipped with the fingernails, leaving the patient a mass of red streaks and feeling "worse than ever."[5] The luckier patient might be given some crude ointment to rub on the affected parts, but the general panacea for all afflictions was opium, an effective painkiller as well as an invaluable source of short-term bursts of energy. Addiction among bandits was general, and at least two foreign captives complained of having the drug pushed upon them for their stomach pains. The chief of one of these gangs chewed opium pills constantly to relieve some unidentified discomfort.[6] By and large, however, bandits accepted their afflictions philosophically, mainly because, apart from the venereal diseases, they were the sufferings endured by most peasants, but also because their lives were usually so full of danger that there was little time for or point in worrying about them.

If it was not physical discomfort or disability, it was the mental anxiety of being permanently on the run that made many bandits' lives a far cry from the romantic ideal. The suspicion and distrust that characterized most bandits often caused what were known in Sichuan province as "brigands' eyes," a swivel effect as if looking everywhere at once.[7] To quote the *North China Herald*, "A Chinese bandit is, at best, as uncertain as dynamite—apt to fly off the handle, at any tangent, at any moment— and a Chinese bandit affected with 'nerves' is doubly dangerous." The correct attitude to take toward bandits was to be "polite—and patient."[8]

Bandits' chief fear was the early-morning attack, as all intelligent army commanders knew. To make up for being outnumbered, their only hope was to sustain a curtain of fire until darkness allowed them to slip away. Midday consequently brought general relief, for they stood a good chance of having enough ammunition to outlast an afternoon attack. Indeed, there was a superstitious taboo in some parts of China against cleaning guns before noon lest that action provoke a sudden attack.[9]

Outlaws, unless members of a well-ensconced gang or one that rarely strayed from its home village, had little time for sitting and staring. Much of their time was spent on the move, especially when they had stirred up trouble through an audacious attack or by taking a foreigner captive, or when they needed to safeguard their boundaries.[10] The anti-bandit forces were well aware of this, and also knew that large gangs given no chance to rest at all came under a lot of centrifugal pressure from their component parts. They therefore strove to make sure that rest was impossible, and observers attributed the defeats of both Bai Lang and Lao Yangren to the effects of harrowing forced marches.[11]

The standard of living of all but the most settled of bandits did not significantly surpass that of the peasants they lived among; indeed, most bandits were comparatively poor. The monetary rewards for all their hardships were slender compared to their income in opium, weapons, ammunition, clothing, and other goods, but both opium and ammunition were used or sold as soon as they were acquired.[12] Instead of trying to accumulate gains, bandits lived from hand to mouth as most peasants did, the difference being that from time to time they were able to indulge in conspicuous consumption: "In fact, it must not be thought that the brigands leave great inheritances behind. If they live comfortably while they are active, the profits pass quickly to purchase ammunition, wine, and opium."[13]

The bandit diet usually consisted of things like raw millet, gaoliang cakes, and boiled corn, or, farther south, rice, eaten cold and often moldy.[14] Among the greatest pleasures of the outlaw life, consequently, was whenever possible to "eat until their stomachs were full." One gang "romped about like little children" at the prospect of good food for dinner, reluctantly provided by the priests of a temple they had commandeered for the night.[15]

Even the least settled gangs were sometimes able to snatch a breathing space and relax for a few hours or days. Those who wished could take time off in the winter when the rewards were smallest, slipping into the nearest city to live it up on what they had accumulated. (This could be more dangerous than remaining in their hideout, for such holidaying bandits, easily recognizable, were regularly arrested and executed.[16]) Those who remained in the camp year-round had various ways of passing the time. Most popular by far was smoking opium, which "seemed to fill their every need. It often took the place of food, sleep and recreation with them. In fact every necessity and all other luxuries were as nothing compared to the indulgence in this one vice. When they had plenty of crude opium, their happiness appeared to be complete. When they were without it, they were demons to live with." [17]

Opium and banditry went hand in hand, opium cultivators turning bandits under official pressure, and bandits adapting their operations to the growing season; both flourished during the slack autumn and winter months. To supplement their meager income from farming, those who could planted opium, others took to banditry, and still others did both, planting the crop in the autumn, then turning outlaw till the harvest was ready, and finally regrouping to guard it as far as the nearest sales point.

As well as providing a highly lucrative source of income, opium played a vital part in the bandits' daily lives—curing illnesses, soothing away pain, and generally relieving the tensions of a hard life. The Lin-cheng captives were "regaled nightly with constant opium smoking"; during negotiations for their release, "on three sides were opium divans upon one of which an opium outfit was kept going constantly." [18] For other bandits opium clearly provided a form of release: on a day of increasing anxiety about the intentions of nearby soldiers, the drug was smoked almost continuously. [19] Parcels sent in to captives, on Chinese advice, were stocked with opium whenever possible so as to appease the bandits during ransom talks, and opium often formed an important part of the ransom itself. [20]

Opium's steadying effect on the nerves evidently increased rather than decreased bandits' fighting ability. As addiction heightened, however, its debilitating effect on the body became more and more marked, especially when the smoker was fundamentally undernourished. It was suggested, for example, that Lao Yangren, finding time heavy on his hands during his stint as an army commander, took to opium with disastrous results for his health. [21]

What was there to do for those bandits who did not smoke opium, or for those who did when the supply ran out? Since most of them were illiterate, reading was out of the question, but talking posed no such problems. Opium, not surprisingly, provided the most popular topic of discussion:

> The majority . . . had a constant fear lest their supply would give out. They discussed various ways and means of getting it, and estimated how much they were likely to receive from this district or that. They also compared the quality of the crude drug that came from different sources. . . . The few bandits who did not smoke were more interested in the market price, and laid plans to get their share delivered to the opium marts in Fuchin or Harbin. [22]

If not opium, it was the ransom money expected for their captives, followed by guns and horses, that dominated bandits' conversation. Though they never referred to their homes and families (it was considered unlucky), they were aware of the dangers of the lives they led, and sometimes talked openly about which of them would be killed next. When these topics were exhausted, "telling smutty stories on each other was one of their greatest joys." More than one gang passed the time by calling on the children they employed as servants to recite nursery rhymes and poetry and sing songs.[23] That illiteracy did not signify ignorance was proved by one captive's observation that his bandits listened every night to recitations from memory of the *Romance of the Three Kingdoms*, learned no doubt from itinerant storytellers in the market places.[24] The standard classics, too, often recited publicly by the authorities to try to impart "respectable" moral and social values, evidently seeped through: "I heard a few bandits in the adjoining hut vieing [*sic*] with each other in displaying their knowledge of the classics. They recited famous poems and the Analects of Confucius by the hour. If one of them made the slightest mistake, he was instantly challenged by his eager listeners."[25] Another popular pastime was singing, followed by feats of strength and agility, mah-jongg, dominoes, cards, and, frequently, poking fun at the prisoners.[26] Quarrels were also a regular occurrence, sometimes even involving clubs and rocks, but the chief would step in before things got too violent, or if one side pulled a gun.[27]

There was practical as well as entertainment value to the shooting practice many gangs engaged in to pass the time. Especially during the long slack season, it was necessary to keep one's eye in, and the Manchurian *honghuzi* in particular often organized marksmanship exhibitions in which bandits would vie for prizes of bullets or opium. Among Kohinata's band this was the most popular diversion during the long, snowy winter when operations were virtually impossible. Wrestling and riding contests were also popular, and they too had their practical side.[28]

What all sources agree on is the importance in bandits' lives of their weapons, and the amount of time they spent looking after them, taking them apart and oiling them with almost superstitious care. The most popular weapon was evidently the long-barreled Mauser pistol, particularly in Manchuria where the design was ideally suited to the technique of "throwing" shots from horseback.[29]

## Bandit Fashions

The ability to squeeze luxuries from the unwilling was an essential part of the bandit mystique, and made up for the evident lack of any long-term monetary benefits. Conspicuous consumption, that is, was a means of asserting the bandits' superiority over the rest, as it is for modern-day gangsters and other underworld groups. This applied to bandit appearance as well as to eating. Wealth, particularly the trappings

of wealth, was vastly important in male Chinese society: "The important
thing for the Chinese great man, is to maintain his distinction from his
fellow men. This is done by ceremonial pomp. . . . In fact, the wider his
distance from the people, the higher is the hero's prestige." [30]

"Ceremonial pomp" for bandits meant dressing up in fine clothes
(appropriated ones, of course) and adopting the habits of the rich, or else
creating an aura about themselves by donning a uniform: "When the
ransom is paid and I get my share, I shall buy myself satin trousers, and a
satin coat, and a horse. And I shall take your silk pants to wear under my
trousers, even if I have to beat you to make you give them to me."
When these bandits were discussing what to buy with the ransom money
they all turned out to be equally dandyish: padded satin coats with fur
collars, sateen trousers, new foreign boots, jewelry, and spectacles were
the most popular items. [31] Bai Lang's followers, too, especially the
younger ones, "dressed in all colours of silks and satins which often give
them a fearful appearance," [32] though Bai himself, as befits a Chinese
rebel's image, continued until the end of his life to wear the simple off-
white tunic of homespun nankeen worn by local farmers.*

When rich garments were not to be had, any brightly colored cloth
was enough to set the bandits apart from the peasants, but foreign
women's clothes were a special favorite. One captive found that they left
most of his possessions intact but took his wife's white shoes and hat;
another observed that they especially coveted her jade-green slippers and
the pink silk tassel on her dressing gown. All in all, the several women
captured at Lincheng provided the bandits with a rare bonanza: "I saw a
villainous looking Chinese with Miss MacFadden's blue georgette hat on
his head, the feather waving in the breeze. . . . He also sported two strings
of blue beads. . . . Mathilde told me afterward that she saw a young
bandit wearing a real-lace brassière of mine. . . . " The brassiere was useful as a receptacle for loot, if for nothing else; women's blouses were also
in high demand, especially if touched with lace. Interestingly enough, it
had already been said of the Nian rebels that their clothes "consist of
women's attire topped by a red turban." [33]

As a rule, any kind of foreign clothing helped create an image, especially if it had been taken from someone, which was an additional
source of pride: "[E]very day . . . the No. 1 jumps below, takes off my
evening dress and puts on Pears' fawn camel-hair dressing-gown with
fancy cording to the cuffs; and placing Blue's uniform cap at a rakish
angle on his head, he jumps on deck and takes command." [34] Parcels of
clothing sent to prisoners had to pass through the bandits' hands first,

---

* *ZGNM*: 287; *BLQY*: 86. Note, however, that eyewitnesses claimed to have seen Bai
wearing a white fox fur hat and fur jacket at the sack of Luan in 1914, and also that he
reportedly liked to be carried in a palanquin (Lü Jiuyu 1980: 316; Xian Yun 1956: 142).

one Henan captive finding that they "especially enjoy putting on im-
ported underwear and then running around like wild men." One of the
most telling items of bandit finery was spectacles, "because they wanted
to look learned and scholarly. If they could beg, borrow or steal a pair
they did so."[35] The image of the "great man" evidently included the
intellectual as well as the bacchanalian aspect.

Uniforms were another popular way of displaying one's identity
as "someone to be respected," and any kind filled the bill: one gang
"dressed in six or seven species of uniform[—]military, police, train
conductors, students, and even boy scouts—no one of them, however,
possessing a complete outfit of any one kind."[36] The prospect of receiving a free uniform probably had much to do with the attractiveness
of the army for bandits in the twentieth century, the aura of authority
attached to braid and buttons signifying to others that the wearer was no
ordinary peasant but one who had "made it" into the ranks of the respected. Nevertheless, more pragmatic bandits were sometimes reluctant
to abandon their old clothes altogether. At Lincheng, the bandits "appeared all decked out in new uniforms which they had put on over their
bandit rags and with their army caps on top of their straw hats which
they refused to part with."[37] Whatever they chose to adorn themselves
with, most bandits appeared extremely proud of the result.

Decking oneself out in weapons, another masculine success symbol,
was a further trait noted by most captives. Essential tools of the bandit
trade, weapons evidently had a decorative function too: many bandits
were described as "bristling with guns, cartridges, belts, daggers and
swords."[38]

A common form of headdress noted by captives from Yunnan to
Henan was the turban, folded around the head until it reached an enormous size; in order to set the wearer apart and to add a dash of finery, it
was often made of silk instead of the customary rough cotton or hemp.
In Henan, at least, the shape differed according to locality.[39]

Despite a shaved head's being most hygienic and least troublesome,
right up to the 1930's some bandits were found, especially in the north
and northeast of China, to be still wearing the queue, the long pigtail
forced upon Chinese men by the Manchus as a symbol of their subjection. Like most symbols of this kind, however, the queue developed over
time into a source of pride, and this evidently applied to bandits, too. In
1925, although most of the bandits in a Heilongjiang gang had shaved
heads, one "had long hair. He had formerly worn a queue and was allowing his hair to grow in order that he might have a queue again."[40]
Even as late as 1933, Manchurian bandits were still reported wearing
their queues. These, incidentally, were the most dangerous among the
bandits,[41] suggesting that the queue was indeed a kind of status symbol
at least among the "village bully" types.

The most vulnerable of the bandits' clothes were their cotton shoes, which gave out continually when they were on the move. Most gangs carried with them a large supply of thread and pieces of leather and cloth with which they made repairs whenever they had a spare moment. If possible the job was given to captives and new recruits. Nevertheless, many bandits were "practically barefooted" most of the time, and would compel local farmers to give them all the good shoes they had. No wonder one gang demanded 200 pairs of socks and shoes to be included among their captive's ransom![42]

## Bandit Attitudes: Some Men Are Brothers

How did bandits view the world and their own position in it? To what extent did they see themselves in the tradition of noble robbers, attacking the rich to help the poor, heedless of the privations imposed by the uncertain life they led? A firm answer to the question is, unfortunately, impossible. The influence of regional traditions, the character of the chief, the nature of the gang, and the personality of the individual bandit all played a part. Though a broad distinction may be made between those areas where banditry blended with community self-defense and those where it did not, even that distinction did not always hold.

There was a "greenwood ethic" in China, comparable to the Robin Hood ideal in Europe, originating in the "Peach Garden Oath" sworn by the three venerable heroes Guan Yu, Zhang Fei, and Liu Pei. Summed up by one writer as "a blend of companionship, morality, and righteousness," this ethic "made personal clashes, secrets, and dissipation unthinkable," and bound those concerned "to disregard their own lives" in the pursuit of justice.[43] It is a constant undercurrent in the *Shuihu zhuan* as well as the basis for the secret societies' world outlook. Attempts have been made to show that banditry embraced this idealistic ethic, too. Unfortunately, however, it was largely mythic, its tenacity over the centuries resulting chiefly from peasant desires for a hero figure worthy of esteem. Bandits who did not actively repudiate this ethic, however, could become heroes, especially when their lives were led in isolation from the everyday peasant routine.

There were undoubtedly a few bandit chiefs who saw themselves as the embodiment of the second aspect of the greenwood ethic: "disregarding their own lives" in the pursuit of justice. Many were burning with anger at the social injustice they had suffered, and some had even extended that anger to include all social ills, and had taken to banditry to put things right. Unfortunately, "putting things right" often meant merely "getting one's revenge." Most of the rank-and-file bandits, however, were involved in banditry because of poverty, and persisted because they could not do otherwise. Some, among both chiefs and followers, were simply psychopaths; others were seeking to prove to themselves and to the peasants around them that the infliction of fear was not the monopoly of the elite. Doling out largesse to the poor—whether in the form of food or of handfuls of coins tossed out as the gang passed— also helped promote a benevolent image as well as adding to the donors' self-satisfaction.[44] Bandits, that is, with few exceptions, were in the game for what they could get out of it, whether it was wealth, prestige, or high position. If they had any motivation toward redistributing the riches that came into their hands, it was only after they had taken their own share, and then only at the discretion of the chief. Justifiable as their attitude may be, these were clearly no Robin Hoods.

In communities that traditionally had to defend themselves against powerful enemies, such as the villages of south Manchuria and the provincial border zones, oral memory of the past tended to concentrate on events such as natural disasters, wars, economic oppression, and anti-landlord struggles—that is, issues that directly affected or threatened the community's survival. In this folk memory popular heroes stood out strongly. As a result, there was almost invariably a current of "social banditry" that fueled the peasants' expectations, and that local gangs found hard to ignore, especially after soldiers became such a murderous nuisance after 1911. In these regions bandits could set themselves up as popular fighters without much difficulty, emphasizing their commitment by assuming names or nicknames borrowed from the heroes who abounded in the songs and folk tales they had grown up with. Chiefs, in particular, "the heroes of many an old tale,"[45] were often regarded by those below them as something akin to gods. Conscious of the kind of ideals they had to live up to, they knew, too, the probable reaction of the local people should they fail to do so.[46]

Traditional rebel slogans such as "Carry Out the Way on Heaven's Behalf" (*titian xingdao*) and "Rob the Rich to Aid the Poor" (*jiefu jipin*) still retained their popular appeal in these areas in the twentieth century, and were often accompanied by promises to level out China's glaring social inequalities and turn the world upside down once the undertaking had succeeded.[47] A song generated by Bai Lang's rebellion, still apparently popular in the 1920's, was typical:

> Bai Lang, Bai Lang
> He robs the rich to aid the poor,
> And carries out the Way on Heaven's behalf.
> Everyone agrees that Bai Lang's fine:
> In two years rich and poor will all be leveled.[48]

Kohinata Hakurō's biography shows clearly the high degree of self-consciousness among the Manchurian village-protection leagues. Listen, too, to another Manchurian chief, identified only as Lin:

"I am a bandit, the chief of an army of bandits. I am a bandit, as are all the great men of Manchuria. Old Chang Tso-Lin, master of the Three Eastern Provinces, was a former bandit; General Ma [Zhanshan] was a bandit. Where would Manchuria be without the bandits? The bandits defend the plain against the warrior tribes of the Mongols, the horse-thieves. The bandits protect the peasants from the injustice of the mandarins. The bandits are the friends of the poor, the enemies of the rich. They are the distributors of wealth. The flower of our youth, the strongest, the most intelligent, the bravest of our young people— what do they become? They become bandits. They dictate their conditions to the governors. Nobody could govern without them. And to-day, who is it that defends Manchuria against the Japanese? Is it the great merchants of the city, is it the cowardly soldiers? Once more it is the bandit who, together with his friend the peasant, will save Manchuria!"

The peasants listened with enormous respect.

A recent study of the "people's revolutionary movement in the Northeast" thus quoted approvingly the popular Manchurian proverb: "When the bandits come, people send out presents of food and drink; when the soldiers come, they point them the wrong way at the crossroads." Similar stories were recalled of Bai Lang's popularity among the villages of south and west Henan, where legends of the exploits of Bai and other past heroes continued to circulate as late as the 1950's.[49]

In such areas it was not too difficult to appeal to bandit chiefs to join a rebellious undertaking, provided the appeal was suitably couched: one could do no better than to feed their egos with praise for the greenwood tradition. Republican activist Wu Luzhen, recruiting south Manchurian bandits in 1910 for the revolutionary forces, pretended to be a bandit chief from the south, and appealed to local chiefs' patriotism in the name of banditry itself! In the militarized environment of twentieth-century China, it was not unusual to find bandit armies bearing such grandiose titles as the "Army of the Self-Governing Association to Relieve the People's Livelihood" (taken by a band that occupied Luan, Anhui, in June 1924) or the "Shandong Self-Government National Reconstruction Army" (assumed by one section of the Lincheng bandits).[50]

The heroic ideal embodied in the greenwood ethic also emerged in the tradition of the "stout fellow" or *haohan*, one who, "seeing injustice on the road, took out his sword to lend help." Resolute, indifferent to wealth, ready to die to defend a friend, the typical *haohan* never surrendered or accepted humiliation, had a "natural exhilaration" born of great strength and courage, and displayed a careless self-confidence and robust humor that were invoked to excuse his frequent excesses.[51]

Not all of these were suitable qualities for a bandit chief; among the educated elite that often provided the leadership for bandit gangs the tradition of armed chivalry predominated, represented by the "knights errant" who abounded in such classics as the *Romance of the Three Kingdoms* and the *Shuihu zhuan*. A proclamation issued by Bai Lang, justifying his becoming a bandit, showed the simple honesty expected of the ideal chief when corruption was all about him: "I would have been an official, but am not adept at intrigue; I could have been an assemblyman, but am not skilled at agitation; hence I have given up everything to be a rebel, willing to risk the most unforgivable deed under Heaven."\* A proclamation issued at Lincheng echoed Bai Lang's politico-moral stance:

> Of late the country has fallen into such disorder that it must surely collapse. Because of supplementary taxation and military requisitions, our people cannot make a peaceful livelihood....[G]reedy and corrupt officials and evil gentry swagger and strut as they please. We heroes cannot rest while all this continues.... Our purpose in assembling all the companions of the greenwoods here is merely to roar like tigers until all these corrupt elements are rooted out once and for all. People of Shandong, rise up! Our concern is for the common people and our aim is communal property. First we must thrash to death all the corrupt and grasping officials and the evil rich, to dig out the roots of China's corruption, thus transforming it into a pure new world!... We are all heroes who have gathered like the clouds. Our food supplies are running short, and we must replenish them, but this [expropriation] will be limited to the homes of the rich; we will make no trouble for the poor. All you army men—if you had not joined up your fate would have been to become bandits. In the end we are all of one class: let us join forces in the common cause![52]

Class feeling then, if not strictly class consciousness, was evidently not unknown, at least in the traditional bandit areas. There are reports of rich Chinese captives being shot, not arbitrarily for their money, but simply out of anger at their having amassed huge fortunes in the midst of the poverty and suffering of the peasants.[53] Another song attributed to the Lincheng bandits expressed these sentiments clearly:

> Upper-class people, you owe us money;
> Middle-class people, don't meddle in our affairs;
> Lower-class people, come without delay,
> And pass the years on the mountain with us.[54]

Unfortunately, this heroic, wrong-righting self-image was largely restricted to gang leaders. For the rank and file, life was harder and the

---

\*Xian Yun 1956: 144. Note the echo of the *Shuihu zhuan*, where the Lianshanpo leader Song Jiang reluctantly declares: "Right now the imperial court is sullied and has fallen into the hands of treacherous officials. Loyal men cannot advance themselves. These corrupt officials and avaricious ministers are harming the people, and I and my men have nothing in mind but to carry out the Will of Heaven." Shi Naian 1952: 1053; see also Shih Nai-an 1963: 840.

prospects gloomier; despite occasional moments of optimism, they often became despondent or nihilistic, longing above all for home. Suggestions that many would be dead within the month, for example, "filled some of them with anxiety, but others only laughed and declared that if they could only kill one or two more soldiers first, they would die happy." [55] Many were evidently, as one missionary put it, "willing and eager to leave their present dreadful life [since] many have been forced [into it] against their will." Hearing that there existed in America "unlimited opportunity for every honest and industrious man . . . to make a good living," one gang declared that they would not be bandits once they got there. Learning that a rival gang had swept through his native village and plundered his home, a bandit proceeded to curse all "bandits" until challenged by a captive, at which point he simply left it that all bandits were "bad—very bad." [56]

These examples, drawn from several parts of China, are extremely revealing. The majority of the rank and file were clearly bandits against their preference, and even the chiefs were forced to find reasons to justify their life-style. The lack of pride among the ordinary bandits and the strong tendency to "return to allegiance" (*guishun*) when the opportunity arose had much to do with the traditional Chinese view of the state and its apparatus as the embodiment of supreme morality. To fight it was to make oneself "immoral," and unless one had a personal reason for doing so, the pressure to bow to it was immense, even for those who had once "fallen into the weeds."

Bandit attitudes toward authority then were often ambiguous. West Henan chiefs in 1911, hearing of the Republicans' plan to install the powerful local chief Wang Tianzong as provincial vice-governor, promptly declared that "When sixth brother [Wang] becomes governor we can all come out into the open. . . . After we have killed the Luoyang magistrate and the Henan viceroy, after the emperor is expelled from Beijing and Sun Wen has taken his place, then we can all become officials, and no one will dare call us bandits any more." *

The influence of state ideology was clearly visible in the way bandits even referred to themselves as having "fallen into the weeds," and described giving up banditry as "washing their hands." [57] Though the

---

* Cited in Wu Cangzhou 1961: 363. The chief's outburst was prefigured almost word for word in the *Shuihu zhuan*, where one of the heroes exclaims: "With our great army, let's start a rebellion! What have we to fear? Elder Brother Chao Gai can be the Greater Song Emperor, and Elder Brother Song Jiang the Lesser. Wu Yong can be Minister of State, and Gongsun Sheng Minister of Education. We ourselves can all be generals, and together we'll seize the capital, occupy the throne, and enjoy ourselves. Not a bad life! Better than staying in this watery marsh, anyway!" (Shi Naian 1952: 682; see also Shih Nai-an 1963: 581). Given the popularity of *Shuihu* among bandits, especially in tradition-conscious western Henan, the 1911 declaration may in fact have been inadvertently lifted.

state condemned them as *tufei*, rural reprobates, however, bandits would never use the term of themselves, except perhaps when they were feeling particularly despondent; they preferred such terms as *dixiong* and *haohan*, reserving the word *tufei* and its like for other gangs. Some particularly self-conscious chiefs, especially, liked to refer to other chiefs as "*fei*" in order to pour scorn on those whom they considered less upright than themselves.[58] As we have seen in an earlier chapter, however, it was difficult for these bandits to give up banditry even if they wanted to, because of the severe penalties awaiting them. Trapped in an undertaking they could not give up, some threw themselves into it wholeheartedly, others resigned themselves to an early death, and still others continued to live in hope of a new, more upright magistrate who would lower taxes and make farming profitable again. Such magistrates, unfortunately, rarely appeared.[59]

As for the other aspect of the greenwood ethic, the "blend of companionship, morality, and righteousness," this too was largely mythic. The exigencies of daily life made its demands hard to live up to, and in fact day to day relations between bandits in the same gang were often a considerable departure from the "merry men" ideal. "Except in time of danger, it was practically every man for himself."[60] Bandits who had been in the gang from its beginnings or who had entered at the same time were naturally close; friendships or elder-brother–younger-brother relationships between individual bandits developed as a matter of course, and could inspire mutual aid; the youngest or oldest bandits often received assistance or encouragement when needed, but the general rule was that gang members coexisted rather than cooperated except when their very survival was at stake.

This applied not only to the larger, less cohesive gangs of soldier-bandits, but also to smaller gangs, where one might have expected sometimes to see the greenwood ethic in action. Of the soldier-bandits of Lao Yangren, a captive noted that they were "usually cheerful and often hilarious...perfectly happy and satisfied," yet he added: "Their treatment of each other is strange and sometimes even mysterious. While acting as sworn friends before each other's faces, they often steal ammunition and various articles from each other, underhandedly. Sometimes they can be seen half-quarrelling and half-jesting about the ownership of a certain garment...that particularly appeals to their fancy."[61]

As for smaller gangs, one that fished near its camp almost every day observed an "unwritten rule" that each bandit had the right to eat all of his catch unless he desired to share it; there was little sharing. When a member of this gang got into difficulties while crossing a stream, it was a captive who was obliged to pull the man out, an action that caused great amazement among the other bandits, some of whom felt he was merely showing off.[62]

## Bandits and Violence

Fear and resentment, two basic components of the bandit psyche, lead most commonly to violence, and among bandits violence and cruelty were everyday affairs. Not that bandits had a monopoly on violence: the harsh behavior of government troops had often created the bandits in the first place, and the expectation of punishments still harsher should they surrender or get caught prevented them from giving up. Bandits, in other words, were caught up in a mesh of violence, and were only one aspect of an overwhelming tendency toward brutalization that, especially from the nineteenth century on, affected Chinese society from top to bottom. The fear of being caught or killed, and the resentment at being unable to break out of the vicious circle except by being caught or killed, underlay much of the cruelty that has characterized banditry everywhere. If many bandits became accustomed to the infliction of pain and even came to see it as a source of delight, such individuals were by no means restricted to the ranks of bandit gangs. Nor were all bandits equally responsible: captives noted "bandits of all kinds," some of them even "quite decent robbers."[63]

Certain general points may be made at the outset. First, most of the violence came from the younger bandits, who had nothing but their strength and vigor to carry them through. Second, since it originated in fear, the violence tended to escalate according to the precariousness of the bandits' own situation—such as when they held some foreign captives:

> In the new junk drawn alongside, was a Chinese prisoner.... Every now and again a bandit gave him a cutting smack across his face, and stamped his foot on the deck and, cursing, spat on him. They whipped themselves up with words and grew mad... their faces white with passion and excitement as they cursed... and threatened us with the same torture that this man was going to suffer.... The man let out a cry.... All the bandits were shouting and cursing like madmen....[64]

Third, violence was most characteristic of the weaker bandits: "Lin Chung... sobbed as though his heart would break. He wanted a friend that night, but he had none. When racked with pain or in times of anxiety, he craved the sympathy and help of others. Yet he treated the captives of his own race with such cruelty...."[65]

Given the characteristics of violence, in the bandits' case it naturally tended to be directed at those unable to fight back: their captives, particularly the Chinese ones. At Lincheng, the "village bully" type of subchief was represented at its least attractive by a man named "Bobo Lieu" (Liu Baobao), who "thinks nothing of tearing children limb from limb and grinding their elders to death under a stone roller."[66] Some bandit violence expressed resentment at the harsh treatment they themselves had received from those stronger than them. Or, since most captives were people deemed rich enough to pay a hefty ransom for their release, the violence they suffered could be deeply imbued with revenge, particularly if the ransom was slow in arriving. He Xiya lists twenty different punishments reserved for prisoners who were recalcitrant or who remained unredeemed, probably just the most horrendous examples he could cull from the sensationalist press rather than a formal list. They included sealing the eyes with plaster; pouring kerosene or vinegar into the nostrils; branding; hanging prisoners up by the thumbs and beating them; forcing prisoners to stand up to their shoulders in water for long periods; and standing prisoners near a fire until their flesh burned.[67] Most common of all were probably beatings or pure neglect, the same sort of malevolent treatment that could be found in any average jail, too. (Significantly, one gang entrusted a former prison guard among its members with overseeing such tortures!)[68]

Traditionally distorted reporting (such as the suggestion that at Lincheng several score Chinese captives were thrown off a cliff to their deaths[69]) has made violence an integral part of the bandit image. In the *Shuihu zhuan*, the heroes slaughter cheerfully with no indications of remorse,* justifying their actions by saying that they are disrupting the traditional order so as to put it right, and that the more disruption they cause the sooner things would improve. Henan bandit slang contained a term for banditry that contained the word *nao*, meaning "to create a disturbance." Instead of combining it with the word *luan* ("disorder") to complete the meaning, it was combined with *zheng* (to "correct" or "adjust") to form the expression *naozheng*: "to create a disturbance in order to put things right." A sentiment commonly heard among Henan bandits in the 1920's was, consequently, "the more trouble you cause, the higher your official rank will be." Sure enough, after the enrollment of Lao Yangren, southwest Henan bandits formed an alliance of more than seventy gangs to get themselves noticed by creating as much trouble as possible.[70]

Bandit violence could be a calculated instrument of policy, but

---

*See in particular the exploits of Li Kui in Chaps. 37 and 39. (I have found no examples among real-life bandits of the kind of cannibalism Li Kui indulges in.) Research into the reality behind the legend of Robin Hood, too, has shown that the "noble outlaw" image portrayed in medieval ballads was in fact deeply hued with blood. See Hilton 1958: 36.

equally often it expressed the desire of the poor for revenge against the symbols of the social and economic inequality that had disrupted their lives: the local gentry and officials on the one hand, and the walled town on the other, particularly those that, like Zhoujiakou in east Henan and Laohekou in north Hubei, were commercial centers or known to house rich residents.[71] The Bai Lang rebel army, whose "cruelties [were] sometimes fiendish," inspired "paralysis" whenever it approached a town, for "when they seize[d] a city they behave[d] like insensate demons."[72]

To the bandits, the walled town represented both a symbol of peasant subservience and a direct threat of retaliation. Whereas most peasants deferred to the town in the hope of keeping their lives on a plane of minimal stability, those who had taken the decisive step into banditry were released into a kind of vicious exhilaration. In true peasant rebel fashion, bandits who managed to break into a walled town (not an easy task, and attempted only by a bandit army) began by destroying official property, and went on to open the prison and free its inmates. The magistrate, police chief, and other functionaries, if they were lucky or farsighted, would have fled long before. If not, they were likely to be found the next day either hanging or, like the mayor of Chenliu in Henan, floating in one of their precious ornamental ponds. Such violent acts, together with the seizure of the police headquarters, constituted for the bandits the symbols of ultimate conquest and brought a chief widespread respect.[73]

Bandit armies rarely sought to occupy towns for longer than it took to complete their ransack, partly because of their irrelevance to bandit strategy, partly because of the danger of being trapped inside by attacking troops. When towns were taken, though, there often followed an "explosion of wrath" in which all social and sexual reservations were cast to the winds and pure violence took control. At Liuhe, Shandong, in 1928, the bandits' methods revealed "unheard-of cruelty." Captives were taken with no distinction between rich and poor; prisoners were retained even after being ransomed, or sent back minus an ear. Captives were killed in the most horrible fashion, boiled or burned alive, ripped apart by horses, and so on.[74]

By and large, however, bandit violence sprang from motives of revenge, sometimes social (e.g. for "crimes against the people" such as indiscriminate suppression policies), sometimes personal (e.g. for the death of a bandit's family, as in the case of one Yunnan chief who gained an unrivaled reputation for savagery after his family was slaughtered by troops in reprisals.* An attack by soldiers was also likely to provoke an

---

*The model was again provided by the *Shuihu zhuan*, where the leader Song Jiang threatens to slaughter a town's entire population if two of his followers held prisoner are executed. See Shih Nai-an 1963: 825.

outburst of chagrined violence, directed not against the soldiers them-selves, but against those most vulnerable: the peasants.[75]

Failure to return the bodies of bandits killed in an attack, or, even worse, the desecration of their graves, could be catastrophic: Kohinata Hakurō killed a magistrate and his underlings and hung their heads on the city wall in retaliation for such a crime (poetic justice, for this was the punishment usually meted out to bandits), and Bai Lang ordered a general massacre in one Shaanxi city for the same reason.[76] A proclama-tion posted near Jingziguan on the Henan-Shaanxi border in March 1914 in the name of the "Great Commander Supporting the Han" rebuked local inhabitants who had violated the graves of bandits killed during a previous raid for failing to demonstrate the correct "etiquette" (*li*) and "righteousness" (*yi*). As a last chance to redeem themselves before violent retribution was enforced, Bai advised them to "be not afraid" when the "Righteous Army" returned, "but to help us with arms and with grain to eat. Those who open their doors and show their al-legiance to me will all be protected, and we will not harm their lives and property."[77]

Another motive for exacting violent revenge was resistance, especially if any bandits were killed or wounded as a result.* Even so, resistance often did take place, usually at the insistence of men with property at stake, or of a magistrate for whom surrender would be equivalent to suicide anyway. Among several cities razed by Bai Lang's army, one re-mained in ruins twelve years later.[78] At Huangchuan (Guangzhou), in the rich farming area of southeastern Henan (particularly renowned for its fine opium crop), everyone was allegedly killed, and elsewhere Bai's followers were said to shoot everyone who ran away, who was found carrying things, or who wore furs or military uniform.[79] Cities that arranged terms, like Nanzhao in western Henan and Tongwei in Gansu, escaped unscathed.[80]

Unfortunately, sources do not make class distinctions when listing the dead and wounded in these attacks. On the contrary, since such sources were compiled by the educated class, they portray a picture of horrific, indiscriminate violence, sometimes to justify calling out the military, sometimes in the hope of profiting from any reparations that might be forthcoming from the government.[81] Nevertheless, there is evidence that the rich and privileged, as the natural objects of the bandits' wrath, were the first to suffer. By swapping her fine clothing for a beggar's rags, a rich woman was able to escape unharmed from a city occupied by

---

*Li Zicheng's regulations, for example, had laid down that cities surrendering with-out a struggle would be spared. If resistance continued for one day, however, one third of the population would be slaughtered; after two days, seven-tenths would die; and after three days a general massacre would be ordered (Parsons 1970: 216–17; see also Shih 1967: 379).

soldier-bandits, leaving the beggar to be shot in her place (according to one popular story).[82] The many landlords and retired officials who had made Huangchuan their home were practically wiped out in Bai Lang's 1913 attack, and reports of his sack of Luan in 1914, in which nine-tenths of the city was allegedly gutted, neglected to mention that the houses left undamaged were in the poorest section of the city.[83] A European inhabitant recalled that when Bai had taken the city "he treated the poor well. If the people were known to be poor, he, like Robin Hood, would have compassion on them and give them assistance."[84]

Bandit violence, in short, was sometimes discriminate, whereas official violence was usually not, unless it discriminated in favor of the elite. Violence is violence, whatever one thinks about it; but at the same time it must be remembered that bandits were not always the initiators, that they were sometimes merely responding to the sort of everyday violence they and their fellow-peasants suffered. Bandit violence must be seen in the context of a social system that was based on violence, and whose principal victims were the poor—who, of course, provided the majority of bandit recruits.

## Bandits, Women, and Sexuality

Most bandit gangs, at least the more or less permanent ones, were all-male fraternities. The idealistic ban on rape was only selectively applied, and the attitudes of rank-and-file bandits did not differ much from those prevalent in male society as a whole. Women's physical vulnerability combined with standard prejudicial notions to turn them into items of property deserving expropriation; rape became a viable means of indirect attack on male enemies, particularly those too strong to be attacked directly. Assaults on women from the privileged classes were especially violent, such women becoming scapegoats for the crimes of their menfolk.

Even those chiefs who banned rape, however, often did so not from humane considerations for women's dignity, nor merely from tactical considerations (though these were probably present to some extent), but from a sheer instinct for survival. A common belief among Chinese men, derived from Daoist notions and passed down in folklore, held that a man was allotted at birth only a certain quantity of life energy, and died when the quota was exhausted. Since sexual intercourse physically weakened a man, chastity could be construed as the difference between life and death. Though men themselves were free to risk their own lives carousing with prostitutes if they wished, women who made sexual demands on men appeared as the enemy, and could be attacked without remorse. In the *Shuihu zhuan*, for example, an "intense theme of misogyny" results in a series of violent attacks on women, but the violence the male heroes employ is not specifically sexual. One of them is criticized for being lustful, which is "not creditable to a hero." The true *haohan* should "waste no time in amorous dalliance, but conserve their energies for feats of valor."[85]

This is not the place for a general discussion of why such obviously dominant men feel threatened by physically weaker and usually submissive women. In China, the paradox was supported not only by the "sexual energy quota" concept, but also by a second Daoist notion of the continuous dynamic between *yang* and *yin*, the male and female elements respectively, such that when one of them waxed strongest it automatically became ripe for decline. Since a man at the peak of his strength became highly vulnerable, the heroes' fear of women was, in other words, their fear of imminent usurpation. In any power relationship, the power-holders are understandably nervous about the ability of the powerless to reverse the relationship, and male-female relations form just one aspect of this classic standoff. The imbalance embodied in such a conception of sexual relations, and the fear of the balance tipping the other way, put definite limitations on the code of male chivalry.[86] Rape was banned not for women's sake but to preserve the life-force and the very lives of the heroes from the threat posed by women.

Although the *Shuihu zhuan* ethic frowned upon the presence of women among the heroes, such presence was never actually condemned. At Liangshanpo there is a clear distinction between the main heroes, many of whose wives and mothers meet with convenient accidents on their way to the camp (thus ensuring the heroes' vitality), and the minor characters, who as the story unfolds turn out to have their families with them. Within the gang itself there are also a small number of female combatants. One achieves the rank of hero after defeating several men in armed combat, and later comes to lead a group of "Amazons" within the band; two others are sent as spies to nearby towns.[87] Both cases are significant. First, male chastity is much easier to sustain when women are absent, and women's presence reminded these men of the limitations of a celibate life. Second, the "Amazons" at Liangshanpo are little more than honorary men, and achieve what power and respect they have in the band as "men," not as women. Whether by enrolling the women as men or by sending them out of the camp on "external duties," the heroes neatly removed what must have appeared as a threat to their existence. The implication is that women as women have no role to play in the camp at all, and are by definition superfluous. Li Zicheng, incidentally, had also banned women from his camps, and the Taipings had sent their female chiefs off to serve as "outposts," simultaneously preserving both the male chiefs' vanity and the movement's basic policy of segregation.[88]

In this sense women are more oppressed in the male-dominated world of the *haohan*, which prescribed no role for them at all unless they became men, than in Confucian society, where at least the male-female relationship was recognized even if it was one-sided. In the *Shuihu zhuan* even wives become extraneous items, whereas in society as a whole they had legitimate, if inferior, social status.[89]

In the early summer of 1911 a dramatic and fatal clash involving two west Henan chiefs revealed that such attitudes were by no means dead. Wang Tianzong, an educated, modern-minded chief, had previously taken the unusual step for a bandit chief of going to study in Japan. There he had met and married a young revolutionary named Mao, whom he later brought back to his hideout on Yangshan, a subpeak of Songshan. The reaction of the other chiefs was hostile, particularly that of Guan Laojiu (Guan Fuen). Guan, known widely for his "great benevolence and righteousness," was a *haohan* who had joined the band after a murder carried out on a friend's behalf, and he had sworn an oath of blood-brotherhood with Wang. To chiefs like Guan, that Wang should go off on a jaunt to Japan was bad enough, but to come back with a woman, particularly a Shanghai intellectual like Mao, and to bring her into the sacred territory of the bandit world was both incomprehensible and impermissible. Guan subsequently demanded that Mao be returned to Shanghai; Wang, he said, had "tricked" her into accompanying him to Yangshan. Most of the other chiefs, also *haohan* types, supported him, and Wang's reputation plummeted. In the end, after a long standoff, a fight ensued in which Wang shot Guan to death.[90]

This pattern, probably more instinctive than ideological, remained strong throughout the Republican period. At Lincheng, for instance, one chief exclaimed, "We despise women above everything, so we never go near them." The Shandong chief Mama Zhao actually divided her forces into separate all-male and all-female units.* As captives, too, women were extremely troublesome and theoretically to be avoided.

Less tradition-conscious bandits, like the rank and file at Liangshanpo, often had wives or concubines in the camp. Mostly noncombatants, they had either been stolen from villages the gang had passed through or chosen from among its ransom victims. Many bandits, oblivious to the paranoia of the *haohan*, had joined the gang principally for the purpose of finding a partner; unable for various reasons to return home, they sometimes stayed on even after doing so. It was also a custom to entice young male captives to stay with the band by offering them a choice of the female captives.[91] Perhaps a major attraction for young men was that

---

*Nagano 1938: 141, 175–76. See also *NCH*, 2 Apr. 1927: 45; Aldrich 1923: 674. North Manchurian chiefs, rather than risk pollution by women, evidently preferred to catch or buy small Siberian bears and live with them instead (Gotō 1928: 37).

they could not only protect their masculine self-respect by acquiring a wife, but sometimes even enhance it by amassing numbers of wives or concubines.[92] Life for the bandit wife herself, though, could be a shaky existence: one chief shot his "number one wife" for being unable to keep up on marches because of her bound feet.[93] Under female chiefs, however, they fared better: one allowed her men to purchase captured women, but with the injunction that such women became the lawful wives of the purchasers, who would be put to death if they discarded them.* Among bandits who had left their wives at home, it was apparently not "good form" to refer to them.[94]

Bandit chiefs could be highly moral with regard to others' behavior, especially that of women. In the *Shuihu zhuan*, the heroes' most bloodthirsty frenzies of violence are reserved for women accused of adultery: that is, those who attempt to kick over the traces imposed on them by the male-dominated culture of Confucianism. Among modern bandit gangs, too, the double standard prevailed: one female captive was severely reproved by the chief for her "indecency" in sleeping under the same quilt as another male captive, but at least two men reported being offered women to sleep with.[95]

Sexuality within the gang was evidently a closed topic. Among the *honghuzi* sexual relations between gang members were strictly taboo; when the men were in need of "entertainment" they would repair as a group to a large town to carouse in its brothels and bathhouses for the day. Prestige-conscious chiefs were more circumspect, and took a room in an inn, outside which they would hang a sword to indicate that they were not to be disturbed. The hanging-sword symbol was popular enough to be instantly recognizable, and to ignore it was a fatal mistake.[96]

As an all-male society, bandit gangs should have had their share of homosexuality, but captives, who were usually given separate sleeping quarters, reveal nothing of this.[97]

## Superstition

As a psychological adjustment to a dangerous life-style, bandits naturally leaned on providence; as we saw, luck was a vital requirement for a successful chief. Among both Manchurian bandits and South China Sea

---

*Outside the gang, however, "bandit wives," like "gangsters' molls," had a mystique of their own, as revealed by a curious lottery organized by Shanxi gentry figures in 1915. To raise money to rebuild a bridge destroyed by floods, they hit on the novel idea of selling off the widows of two well-known bandit chiefs captured and executed a few months before. The lottery was "immensely popular" even at 1,000 strings of cash per ticket, and the necessary funds were raised with no difficulty at all (*NCH*, 13 Nov. 1915: 525).

pirates, great faith was placed in palmistry for predictions of what the future held for the gang. Some chiefs carried divination books whose prognostications were weighed against the results of practical investigation before an attack was carried out; pirate fleets never set sail unless the omens were auspicious.[98] The traditional ties between the *honghuzi* and local Daoist centers imbued local bandits with a strong belief in divine intervention, and they frequently stopped to pray at wayside shrines.[99] The area where popular Daoism blended into superstition is a very shady one, however, and here I will concentrate on those superstitions that may be considered peculiar to bandits.

Most bandit argot grew out of the need to cope with various specific superstitions. A common practice was the substitution of alternative words for those of bad import. Certain reports have suggested eight principal taboo words—dream, tiger, wolf, tooth, spirit, pagoda, ghost, and pig—but the full list was much longer.* One observer made a bandit start in fear by asking him if he were eating *baogu*, meaning either maize or Indian corn. The use of the word *bao*, meaning "to wrap up," was thought likely to cause an encirclement (*baowei*) by soldiers.[100] Another expression to be avoided was *xiexie*, meaning "thank you" in its commonest usage but homophonous with another word meaning "to

---

*C. Y. Chang 1937: 498; Swallow and Lu 1934; Mantetsu chōsaka 1930: 45. One may speculate on the origins of these word taboos. Dreams (*meng*) had an annoying tendency to come true, or at least to suggest portents of dark days to come, and were generally considered unlucky; opium dreams may well have been particularly anxiety-provoking. Even bandits whose name was Meng were referred to as "Ming" (Tanaka 1934: 162; see also Yao Xueyin 1981: 13). Avoidance of the words "tiger," "wolf," and "tooth" probably reflected the overall taboo on mentioning potentially dangerous adversaries. The ban on "tiger" (*hu*) may have come from the traditional geomantic association of the Chinese word with the female principle, but it more likely arose from the practice of referring to the magistrate's *yamen* or office as "the tiger's mouth" (*hukou*), implying that those who entered were unlikely to come out alive. The word for "tooth," *ya*, is also a homophone of the first syllable of "*yamen*." Direct mention of the place was thought liable to result in the appearance of the magistrate with his soldiers. The taboo on "wolf" (*lang*) must have stemmed either from the bandit custom of calling government troops "weasels" (*huangshulang*), or from fear of the real wolves that still haunted many remote areas. When it became necessary to introduce such words into a conversation, therefore, alternatives were preferred, such as "wide-opened mouth" (*haizuizi*) for tiger, "gaping mouth" (*liezuizi*) for wolf, "broken sword" (*zhedaozi*) for tooth, and "yellow millet" (*huangliang*), an obscure classical reference, for "dream" (Mantetsu chōsaka 1930: 45). The problem with "spirit" was its association with death, a taboo subject whose mention invited death within the gang. A bandit killed in action was thus said to be merely "asleep" (Howard 1926: 105; He Xiya 1925a: 68). Another reason for avoiding "spirit" was that the Chinese word, "*ling*," is homophonous with those meaning "prison" and "fragment," raising grim visions of a future spent incarcerated or, even worse, of being sliced into pieces following execution. "Pagoda" (*ta*) was possibly taboo because the same word was used to mean a grave marker, another death-related concept. "Ghost" (*gui*), like "spirit," both reminded the bandits of their own imminent extinction and had the potential of conjuring up the avenging specters of their victims. The taboo on "pig," finally, almost certainly resulted from its Chinese equivalent *zhu* being homophonous with another word used to refer to the execution or extermination of rebels and bandits.

cut in pieces," the punishment reserved for bandits and rebels. Although many bandits "caught" ransom victims for a living, the usual words for "catch," *zhuo* and *zhua*, because they were also used to refer to captured bandits (*zhuozei*, etc.), were replaced by *jia* in the traditional term for kidnapping, *jiapiao*, or by *shi*, similar in construction to *zhuo*. To kill someone was for similar reasons referred to circumspectly as to "release" (*fang*) them. A bandit not yet fluent in or neglecting these taboos was regarded askance by the other bandits, most of whom took them very seriously. To put a nonchalant veneer on their activities, to be wounded was referred to as "wearing colors" (*daicai, guacai*) or as "receiving a decoration" (*tiejin*). Banditry itself was glossed over as merely "playing" (*wanwanr*) or "business" (*shengyi*), or, in more practical vein, as "to climb on a horse" (*shangma*) or "to take up a stick" (*daigan, laganzi*).

Because of the superstition against the direct mention of enemies, certain terms grew up as substitutes. The magistrate, for example, became simply "the enemy" (*diren*) or "the ancient" (*guzi*), his yamen and the police station "brothels of power" (*weiwuyao*); a jail was the "brothel of the magistrate's runners" (*kuaiyao*); a deserted temple, where bandits might be executed, was the "brothel of the dumb" (*yabayao*). Soldiers and policemen became "locusts" (*zhameng*) or "rabbits" (*tuzi*), and also "sleet" (*lengzi*) or "wind" (*feng*), all terms that implied not only their large numbers but also their general unstoppableness when resolved to advance. When attack loomed, it was said that "the wind was pressing" (*fengjin*).* A county seat, since it was surrounded by four walls, was referred to as the "circle" (*juanzi*).[101]

Certain actions were also against the rules, such as whistling, which was thought to bring bad luck.[102] The kowtow—prostrate with head pressed to the ground—was forbidden, either because it reminded bandits of the kneeling person waiting for the executioner's sword to fall, or because it represented surrender and was therefore repugnant (bandits, remember, generally preferred people who put on a bold front). The usual word for "kneel down," *xiabai*, was replaced by another, *jianfu*, literally meaning "trim and brush." Clasping the hands behind one's back was taboo because it resembled a trussed prisoner's posture.

Chopsticks were to be laid flat on the table, not across the dish, which would look like a pair of gun barrels pointing at the person opposite; nor

---

*He Xiya 1925a: 72–75; Inoue 1933: 60. According to Inoue, the word "wind" was brought into underworld slang by pirates, especially coastal salt smugglers. Since their success depended on the wind, a good one was life-giving, whereas no wind threatened disaster. *Pufeng* was "to sail against the wind"—hence to resist arrest: *shifeng*, "to lose the wind," meant being arrested; to successfully repel an attack was *defeng*, "to get a good wind." For very similar speech taboos on the part of mine workers, another dangerous profession, see Sun 1967: 66. Yao Xueyin 1981, incidentally, provides a wealth of slang terms used by Henan bandits, only a small number of which could be introduced here.

were they to be leaned diagonally against the dish, which would resemble the position of an individual awaiting execution. Any tearing or breaking was also frowned upon because it reminded bandits of the punishment that had in past days frequently greeted those who were captured, that of being stretched or torn on the rack. Bread, in particular, was never to be sliced from the side in the usual fashion since the word *heng* meaning "side" was also used in the construction *hengsi*, meaning an "untimely death." Slicing was also the supreme punishment reserved for rebels and recalcitrant bandits.

Among other actions designed to improve or protect the gang's fortunes was the practice of sprinkling five drops of wine on the floor with the middle finger before a meal to signify respect for Heaven, earth, the emperor, and both parents. Whereas Manchurian gangs allegedly carried out attacks only on days with odd numbers—3, 5, 7, or 9—some Sichuan bands refrained from activity when it was raining, according to travelers' tales. As for food of good and bad import, though some bandits would not eat the heads of fish or chickens because these brought misfortune, others sought out the heads of chickens to eat so as to increase their intelligence, the intestines to preserve a healthy appetite, and the feet so as to be able to run away from the soldiers. Only one side of a fish could be eaten, presumably because to eat both sides would expose the bones and trigger off unwelcome associations.[103]

## Conclusion

The life of the average rank-and-file bandit was a hard one far from the world of the sentimental ballad. Most of them remained unwilling recruits from beginning to end, and their day-to-day attitudes reflected that fact of life. Few apart from the chiefs had any illusions about what they were doing, but they made the best of a bad job, inventing words and actions to put the future out of mind, enjoying themselves whenever possible, and taking to opium dreams when the anxiety became unbearable. The violence that surrounded and threatened them was echoed in the cruelty they practiced toward their weaker fellow-humans, particularly women. Meanwhile, the harshness of their lives was recompensed somewhat by the healthy respect they managed to garner as people who had stood up and out of the peasant mass.

Bandits, when they have engaged the attentions of serious investigators, have all too often been seen purely in terms of the explosive acts of violence sometimes committed by the gang as a whole. Not only have the long periods when a band was on the run or lying low to enjoy its spoils been ignored; the fact that it was in the end a collection of diverse individuals each with his or her particular dream or ambition or anxiety has been more or less forgotten. Bandits, that is, have been judged by the violence they sometimes wrought, but equal consideration must be paid to the frustrations which provoked that violence, and to the anxiety encouraged by the fugitive life. In the turbulence of action and the confusion of retreat, individual concerns are obliterated. Yet a close empirical look at the daily lives of bandits indicates that in their resort to direct predatory action bandits were often voicing the dreams or anger of the inarticulate poor. Cutting through the opaqueness of the official data permits a perspective on the Chinese bandit that, though it reveals the workings of treachery and vindictiveness as much as those of courage and magnanimity, reminds us that in the end bandits were just people.

## CHAPTER SEVEN

# "Prevailing Winds, Adverse Currents": Bandits, Power, and the People

*"We have an old Chinese saying, 'Big fish eat little fish, little fish eat shrimps, shrimps eat mud!' That's sure true here, my friend. . . . The peasants are the shrimps, the little fish are the bandits, the big fish are the officials!"*                                            —*Snow 1972: 49*

*"The bandit appeared both as the enemy of all the people and the helper of the oppressed. He was described as cruel and bloodthirsty, as helpful and noble, as brutal, brave, tender, cowardly, extravagant, immoral, depraved, generous and free."*          —*Cited in Tiedemann 1982: 395*

ACCORDING TO THE writer and anthropologist Elie Reclus, the origins of the state and its police force lie in an agreement among bygone brigands to substitute the collection of tolls for outright robbery, obviating competition among themselves and ensuring a peaceful division of the spoils.[1] Likewise, modern professional gangs that sought to acquire for themselves a niche in the local power structure were quite often welcomed by a less-than-vigorous local elite. The precondition was the inability of the "legitimate" authorities to monopolize power on their own terms.

In regions where the capacity of the center to enforce its will was diluted by distance or poor communications, local officials and military figures and their allies the landed gentry were often left more or less to their own devices. Local officials, knowing that banditry would persist so long as the conditions that produced it remained unchanged (and not usually caring much either way), concentrated on keeping it to a permissible level or edging it into another's jurisdiction. The military, apart from having much in common with the bandits, usually had more to gain materially from tolerating them than from suppressing them. Landed gentry figures, with more at stake, adopted a posture appropriate to the relative strength and behavior of the bandits, sometimes moving to suppress them, sometimes arriving at mutual agreements to avoid hostilities.

Unquestionably, banditry was a hard and dangerous profession. Since most bandits were ultimately out to enrich themselves, the prospect of getting themselves killed before they could spend their gains was hardly appealing, and they were alert to chances of reducing the risk. Although some. of them were genuine "social bandits" who took an implacable stance toward the local establishment, the majority were pragmatists who understood instinctively that the only road to realizing any of the dreams that moved them was to come to terms with whoever was ready to parley. Their close ties to their native area gave them a strong bargaining tool. The typical bandit gang was thus prone to shifting allegiances, now standing for the poor and landless, now in the pay of the rich with a mission to put down upstarts of the sort they themselves had once been. In contrast to the uncaring attitude of the officials and the military, however, the bandits' local ties gave them a certain influence. Their presence, though not always visible, was felt much more strongly than that of local officials, and often earned them the loyalty of the poor and even the grudging respect of the rich. Local officials tended in practice to reconcile themselves to this political reality. In the interests of a quiet life bandits were often left to themselves, or even transformed into a legitimate "local defense" detachment. When things did not go quite so smoothly, a gang could still offer the only available source of informal protection for a locality despite the presence of those, like the soldiers and the elite-controlled militia, for whom protection was their reason for existence. The pattern varied according to time and local conditions, but as a general rule it can be said that banditry in practice was an adaptation to, not a protest against, the local power structure. Except in troubled times it tended to reinforce rather than disrupt the status quo, for the reverse side of the "protection" bandits offered was coercion, preventing local people from controlling their own destinies in the same way that the state apparatus did.

The relationship between bandits and the people of their home area was not always one-sided. Although ties to the elite were a powerful factor in a gang's ability to survive, there was no shortage of rivals, and chiefs had to keep one eye on their local rapport. The ability to earn at least the blind eye if not the positive support of local people was thus another important factor in a gang's potential to remain uncaught. The stronger those popular ties were, the more difficult it was to catch a gang without the use of terror.

## Patriarchs, Patrons, and Patrolmen

The county or *xian* magistrate was traditionally recognized by security-conscious imperial officials as the most important link in the government's chain of control, for his jurisdiction lay closest to village society where the vast majority of Chinese dwelt.[2] In practice he played no part in the peasants' everyday lives that could not have been easily dispensed with, and experienced few qualms about the contrast between the splendor of his own surroundings and the destitution of his "children people," as the peasants were patronizingly called. As an outsider, unfamiliar with local customs and certain to be transferred before very long, a magistrate usually concentrated on making his fortune by the imposition of various unofficial levies. At the same time, a network of poorly paid and notoriously corrupt clerks, secretaries, and runners made approaching the magistrate's office or *yamen* akin to "entering the tiger's mouth."[3] In materials on rural China, the magistrate, for all his theoretical importance, is conspicuously absent.

Although officially charged with settling local disturbances, from the military point of view the county magistrate was ill-equipped for the task. Commanding no more than a few hundred barely trained and poorly armed men, at the best of times he could hope to deal with no more than scattered incidents of unrest.[4] At worst, attempts to suppress bandits might escalate the trouble, for *yamen* employees and constables would exploit the situation to their own ends, making false arrests so as to extort money from the victims, inciting vagrants to cause trouble and prolong the crisis, and so on. Someone in the magistrate's office itself might even be in collusion with the bandits, selling them information about suppression plans. In any case, from the viewpoint of the average local official, for whom the slightest hint of trouble could mark the end of his career, any attempt to suppress bandits actively was extremely perilous; unless sure of success, most magistrates sought to ignore the suppression directives that periodically descended upon them from their less vulnerable superiors:

> The county magistrate turns a blind eye,
> Playing mah-jongg and carousing in the brothels.
> No cares for the people, no plans against bandits—
> Who'd imagine he's on an official salary?[5]

Understating local unrest was a misdemeanor of which local officials were frequently accused. This was understandable, for to recognize the existence of a disturbance was to assume the burden of settling it, and many an official career had been shattered on the rock of failed responsibility. "When the forces of order heard the word *t'u-fei* [bandits]," went the popular saying, "they jumped like a mouse who had heard a cat meow."[6] A mid-1920's newspaper report consequently pointed out that, although Henan was already well on the way to becoming the principal "bandit province" of China, in the absence of truthful official reporting it appeared to outsiders quite peaceful and bandit-free.[7] The intelligent local magistrate, hearing of an impending bandit attack, would immediately make preparations not for defense, but to receive the gang as conquering heroes: sending out a welcome party to escort the gang into town amid great fuss and fanfare was particularly effective in keeping the chief in a good humor, and communities that took such steps often escaped relatively lightly.[8]

Given the important role of self-enrichment in the average official's outlook on life, an agreement with local bandits to turn a blind eye in return for a cut in their profits could appear extremely attractive: "The universal complaint of the common people is that the robber bands are immune from attack because of a plain business arrangement with the nearest official, who shares in the spoils. It is also firmly believed by the common people that arms and ammunition are furnished the bandits by the officials themselves, at prices [from] which the latter make an enormous profit." No wonder then that many local functionaries themselves became known as "official" or "legal" bandits (*guanfei, fafei*).[9]

Yet, as Bai Lang's lethal revenge on the unpopular Yuxian (Henan) magistrate in June 1913 showed, it was more than mere politics or profits that prompted magistrates to appease local bandits. One Shandong official changed his sleeping quarters every night out of fear of revenge by friends of the bandits he had had executed. By the 1920's, the majority of local officials had become the puppets of local warlord patrons, and rampant corruption reduced the stock of the county magistrate to rock-bottom. One North China bandit chief even offered a reward of 100,000 dollars for the head of the local magistrate (plus 30,000 each for those of the three local police officials).[10]

When it became impossible for the magistrate to procrastinate any longer, his usual tack would be to arrest a few of the bandits' leaders (if they could be found), or else, if there was no chance of being exposed, to arrest some of their accomplices and claim they were the leaders, then report the affair settled. If the remaining bandits could be persuaded to hop over the border into another official's jurisdiction, so much the better. In the report the scale of the disturbance and the number of participants would be played down and the whole affair made to appear as a trivial matter that the magistrate had settled skillfully and with a minimum of fuss. Unsuspecting individuals arrested as "bandit accomplices" would find themselves in jail until a suitable bribe was raised. All in all, it was difficult to say which caused more trouble for local inhabitants, bandits or corrupt officials, and not a few observers have come down against the latter.[11] In short: "Local officials began by concealing bandits; continued by conniving at them; and their mutual cooperation soon became second nature."[12]

With no more than a small constabulary at their immediate command, most magistrates were not equipped to deal with large, well-armed bandit gangs. Though laws passed after 1911 empowered them to take command of local troops when the situation required,[13] the army, for its own reasons, was as reluctant to come to grips with a bandit problem as the magistrate was. When troops arrived in a neighborhood, it was traditionally said, "while the villagers wept, the bandits were all smiles."[14]

The average county garrison numbered between 150 and 300 soldiers raised from among the young men of the county, whose main responsibility was to ensure security within the county boundaries. When bandits were reported in outlying areas these troops were supposed to take independent action to suppress them. As the old proverb went, however, "good iron is not made into nails; good men do not become soldiers": the local garrison, apart from a few well-meaning youths who volunteered to protect their home county, generally attracted the same rough sorts who would join bandit gangs or the government army (whose reputation was the lowest of all).[15] Indeed, it was often no more than the relative proximity of the nearest garrison as compared to the nearest bandit gang that governed an individual's choice. The same man could even be bandit one day and soldier the next, and few on either side were willing to fight against people with whom they had once shared a campfire: "When I returned," wrote one former captive, "I found that two soldiers in full uniform had come in during my absence. Their presence surprised me, but not so much as did the evidence of cordial relationship which I observed existing between them and the bandits...."[16] Bandits also provided a constant pool of cost-free reserves, many of whom, like the Shaanxi *daoke*, were able to be either bandit or soldier according to taste and the local military situation.[17] As yet another proverb put it, "bandits and soldiers were breath from the same nostrils."

The troops had ample reason to avoid serious clashes with the bandits. Most had joined up for the economic security the army offered, not for the joy of fighting, and sought no more than a quiet, steady life with the occasional chance to let their hair down. Their officers were primarily concerned with reaping a profit and achieving regular promotion through the skillful manipulation of "connections." Soldiers of this sort were not likely to risk their lives in a fight with bandits when they could just as easily avoid one. Moreover, by defeating the bandits they themselves would become redundant. Even a commander with loyal intentions often found himself thwarted, for the bandits would seek to persuade the soldiers at least to ignore them if not actually to join them, and the military's bleak living standards ensured that their appeal found ready listeners. The difficulty and expense involved in acquiring ammunition also made bandits reluctant to expend it unnecessarily. To induce the soldiers not to fight, therefore, Bai Lang's vanguard fighters would call across the land dividing them from the army lines that "we never kill our brothers, only officers of company-commander rank and above."[18] At the first sight of bandits Henanese troops were said to fire blanks to give warning of their approach. A soldier participant later confessed that, since the troops sent against Bai Lang were all his fellow-provincials, despite several apparent clashes there had been no real fighting at all.[19] During the sweep through fertile southeast Henan and Anhui in January 1914, for example, the 25,000 men sent to "exterminate" the band busied themselves raking over the countryside in the wake of its passage for anything the rebels had left behind. Similar accusations of military venality were leveled after Lao Yangren's spectacular and unopposed circuit of Henan in late 1923.[20]

This traditional bandit-soldier intimacy increased after the appearance of antibandit village defense leagues like the Red Spears. Because the successful eradication of banditry would put the soldiers themselves out of a job, the latter often stood by and watched while bandits and villagers fought. Should the villagers appear to be gaining the upper hand, the soldiers might even open fire on them to permit the bandits to escape. At the very least it was usually a simple matter for bandits to "borrow the road" (*jiedao zou*) from soldiers in order to pass by their strongpoints unhindered.[21]

Bandits and local "defense" garrisons thus played more or less complementary roles in the local military structure, and had more to gain from tolerating each other than from fighting. With the loot acquired from the people whom the troops were supposed to protect, the bandits were able to buy from the soldiers guns and ammunition, plus the freedom to operate. In return the soldiers augmented their meager pay and at the same time attained a certain security by demonstrating the continuing need for "bandit-suppression" forces. In bandit slang, this was the "double convenience" (*liangbian*), denoting any arrangement by which bandits and soldiers reached agreement to avoid hostilities.[22]

The connection could be made in a number of ways. The bandits might pass word to the soldiers that part of their loot was buried in a certain place (prostitutes in the local brothels often served as useful and willing go-betweens).[23] The soldiers would then proceed to the appointed place and, after expending large amounts of ammunition into the air to give the semblance of a fight, dig up the money and bury guns and bullets in its place, later reporting the munitions "lost in battle." Occasionally direct commercial exchanges took place. Lao Yangren offered defense garrisons on his route of march $100 for every rifle they allowed to reach him, and accusations of a garrison's having "sold" its town to the attacking bandits became rife after 1920.[24] (An enterprising chief who aimed at more than just a stake in the local power structure could take advantage of this venality. Bai Lang's band, like the Nian rebels fifty years before, would leave a trail of loot for "pursuing" soldiers to find, then double back and wipe them out while they were absorbed in gathering up the spoils.)[25]

The facts of this traditional bandit-soldier relationship were fully known to the authorities, and it was probably no more than a public relations exercise when, in January 1914, the Henan provincial government ordered magistrates to take a census of all publicly and privately owned weapons in their districts after finding that the majority of the guns captured from bandits were official issue. The problem assumed more seriousness, however, when it became impossible to employ Henan troops in a joint anti–Bai Lang campaign mounted by the authorities of Henan, Hubei, and Anhui in the spring of that year. According to one correspondent's blunt explanation, the soldiers' guns were all in the hands of the bandits. People ironically labeled the bandit-suppression commanders the "transportation commanders" because so much of their ordnance fell into bandit hands.[26]

The balance of forces determined the precise nature of the bandit-soldier relationship. Where bandits had the edge over the soldiers, the latter might buy their cooperation so as to avoid recriminations from higher up. Of the one dollar per ton of coal paid to the military for protection against bandits by the owners of the big Zhong Xing coal mine in Shandong, half, it is said, went to the bandits themselves.[27] Where the scales were weighted the other way, racketeering soldiers could demand "protection money" from the bandits in return for giving them a free hand, a device that the "victims" agreed to readily. There are even cases recorded of soldiers doing nothing while another regular military unit received a drubbing at the hands of bandits, usually because the unit in question, by taking its antibandit mission too seriously, had endangered the all-important racket.[28]

Since officials were primarily concerned to keep a lid on things, the object of a "country-cleansing" (*qingxiang*) campaign was not so much the physical extermination of the bandits themselves as the removal of the problem the bandits were causing. Energetic suppression methods generally gave way to arbitration in the so-called "bandit provinces." To avoid retaliation, the affair would be handed over to former bandits if possible, or else to people with close bandit contacts. With their expert knowledge of what was needed, the latter could use friendly persuasion instead of force, an approach neatly encapsulated in the phrase "simultaneous suppression and pacification" (*jiao fu jianshi*).[29]

When soldiers did move against bandits, the ideal solution was not to eliminate them physically but to drive them over the border to become someone else's responsibility. Even when an attack was eventually pressed home, the bandits were often first allowed long and fruitful forages, for the longer they operated the richer they became, and the greater the profits from the final roundup. Hence the "cleanup" campaign rarely had much effect on the bandit problem itself, and brought most benefits to the military garrison: the soldiers received a rake-off from the long-departed bandits, together with whatever they had picked up themselves; the officers and the local official, as well as taking the lion's share of the profits, were rewarded for successfully "suppressing" the bandits; and the authorities higher up were relieved because a troublesome district had been effectively "pacified."[30] No wonder, then, that villagers called soldiers the "second *tufei*."

The gentry, unlike the magistrate, had their roots in the area where they lived. When they mobilized, they did so in defense of their own lives and property, not out of loyalty to some abstract notion of "the state." Hence they were obliged to face up to the fact of banditry, a constant reminder of the violent fate that awaited them should their power begin to slip. The magistrate, on the other hand, was interested primarily in maintaining peace and quiet, preferably through ensuring a stable balance of power. In the long run, the magistrate's interests naturally paralleled those of the gentry, whose fortunes equally depended upon maintaining the status quo. In the event of a bandit-suppression campaign, the gentry forces were obvious allies. Frequently, however, official suppression was not attempted, magistrates merely closing the gates of their city when bandits were reported nearby.

Rich families living in or near the bandit areas had two choices if they wanted to remain where they were: take steps to guard their property against attacks, or, especially if they lived in isolated houses, find some means of preventing attacks altogether. The front entrance of the main living quarters remained permanently closed, and sleeping quarters were changed regularly. Even in the daytime gatemen would not open the door without a satisfactory reply to their challenge; shooting first and asking questions later was the fundamental rule of thumb.[31] With the right connections the family might be able to keep a small force of regular soldiers at its personal disposal, but usually self-defense meant diverting funds to maintain a private militia. The latter were not only expensive but also unreliable: many were former bandits and remained in touch with their old comrades; others were the very type who would otherwise have drifted into banditry. Effective against smaller gangs, these private retainers were rarely able or inclined to stand up to a major attack, and in a crisis their most valuable function could be to act as a pipeline between the beleaguered family and the bandits through which the former could attempt to come to terms. In the long run it was usually better to seek to remove the danger of attacks altogether, either by paying a regular toll to the gang or by implicitly recognizing its local hegemony.[32] Many North China chiefs, particularly along the troubled border districts of Henan, Shandong, and Anhui, were able to mix freely with local elite figures, treating them as their social equals and even "inviting" them to marriage feasts and other festive occasions.[33]

On the whole, the rich rural gentry in the bandit areas took issue only with gangs that directly threatened their own specific district. In the case of major upheavals such as that of 1911 they might join forces, forming militia across a considerable geographical area to protect the interests of the system they represented, as the bloody example of the "Future-Safeguarding Society" of Henan showed.[34] Otherwise, their local affiliations allowed accommodation with gangs that did not pose a direct danger.

An event that took place at the height of the Lincheng crisis was typical. Two weeks after the derailing, with negotiations over the captives' release stalled by the military siege of the bandits' hideout, local gentry sent three representatives of their own to speed matters up. These gentry delegates, men of some local prestige, nevertheless submitted to being led on a deliberately contrived wild-goose chase from mountain village to mountain village under a hot summer sun. The bandits having made their political point, the talks finally began, and the reason for the delegates' tolerance was made clear: in just two weeks the troops billeted on the local countryside had reduced the area to such desperate straits that soon it would be financially incapable of supporting an expanded provincial army. If the bandits were serious in their intention of becoming soldiers, the delegates insisted, it was in their own interests as well as those of local people to reach an agreement with the government negotiators without delay.[35]

Unfortunately, gang fortunes waxed and waned, the balance of power shifting constantly as new leaders emerged to take the place of those who had been killed or bought off. The replacement of "their" gang by a new one and the expensive renewal of the contract could spell disaster for even the richest family if repeated too often. Most, however, were resigned to it, counted carefully those blessings they did have, and accepted that "disaster comes at three-yearly intervals."[36]

When the struggle for ascendancy between rival gangs reached the merciless heights it did in many parts of China in the early twentieth century, the only thing left for many once-powerful lineages was to set themselves up as political bosses in open alliance with some nearby gang leader.[37] The strong possibility that the latter might actually come to supplant their patron altogether, or, alternatively, that the patron might abandon his statist alliance once and for all by setting himself up as an independent military potentate, made such alliances a severe headache for the outside authorities.

## Bandit Power—Power to the People?

If the local elite, as described in the previous section, had a vested interest in reaching agreement with a powerful bandit chief, the bandits themselves, contrary to the popular image, were rarely in a position to turn their backs on the straight world altogether. An alliance with a local elite figure was thus a fairly logical decision. For the chiefs it could be a step up on the ladder of local respectability and a means of gaining formal sanction for the power they wielded; for the rank and file, any offer that improved upon or at least equaled the rewards to be expected from predatory banditry, minus the opprobrium and constant danger, could not be sniffed at. It was not unusual to find ex-bandits and other propertyless individuals serving as strong-arm retainers in rich households, and a Shandong businessman captured at Lincheng was able to effect his release through a relative who had formerly engaged one of the bandit chiefs as a bodyguard.[38]

The economic factor also played its part, for self-enrichment from banditry was a touch-and-go affair: one had to obtain arms and ammunition from somewhere, which usually meant from the "local bullies and evil gentry" (*tuhao lieshen*)—the Chinese term for elite figures who abused their privileges to oppress the poor—or from the local military garrison. These could of course charge what prices they liked, knowing that it was a seller's market.

Bandits also had to find someone to dispose of their surplus income. Though big gangs could set up front organizations in nearby cities (one had at least two "bank accounts" from which they regularly drew money to buy supplies[39]), most had to depend on local "fences"—once again, usually the "local bullies and evil gentry," who thereby ensured their own immunity from attack. One well-heeled Chinese captive came under considerable pressure to allow his house to be used as the gang's new headquarters. In return he and his family were promised protection plus a share in the profits. If discreet, the chief insisted, they could go undetected for years. Another landlord, who had acted as trustee for the large fortune he had permitted a local chief (his former hired hand) to store in his house, grew rich overnight when the chief was killed. On the other hand, if they were not careful gangs could eventually find themselves at the mercy of such people, for this time it was a buyer's market. Relations between bandits and the rural elite were thus a fairly complex affair. The writer Yao Xueyin's experiences provided a revealing sidelight on this situation, for after his gang was defeated the remnants found refuge in the home of a local landlord.[40]

A chief who had managed to secure such vital elite contacts was also in a strong position to dictate terms to others who had not managed to do so, acting as go-between, arranging the disposal of their gains, supervising (for a commission) their purchase of weapons, and so on.[41] Chiefs who rose to positions of supremacy in the "bandit kingdoms" had usually done so by at least some degree of manipulation of clandestine links with the elite rather than by mere physical prowess alone.[42] Since both sides were equally interested in maintaining the arrangement successfully, from the chiefs' point of view it could be interpreted not only negatively, as a survival technique made necessary by unfriendly circumstances, but also positively, as a demonstration of their ability to bring even the all-powerful elite to terms. Such chiefs, therefore, as long as their actions did not alienate the local population in other ways, could remain heroes despite what purists might see as an unattractive compromise. Bai Lang's connections with both the Republicans and the Royalists, whatever ideological basis they might have had, had at least an equal basis in this need for elite contacts.

In the "bandit kingdoms," consequently, it was an easy transition to the "racket," sometimes known as the "private government of crime." The criminologist Mary McIntosh has put it in a nutshell: "If the state has a monopoly of the legitimate means of force, the racket strives for a monopoly of the illegitimate means of force."[43] Though no ideological threat is posed to the state, the state can in fact be weakened as the racket subverts its underlings, disrupts communications, and provides an alternative, often preferable mode of social control. Consequently, such terms as "bandits' kingdom" and "brigands' paradise," so often and so scornfully bandied about by the foreign and native press in China, contained more than a grain of truth. The state, of course, was the last to admit it—hence the derogatory label "bandit"—but was nonetheless anxious lest the situation get out of hand.

Bandit power flourished in marginal regions where outside authority was difficult to enforce. In Sichuan, where "the political situation was the most complex in all China and warlord intrigues the most devious," bandits were strongest precisely where the territories of rival warlords met or overlapped, sometimes attacking, sometimes merely levying a toll on passersby, but taking violent retribution against all who sought to evade their turnpike.[44] In neighboring Yunnan, it was said that the "Chinese own the plains, the tribesmen own the mountains, the bandits own the road."[45] Bandit gangs actually controlled extensive tracts of territory, particularly along the border zone between the two provinces. Many of the main roads as well as several vital mountain passes were impassable even to the military unless they were accompanied by ex-bandit officers. Here, as in the eastern province of Jiangsu, explorers and missionaries found that powerful local bandit chiefs could be effective protectors.[46]

The system of established rural markets described by Skinner and the complex communications network that had crisscrossed China since imperial times thus gave bandits two lucrative sources of income: the markets themselves and the shipments of goods to and from them. And, since the racket was so much less strenuous than raiding, the transition from bandit gang to armed protection group was a fairly common occurrence. In Guangxi, for example, by the 1920's bandits had come to control many of the rivers that served in place of roads in that mountainous province. Because of the tolls imposed by each gang along its particular stretch of river, waterborne trade had almost come to a stop. A bandit representative known as the "Peace Delegate" would sail with a boat the length of a gang's territory to inspect the value of its cargo and passengers, and to discuss a suitable price with its captain before allowing it to sail on to the next barrier. The negotiations could take hours or sometimes even days.[47]

The state's implicit acceptance of the transformation of bandit gangs into armed protection groups, like the routinization of the Mafia in Al Capone's Chicago, was the most obvious example of the congruence of the "overworld" and the "underworld" in China. Many a gang, like the original inhabitants of the Communist base on Jinggangshan, made a living from tributes exacted from local merchants or landlords as a guarantee of nonbelligerence. One Shandong gang even reached the stage of exacting regular land dues from peasants.[48] In Manchuria, because of the insecure frontier or outback conditions, every farmstead had a rifle, either to fight off bandits or because the occupants themselves were bandits.[49] The result was the most comprehensive protection system in China. Those who took on this job, known as *baobiao*, were usually expert fighters and well-versed in local conditions. Some, like the young Zhang Zuolin, were themselves the leaders of local bandit gangs; others were simply people who had made themselves respected enough to ensure their safety against attack. They undertook to provide armed escorts for commercial convoys, and guaranteed the complete safety of all trade goods carried under their protection. Since they also reimbursed faith-fully all losses incurred, the reputation of the *baobiao* was often consid-erable. Even government cash deliveries (unofficially, of course) some-times came to depend on their services.*

In such areas, where the distinction between "troubled" and "peace-able" times was as elusive as the bandits themselves, people acting as armed guards could become local potentates, independent of both the authorities and the bandit gangs, but equally tolerated and respected by both. Bai Lang, until the political events before and after 1911 changed his mind, was mildly resented by local chiefs because he refused to "climb Mount Liang," yet remained respected and was able to conduct trade shipments unscathed through one of the oldest "bandit kingdoms" of north China.[50]

Traffic in illicit goods, by definition illegal and therefore classed as "banditry" (*yanfei*, etc.), was another example of the racket. One Manchurian gang not only kept a number of Chinese hostages to ransom off at regular intervals, but also engaged in another racket: collecting, with the connivance of soldiers, a regular opium tribute from local farmers.[51] By the late nineteenth century the north China opium trade had come to be dominated by big bandit gangs, some of which doubled as salt-smugglers.[52] Henan was an important center: from clandestine marts in the railway town of Zhengzhou, opium moving north to Shanxi was guarded by heavily armed gangs and connived at by local officials; southward traffic bound for Hankou passed through the bandit country of southwest Henan only on the sufferance of local chiefs, who often levied a tax on the bandit-escorts. In 1923 between thirty and fifty cartloads a month were recorded along this route.[53]

Even after the superior force and organizing power of the military wrested control of the lucrative opium trade from the bandits, gang ac-tivity continued to focus upon opium districts. Since the local military was itself largely recruited from bandits, the two could easily reach agreement. In return for a cut of the profits, bandits might guard opium

*Lee 1970: 95. See also Mackay 1927: 188, 192; Liu 1967: 53; "Guanzhong daoke"; *STSB*, 11 Sept. 1912: 4, 12 Sept. 1912: 4. On Zhang Zuolin, see Li Xin et al. 1978: 179. According to Kohinata Hakurō's memoirs (Kuchiki 1966: 415–16), it was impossible to do any business in Manchuria unless one had a bodyguard. One American tobacco mer-chant hired "the worst robber [he] could find" to protect his property, conduct large bank transactions, and guard the premises in the owners' absence. To warn off intruders, this man would stand all-night vigil outside the house, shouting that he was a "robber" guarding a friend. His "organization" even provided a small flag to be displayed on the company's carts to ensure unmolested travel (Thomas 1928: 172–76; see also Kuchiki 1966: 133–34. For a photograph, see Rock 1925: 333). By the 1930's journalists were actually nostalgic for this old predictable pattern of banditry, speaking wistfully of the "good times" twenty years before when "those sturdy fellows known as *pao piao*" al-lowed bandit territory to be crossed without difficulty (Swallow and Lu 1934).

in transit from attacks by other gangs, or else act as strong-arm men, collecting fines and persecuting peasants who refused to cultivate the crop. Opium thus flourished in much the same way that illicit liquor flourished during the Prohibition years in the United States, the control of the underworld supported and connived at by representatives of the overworld. By imposing their role as middlemen in this way, however, bandit gangs deprived many peasants of a large proportion of the profits of their labor.[54]

Another essential element of racketeering is that the victims do not usually cooperate with the state to prevent it. Advice given to Edgar Snow when he left Kunming, Yunnan, for Burma was telling: "Don't forget... bandits are just people in business for money. Don't argue, give them your money, and they won't hurt you."[55] In short, since racketeering flourishes wherever the state is unable to enforce its own set of rules, it pays to conform to the rules of the immediate masters—the "ministate" effectively represented by the "bandit kingdom." This passive cooperation by victims explained the profitability of kidnapping for ransom.

## *Kidnapping for Ransom*

Kidnapping was the most lucrative and practical way of making a bandit living, as well as imposing a sort of unofficial wealth tax on local property-owners.[56] After the early 1920's the practice of taking captives (*roupiao*: "meat tickets") attained a new notoriety when someone hit on the brilliant idea of taking "foreign tickets" (*yangpiao*) instead of Chinese or "local" ones (*benpiao*). With this development, ransoming or "stealing the ticket" (*jiapiao, bangpiao*) became for the foreign community the latest symbol of "bandit-infested" China. For prosperous Chinese, however, it was neither new nor exciting:

> Since it is in the programme of every wealthy Chinese to be kidnapped sooner or later, there is always a certain sum of money laid aside to be used for ransom. This fact the pirates know well. So it happened that Ko Leong Tai fell into the hands of pirates. The merchant did not worry over much, but promptly sent one of the bandits to his brother with a letter asking that the requested sum be paid. He was certain that the matter would be attended to without delay.[57]

Chinese captives not only were resigned to their fate, but were mostly greeted with indifference by the people of the villages they passed through. Since most were from prosperous families, to the poor their fate must surely have appeared richly deserved, and hardly warranting sympathy. The capture of a Chinese aroused little public attention either, media reports treating it as a matter of course. A survey carried out in southwest Henan's Lushan county in 1914 showed that during the nineteen days between August 14 and September 2 at least 230 people were kidnapped and either ransomed or killed.[58]

In those early days of the Republic, ransom targets were almost always the rich. As late as 1923 major chiefs like Fan Mingxin were said to sniff at individuals worth less than 10,000 dollars.[59] Later in the 1920's, as war-induced disruption swelled the number of bandits, the rate of kidnapping went up too. Many rich families, after experiencing four or five kidnappings, were reduced to near-poverty. By the end of the decade robbery had "gone out of fashion"; instead, kidnapping for ransom was being mentioned at least as often as banditry, and the two seem to have become more or less synonymous.[60] Since almost everybody with money had fled the rural districts, bandits were forced to lower their standards, kidnapping first the middle-rich, then, when those too began to move out, even local miners and peasants. The price of the victim also plummeted to around twenty dollars in the late 1920's, and to as low as five or ten dollars or even a few pecks of wheat in the 1930's. By that time, practically anyone remaining in the worst-affected areas had become a prospective victim; those who had not moved out were assumed, usually correctly, to be either directly involved in banditry themselves or paying protection money.[61]

Ransoming was an old and tried practice, with three obvious advantages over plain robbery. First, the risks were smaller since it was on the whole accepted by its victims. Second, whereas loot was difficult to dispose of, a captive's family could usually be relied upon to redeem the victim.* Finally, captives, being mobile, were more convenient when a gang was on the run.

The kidnapping itself was a calculated and elaborately organized affair, reflecting above all a gang's familiarity with local conditions. Many big Manchurian gangs even had special kidnapping units that operated independently of the main fighting force.[62] On the whole, bandits preferred to kidnap the very rich, particularly those whose avarice and opportunism had alienated them from the local people, and whose capture might perhaps even throw a positive light on the bandits themselves.[63]

Great care was taken before a kidnapping to ascertain the wealth of the family in question, and thus whether the anticipated ransom justified the risk involved. Some prospective victims were kept under surveil-

---

* Though not always: one captive's brother decided "that it would be to his interests to see to it that Ko Leong Tai remained a captive. So he appropriated all the unfortunate man's property and wrote a letter to the bandits requesting them to keep his brother a prisoner, and promising to pay a certain monthly sum for his upkeep" (Lilius 1930: 136).

lance for weeks.[64] The best arrangement, since the victims were usually compliant, was to save effort by running an extortion racket: sticking notices on the doors of wealthy households ordering them to hand over so much money by a certain day or else have their houses burned. One brutal method of persuasion was to hang the headless, limbless torsos of those who had failed to pay from trees in the village during the night.[65] At any rate, once a rich person had been earmarked as a victim there was little chance of escape, except by the regular payment of "squeeze."[66]

In some places, such as Guangdong, gangs with little organization and insecure hideouts sold their prisoners to better-endowed gangs at secret, specially organized markets. Certain individuals operated as dealers, and captives might travel far and change hands several times. With each change the ransoming process had to begin all over again. Around Canton ransoming became a thriving business:

> Sometimes it happened that some other pirate chief also wanted to get hold of the same man, and when this chief learned that his proposed victim had already been kidnapped, he often bidded for the purchase of the prisoner. The fact that there is an actual traffic in kidnapped victims has given birth to a spy system.... Whenever a name is mentioned as a prospective "customer" there is very little doubt that the information will leak out, and there will be a general rush for possession of the victim. The first gang to lay hands on him usually benefits most, and it is to the interest of the victim to have himself ransomed as soon as possible....[67]

The sale of captives was common elsewhere, too. Three British seamen captured in Manchuria in 1933 found themselves up for sale when a neighboring gang offered two million dollars plus 150 rifles for them, but the chief demanded double the money and 400 rifles, and the deal was forgotten. In Fujian, on the other hand, it was forbidden to capture the same person twice.[68]

Sometimes when a raiding party arrived at a town the bandits already knew which houses most warranted a visit, for individuals in towns expecting an attack commonly used the opportunity to even scores with personal enemies by secretly reporting their wealth to the bandits; another device was to join a gang after discovering a prospective ransom victim, then lead it to the victim's house. Otherwise, the bandits' choice of victim followed certain set patterns. The obvious candidate was an eldest son, whose family would then be forced to produce the ransom quickly to ensure the lineage's survival and so placate its ancestors. If this was impossible, the next most important member of the family was chosen, but it was essential to ensure that someone capable of decisive action remained behind to handle arrangements. Sometimes an entire family was captured, and the most able member released to rake up the ransom money as quickly as possible. On occasion whole villages were carried away: during a traveling play or fair when the villagers were all gathered together in one place and off their guard, they were highly vulnerable to the gangs which often followed in the wake of itinerant drama groups.[69]

The capture of women was a delicate affair. Whereas in Europe chivalry might have ensured a quick release for a girl taken by bandits, in China such considerations were less important. At the same time there did operate a clear set of bandit rules that proscribed the capture of women and children, the former known in bandit slang as *caihua* or "plucking flowers" (also, significantly, a metaphor for the act of "deflowering" a virgin girl). Even among the small-time, often wilder bandits to whom such moral niceties did not apply, there were solid reasons for not choosing women as ransom victims: in a patriarchal society like China a woman kept outside her home overnight lost her moral reputation, her marriageability, and in effect her reason for living. The prospects of a ransom dwindled accordingly. As far as bandits were concerned, women, especially unmarried ones, were "quick tickets" (*kuaipiao*) or "earthly tickets" (*dipai piao*), whereas men were "heavenly tickets" (*tianpai piao*).* Another problem with women captives was that their bound feet made them a liability on the march.

The evidence thus suggests that women taken as ransom victims were likely to be the daughters of families known to be rather modern-minded, often either schoolgirls or schoolteachers, for these types had more prospect of being ransomed than did the daughers of traditional families. Older women, having exhausted their sexual attractions, were the least promising of all.[70]

Cases of women falling into bandits' hands are, all the same, legion (Hunan was particularly notorious in this respect).[71] The object, though, except in the case of the Moslem bandits active in some parts of North China, was evidently not the extraction of a ransom but the acquisition of the women as slaves or for sexual purposes. In the 1923 attack on Hai-yang, Shandong, for example, some forty-odd women were captured while watching a village play. After the old and "ugly" were weeded out, more than twenty were taken away, presumably to serve the gang as its wives and concubines.[72] Bandits were frequently allowed to keep their female victims even after they had been taken into the army. Lao

---

*He Xiya 1925a: 71; Inoue 1933: 63. The distinction had its origins in the Daoist text *Taiping jing* (Scripture of Great Peace), according to which the female element was the "spirit of the earth" (*tudi di jingshen*) and the male element the "spirit of Heaven" (*tian di jingshen*) (Kaltenmark 1979: 38). In bandit slang a young girl, especially an unmarried virgin, was referred to as "two-five" (*erwu*) (He Xiya 1925a: 76). The term came from the scores on a gambler's dice. Men, the most valuable captives, were rated six, while married women, the least valuable, rated only one; young girls, though they were less valuable as captives, scored for their sexual attraction, and came midway between the two: hence the term "two-five" (Inoue 1933: 63).

Yangren had several hundred female captives with him both as a bandit and during his spell in the military. Many were later killed or committed suicide.[73] The Nian rebels, however, had preferred to either sell their female captives outright or ransom them quickly in exchange for horses, and the Lincheng bandits also insisted that "Because women are troublesome at times of fighting, since long ago we have never kidnapped women. Once we caught two or three, but we sent them home."[74] The women among their foreign captives too were released at the first opportunity.

Children, despite an ostensible ban on their capture, also featured commonly among ransom victims, a practice known in bandit slang as "enfolding a child in one's arms" (*bao tongzi*); selling children was referred to as "transporting stones" (*ban shitou*).* A little higher up the mountain from where the white captives were kept at Lincheng another camp allegedly contained a large number of Chinese children aged between two and fifteen. Most had been there between one and three years awaiting ransom; rags of silk and satin testified to their social origins.[75] Bandits also controlled the traffic in female slaves across the China-Vietnam border in the nineteenth century, and in the Shanghai area the capture of women and children for sale as servants to big city families was evidently a flourishing business.[76]

Once taken, a victim was blindfolded and led off to the bandits' camp, and the ransom demand sent out immediately. The simplest way of informing the unlucky family was to send a message or nail one to their gate, together with items to prove the captive's identity. A letter either from the victim or from the chief stipulated that such and such a sum, along with so many guns and other required commodities, be brought to a certain spot at an appointed time, after which the prisoner would be released.[†] Should the appointment not be kept, or should the family notify the authorities, fail to pay the full amount, and so on, the captive was threatened with dire revenge and the entire family was promised severe retribution. The bandits insured themselves against vengeance by finding an individual closely related to the victim's family to act as go-

---

*Inoue 1933: 63. Inoue states that these were specifically Shanghai terms. The origin of *ban shitou* lay in the expression *shitou zier*, "stone child," a certain variety of gem or polished stone. Bandits substituted the first half of the phrase for the second when referring to children.

†See, for example, Ueda 1924: 6–7. The language used for such communications was highly allusive, as the following example shows: "I have been spending a few days with friends and have exhausted all my spare cash. Please send a little more to tide me over." To avoid misunderstanding, the letter would then add something like, "as much as possible, and within five days." The family's response, too, was appropriate: "Mr. _____ has been presuming on your hospitality for a long time and all his family are grateful ..." (*ibid.*: 62, 66). For more examples of ransom letters, see He Xiya 1925a: 51; Kurushima 1952: 182–83, 198–200, 207; Howard 1926: 254–55; Gotō 1923: 55; Mackay 1927: 189 (including a photograph); *NCH*, 5 Feb. 1927: 212.

between. If the family took any action against them, the force of the law immediately fell upon the go-between on suspicion of being an accomplice (which according to the law was tantamount to being a bandit).[77]

The family that responded too readily to the bandits' demands, however, could make things still more difficult for itself. Although bandits usually adjusted their ransom demand according to the family's wealth, the initial demand was upped several times in the opening stages of negotiations to test the original assessment's accuracy. A family not knowing the ropes and paying the stipulated sum without question was suspected of having unlimited funds, and usually ended up paying three or four times what was first demanded. If they were wise, therefore, they consulted friends on the customary procedures before making any moves. First of all, a go-between known to be acceptable to the bandits had to be found and sent out to begin negotiations (*shuopiao*). When he arrived at the designated spot there would be nobody in sight, though he himself (it was not a task for which women were selected) was being carefully watched from hiding. As soon as those watching were sure that no soldiers were following along behind, they would appear and take him to the site set for the talks. The family was expected to provide everything required, principally tobacco, tea, and food, as well as towels, shoes, hats, and other gifts for the bandits, plus a good supply of opium.

While the go-between tried desperately to get the ransom price reduced, the bandits sought to milk the family for all it was worth. It was a kidnapper's market, and sometimes they would raise the price or change the terms, or take the captive deeper and deeper into the mountains so as to irritate the family still further and persuade them to pay what was demanded. Usually, though, a sum was agreed upon after several bargaining sessions. On the first visit of the go-between the bandits were generally polite, displaying the captive and treating him kindly while remaining firm about the ransom sum. On the second visit, however, they often treated the victim with excessive cruelty, whipping or even bayoneting him so as to ensure rapid progress while simultaneously expressing willingness to discuss the terms of release.

This sort of procedure was generally effective, but it occasionally became necessary to speed up the talks: the commonest method was to send the family a finger or an ear of the victim, known in bandit slang as "clipping the ticket" (*jianpiao*).* Even so, negotiations tended to be long

---

*Grafton 1923: 600. One pair of English captives was shocked to be told by their bandits that "our ears are just right for sending in a parcel to Yinkow" (Johnson 1934: 59; see also 119–20, and Kurushima 1952: 141). For a horrifying description of one "clipped ticket," minus nose, ears, eyelids, lips, and testicles as well as fingers, see Ueda 1924: 44–45; also 37–38. These bandits had a special medicinal herb that stopped bleeding and prevented death from blood-loss, allowing the hapless victim to be kept alive as an object lesson to the other prisoners.

and circuitous, and the length of captivity might stretch to nine or ten months. Many a family went bankrupt in order to rescue a relative and ensure its future continuation. Should the ransom fail to arrive before the bandits grew bored or angry, the captive was classed as an "unredeemed ticket" (*qipiao*) and killed without mercy, a final solution known as "tearing up the ticket" (*sipiao*),[78] after which his severed head would often be returned to his family.

Treatment of Chinese captives varied according to their ransom potential. The first encounter was joyfully referred to as "welcoming the God of Wealth" (*jie caishen*), and violence was kept to a level sufficient to persuade those with money to reveal its extent and whereabouts.* While the least valuable prisoners were often killed, the richest victims were carefully preserved as long as the ransom seemed likely to be paid. The acquisition of such rich captives was known as "pulling in a fat pig" (*la feizhu*). A protracted stay, however, indicated that a victim was unlikely to be redeemed, and such unfortunate individuals became the targets of all the pent-up fears and frustrations or repressed sadism of some of the bandits. To "encourage the others," the fellow-prisoners of one condemned to be killed or beaten were required to watch the victim's agonies.[79]

Although wealthy-looking people were the preferred targets, the poor would be taken when nothing better was available (particularly in the case of the soldier-bandits).[80] However, the bandits knew that many rich people wore beggar's clothing so as to appear poor. To persuade them to reveal their true wealth, captives were first put through a "third degree" interrogation session, usually conducted by the chief, a procedure known as "coaxing the goose to lay its eggs" (*yang e shengdan*). The object was to frighten them into a confession, and many collapsed or even died without being beaten. If this mild strategy did not work, the violence would begin, the victim being stoned or beaten with sticks or rifle butts. The camps of the soldier-bandits, who rarely bothered to observe the traditional practices but simply took every likely looking victim they could find, consequently echoed throughout the night with the screams of such unfortunates. Most victims gave in quickly under this kind of treatment, but sometimes the bandits could work themselves up into a fury over a captive who remained silent. The ultimate penalty was always death.[81]

---

* Because of the practice of burying wealth in the ground for safe-keeping, a captive's fortune was often hard to ascertain unless he or she could be forced to reveal its hiding place; hence the need for violent measures. Bandits referred to such hidden caches of treasure as the "earthworm" (*dilong*)—literally "earth dragon," "dragon" (*long*) being a standard underworld term for treasure; readily available cash or silver was consequently known as the "living dragon" (*huolong*). The spot where the treasure was buried was referred to in bandit slang as "the grave" (*fen*), so the act of burying the cash was called suitably "interment" (*zang*) (Inoue 1933: 60, 63).

The prisoners, including children, were usually tied together in long lines and hurried along with sticks if they lingered. Anyone unable to keep the pace—or who attempted to escape, or who stepped out of line—was automatically executed. By the 1920's Henan bandit slang had come to substitute the word "pull" (*lao*) for the usual one meaning "march," since the captives were bound together like oxen before a plow.[82] To avoid the dangerous precedent of allowing a captive to get off without paying a ransom, a sick prisoner would be shot rather than left behind. The sound of shooting when a soldier-bandit army was on the march often signified not a brush with troops but the executions of those unable to keep up. One missionary estimated that over the first six days of his captivity more than two hundred captives were killed as the bandit army struggled through an area crisscrossed by swamps and rivers.* To lessen the possibility of escape, captives were deliberately kept short of sleep; most were also obliged to act as servants. They survived on whatever the bandits left in their bowls.[83]

Captives who cringed or whined were sometimes shot out of contempt, for in the "man's world" of the bandit gang those who stood up to their tormentors, especially if they were young, often received favorable treatment. They might even, like Kohinata Hakurō, be invited to join the gang, or, like Yao Xueyin, be adopted as foster-sons of the chief.[84]

Memorizing the bandits' "dark language" and observing the taboo on mentioning their personal names were obligatory for all captives, including foreign ones. Since much of the bandits' vocabulary was derived from superstitions originating in fear, the bandits were just as shocked to hear the taboo words pronounced by captives as by their fellow-bandits. Captives who slipped up put themselves at great risk, and were sometimes even killed if unable to memorize the "robber tongue" quickly enough.[85]

A gang possessing a valuable captive acted as a magnet to other gangs, who would flock to join it in the hopes of a share in the spoils; the longer it held on to its prize, the larger it tended to grow.[86] Although the ransom would have to be divided more ways, the stronger the gang became the better its bargaining position and the higher the potential rewards, so the lucky gang did not usually object to the appearance of newcomers. In the case of the soldier-bandits, whose aim was generally military induction rather than material reward, this applied all the more.

A captive's release (*shupiao*) was as carefully conducted as the original

---

* *Hankow Herald*, 29 Oct. 1926, in SD 893.00/7963 (Hankou to Washington, D.C., 15 Nov. 1926). In bandit armies like this, component gangs had their own hostages that they guarded carefully; presumably they could also expect to pocket most of the ransom received for them, if not all. See Lundeen 1925: 40; Ueda 1924: 83; A.N. 1923: 162; *NCH*, 12 Feb. 1927: 257.

capture had been. Every captive has noted an atmosphere of tension prior to his or her release,[87] for the possibility of official treachery was always present. What the bandits most feared was an attack by soldiers after the captive(s) had been handed over. Hence they would first send out scouts to look for evidence of soldiers in the vicinity of the spot chosen to pick up the ransom. Only if no suspicious signs were found would the ransom be collected. Even if this stage went smoothly, however, the captive was not released immediately. The collection spot was always fixed far away from where the captive was held to guard against surprise attacks, so it would take time to return with the money, which then had to be checked lest it be counterfeit or in unusable denominations. Having made sure that the money was acceptable, the gang would then flee, leaving behind the captive. Not until they had reached a safe place beyond pursuit would they announce where the captive had been left. In the meantime the family waited on tenterhooks to find out whether the bandits had fulfilled their part of the bargain, or whether their relative had been killed.[88]

If the bandits' prisoners included someone with local influence, things could go extremely smoothly. Among the prisoners at Lincheng, for example, was the son-in-law of the pre-1911 Governor of Shandong. This man had previously served as an officer under the warlord Zhang Xun, and was able to renew many old acquaintances among Zhang's former subordinates operating with the bandits. His influence allegedly accounted for the harmonious relations between the bandits and the Shandong authorities.[89]

In any case, the length of time that a captive could be kept was limited by the gang's operating season. When it ended—except sometimes in Manchuria—all but the most important and valuable captives would be shot rather than released. After the Henan soldier-bandit chief Niu Shengwu had spent the autumn of 1926 selling off as many as possible of his gang's captives, for instance, the eight hundred that remained when Niu decided to disband for the winter—unlikely to be redeemed however long they were kept—were allegedly massacred.* Only when a gang needed to raise money quickly, such as to buy fresh ammunition after a battle, was it permissible to let captives go cheaply.[90]

The practice of kidnapping for ransom could only be carried out successfully close to population centers, and this itself made it a highly

---

*NCH, 16 Apr. 1927: 136. This report has to be considered in the context of traditionally biased official reporting. It is worth mentioning, however, that Fan Mingxin was said never to shoot unredeemed hostages (*Relations de Chine* 7 [May–Aug. 1923]: 111). Whether this means that he hung on to them indefinitely or that he let them go without a ransom is not clear. In most gangs the latter would have been unthinkable, but it should be added that Fan was a rarity among the powerful soldier-bandit chiefs in that he possessed strong "social bandit" qualities.

suggestive aspect of "bandit power." Most captives were kept but a few miles from their homes, and bandits frequently had their camps within easy striking distance of military garrisons in the cities. Some chiefs, like the aforementioned Niu Shengwu, were even powerful enough to set up temporary camps to sell off their captives openly,[91] the latter's social standing and the military's notorious venality combining to render them more or less immune to all-out attack.

From the 1920's on, particularly following the emergence of the soldier-bandits, the plight of Chinese ransom victims was rapidly forgotten as foreigners (Europeans, Americans, and Japanese) became the increasingly frequent victims of daring bandit assaults.

Prior to 1911, the aura of impunity that surrounded foreigners had generally been enough to deter bandit attacks. The slightest harm to any of them guaranteed a rapid and forceful reaction from their government, and was likely in turn to trigger the wrath of the Chinese authorities against the bandits. There were plenty of precedents to refer to. The murder of two German missionaries in Shandong in 1897 had led their government to seize the vital harbor of Jiaozhou (Kiaochow) Bay, assert its rights to exploit nearby mines, and build a railway through the province; and attacks on foreigners during the Boxer Rebellion had led to full-scale foreign intervention. The lessons were well-taken by all concerned. Not only did bandits steer clear of foreigners, who were thus able to live tranquil lives in the otherwise unsettled interior; Chinese officials too made sure not to burn their fingers, permitting foreign residences and missions to develop as places beyond the reach of the law, and often allowing their inhabitants to become local potentates.[92]

Attacks on foreigners began to increase after the 1911 Revolution,[93] and by the 1920's had become commonplace. Xenophobia was not usually the motive, though there was a strong groundswell of antiforeign feeling, particularly against missionaries, in places like Henan where the influx of foreign evangelists in the post-Boxer years was associated with the government's unpopular modernization policies.[94] Nor, at first, were these attacks inspired by the desire for ransom, for no payment is recorded for any of the 38 foreigners who passed through Bai Lang's hands.[95] Most important was the realization, amid a new mood of national confidence, that the very aura of sanctity surrounding foreigners could be turned to the attackers' advantage. The possession of a foreign hostage, that is, ensured the rapid and effective satisfaction of one's demands, as the soldier-bandits soon made clear.

Lao Yangren's policy of kidnapping foreigners was the first example of this new trend, and it paid off richly. On June 9, 1922, a month after beginning operations, his forces looted a mission station and carried off a Norwegian missionary. On August 24 they took a Frenchman and a Greek, then an Italian. On October 13 they attacked an American mission, taking one American and one Swedish missionary captive. In the same month three Britons were taken, and in early November another American and his six-year-old son. By the end of the month Lao Yangren was holding a total of fourteen foreign hostages. On November 16, as he (or Zhang Zuolin, said to be sponsoring the mayhem) had perhaps calculated, the Beijing representatives of countries whose nationals had been captured issued an official warning to the Chinese government* and announced their intention to send an international commission of inquiry to Henan to report on the sincerity of the provincial authorities' suppression efforts.[96] The threat was highly effective. By the middle of December all the foreign captives were freed and Lao Yangren was given high military rank at the head of his followers.[97]

The lesson was well taken by the bandits, for May 1923 saw the Lincheng Incident, in which more than a score of foreigners were taken hostage, and Lincheng was followed by a spate of similar kidnappings and train holdups all over North China that eventually made foreigners afraid to use the trains at all. Ransoms demanded by Shandong bandits during 1923 precisely equaled that province's total tax revenue for the year, according to one report; another noted 92 separate "outrages" involving foreigners on the books of the Chinese Foreign Ministry for the same year. By this time the tactic's popularity had spread south, particularly to the Yangzi Valley where most of the 41 Americans, 23 British, and 14 Japanese captured during that year were taken. As exemplified by the Lincheng episode, the most notorious and influential of them all, few court settlements were ever achieved.[98]

In this way, soldier-bandits, made more politically aware by changing social conditions than their predecessors, contrived to use the government's fear of foreign retribution to their own ends. A foreign captive, referred to as "insurance" (*baoxian*), became the trump card in all dealings with the authorities, whether for negotiating enrollment terms, seeking high ransoms, or merely fending off the military.[99] Whereas foreign journalists bewailed the "loss of respect for the white man" these new developments seemed to prove, the bandits' own pronouncements

---

*Only one commentator seems to have noted the irony of such diplomatic threats. Writing soon after the Lincheng episode, he pointed out that among the captives were natives of the United States, Italy, and Mexico, where "train robberies and bandits are just matters to be read about and forgotten" (*NCH*, 19 May 1923: 467). What was more, those who complained of the lack of protection for foreigners in China neglected to mention that their own governments extended little or no protection to Chinese living under their jurisdiction: immigrants to California, for example, suffered far more than foreigners in China did. For an alarming report from California strikingly similar to the denunciations of bandits appearing in the China treaty-port press, see MacNair 1925: 233.

revealed quite the opposite:

> Having been made destitute and loneless [*sic*] through incessant civil wars, we are obliged to invite a few foreigners to come up the hill, so that we may make use of them to enforce certain demands and secure certain guarantees.... We have no intention of ill-treating the foreigners or bringing about diplomatic complications. As money is not our object, it is useless for you to talk to us any more about having them ransomed.[100]

Foreigners were also expected to be able to intercede with the Chinese government in securing military commissions for the bandits and protection for their families, qualities that added to their luster.[101] Soon gangs were vying with one another for foreigners to hold, as they had previously done with rich Chinese, and by the 1930's, following the violent deaths of several captives, many of the foreign missionaries who had formerly lived and worked unscathed in the interior had been recalled.[102] As Fujian bandits explained to a British lumberman they had captured, "This branch of the bandit industry . . . was much more profitable than carrying off other Chinese, who could not pay big ransoms and who frequently had to be killed after capture." Lao Yangren's bandits were said to be "fearfully proud of [their] foreign victims," and Hunan bandits referred to a missionary captive as the "fat sheep with the precious wool."[103]

Given the importance attached to foreign captives and bandits' awareness of the power that lay behind them, it is not surprising that the majority were accorded preferential treatment. Although a mission magazine was already complaining in 1918 of a growing disregard for foreign lives,[104] in fact it was merely the "untouchability" of the foreigner that was gone; bandits very rarely killed foreigners except by accident or in self-defense. Those who died during Bai Lang's rebellion—a French Catholic priest at Luan and a Norwegian missionary at Laohekou—and the woman missionary raped at Zaoyang, were all the victims of local bands acting under Bai's umbrella.[105] Astute chiefs realized that to kill a foreigner, particularly a white one, was the surest way to incur the wrath of the Chinese authorities, however reluctant the latter might be to take action; they knew too, of course, that a dead foreigner had no "insurance" value.*

Nevertheless, a number of white captives did suffer the "third degree," consisting of harrowing stories of their likely fate should the ransom not arrive, of the terrible privations earlier captives had suffered,

---

* See Howard 1926: 63–64; *China's Millions*, Sept. 1918: 95. Note also the following passage, from Hall 1919: 1019: "[The bandits] were stricken with a deadly fear when they discovered my passport. . . . Now they dare not turn the captive loose—they dare not kill me—they dare not let me live to tell of their existence!" Japanese, incidentally, were often exceptions to this rule. See Gotō 1928: 77–94 for an example.

and of the bandits' torture and execution methods. "Cut his ears off, kill him!" was the reaction to one missionary's uncooperative attitude. A second captive heard one bandit "confess" how he had become ill through eating too many human hearts and livers, and another relate in gruesome detail how he killed a prisoner whose ransom was insufficient. There followed a discussion about which of the present captives to kill first.[106] This sort of petty cruelty toward white captives, though nothing compared with the fate of their Chinese counterparts, evidently recompensed the more psychopathic characters among the bandits for their inability to actually kill them.

Apart from such minor annoyances and the inevitable torments of prolonged captivity, such as vermin (summed up by one genteel sufferer as "what lice don't get the bedbugs take; what the bedbugs don't get the fleas take"),[107] few foreign captives have recorded deliberate mistreatment. On the contrary, their captors were as a rule extraordinarily well-disposed toward them. Bai Lang, despite a decade of anti-Christian feeling among south Henan's peasants, executed six members of his band reported to have roughed up some of his missionary captives. Despite paranoid assertions that Bai had "declared war upon the persons and property of missionaries," his proclamations actually announced protection for all foreigners.[108]

For all the furore surrounding the Lincheng Incident, the captives admitted receiving no serious ill-treatment from the bandits, and indeed seem to have regarded their experience as a huge joke. After their release and arrival at Shanghai, the journalist George Sokolsky observed them to be "so healthy and fine-looking a lot of men... that many a... foreigner envied them their rest on the heights of Paotzuku."[109]

Generally speaking, a captive's treatment depended on the gang's own prospects. As long as a successful outcome seemed likely, tempers were mild and treatment genial, but when danger loomed in the shape of pursuing soldiers, the captives, including foreign ones, bore the brunt of the bandits' anxiety.[110] All the same, threats to kill the foreign captives remained just that for many years. Only the growing rivalry among the increasing numbers of soldier-bandits all seeking military enrollment changed this situation. Toward the end of the 1920's treatment was being criticized as less "respectful" than before, and missionaries were being killed, usually out of resentment when the military spurned the bandits' demands. Japanese captives continued to fare the worst.[111] Considering the number of foreigners who were taken, however, cases of death or injury were rare.

The authorities rarely took direct measures to rescue Chinese captives, and they did not always go free even after the bandits were "pacified." Following the conclusion of the Lincheng case, those wishing to continue as bandits instead of joining the army were permitted to escape with their Chinese captives.[112] Where foreigners were concerned, however, energetic representations from the appropriate consul and the threat of wider repercussions spurred the Chinese authorities to secure the victim's release at any price. In October 1913, for instance, Hubei governor Li Yuanhong was pressured by foreign consuls into conceding that local military authorities might "grant freedom and safe conduct to all the bandits to secure the release of the missionaries [captured by Bai Lang] unharmed."[113] Alternatively, soldiers were sometimes offered premiums for rescuing foreign captives unscathed, even if they had to make a show of force to preserve the façade of a genuine battle. In fact, since the chances of their being allowed to escape with a foreigner's blood on their hands were remote, bandits tended to discard their captive and flee if there was no chance of successful resistance. The danger of a captive's being killed in an attack by soldiers was thus calculated at no more than five percent.[114]

Nevertheless, the life of a foreigner made even a five percent risk impossible, and the release procedure became an intricate dance between the bandits and the troops assigned to suppress them. The bandits knew that release without a ransom would bring loss of face and create a bad precedent. The military knew that too much pressure on the bandits not only would demonstrate the ransom value of their captive but also might provoke repercussions. So each side hedged and deferred, constantly alert for the other's treachery. Actual military clashes were rare, and the release was finally effected either after long bargaining between the two sides or after "fifth column" work within the gang.[115]

The capture of foreigners in China was thus blown up out of all proportion by the blustering treaty-port media, especially in comparison with the far worse plight of their Chinese counterparts (which was, paradoxically, almost ignored).* Few were in any real danger of coming to harm, being usually kept carefully in the rear. Much of the uproar that accompanied this new development in banditry was generated by paranoia, both the outraged self-righteousness of the expatriate white community and the exaggerated fears of the Chinese authorities— particularly the warlords, always afraid of losing a trick to their rivals. The soldier-bandits played skillfully on this two-sided fear, and succeeded in raising banditry to a new stage.

---

*Duxiu 1923: 189. The aura surrounding white foreigners sometimes attached itself to their Chinese employees and converts, too. Bandits who captured and beheaded a Chinese employee of the Standard Oil Company, for example, reattached the head and returned the body to his parents when they discovered his identity (Hedges 1923: 609). In early twentieth-century Henan, despite virulent anti-missionary feeling, Chinese converts were often exempt from attack (see *The Times* [London], 3 Apr. 1914, 23 Mar. 1925; Augustana Mission 1925: 197–99; Borst-Smith 1917: 213–14; *China's Millions*, June 1922: 88).

Nevertheless, it remains true that foreign captives introduced a new, dynamic element into the old art of kidnapping, as well as accentuating the tempestuous relationship between China and the foreign powers. Astute captives soon saw the implications of poor Chinese peasants seeing the once-mighty foreigner being driven along like a beast by a scruffy gang of bandits. One found that villagers would burst into laughter when he and his fellow-captives were marched by.[116] In this sense at least, the kidnapping of foreigners probably had a more significant effect than is generally realized.

The racket was the supreme example of the institutionalization of banditry. Where conditions were right it was possible, if not terribly common, for bandits to acquire land and become landlords. One former bandit became the only person in his village (in Guangdong just before the Japanese invasion) with access to officialdom because his former chief had, through a series of political alliances, become the local military commander. This man eventually became the head of a prosperous family founded on the riches he had stashed away during several years of robbery and opium smuggling. The combination of social, economic, and political power made him a formidable force in his home area. Like most of the new power-holders, moreover, he was almost totally illiterate—having, as the expression went, "not a drop of ink" in him.[117]

What was most interesting about such characters, as one Communist organizer discovered in the 1940's, was their extreme conservatism. Desire to protect their landholdings often made them the most recalcitrant reactionaries. But whether this kind of attitude should be condemned as mere "compromise [of] political principle"[118] is less sure. Their conservatism most often combined their desire to demonstrate to the authorities what loyal, anti-Communist citizens even former bandits could be, and their fear of losing the property they had gone through such hardships for—hardships the hereditary rich could not usually claim to have shared!

Bandits, then, could come to constitute a level of control independent of that offered by the "authorities." When times were peaceful, "arrangements" ensured a stable balance of force; but when those arrangements broke down, the standard bandit–armed-guerrilla tactic of avoiding head-on clashes provided no guarantee of stability to the people living under their control (not that those living at the whim of legally constituted authorities always fared much better). Fujian bandits, for example, could do nothing to prevent newly arrived northern troops from burning the homes of two families charged with sheltering them. On the other hand, since the bandits had forced their presence on the families, they appraised the damage and fully reimbursed the victims without equivocation.

Such acts of justice, compared to the uncaring attitude of the "legitimate" authorities—whose presence was equally forced upon the people —made bandit control in many areas both accepted and respected:

One chief I visited held regular courts in order that the people, who could get no semblance of justice in the regular courts, because they could not engage the necessary influential scholar [to] play lawyer for them, could get fair play. . . .

In all such instances where I had occasion to investigate I learned of no case where the bandit acted counter to the merits of the testimony given. Notwithstanding the terrible suffering caused by the presence of so many bandits abroad, one often heard the people expressing a preference for the bandit courts to the regular tribunals. Never once did I hear a suggestion of bribery entering into a decision by a bandit judge.[119]

When the need arose to reassert bandit control, though, there were no half measures. The theft of a 30,000 dollar tribute from the townspeople provoked the same Fujian chief-cum-judge to send down a raiding party that burned more than three hundred homes. A placard called the raid an object lesson to any community daring to defy a bandit chief.[120] Bai Lang, too, as we have already seen, could be equally vicious when defied. No one, however, appeared surprised that the chief sought such violent retribution, and the people at least benefited from what justice they did receive.

Even the so-called "bandit villages" were not always spontaneously generated. The need for a secure base commonly led gangs to ensconce themselves in a certain promising border region or mountain redoubt as "guest bandits." The people already living there either moved out or, more often, stayed for lack of anywhere else to go. Though they might become no more than the bandits' servants, in many cases they came to function, in return for protection against outsiders, as the gang's "ears and eyes," quietly keeping track of the movements of the police and military, and sending word of ominous developments. Regarded by the authorities as bandits themselves, they acquired a natural interest in securing the gang's protection against the state's incursions, which were usually more disastrous than everyday life spent under the bandits' dominion.

When necessary, bandits had no qualms about compelling poor families at gunpoint to look after their stolen goods or captives until they returned to collect them. If found in such compromising circumstances by the soldiers, such people would be shot as "bandit confederates" regardless of their pleading explanations. Though they were aware of the real nature of the relationship, the authorities nonetheless took a ruthless stand, knowing that without such contacts the bandits could not operate effectively.

Bandit rule, like the officially sanctioned variety, was fraught with contradictions. Though rulers of both sorts assumed sole responsibility for the "well-being" of those under their control, they reserved the right to support themselves by means of exactions forced upon those same people, however unwilling. In the *Shuihu zhuan* the claims of the heroes to represent superior morality mesh badly with the physical threat they present to local peasants. Though they reject the exploitation of the common people by town, gentry, officials, and so on, they themselves, since they are not producers, are equally parasitic—most of what they gain for the peasants by robbing government convoys they have to take themselves in order to live.[121] In the twentieth century, too, the complaint was often heard that by taking over the roads and rivers bandits stifled progress toward commercialization: "... at no time during our tour of northern Shensi [Shaanxi], did we meet a single load of merchandise or a single traveller of the better class, so utterly has all trade and traffic in that region been destroyed by the brigands."[122] Another grumble was that bandits, by stealing draft animals, made peasants reluctant to invest in such animals and ultimately reduced their enthusiasm for farming altogether.[123] On the other hand, since bandit exactions were usually imposed after the official ones had already been extracted, to saddle them with the whole blame for bringing impoverishment to an area already reduced to near-penury by the forced payment of taxes and rents, by the corvée, and so on seems demonstrably one-sided.

## Bandits and the Common People—Fish in the Water?

By fitting into the gaps of power left by the representatives of the established ruling class, bandits were ultimately just one of the many nuisances that the long-suffering people had to put up with (others included natural disasters, soldiers, and tax-gatherers). Lacking the power to control their own destinies, local people made the best of a bad job: seeking protection where it was available, clinging to what self-respect they had, but appreciative of the smallest mercies. At the same time, bandits' local origins sometimes permitted a special kind of relationship with the people of their home area.

Though bandits naturally preferred rich targets, it was not unknown for the poor to be attacked—seasonal migrants returning from Manchuria with their wage-packets, peasants taking their produce to market, and so on.[124] Indeed, banditry has sometimes been unquestioningly regarded as preying largely upon the defenseless poor: "There is a case, no doubt, for the bandit, though it is seldom stated.... Unfortunately, it is easier to sheer sheep than wolves, and, though popular sympathy is sometimes with him, the majority of his victims are worse off than himself."[125] On the whole, though, this view was mistaken. Whenever possible, bandits took what they needed from the classes upon which official exactions fell lightest: those with property to spare. In this sense they could be seen as an objective leveling influence. If they did take from the poor it was usually because of specific intervening factors. Generally it was the smaller, poorly armed gangs that did so. As gangs grew larger their horizons expanded accordingly, and though much of their time was spent in flight their ambition was ultimately to replace the local hierarchy by putting themselves in the seat of power. In their own eyes they were presenting an alternative image to the official hierarchy, even if the end result for those who lived under them was the same.

As various captives have noted, there were many kinds of bandits, some good, some bad, some erratic. A permanently established gang would include some men whose ambition or recklessness had made village life impossible, and others who were unable to return home because their faces were known to the authorities. Their attitude toward the village was a mixture of scorn and resentment, tempered perhaps with condescension and romance. Seasonal gangs, however, which expected to return to village life as soon as the current crisis was over, were much closer to the local community and behaved quite differently. Gangs led by particularly sadistic chiefs would also show less mercy to the defenseless than those enjoying more stable leadership. Above all, bandit chiefs had their "off" days like anyone else. If a gang's behavior was unpredictable, this was not really so surprising: "The Chinese bandit is a paradox. He is at one and the same time the terror of the countryside and the guardian of the people. He is an erratic Robin Hood. He protects some at the expense of others. The country folk curry his favour, bribe him with revenues, use him to fight out their differences with other villagers. . . . "[126]

The nature of bandit activity was also strongly influenced by environmental factors. Amid rampant starvation caused by crop failure, bandits invariably multiplied and their activities became reckless. When personal survival is at stake, social banditry is rarely at a premium, especially when the most prosperous families have fled behind city walls. At such times attacks on those previously too poor to warrant notice stood out precisely because of their unusual nature. They also tended to overshadow the permanently established racket, which, because of the victims's reluctant acquiescence, was often invisible. Whereas one kidnapping of a rich victim might be enough to sustain a gang for some time, the amount that could be extracted from a poor family was minimal, and only by constantly seeking new targets could a starving gang keep its head above water. When this situation was reported in the press and in official memoranda, the impression was that bandits always lived off the poor, which in the long term they neither did nor could.

The strongest influence upon a gang, however, was its local affiliation. Toward people of their own locality bandits generally behaved with consideration—even soldier-bandits, in Henan's case. Local villagers would not be attacked unless the gang was really desperate or starving, or its chief unusually wayward. After all, they were the people among whom the bandits had been living until a short time before, and among whom many members of the gang would hope to resume living in the future; they would also include not a few blood relatives. Even the wealthy, to some of whom the chief might conceivably be linked by lineage or other ties, would stand more chance of reaching an accommodation with the bandits than their counterparts elsewhere. Those who were attacked were probably those whose avarice not only made them widely hated but also prevented their reaching a suitable financial arrangement with the bandits. Only if the gang felt sufficiently secure, or if the chief possessed social-bandit characteristics would the local rich be attacked indiscriminately. On the North China Plain in particular, because so many of its inhabitants moved regularly in and out of banditry according to economic circumstances and because of the relative lack of secure hideouts, gangs tended to maintain good relations with the villages, and chiefs were frequently either representatives of major clans or village leaders.[127]

As the proverb went, "a rabbit does not eat the grass around its own burrow." A bandit acquaintance of Agnes Smedley, for example, told her the story of one of his uncles. The man had belonged to a gang of bandits that hid out in the mountains commanding their home village: "about their names was woven a subtle web of mystery and of unexpressed approval." This uncle would descend to the village at night and leave at dawn, leaving behind money and valuables. Though the local bandit might steal a chicken or a little grain, this was probably only to satisfy some private fantasy, or because of need. It was tolerated by neighbors, who with the memory of the last military foray in mind were no doubt thankful for small mercies. More serious operations were conducted further afield.[128]

A gang's attitude toward home reflected the cell-like nature of rural Chinese society. Just as one village (or sometimes marketing area) was isolated from others not only spatially but also emotionally, so too the local bandit gang instinctively identified the world with the village or villages that gave it birth. In many parts of China villagers automatically referred to inhabitants of other villages as "bandits" (*fei*), and when conflicts broke out would request the intervention of troops against the other side in the name of "bandit-suppression."[129] Gang behavior, too, naturally reflected such extreme local particularism. When a gang moved beyond its own local boundaries it often behaved as an enemy, and was automatically regarded as such, regardless of its origins and allegiances. In short, though in its home area a gang might provide a model for heroism and youthful rebellion, outside that area it was subject to being hunted down and exterminated by people who might simultaneously be protecting their own "bandits." Thus, along the Sungari River in northern Manchuria, "... the common people consider that the bandits of their own side are a nuisance, but part of the natural social order and usually amenable to diplomacy and reasonable arrangement; while the bandits from the other side of the river they loathe and dread."[130]

Behind the contrasting popular attitudes toward "bandits" there was more than met the inexperienced eye. When Wang Tianzong's band set out to attack Luoyang in October 1911, local people saw it off with refreshments; the Lincheng bandits, fleeing from the scene of the train wreck, enjoyed a breakfast of hot water and bean soup left for them by local villagers (afterward the dishes were carefully stacked by the side of the road); Fan Mingxin was extremely popular not only with the poor but also with the middle peasants of his locality; and in Caozhou (Shandong) the local poor were able to enter and leave one bandit camp as they pleased, especially if they brought things to eat.[131]

Apart from merely behaving better, under the right conditions and with the right sort of chief the local gang could also play a positive role in protecting the community against outside attacks, either by undisciplined troops or by predatory nonlocal gangs. Communities could solve their bandit problem either by paying the gang to take its activities elsewhere, or by hiring it as an unofficial militia, a role into which it could sometimes settle easily and naturally:

> Since we were reorganized [as a militia, said one chief] my income is only one-tenth what it was from robbery and ransoming. On the other hand, as a bandit I was always beset by hunger and cold. There was danger too, not only to my own life, but to my family, who could be made to take the blame for my misdeeds. Banditry has no long-term guarantees; today, however, we are the equals of the military, while our homes and persons are safe and sustained by society. We must repay our debt to the community by carrying out our new tasks with great vigor.[132]

Whatever the arrangements, a powerful local gang could at least check the ability of corrupt gentry to ride roughshod over the people's lives. At times it could even stand up to the military.

Although in a head-on clash bandits were rarely a match for trained soldiers with a will to fight, certain factors worked in their favor. The first was familiarity with the local terrain. By darting in and out of the hills they knew so well, bandits were able to tire and disorient regular troops. Only when faced with fellow-irregulars from the same area, or when numerically overwhelmed and cut off from their avenues of escape, did they lose this advantage. Second, troops were rarely paid enough to induce them to fight with conviction. Third, knowing their fate to be torture followed by execution, bandits fought like demons to avoid capture. Fourth, bandits were not tied down by the military rulebook in the way so many regular commanders were, but could scatter and regroup at will. Fifth, the soldiers often vied among themselves for rewards, as shown by the squabbling over the credit for killing Bai Lang. Finally, the soldiers' sheer ineptitude through lack of training and battle experience could give bandits the upper hand.[133]

From the economic point of view, too, since a part of the bandits' proceeds found its way into the village, a successful gang could bring the villagers certain benefits even without being formally enrolled on the village's side. In this sense, although the "cash and notes [thrown] out to the poor" by Bai Lang's followers[134] may have represented no more than a minuscule part of the gang's total income, to a peasantry reduced to periodic begging by an uncaring officialdom such "pittances" were substantial. The traditional view of bandits thus demands qualification. Bandits could be quite welcome in a community, particularly when the requirements of local defense were insufficiently satisfied by other local power-holders. Most villagers, we can conclude, "were glad to have a few resident robbers among them."[135] To see how the relationship between bandits and local people worked in practice, let us return to the case study of Bai Lang, whose rebellion revealed not only the depth of popular feeling available in the old bandit areas for a chief who satisfied the social-bandit criteria, but also the contradictions and limitations that seem to have hamstrung all rebel movements as well as bandit gangs.

Although Bai Lang's decision to be an outlaw was not taken until the late summer of 1911, the kind of bandit he would become was already clear. Even while driving a government-owned salt cart through his native Baofeng (an occupation that frequently served as a stepping-stone to banditry) he had come to be regarded as the leader of the carters because of his way of sticking up for his fellow-haulers. Soon he became known throughout the region as a popular champion who would take on anyone's problems as his own, attracting the nickname "everyone's big brother" (*guan dage*).

Putting into action the time-honored slogan of peasant rebels, "kill the rich, succor the poor," and observing strict discipline, Bai and his fledgling band quickly achieved local fame. Their attacks concentrated on official property and the houses of big landlords, usurers, and rich merchants; they threw open government granaries and rich residences, and distributed the grain and money among the people. Every time they returned to their old haunts from raids elsewhere, the poor came out to greet them "supporting the old and carrying the young," and setting out along their route tables laden with presents. Many wore the garb and makeup and sang the melodies of popular local operas, whose heroes were usually the same sort of local peasant leader that Bai himself had become.[136]

As Bai's forces gathered more and more strength by absorbing famine refugees, survivors of anti-radical pogroms, and disaffected soldiers, their popularity became "unlimited." According to newspaper correspondents, some counties supplied all their needs, others simply enjoyed their protection, and "all agreed [Bai Lang] to be the future successor to the Ming emperors."[137] The poor provided Bai with "ears and eyes" by voluntarily acting as scouts and spies as well as by donating food, and Feng Yuxiang, in command of a detachment of the suppression force, complained of receiving nothing but false information. Scouts, though their identity was known to all, were never given away. Even suppression commander Duan Qirui admitted in an interview "the support which [Bai Lang] is receiving from the people...."[138]

From the middle of 1913, however, Bai came increasingly under the influence of Nationalist Party advisers sent to win him over to the revolutionary cause. After January 1914 his forces spent less and less time in their old haunts, and in March they set off on a long westward trek in search of a new base area. In the process, the nature and extent of their support changed, dwindling in proportion to the widening physical gulf between them and their homes. In eastern Henan Bai Lang came to be considered an "ex-coolie gangster" whose name was invoked by local mothers to frighten naughty children; as the band moved into Shaanxi, although "the four words 'Pai Lang Chao Liang' (White Wolf is recruiting) passed secretly up and down the Han Valley, and recruits from all quarters flocked to join the band,"[139] these were people who would have joined any popular army in transit—not peasants but marginals, members of preexisting bandit gangs and secret societies, and refugees starving from three consecutive famine years. Although Bai sought to appeal to the legend of Liu Bang, the farmer who became the first Han emperor, the deep-rooted support and trust he had enjoyed from the peasants of west Henan no longer came his way. Thus there is no record of the success of a scheme to persuade Shaanxi peasants to tear up the railway tracks to impede pursuing troops, although one peasant at least recalled later that Bai's army had been a "very good" one that "never entered people's houses and never stole money...." The press claimed that when the band recrossed the province a month later stragglers were set upon by local vigilantes and killed since they had been so brutal toward towns that had resisted.[140] Of the only two songs about Bai Lang to have come out of Shaanxi, one was actually made up by his gentry opponents pouring scorn upon the band's fighting ability (the other song is more sympathetic).[141] This lack of popular songs is as good an indicator as any of Bai's failure to achieve any lasting acceptance in Shaanxi.

If Shaanxi had failed to respond to Bai Lang's appeals, Gansu was a disaster. Though Moslems formed a considerable minority in Bai's home county of Baofeng, and might well have been represented within the band itself, the largely Moslem province created additional problems that Bai found insoluble, despite the fact that a rising was considered imminent.[142] Many of the band, homesick after "turning their backs on their native places," lost the will to fight. The Shaanxi recruits may even have tried to settle scores with the Moslems, whose grandfathers had laid waste their province in the great Northwest Rebellion fifty years before. In this fashion, the localism of Bai's own followers came up against that of the Gansu peasants, fostered by centuries of Han domination and naturally encouraged by a nervous local elite. The army's very arrival must have appeared the forerunner of a new Han invasion, and language problems made it difficult for the rebels to present themselves otherwise. Yuan Shikai, who had already rejoiced recognizing Bai's mortal error in abandoning southwest Henan, now rejoiced anew, stressing that the danger of a secret-society uprising provoked by the rebels' passage was henceforth far greater than the threat posed by Bai Lang himself.[143]

The support that the band did receive came once again not from the peasants but from the traditional marginal quarters: disbanded troops of the reactionary Moslem general Ma Enliang; "New Religionists" seeking to exploit the emergency to foment a Moslem uprising; and the Elder Brothers Society, which, being predominantly Han in its membership (Bai Lang himself may well have been a member), was no index of popular Gansu feeling as a whole.[144] Even the post-1949 investigation into Bai Lang's movement confirmed that his support did not extend to the average Gansu peasant and noted that when the rebels returned to Henan the Gansu recruits remained behind as ordinary bandits.*

This mistrust for the natives of other provinces evidently extended even to relationships within the rebel army itself. The large Hubei component was always treated disparagingly, for example being ordered to cross rivers first to test the current; the only people Bai completely trusted were those from his own village of Daliu. Needless to say, such discrimination created considerable discontent within the ranks, and was

---

*BLQY: 92–93; Huang Guangkuo 1960a: 26–27. This Gansu episode had been prefigured fifty years before when the Western Nian army marched through Shaanxi into the province in the spring of 1867, sacking the same centers Bai Lang's rebels would later attack. The Nian, too, had problems with the Moslems, who were also in rebellion at the time (Teng 1964: 163–64). The Taiping rebels also tended to be callous toward local inhabitants as they expanded beyond their original base area (Perry 1980: 80).

allegedly responsible for the high desertion rate that followed the return to Henan. As a survivor recalled, "Bai Lang couldn't use people from other provinces. That was an important reason for our failure."[145]

The experience of Bai Lang's rebellion demonstrated clearly the restrictions local affinity placed on a bandit chief's wider ambition. Simply by being the leader of a military force—and thereby a potential if not an actual oppressor—the most social of social bandits were rarely able to extend their popularity outside their home base. Authority spontaneously accepted at home had to be enforced by might elsewhere; in the process it was transformed into naked power, and thereby announced itself as the enemy. Only by overcoming this local bias could any social movement hope to lay a basis for broad popular appeal. For bandit gangs, even rebel bands like that of Bai Lang, the majority of whose members had taken to predatory activity to overcome economic insolvency, restore lost pride, and so on, such an achievement was virtually impossible.

But it was not merely admiration that caused local villagers to support and protect a bandit gang. Their feelings were much more ambivalent, reflecting simultaneously the need for protection in a violent world and the knowledge that at any time the protectors could become aggressors. What they felt, that is, probably even toward gangs like Bai Lang's, was respect built on fear—the mix that kept them subdued whoever the master—tempered with local affinity that identified the local chief as "one of us": In short, "Brigands live by love and fear. When they inspire only love, it is a weakness. When they inspire only fear, they are hated and have no supporters."[146] Though an exceptional character like Bai Lang might have awakened some deeper emotion in the breasts of the peasants of southwest Henan, even there the threat of violence was never entirely absent, for Bai led a force strong enough to repel the attacks of increasing numbers of soldiers. In a violent society, the capacity for inflicting violence assured bandits respect of a kind: "Hao! When a hunghutze wants a thing he takes it. That is as it should be!"[147] Like it or not, the "social bandit" could not live on love alone, but needed to push the message home at least by implicit threats. The result, nevertheless, was often a bond much stronger than that which tied the peasants to the legitimate authorities, who ultimately inspired only fear without the love.

At the very least, the bandits were an improvement on the traditionally rapacious soldiers: "when bandits come, they steal and burn; when soldiers come, they devour us wholesale"[148] went a popular village rhyme. As far as agriculture was concerned, bandits caused far less trouble than is generally assumed, the biggest problem being perhaps their seizing of draft animals for food. They would not normally damage crops deliberately, especially since many were themselves farmers for much of their lives; farming evidently continued regardless of a gang's presence. The passage of a large body of soldiers, on the other hand, no less hungry than the bandits but unconcerned about the outcome of the next harvest, was usually much more devastating. Li Zicheng had consequently managed to garner strong public support by taking the old cliché "pacify the bandits and settle the people" (*jiaofei anmin*) and changing the word "bandits" to "soldiers."[149]

At the height of Bai Lang's rebellion, too, even while officials were reluctantly conceding that local people saw the soldiers as "enemies" and the bandits as "family,"[150] Bai sometimes found it necessary to justify his activities by referring to the villagers' fate should they be left to the military's mercies. The long-established "combing" rhymes were the most popular way of persuading the powerless to be grateful for what they did receive, and Bai was locating himself in a tradition going back at least to the seventeenth century when he pointed out that though he was admittedly a *shu* (an ordinary comb), the soldiers were a *bi* (a fine-toothed comb that caused bleeding if it came into contact with the scalp) and the local bullies *dipi*: veritable razors.[151]

The relationship between bandits and the local people was not always one-sided, however. A gang's attitude toward its home area was more than mere local solidarity, for its fate lay ultimately in the hands of the people who chose not to give it away to the officials. Its activities were calculated to ensure the area's preservation as a base and refuge, and no gang that alienated itself completely from the peasants of its own locality lasted very long. Sometimes those peasants actively supported the gang, sometimes it was mere apathy or self-interest that kept them silent. Whatever the motive, however, when a gang lost the protection such attitudes offered it was lost.

How long that relationship lasted depended upon the behavior of the gang. Though Hobsbawm, citing the bandits of northeast Brazil, has suggested that through the sheer scale of his ferocity the most villainous chief could secure a place in legend, in China only those who unequivocally identified themselves with the people did so. Henanese "bandit ballads," for instance, omitted not only those chiefs who had been too weak to survive for any length of time, but also those who had been lax in keeping discipline and those who, though powerful, took a vacillating attitude toward the authorities: joining the state instead of fighting it, becoming "bandit suppressors" instead of popular fighters, and so on.[152]

How might a band lose popular sympathy and support? An Anhui case provides an illustration:

The explanation was simple. . . . During their early patrol, the guerillas' efforts had been confined to the looting of more or less wealthy families. . . . Then, for reasons unknown, the bandits failed to discriminate and began raids on ordinary peasants and tenant villagers, often burning the houses of their victims.... The peasantry kept tabs on the location of the bandits and informed the local authorities.[153]

As this example suggests, bandit rule was not always endured in silence. On the North China Plain, "rustic fortresses" indicated a tradition of community defense dating back at least to the mid-nineteenth century. Many of these fortresses, together with walled villages, remained in general use into the next century; others were restored to meet the threat of declining social conditions in the 1920's. The advent of darkness saw everyone manning the walls in vigilance.[154]

When local order broke down more or less completely, these fortresses became not only refuges but focal points for resistance, functioning equally well against predatory bandits and against those who were supposed to be on the people's side, like soldiers. For every tale of "bandit atrocities," there was a comparable story of the violent bloodletting that inevitably accompanied the state's response to uprisings against its authority, and from time to time enraged inhabitants sallied forth on the attack. In March 1868, for instance, during the Nian Rebellion, there had been a general uprising of people in eastern Zhili sick of being attacked not only by bandits but also by imperial troops and other official levies, of having their children kidnapped and their women outraged, their houses burned, and so on; both rebels and soldiers were massacred indiscriminately. Half a century later the fortresses and walled villages again furnished strongholds for the Red Spears, the prime example of a new spirit among rural inhabitants to refuse to accept any longer whatever was dealt out to them.[155]

The peasants did not expect the bandits to be kind, for masters were not like that, but they did expect them to be discriminating. This was what distinguished the bandits from the outside authorities, and was the source of their local acceptance. Those who were both became the peasants' champions, and, like Bai Lang, were remembered for generations. Others, like Bai's contemporary Sun Yuzhang, were feared and respected enough to be called upon to defend local people against gentry aggression, and shrewd enough not to refuse.[156] But men like Sun have not come down in legend. Respected for their rejection of straight society and feared on account of their strength and unpredictability, they were rarely loved for any outstanding deeds.

"Love and fear," from the Taurus Mountains of Turkey to the bandit kingdoms of China, held the keys to a successful career in banditry. Neither could supplant the other totally. Though plenty of chiefs were ready to rely on the latter to cudgel the peasants into submission, such chiefs did not last long, betrayed either by the people whose cooperation they had flouted, or by their own followers, who foresaw for themselves a violent end even closer than otherwise likely. On the other hand, a bandit who attained a "Robin Hood" reputation, who was called upon like Bai Lang to right wrongs and avenge the poor, was equally vulnerable. Those individuals who simply asserted their independence from and contrast with "the rest" were usually ready to succumb to the wiles of the establishment, for their kind of banditry was above all a kind of masculine self-assertion, and what better status symbol in a hierarchical, patriarchical world than official appointment? But the people's bandit, the rebel and subversive, who in addition to the usual qualities possessed a strong sense of mission, was a different matter. These types were best eliminated, for their mere existence, even in the unlikely event of their joining the authorities, was a permanent political threat and an inspiration to the people. Their real valor would be swollen by the growth of mythical stories about their strength and exploits, so that those detailed to catch them dragged their feet in fear. Their survival of repeated "victory" announcements made their eventual capture and death, like that of Che Guevara, seem unreal. Yet caught they always were, though rarely by direct means.

Knowing that the people would not willingly surrender one of their own any more than they would protect one who rejected their good will, and knowing too that outlaws would not voluntarily place themselves upon their enemies' mercy with only the prospect of the executioner's sword or worse to look forward to, the powers-that-be set about alienating the bandits from the people. First, suppression troops were stationed in the villages so as to deny food and shelter to the bandits, who were thus forced to take to the mountains permanently. These soldiers would be under orders to make the lives of the villagers so miserable that they would question the sense of protecting the bandits further when doing so threatened their own and their children's lives. Sooner or later, someone, either a gang member seeking to save his own skin, or a peasant driven beyond the limits of endurance, would decide to sell out the gang and bring the troubles to an end. Consequently, social bandits everywhere have almost always met their ends as the result of a betrayer's perfidy.[157] For the local poor, though many of them may have harbored the same wavering feelings, any other end to a chief who embodied their own resentment and aspirations would constitute an intolerable victory for the forces of corruption and evil.

If sporadic terror has been the hallmark of certain bandits, *total* terror is the prerogative of governments. In the wake of Bai's Lang's death in August 1914, although official figures reveal no evidence of reprisals (only 61 bandits reported killed in Henan in July, 112 in August),[158] local people confirmed that, to extinguish whatever spark of resistance remained, "kill and burn" became the order of the day. Bai's home village of Daliu, once the soldiers had finished plundering it, was put to the torch and the family property confiscated (Bai's married sister's home in a neighboring village received the same treatment). According to the *Central China Post,* "The order to the troops is to exterminate the robbers' relatives, confiscate their farms and burn down their homes to prevent uncaught brigands from returning to their homes and at the same time to serve as an object lesson to others."[159]

The more entrenched the bandit tradition and the greater the eliminated chief's popularity, the more difficult the authorities' task became. Terror could not usually be sustained indefinitely, because even those on the inflicting side became sickened with their atrocities. In southwest Henan, despite the terror and despite a policy of absorbing Bai Lang's remnants into the provincial forces, it was not long before people began to regroup and new leaders came to the fore. In September and October 1914 bands still claiming allegiance to Bai Lang were reported active south across the border in Hubei and east along the Beijing-Hankou Railway. Many of the chiefs who in the next decade would raise again the flags of recalcitrance had already been fighters under Bai.[160] In short, Bai Lang's memory refused to die,* and the Henan authorities were forced to try a simultaneous policy of mass-manipulation: commissioning special plays in which Bai appeared in the garb and white makeup traditionally worn by Chinese stage villains. At least one performance, however, saw angry peasants riot and force a different play to be performed; other performances were boycotted. The people finally replied by writing their own plays, in which Bai Lang appeared in a guise more closely fitting his true memory: wearing the traditional red makeup of heroes.[161] As a result, when the Communists began moving into nearby areas a decade and a half later, they found that the memory of "the White Wolf" still lingered, recalled along with the White Lotus and the Red Spears as a "revolutionary group" of the past.[162]

Far from digging up or covering over the roots of the problem, the authorities' ironfisted tactics merely succeeded in pressing the earth down more firmly around them. The shoots that did subsequently come through were the stronger for it. Let the last word go to the bandit-judge of Fujian, who confronted a military commander with the follow-

---

*See, for example, Tao Juyin 1957–58: II, 46. As late as December 1915, some sixteen months after Bai's death, a Japanese news story claimed that "in Honan Province, the White Wolf, whose death has repeatedly circulated, is active, rallying to his colors as many bandits as possible" (cited in Friedman 1974: 216–17). Some years later an American traveler in Shaanxi would confide to his readers that "the brigand chief lived on under secret agreement with Yuan [Shikai] whereby the authorities respected his incognito on condition of his keeping the peace" (Close 1924: 193). Even in the 1930's, such rumors continued to be reported and, evidently, believed (see Martin 1938: 174, 175).

ing ringing condemnation: "General Wang, you people have within the past months executed more than three thousand people. In all of your cutting off of heads you have not caught ten bandits. In this matter it is impossible that a bandit chief be mistaken."[163]

## Conclusion

In many parts of China a bandit gang was a fact of life, perhaps permanent, perhaps transient, but never quite forgotten. A gang's sense of identity was strong, and when a village's own strong local affinity put it at loggerheads with other communities, such gangs could become the vanguard of village solidarity. This relationship, drawing the loyalty of the poor and sometimes the acquiescence of the rich, could also give a gang political punch, which local officials and their elite allies had a natural interest in accommodating themselves to. To request outside suppression troops was to invite more trouble than the bandits themselves caused. So, in the interests of a quiet life and a steady career, officials often suggested terms whereby the gang found itself representing legal authority as either a local defense detachment or a militia under gentry leadership. The effect was to legitimize its previous activities, keeping robbery below a level that would attract attention in the capital but at a level sufficient to justify maintenance of the new "suppression force." Other gangs either submitted to their new masters or were forcibly repressed until a new one (or combination) arose strong enough to challenge the balance of power, when the process began all over again. In the meantime, "crime" meshed with "law enforcement" in such a way as to make the two all but indistinguishable.

Bandits could, therefore, sometimes lay claim to a significant role in the local power structure, reinforcing their claim by force if necessary. Suppression troops rarely risked their lives without a fair chance of an easy victory. If locally recruited, they were naturally on good terms with the bandits (sometimes they actually were the bandits), and hardly willing to suppress them since their own livelihood demanded the existence of a "bandit problem." External troops faced the additional difficulty of being strangers in a land where "stranger" equaled "enemy," and their motivation and tactics suffered accordingly.

Though local gentry often organized militias to fight the bandit threat to their lives and property, they were chiefly concerned with the danger to their homes, and only in the case of a major disturbance joined forces to defend the status quo. Hence bandits presented a viable alternative to official control, and in their capacity as local protectors sometimes developed strong regional ties that had to be destroyed before the legitimate authorities could reassert themselves. Frequently the latter did not bother, but took the bandits to their own, for they were often the most effective of peacekeepers.

Although the bandit was basically looking out for "number one," rural class differences were generally stark enough to remove any doubts about where the best profits were to be had. To the extent that they exploited the rich for their income, bandits, in the absence of more constructive heroes, could be regarded as representing the interests of the poor. As we have seen, however, certain qualifications are necessary. In the first place, the relationship between bandits and the common people was one explicitly based on power. People regarded them first and foremost as rulers, to whom a debt of gratitude might be owed for the relative protection they did bring, but who still demanded tribute and other ritual obeisances in return, and who took harsh revenge when these were not forthcoming. This in itself was not surprising. In a society gripped by recurrent starvation and sporadic violence, permeated by the dulling effect of the agrarian cycle, and dominated by the logic of machismo, there is no reason why a libertarian attitude toward the wielding of power should have spontaneously emerged.

Nevertheless, we do not have to accept the usual denunciations of bandits, for we have seen that under the right circumstances it was possible for a special kind of relationship to pertain between them and the people who lived under them, one that enforced itself on both sides. Whereas the state, being supreme, can simply suppress minority dissent if it so desires, bandits controlled at best only the local, illegitimate means of power. Hence, if the people themselves were obliged to recognize their local "protectors" as champions, the latter too were to some extent forced to live up to this expectation by the threatening posture of the state. Those who did not do so soon disappeared, and it is their kind that has featured most commonly as infamous representatives of "banditry." But there were also genuine protectors, who rarely made headlines on their own account (such famous chiefs as Bai Lang were an exception, of course). Just as "good news is no news" for the press today, so parts of China that suffered their bandits in relative peace did not attract the attention of journalists. The popular image of the bandit has been considerably colored by one-sided reporting both in the press and in the history books, and has given the average gang a bloodthirsty reputation. To some extent the image fit, but no more than it did any other group of men with power that they wished to preserve. Behind the bloody exterior could often be found a presence more complex than is generally realized.

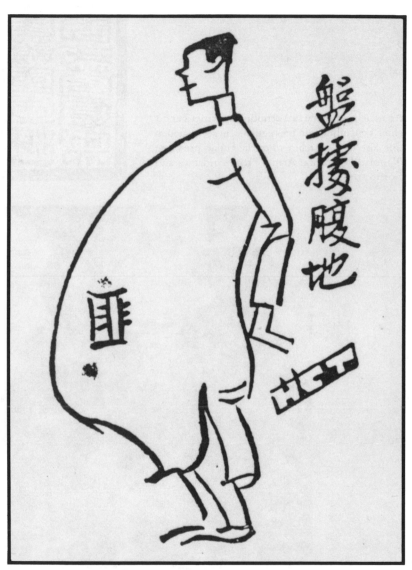

A Japanese propaganda cartoon of the 1920's depicts a fat man, China, unable to move because of his swollen belly. The *fei* character on his stomach, meaning "bandits," is a homophone of the word meaning "fat." The cartoon reflects the Japanese view that the bandits who permanently infested the interior provinces were a natural corollary to China's overspread empire, and hints at Japan's desire to annex parts of China. From *Shina meibutsu hizoku monogatari.*

An official military seal denoting a former bandit chief's enrollment in the regular army—issued in this case by a detachment of the Fujian province National Protection Army. From Andrews and Borup 1918.

Two Manchurian bandit chiefs. One was later enrolled as a colonel under Zhang Zuolin. From Mackay 1927.

"The White Wolf's Transit of Shaanxi and Sichuan." A sympathetic contemporary woodcut by a local artist shows Bai Lang's attack on Fengxiang, Shaanxi, in April 1914. The upper section shows Bai Lang himself, under a banner reading "Generalissimo Bai," supervising the cavalry attack on the city's walls. Below, foot soldiers await the signal to storm the city. From Wang Shucun 1964.

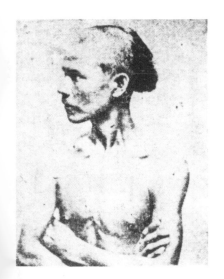

A Manchurian bandit chief, photographed after capture. From *Manshū nichinichi shinbun*, Nov. 26, 1922.

The heads of Bai Lang and several of his followers are suspended in cages on the south gate of Kaifeng city. Bai's head is in the cage second from right, according to the inscription. From White 1966.

A flag issued by Yunnan bandits signifying that the bearer is authorized to cross the territory under their jurisdiction. From Rock 1925.

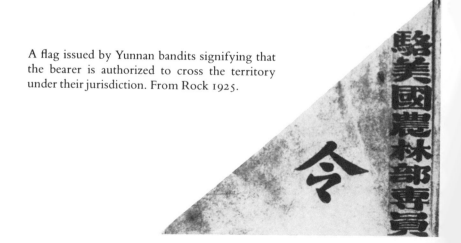

## CHAPTER EIGHT

# "Apotheosis of Banditry": China Becomes a Bandits' World

*Let every day be a Happy New Year, and get a new wife every night.*
*You wish to become high military officers,*
*Then aspire to be bandit ring leaders.*
*You wish to have plenty of food, then set Nanyang city on fire.*
*You wish to make plenty of money, take a young girl captive.*
*You wish to get a beautiful wife, take her home.*
*It is better to be married to an old bandit chief,*
*Than to be a worse half, though he be rich and young.*
　　　　　　　　　　　　　　　　　　　*—Swallow and Lu 1934*

*"A monkey dressed up in the robes of Chou Kung will be miserable*
*until it has torn them off. If these men really have the nature of Chê*
*the robber, they can hardly be comfortable in the role of pillars of*
*the state." (Zhuangzi)*　　　　　　　　　*—Quoted in King 1927: 173*

POLITICAL INSTABILITY, whether in far-reaching empires or in fledgling nation-states, always brings the army to the fore. When civilian control is ineffective the military tends to take over as a matter of course, both because it is the only organized force available, and because soldiers' instinct for "order" makes "chaos" intolerable. Ambition and an ingrained respect for hierarchy play their parts, too. In China the warlord period made military capability the new key to power, while simultaneously blurring the distinction between official and unofficial mobilization.

Bandits, with their fighting experience, were a potent force in the highly militarized Chinese Republic. The revolutionary movement of 1911, the conflicts between rival warlords, the competition between the Nationalists and the Communists, and the increasing pressure from Japan all created new possibilities for aspiring bandit chiefs to exploit the straight world to their own ends. Since banditry was a means of survival and of masculine self-assertion rather than of explicit social protest, it was inevitable that sooner or later bandits would become closely interwoven with the country's new military rulers. At the very least, militarization's destructive effect on the local distribution of power gave a gang much more freedom to operate. At best, the capable gang leader could aspire to the highest echelons of national power. In between, local and provincial power was available to the individual able and lucky enough to take it.

As long as bandits were needed as reserve forces for military conflicts or as retainers for local bosses' private feuds, their profession survived and they thrived. The patron-client relationship between the two sides brought equal benefits to both, and the inability of the authorities to extend their control throughout the country nourished that relationship. Only when the state with its superior resources was able to mount coordinated and large-scale campaigns to remove both the economic and the logistic basis of banditry—building roads, using airplanes, establishing strong garrisons, etc.—did the relationship falter and die. The inevitable consequence was the demise of banditry itself.

The fact that power-holders of all kinds sought to manipulate bandits to their own purposes suggests that the latter had become no more than expendable pawns in other people's military chess games. Yet it also indicates that bandits, having become a part of the local power equation in many parts of China, could not be ignored. Though it was precisely the division of sovereignty between competing warlords, revolutionary forces, and foreign imperialism that did so much to create the preconditions for the growth of banditry, in their efforts to influence or control China's future these forces also had no choice but to take those bandits into consideration. For just as the multiplication of power sources made it more imperative than ever for bandit chiefs to create political alliances for self-protection, so too it became increasingly clear that if you did not use bandits in your own army someone was going to use them against you. In such times even a bandit army with all its faults was better than no army at all.

## Bandits as Soldiers: The Apotheosis of Banditry

The practice of enrolling bandits as soldiers (known as *zhaoan*, "summoning peace," or *guishun*, "returning to allegiance"), was not in itself new, dating back at least to the late Ming rebellions and enshrined in principle in the *Shuihu zhuan*. Government forces employed the tactic during the mid-nineteenth-century rebellions and in the defense of the Manchurian frontier,[1] exploiting local ties so as to allow the bandits' subjective interests to be mobilized for the defense of hearth and home. The Manchurian case was especially significant: irregular units fought bitterly in all the conflicts that racked northeast China during the decade 1895–1905—the Sino-Japanese War, the Russian intervention against the Boxers, and the Russo-Japanese War. It was during the same period of political turmoil that the Dowager Empress Zi Xi exhorted "desperate men who have turned into bandits and robbers to 'reform' themselves and enlist in the various regiments, where brave and strong men are required, instead of risking their lives in robbing and pillaging."[2]

Warlords, always in need of recruits for their armies, also made a regular practice of absorbing bandits, in line with the age-old strategy of "simultaneous suppression and pacification."[3] There were numerous reasons for doing so. For one thing, it eliminated the need for troublesome suppression campaigns—an important consideration, since enemies were always quick to take advantage of a rival's absorption in internal affairs to launch surprise attacks. For another, it prevented the same bandits from being enrolled by opponents or from being incited by them to cause trouble. Third, it was easier than carrying out official recruitment drives, especially since the bandits often possessed their own weapons and had battle experience. Fourth, roping in large numbers of bandits gave an impression of strength and justified high levels of taxation, military requisitions, and so on. Finally, it enabled the warlord concerned to convince his superiors with the minimum of effort that a bandit-troubled area had been effectively pacified.

Alongside the institutionalization of the military, therefore, the warlord period also saw the institutionalization of the bandit as soldier. As one observer put it, "officially recruited bandits are soldiers; privately recruited soldiers are bandits."[4] Though the soldier-bandits, as we shall see later, demonstrated how the application of military principles to banditry could take that activity onto a new plane, bandits as soldiers added little if anything to the military textbook, at least until the advent of guerrilla warfare. Subjected to enemy fire in conventional battle formation, ex-bandit troops usually turned and fled.

This inability to stand up to regular troops was noted by, among others, the Communist general Zhu De. Even Zhang Zuolin, though himself of bandit origins, began weeding out the ex-bandits from among his troops after noting their poor performance in battle, a measure which improved his fortunes considerably.[5] Other warlords learned the lesson equally painfully. The huge bandit army of the Shandong warlord Zhang Zongchang, despite its description as "countless hordes of hardfighting bandits who are, beyond cavil, China's finest fighting material," totally disintegrated before troops of the Northern Expedition in 1928. The Second and Third Divisions of Feng Yuxiang's National Army

(*Guominjun*), consisting of a hundred thousand or more former bandits recruited in Henan and Shaanxi, also crumpled when forced to face the trained armies of Wu Peifu and Zhang Zuolin in 1926.[6]

For the bandits themselves, unless their unit was a particularly rapacious one, enrollment rarely proved as attractive as they had expected. Though the chiefs might hope for promotion if they survived the assassin's bullet, for the rest there was little more than the soldier's life, which, though perhaps more regular than the bandit's, generally brought smaller rewards. On their meager wages—often delayed or withheld—they had to buy what they needed, including food. They also had to undergo tiresome drill sessions. Since ex-bandit troops were always considered the least reliable segment of a warlord army, their primary function was that of cannon fodder.[7] It was common for such units to be transported to some far-off province to fight against an obscure enemy in the name of unexplained objectives or ideals. Consequently, after a quick breather, many bandit-soldiers began to hanker after the old life again. The subchiefs in particular, more ego-conscious than the others, began to dream of further promotion, of becoming chiefs again and being enrolled in their own right after causing a bit of trouble to get themselves noticed. Thus it was often not long before "pacified" bandits returned to their old ways. The main attraction of the military life was the possibility of licensed plunder, and even this could be used by the authorities as an excuse for suppression.

Treachery was a constant hazard for those who dreamed of a military career, for the authorities were fully aware of bandits' military shortcomings. One ex-bandit officer in the Anhui provincial army, ordered to suppress the remnants of his old band, soon captured the new chief's wife and held her against the band's surrender. Her husband, however, contacted the authorities, suggesting instead that the bandit-officer himself be killed, the woman released, and he and his followers taken into the army with good pay, new uniforms, and food. Being a relatively painless way of restoring peace and quiet, the plan was agreed to and executed within the hour.[8]

At Lincheng, the "professionals" in the gang refused enrollment because the previous year 40 of their number who had surrendered to the army had immediately been murdered and had their heads publicly exposed.[9] Such fears were well-grounded, for only six months after receiving their commissions Sun Meiyao and several of his subordinates were dead. Since the Shandong military authorities had been reluctant to enroll the bandits anyway, pay and weapons were withheld and they were encouraged to live off the surrounding countryside. In a series of mysterious incidents, Sun Meiyao's mother and two sisters were kidnapped by the very bandits Sun was supposed to be suppressing, and one sister and a nephew of Sun's were killed. Rumors began to spread that Sun's own days were numbered, encouraged no doubt by the military. Finally he was lured into a trap along with several of his subordinates and executed on the grounds of failing to control his followers and refusing to obey orders. The remainder of the bandits were disarmed and sent home, save for a few officers who, for their complicity in the murders, were allowed to retain their commissions. Clearly there was no honor among the thieves, let alone among those who sought to exploit them. In contrast, chiefs among the anti-enrollment faction were still operating two years later.[10]

The treachery that followed the Lincheng affair became a cause célèbre along the North China bandit grapevine and even as far as northern Manchuria:

The results of that episode were well-known to "my" bandits. . . . More than once I heard them discuss that affair as a precedent and an example of what might happen to them if they should let me go free. It was quite an important factor, I am sure, in prolonging my captivity, and in forcing the bandits to keep well out of the reach of the soldiers who were sent to take me from them.

These bandits, too, had their apprehensions fully borne out: 38 of the original band who surrendered on the promise that they would be taken into the army were later put up against a wall and shot. Another band that had inherited this captive, though it refused to treat with the soldiers, still received nothing in return for his release save the freedom to escape unmolested.[11]

Thus, though military instatement was the most obvious and most attractive avenue of advancement for ambitious individuals in Republican China, there was often more security even in the uncertain life of the bandit. That a career in the army remained popular reflects not only the warlords' almost infinite hunger for recruits, but also the steady institutionalization of the military as a vehicle for predatory as well as protective violence.

Taken on their own terms, however, bandits could be fairly effective. Mao Zedong, for example, considered them doughty figures given correct leadership and something to fight for, and so did He Long.[12] By far the most potent motivation was keeping the peace in their home districts. Sun Meiyao's men, for example, were originally organized into a brigade to protect the Tianjin-Pukou Railway at the Shandong-Zhili border, not far from the site of the Lincheng Incident itself.[13] The most significant illustration of this principle, however, in North China at any rate, was the Songxian Pacification Force (*Zhen Song jun*), organized in 1912 from the mainly bandit irregulars who had fought to overthrow Qing rule in Henan.

The nucleus of the SPF was a complex bandit gang several hundred strong based on Yangshan, a formidable peak located in the mountainous west Henan district of Songxian. This force had been mobilized by Republicans in 1911 and reorganized initially as the Henan-Shaanxi Allied Army. When hostilities ended, the close ties between the Army's Republican advisers and the local elite allowed it to be formally instated as a regular military unit. Although the former Yangshan chiefs were retained as second-level officers, supreme control was given to the ambitious, conservative Republican Liu Zhenhua.[14] At one stroke the proud and respected bandits of Yangshan were transformed from revolutionary guerrillas into antipopular levies, for the SPF's role was clear from the outset: to restore "order" to the traditionally unruly bandit districts of west Henan in the interests of the local elite. "Their first responsibility," it was announced, "was to protect local people's lives and property." In Baofeng and Lushan vicious pogroms razed villages and sent survivors fleeing to the mountains. So impressed with their "pacification" campaign was the corrupt Henan military governor Zhang Zhenfang that he promptly drew up a report for the purposes of future military instruction.[15]

In Songxian, despite the gentry's enthusiasm for the slaughter of upstart peasants, it was with the traditional method of "summoning bandits to form an army" (*zhaofei chengjun*) that the SPF had most success. Liu Zhenhua, in the process of building up his own power base, had a vested interest in winning over as many of the bandits as possible. A combination of lingering local support, familiarity with the region's topography, and the SPF's own bandit origins brought Liu's efforts considerable success. Despite his and his fellow officers' vow to "consider the extermination of Songxian's bandits as their sacred duty," in fact it would not be by outright suppression but by "cleansing their hearts and changing the skin of their faces" (*xixin gemian*) that their "extermination" would take place.[16]

Known to local peasants as the "Grey Rats," the SPF participated energetically in the suppression of Bai Lang's rebellion, earning people's hatred everywhere but perhaps in its native Songxian. At least two of the officers credited with Bai's death were former Yangshan chiefs,[17] and it was their 1911 ally Zhang Fang who was responsible for denying Bai a route into Sichuan in mid-1914.* There could be no more turning back.

---

*Zhang's complicity is more or less confirmed by the fact that on the day of the battle that drove Bai's forces farther west into Gansu he was promoted to the rank of South Shaanxi Defense Commissioner, a move clearly designed to keep him loyal (*NCH*, 13 June 1914: 850; *DFZZ* 11, no. 1 [1 July 1914], "Zhongguo dashi ji": 32). Bai Lang had sought to win Zhang over by using his personal ties to Wang Shengqi, a former Shaanxi provincial army officer who had defected to the rebels with his men shortly before. While Bai boasted publicly of his intent to attack Xian, Wang and a few others were sent

For more than a decade the SPF retained responsibility for local peace-keeping, putting down Shaanxi rebels as well as west Henan bandits, while Liu Zhenhua steadily increased his control over both provinces. By 1924, more than 50,000 strong, it had become the mainstay of Liu's power.[18]

The SPF's debacle came in 1926 with the unsuccessful siege of the Shaanxi capital of Xian. Ordered into action against the "bandit" Feng Yuxiang, Liu supplemented the SPF with another division of Songxian bandits and Red Spear defense units and chased Feng's men out of Henan into Shaanxi, finally forcing the latter to shut themselves up in Xian. For the nine months that the SPF besieged the city they laid waste the surrounding countryside, occupying towns and villages and requisitioning all the women they could find as concubines. Ironically enough they were still referred to by Shaanxi peasants as the "Henan-Shaanxi Allied Army," but fighting was by now evidently not their strong point. When Feng Yuxiang's reinforcements arrived in November, the besiegers were easily scattered. By the end of the year those who had not been killed or defected to Feng's side had been driven back into Henan.[19]

The extent to which the SPF had alienated local popular opinion even in its native districts now became painfully clear. As the defeated soldiers streamed back over the border, west Henan Red Spears said to be a million strong launched a general uprising. Foremost among their demands was that Liu Zhenhua and the SPF be forbidden from entering the area; they even promised to expel Liu's subordinate Zhang Zhigong, another once-popular Yangshan chief, if he tried to negotiate the issue, though Zhang had not joined Liu's expedition to Shaanxi and had been considered relatively trustworthy.[20] After this debacle the Songxian Pacification Force seems to have disappeared as an independent military entity.

Several lessons stand out from the examples considered here. First, bandits could easily be transformed from fighting for revolutionary ideals to putting down popular rebellion, for the combination of strong personal loyalty to their leader and their parochial horizons made them pliable tools in the hands of calculating power-seekers. Second, bandit troops were most reliable when defending their own territory, and often disintegrated when this tie was removed. They could not be enrolled and turned into disciplined soldiers overnight. Third, such troops were on an

---

quietly down to Hanzhong to negotiate a passage across the border. They were never seen again. A series of mutinies in the city followed, however, suggesting that Wang's pleas for a renewing of revolutionary commitment did not go entirely unheeded (Wang Zongyu 1964: 21; Qiao Xuwu 1956: 138; Du Qunhe ed. 1980: 164–65; *STSB*, 26 Apr. 1914: 9). One source, incidentally (Wu Rui 1970: 22), claims that a small force of about a hundred rebels did in fact manage to slip across the border, only to be cut to pieces by defending troops and peasant vigilantes in the vicinity of Wanyuan.

unwritten code of good behavior in the districts they served, and lost whatever support they had if they ignored it. Difficult as it was for a gang to sustain that relationship once it crossed the line into the official world, only thus did individuals hoping to use bandits stand much chance of success. Fourth, the sharp contrast between the traditional methods used in Songxian and the bloody repression unleashed elsewhere revealed starkly the polarization of rural communities, where the dividing line between "bandit" and "hero" was often also a regional boundary. The fact that the "bandits" of one side could be effectively used to control the "heroes" of the other simply by reversing the terms of reference was a lesson not lost on those in power.*

## The Prospects for a Bandit Chief

Songs and rhymes current under the Republic, like the one that follows, lamented sardonically the rise of banditry as an avenue to power and privilege:

> Just pull back the trigger of your rifle
> And you've two or three thousand silver dollars;
> One who was "carrying a stick" in the morning
> Will be an official by nightfall.[21]

There was indeed a future for the bandit chief in warlord-period politics, but it was one fraught with pitfalls. Most chiefs were pragmatic, with a good eye for the main chance (those who were not soon died), but frequent political changes at both local and national levels and the difficulty of living down one's bandit origins meant that long-term survivors were few. On the whole, ex-bandits who achieved lasting recognition under the Republic tended to hail from the border provinces of Mongolia and Manchuria, Guangdong, Guangxi, Sichuan, and Yunnan[22]—not surprising, really, when one considers the rich bandit tradition the border zones nurtured and their politically crucial location. Among them, the majority were from Manchuria and owed their success to the patronage of Zhang Zuolin, the supreme example of the bandit-warlord. Other former bandits to achieve national prominence included Lu Rongting, for a time the most powerful warlord of South China; Yang Hucheng, the one-time Shaanxi "Sword-fighter" who achieved fame when he helped engineer the 1936 capture of Jiang Jieshi known as the "Xian Incident"; and Li Fulin, a Cantonese chief who rose to become an important figure in the Nationalist Army. By the mid-1920's, ironical

---

*The pattern was furnished by the *Shuihu zhuan*, where the heroes, many of them from the privileged classes, are ultimately reconciled with the authorities and sent to fight the genuinely subversive antidynastic revolt of Fang La. See Chesneaux 1971a: 19.

commentators were speaking of "the Red Beards in the north and the bandits in the south," [23] meaning Zhang Zuolin and Lu Rongting, respectively. What stands out about almost all these characters is their conservatism and opportunism, properties that reveal as much about the nature of warlordism as about bandits.

Success stories on a national level were not the norm for bandit chiefs, however. Most spent their political careers much lower in the ranks, and submerged leaving hardly a trace. Sometimes it was treachery that stopped their lives short, as with Sun Meiyao and Lao Yangren, and also the Shaanxi bandit-rebel Guo Jian, murdered by Feng Yuxiang in 1921.[24] Bai Lang's failure to employ the traditional ruse of submitting to the government when pressed undoubtedly reflected a lesson learned from the execution of those eighteen fellow-chiefs who had tried it in October 1912. Even Zhang Zuolin, after twenty years at the forefront of national politics, died an ignominious death at the hands of his former Japanese patrons.

Many other chiefs who staked their lives on a military career died fighting before they could make a name for themselves. Often it was because they were thrown into the thick of battle as expendable human matériel. Wang Laowu (Wang Zhen) and Ren Yingqi, Lao Yangren subchiefs who survived the defeat and secured military commissions, were typical. Wang, demobilized in 1925 following political changes in Henan, somehow (with a secret brief from Communist agents?) managed to drift up to Manchuria, where his activities are shrouded in mystery. By 1929 he was back in Henan recruiting a bandit army 30,000 strong to support Feng Yuxiang's northern warlord coalition, but in the government's counterattack in 1930 his force was roundly defeated and Wang himself was killed.[25] Ren Yingqi, who, like Wang, had also fought with Bai Lang as a youth, had a more steady career in the army after 1923, serving sometimes with Feng Yuxiang, sometimes with Wu Peifu, always maintaining a fairly radical position, until his capture and execution in 1930 while fighting for the same northern warlord coalition.[26] The former 1911 hero Wang Tianzong led a similar career until his death in battle in 1917.*

How such bandit-militarists fared depended to a large degree on their personal astuteness. To entertain any illusions about the military's atti-

---

*There are contrasting accounts of Wang's later career. The standard version claims that he distinguished himself resisting Zhang Xun's ill-fated imperial restoration attempt in 1917, but then, after falling out with the government, went south to join the anti-Beijing "Constitution Protection Army" (*Huguo jun*). In the midst of his successful guerrilla campaign against the government he became ill and died (*XHSY*: II, 45; Zhang Xiuzhai 1961: 374; *ZHMG*: 153). A recent Taiwan account, however, has denied Wang's heroic role in these events, citing eyewitnesses who allegedly saw him living quietly in Beijing in 1917 and 1918 (Wang Tiancong 1971: 13).

tude was a fatal mistake, for the slightest technical slip on the ex-chief's part could provide the excuse for elimination. The most successful chiefs were consequently those who paid careful attention to the prevailing wind and allowed themselves to be blown along with it, never afraid or ashamed to return temporarily to banditry when necessary. Throughout the nineteenth-century rebellions, for example, many bandit chiefs repeatedly switched from government to rebel allegiance and back again according to the fortunes of war. Likewise, He Long shocked his new-found Communist friends in 1928 by openly admitting that as a bandit chief he had naturally allied himself with whoever was most powerful or offered the most benefits, maintaining the alliance for as long as it suited him and breaking it at will.[27] This piece of bandit wisdom was borne out by the careers of several North China chiefs.

First was the powerful west Henan gang leader Zhang Juwa, better known as Zhang Guafu or "Widow Zhang." Successor to the local social bandit tradition, Zhang was said by local missionaries to plaster the towns she passed through with brightly colored posters bearing slogans like "Rob the rich and save the poor!" A woman of great charisma, she commanded the loyalties of some 5,000 followers, mostly from the mountain counties of Luoning, Yiyang, Yichuan, and Luoyang. This was a considerable force even in the conditions of the late 1920's, and she soon graduated from banditry to fighting for the government against independent warlord units in west Henan until attacked and disarmed by fearful local militarists. Recruiting anew, she quickly recovered most of her former strength and saw service with the government again as a divisional commander under the 1911 veteran and former "Sword-fighter" Zhang Fang, now a Nationalist general. For unexplained reasons—probably she sniffed fresh treachery in the wind—she turned bandit once more, trying to join He Long's Communist units in Sichuan, but was finally captured and executed by Henan Bandit-Suppression Commander Liu Zhenhua at Luoyang in 1931. Before she died she allegedly confessed details of a conference held that spring by Henan chiefs to consolidate their forces into a political army.[28]

Fan Zhongxiu was yet another peasant leader to emerge from the villages of southwest Henan. Even before 1911 he was leading his own local band, highly regarded by villagers for his combination of military ability and moral scruples. The confused years after the revolution eventually found him commanding a thousand or so irregular soldiers in Shaanxi, whom he led through the 1916 rising against Yuan Shikai and the 1918 declaration of independence from the warlord government in Beijing. As a "leader of the Henan popular forces" he was singled out for attention by revolutionaries in the Nationalist Party and finally given a command in the progressive Nation-Pacifying Army (*Jingguo jun*) under his former superior Zhang Fang, whom Fan and other irregular leaders had insisted be put at their head in place of the Republican Yu Youren.[29] At this point in his career Fan clearly trusted his old outlaw contacts more than he did unknown quantities like the Nationalists.

Although the Nation-Pacifying Army was an independent force, it was not long before Fan managed to get himself recognized by the regular military. In 1921 he was absorbed into Feng Yuxiang's forces and subsequently sent back to garrison Henan,[30] where his bandit background made him a natural if reluctant candidate for dealing with the soldier-bandits of Lao Yangren, holed up with several foreign captives and pressing for military enrollment. Lao Yangren had gained a reputation for slaughtering government emissaries unless they came with concrete proposals, but Fan had one special point in his favor besides his common bandit background: the presence among the gang's subchiefs of his former schoolmate and outlaw colleague Ren Yingqi. With Ren as intermediary, Fan not only persuaded Lao Yangren to accept the terms of surrender he brought, but also surreptitiously recruited the two chiefs for the revolution, requesting them to bide their time until the arrival of a northern expedition from Guangzhou set for the following year.[31]

The next few years of Fan's career were a kaleidoscope of action as he first obeyed a summons to help defend Guangzhou against the local warlord Chen Jiongming, then, at Sun Zhongshan's request, returned north to prepare Henan for the planned military expedition against Beijing.[32] As one of Sun's leading generals, Fan operated under a flag announcing him as "Commander of the National Construction Army of Henan."* After the expedition's failure, he became embroiled in one warlord intrigue after another, now fighting for Feng Yuxiang against Shanxi warlord Yan Xishan, now operating as a vanguard for Wu Peifu against Feng Yuxiang.[33] In the intervals Fan returned temporarily to the wilderness as a bandit, but he had not forgotten his capacity to raise a large army in a short time, nor his links to the west Henan peasant community. When Wu Peifu double-crossed and began slaughtering Red Spear units in 1926, he once again climbed down on the right side of the

---

* Wilbur 1976: 361. It has been suggested (*BLQY*: 91, 100) that the Nationalist Party intermediary between Fan and the Guangzhou forces was none other than Bai Lang's former strategic adviser Shen, who had attached himself to Fan's forces in Shaanxi after Bai's defeat. Contemporary accounts differ on whether Fan was in fact ordered south by Sun's agents or went there first under orders from his superior Wu Peifu to aid Chen Jiongming. Li Xiaoting, for example, a Sun Zhongshan envoy who was in secret contact with Fan, takes the second position, adding that he himself was responsible for persuading Fan to defect at a crucial moment in the battle, allowing Chen's forces to be routed (Li Xiaoting 1969; see also Wen Gongzhi 1930: III, 134). Other reports have added to the confusion by suggesting that 4,000 of Lao Yangren's men were sent south against Guangzhou (Nagano 1924: 86), and even that Lao Yangren himself was leading them (Dailey 1923c: 245). One likely possibility is that Fan's troops included units recruited from Lao Yangren's followers.

fence by joining with the Red Spears against the Wu military machine. Within a few weeks, in coordination with a new northern expedition then marching out of Guangzhou, Fan had expanded his forces to 50,000 irregulars and, with Red Spear cooperation, was holding the vital Nanyang area dominating the main military gateway to the south.

Fan's moves at this time suggest that he had already received orders from Guangzhou to put into action the mission assigned him by Sun Zhongshan two years before. During the summer of 1926 his attacks on vital Henan cities and on the Beijing-Hankou Railway forced Wu Peifu to divert almost all his forces in the province from meeting the southern threat to suppressing Fan's revolt. By September, vanguard units of the Northern Expedition had already taken Hankou, had established contact with Fan's units, and were poised for the thrust across the border from Hubei. Meanwhile, a large segment of Wu's army, perhaps also following a prearranged plan, declared "independence" under the leadership of Ren Yingqi and his 9,000 men, still listed as "former Fan Zhongxiu units." Both Fan and Ren were promoted to Army Commanders and given commands in the National Revolutionary Army. By October, bandit armies and Red Spear units (at this stage it was often difficult to tell the two apart) armed with huge banners bearing the single inscription "FAN" were operating alongside one another and dealing crushing blows to Wu Peifu's forces all over the south of Henan.[34]

At the end of the year, as the southern armies crossed the border and struggled painfully across Henan, "large brigand bands" under Fan's control provided them "valuable assistance." Many also cooperated with local Communist Party activists trying to establish a revolutionary presence in the province before it was taken over by Feng Yuxiang.[35]

The seesaw pattern of Fan's career continued unchanged despite the country's nominal unification in 1928. In the spring of that year his personal ambition evidently won out over his "greenwood" instincts as he sought to occupy Luoyang and Zhengzhou while provincial governor Feng Yuxiang was absent fighting Zhang Zuolin. Although formally allied with Feng, his probable intention was to establish a progressive independent regime in western Henan based on his still-massive popular support: the press referred to him and his followers as "more or less a communistic group." Routed by Feng's crack units, however, Fan's irregulars fled, and Fan himself went underground once more.[36]

After almost a year of desperate predatory banditry along the borders of Henan, Hubei, and Anhui, the scattered units formerly under Fan's leadership were approached once again by agents of Feng Yuxiang the following June. Feng was planning a new struggle against the government for October, and these men had been sent to whip the irregulars into shape. By mid-1930 Fan was no longer the "free-lance brigand general" of a year before but a full-fledged "army officer," and his continuing local popularity enabled him to recruit an entire division of bandits, the Twelfth Division, to be stationed at Zhengyang.[37]

Unfortunately, this was Fan Zhongxiu's last trick. By the summer of 1930 he was dead, killed by an exploding aerial bomb in the same battle for the city of Xuchang that resulted in the death of his fellow-Baofeng chief Wang Laowu. His 10,000 followers, fearing disbandment, mutinied and were eventually incorporated into the forces of the nearby Eyuwan Soviet Area.[38] Fan would no doubt have been happy with that result.

The almost bewildering array of causes and personalities with which Fan allied over the years is testimony to the number of roads open to the able and aspiring bandit chief during the Republican period. It also shows how difficult it had become to maintain one's position, unless one were very lucky, after 1911. Those like Zhang Zuolin who were successful politically had already established positions of local power when the Revolution broke out; with fewer rivals they were able to stake an early claim to legitimacy. As the contenders for power multiplied, it became more and more difficult to maintain a hold on the ladder.

Fan Zhongxiu was not a typical militarist, though, for his reputation as a popular leader, however he or his superiors chose to exploit it, endured up to and after his death. In 1959 people in Baofeng continued to hold him in considerable esteem as a flag-bearer of Bai Lang's rebellious heritage.[39] If anything, this particular characteristic probably stood Fan in good stead, for it meant that unlike many other militarists he was never without a popular base so long as he stayed in his native west Henan or in Shaanxi. He was thus not afraid of "falling into the weeds," for on the one hand the fall was sure to be a soft one, and on the other the rebound was almost guaranteed. Few twentieth-century bandit-militarists managed to match his combination of resilience and moral scruples.

## Soldiers as Bandits: The Phenomenon of Soldier-Banditry

By the early 1920's, traditional old-time banditry (*tufei*) had been swamped in many parts of China by the tide of what most commentators called "soldier-banditry" (*bingfei*). Substantially, the term referred to a joint process by which, on the one hand, former soldiers deprived of their military status sought to retrieve it by the use of predatory bandit techniques, and, on the other, regular bandit gangs strove to utilize their customary activities to acquire regular military status otherwise unattainable. In short, a dialectical process was operating by which the military became "banditized" and the bandits became "militarized": "If the policy is disbandment, soldiers turn bandits. If it is recruiting, bandits turn soldiers. Therefore there is no brigand who is not a soldier and no soldier who is not a brigand." *

The soldier-bandits differed from traditional bandits in seven principal respects:

(1) Their activities were aimed not at survival outside the law, but at the achievement of legitimacy through instatement or reinstatement in the military.

(2) Their operations, instead of centering upon a given locality and depending on local sentiment, were harsh and wide-ranging, calculated by the generation of maximum distress to ensure a rapid reaction from the authorities. A base was used only when hard-pressed or while awaiting the result of negotiations.

(3) This abandonment of local ties, coupled with the military experience of the most prominent bands, resulted in the brutalization of banditry relative to previous years, with effects felt most painfully by the peasants.

(4) The maximum-impact strategy required that large towns and cities, normally outside the scope of gang operations, become the principal objects of attack.

(5) To make this strategy a practical proposition required much larger numbers and better organization than had been required for local banditry. This in turn had a reciprocal effect, increased size not only making new modes of behavior possible but simultaneously making the old ones defunct.

(6) For the same reason, speed of movement was essential. The surprise night attack thus became a standard feature of soldier-bandit raids, and when a town could not be taken easily the band would usually move on.

(7) Finally, the strategy was greatly improved by the capture of foreigners, which ensured not only that publicity would result for the gang's chief, but also that pressure would be exerted on the Chinese authorities to accede to the bandits' demands.

In practice, then, soldier-banditry was a fairly complex phenomenon with its own rules of operation. To see how it actually did operate let us look more closely at the man who started it all: Lao Yangren, "The Old Foreigner."

The name of Lao Yangren first began to appear in anxious dispatches

---

*Close 1924: 18. Note also the following despairing comment from a longtime missionary: "Robbers—soldiers. . . . You meet a man in the uniform of a soldier, and he tells you that he used to be a soldier but no longer is one. Now he is a robber since deserting the army, and he wears the uniform just to have something to wear. Then you meet a man in a padded jacket and baggy pants and he tells you that he is a soldier, that he has no uniform because the army ran out of uniforms" (Jurgensen 1965: 134–35).

from Henan in the summer of 1922. In May, at the height of the First Zhili-Fengtian War, Henan military governor Zhao Ti turned against his Zhili superior Wu Peifu in support of Fengtian leader Zhang Zuolin, only to be heavily defeated at Zhengzhou. Feng Yuxiang, appointed Zhao's successor, stripped him of his rank and ordered his troops disbanded. These soldiers, however, possibly under direct orders to cause trouble for Feng, then broke up into small bands and fled with their weapons into the mountains and forests of west and south Henan, where they were joined by ex-subordinates of Bao Dequan, one of Zhao Ti's generals recently executed by Feng Yuxiang.[40] Thus did "soldier-banditry" come to Henan's "bandit kingdoms," and the effect was akin to that of upsetting a beehive. "Since that time," sighed the compiler of a local gazetteer, "the situation in Henan has been chaotic."[41]

Within weeks, the rich rural gentry had begun to remove themselves to the walled towns, following the old adage "live in the cities during a minor disturbance; live in the countryside during a major rebellion." Clearly, no one had foreseen the scale of the disruption the soldier-bandits were going to cause, nor the difficulty of dealing with them once they had blended into the old bandit districts. By June, only a month after the Zhao debacle, 30 counties had been overrun and three major cities of southwest Henan—Lushan, Baofeng, and Fugou—left smoking ruins. Lushan, after a long siege, was finally sold out by its garrison. A local Chinese newspaper described the scene:

> Among the plundered cities Lushan suffered most. The magistrate, the judge, the prison warden, the secretaries and clerks in the magistrate's yamen, and the employees of the other government offices were carried off by the bandits. All the foreign missionaries were taken captive.... Over 2,300 of the inhabitants, men, women, and children, were carried off, and seventy cartloads of booty were hauled away. The magistrate's yamen was destroyed by fire, the prison was broken open, and the prisoners were released. Not one house in the city escaped being looted.[42]

The mastermind behind this attack, which demonstrated many features typical of soldier-bandit raids—official targets, opening prisons, collusion with defending troops, taking foreign captives for ransom, and maximum destruction—was Lao Yangren. For almost two years this man personified soldier-banditry in North China as he and the other leaders of his powerful bandit army—Wang Laowu, Ren Yingqi, Zhang Desheng, Li Mingsheng, Fan Zubao, and Wang Yuedong—set out to put Henan's bandit subculture on the twentieth-century Chinese political map.[43]

As far as can be ascertained, Lao Yangren was not serving with Zhao Ti in 1922. The most plausible explanation for his meteoric rise to fame is that, as the best known and most capable of all the chiefs then en-

sconced in the mountains of southwest Henan, he became a natural rallying point for the thousands of soldiers who came flocking south from the
battlefields of Zhengzhou. Whether he now saw a rich opportunity to
"raise the flag of rebellion," or whether he was secretly contacted with
a promise of a military career is yet to be confirmed. Whichever is true,
Zhang Zuolin's recently defeated Fengtian faction, which now included
Zhao Ti's swashbuckling younger brother Zhao Jie,* seized upon Lao
Yangren's activities as a golden chance to discredit its triumphant Zhili
rivals.[44]

In October Lao Yangren commenced a strategy of wide-ranging destruction intended to make a name for himself as both a military leader
and a ruthless adversary. After gathering his 10,000 or so followers
around the village of Daying in the heart of "Robberland," he moved
them out, in tight military formation, through the foothills surrounding Yexian down toward the prosperous agricultural counties of southeastern Henan, along a route not far from that taken by Bai Lang ten
years before. A missionary captive observed the contrast between the
bandits' behavior in Robberland and that elsewhere:

> The whole country is swarming with bandits, and everybody moves east-
> ward. Robbers continue to come from every direction.... The throng is
> growing more and more hilarious.... Several of the men carry horns and
> trumpets... blowing them to their heart's content....
> We have just emerged from the robber district. Our idea of the bandits
> is now suddenly changed for the worse.... The work of ravaging is at its
> height.... On every side villages are destroyed. Smoke and fire are unmistakable
> signs of the robber trail.[45]

Over the next two months, as these pioneer soldier-bandits cut a
swath of mayhem across much of Henan and western Anhui, almost a
dozen major walled towns and hundreds of smaller ones were reduced to
charred ruins, thousands of captives were taken (including fourteen
foreigners), and the biggest suppression operation seen since the days

---

*Zhao Jie was a well-known opium addict, and used his bandit contacts in western
Henan to enforce cultivation of the opium poppy while his brother was governor, be-
coming very rich in the process (*China's Millions*, Jan. 1923: 14–15; *NCH*, 27 May 1922:
595; Ide 1921: 35, 45). In the spring of 1922, shortly before the Zhengzhou debacle, Zhao
Jie had abruptly disappeared following a military setback, raising fears that he would
become a "second White Wolf" (SD 893.00/4522 [Hankou to Beijing, 11 May 1922];
*Central China Post*, 17 May 1922, in 893.00/4524 [Hankou to Beijing, 17 May 1922]. After
Lao Yangren's death in January 1924 he reemerged in Mongolia, and was soon being
referred to as a "well-known bandit" (McCormack 1977: 118; see also *Gendaishi shiryō* 32:
583–84). His later career is a mystery. In 1927 a man with the same name was listed as a
Guangdong bandit chief (Shibuya 1928: 136), and three years later one "Zhao Jie" was
being criticized for his policy of absorbing bandits into his local defense detachment
in Xuzhou, north Jiangsu (*ZGNC*: 333). If these references were indeed all to the same
man—not at all impossible—Zhao Jie's passage from warlord to bandit chief and back
again in a career spanning the length and breadth of China would furnish a fascinating
illustration of the permutations of twentieth-century banditry.

of Bai Lang was mounted against them. In December agreement was reached, and Lao Yangren was taken into Wu Peifu's army along with six or seven thousand of his men.[46]

If Lao Yangren had established a new pattern for banditry, the methods employed to deal with it were nothing new. His army was broken into four sections, only one of which was allowed to remain behind to garrison its old haunts in western Henan. One was sent south to bolster Wu Peifu's defenses, but the main body was dispatched to the Anhui border far away from Wu's main headquarters in Luoyang.[47]

Only six months after these events the beehive was overturned once more when Wu Peifu botched an attempt to eliminate the former bandits. As Wu's five-province army closed in, Lao Yangren and his 20,000 followers, outnumbered two to one, broke out toward their homes in southwest Henan. Towns along the way recorded their passage in tones of sadness and shock.[48] By the middle of October Lao Yangren was a bandit again, holed up in the mountains he knew so well. After failing to break through into Sichuan to join the pro-Nationalist general Xiong Kewu,* he and his followers set off on a repetition of the previous year's campaign, weaving and crisscrossing along the borders with Hubei and Shaanxi. As town after town fell to their onslaught they were described as more formidable than ever before. Not until Lao Yangren was treacherously murdered by a mercenary subchief did his rampage come to an end.[49]

On this second bout of mayhem, Lao Yangren again used the tactic of employing foreign captives to create leverage. One recorded that, despite their earlier experiences, the bandits continued to talk openly about joining the army. At the end she overheard them talking in whispers about the chief's death, and after she had been handed over to the soldiers noted that some bandits were still with her, though a compromise was denied.[50]

Lao Yangren's movements created the basic pattern for soldier-banditry. As "the first man to introduce the sport of kidnapping foreigners,"[51] he showed clearly his ultimate aim to be his and his followers' enrollment in the army. Many were indeed formally instated after his death—some, like Ren Yingqi, leading relatively successful careers. The remainder resumed banditry in their old haunts. Thanks to this example, there were now few large North China gangs not dominated by soldiers; most followed the same strategy Lao Yangren set out: quick movement, great destruction, and foreign captives. The raid of one "Captain Sun" (Sun Dianying) provided an exemplary case.

---

*It may well be that Lao Yangren, already given the signal by Fan Zhongxiu half a year earlier, had been contacted by Party agents in the same way that Bai Lang had been, and advised on the basis of Xiong's presence there to try to set up a base in the mountainous border areas of Sichuan.

Sun, also known as Sun Kuiyuan, was a former message-carrier for the Yangshan chief Zhang Ping. Absorbed into the Songxian Pacification Force, he rose to minor command under Han Yukun, but by 1926 had returned to banditry. That spring Sun led his forces at top speed across the breadth of Henan from the western mountains to the Anhui border. No pillaging took place, and the band captured the important city of Bozhou at the end of their journey completely by surprise and almost without a fight. Having successfully established his ability as a military commander, Sun was given high command at the head of his men. He subsequently had a long but quite undistinguished military career, becoming a commander in the armies of the Nanjing government, and eventually going over to the Japanese after their occupation of north China.[52]

Although the capture of cities was a fundamental part of the soldier-bandits' strategy, it was not an easy task to fulfill. Most had walls some 35 feet high and ten to twelve feet thick, with massive doors of heavy wood bound with iron. According to the pattern perfected by Lao Yangren and his successors, the first ploy would be a surprise attack staged in the small hours of the night. It was usually carried out by an advance force of several hundred to a few thousand bandits who would ride ahead at top speed, often covering some fifty miles a night, to achieve the element of surprise. Often the defending garrison had been bribed beforehand or was won over by ex-soldiers operating with the bandits. If both methods failed, bandit agents planted in the city would begin the attack from the inside.

This advance force did the work of intimidating the city's inhabitants before the arrival of the main contingent. After that, amid what one journalist described as a "howling inferno of blood, lust and crime,"[53] the town was stripped clean, the prisons opened, official functionaries killed and their womenfolk raped, often to death. By the following afternoon the work was usually finished, and, sometimes by prior arrangement, the bandits left just in time to avoid "pursuing" troops. The methodical way in which the soldier-bandits stripped large towns (Lao Yangren's three-day sack of Shangcai left it a total ruin with losses amounting to some five million dollars) also indicated their object of making the maximum impact. One Shandong gang in late 1922 made 200 scaling ladders and purchased kerosene, candles, resin, rope, and all kinds of combustibles in preparation for its planned attacks on a series of local towns.[54] Sometimes, however, instead of simply burning at will and taking prisoners indiscriminately, they would raze only the official or commercial sections and carry off only the most valuable residents. The 200 Chinese captives released at the end of Lao Yangren's first campaign, for example, constituted *almost all* the leading citizens of south and west Henan.[55]

Soldier-bandit armies rarely numbered less than several thousand men (though they often broke up to operate temporarily in smaller contingents), and sometimes counted as many as twenty or thirty thousand. Organization was along tight military lines, and for the outsider it was often quite difficult to distinguish these formations from regular military ones. The chiefs were usually referred to as "generalissimo" (*zongsiling*) in place of the traditional bandit titles. When crossing flat land the soldier-bandit armies often spread out over the entire plain in subdivisions several thousand strong, and captives have recorded that "sometimes one arm of the procession [was] a mile long." Orders were issued and obeyed with military precision. Most of the bandits would be on foot, but mounted units effectively carried out advance, flank, and rearguard duties, while scouts scoured the countryside one day ahead for signs of enemy troops.[56]

From the inside, the great soldier-bandit armies appeared less cohesive. Their enormous size created the preconditions for the success of their strategy, but at the same time made them prone to constant centrifugal pressures. In particular, the chiefs' position was more vulnerable than in any other type of bandit outfit. The size of their command made it difficult to exercise personal sway, exposing the subchiefs to the temptation of making their own deal with the authorities, and encouraging the rank and file to let their hair down when they chose. The vast geographical area from which recruits were drawn, by reducing the local affiliation that had provided the strongest cement for bandit gangs, weakened internal ties still further. All in all, the comment of one of Lao Yangren's missionary captives seems to have been pretty near the mark: "While organized well enough for their purpose, a lack of respect for their leaders, *especially of other divisions*, is very evident. A feeling of independence, self-satisfaction and arrogance prevails."[57]

What was more, a large proportion of a soldier-bandit army on the move consisted of people who were bandits only in a nominal sense. Many had been coerced as porters for the gang's vast quantity of expropriated property; there were also numerous prisoners as well as women shanghaied to replenish the gang's harems. Sometimes an area was deliberately despoiled so as to leave local inhabitants no choice but to join, for their presence provided a useful cushion against attacks. Lao Yangren's army devastated a strip of country a mile wide, burning houses and supplies and killing all who resisted so as to make people join. Of the 20,000 or so "bandits," only 8,000 had guns and could be considered regulars. Five-figure estimates of a soldier-bandit army's strength invariably included such "recruits," most of whom stuck to the gang from fear of the pursuing soldiers rather than from any desire to become bandits. They usually brought up the rear of the march along with the captives and played little or no part in the fighting.[58]

Many of these soldier-bandit armies assumed political titles, an indication not only of their desire to present themselves as worthy of military instatement, but also of the new ideas slowly filtering through to the provinces. Lao Yangren's army referred to itself at various times as the "Henan Self-Governing Army," as the "National Construction Army," and as the "Relieve Henan Army."* Fan Mingxin called himself the "People's Revolutionary Commander of Henan and Anhui to Relieve Shandong," and the Lincheng bandits adopted the titles of "People's Self-Deliverance Army" and "Shandong Self-Governing National Construction Army." [59]

As militarization increased, the martial pride characteristic of bandit chiefs was also transformed into acute rank-consciousness, reinforced by the examples of former bandits who had become powerful warlords like Zhang Zuolin and Lu Rongting. Niu Shengwu, for instance, when negotiating his enrollment in the Henan army in 1926, rejected the proferred colonelcy and demanded a full generalship; Feng Yuxiang reported capturing a Manchurian chief who refused to answer Feng's questions on the grounds that he was of insufficient rank. [60]

For all the grandiose titles and martial pride, the ones who suffered most from the soldier-bandits' strategy were the peasants through whose midst they had to pass. The unwritten territorial agreements between gangs that had brought relative security for people with no possessions worth stealing were made more or less redundant. Captives deplored the "desolation of all the district[s] through which we were taken," adding that "the people are truly like sheep for the slaughter," and noting that dead men and horses lay all along the route of march. [61] Even when a gang had been instated as a military unit, its passage was usually recorded by local gazetteers alongside bandit raids. [62]

When arriving in a village where they proposed to stay, the bandits would first be divided up into small groups, each of which went to a different house to demand food and shelter. After eating in a house they would sometimes set it on fire: "I have seen them take their meal in one farmyard, and set fire to the buildings opposite so as to provide light and warmth as they partook of their food." [63]

Nevertheless, soldier-bandits never completely transformed traditional patterns. Although many were ex-soldiers, many more shared motives common to banditry in any era, not the least that of "amassing wealth and making a name for themselves as robbers." Others were there simply because no other livelihood was available, still others in

---

*DFZZ 19, no. 23 (10 Dec. 1922): 129. These were the titles bestowed upon Fan Zhongxiu and his followers by Sun Zhongshan. It is not clear whether Lao Yangren had Fan's authorization to use them or whether he was merely trying to steal some of Fan's thunder.

order to repay heavy debts or escape their creditors. Revenge was another common motive, but many of the rank and file were merely young boys out to see the world.

Not all of the soldier-bandits sought military enrollment, either. Though the enormous ransoms they demanded were often designed "to compel the Central Government to re-enlist them in the army," other gangs, including even sections of Lao Yangren's band as well as part of that at Lincheng, were primarily interested in the ransom itself and had no intention of joining the army. Numerous chiefs, especially those from the old bandit regions, displayed the traditional social bandit qualities or had taken to soldier-banditry to work off their grudge against the authorities. The majority also retained their local ties, returning after each raid or spell in the military to the same small section of "Robberland" from which they had set out. For all their excesses, Lao Yangren and many of his southwest Henan contemporaries are still regarded locally as native sons and popular heroes.[64]

Soldier-banditry began in North China and, as the remorseless militarization process went ahead, set the trend for the rest of the country. One by one the old bandit areas became primary targets of militarists in search of recruits, and bandits were drawn willy-nilly into the new era. Whole armies were formed from preexisting gangs, and a career in the military became the new means of achieving "respect" as a *haohan* or hero. Few chiefs could escape this trend, and those who sought to do so sank without trace. The numbers of ex-soldiers who came flocking to their calls for recruits made sure of that—by sheer fighting power and experience pushing into the background those who had joined the gang for the traditional reasons. This development signified a further break with the past and paved the way for the complete politicization of rural banditry.

With the emergence of the soldier-bandits, rural banditry became more predatory and violent, less discriminating in its choice of victims, and therefore less predictable. As overall social decline made survival a more and more imperative anxiety, even in the traditional bandit areas ambitious chiefs found it impossible to stake out a career without leaving a trail of ruin to mark their passage, and bandit morale in general plummeted. In south Manchuria, for example, the traditional village-centered armed self-defense groups began to lose their cohesion and to appear more and more like the predatory bandits they had always been decried as. In the old days people who stood out as heroes enjoyed tremendous local popularity. Village heads needing help against aggressors had only to pay a visit to the Daoist temples on Qianshan, explain their case, and ask the priests to use their influence to persuade a suitable local chief to help them repel the attack. Although such villagers paid for the protection they received, they preferred that to paying taxes to the "bandits in office." A gang on the run from soldiers, provided it was not given to excesses, could find a welcome in almost any village where it was known, and when not made welcome usually moved on without demur.[65]

In the new conditions this relationship began to disintegrate. Peasants living along routes regularly used by raiding parties had to be forced to provide shelter when required, especially in Heilongjiang. It became normal for a gang in need of food or shelter to descend upon a village and occupy it without asking leave, often at gunpoint (though a particularly poor village might be spared). The gang would arrive in the late evening or night and often remain there all the next day, expecting to be provided with food throughout its stay. Sentinels were posted, and no one was allowed to leave lest they take word to the soldiers. Anyone happening to arrive was held captive until the gang moved on. Peasants working in the fields when the gang passed looked down and pretended not to notice. In many villages only those who were too old to flee remained, and the elders of a village that declined hospitality were liable to be shot. As one expert observer put it, this transformation in Manchurian banditry marked the passing of the "frontier phase" with which banditry had traditionally been associated, and the extension to the area of "normal" administration.[66] The "norm" was the militarization of Chinese society as a whole.

All in all, those who sought to exploit bandits' military potential did not find them very reliable. A far less hazardous way of exploiting the "bandit problem" to one's own ends was to send representatives to arm and encourage gangs in a rival's territory. In addition to preoccupying the rival with domestic affairs, this was also a useful means of discrediting him in the eyes of observers, especially when the two were competing for coveted foreign aid. Bandits could thus be exploited for their nuisance value where it was not possible to weld them into military units—a device that, since it allowed the manipulators to dissociate themselves from the bandits should anything go wrong, was also much safer. The more bandits there were, the commoner this tactic became, beginning in Henan in the summer of 1922 with the attempt to embarrass Wu Peifu and Feng Yuxiang by kidnapping foreigners.[67]

Allegations of political involvement behind Lao Yangren's strategy, though denied by Henan overlord Wu Peifu himself, included suggestions that the bandits' operations had been encouraged, if not actually financed, by Wu's political enemies—i.e. Zhang Zuolin—in an attempt to discredit him by exposing his inability to preserve order even around his own headquarters. According to "unquestioned sources in Kaifeng," the policy of kidnapping foreigners was designed to force Wu to come to terms with the Fengtian leaders through fear of foreign intervention. Reports circulating later in 1922 also suggested that the same bandits were planning to kidnap the U.S. minister to China during his scheduled trip through Henan. Though these reports were never confirmed, a missionary stationed in the south Henan city of Biyang claimed that three men had been arrested carrying documents from Zhang Zuolin authorizing them to organize the local bandits into an army to cause as much trouble as they could.[68]

The timing, organization, and conduct of the Lincheng Incident also convinced many observers that it, too, was no isolated bandit incident but originated in warlord intrigue. Allegations continued to fly long after the dust settled on the affair. Sun Meiyao's execution six months after his enrollment in the army was attributed to his failure to cut his links with the Fengtian faction. With Lao Yangren's late 1923 return to banditry and Fan Zhongxiu's defection to the Sun Zhongshan camp soon after, Wu Peifu allegedly decided to eliminate Sun before anything similar could happen in Shandong.[69] As we will see later, southern contacts with the bandits gave Wu ample cause for anxiety.

Gunrunning rather than direct manipulation was the more common relationship between bandits and the foreign powers, most often involving Germany, Italy, and Japan. Russian troops and deserters, too, both "Red" and "White," allowed many of their weapons to slip through to the *honghuzi*.[70] That bandits themselves regarded foreign countries as the direct or indirect source of munitions is left in no doubt by certain instances of underworld slang. Bullets, for example, were referred to as "sugared lotus-seeds from abroad" (*waiguo tanglianzi*).[71] When it came to the actual exploitation of bandits to its own ends, however, Japan reigned supreme. Apart from its activities in Manchuria, evidently considered a virtual extension of the Japanese islands themselves, and in Shandong, which after the First World War became a Japanese sphere of influence, Japan was also accused of aiding Bai Lang, running guns to bandits in northern Fujian, and a host of other provocative activities.*

## The Japan Connection

Together with the revolutionary movement discussed in the next chapter, Japan's twentieth-century emergence on the Chinese political

---

* On the Bai Lang connection, see *STSB*, 18 Mar. 1914: 9; *NCH*, 15 Nov. 1913: 490. On northern Fujian, see Caldwell 1925: 145. The same 15 Nov. 1913 issue of the *NCH* (p. 490) also asserted "as a fact" (though without any evidence) that Bai Lang's name itself was a Japanese one. *La Politique de Pekin* 13 (12 July 1914): 3, insisted, again without evidence, that a Japanese military officer was advising the rebels.

scene offered bandit chiefs a perfect opportunity to mount the political stage. For the Japanese, bandits provided the ideal means of sowing mayhem and of justifying its persistent carping on China's inability to govern itself. For the bandits themselves, Japan must have seemed a dependable ally compared to warlord patrons, with their frequent ups and downs. The influx of Japanese agents seeking to manipulate the leadership of the most powerful gangs was also crucial. Skilled fighters, often with military training and possessing access to sources of guns and cash, these agents filled all the requirements of a successful bandit chief, so their ability to use the gangs they led in the service of a foreign imperialist power was not surprising. As in the case of connections with the local elite, the decision of a bandit chief to ally with Japan, though it engendered accusations of treason and opportunism, was logical in terms of the balance of power.

Periods of war and unrest were traditionally times when bandit chiefs came into their own. In the 1895 Sino-Japanese War and the Russo-Japanese War, for example, both of which were fought largely on the plains of Manchuria, much of the fighting consisted of clashes between gangs of *honghuzi* armed and incited by the rival powers. In the latter conflict, particularly, Japanese adventurers backed by the Imperial Army contacted such gangs and led them on harassing missions behind the Russian lines, blowing up bridges and destroying railway lines in the name of the "Righteous Army of Manchuria" (*Manshū gigun*). Among the many chiefs to come to prominence at this time was Zhang Zuolin, who first "entered the greenwood" following his experiences as a soldier in the war of 1895. When fighting erupted again ten years later he threw himself into the thick of it, first (under pressure) for the Russians, later for the Japanese. His lieutenants included many of the men who would later become his trusted warlord subordinates, and the ties he struck with the Japanese played a large part in his successful rise to the position of Manchurian dictator.[72]

The 1911 Revolution, too, sent ripples of excitement through Japan. Politicians, military men, and Pan-Asian swashbucklers all saw new vistas open up for their particular field of action, just as did many bandit chiefs in China itself. Bandits featured strongly, for instance, in a series of Japan-sponsored Mongolian independence movements.[73] As was usual with Japan's less respectable intrigues on the mainland, the government's attitude was two-faced, and most of the day-to-day wheeling and dealing was left to the military—here, too, lower-level officers often acted independently of or as proxies for their superiors—or to the growing band of "mainland adventurers" (*tairiku rōnin*).* Although the attempts

---

* Not every case of Japanese involvement with bandits in Manchuria was conducted at a political level. One of the most interesting characters to emerge on the Manchurian

to sever Manchuria and Mongolia from the rest of China came to nothing, Japanese merchants and military agents, according to Prime Minister Terauchi in 1917, continued to supply bandits with arms, and almost all the weapons captured from Manchurian bandits were subsequently found to be of Japanese make.[74]

A new arena for Japanese involvement was opened up by the 1919 Treaty of Versailles, which officially recognized Japan's 1914 takeover of the former German port of Qingdao in Shandong. The Chinese protested, citing evidence of Japan's intent to use bandits and revolutionary elements to furnish an excuse for large-scale military intervention, but to no avail. Yet villagers in nearby Taitou claimed later that bandits were indeed allowed to operate unhindered from bases in Japanese territory. Lootings and kidnappings along the Qingdao Railway increased sharply after gangs were purportedly encouraged to move their headquarters from the mountains down to the Japanese-controlled area. By the end of the decade Shandong's estimated 30,000 bandits were all said to be organized and supplied by Japan.[75]

Even after the Japanese began reluctantly withdrawing from Qingdao in April 1922, the Shandong authorities continued to assert that bandits formerly ensconced in their territory were being sent back to cause trouble for the Chinese. By December, when the Japanese withdrawal was almost complete, telegrams indicated that the former leased territory was more or less in the hands of bandits, who robbed merchants and blackmailed officials at will. The few remaining Japanese soldiers took no steps to control them, and the Japanese themselves were never attacked.[76]

Most contemporary observers also assumed (often with no more than circumstantial evidence to go on) that Japan was involved in the planning of the Lincheng Incident, allegedly intended as the climax of a campaign to discredit the Chinese following the evacuation from Qingdao. It was reported that a party of Japanese traveling on the ill-fated train got off at Suzhou, fifty miles south of the ambush site; other Japanese (secret agents?) were said to have been seen warning their compatriots not to buy tickets for stations beyond that city. Three Japanese were reported in

---

frontier at this time was the former bar hostess, army prostitute, and concubine to high Chinese officials Yamamoto Kikuko, alias "Han Taitai." After rescuing the powerful Jiandao chief Kaoshan (alias Sun Huating) from a Japanese execution party, she went off to live with him and his gang in the mountains. When he became ill she assumed leadership of the gang herself, and by introducing her knowledge of Imperial Army methods made it one of the best organized in south Manchuria, even managing to persuade numerous other chiefs to join her with their own forces. With these reinforcements she was able to put together one of the strongest and most reliable protection systems in all Manchuria. Commercial traffic moving north from Korea through Jiandao could ensure safe passage by displaying a flag (*baobiao*) to show that it had bought the protection of Yamamoto Kikuko (Watanabe 1964: 55–56. See also Tsuzuki 1976: 316–23).

the bandits' camp following the holdup, one of them said to be a gun-runner; captives also noted that most of the bandits' weapons carried a Japanese mark.[77]

Japan's government did not join the Western chorus demanding sanctions, but did suggest that the incident might never have taken place had its forces been allowed to remain in Qingdao. Ideologists like Gotō Asatarō held up the affair as vindication of the view long held in some Japanese quarters that China was incapable of governing itself, and hoped the Western powers would regret forcing Japan to abandon its positions in Shandong.[78] In the wake of the incident a veritable rash of books, pamphlets, and articles appeared both in Japan and in the Japanese-sponsored press in China upholding the same basic position.

Another factor tending to implicate the Japanese was the complexity of the bandits' demands, one of which was for a portion of territory several hundred miles square to be neutralized under international decrees and administered by the bandits themselves. Other demands, involving collecting taxes, exploiting coal and other resources, and expanding communications,[79] bore a strong resemblance not only to the Twenty-one Demands of 1915, but also to what Japan had itself tried to do during its brief occupation of Qingdao, and prefigured the kind of demands that would later be made in Manchuria.

The alleged connections between the Japanese authorities and the Anfu warlord clique also hinted at involvement. General Zhang Jingyao was said to receive Japanese visitors daily at his refuge in Tianjin, and his former subordinate Sun Meiyao, who evidently came from there on the day of the attack, traveled back and forth constantly while the negotiations were in process. It was further alleged that all the Anfu generals had their personal funds deposited in Japan ready for a quick getaway.[80]

Naturally enough, the Japanese authorities denied all the allegations leveled against them. As the following pages will make clear, however, Japan's clandestine activities in China were frequently ideal examples of the right hand not knowing what the left was doing, or not caring to know. The chances are strong either that profiteers were running guns to the Lincheng bandits, or even that a faction within the Imperial Army with personal links to Chinese warlord figures was involved. On the other hand, the bandits of Lincheng had ample reasons of their own for launching the attack, and were powerful enough to take autonomous action when the situation demanded, so it would be wrong to lay as much weight on the Japanese connection as did paternalistic Western observers.

Although there is no clear evidence of "mainland adventurers" being involved in the Lincheng Incident, then, back in Manchuria such men continued to attract reputations as leaders of bandit gangs. Their exploits, read about in luridly printed pamphlets and newspapers, made the dream of "fighting for China" a compulsive one: "From time immemorial, China's history has been the history of the mounted bandits [*bazoku*]. . . . So off to Manchuria, and let's become *bazoku* ourselves!"[81] Gradually, large numbers of young Japanese began to cross over to the continent with nothing in mind but to put their romantic dreams into action by gaining command of as many "*bazoku*" as they could. Along with the dream, then, went a strong element of the patronizing attitude toward China that would later make the *tairiku rōnin* one of the symbols of Japanese expansion:

> I'm getting out, how about you?
> This poky Japan is too tiresome to live in.
> Beyond the waves China lies,
> And 400 million of its people are waiting.[82]

Most of these naive adventurers, however, dreams notwithstanding, were unable even to get near the *bazoku* bands, let alone take over their leadership. Instead, many took on regular jobs as merchants, or worked for the newly formed South Manchuria Railway Company helping to promote the Japanese economic invasion of China. Others were transformed from idealistic "mainland adventurers" to troubleshooting "mainland gangsters" (*tairiku goro*), becoming mere pawns in the various unsavory episodes that were to unfold over the next few decades.*

Two of the most notable among these men were Date Junnosuke (alias Zhang Zonghuan) and Matsumoto Yōnosuke (alias Xiao Tianlong), the former a naturalized Chinese and a blood brother to Zhang Zongchang. Both came to receive the full protection of the Japanese military, already beginning to assert itself in Manchuria as a force not always answerable to government control. Date had fought with the 1916 Mongolian Independence Movement, and when it collapsed had become a bandit on the Manchuria-Mongolia frontier with his twenty or thirty followers. Matsumoto was a young hell-raiser who, after a brief period working for the military, had drifted into a Chinese bandit gang active in the same area as Date's.[83] Links between the adventurers and the Japanese civil authorities at this point in time were far from official, perhaps even nonexistent. Presumably the Guandong Army, as the Japanese forces in Manchuria were known, was keeping them in reserve in preparation for events still to come.

The process by which such men came to be accepted as chiefs by the

---

* Andō 1963: 7–9; Jansen 1954: 125; Watanabe 1964: 107. Nevertheless, the attraction of the *bazoku* bands lasted. In 1934 one writer felt the need to preface an article about gang organization with the hope that his research would serve to dampen the ardor of young men who still cherished romantic dreams of joining such gangs. See Tanaka 1934: 153.

rank and file is not clear, though it must have had a great deal to do with their fighting ability: both Date and Matsumoto were ranked among the best marksmen in Manchuria, and must have offered attractive prospects for lesser chiefs needing some powerful figure to attach their fortunes to. Date's band, though lacking strong village links, maintained the discipline that distinguished "social bandits" from the rest, though it could be as rapacious as any when necessary. Matsumoto's usefulness seems to have lain in nothing more than causing trouble by kidnapping travelers, seducing women, and so on.[84] According to Chinese reports the Japanese concessions along the coast, the South Manchuria Railway Zone, and the Guandong Leased Territory (the name for the southern part of the Liaodong Peninsula, including Port Arthur and Dairen, administered by Japan since 1906) became "veritable meccas" for bandits and smugglers, who could easily slip over the boundary out of Chinese jurisdiction when challenged. The increase in banditry along the peripheries of these areas (nine cases in 1906; 368 cases in 1929; 1,600 cases involving 232,000 bandits from September to December alone in 1931), say these reports, was directly proportional to the growth of Japanese influence. Many of the gangs were actually led or advised by Japanese.*

With the Mukden Incident of September 1931, Japan's strategy toward China reached a turning point. The incident itself was a good illustration of the basic pattern of activities already established by the military. First, a gang of sword-wielding "mainland gangsters," posing as anti-Japanese provocateurs, was ordered to attack the Japanese army barracks, and local bandits were instigated to create disturbances in the surrounding countryside. This allowed the Japanese garrison to be called out to "quell the disturbances," and the complete occupation of Manchuria soon followed. Given at last the free hand it had always coveted, the military promptly set out to rid Manchuria of the bandits whose existence it had hitherto been content to exploit and foster.

As the Japanese evolved from challengers to incumbents of the seat of power, a subtle terminological change took place with regard to bandits. The word *bazoku*, with its positive connotations of village defense and its romantic aura of adventure, disappeared in favor of *hizoku*—"robbers" —applied indiscriminately to all armed groups not under full Japanese control. This included everything from simple marauders and secret societies to the village-defense leagues, and even to the nationalist guerrillas who put up a last-ditch resistance.[85] The repression was brutal:

---

* "Fostering Banditry in China": 491, 496–98; *Gendaishi shiryō* 31: 584. For photographs of documents taken from the body of one such adviser, see "Creation and Organisation of a Bandit Army." On the other hand, it is clear from one account (Shimamura 1973: 159) that Chinese gangs did not always welcome these individuals, one of whom was forced into flight by a joint force of local bandits and Red Spears who resented his intrusion.

unable to catch the gangs, most of whom had fled to the mountains, the Guandong Army adopted a scorched-earth policy designed to scare the Manchurian population into submission. Even gangs formerly allowed to operate freely from Japanese territory were suppressed unless they were under direct Japanese control (which usually meant having Japanese chiefs or at least advisers). Those that continued to be tolerated for their nuisance value were supplied from funds captured in the takeover of Mukden, and were encouraged to cause as much disruption as they could for the Chinese.

Japanese-led bandits played significant roles in various historical episodes. During the 1932 abduction of the deposed Manchu emperor Pu Yi in preparation for his installation as emperor of "Manchuguo," the powerful gang led by Matsumoto Yōnosuke was employed to provide cover. The vanguard of the subsequent invasion of the northernmost Chinese province of Rehe, too, was commanded by former bandit chiefs advised by Date Junnosuke. Not surprisingly, the old dream of an independent Manchuria-Mongolia was also rekindled in these early, more romantic years of Japanese hegemony, but this time such prime movers as the Mata Hari–like Kawashima Yoshiko found that the only forces she could recruit were bandits.[86]

Not even guntoting *tairiku rōnin* or charismatic intriguers like Kawashima Yoshiko could bring all the bandits of Manchuria under the imperial flag, however. Those who found Japanese control too oppressive began, with or without official Chinese recognition, to spread mayhem in the Japanese areas too. Amid such early resistance activities were sown the seeds of the North-Eastern Anti-Japan Volunteer Army (*Dongbei Kang Ri yiyongjun*), whose initial leadership consisted almost entirely of former bandit chiefs.[87]

Japanese hopes of eliminating bandits throughout their jurisdiction were convincingly dashed by a famous kidnapping case of September 1932, in which one of the victims was Tinko Pawley, the eighteen-year-old daughter of an English doctor (some said spy) living in the south Manchurian treaty port of Yingkou (Niuzhuang). The gang demanded a ransom from the Japanese of one million dollars plus guns and ammunition, adding that the captives would be returned unconditionally if the "Japanese devils" evacuated Manchuria within a week. In Japan rightist groups seethed at this besmirching of national pride, and the government, which was about to put its case for recognition of Manchuguo to the League of Nations, was appalled. The Guandong Army authorities finally appealed to the only person in Manchuria capable of effecting the captives' release without aggravating the incident still further: Kohinata Hakurō, alias Shang Xudong and Xiao Bailong, a mainland adventurer of long standing.

Kohinata's case was rather different from that of the other Japanese adventurers, for by covering up his true identity he had managed to become the most powerful chief in all of south Manchuria, regarded with extraordinary adulation by local gangs and the villages they defended. Although he simultaneously maintained his ties to the Japanese military, and was even linked to protofascist right-wing groups, he had been appalled at the Guandong Army's heavy-handed methods of establishing Japanese rule.* At the time of the Pawley Incident, therefore, he was secretly in overall command of the North-Eastern Anti-Japan Volunteers. In exchange for securing the release of the English captives, he insisted upon and obtained agreement from the Guandong Army to cease its crackdowns against the resistance movement. He then showed the power that bandit chiefs could wield over their followers by actually persuading the Volunteers to cease resistance activities so as to avoid provoking further Japanese atrocities. Afterward he went into the bandits' camp and brought out the captives unharmed.

Even stranger was the second half of the deal. In the spring of 1933 began what is best called the "Great *Bazoku* Migration." On the guarantee of supreme leader "Shang Xudong," powerful gang leaders and former officers of the Anti-Japan Volunteers led their followers and families in a great column some 70,000 strong south of the Great Wall to Beijing, where Kohinata had already made arrangements for finding them homes and employment (some in fact returned to predatory banditry in their new locales). In this way Japan's "bandit" problem, at least in the areas to which Kohinata's authority extended, was solved by moving the bandits to China—hardly original, but as effective as ever in the short term. Where that authority did not extend, however, such as

* Since Kohinata was always known by his Chinese name, Shang Xudong (as well as by various nicknames given him by local people, such as Xiao Bailong), it appears that most Japanese and Chinese were ignorant of his real identity. See, for example, Dairen Chamber of Commerce and Industry 1931: 38; Chou Tsun-shih 1969: 13. Qu Qiubai (1953: I, 307–9) described him bitterly as a bandit chief who did nothing to resist the Japanese. A recent biography (Tsuzuki 1974) revealed that he was in fact on the payroll of Japanese military intelligence from the first, and remained in constant contact with the powerful Beijing agent Banzai Rihachirō (*ibid.*: 88–89, 121–22). Befriended by a circle of Japanese military officers later to feature as the architects of Japan's war strategy in China, he spent some two years learning how to shoot as well as becoming proficient in the martial arts of *jūdō* and *kendō*. When he finally set out from Beijing to do reconnaissance work in Manchuria, he was wearing military uniform and was well armed, bearing suitable letters of introduction addressed to the people he might meet on the way (*ibid.*: 23–26). He was consequently not the innocent young traveler he is presented as in Kuchiki's biography. Numerous other details appear in a different light in Tsuzuki's book, since Kohinata himself (who is still alive today) has chosen to hold back many delicate revelations until those likely to be affected have passed away. Each successive biography, therefore, tends to reveal a little more than the last, particularly concerning his connections with Japanese intelligence. Still more revelations may be expected in the future. Nevertheless, Kuchiki's detailed work remains the major one and has been relied upon here for most of the information about Kohinata's bandit career, with Tsuzuki 1974 for backup.

farther north in Jilin, on the Korean border, and around the Chinese Eastern Railway zone, resistance banditry continued to plague the Japanese up to the outbreak of full-scale war.[88]

Only six months after the Pawley case, another international incident reminded the Japanese that resentment against them remained strong. This was the kidnapping of four British merchant marine officers, again near Yingkou, in March 1933. Though the culprits were no more than a small-time local pirate gang, they too demanded explicitly that the ransom should be paid by Japan, not by Britain, and urged the latter to take active steps to drive the Japanese out of Manchuria. After five months of negotiations, the captives' release was eventually effected by the Guandong Army itself, supported by "two Japanese officials... [who] had originally been bandits themselves, so they would know the type with whom they would have to deal."[89] Whoever these two "officials" were, their participation in this episode showed clearly the role being played by the "mainland gangsters" in the "pacification" of Manchuria—at least until 1937.

As long as the Guandong Army needed excuses to justify its persistent encroachment on Chinese territory, bandits continued to enjoy a useful existence. The step-by-step advance south of the Great Wall after 1933, for instance, was spearheaded by bandit gangs encouraged to cause chaos and provide an excuse for Japanese intervention (at least one was said to be led by a woman). In 1935 Liu Guitang (Liu Heiqi) and other ex-bandit militarists with Guandong Army backing formed the splendidly titled "East-Asian Allied Self-Governing Army" with a similar mission in mind. All over North China, other local militarists, mainly those with bandit backgrounds like Sun Dianying and Pang Bingsun, began throwing in their lot with the Japanese and were transformed into vicious enemies of the Chinese resistance.[90] With the full-scale invasion of July 1937, however, the need for such allies became virtually a thing of the past.

Though the disruption caused by total war made the bandits themselves more desperate than ever to find the powerful patrons that survival demanded, their unreliability and irregular tactics had little appeal for the Japanese military, which was highly elitist and anxious to extend its occupation as quickly as possible. Like the warlords before them, the Japanese had considerable difficulties with the *bing fei bufen* ("bandits and soldiers cannot be distinguished") problem, finding that the ex-bandits would obey orders only when it suited them; consequently, bandit-suppression became a constant theme of the occupation.[91] Japanese popular singers now crooned not of the romantic life on horseback but, as in the plaintive hit songs "Off to Catch Bandits" (*Tōhikō*) and "Ballad of Bandit Suppression" (*Tōhi no uta*), of the miserable lives of the soldiers sent to bludgeon China into the Japanese Empire.[92] New arrivals still in search of the "dream of Asia" subsequently found themselves not hard-riding bandits but hard-nosed propagandists or teachers in the pay of the army. Those already there with experience of riding with or organizing bandits were either transferred or put to work training puppet troops.

In the autumn of 1938 the former *bazoku* whom Kohinata Hakurō had led to North China were brutally suppressed. Matsumoto Yōnosuke was arrested as a bandit chief, was channeled into the military, and subsequently disappeared. Date Junnosuke had more success, using his army connections to have himself transferred to Shandong, where he emerged as commander-in-chief of the "Shandong Self-Governing Allied Army" with a mission to keep the local Chinese population subdued. He and other veteran adventurers, together with former chiefs once with the army of Manchuguo, recruited local bandits and degenerated Red Spear fighters until the total strength of the "Allied Army" reached some 10,000 men. These forces, plus the support of local potentate Liu Guitang, allowed Date to occupy the provincial capital of Jinan and establish his headquarters in the city. Date's reign as "king" of Shandong was a brief one, however, and in 1940 his forces were ordered by the Japanese Imperial Army to disband.[93]

With the Japanese collapse in 1945 the long history of that country's involvement with China's bandits came to an end. Those who had been reorganized into puppet armies were mostly absorbed by the Chinese government forces in the civil war with the Communists that began in 1946. Many gangs had already been bought over by the government to cause trouble for the Communist Liberated Zones, and the progressive writer Zhao Shuli was only one of many to be kidnapped and handed over to them.[94] Easily defeated, most of these gangs either surrendered or escaped, to be eliminated in mopping-up operations after 1949. Many of their chiefs who had been able to return with the government forces and set themselves up as county or village heads were overthrown by guerrilla forces or met a bitter end after Liberation.[95]

## Conclusion

All in all, bandits' involvement with Japan underscored the role they had begun to establish for themselves under the warlords. Increased confusion and uncertainty accelerated the process by which bandits were created. At the same time, fresh opportunities were held out to aspiring chiefs to take their activities onto a new plane, one that brought them both legitimacy and respect. Whether spearheading the Japanese advance into North China or simply bringing local gangs together as a formal constabulary, they could be seen, through the legitimate status conferred upon them by their Japanese masters, as having "made it" into the ranks of the powerful. The self-respect this brought them perhaps even outweighed the criticism heaped upon them by their Chinese compatriots (most of whom belonged to a different world anyhow), underlining not only the fickle nature of bandit allegiances, but also, and far more importantly, the role "respect" played in all their dealings with the world around them. (Many other bandits, it should be added, chose to acquire their "respect" through participation in the anti-Japanese volunteer forces.) In this sense the bandits' involvement with Japan can be seen as another stage in the process of politicization that had been at work since the early years of the century, and as the penultimate stage in the "apotheosis of Chinese banditry." In the following chapter we will seek to throw some light on the ultimate stage: the role played by bandits in the modern revolutionary movement.

CHAPTER NINE

# "Levelers or Liabilities?": Bandits and the Revolutionary Movement

*The brigand is always the hero, the defender, the avenger of the people,
the irreconcilable enemy of the entire State régime, both in its civil and
its social aspects, the life and death fighter against our statist-aristocratic,
official-clerical civilization.*

—Michael Bakunin, quoted in Venturi 1966 : 369

*The bandits are the lumpen proletariat, [but] they possess various
accumulated habits. In the struggle for the land revolution they can
be considered merely an auxiliary force.*

—Zhongyang tongxun *no. 30(3 July 1928),
quoted in Pak Hyobom 1971 : 400–401*

THE TIDE of revolution as it rolled back and forth across China for
half a century affected everything in its path. Bandits were no exception.
The revolutionary movement, dominated as it was by intellectuals, displayed an attitude toward bandits little different from that of previous
contenders for power. For many years the rural hinterland was regarded
as a mere backup area for the "real" revolutionary environment, the city.
Its irregular forces, principally bandit gangs and secret societies, were
auxiliaries, last resorts when more acceptable revolutionary elements such
as workers, soldiers, and students were not available. As auxiliaries, moreover, such forces were often considered expendable.

The bandit, in other words, was a world away from the revolutionary
militant. Whereas the development of a revolutionary force implicitly
demands coherent organization, bandits came together for survival, and
any rational, long-term organization had to be grafted on by outsiders
working with them. Perhaps more important, revolutionaries begin

from an awareness of the need for an alternative, better society, and all their actions derive from the strategy for realizing that vision. Bandits, however, saw better prospects in the world they knew, and organized and behaved in accordance with its values. Bandits, consequently, were not bound to join a revolutionary movement, regardless of the hopes it held out for the poor. This lesson, never really learned by the Republicans who sought to involve bandits in their various attentats before and after 1911, was absorbed slowly and painfully by the Communists as a result of their attempts to establish guerrilla bases in the old bandit areas.

Though major bands that seemed to have the potential to become a political force in their own right had sometimes been assigned political advisers to keep them on the right track, the idea of actually learning from the bandits in the sense of adopting their tactics and strategy, while at the same time seeking to remedy the more destructive aspects of their behavior by the application of guerrilla principles, had to await the Communist movement. In the process of the civil war with the government and the revolutionary war against Japan, the Communists finally managed to create enough momentum of their own for the bandits to be swept along whether they liked it or not, and enough strength to eliminate with relative ease those who remained recalcitrant. As before, it was usually a matter of necessity: if you failed to do something about the bandits yourself, someone else was going to, with less than beneficial results for your own side. Accordingly, right up to Liberation in 1949 the problem of dealing with bandits was a preoccupation of revolutionary strategy.

As for the bandits themselves, the arrival of Republican revolutionaries and later Communists often did no more than add a new, complicating factor to the existing pattern of elite-oriented relations. Fundamental differences in outlook and in breadth of horizons made bandits and revolutionaries questionable partners whatever their short-term similarities, yet convenience often overcame suspicion. Increased confusion and insecurity created bandits in larger numbers than ever, accentuating the competition for powerful patrons. When the revolutionaries held out better prospects than those offered elsewhere, it was not unusual for bandits to make at least temporary alliance with them. In the process, some acquired a new vision, others retained their traditional outlook. At any rate, for the bandits themselves as well as for those who had to treat with them, the possibilities of their being ignored by or left out of the revolutionary process shrank progressively as the years went by.

"After the revolution" was another concept that appeared differently to bandits and to revolutionaries. For ordinary people, it made no difference that the new "revolutionary" government claimed to rule on their behalf when bullies continued to bully, taxes continued to be demanded, and so on. After the establishment of the People's Republic in 1949—despite the elimination through land reform of the most glaring social inequities, the removal of the contending centers of military force, and the expulsion of foreign influence—the new government found in areas with traditions of predatory self-help that banditry continued to be an instinctive response to natural disaster and unjust policies.

## The Bandit as Revolutionary

When reactionary pogroms drove dissident intellectuals from their city havens to the safety of the villages, the search began for fresh allies to supplement their struggling cause. To these militants fell the task of "undermining the old sense of inevitability" and transforming local grievances and latent anger into an all-encompassing sense of imminent retribution. In practice, however, transformations of the peasantry as a whole were seldom easy, rural communities being past masters of the art of avoiding or deceiving strangers. As a result, revolutionaries could hardly have failed to be attracted by the apparent revolutionary potential of bandit gangs and secret societies, rising as they so conspicuously did above the "thickets of social life." By contrast with the passivity and suspicion characteristic of peasant society as a whole, the heroism of such groups must have seemed well suited to the putschist revolutionary orthodoxy of the early twentieth century. The appeal was probably heightened by the congruence of the elite-oriented *wuxia* ("knights-errant") and the more earthy *haohan* ("stout fellow") traditions. Local forces, for all their shortcomings, thus remained very attractive as a source of revolutionary recruits throughout the first half of the twentieth century, and won the praises of a range of radical militants.

The most unsparing in his applause for bandits' revolutionary potential had been the Russian anarchist Bakunin, to whom the bandit was "the genuine and sole revolutionary—a revolutionary without fine phrases, without learned rhetoric, irreconcilable, indefatigable and indomitable, a popular and social revolutionary, non-political and independent of any estate"[1]—in short, an anarchist. For Bakunin revolution began from the destructive impulse, which in turn led naturally into the creative urge. By using the existing "forces for revolt"—that is, bandits—he envisaged not merely tapping their enthusiasm for destruction, but also uniting them into a "single calculated and ruthless popular revolution."[2] Decentralization of political control, the first requirement of a genuine revolution, would also allow optimum exploitation of the bandit's best tendencies, summed up in the stirring phrases that opened this chapter.

Unfortunately, as the preceding chapters have shown, Bakunin's characterization of bandits as "irreconcilable," "independent of any estate," and so on was often far from the truth, and was in most cases an impossible ideal. As an aristocrat, his personal contacts with bandits were more or less nil, and his approach as a whole reflected his preoccupation with violent insurrection and his tendency toward romantic idealization. At the same time, much of the blame for his idealization of the bandit has to be laid at the door of the increasing intellectualization and consequent loss of spontaneity in the European revolutionary movement following the ascendancy of the Marxists over the anarchists. To Bakunin it must have seemed that "revolutionaries" themselves were a lost cause, and brigands the sole remaining source of the energy required to turn the world "rightside up."

In many ways Mao Zedong was similar in character to Bakunin despite his very different background, and he had in fact fallen under the Russian's spell for a few months in 1918. He too was tired of the purely intellectual commitment to socialism that prevented its mainly city-based espousers from seeing the potential of the countryside, particularly the "forces for revolt" that existed there. Through the medium of human will, Mao insisted, any rural vagabond could be transformed into a representative of the vanguard of the proletariat.[3]

Just like Bakunin, Mao's vision for bandits in the revolution was not merely to leave them to their own destructive devices, but to appoint political agitators to unify and organize them. His 1926 report on the Chinese class structure, for example, insisted that "These people [soldiers, bandits, robbers, beggars, and prostitutes] are capable of fighting very bravely, and if properly led can become a revolutionary force."[4] During the early years of the Communist movement he accepted the support of bandit and secret society chiefs with a great deal of sympathy, not merely with resignation, as the official editions of his writings suggest. This is not surprising when we recall that the *Shuihu zhuan* had been among the most popular books of Mao's youth and a constant source of revolutionary inspiration for him. Asked about his solution to the country's ills, for example, he replied briefly: "Imitate the heroes of Liangshanpo!" And it was to the *Shuihu* hero Song Jiang that he referred to illustrate a philosophical point in his essay "On Contradiction." The close connection between the bandit tradition and the long history of China's peasant rebellions was clearly recognized by Mao when he referred to himself in later years as both the last in a long line of peasant leaders and also a "graduate of the university of the greenwoods."[5]

Other Communist leaders also found positive qualities in bandits. Zhu De, Red Army commander-in-chief during the movement's earliest years, had previously been an officer in the Yunnan provincial army. In 1922 he had fallen into the hands of the Sichuan chief Lei Yongfei, who "was a bandit all right. . . . Compared with the warlords, he was a righteous and honorable citizen." On the other hand, with more experience of actually working with bandits than Bakunin had had, Zhu observed that bandits' revolutionary potential was limited by their tendency to either defect or retreat under pressure.

It was Zhu's fellow-general He Long who spoke of bandits with the voice of personal experience:

> Though they were barbarous all right, they also had their merits: they were sincere, spirited, and hard-nosed. If they don't want to talk and fraternize, they'll never talk and fraternize. Once they trust you, then neither death nor earthquake can change [them]. No matter what you bring, an official [rank] or money, you cannot buy them off. And they were so brave—many people sacrificed themselves by following me alone.[6]

How did bandits measure up in practice to the expectations invested in them? Though bandits were not the hopeless social rejects that many arrogant, urban-educated revolutionaries considered them, neither were they the natural revolutionaries they often appeared to be to more sanguine militants. As the Communists found when they began moving into the long-seething border areas to lay the foundations of the first revolutionary bases, the relationship between "banditry" and "revolution" was far more complex than had generally been thought. Though as individuals bandits and revolutionaries may have sometimes shared a number of common properties, in the end there was a fundamental divergence of perspectives.

Banditry grew as an adaptive response to rock-bottom socioeconomic conditions, but did not seek to alter those conditions for the better; a revolutionary movement rested on the premise that the structure of society itself had to be overhauled. Banditry gave its practitioners an identity as beings apart from the general mass, with the implication, natural in a society based on inequality, that this status gave them certain prerogatives; the revolutionary movement, with its roots in a struggle for equality, insisted that its fighters not put themselves above peasants and reap no personal rewards for the hardships and dangers they faced. Banditry was for many a temporary occupation, part of life's natural cycle, not usually involving any deep commitment to political opposition; joining the revolutionary movement, on the other hand, was a fundamental decision to work actively for social change. Bandits provided an alternative and contrasting status quo parallel to that of the legitimate authorities without altering the basic social structure; the revolutionary would turn all values on their heads so as to rebuild the status quo from bottom to top. Bandits, therefore, could work with the prevailing power structure as easily as they rejected it; the revolutionary movement, in principle at least, was committed to opposition.

Although bandits did little—at least intentionally—to raise the consciousness of the peasants they lived among, in the absence of an ideologically motivated movement banditry became for the peasants the approximate equivalent of political activity. Traditionally it formed the rudimentary stage in a process that could lead under the right conditions to the formation of a rebel movement whose objective was to gain the "Mandate of Heaven." In itself, though, it was not rebellion, and certainly not revolution. As we have seen, the people who became bandits did so for a variety of reasons, but all involved either self-preservation or self-advancement. No change of values was involved, and their decision constituted at best an undermining of the sense of futility which most peasants shared. Whatever aspirations were evoked were those of the peasant world: for the poor, enough food to last until the next harvest; for the chronically unemployed, a life of relative security; for the landless, an alternative to hiring land or working another's plot; for the ambitious, a chance for martial status and perhaps political advancement on a local scale. Only when the conditions generating hunger failed to be removed; or when the opportunities to "earn an honest living" failed to materialize; or when chiefs came into contact with already rebellious groups and saw chances of even greater advancement—only then were the first seeds of rebellion sown.

As it stood, then, banditry did no more than notify whoever cared to notice that conditions in specific localities were out of joint. It did not demand change in the highly stratified natural order; it merely underlined the fact that those at the bottom of the pile were getting a raw deal. When bandits turned to the offensive, therefore, they attacked not their superiors as such, but only their oppressors: people who had reaped the advantages of high position while abusing the responsibilities.

Above all, bandits were avengers, fighting not the system that oppressed them but the individuals who abused the system. If they demanded change—by no means always the case—it was only of the individuals at fault. More often, though, it was not change at all they wanted, but merely payment in blood or silver for the injustices they (and by implication their fellow-villagers) had suffered. In their own terms, bandits had lifted themselves up out of the peasant mass; but without the aid of a new kind of vision, their political horizons stretched at most as far as the county seat. Their outlook was therefore reactive, localized and particularistic, "incapable of the kind of abstract hatred that motivates [violent] revolution."[7] Rarely could they distinguish between different kinds of enemy; and even the difference between enemy and friend was sometimes less simple than might be expected. Where self-interest so dictated, it was quite feasible to join the very militarists and "local despots" whose oppression had been responsible for their hunger or rage in the first place; bandits could switch allegiances with bewildering rapidity as the pendulum of power swung back and forth. When their rage did come to be expressed in deeds against the oppressors, it was often in terms of a blind, retaliatory violence. Though an effective measure of peasant discontent, it did no more than provide a kind of ritual cleansing, satisfying a desire for revenge that usually soon subsided, leaving in its wake a trail of blood that did not always lead only to those responsible.

Similar conclusions could be reached, incidentally, about village-defense associations like the Red Spears, which, though basically defensive where bandits had to be aggressive to survive, nevertheless because of limited horizons shared the fundamental trait of conservatism. Mere anger at the status quo could only result in banditry, and even the awareness that the authorities were unable or disinclined to provide protection led only to local defense; in both cases the wider perspective essential to an overall critique of society was impossible. In short, banditry, local defense, and social revolution constituted three distinctly different stages of development. Though both local militancy and social revolution assume extreme social disruption and disillusionment, perception of the means of change must be added to raise that militancy to the higher stage.

This applied particularly to areas where predatory banditry and village defense had blended into a mutually accepted system of protection. Being a time-tested and reasonably successful solution to the problem of survival, this system's practitioners strongly resisted the introduction of new techniques, especially since it was usually outsiders who brought them. The so-called "bandit worlds" generally had some geographical advantage, such as high mountains or dense forests, which allowed a gang to hide. As far as personal survival was concerned (which was, after all, the bandit's main preoccupation), this was fine. As a long-term strategy, however, it had few prospects, for merely hiding in the mountains or forests would not subdue or weaken the enemy.

An added problem that this kind of environment tended to promote was the development of "professional" or full-time bandits, difficult to integrate into a disciplined revolutionary organization without military persuasion. They probably drew enough sustenance from the bandit life to satisfy themselves, and their chiefs usually possessed sufficient prestige as well as real local power to make them contemptuous of the advances of a revolutionary movement that was, under the circumstances, probably weaker than themselves. As a result, as Hofheinz has put it, in areas with traditionally high levels of banditry, "rivalry may have been a more typical relationship than collaboration."[8]

The "occasionals," on the other hand, those who had been driven into banditry by short-term factors, were more susceptible to revolutionary promises. According to circumstances, such people were as likely to become the rank and file of revolutionary armies as of bandit gangs. Once again, however, it was survival not revolution that prompted their decision to join. Like the city mob, they could be exploited by any group offering satisfaction of their demands for food and work, and were highly volatile. As a professional Communist organizer concluded, such people were capable of joining the revolutionary movement, but only if their "romantic and undisciplined nature" and tendency toward recklessness were curbed. (Significantly, the bandit term for militant activity in Henan was "to stir up" [*nao*] revolution.)[9]

In any case, the bandits' participation in a revolutionary movement could be as much fortuitous as deliberate. The opportunities offered to the strong and energetic in a revolutionary situation were many. Young toughs who might otherwise have remained a traditional village gang often found new vistas for heroic action opening up before them. The potential for proving one's bravery and inspiring new legends was something not lost on young people chafing at the boredom of village life. In the course of their practical revolutionary involvement, many such people would be brought around to an understanding of the political factors involved by reading propaganda. Others might simply satisfy their yearning to emulate the deeds of the old *wuxia* heroes by identifying the movement's aims as a "worthy cause to fight for." Meanwhile, for chiefs who had already put themselves at risk, especially those backed by popular approval, it was a natural step to become the advance guard of a revolution that many of their oppressed followers had come to see as a once-and-for-all day of reckoning.[10]

All in all, though, the bandit's world was not the revolutionary's world. When bandits and revolutionaries eyed each other, it was with a feeling of reluctant admiration tinged with mutual distrust. From the bandits' point of view, militant revolutionaries appealed to their aggressive masculinity by having taken up arms against the authorities, especially if they had elected to live the hard life of the rural fugitive. Clandestine revolutionary activities in the wake of a government purge, for example, thus gained bandit respect and support fairly easily. Having a "price on their head" became a bond, confirming the revolutionaries' antipathy to the same powers that threatened the bandits' own lives. On the other hand, the revolutionaries were plainly outsiders, often with alien middle-class habits, and with the annoying tendency to try to dictate terms.

From the revolutionaries' point of view, too, I suspect, there was a good deal of romantic respect for the bandits' masculine life-styles, especially at the lower levels. Bandit chiefs, meanwhile, were often intelligent and educated, and thus amenable to having their ideas altered in the direction of social change. Since bandits usually lived by expropriating the property of the rich, the basic direction of their activities was acceptable even if their ultimate aims were obscure. In the initial phases of setting up revolutionary bases in the hinterland, there was consequently little to distinguish between "bandit activities" and "revolutionary operations."

He Long's first months with the Red Army provide a good illustration of the gulf between banditry and revolutionary ideals. According to Zhang Guotao, his "cooperation with the [Chinese Communist Party] was beyond question, but he was not like a Communist in his way of living." He surrounded himself with a huge staff of personal advisers, liked to be carried in a four-man sedan chair, and insisted on the best Chinese and Western food being prepared for him by his own cooks. Not surprisingly, he and his officers got on badly with the Communist officials; even on the eve of He's admission into the Party, he and his men were being referred to as "bandits" by top Communist generals. Because his defection was considered imminent, He Long received constant visits from Party propaganda experts to ensure his continued loyalty.[11]

Ultimately, though, bandits were not bound to join or remain loyal to a revolutionary movement, no matter what its scale. Just as some South China chiefs had refused to join the Taiping Rebellion in its early days because it was "not very strong and unlikely to come to anything," during Bai Lang's rebellion three local chiefs set up an organization to support President Yuan Shikai. Likewise, the decision of the Jinggang-shan bandit chiefs to unite with the Red Army in 1928 was taken mainly because the latter had monopolized the "bandit environment" through its superior organizing power, not because of any immediate conversion; the chiefs' allegiance, moreover, was relatively short-lived.[12] "Authority" is never wrong, and many bandits, seeking to escape the confines of peasant society, identified power and prestige with the establishment. Rather than join a disciplined revolutionary movement and lose whatever autonomy they already possessed, they chose the less strenuous and seemingly more rewarding course of becoming the "fangs and claws" of the reaction. In the name of "bandit suppression," ironically enough, they could then put down with gory enthusiasm those who threatened their new-found status—particularly revolutionaries. For the latter this was an even bigger problem than the bandits' limited horizons and loose organization.

## Bandits and Revolution, 1911–28

In November 1911, following a decision to seek the cooperation of local popular forces for the insurrectionary movement against Manchu rule, three young militants of the revolutionary organization known as the Alliance (*Tongmeng hui*) arrived quietly in Luoyang from Kaifeng. Their task was to contact the "Robber King of Honan," Wang Tianzong, and recruit his band of "Sword-fighters" for the revolution.

Wang's was a classic example of the professional bandit gang. In 1907, four years before the events about to be described, a group of self-styled heroes known as the "Ten Big Brothers of Different Surnames" * had assembled on a peak named Yangshan in the foothills of Songshan in Songxian, west Henan. All were young, educated, of relatively wealthy origins, and fugitives, having fled to the mountain to avoid punishment after "committing crimes to right wrongs." Sworn to regard each other as blood brothers, they set about protecting the district from the depredations of "bandit gangs" from outside (like that of Song Laonian which swept through the area in 1908). Before long they had expanded their influence to cover several counties of west Henan. Their organization was tight and their numbers strong, and even before 1911 they had repulsed a series of government attempts to dislodge them from their mountaintop headquarters.[13]

Of the agents sent in 1911 to sound out this promising force of irregulars, two, Wu Cangzhou and Liu Qunren, were entrusted with the task of making direct contact with the band; the third, Liu Zhenhua, provided them with a letter of introduction to his friend and benefactor, the radical schoolteacher Shi Youjian (Shi Yan). Shi was not only an avid supporter of Sun Zhongshan and an advocate of revolution, but also a

---

* The Qing legal code explicitly linked gatherings by "people of different surnames" with the crime of collective rebellion, since such gatherings implied rejection of the *wulun*, or "five traditional relationships," and were thus unfilial and by extension treasonable. The free mixing indulged in by the heroes at Liangshanpo, in addition to being a major irritant to the government of the time, made many of the heroes themselves initially reluctant to join. See Chesneaux 1971a: 10–11. Hsiao Kung-chuan 1960: 472, cites a nineteenth-century rhyme showing how socially mixed such a brotherhood could be. See also Yuan Shikai's mandate on "Suppression of Secret Societies" of 1912, quoted in the *China Yearbook*, 1913: 528.

The order of precedence among the ten chiefs, according to one account, was as follows: (1) Li Yongkui (Li Laoda); (2) Zhang Ping; (3) Jin Hengzhao; (4) Lu Jingbo; (5) Sun Guan; (6) Wang Tianzong; (7) Tao Furong; (8) Zhai Yunsheng; (9) Guan Fuen (Guan Laojiu); (10) Han Yukun. Following Guan Fuen's death, the band split according to geographical and personal loyalties: the eastern faction, commanded by Wang Tianzong, included Li Yongkui and Tao Furong (d. 1910); the western faction, led by Han Yukun and Zhai Yunsheng, included Zhang Ping, Jin Hengzhao, Lu Jingbo, and Sun Guan. The two factions were temporarily reunited by revolutionary agents in 1911, but the split was fundamentally irrevocable: it was reflected not only in the formation and organization of the Songxian Pacification Force, which excluded the Wang Tianzong faction, but also in Liu Zhenhua's ruthless suppression of Wang's ally Li Yongkui in 1912 (see Wang Tiancong 1971: 9–10). Wang Tiancong's account, by the way, inexplicably omits Zhang Zhigong from the list of ten, although Zhang is one of the few specifically mentioned in Wu Cangzhou 1961. The youthful Zhang's star must have risen considerably between 1910 and 1911. On the suppression of Li Yongkui by Liu Zhenhua, see Wang Tiancong 1971: 15; *MLB*, 27 Jan. 1913: 8; and Shimamoto 1974: 53–54.

man close to and evidently respected by local chiefs, including those on Yangshan. He was able to give the emissaries detailed information about current conditions in the Yangshan hideout (including the breach between Wang Tianzong and Han Yukun's factions over Wang's killing of fellow chief Guan Laojiu that summer) and about how to get there, as well as furnish a few words of advice about how to approach the chiefs. In particular, he advised them to learn the gang's "dark language." Thus prepared, and carrying papers identifying them as Kaifeng officials come to assess the Yangshan bandit problem, the two radicals set off bearing Shi's letters of recommendation to carry out their mission.

Despite the strict security precautions they encountered as they made their way up the slopes of Yangshan, it was enough to mention the name of Shi Youjian and show their credentials to earn themselves a hearty welcome. The first person they met was none other than Wang Tianzong himself. Liu Qunren immediately explained the Republicans' desire to join forces with Wang and his band to carry through a revolution in China, adding that, if successful, "we hope that you will agree to becoming governor of Henan." Wang, highly pleased, promptly introduced them to his fellow chiefs, who were then treated to a lecture by Liu on the infamous history of the Manchu dynasty, the oppression of the common people by corrupt officials and local tyrants, the revolutionary movement led by Sun Zhongshan, and the success of the Wuchang uprising. Liu then explained to all of them the purpose of their mission to Yangshan. The chiefs, it is said, sat wordlessly through Liu's monologue; only when he proposed joining forces to take Luoyang and bring Henan over to the revolution so that the people might live and work in peace did they join him in his enthusiasm.

That night was the occasion for a great banquet featuring dishes of pork, mutton, chicken, duck, and other delicacies, a good illustration of how well Wang and his forces had set themselves up in their hideout. Wu and Liu each sat at the head of a great table, flanked by the gang's principal chiefs. When the food was gone they drank cup after cup of wine. Remembering Shi Youjian's advice about how to heal the breach within the gang, Wu singled out Guan Laojiu for special praise, until Han Yukun jumped up to take him off to meet Guan's sixty-year-old mother, now venerated as the band's elder presence. Her first words to the half-tipsy Wu Cangzhou, after giving him some sugar and water to sober him up, were: "You look like a young man of good breeding. What brings you to Yangshan of all places?" She went on to tell him how the various chiefs had all ended up fleeing to the mountain as a result of having caused trouble by repaying blood debts or killing tyrants and urged him not to end up the same way. "Study hard and carry out the Way as it should be carried out!" When she had finished speaking

Wu kowtowed respectfully and replied:

I lost my mother at thirteen, my father at fourteen, and became a wanderer when I was seventeen. Hearing of the bonds of righteousness sworn by the friends of Yangshan, I expressly took the liberty of paying a respectful visit to you. It is my plan to join the revolution together with you, overthrow the corrupt officials and local tyrants, and carry out the Way on behalf of Heaven.

The next day Wang Tianzong gathered all eight hundred of the band's members together and asked Liu and Wu to give their speeches once again, after which they were asked to inspect the fighters and their weapons, the latter mostly purchased from local soldiers. Following the inspection it was time for another banquet, attended this time by the entire band. At the end of the banquet Han Yukun and another chief named Zhang Zhigong took Wu Cangzhou once again to meet the old lady, before whom the ceremony of swearing blood brotherhood was finally conducted. Before a small carved wooden image of the God of War, Guan Di, and other revered statues, the old woman told the three men: "These are my family's ancestors. They too became brothers after tying the bonds of friendship. Now do you also swear, before the Sage Emperor, to live and die as one, to share together all good fortune and suffer together every tribulation." Wu indicated Han and Zhang with his finger and replied: "These two men are as your own children. I beg you to accept me too as one of your children. Please permit me to pay you my respects." The old woman smiled faintly: "Now you three brothers: set some incense to burn." Han and Zhang instantly lit candles and burned incense and yellow papers (*huangbiao*: used to beseech Heaven to recognize the initiation of new members), then poured drops of blood from a freshly killed cock's comb into a bowl of wine. First they performed the traditional "three prostrations and nine kowtows" in homage to Guan Di. Next they turned to Old Mother Guan, bowed, and took the oath of blood brotherhood with the newcomer. Finally, as required by the ceremony, all three drank together of the wine mixed with cock's blood to symbolize their union. Han was then 24, Wu 25, and Zhang 20. When the ceremony was over, Old Mother Guan presented Wu with the Browning pistol that her son had treasured when he was alive.*

As the foregoing account suggests, in allying themselves with ban-

---

* Wu Cangzhou 1961: 358–65. It was also at the visitors' suggestion that Wang changed his given name from Tiancong, meaning "one who follows Heaven," to Tianzong, "one who is endowed without limits by Heaven," a reference to Confucius taken from the *Analects*. The intention was to transform him from a simple local fighter to a revolutionary hero. See Des Forges 1979: 13. This is the name by which Wang became known thenceforth, and by which he has been referred to throughout the present text (even for pre-1911 mentions) to avoid confusion. Incidentally, the author of the essay cited here as Wang Tiancong 1971 bears no relation to the Wang who appears in the text.

dits and other popular forces, the Republicans, like later revolutionaries, faced three major problems. One was that of expressing themselves in terms the outlaws could understand—such as Wu Cangzhou's description of himself as a homeless, wandering *haohan* and Shi Youjian's advice to him to learn the bandits' "dark language"—and in ways they could appreciate, which meant throwing themselves wholeheartedly into the life of the band. They were thus compelled to involve themselves in popular local issues, such as the overthrow of local officials and attacks on the land rent, even in mere "bandit" activities such as kidnapping rich gentry figures. Revolutionaries also had to present personal evidence of their integrity, sharing the dangers of the bandit life and often, as at Yangshan, participating in traditional blood rituals, however distasteful.*

The second problem revolutionaries faced was overcoming the bandits' local bias. The Yangshan band saw the capture of Luoyang as the culmination of the revolution and had little interest in other aspects of Liu Qunren's monologue.† The difficulty of overcoming this problem aggravated the Republicans' tendency to view local forces as expendable.

The third problem was that of maintaining ideological credibility as revolutionaries untainted by the connections with "bandits." Liu Zhenhua, for example, because of his activities with popular forces in 1911 and his subsequent control over the ex-bandit Songxian Pacification Force, was still being referred to (inaccurately) as a "Songshan bandit chief" or as having held a "lieutenancy under White Wolf" as late as the 1920's.[14]

There were both advantages and drawbacks to this coalescence between bandits and revolutionaries. On the one hand, underworld groups like bandits were both tactically and psychologically prepared for the kind of covert behavior associated with a revolutionary movement in its germinal or defensive stages, and many natural alliances were set up on such a basis. On the other hand, unless the alliance could extend the social basis of its control by enlisting support from various classes, it was

---

*Note Esherick's statement: "insofar as radicals of this era...succeeded in allying with the peasantry, they did so on the basis of rather traditional formulae which answered long-standing peasant demands. Conversely, insofar as radicals were 'modern,' they cut themselves off from the peasantry" (1976b: 156). See also Gao Jing 1939 for an example. Bai Lang's Republican adviser apparently enjoyed great popularity within the band for not shirking any of the hardships faced by the ordinary members, despite being somewhat resented because of his extravagant whiskers (*BLQY*: 90–91).

†In Guangdong, too, the political horizons of the Republicans and the peasant bands they recruited to the revolution diverged considerably. Whereas the former focused upon the provincial capital as the movement's minimal target, the latter, like many local bands that had supported the anti-Ming rebels three hundred years before, were prone to go home after the local county seat was taken, assuming that the revolution had been won (Hsieh 1969: 90; on the anti-Ming bandits, See Dardess 1972: 108).

fated to remain forever at the government-labeled level of mere "banditry," and could never consolidate its political authority.

Similar ceremonies to that described above were taking place between bandit chiefs and Republicans all over China during the feverish last months of 1911.[15] Despite the difficulty of bridging the social and ideological gulf between them, the Republicans, hard-pressed for allies in their heavily outnumbered cause, almost everywhere turned to bandits or secret societies, especially where troops were insufficient or could not be won over. In North China, where most of the troops were loyal to Yuan Shikai and secret societies were weaker than in the south, the revolutionaries' approaches to bandits were particularly urgent.

The first fruits of this new strategy came in Manchuria in the spring of 1907 with a plan to mobilize local *honghuzi* to occupy the city of Fengtian so as to distract Beijing from an uprising planned farther south. The mastermind of the plan was Song Jiaoren, a longtime advocate of recruiting the *honghuzi* to the revolution. Unlike many "progressives," Song took a positive view of the heroic outlawry represented by the *Shuihu zhuan* and other knight-errant novels, and saw the *honghuzi* as being in the direct line of descent from that tradition. As early as 1905 he had written a short article titled "Twentieth-century Liangshanpo" dealing sympathetically with the armed communities of Manchuria, and by 1907 he had determined to try to enlist their fighting experience for an antistate uprising. Overtures to chiefs active in the coastal Jiandao area were initially successful. In his letter to them Song was careful to praise the *honghuzi*'s tradition of resistance to Manchu despotism, noting only that, with the passage of time, that resistance had become dispersed and little better than outlawry. The tone of the letter suggested that the alliance between bandits and revolutionaries would be one among equals, the revolutionaries' task being to add guidance and assistance to ensure the insurrection's success. On the day set for the rising, however, plans were leaked, the chiefs failed in their task of recruiting all the area's bandits, and the enterprise collapsed. Song himself was forced to flee to Japanese-controlled Dairen.[16]

Despite the failure, and despite the continuing distrust for the *honghuzi* among the Republicans as a whole, contacts continued. Huang Xing, another revolutionary leader, told Sun Zhongshan in a letter of May 1910 that in the previous year the Japanese adventurer Kayano Nagatomo had brought a group consisting of Manchurian mounted bandits and Yellow Sea coastal pirates to see him in Japan for the purpose of using them to hamper government troop movements in North China. In 1911, too, the militant army officer Wu Luzhen was creating links with south Manchurian gangs for the same purpose,[17] though no effective alliance was ever realized.

Henan's long rebellious tradition and obvious social contradictions, according to one Chinese historian, created the "objective conditions for revolution." In combination with its strategic importance as an avenue to Beijing, these made it a natural candidate for Republican attentions in 1911. As early as the spring of 1907 four fronts had already been tentatively formed to mobilize the groups felt to be most susceptible to revolutionary stimulation: the army, the students, a local secret society (called the *Renyi hui* ["Society for Humanity and Righteousness"]), and the bandits. Whichever front had the most success was to be allowed to provide the province's new governor after the revolution. Some elements, like the Yangshan bandits, were contacted and persuaded to join the rising by Republican agents; others rose spontaneously.[18] Symbolic of this switch in revolutionary attitudes was the abrupt transformation in the terminology used by Republican organs such as the *Minli bao*, in whose pages the one-time "bandits" (*daofei*) became officially acknowledged now as "heroes" (*jianer*).[19] Even without the political factors that made Henan unique, however, the inexorable increase in rural violence, marked by a series of local riots between 1902 and 1911, would probably have forced the Republicans to pay attention to irregular forces, for there was no sign of the militant trend abating even had 1911 not erupted into revolution.

The revolutionaries concentrated their attentions on three main routes: an eastern route that would mobilize the *Renyi hui* to occupy the Yellow River valley; a southern route aimed at winning over the peasant bandits of Baofeng, Lushan, and Jiaxian; and, most promising, a western route intended to bring about an alliance between the bandits of Yangshan and the *Zaiyuan hui* ("Peach Garden Society"), another secret society concentrated around Luoyang, with the aim of securing that city for the revolution. In the end it was the forces of the last-named route that made the most significant rural contribution to the revolution in Henan, for almost all of the principal chiefs, after the initiation described above, gave their support to the revolution.[20]

Toward the end of 1911, following their recruitment by the Republicans, Wang Tianzong and the rest of the band were reorganized as the Henan People's Army. After killing the Songxian magistrate they managed, in alliance with the *Zaiyuan hui*, to mobilize some 10,000 to 20,000 west Henan peasants and lead them against the city of Luoyang. Local peasant bands helped by harassing pursuing government troops. The attack failed because of unexpected resistance, and the band fought several protracted battles before retreating west toward Shaanxi. On the border between the two provinces they met and joined forces with a similar band of militant irregulars, the Shaanxi People's Army, commanded by another Henanese named Zhang Fang (also known as Zhang Peiying).

From then until the announcement of peace negotiations between the Qing court and the revolutionaries, the "Henan-Shaanxi Allied Army" maintained its position in counties straddling the border, surviving several major clashes with soldiers and attracting strong popular support.[21]

Yet, despite the bonds that were forged in so many isolated parts of the province, and despite a number of heroic actions comparable to those of the Henan People's Army, the projected central command of Republicans and popular forces never materialized. Neither the latter, often armed with no more than desperate courage and enthusiasm, nor the former, none of whom had any practical experience of organizing a revolutionary fighting force, made any attempt to coordinate their actions. One reason was the mutual mistrust that, despite everything, lingered on both sides. Wang Tianzong, for example, naturally blamed the Republicans for the failure of the Luoyang raid since the plan had been leaked by a young Republican conspirator. On the other hand, the failure of an early coup against Kaifeng involving the *Renyi hui*, according to one opinion, resulted from the Republicans' reluctance to put their faith in such irregulars.[22] When banditry resumed after 1911 in many parts of the province, both as a survival technique and as a substitute for the excitement of recent months, Republicans chose this time to ignore it, and their journals reverted once again to labeling those popular heroes who had not surrendered to the new authorities as "bandits."[23] The wheel had come full circle. Irregulars that were not, like the Songxian Pacification Force, absorbed into the military system were either disbanded by the Republicans themselves in a naive display of goodwill, or else forcibly dispersed by Yuan Shikai and allowed to return to banditry; still others, on the instructions of official telegrams ordering local loyalists to "kill all troublemakers as bandits," were summarily slaughtered.[24]

Clearly then, the Republicans in 1911 never managed to see beyond the alliance of convenience they had forged with the bandits. As for the bandits themselves, those with a clear sense of mission like Wang Tianzong and his fellow chiefs saw the uprising as a golden opportunity both to gain revenge on a system that had slighted them and to prove that they were a cut above the general run of "bandits." Smaller bands, too, active all over south and west Henan amid a growing economic crisis, saw various possibilities in the revolutionary fighting. For some it was a case of staking everything on a last-ditch effort to restore the world they knew, with themselves as a retributive vanguard. For others, already isolated from agrarian life, there was the promise of securing a foothold on the ladder of power by gaining official recognition of their military abilities. In either case, the perspective was that of the rural, local hero, and was sooner or later bound to clash with the more political, pragmatic outlook of the Republicans. The trust inspired by such idealists as Liu Qunren and Wu Cangzhou was purely personal, and did not extend to revolutionary militants as a whole as long as the latter remained basically outsiders. Not for two or three decades would that situation show any sign of change.

## Bai Lang Joins the Revolution

In the summer of 1913 the Republicans launched a new armed struggle in an attempt to wrest power back from the "usurper" Yuan Shikai: the "Second Revolution." Being militarily as weak as they had been two years before, they naturally turned to the rapidly growing peasant band of Bai Lang on the Henan-Hubei border. For the latter, too, it was an ideal opportunity to bolster his prestige and secure a powerful patron in place of the declining Royalist Party.

The earliest contacts between Bai Lang and the Republicans were initiated by the Nationalist Party's agent in Wuhan, Zou Yongcheng. Following a secret conference with other Party agents, Zou recalls in his memoirs, he met with two Bai Lang emissaries* and sent them back to Henan with seals appointing Bai Lang to the post of "Vanguard Commander, Hunan-Hubei-Henan Allied Army." Although the date of this event is not clear, it probably took place in the middle of June 1913—a month, that is, before the new insurrection was declared.[25]

It seems unlikely that this was Bai Lang's first knowledge of the Republicans' existence and the meaning of the events of 1911. Despite his links with the Royalist Party, during the previous winter spent in the mountains of north Hubei he had already come into contact with the "Rivers and Lakes Society" (*Jianghu hui*), a network of local secret society groups that not only had traditionally maintained close contacts with the Henan bandit gangs constantly filtering through in search of refuge, but had also responded readily to the Wuchang uprising thanks to the activities of local revolutionary instigators. Whether Bai Lang was actually contacted by any of these agents has yet to be proved, but that

---

*One of them at least, Xiong Siyu, was a veteran intriguer, having first established contact with Bai as an agent of none other than military governor Zhang Zhenfang in a March 1912 attempt to have Bai submit to the authorities. His experiences convinced him of the basic worth of the bandits compared to the corruption of their rulers, and, although there is no firm evidence of his having been a member of the Nationalist Party at that time, by 1913 he had left Kaifeng and slipped back into the mountains to act as go-between for Bai and the revolution (*BLQY*: 90)

Not all the radical leaders seem to have been aware of the Bai Lang connection, incidentally. Chen Qimei, for example, included among his stated reasons for opposing Yuan Shikai's government the fact that Yuan was unable to suppress "the White Wolf [who] causes trouble in Honan" (cited in Friedman 1974: 144–45n).

he was swayed by the insurrectionary enthusiasm of the societies themselves seems highly likely, particularly if, as one newspaper suggested, he
was himself a member of the local "Big Sword" society.[26]

Bai Lang's contact with Zou Yongcheng came precisely at the time
when Yuan Shikai, having got wind of the revolutionaries' plans through
his spies, was pouring troops southward to forestall the planned insurrection. It was essential for the revolutionaries to delay these troops before
they could reach the Yangzi Valley where the friendly armies were concentrated, and the decision to contact Bai Lang was undoubtedly made
in the light of this need. Zou's instructions to the two emissaries were
therefore to return to Henan and try to blow up the railway bridges over
the Yellow River. Unfortunately, both were caught and executed before the mines could be laid.

It is not clear whether Bai Lang's band was also to join in the attempt
on the bridges, but by July Zou's message had certainly been received
and his initiative was being followed up. Although large numbers of
northern troops had already been successfully transported south, the
band still retained a vital role in the revolutionaries' plans: to create
havoc in the vacuum left behind by the transfer of so many troops, and,
more importantly, to occupy the Beijing-Hankou Railway zone to hamper the passage of further supplies and reinforcements—a task they
carried out with some success for the two months that military operations lasted.[27] Vital as it may have been, however, it has to be noted that
Bai Lang's role was intended to be a supportive one for the "real" forces
of the rebellious provincial governors.

Nevertheless, the Republicans were clearly prepared to go to some
lengths to ensure Bai's cooperation. Like Wang Tianzong two years before, Bai, in a personal letter from revolutionary leader Huang Xing,
was offered the governorship of Henan after the revolutionaries seized
power.[28]

At the same time the revolutionaries created difficulties for themselves
by the alliance with Bai Lang, since Bai was already known as one of the
most formidable and implacable of all the south Henan chiefs as well
as a committed foe of gentry control. In a desperate attempt to avoid
an upper-class backlash should Bai eventually become governor, they
therefore launched a separate attempt to win support for him by enlisting the services of Yan Zigu, a long-time Henan activist.

After the revolution Yan had been appointed magistrate of Linru in
west Henan with an implicit brief to use his contacts with local bandit
chiefs (many of whom he had personally brought into the insurrectionary plans in 1910) to create an irregular force that could be called upon
when needed. Yan's new task was to use his elite connections to mollify

local gentry and political figures and somehow win them over to sup-port Bai Lang as the province's military governor. Although the task was probably hopeless from the beginning, Yan was summoned in the early summer of 1913 and ordered to contact Bai Lang, then start a sepa-rate uprising on his own behalf in the Huai region near the province's eastern border. It was hoped that his participation would win for the movement the gentry support it needed. After the Second Revolution got under way, Yan received his final instructions in Nanjing and re-turned to Henan, but he was dragged from his train immediately upon arrival and summarily shot together with nine other conspirators. Many of the survivors fled to join Bai Lang, and the rising collapsed.*

The official terror that followed the declaration of hostilities drove activists from various quarters into Bai's band. Some of them were refu-gees from the pogroms in Wuchang, others from the recently suppressed rising at Shayang, north Hubei (including its organizer Ji Yulin, said to be a "good friend" of Bai Lang). At the end of the year the Shayang refugees were reported to be trying to bring local bandits under Bai's banners for a joint attack on Wuhan.[29]

Meanwhile, a parallel reign of terror was being carried out through-out Henan on Yuan Shikai's orders by military governor Zhang Zhen-fang. Martial law was declared in the province in August following re-ports that it was "strongly in sympathy" with the anti–Yuan movement. Local magistrates, many appointed by Zhang himself specifically to eliminate Yuan's enemies, were empowered to conduct summary punish-ment of bandits without awaiting authorization from above, and for several months mass executions became the order of the day. Many of the refugees had little choice but to join Bai Lang's followers in the hills.[30]

In this way Bai Lang's poor-peasant band was swollen by the addition of many people with Republican sympathies and began to take on a po-litical hue of its own. At the same time, "countless" representatives were

---

* *XHGM*: VII, 355, 359; Feng Ziyou 1969: 22, 24; *XHSY*: IV, 86; *ZFGB* 528 (23 Oct. 1913); *STSB*, 10 Oct. 1913: 8, 17 Oct. 1913: 8, 13 Nov. 1913: 8; Shimamoto 1974: 47. See also *Central China Post*, 31 July 1913, in SD 893.00/1906 (Hankou to Washington, D.C., 6 Aug. 1913). Li Shican, the contact in Zhang Zhenfang's office through whom Yan had acquired his position as Linru magistrate, may also have had something to do with his exposure. Li evidently got off scot-free despite the appearance of his name in official records. A book that appeared in 1926 entitled "A Complete Record of Suppressing Endemic Banditry in Tangyin and Qixian Counties, North Henan," however, was authored by none other than Li Shican himself, suggesting that Li, in return for betraying Yan Zigu, was pardoned and put in charge of bandit suppression. His officers would no doubt have been those former followers of Yan Zigu who betrayed him to save their own skins. Li later became Zhang Zhenfang's personal secretary and "brain" (Shimamoto 1974: 30).

being sent up from the south to make contact with him, bringing instructions, carrying supplies, and so on.* Most of these representatives made contact with Bai through the 1911 activist Ling Yue, a former provincial assemblyman who had been expelled during a purge of radicals. Ling himself had been sent to Bai Lang with letters of greeting and instructions, and had been authorized by Sun Zhongshan to acknowledge Bai as provincial governor.[31] Numerous other Republican agents were also said to be working with Bai Lang, the most influential among whom, an emissary from Sun Zhongshan named Shen, was apparently held in such esteem that he was allowed to devise all the major military strategies after January 1914. Veterans of the rebellion recalled later how popular Shen had been, but stressed that he had had no power to give direct orders, only to make proposals for Bai to act upon as he saw fit. Nevertheless, subchiefs were said to resent Shen's influence upon Bai Lang, especially when it did not coincide with their own desires. Shen's role was purely a military, not an ideological one: the only time he was heard to use the word "revolution" was when he chided someone who had come to apply for acceptance as a "bandit" (*tangjiang*). Other agents, usually disguised as merchants, were sent for the purpose of delivering munitions, though few managed to find the band in the thickly forested mountains of south Henan.[32] In any case, once Bai decided on a roving strategy at the end of 1913 he effectively put himself out of range of any further supplies.

All in all, therefore, the evidence is overwhelming that by the mid-summer of 1913 strong links had been forged between Bai Lang and the anti–Yuan Shikai revolutionary movement. Proclamations already announced him as "Great Military Governor Bai, Commander of the Chinese Republic to Support the Han and Overthrow Yuan Shikai." During July the band launched a series of attacks on south Henan cities to keep government troops pinned down, defeating a whole regiment of soldiers at Tangxian, then moving on to Yuxian (Yuzhou), famed for its

---

*For examples, see *STSB*, 21 Aug. 1913: 8, 24 Dec. 1913: 8–9, 30 Jan. 1914: 10, 8 Mar. 1914: 9, 6 June 1914: 11; *ZFGB* 624 (14 Mar. 1914), 720 (9 May 1914); *Shibao*, 4 Dec. 1913, quoted in *XHGM Hubei*: 724–25; *Da gonghe ribao*, 25 Nov. 1913, quoted in *XHGM Hubei*: 732; Li Xin et al. 1980: 155, 160; SD 893.00/2154 (Hankou to Washington, D.C., 3 June 1914). One notorious case involved a young Chinese living in Canada, Jack Kong, who was accused of murdering the wife of his Canadian Pacific Railroad employer. He had allegedly been stealing from the family in order to provide funds to send arms to Bai Lang, presumably at the instigation of revolutionary agents, and had been caught in the act. One £800 shipment had already been sent in December 1913, and the Hong Kong authorities were requested to hold up all further consignments (*The Times* [London], 8 Apr. 1914, 13 Apr. 1914; *STSB*, 21 Apr. 1914: 9). In Great Britain the impact of Bai Lang's activities was sufficient to cause a revival of anti-Chinese hysteria, hotels being obliged to dismiss their Chinese waiters and so on (*The Times* [London], 7 Apr. 1914).

prosperous inhabitants.* The campaign also brought in large numbers of recruits as well as weapons and other supplies. Meanwhile, a second force was sent to launch a surprise attack on the Beijing-Hankou Railway garrisons. One Republican newspaper announced: "Bai Lang's soldiers are already cooperating with the people's armies; they are strong and well-disciplined." Another even stated: "These soldiers [of Bai Lang] are enough to ensure Henan's independence; in future it will be simple to send troops to attack Beijing."[33] European prisoners taken at the time also attested to the band's "political tendencies": some members had wanted to know "how the rebellion was proceeding," and "appeared to hold Huang Xing in the highest respect." Yuan Shikai responded by putting a price of five thousand dollars on Bai's head.[34]

To the consternation of the authorities in Wuchang, Bai Lang's next move was south to Zaoyang in north Hubei, but the news received from the thirteen missionaries captured there was shocking and depressing: the insurrection had failed and its leaders had fled (at which news Bai was said to have shown "considerable signs of vexation"). At the beginning of October, therefore, Bai and his forces abandoned the city and returned north to Henan, which was immediately declared to be in a state of "no policing, no government."[35]

Like it or not, Bai Lang was now the main hope of the revolutionary movement, no longer a mere support for the "real" revolution conducted by regular troops. He was also Yuan Shikai's main enemy in North China, as well as being a daily figure in both the Chinese and the treaty-port press. The lesson was not lost on Yuan, who proceeded to issue orders for Bai's immediate suppression, or on Zhang Zhenfang, who intensified the purge of "undesirables" around Kaifeng. Many of these latter, rather than wait around to be slaughtered or incarcerated, once again crowded into Bai Lang's army, advising him at the same time that "if you want to make revolution, you must go south and seek Sun [Zhongshan]."[36]

By this time Bai Lang also seems to have become personally committed to the revolutionary cause (not least because of the prospect of becoming Henan's military governor, one might add). According to a captured subchief's confession, he remained in constant touch with the revolutionaries, including both Sun Zhongshan and Huang Xing (though

---

*The authorities' deliberate attempt to hush up the attack on Yuxian, center of Henan's traditional pharmaceuticals industry (Wu Shixun 1936: 118), was a good example of the concealment policy then in force. Though the governor's office denied their reports as no more than "dangerous talk," Beijing correspondents confirmed that the city had been looted of almost everything from medicines to guns, and concluded that the real purpose of the hush-up was to conceal the official ineptitude that had left the important city undefended. See *STSB*, 2 Mar. 1914: 3; Wang Canli 1979.

the two leaders seem to have offered him conflicting advice). He had a core of educated advisers, both students and military exiles, who no doubt put continuous pressure on him to keep the fire of revolution burning, and who gave him the beginnings of a concrete political platform. He also improved his military strength by attacks on armories, absorbing ex-soldiers and forging local alliances.[37] This, together with the strong popular support he was receiving as leader of the strongest band the region had seen for some decades, boosted his confidence considerably. Finally, at the end of 1913, Bai decided to overrule his subchiefs (who preferred a defensive campaign in the "pell-mell tumbled mountains of West Honan")[38] and to lead the army out of those mountains to rejoin the revolution. The numerous titles that he and his army adopted in the ensuing months all showed his commitment to the anti–Yuan Shikai cause. Bai is referred to sometimes as "Military Governor and Citizen Commander of the Han Army," sometimes as the "Commander of the Army to Punish Yuan Shikai"; banners naming him "Universal Marshal Bai" were hoisted alongside those proclaiming "President Sun of the Republic of China." The rebel army itself was announced as the "Citizens' Army to Exterminate the Bandits" or the "Citizens' Punitive Army," a reference to its anti–Yuan Shikai mission. On one occasion banners proclaimed the rebels as the "Second Punitive National Construction Force"—clear evidence of their links to Sun Zhongshan, since "National Construction" was one of Sun's favorite slogans. Posters put up on the way through Shaanxi rebuked Yuan's government as "an autocracy masquerading as a republic," for whose overthrow Bai Lang was "gathering together heroes to request the Mandate of Heaven on behalf of the people." As soon as his preparations were complete, his army would return from the northwest to destroy Yuan's dictatorship and "set up a perfect government."[39]

Bai's roving strategy, begun at the end of 1913, also stemmed from his revolutionary connections. Although his followers were reportedly reluctant to join him on his first move down to Anhui, Bai pulled them all along with him, his aim being apparently to join Huang Xing near Nanjing. Huang, unfortunately, had long since fled, and when it was decided to trek west to Sichuan instead, it was almost certainly at the urging of advisers closer to Sun Zhongshan than to Huang Xing, for whose "cowardice" Bai now reportedly felt "contempt."[40] Nevertheless, whatever support the band was receiving from the Republicans at this stage was mostly of the moral variety. One emissary who was found wandering in the mountains near Lushan told peasants that he had come to deliver arms to Bai Lang, but could not find him. The statement of a former subchief that the band never received any support in the form of munitions suggests that the emissary went home without achieving his mission. Other reports that the band at this point was stealing mostly weapons and horses reinforce the subchief's claim.[41]

It was perhaps this failure to receive more concrete aid in the last stages of the campaign that clinched the decision to flee back to Henan instead of trying again to force a passage from Gansu into Sichuan. Bai had previously been able to override his subchiefs' natural inclinations to stick close to their Henan base by the promise of material aid and military support from the Republicans; now, in far-off Gansu, hemmed in by hostile troops and an angry populace, it was not so easy. When his followers refused to go any farther he turned in desperation to his adviser, Shen, whose reply was brief: "If none of them wants to go, so be it. All we can do is turn back for Henan."[42] The disintegration when they got there could not have been foreseen, and in fact left the Republicans wrong-footed:

> The devoutest hope a Socialist can express at the present time about China is that the bandit "White Wolf" may turn out as successful a bandit as Pancho Villa.... [H]is army of bandits looms up an ever greater menace to the tottering peace of the Chinese Republic.... [I]t is an open secret that his military operations have the support of a national revolutionary organization....[43]

When this optimistic report appeared, unfortunately, Bai Lang's headless body was already rotting in its grave.*

* As late as November 1914 the following curious claim by an individual purporting to be Sun Zhongshan's secretary was recorded in the local press: "Another army opposed to Yuan Shih-k'ai and despotism is already in the field, although they are termed bandits and murderers by the Yuan Shih-k'ai subsidized press. That is the army led by the quiet, studious American college graduate, formerly a general under Yuan Shih-k'ai, and now called by him 'The White Wolf.' ... The White Wolf and his army, more powerful than the world realizes, are ready to step in under the flag of Sun Yat-sen when the word is given." (*Central China Post*, 2 Nov. 1914, in SD 893.00/2233 [Hankou to Beijing, 2 Nov. 1914]). For a photograph corresponding to this image, see *STSB*, 9 Aug. 1914: 2.

The Republicans' involvement with Bai Lang's rebellion did not end here. Later in 1914 a Chinese Revolutionary Party organizer in Shaanxi (perhaps the same Shen who had served Bai Lang) enrolled the leader of a group of remnants (Fan Zhongxiu? Song Laonian?) into the Party with the hope of turning the group into anti-government guerrillas. Sun Zhongshan's letters in 1915–16 continued to voice his hope for CRP risings in Shaanxi, perhaps anticipating that these bandits would return to the glory of 1914. See Friedman 1974: 163, drawing on a handwritten manuscript by CRP member Xu Chonghao. See also Borst-Smith 1917: 187. Recent materials from Taibei, meanwhile, have drawn attention to a curious legend according to which Bai Lang's only son, Bai Zhendong, after serving as an officer in Fan Zhongxiu's National Construction Army, went on to become a popular anti-Japanese guerrilla leader under the nickname "Xiao Bai Lang" (Little Bai Lang). In return for his services to the Nationalist Revolution, the family's land, expropriated following his father's death, was restored, and, the legend continues, memorial services were held attended by several notable figures (Wang Tiancong 1978: 29–30; Cheng Yufeng 1978 [Oct.]: 32). These articles, part of a spate of Bai Lang–related materials carried in the magazine *Zhongyuan wenxian* in recent years, indicate a change in the Nationalists' assessment of Bai Lang. From being once regarded as no more than simple banditry, his movement is now rated positively for its anti–Yuan Shi-

No effective relationship between bandits and the revolutionary forces was ever worked out during the warlord period, primarily because of their divergent outlooks. The record shows that to the Republicans such forces were auxiliaries subordinate to the role of the regular military. Only when the latter was inaccessible or defeated did the Republicans commit themselves fully to bandits—and even then with the attitude that doing so was only a temporary expedient and that the bandits themselves were therefore expendable. It was consequently as shock troops that bandits and secret societies were most often recruited, or else as diversionary targets to blunt attacks on the precious regular army—roles that fortunately suited their natural enthusiasm and ignorance of the nature of modern warfare. Though their usefulness for such purposes was never denied by the revolutionaries, in China, after all, there were always plenty more to be found. It was no accident, surely, that as one 1911 veteran recalled, "In the revolutionary struggle, nearly all the dangerous and perilous tasks were carried out by members of the Elder Brothers Society." Neither should we be surprised to find that most of the "revolutionary martyrs" of the 1911 troubles in Henan were members of the *Renyi hui*, or that revolutionary strategists elsewhere actually called for the formation of a federation of "bandit commandos" for suicidal attacks on government positions,[44] a rarely equaled expression of elitist arrogance. Popular forces were primarily useful as cannon fodder.

For their part, bandits approached revolutionary alliances with equal ambivalence and pragmatism. As rural forces, their horizons were extremely narrow, limited by their own experience. Thus Bai Lang's followers preferred killing Henan magistrates to opposing Yuan Shikai; Wang Tianzong's band saw its target as Luoyang, not Beijing; and the "people's armies" of Guangdong packed up and went home after sacking the county seat. Their lack of trust of the revolutionaries showed itself on many occasions, as in Bai Lang's sudden change of attitude toward Huang Xing; the "Sword-fighters'" accusation that the Alliance was to blame for the failed attack on Luoyang; and Fan Zhongxiu's preference for the "local hero" Zhang Fang over the "revolutionary hero" Yu Youren as his commander in the "Nation-Pacifying Army." Nonetheless, Bai Lang's followers were swayed by exaggerated accounts of the Republicans' strength to follow their leader all over North China;

---

kai position. That the legend of Bai Lang's descendant was no more than legend was underlined by the absence of any mention of a son in the 1959 Kaifeng investigation. Another cause for skepticism is the strong similarity between the nickname "Xiao Bai Lang" and that of Kohinata Hakurō, "Xiao Bai Long," as well as the coincidence of Kohinata's given name Hakurō, whose Chinese pronunciation would be "Bai Lang." The legend probably arose from a confused identification of the equally legendary activities of Kohinata with the memory of Bai Lang.

and Bai Lang and Wang Tianzong themselves were brought over to the revolution by promises of substantial power. Bandits and other rural forces were in constant need of powerful patrons, and turned to the revolutionaries when they seemed likely to fulfill that need.

   After 1917, following Sun Zhongshan's establishment of a Provisional Government in Guangdong, the center of revolutionary activity shifted to the south, while in the north the army became the prime source of patronage and prestige. With the exception of the organization of the Nation-Pacifying Army in Shaanxi, revolutionary contacts with north China bandits tended to take the form of stirring them up in the territory of reactionary warlords to create confusion. In 1922–23, while preparing for the First Northern Expedition, Sun Zhongshan reportedly contacted west Henan soldier-bandits with the idea that they might serve as a possible disruptive force behind Wu Peifu's lines (presumably a reference to Fan Zhongxiu and Lao Yangren). His agents are also alleged to have remained with Lao Yangren's band after they were enrolled in the military in 1923, and to have courted Fan Mingxin the following summer as a potential ally should the southern forces then in Hunan break through into North China.[45] The Lincheng bandits, according to a letter from one of Sun's associates, also received encouragement from the south, as their assumed title, "Shandong Self-Governing National Construction Army," indicated. They were urged to delay a settlement and the release of captives for as long as possible so as to cause the maximum embarrassment to the Beijing warlord authorities.[46] Even the Communist Party's Henan branch reported in 1927 that it was "concentrating" on agitating among bandits near Kaifeng to cause problems for the warlord authorities.[47]
   Whether seeking to coordinate the bandits as guerrillas or merely to manipulate them from afar, the nature of these revolutionary approaches was essentially identical: bandits were to be "used" for the revolutionaries' own purposes—to "distract attention," "cause trouble," "hamper troop movements," and so on. Nowhere is there any sign that the revolutionaries had considered the bandits' own fate.

### Bandits and Revolution: The Communist Movement

   Early encounters between Communists and bandits were rooted in the same mixture of romanticism and mistrust that had characterized previous approaches. As the Communist movement itself gathered strength, the mistrust remained—with reason—but the romanticism gradually became tempered with pragmatism. Committed to a revolutionary program that envisaged fundamental social change achieved through violent struggle, the Communists in their contacts with bandits had to cope with patterns of violence that were aimed first and foremost at survival. As the revolutionary movement developed from aggressive expansion to the creation and consolidation of soviets, its attitude toward bandits hardened and matured. At the same time, the bandits, caught up in a rural revolution that made their traditional heroic role increasingly redundant and a life of robbery increasingly difficult, had no choice but to come to terms with a fast-changing reality.

When it came to frontal approaches, the Communists encountered the same problems as had the Republicans in 1911: how to present themselves effectively to the bandits while maintaining their own ideological credibility, and how to overcome the bandits' local bias. He Long, for example, used the traditional method of swearing blood brotherhood to gain bandits' confidence and bring them over to the revolutionary side, and Zhu De owed his life when captured by bandits in 1921 to his having been, like the chief, a member of the Elder Brothers Society and thereby a fellow member of the underworld.[48]

This could also present problems. Bandits in the counties surrounding Haifeng in Guangdong, where the first peasant association was established in 1923, saw the organizers as "kindred souls" thanks to their opposition to the authorities and abstained from rustling the cattle belonging to villages within the association. Before long the association came under fire from above for its "symbiosis" with the bandits, and, thanks to the government's monopoly over the media, came to be regarded as no different from the bandits themselves. Peng Pai, the main organizer of the peasant association, was dismissed as a "bandit chief" planning to instigate trouble.[49]

In these early stages of the Communist movement, however, there was rarely the time or the opportunity to consider the niceties of public opinion. Even allowing for distortion by government propaganda seeking to discredit their political program, certain of the Red Armies behaved much like predatory bandits themselves or else allowed independent gangs "to act in the name of the Red Army and under our slogans." * Tactical decisions like these caused subsequent strategists to sigh ruefully: "The masses completely failed to understand what the Red Army was. In many places the army was even attacked, like a bandit gang. The army had no support from the masses. . . ."[50]

---

*Tang Leang-li ed. 1934: 67–68; Nagano 1933: 210–11; *Bukan hōmen*: 11–12; *Shina meibutsu*: 8–9. The activities of the various Red Armies evidently tended to differ according to their internal makeup. Where peasants predominated (a rare case), the land question was uppermost; those in which former soldiers were the majority were apt to develop "warlord tendencies" toward carving out territory and cliquishness; units dominated by bandits or vagrants were often noted for their propensity for expropriation and violence accompanied by a tendency to compromise with the enemy (Nagano 1933: 208–9).

If the Communists suffered from their alliances with bandits, they also learned many tactical and strategic ruses from them. The most obvious lesson was the siting of soviets along remote provincial boundaries where administration was weakest, where hideouts were often impregnable, and where retreat was a simple matter. The guerrilla methods learned by Zhu De during two years spent fighting French-sponsored bandits in Yunnan stood him in good stead when devising tactics for the Red Armies in later years. He also admitted that in seeking effective ways to defend the Jinggangshan base from government troops he had consulted the two bandit chiefs who had occupied the mountain earlier, Wang Zuo and Yuan Wencai.* They in turn had passed on the advice of a veteran bandit named "Old Deaf Chu": "You don't have to know how to fight; all you have to know is how to encircle the enemy." Wang and Yuan had followed this cryptic advice and their hideout had never been breached, even though their followers were armed with only primitive bows and arrows and cannon fashioned from tree trunks.[51]

Mao Zedong also incorporated bandit techniques into his repertoire, stressing the possibility of guerrilla campaigns on the plains using the "green curtain" of gaoliang. He also noted that the river-lake regions had long been the scene of "dramatic battles fought by 'pirates' and 'water-bandits' (*shuikou*), of which our history is full."[52] However, Mao added, such techniques could be no more than one aspect of revolutionary strategy, a tactical borrowing rather than a strategic one—for in the last analysis tactics alone could not achieve revolutionary change and were useless except as part of a long-term overall strategy.

Behind the early cooperation between Communists and bandits was the dire state of the revolutionary armies themselves. Outnumbered by government forces and almost obliterated by futile attacks on major cities, the Communists in South China had been forced to seek the aid of south Hunan bandit chiefs. On the latter's recommendation, they were then able to retire to the mountains straddling the border between Hunan and Jiangxi, the famous Jinggangshan base already occupied by Wang Zuo and Yuan Wencai. In other parts of China, too, initial weakness had obliged revolutionary armies to seek similar country in order to develop their strength beyond the reach of government repression. These were the areas, needless to say, where bandit gangs had maintained rarely disputed sway for centuries. Local partisans selected them for the same reason that the bandits had used them: safety. Nevertheless, though he

---

* Both Wang and Yuan were poor peasants brought up on the *Shuihu zhuan* and the *Sanguo zhi*, heard from storytellers in the marketplaces. They had become blood brothers and formed a small army of former militia members and bandits. Though loyal to each other and to their followers, they were merciless to their foes, especially landlords who broke prearranged agreements on the division of power (Smedley 1934: 64–66).

stressed the importance of such border areas for resting the "buttocks" of the revolutionary movement—that is, for providing an opportunity to sit down to catch its breath—Mao Zedong pointed out that they were not normally secure enough for long-term occupation.[53]

Although bandits furnished both the nucleus of a preliminary fighting force and the tactical experience appropriate to guerrilla warfare, the conditions that produced and perpetuated endemic banditry did not constitute a revolutionary environment. Promoting a revolutionary movement meant mobilizing peasants to participate in land redistribution and self-defense, whereas bandits, as Zhou Enlai pointed out in a 1930 address, had little interest in such objectives.[54] A land revolution, moreover, did not usually appeal to any of the original inhabitants of the regions where the revolutionary bases were sited. Because of the isolated, self-sufficient nature of such regions, there were often already well-defined power networks based on an agreement by all concerned to live and let live. Bandits and landlords, as in the mountains of Jiangxi prior to the Communists' arrival, had probably reached agreement on division of the available spoils, with the landlords, for example, making a regular "tax" payment to ensure immunity. Officials were often turning a blind eye to smuggling in return for a rake-off and a degree of peace and quiet. Being closely inbred, such communities often resented the intrusion of outside political forces trying to reorganize social relationships, and were even likely to unite across class differences to resist.

As long as the existing power structure remained intact, revolutionaries found it hard to establish themselves except by winning over the local bandits by promises of material support and financial gain. The nature of the alliance, however—which often saw the bandits vacillating between support for the Red Army and the enticements of established local figures—did nothing to promote local security, without which peasant support could not be achieved. Even after the revolutionaries gained preeminence, there was a constant tendency for rich peasants and landlords to take to the hills and form bandit gangs of their own[55] (an interesting development in itself that one might refer to as the "embourgeoisement" of banditry).

On the whole, therefore, areas in which the revolutionary movement was forced to rely geographically and logistically upon existing bandit subcultures did not provide the means for developing new forms of social organization. The potential of such regions for revolution was therefore much weaker than their tendency to produce banditry, which only operated outside its home area and which, unlike the revolutionary movement, could be connived at by those able to pay. In the eyes of the peasants, as one local Communist organizer reported, "If there is still banditry, it will bring no benefits to us no matter how many rent reductions you have carried out. One kidnapping is enough to ruin me completely." [56] Not surprisingly, the major successes of the Communists in Henan came not in the economically undeveloped zones where poverty was rife and banditry endemic, but in the newly developed and degenerating zones, such as the towns along the Beijing-Hankou Railway, where local self-defense was more typical than banditry. Even those successes were extremely short-lived.[57]

As long as the provincial border zones remained self-supporting and nonexpansive, they were usually safe against concerted suppression attempts. As we have seen, local banditry was largely tolerated by the authorities so long as it posed no overt threat to regional security. The arrival of the Communists, however, changed the picture entirely. The presence of an aggressively expanding military force backed up by a subversive ideology turned such regions into prime targets for government intervention. For the Communists, the resulting need to stress military organization increased the difficulty of conveying their egalitarian message and inspiring peasant allegiance. This in turn prevented extensive mobilization and forced them to rely still more heavily on bandits. Shaanxi province in the early 1930's and the Eyuwan Soviet farther east were good examples of areas that, like all the border regions occupied by the Communists, presented major obstacles to the consolidation of revolutionary power, and made Mao Zedong insist on the need for *mobile* base areas.[58]

The story of the Shaanxi revolutionary movement—a movement that was central both to the struggle against Japan and to the final consolidation of Communist control—began early in the 1930's. Its main instigator was a young Communist named Liu Zhidan, a veteran of the Northern Expedition and a former party organizer. In 1928 he had returned to Shaanxi in an attempt to mobilize the soldiers of Feng Yuxiang's *Guominjun* army, and he then led a peasant rising in the south of the province that, though quickly suppressed by Feng with great bloodshed, furnished from among its survivors the first Shaanxi guerrillas. From that point on Liu led a career remarkably similar in its early stages to that of Fan Zhongxiu, described by Edgar Snow as "a kaleidoscope of defeats, failures, discouragements, escapades, adventure, and remarkable escapes from death, interspersed with periods of respectability as a reinstated officer." By 1931 Liu was ready to inaugurate the province's first Communist force and to take over two whole counties in the north Shaanxi mountains as a base. Government troops sent against him changed sides; legends flew of Liu's "invulnerability to bullets." By 1932 the revolutionary army was occupying eleven counties, and in the following year the Shaanxi Soviet was proclaimed.[59]

"In the mind of the average Chinese of the eastern provinces," wrote an American observer in 1912, "...North Shensi [Shaanxi] is a nest of plunderers lost in a wilderness; and South Shensi...little better."[60] From the beginnings of the movement, consequently, Liu Zhidan was forced to rely (perhaps, like Mao Zedong, not altogether reluctantly) on north Shaanxi's bandit subculture for his major source of recruits. The tactics that the movement adopted, moreover—taking from the rich to give to the poor, raiding and retreat to the hills, passage in and out of the military—were identical to those of the outlaws who had occupied Shaanxi's hills for centuries. Liu himself, like He Long and Zhu De, was a member of the Elder Brothers Society, always strong in the region and a necessary ally in any militant cause. Even as late as 1931, when the army (600 strong, but only half of them armed) adopted the title of "North-West Anti-Imperialist Allied Army," it was said that the Red Army's flag could not be raised because of the preponderance of bandits. The peasants who joined were acting out the pent-up fury of generations as they killed landlords, tax collectors, and local officials, carried off rich captives for ransom, and "expropriated the expropriators" much like bandits anywhere. To those observing this behavior it was virtually impossible to distinguish the "guerrillas" from any other bandit gang.[61]

The biggest difficulty lay in carrying out land redistribution in favor of the poor peasants and landless villagers. There were obvious reasons for *not* doing so, for the area's reconquest by government or warlord troops was always an imminent possibility, and defenseless poor peasants naturally held back for fear of reprisals. Instead, the partisans applied themselves to problems that they saw as more pressing: famine-induced starvation, high taxes, and inextricable debt. As a result they came to appear not as modern-day revolutionaries but as akin to the bandit heroes of legend: seizing grain and other produce from the landlords for redistribution to the poor, who were thereby freed of the fear of retaliation. No doubt such tactics earned the partisans rapid acceptance among the tradition-conscious peasants of the northwest; but from a revolutionary point of view the problem was that the peasants themselves were excluded from the struggle. They were able to sit back and passively receive redistributed grain without becoming actively involved in the movement to change social relations. Unable to guarantee military security—as in Jiangxi, a series of defeats had seen the base switched from one border region to another—the Shaanxi Communist partisans were forced to follow a line hardly distinguishable from that of social bandits. As late as 1934, when a base area was consolidated in a well-known outlaw hideout, the army was being reinforced by bandit refugees from Shanxi governor Yan Xishan's current anti-opium drive. By that time, however, the partisans had grown in numbers and were gradually creating the basis for a genuine revolutionary soviet that, by bringing security to the villages within its control, would make a radical program of peasant mobilization possible for the first time in the Shaanxi movement's history.[62] With the arrival of the Long March from Jiangxi in 1936, north Shaanxi's role as a revolutionary base was confirmed, and it went on to become the center of Communist operations against Japan after 1937.

Nevertheless, the movement's successful metamorphosis owed a great deal to Shaanxi's being a power vacuum because of its remoteness from major political centers, the same precondition that underlay the region's age-old bandit subculture. The Communists, that is, given the right political conditions, were able to build upon the tradition established by bandit-rebels of the past. The history of the Eyuwan Soviet, seen in these terms, was rather different.

The creation of what was to be the Eyuwan Soviet by Communist military units fleeing Jiang Jieshi's anti-Red purge was another example of the obligatory reliance on bandit subcultures to rest the "buttocks" of the revolutionary movement. The name "Eyuwan" was formed by combining the ancient titles of the three provinces of Hubei, Henan, and Anhui. Located athwart the traditional bandit country straddling the mountainous region where the three provincial boundaries converged, the Eyuwan Soviet after its formal inauguration in 1930 was regarded as the "most important Communist political organization north of the [Yangzi]."[63] For five years, from 1927 until the summer of 1932, the Communists gradually expanded the area under their control until, under pressure from almost half a million government troops, they were forced to undertake what became the first "Long March." During that time they fought off four major suppression campaigns and increased the population of the soviet area from the inhabitants of a few villages in north Hubei to a total of two million people spread over three provinces. By early 1932 all mail and freight traffic through the region passed on the sufferance of Red troops unless escorted by well-armed regular government soldiers.[64]

In the early stages of the soviet the Communists drew upon the same traditional sources of recruits that the Shaanxi movement was tapping farther to the west: poverty, disaffected troops, and of course bandits. This part of Henan, according to American consular reports, currently sheltered "some 100,000 bandits, mostly troop remnants or deserters equipped with rifles." It was a force, however disorganized, that the Communists could ignore only at their peril; by 1930 large numbers of these bandits had been "communized," and the remainder had joined the forces of reaction or disappeared.[65]

The same Henan party branch decision of July 1928 that formalize the decision to create a local soviet also made the following statement:

Bandits constitute a very great multitude in Honan. The bandits are dis-possessed, landless peasants.... Our party should wage the following pro-paganda to the bandits to call upon them to participate in the peasant struggle: "Return the land to the peasants, soldiers, and revolutionary bandits," "Oppose sending the bandits to death, oppose regrouping by the leaders." The bandits are the lumpen proletariat, [but] they possess various accumulated habits. In the struggle for the land revolution they can be considered merely an auxiliary force.... We can never rely on them without spurring [*sic*] the rank-and-file. At the same time, we should never attack the rank-and-file bandits who do not impede the land revolution....[66]

The Red Armies of the Eyuwan Soviet, as in Shaanxi, themselves behaved like social bandits, robbing the rich to support their activities and so on. When attacking a district they would take only what they needed, and leave after killing certain "enemies of the people" such as county magistrates, government officials, police chiefs, and tax offi-cials.[67]

About March 1, 1931, some 10,000 ex-bandit soldiers of the 12th Henan Division mutinied at the important railway junction of Xinandian on the Beijing-Hankou line, following the deaths of Fan Zhongxiu and Wang Laowu. The next day they captured Liulin, a city near the Red districts, which apparently sent several thousand troops to support them. Many of the government contingents sent to suppress them also changed sides, including one whole division commanded by the former Henan warlord Yue Weijun, which defected with its entire strength of 10,000 men. Although Liulin was retaken by the government on March 5, the incident was a major windfall for the Communist armies since many of the mutineers and defecting troops took refuge in the Soviet.[68]

Poverty added the final ingredient for the growth of Red power in Eyuwan. The independent newspaper *Dagong bao* reported during the winter of 1931–32 that "appalling suffering"owing to poverty was driv-ing people into the hands of the Communists, and warned that "if fun-damental assistance is not given quickly it is to be feared that the whole province [of Henan] will become a second Kiangsi [Jiangxi]."[69]

The similarity with Shaanxi is striking: lack of security making it impossible to effect land redistribution, and peasants resisting Com-munist programs for fear of reprisals. Atrocities by government troops were appalling, villages being bombed merely on suspicion of being Red. The same General Zhang Fang who had played a hero's role for the Republic in 1911 (and then betrayed Bai Lang soon afterwards) now reappeared as a government general fighting the Communists with a reputation for atrocities as bad as any ex-warlord general.[70] As a result of this insecurity, right up to the very end of the Eyuwan Soviet there was no concerted attempt to redistribute the land, though the alienation of many local residents caused by the social-bandit-type policies pursued in the early days did force the Communists to switch their emphasis to agricultural production and local defense, a change that apparently attracted some support from rich peasants and even gentry figures.[71] By and large, however, as in other areas where the gentry kept a firm grip on local control, the peasant movement floundered until the Red Army arrived in sufficient force to counteract gentry power altogether. Often it was organizations like the Red Spears that became the cutting edge of landlord retribution, even while some Red Spear units were still serving as the mainstay of the Red regime.[72]

Like the Shaanxi movement, Eyuwan was forced to rely upon the personnel, tactics, and base areas of local bandits and soldier-bandits, and to adapt to the sociopolitical conditions that went with them. The number of those bandits made the formation of an irregular armed force comparatively easy, and bandits who could not be recruited were probably eliminated along with local warlords and other minor officials through mutual nonaggression pacts.[73] However, the ultimate fragility of the area—despite its having been almost impregnable as a bandit hideout for centuries—was shown by the speed with which it fell to a concerted government onslaught. Part of the reason bandits had been able to survive in isolated areas like Eyuwan was, of course, official reluctance to mount strong extermination campaigns, but such was not the case once the "bandits" became an openly political movement. Both Shaanxi and Eyuwan demonstrated to the Communists that going beyond the strategies of bandits to create a stable revolutionary base area in such a region was a very difficult undertaking.

The key to winning bandits' respect was establishing military dominance over them, and the Communists had to confront this problem just as their predecessors had. A good example was the case of Wang Zuo and Yuan Wencai. Though they controlled only a few hundred poorly armed peasants, Wang and Yuan still outnumbered the battered remnants of the Red Army when it sought to take refuge in the bandit hideout of Jinggangshan in 1928. For the first month they demanded (as a similar gang had done farther north in Eyuwan) that the Red Army be put under their command rather than vice versa. The superior organization of the Communists, however, convinced them—or, more likely, their followers—of the need to cooperate if only to avoid annihilation, and they finally agreed under certain conditions to be absorbed into its ranks. The granting of commissions mollified their hurt pride, and the two chiefs eventually became commander and battalion commander, respectively, in the Red Army. Both were in charge of their original followers, though industrial workers and political commissars were mixed in to improve discipline. Wang was subsequently involved in party committee work, and Yuan was for some time ranked alongside general Peng Dehuai as a commander of Red forces in Hunan.[74]

Despite these hopeful beginnings, both Wang and Yuan defected within two years. Wang, already under a cloud because of numerous breaches of discipline, was chosen because of his familiarity with the local terrain to stay behind as a rear guard with Peng Dehuai when the base was moved farther south at the end of 1929. After Peng, under pressure from government troops, led his men south to rejoin the main force, Wang and his old followers remained behind as bandits. Later, interestingly enough, his followers rebelled and handed him back to the Communists, who promptly shot him for desertion. Yuan Wencai, too, was eventually shot—but by one of his old band while he was trying to lead it over to the government. The Communists subsequently established the policy that bandits might still be taken into the Red Army, but instead of operating as a separate unit they should be amalgamated following rectification.* This was a new departure in the recruitment of irregular forces, and marked the real birth of the Red Army as a revolutionary fighting force.

The local success of this new policy was soon noted by an observer of Peng Pai's peasant movement in the Haifeng-Lufeng area of coastal Guangdong: "... with their wounds smarting and their ranks filled with the rag-and-bobtail of soldiery and outlaw bandits, the first Red groups carried on their fight against the existing order with an unrestrained savagery that exercised but little discrimination in its incidence." By 1930, however: "The communists today employ means other than violence and death. For two years Hai Fong and Lon Fong were occupied by brigands and terror reigned supreme.... However, for some months... the communists have changed their methods.... The brigands which they command are very well disciplined, if one is to believe P'ong K'i Piao, who is in command of the suppression of brigandage...."[75]

Experiences like these underwrote Mao Zedong's determination to stand up to party reluctance to distinguish between bandits and the guerrilla outfits he recommended. The party's Central Committee had written to Zhu De in December 1927 accusing Mao of "behaving like the bandit heroes of Water Margin, sallying forth to carry out heroic exploits on behalf of the masses, instead of rousing the masses to under-

---

*Schram 1966: 138; Smedley 1934: 140–41, 109; Clubb 1968: 69. See also Lötveit 1970: 168. The Taipings had had similar problems with the numerous bandit gangs that locked to join them in the early stages of the movement. Rather than fall afoul of the trict Taiping disciplinary code, many of these preferred to defect to the government side, seeing more prospects under lax officials than under self-righteous rebel chiefs (Curwen 972: 69; Jen Yu-wen 1973: 68).

take a spontaneous armed insurrection." Mao's model for the guerrilla unit, however, though superficially resembling that of bandit gangs, was an integrated structure of leadership: that is, "centralized strategic command and decentralized command in campaigns and battles." The strategy, however, required overall comprehension at all levels of the army of all the issues at stake in the struggle—hence a need also for "intensified education."[76] These were the crucial factors distinguishing Mao's revolutionary guerrilla program from the activities of a bandit gang. Whereas purely local or short-term considerations could convince bandits to seek temporary détente with the enemy, for instance, such a policy was inadmissible for guerrillas until its long-range implications had been analyzed and the most opportune moment for its implementation selected. Whereas bandit subchiefs had always retained the option of unilateral action when their own interests so dictated, Mao's integrated structure of leadership made such instability a thing of the past.

In this way, understanding derived from experience enabled the Communist movement to arrive at a happy compromise concerning bandit recruitment. Though it took full account of the suspicions of those least inclined to give bandits the benefit of the doubt, the policy was nevertheless founded upon the sanguine expectations of people like Mao Zedong. By 1944 an American diplomatic official stationed in Yan'an could report of the Communist leaders he interviewed that "They found it very funny to talk about the old days when they had a price on their heads, or when they were chasing and kidnapping missionaries."[77]

After the full-scale Japanese invasion of July 1937, the bandit issue became more pressing than ever before. The sudden withdrawal of government administrators from eastern China to Sichuan in 1938, the large numbers of fleeing or disbanded government troops (who often sold their weapons to keep themselves alive), and the agricultural chaos created by the fighting led to a resurgence of banditry in many parts of the country. The chance to use these gangs to raise havoc behind an enemy's lines was not ignored by any of those involved, and within a short time bandits became the targets of mobilization efforts by all three contenders for power: the government, the Communists, and the Japanese.

How a gang reacted to the incursion of Japanese forces depended first upon the inclinations of its chief. In Manchuria, where banditry and local armed defense were permanently intertwined in a long resistance tradition, socially conscious local chiefs were the first to resist. In adjoining Shanxi, too, which had also been under prolonged Japanese military pressure, many bandits apparently hated the Japanese and "were willing to combine fighting them with a little looting-for-a-living" on the side.[78] In other regions, most chiefs reacted pragmatically—and Communist Party organizer Liu Shaoqi sarcastically characterized them as the "resist-Japan-and-get-rich bandits": "Some bandit groups are sincerely interested in resisting Japan, but most raise the banner of resistance only to camouflage their true intentions of plunder. Others actually fight on the side of the enemy."[79] For bandits, however, survival loomed as supremely important, and political considerations were an almost impossible luxury. In the face of a seemingly unstoppable Japanese advance, the Communists, too, were forced to be pragmatic: "If local bandits active in the enemy-occupied area are adequate for the task of wrecking the enemy's order, and if the anti-Japanese forces are relatively weak there, then we should persuade and unite with the bandits."[80] By and large, however, the level of politicization among the bandits was low: most reached an agreement with the nearest power center, becoming either Japanese puppet forces, government guerrillas, or Red Army irregulars.

Although the government and the Japanese were content to leave the bandits to their own predatory devices once their services had been successfully purchased, the Communists' approach was radically different. From the point of view of their revolutionary vision, and as a result of their being the minority force among the three contenders for power, the Communists could not regard bandits lightly. Both to prevent their being bought out by the reaction and to reduce the numerical imbalance between the Communists and their opponents, it was necessary to develop a creative bandit policy. Where the Communists possessed military superiority they could seek public support by suppressing bandits (as long as the latter enjoyed no public support of their own). Gangs that had already established some sort of local ties, however, as well as those with links to the government or the Japanese, created difficulties. Under such circumstances the Communists preferred a political solution to a military one. On the one hand, local communities were encouraged to organize to defend themselves against bandits (instead of accepting them as masters) as a means of raising local consciousness; on the other, a direct political approach to the bandits was attempted. A chief was offered the choice between coexistence on the Communists' terms—no collusion with the Japanese, no anti-Communist activity, no predatory activity within Communist territory—and moving the gang's operations into enemy-occupied areas. However, the "very suspicious and belligerent" nature of bandit chiefs meant that they could never be forced to reorganize. Cadres were accordingly instructed to be patient and show respect for bandit life-styles.[81]

The early years of the war saw numerous attempts by brave volunteers to penetrate and win over bandit gangs in various parts of the country. The account that follows of one of those attempts reveals as much about the attitudes and behavior of bandits during the Resistance War as about the successful tactics of the Communists. It also shows that bandits had not made any substantial progress since Wu Cangzhou and Liu Qunren ascended Yangshan to court Wang Tianzong some thirty years before.

Early in 1938 a group of west Shandong students surrendered voluntarily to a local bandit gang and applied for permission to join its rank and file. The gang, some 4,000 strong, had opportunistically adopted the title of "North China Anti-Japanese Alliance." Joining it was not easy, especially for a group of young students. The first problem they had to deal with was the suspicion of the gang's top echelons, who ordered them kept in solitary confinement for three days and constantly questioned them about their true motives. Knowing that their first task was to persuade the chiefs to trust them, the students adopted time-honored techniques of total obedience to all instructions combined with gentle flattery. Like Liu Qunren and Wu Cangzhou at Yangshan, they were also careful to present themselves in a light the bandits could understand by maintaining the distinction between leaders and led within their own group. Insisting that they had surrendered to the gang because of its patriotic attitude, they declared that "if bandits are anti-Japanese, we are willing to become anti-Japanese bandits."

With the chiefs' egos thus soothed, the group was at last allowed a little more freedom of movement, and its members scattered quietly among the gang's subsections to begin the slow process of conversion.* After reluctantly taking part in several armed actions against local peasant militias, they found themselves in a position to point out the bandits' inefficient methods and organization, beginning with the high rate of injuries and low rewards, without seeming to be forcing their own opinions upon them. While sharing the bandits' hard lives, they also brightened up the hours of inactivity by composing songs, plays, and stories based on local melodies and folk knowledge but subtly adapted to convey a message of cooperation between bandits and peasants against the Japanese. It was a message that no self-respecting hero could ignore, and by reducing the amount of sheer wanton robbery the students' first task was achieved. A clear demonstration of their success was given

---

*Among the gang were evidently some former members of the Manchurian Anti-Japan Volunteers. They may well have been participants in Kohinata Hakurō's "Great *Bazoku* Migration" of five years before, many of whom had returned to banditry when they were unable to make a living as farmers. Such men could not be considered pure examples of Liu Shaoqi's "resist-Japan-and-get-rich bandits."

when the chief drove off an agent of the Japanese sent to win him over with promises of a cash reward.

Having come so far, the next problem was how to induce the gang to surrender formally to the Communist forces and be instated as an official guerrilla unit. For the rank and file this posed no problem, since they were concerned merely with survival, but the chiefs presented two major difficulties: first, their desire to "become a big official and get rich"; and second, their excessive confidence in their own strength. To get around both these problems at the same time the students adopted a mixture of sweet talk and hard politics. By allowing the gang a glimpse of nearby Communist forces they were able to induce the subchiefs— who had less prestige at stake—to talk the main chief around. To mollify the latter still further they held out the possibility of personal enrichment even after the gang's surrender, in terms he could readily understand:

Although the political worker can't make you a big official or bestow great wealth upon you . . . at least after being reorganized there will no longer be the problem of food. Also, though the political worker is low-ranking and poor, this is not necessarily a permanent state of affairs. At the moment he is resisting Japan . . . but in the future there are good prospects of his becoming an official. If we surrender to him and resist Japan together with him, after victory, when he has become a big official, of course our own status won't continue to be as low as it is now.

After three months of similar persuasion the students were finally able to persuade the chief to lead his followers over to the Communists and be reorganized as guerrillas.[82]

The condition for such alliances, in principle at least, was that the bandits adhere to certain rules of behavior, such as abstaining from atrocities and ceasing to levy protection fees. In return they were given material support. In this way the Communists were able to gain popular acceptance without alienating the bandits themselves.[83] Unfortunately, such severe conditions, however necessary, were often most effective in persuading the bandits to join the reaction. One chief, for example, tested and rejected by the Communists, was subsequently taken on by the government as an anti-Red commander, with the promise of control over all of western Fujian if he moved against his former comrades. Many Communists with responsibility for local security were forced to bear the brunt of popular wrath when the terms of the alliance were broken by the bandits. Some gangs rejected the agents sent to win them over, preferring to cause trouble and so win enrollment in the government army. The latter, needless to say, could usually be relied upon to accept the bandits without conditions, and to lavish upon them the grandiose titles and territorial control they generally cherished. It was not unusual for chiefs to accept the Communists' terms but flout them in practice; neither was it unknown for gangs to fly red flags and begin looting in the name of the Red Army.[84]

By the early 1940's, the Communists had learned to be hardheaded despite their confessed need of the bandits. The last straw was the betrayal by a Fujian chief of a local cadre who had even sworn blood brotherhood with him. As a result of this betrayal, nine other Party cadres were also caught and executed, an event that provoked the following warning from a high-ranking Party official:

> As for the work on bandits, particularly those with political ties [with our enemies], I have always told you to "use them, but never trust them." When we try to use them, we should remember that we will have no trouble only if we have sufficient strength to control them. Their progress [to Communism] can only be slowly, gradually accomplished over a long [period of] time.

To those who still clung optimistically to the heritage of Mao Zedong's early romanticism, another local organizer reiterated firmly: "Despite their peasant origins, bandits change their political character the moment they undertake looting. Some even collaborate with local bullies to repress their fellow peasants. They are a reactionary social force."[85] The gulf between the Communists and the bandits was thus not one that could be bridged easily. The first priority for the former was therefore to consolidate their own strength so as to make bargaining with the bandits unnecessary.

As the scales became weighted more and more in the Communists' favor, bandits who interfered with the mass mobilization of the peasants against Japan began to find themselves condemned as "unpatriotic elements" and consequently found it more difficult than before to gain popular sympathy. With the peasants in arms to defend themselves, predatory activities became a risky business. What was happening was that the social environment that created the wherewithal for banditry—a defenseless, alienated, isolated peasantry—was gradually being removed. When things went well the bandits could be offered an amnesty and provided with an alternative channel for their aggressive energies, a chance to fight for social gains rather than mere survival. Even where the social gains in themselves were not attractive, a chief's political ambition could be exploited to bring him or her over to the side of a strong Communist force. As a popular representative that chief then had the responsibility to ensure that predatory activities ceased, and could be punished for failing to live up to that responsibility.[86]

Bandits who joined the Communists in the 1940's found themselves operating under far stricter conditions than those of the previous decade. Most significant was the destruction of the group ties between chiefs and followers. Unlike the early Jinggangshan days, now when bandits were admitted into the Red Army they were scattered throughout the ranks of ordinary soldiers, with political officers to keep them under permanent surveillance. No chiefs were allowed to control their old followers. To ensure discipline, bandits recruited into the guerrilla columns were sent immediately to combat zones.[87] (Presumably this policy was additionally helpful in eliminating a large number of the bandits, whose most useful role thus became once again that of providing cannon fodder in place of the regular troops.) Bandits admitted to militia groups, meanwhile, were obliged to hand their weapons over to politically reliable peasants.

Although bandits who continued to operate inside Communist territory were ruthlessly suppressed (including the notorious Liu Guitang, or Liu Heiqi),[88] many, following the traditional pattern, were able to set up their own spheres of control in the twilight zone between Communist and government or Japanese positions. Bands like these, far from being suppressed, were encouraged so long as they did not attack Communist forces, and many became an effective guerrilla-type fifth column behind enemy lines. Those who accepted the Communists' conditions were even given military rank, a sure way of gaining their support provided the enemy did not improve upon the offer.[89]

By the end of the Resistance War the contrast between Communist-controlled areas and the rest of the country had become startling. In the government areas, predatory banditry actually increased during the war. Harsh military conscription quotas left farms without labor, heavy taxation and merciless grain requisitions caused widespread impoverishment and frequent famine, and half-starved soldiers deserted in huge numbers. Military suppression merely heightened the problem, and most of the old "white areas" the Communists inherited after 1945 were rife with predatory activity. In the Communist areas, on the other hand, reports both from the Communists and from travelers passing through had by 1944 ceased to mention banditry at all, even in the "nest of plunderers" of northern Shaanxi.[90]

## *After the Revolution*

All revolutionary movements, local as well as national, tend to go through a dialectical process of expansion and consolidation. In the expansive phase, bandits' disruptive energy and iconoclastic impulses have an important role to play (with reservations as noted already). In the consolidation or bureaucratic phase, especially after a Leninist-style putsch as the new revolutionary authorities seek to establish their legitimacy, such energies are counterproductive. Bandits who have not been

"reformed" are mostly left isolated and helpless, targets for the enticements of the revanchist old guard, and always a potential motive force
for the next revolution to come.

Behind this dialectic is the fact that revolutions rarely or never achieve
all their aims. It is not easy to sustain revolutionary energy for long
periods unbroken, and the usual tendency in the aftermath of a Leninist
revolution that has achieved local or national power is for old and new
oppressions to coalesce. Once a revolution is seen to have achieved even
its minimal demands, momentum decreases as the natural conservatism
of many revolutionaries prods them into defending those achievements
rather than expanding the movement's scope still further. The first concern of the new authorities, moreover, from the center down to the new
local functionaries, is stability—defending their newly won power. The
elimination of bandits, with their capacity to cause trouble and their
openness to manipulation, comes before settling the local injustices that
created them.

"After the revolution" means nothing for the ordinary people as long
as landlords remain landlords and officials remain officials, as in post-
1911 China, or as long as hunger pangs remain unassuaged, as was sometimes the case even after 1949. In such circumstances the revolution itself
becomes an enemy, along with those who support it and now seek
to defend it. In short, "after the revolution" can also be "before the
revolution" for some people, depending on their relationship to that
revolution. Banditry "after the revolution" is as natural a response to
oppressive conditions as it was before, but this time the new authorities,
instead of harnessing it to their own purposes, have to crush it in the
name of their claim to legitimacy. In the process "revolutionary armies"
become "bandit-suppression armies," former "heroes" become "villains"
or "bandits," those who prefer to remain "popular heroes" rather than
become public bureaucrats are cruelly slaughtered as "traitors," and the
world turns upside-down once more.

Not surprisingly, then, liberation of the country in 1949 did not eliminate reports of banditry. The objects of the new government's extermination campaigns, however, were not only bandits as we have come
to know them in these pages, but all forms of armed resistance, including
Red Spear chapters as well as former Nationalist guerrillas. In short:
"After twenty years in which they themselves had been often known as
'bandits' . . . the Communists now used the same indiscriminate term to
describe all forms of armed opposition against them." [91]

Shades of *Animal Farm* indeed. According to Communist usage after
1949, the term "bandit" (*tufei*) applied to all forms of armed resistance in
a given area after it had been "liberated," with the result that it became
as difficult as ever to get a clear picture of who all these "bandits"—

more than a million were reported suppressed by May 1951—really were.[92]

For all the achievements of the Communists, a bandit tradition is not destroyed simply by removing the physical factors behind it. Henan, with its age-old bandit subculture, was one of the most Maoist of all provinces after 1949, but it also saw reversions to banditry as a stock response to renewed conditions of poverty and insecurity. The first was the formation in 1955 of the Jiangsu-Shandong-Henan-Anhui Border Region Guerrilla Column,[93] reminiscent of the high-flown titles assumed by the soldier-bandits thirty years before. Five years later local administration was rocked once again by peasants who took direct action to resist the threat of starvation.

Widespread crop failures in 1959–60, together with rushed implementation of the communization process, had by the summer of 1960 again brought forth a combination of economic disaster and deep popular discontent. Though many peasants had perforce adopted the time-honored strategy of flight, as always there were those who preferred to fight. Now as ever before, in the words of the old proverb, "hunger and cold bred the bandit spirit." The outcome was the "Henan revolt."

In Xinyang, Kaifeng, and other regions, peasants with access to weapons as members of the militia organized themselves into gangs and engaged in "armed banditry." In Shangcheng, the militia leaders of thirteen communes led armed groups to search houses, rape women, and rob peasants at gunpoint. Though details of the disturbances are not available, the government obviously thought them serious enough to send in troops and launch an all-out drive to "suppress the counter-revolutionaries and pacify the countryside" (expressions with an ironically familiar ring). In some places the militias had to be forcibly disarmed and their weapons given to trusted peasants in a replay of the party's bandit policy of twenty years before. In January 1961 even Mao Zedong would finally heave a sigh of relief: "The situation was grave. . . . [Xinyang], Honan, *which we were all worried about,* has now become a good area, a revolutionary area that has turned over a new leaf. . . ."

The subsequent report on the affair by General Fu Qiudao, commander-in-chief of the national militia system, placed most of the blame on the rapid and undiscriminating expansion of the provincial militias in the wake of the outbreak of hostilities with Taiwan in 1958. Many of the cadres were from "well-to-do middle peasant, . . . landlord, rich peasant, counterrevolutionary, bad, and rightist elements." In one commune in Jiayi county, the militia commander and other officials were all "descended from ruffians, bandits, puppet troops, and rightist elements." Local people referred to the militia in such terms as "gangsters," "little bosses," "bandit kings," and "living bandits." In one county during the height of the crisis a group of militia members even set up a machine gun post on a key highway to hold up passersby.[94]

Fu Qiudao's description of the people who made up the recalcitrant militia units in Henan at this time is so all-embracing as to offer little chance of analysis. Though his allegation that people of the richer classes loyal to the old regime had wormed their way into leadership of the militia may have been true, political opposition to or resentment of the authorities has always been a feature of bandit chiefs' origins. What is more important is that, although the reaction of the majority to the disasters was flight to avoid starvation, the strong-willed took apparently instinctively to banditry. This situation, coupled with the revelations of the violent reality of the 1966 Cultural Revolution, suggests that bandit tactics will continue to be a standard reaction to turmoil and insecurity for a long time to come. A 1967 report, for example, referred to a "handful of class enemies...engaged in corruption, theft, and speculation" who had set up a gambling racket in one production brigade:

> Later these bad people hid themselves in a small valley on the border of Chekiang [Zhejiang] and Kiangsi [Jiangxi], and they thought it was safe there. When the masses of Chekiang province went to arrest them, it took them half a minute to run over to the Kiangsi side, where they claimed to belong to Kiangsi. When the masses of Kiangsi came to arrest them, it took them half a minute to run over to the Chekiang side, where they claimed to belong to Chekiang.[95]

The time-honored practice of border-hopping thus remains much alive.

The social historian Sa Mengwu, in an essay concerning the relationship between the *Shuihu zhuan* and Chinese society at large, has distinguished two ethical systems in China: that of the gentry, stressing loyalty to family and superiors, that is, Confucianism; and that of the underworld, idealized in the *Shuihu zhuan*, based on blood brotherhood and stressing loyalty to friends, mutual aid, and indebtedness arising from favors rendered.[96] The heroic element in the novel can hardly fail to appeal to anyone who reads it, and it is unimaginable that Red Guards, aware of its significance in Mao Zedong's own political development, were unmoved by its appeal. As they boldly took on the entire Chinese government party bureaucracy, the similarity of their position to that of the lonely outpost of righteousness at Liangshanpo, and the assurance that their cause, like that of the *Shuihu* heroes, would eventually triumph, must have had a deep impact on the thinking of many young people. Bandits in the past reacted to an uncaring establishment and an arrogant bureaucracy by forming their own organizations based on the underworld's code of values. In the future, should the government stray too far from its socialist ideals, renewed reports of "bad elements," "counterrevolutionaries," and border-hopping, as the state seeks successively t smother its enemies' aspirations, may well indicate that that code, albeit in more modern guise, has found new acceptance.

## Conclusion

When bandits and revolutionaries came together, it was for both sides an alliance of convenience. Despite certain factors that could provide the basis for a temporary coalescence, the fundamental difference in their perspectives made a lasting relationship impossible. Only when one side was persuaded to join the other in substance as well as form was there any chance of transforming the nature of the alliance. In practice it was always the bandit side that made the necessary adjustments, usually as a result of the balance of power, though the bandits' new identity rarely outlasted for long the restoration of stable conditions. Though their revolutionary allies often complained that bandits were wont to renege on agreements when it suited them, from the bandits' point of view the same could be said of revolutionaries once the need for bandit allies had passed. Admired for their fighting ability and capacity to hold down at least their own locality, at the same time bandits were regarded by all but the most romantic idealists as mere auxiliaries to the main revolutionary movement. The use of bandits was a stopgap in the absence of an organized revolutionary network, in the same way that warlords recruited bandits in lieu of formally trained soldiers. In Henan, for example, despite the time-tested bandit subculture for which the province was known, there was no comprehensive attempt to consolidate an alternative power center before the establishment of the Eyuwan Soviet.

Unlike their predecessors, the Communists sought not only to employ but also to adapt the methods and resources of the bandits, meanwhile seeking by the application of radical organizational principles to wield bandits into a cohesive force and so erase the bandit-revolutionary distinction altogether. In contrast to official reports that endeavored to place the Communists alongside local bandits and secret societies as just one of the nuisances troubling the central authorities, the Communists saw themselves as being in the process of building a new society. Whereas the authorities saw their alliances with and absorbing of such irregular forces merely as evidence of their urge for total control over illegitimate violence, the Communists saw that control as part of a strategy designed to turn all rural fighters into agents of social change.

Other things being equal, this vision, put into practice effectively, would have worked. Unfortunately, the very condition that most typically produced banditry—the fragmentation of power—tended to dangle so many different opportunities before bandit chiefs that few could settle down to one option for long. Economic crisis, another key factor, also tended to create fresh bandits to replace those who had been successfully wooed. In the end, as the Communists found through a process of trial and error, the most effective method turned out after all to be to wield a big stick and to be prepared to use it when necessary. This was language the bandits understood. The unfortunate effect was to make any alliances that were realized more transient than ever.

# CHAPTER TEN

# Conclusion

LOOMING LIKE a dark shadow through the pages of historical writing from antiquity to the present, China's bandits have by sheer weight of numbers refused to be ignored. And yet, for reasons this book has sought to point out, they have remained among the most elusive characters of all. Isolated both geographically and emotionally from those who set themselves up as framers of public opinion or overseers of social mores, bandits have generally been rejected as cruel, self-seeking, ruthless men bent on rapine and murder, robbing those least able to defend themselves and fleeing like curs from retribution. There were, of course, bandits who behaved in just such a way, but to tar them all with the same brush is both insensitive and shortsighted social analysis, and a calumny upon those for whom banditry was the result not of bloody-mindedness or sadistic whimsy, but of extreme frustration and anger or hunger, involving a grim and painful existence in the constant shadow of the ultimate penalty.

With respect for both the conditions that produced and characterized banditry and the hopes and fears of those drawn into it, this book has sought to explore the subject not only by pointing out its relationship to social and political realities in the twentieth-century Chinese countryside, but also by describing, as far as sources allow, the emotional patterns it encouraged. In short, this has been a study not merely of banditry but also of *bandits*; not merely of bandit suppression and pacification, but also of the fear and despair of those to whom the elimination of banditry meant the difference between life and death; not only of the violent scourge a bandit gang could become in the villages of the interior, but also of the implications of that violence for both executors and victims.

In terms of fundamental motivations, patterns of banditry throughout China demonstrated great similarity. On the surface, bandits adapted to local conditions by developing water-based techniques, mountain hideouts, highway robbery, permanent movement between mobile bases, border-hopping strategies, protection rackets, and so on as required. In the name of survival whole villages might turn to attacking travelers as a permanent sideline. Border communities might gain reputations as dens of predatory raiders, coastal villages as nests of wide-ranging pirates.

What all these areas of banditry had in common was the fact that they were peripheral, in the sense of being least eligible for official handouts and attention. The hills of west and south Henan, the loess ravines of north Shaanxi, the ecologically unstable Huaibei region, the mountainous border between Hunan and Jiangxi, the volatile Manchurian frontier zone, and the other areas singled out for analysis in this study were all traditional centers of illicit or insurgent activity, dominated by the struggle over scarce material resources. The power relationships thrown up by that struggle, the consequent preeminence of the aggressive instinct, and the tempting appearance of better-endowed regions adjacent to the peripheral zones provided a constant theme for bandits over the generations, and were an important factor in the militarization of Chinese politics in the early twentieth century.

Bandits and banditry, however negative or insignificant they may have seemed to lawmakers or opinion leaders at the national level, were a fact of life not only for their potential supporters the poor, but also for their bitter enemies the rich. How each side adapted to the bandits' presence, and how the bandits responded to the expectations of those around them, were crucial factors affecting the quality of life in a given locality. Even in the chaotic years of the Chinese Republic, dominated by lurid tales of bandit atrocities and warlord conflicts, a certain order nevertheless existed at least below the level of the county seat. As the capture of whites for ransom became almost commonplace in some notorious parts of China, Western observers began to build "The Chinese Bandit" into a figure of awe. In a leader entitled "The Peasant and His Master," the Shanghai *North China Herald*, reflecting the paranoia of the foreign community in a world slipping away from them faster than they could comprehend, even acclaimed the bandit as the supreme ruler of China.[1] Reality was far closer, as we have seen, to the image suggested by the common expression "officials and bandits share control" (*guan fei fenzhi*). Intended to be ironical, this expression often accurately summed up a local situation in which the nominal authority of the official side was balanced against the effective if limited control of local bandits, a relationship from which each side could draw benefits.

Bandit activities were frequently the precursors of rebel movements, growing and combining until a leader emerged with a vision that transcended local horizons. Mao Zedong's endorsement of China's history of peasant rebellions as "without parallel in world history" and the frequently heard dismissals of China as "the world's number one bandit country"[2] had more in common than has generally been recognized. Yet we have to beware of confusing our categories. Banditry *could* be an expression of protest, at least on an individual level, but in many cases it was no more than a reaction to the destruction of human relationships and the collapse of social conventions in a world racked by poverty and conflict. Troubled times naturally provided the perfect opportunity for those in a rebellious frame of mind, but, equally important, they also brought about a moral collapse in which adherence to traditional forms became less imperative. Even in untroubled times, banditry furnished an outlet for high spirits, but it also catered for those who bore a grudge, and for those whose sadism made cooperative life in the village impossible. In troubled times these two types tended to increase.

Though accepting that "social bandits" were less than typical, and acknowledging the role of sadism and demoralization in the everyday makeup of bandits, we also have to understand that one's view of bandits depended on who one was.* A landlord or rich peasant was hardly likely to see in them what the poor peasant saw. Memories of Bai Lang's rebellion, for example, were clearly colored by class distinctions: the only informant to speak critically of the discipline of Bai's army to local researchers in 1959 was later found to be a member of an ex-landlord family; the others, all peasants or former landless laborers, described it as impeccable.[3] The word "banditry" was one of the formulations that helped disguise the reality of life in the countryside, founded as it was on the unequal distribution of wealth and power. Whereas a landlord's seizure of 50 percent or even 75 percent of a tenant's crop as rent was accepted as normal, the attempts of hungry and desperate peasants to retrieve what had been taken were condemned as banditry, and the peasants themselves subject to ruthless "pacification." As the Red Army general Zhu De remarked to Agnes Smedley, "banditry is a class question."[4]

On the other hand, it is clearly impossible to accept unequivocally He Long's definition of banditry as "acts of bravery by fearless people who were simple, loved preeminence, had real fiber, and valued friendship."[5] A poverty-stricken peasant society in which the fight for survival had become routine would hardly produce such perfect specimens with regularity. The punishments reserved for the bandits' ransom victims, even allowing for journalistic exaggeration, were sadistic enough to

---

* A popular song that circulated during the Nian Rebellion went as follows: "When the Nian kill, they kill the wicked; the poor folk they love tenderly./The poor say always that the Nian are beyond compare;/The rich cry that they will go to Hell." (Jenner 1970b: 218.)

dispel any illusions of an untainted "greenwood ethic." The cynical and un–Robin Hood–like realism of much bandit slang helps balance any tendency to stress too strongly the social over the antisocial aspects of banditry. Heroes to some, bandits, like the soldiers with whom they were frequently interchangeable, like the patriarchal magistrate or gentry-member whose traditional adversary they were, were as pragmatic and imperfect as anyone.

As a result, it is as difficult to describe the "typical bandit" as it is to describe the "typical man." Bandits were, it is true, predominantly male, and their operations as a rule represented the triumph of male values, but like men in any other walk of life the range of individual types encompassed by the "bandit world" was wide, and any one individual could contain within himself a host of conflicting personal traits. Depending on his mood, the same man could be a mild benefactor one moment, a grim avenger the next. For the same reason it is very difficult to isolate an ideal type of "social bandit." Bandits were part of a structure of violence and power, and obeyed its rules. Within that structure there was "good" violence and "bad" violence, the former corresponding to that which represented or seemed to represent the interests of the common people, the latter corresponding to that which was clearly directed against the people. Whether or not those people reaped any benefit, "social banditry" could often amount to no more than violence that was perceived to inflict damage upon the oppressors. Any bandit who fulfilled such a role for at least half the time could qualify for the support and protection generally accorded the "social bandit," and only those who turned their weapons too regularly on the defenseless would be identified permanently with the oppressors. No one was perfect in such an environment, and a bandit who struck even one blow "for the people" could at least temporarily join the ranks of the heroes.

The peasants were well aware of the relationship that ultimately prevailed between them and the bandits when times were hard, preferring to accept the gang as a lesser evil to be swept away, perhaps, at some future date along with the rest. When the countryside was at peace the bandit gang provided peasants with a model for rejection of the status quo, defining the limits of what was possible and conceivable under the given circumstances. However, its assumption of the trappings of power in the form of control over the local countryside made it always a potential target for the peasants' leveling anger. On those special occasions when insurgency overwhelmed the villages, the bandits would have to learn to adapt themselves to it, or else join the opposition.

The bandit worlds of the peripheries demonstrated the intrinsic ambiguity of the "social bandit" concept. What Hobsbawm has called "primitive rebellion"[6]—perhaps better described as "fundamental rage"

—was represented in the form of attacks on the rich, handouts to the poor, the desperate idealization of such acts by the defenseless, and so on. At the same time, the repressive, conservative features also mentioned by Hobsbawm but stressed more by Blok* were equally well represented and, under the circumstances, often predominated. In the name of power, survival, or both, the bandit gang could treat the poor, the women, and even the children outside its own territory as sadistically as it treated the rich; as paid killers for the powerful, bandits could turn against rebels, revolutionaries, and all who less ambivalently represented the poor's interests. The gang's acts were often calculated: since fear was an essential element of respect, the gang had to make itself feared not only among the rich but also among the poor; it often attacked the rich not because of class hatred but because only they possessed resources worth stealing. Many chiefs complained about social injustice and economic inequities, but their ultimate solution to the problem was often to open a chink in the system wide enough to allow entry, not to turn the system itself inside-out. For such chiefs, banditry was a mode of personal advancement and of gaining for themselves alone the degree of dignity or justice they craved. Their followers, meanwhile, had even fewer illusions about what they were doing. Though it may have been more profitable to rob the rich than to prey upon the poor, bandits soon learned to avoid the families who defended themselves too rigorously. Poor pickings were preferable to leaving your own corpse behind to be picked up. In any case, when banditry itself multiplied or the best victims fled to the towns, there was often no choice but to broaden the field.

Yet those who seek to maintain themselves in power indefinitely can only do so by the infliction of total terror—historically proved to be a short-lived expedient—or by convincing the powerless that it is in their interests not to rock the boat. The latter policy is more effective, but it also implies certain conditions, such as giving concrete proof of the benefits that a particular ruling group alone can bring. This rule applied to bandit chiefs as much as to gentry bosses, military commanders, and national leaders. Though the nonbandit local figures were confirmed in their positions by tradition, heredity, or their capacity to call in outside force, bandits' claims to stand alongside them were far more fragile because they were based on a chief's *personal* ambition. The rise of another chief with similar ambition and superior resources could easily result in a

---

* See Blok 1972. What seems to be at stake here is not the facts themselves but their selection and interpretation. Both Blok and Hobsbawm, that is, are basically following their own personal predilections. Bandits, as we have seen, had perforce to form ties with both the powerful and the powerless, and to emphasize the one at the expense of the other is misleading. The present study has preferred to stress the element of power play in bandits' dealings with all comers, and focuses on the kinds of social relationships it encouraged.

turnover. Elite patrons cared little one way or another, because foremost in their calculations was the effective safeguarding of their special status.

To offset their one-sided dependence on such patrons, gangs had to create some sort of relationship with local villagers, who themselves were only too aware that a stable future depended on the continuation of their patronage ties through the gang to the local elite. Depending on the chief, the gang's arrangement with the villagers may have amounted to little more than simply taking its predatory activities elsewhere; and since a gang's existence in a neighborhood also to some extent deferred attacks from outside, even such a negative blessing could be enough to win the gang at least neutrality, if not support. Given the importance of heroes for people whose lives are permanently undermined by insecurity, such gangs, regardless of whatever else they did and of their fundamental aspirations, could easily appear as "social bandits." Their ongoing war with the local garrison, proving their ability to return violence for violence, was itself enough to generate a strong current of admiration even if they were not absolutely regarded as "good" bandits. Chiefs who were strong or intelligent enough to establish their gangs as the main arbiters of justice in their own small localities—no matter that their motives were little different from those of the local police chief or garrison commander—could often take on the appearance of reborn Robin Hoods simply because they did not wear a uniform. All in all, then, it is doubtful whether there was ever such a thing as a pure "social bandit." Perhaps more significant about the whole concept was what it revealed about the needs and aspirations of those without power—for example, that people were not contented with their lot, that they dreamed of returning some of the blows they received from their oppressors, and that they did so, vicariously, through the activities of their "representatives," the bandits. The emphasis on good deeds, courage, and refusal to compromise, and the myths of invulnerability and rebirth, all suggest that even the most hopelessly oppressed dreamed of a world in which power was not always something to be used against the weak, in which the brave did not have to keep their heads down and their eyes averted, and in which, finally, even the dream itself did not come to an end with the extinction of a particular individual.

This aspect of "social banditry" had contradictory implications. On the one hand, it provided evidence of a dormant protest element among the powerless peasantry that was always capable of bursting into eruption. Paradoxically, however, the peasantry's very faith in its time-tested and more or less effective patterns of resistance—such as banditry— ultimately blocked the efforts of those who came from outside with a social vision powerful enough to channel the occasional eruption into profound and lasting social change. Tied to the conservative vision of local bandits, that is, the pressures generated by the peasants' dream of Utopia were bound to spin uselessly in a continuous cycle of empty violence. To overcome the problem meant, first of all, neutralizing or eliminating the established elite power-brokers whose patronage was largely responsible for the bandits' ability to survive. Without that patronage, the bandits themselves became extremely vulnerable, and their ability to exercise the trappings of power over those beneath them diminished accordingly. Freed from the circumscribing influence of local banditry, the peasants' latent anger could then be transformed into an inexorable flow of molten energy capable of sweeping all before it.

No one with a secure foothold on life and a predictable future became a bandit. Consequently, those who did become bandits were those for whom survival, for various reasons, had suddenly become more precarious than before. In short, insecurity—political, economic, or both—can be isolated as the first unifying factor in banditry. For the chiefs it was usually political, some sudden reversal having undermined the comfortable niche in society they had hitherto occupied. Even for those who became bandits as a result of domestic problems like the loss of landholdings, some political factor was usually involved—for example, a clash with a rival family that had managed to get the law on its side. For the rank and file the insecurity was more often economic—inability to pay rent or meet debts, or some sudden disaster that destroyed the fragile foundations of their existence.

There was also a regional dimension to this general state of insecurity. Areas farthest from established political and cultural centers were usually less blessed with natural resources, resulting in a lower standard of living all around, especially if, as was often the case, the area coincided with a range of mountains or hills. The relief reluctantly doled out when living standards fell below the level that persuaded people to keep quiet tended to reach these peripheral areas last of all, not only because of the problem of physical access, but also because of their emotional and spiritual isolation. Far from the interfering gaze of the capital or the administrative centers, the local hierarchies in these peripheries tended to operate in a world of their own, the official militia thin on the ground and open to bribery, and even officials either joining in the corruption or turning a blind eye to it. A power struggle between elite gentry families over the allocation of scarce resources involving the grossest breaches of law and accepted custom could and often did take place with little danger of the force of central or provincial authority being brought to bear on the guilty. The victims sometimes had little choice beyond that between a life behind bars and a life beyond the law, and in the case of young people the latter was eminently more attractive. The marginal peripheries, where the struggle for survival intrinsically encompassed both political and economic factors, were consequently traditional centers of banditry.

The central or core regions where administrative and population centers were located, on the other hand, were a dramatic contrast. Higher economic levels, better prospects for spontaneous recovery from disasters, and prompt access to relief when necessary meant that the insecurity that traditionally created banditry was much rarer than on the peripheries. The rapidity with which military units could be deployed and the vulnerability of officials to centralized supervision also contributed to their stability. Village structure tended to be more cohesive, and self-help a less urgent priority. Without the need to struggle for their survival, the populations of such regions were more likely to resort to protection strategies than to aggressive banditry when their standard of living was threatened. Even then, such strategies were a response to sudden necessity, and atrophied when the threat receded. With more to lose than to gain from violent conflict, the people of the core regions did not drift into confrontations unless seriously provoked. Generally more prosperous than the inhabitants of the peripheries, their attachment to their property and to the patrons who had traditionally guaranteed them work and security made their outlook on life basically conservative and defensive, and their relationship to the local elite sometimes less brittle.

In regions dominated by the struggle for survival, where strength and ruthlessness are at a premium, it is almost axiomatic that men are the dominant sex. A good illustration is the fact that on the peripheries (and anywhere where the conditions of life were strained) such misogynistic customs as female infanticide and foot-binding were much commoner than in relatively better-off areas. The link between this tradition of male dominance and the violent methods that often characterized the peripheral regions' survival methods was an intimate one. Mutual aid, for example, tended to be practiced less than in villages closer to the centers, and a masculine code of rugged independence encouraged the ideal of self-help. In such circumstances, falling into financial debt and thence into the "weeds" was a fate preferable to falling into the personal debt of another man. Where strength itself was a prized possession, relative degrees of strength naturally accorded relative degrees of status. Passage up through the status hierarchy could thus be achieved by feats of strength, which may or may not have involved others as their victims.

Though strength alone does not intrinsically imply violence, the combination of strength and insecurity often does. It is no accident that the phenomenon of the blood feud featured predominantly in the fragile peripheral areas dominated by men and by stark insecurity. Whether in Sicily or in China, relationships between families were characterized by incipient rivalry, not only because of the scarcity of material resources, but also because of the need felt by men as a whole to be able to hold their heads up high amid conditions that were basically humiliating. This was the origin of the high premium put on "honor." The reason why its assertion tended to be violent lay in the tradition of insecurity-induced male dominance.

Relations with outside communities reflected the same conditions. If strength exerted to assert one's "honor" within the community was often sacrificial and led to the extinction of whole families, strength asserted to ensure survival was, logically enough, directed against those whose retaliatory power posed the least risk of retribution. In most cases this meant those nonperipheral regions mentioned above, which, being more secure, traditionally organized not for predation but for protection, and which, since they did not usually maintain a permanent state of military readiness, were extremely vulnerable to the surprise attack. Yet the attractiveness of such communities as victims went deeper than just their supplies of scarce material resources.

First, the relative ease with which life could be sustained there without struggle pricked the masculine self-respect of the men of the peripheries, tempting them to settle by violence the issue of which was really superior. Second, the fact that life in such areas tended to lack the aggressive life-style associated with areas of greater insecurity provoked scorn for their male inhabitants as "less than men," and this too sparked off exhibitions of masculine wrath. All in all, the sporadic raiding and defense that characterized the relationship between periphery and center reflected not only the economic survival factor but also the dominant influence of male aggressiveness.

This analysis does not go all the way to explaining the consistent affinity between banditry and the peripheral areas, but it does take us a considerable distance. We can go still further by next examining the kind of societies usually thrown up by the social, political, and economic conditions of such areas. In centralized societies, the values propagated by the ruling elite have most impact in the national center and gradually lose their persuasive power in relation to the distance traveled from the capital. The pattern recurs in a wavelike progression, the mores of the capital being revived—or revised to suit local conditions—in each regional capital, but losing their tenacity once again according to the distance traveled toward that region's own periphery. The consequence is that the value systems espoused by the peripheral areas are frequently at odds with those prevailing in the capital areas.

In China's peripheries, therefore, there was a tendency to turn values on their heads, to define the conditions of life in terms quite different from those used in the capital. A prime example was the definition of "respectable" behavior: in the peripheries, "outlawry" could fall easily within the scope of acceptable conduct; violence was widely accepted as a rational alternative to death from starvation, or as a natural right in defiance of the state's monopoly on power. Under such conditions, the decision to become a bandit was not one undertaken only by those "of a natural criminal bent," nor merely by those who "liked a good fight"; on the contrary, it was a highly rational course of action whose effectiveness, if temporary, was confirmed by the experience of generations. The question of banditry's "legality" did not arise as a primary consideration: sanctified by custom and ignored by officials unless it got out of hand, it provided an outlet for many of the pressures that built up in the ecologically insecure peripheries. That being the case, the decision of a young man or woman to take to the hills could be much easier here than elsewhere, since it was relatively untrammeled by the qualms of legal conscience. People knew, of course, that they were putting themselves outside the bounds established by those in control of the ultimate sanctions; they knew, too, that the rest of their days might be a repetition of giving or receiving violence, and that they might well have far fewer of those days than if they stayed at home. The fact that it was "against the law" to arm oneself to control one's own destiny, however, shrank to minuscule proportions relative to the alternative, which was usually annihilation.

The distinction between "criminal" and "respectable" behavior was further blurred in the peripheries by the issue of social class. Whether or not banditry was an expression of the class struggle, the very real nature of class differences for those involved in banditry has been pointed out frequently in these pages. Those differences were as stark on the peripheries as in the centers—perhaps starker, since those in positions of power sought to gather into their own hands as much as they could of the meager available resources, leaving the weak to fend for themselves as best they could. Isolation from established legal and political processes, moreover, made this local elite to a large degree independent of outside control. Its capacity to take both the interpretation and the execution of the law into its own hands was another important feature of politics on the peripheries. A rich family's hiring of armed guards for personal protection or for feuds against rival families was the equivalent of the resort to banditry for those unable to hire others to do their fighting for them. In practice, the empirical distinction between bandit gangs and these armed retainers of the elite was often an extremely tenuous one. A gang could easily pass over from "outlawry" into "respectability" by persuading some local political boss to take it on as his personal retinue; it could just as easily pass back again if the rewards fell below expectations, or if its employer was toppled from his seat of power. For both retainer and retained under such circumstances, the legal definition of "respectability" meant little. To the state, meanwhile, even the elite's hiring of armed guards for forays against rivals was a threat to its monopoly on force.

The peripheries thus operated largely according to their own rules, the rules of power and survival, the two usually running parallel. For a strong person forced into banditry and emerging at the head of a gang, the first priority was acknowledgment of that gang according to the local rules: establishing a viable relationship with other local power-holders who recognized the gang's existence, or else using popular acceptance to give the gang enough muscle to outflank its rivals. From this starting point the gang could develop in a number of directions: into free-lance raiders relying on the protection of certain local bosses; into paid retainers operating only at a particular patron's whim; or into a regular military unit after bringing itself to the notice of some local garrison commander. All these possibilities fell within the rules of power of the peripheries, and the frequent physical clashes between gangs or former gangs did not usually imply any clash of values. All were armed bands operating under different guises and in the name of different sponsors, but the rules they operated by were ultimately the rules of power, according to which the strong rose to the top of the pile and the weak fell by the wayside. The key was the strength and astuteness of one's patron.

If the rules of power demanded that one attach one's destiny to that of the most promising patron available, so did the rules of survival. According to local conditions this might be a powerful bandit chief, or a respected local garrison head, or a strong-minded gentry figure who kept the neighborhood pinned down through a strong force of retainers. Although some villages or village-clusters had a tradition of scorn for the antipopular repressive forces, the rules of survival usually required hitching oneself to whoever offered the opportunity for a full stomach and a reasonably stable existence. Here, too, the element of chance predominated over any clash of values.

Political turmoil in the twentieth century, far from destroying the pattern whereby insecurity bred parallel struggles for power and survival, on the contrary expanded the geographical boundaries of those struggles and deepened their political implications. In warlord China the traditional distinction between centers and peripheries steadily broke down, until in some parts of the country everywhere outside the walls of the cities became in a sense the periphery, responding to the same priorities and repeating the same patterns of power-sharing and violence that the traditional peripheries had established. As a result, banditry too spilled over its traditional boundaries onto the national stage. Bandits remained the proxies of the powerful, but now local power-brokers and garrison commanders were replaced by ambitious politicians and their patrons, the warlords and superwarlords.

Essentially, however, the basic pattern had not changed; what had changed was the level and extent of the bandits' patronage. Soldier-bandits allowed to run amok through large stretches of territory were repeating the pattern whereby gangs had operated as free-lance raiders at the end of a long leash held by some local power boss; bandits absorbed into the army inherited the tradition of gangs' being taken on as personal retainers; and the frequent passage in and out of the military's ranks reflected the always tenuous distinction between bandits and the armed bodyguards of the rich. Though some sought to keep alive, as far as circumstances allowed, the utopian vision invested in them by those unable to live out that vision directly, the scope for putting that vision into practice became, if anything, narrower not wider as the need to confirm and reconfirm one's political-military patronage grew stronger. Whatever loyalties some bandits may have felt to the common people, the logic of power that controlled their very existence as bandits took priority, because to ignore that logic meant an even quicker death than could have been expected in the old days.

If anything, therefore, the expanded geographical and political horizons of twentieth-century banditry confirmed the unlikelihood that bandits on their own would ever become the coordinators of peasant wrath, or even an independent vanguard of peasant resentment against their oppressors. In troubled times bandits turned to those very oppressors, not to the peasants, to sustain their existence. The greater their need to confirm their elite ties, the looser bandits' peasant connections became. The role of bandits in warlord China by and large confirmed Blok's observation[7] on the negative correlation between banditry and peasant mobilization. Not only were bandits effective in putting down by terror a growing tide of collective action; their own success as paid underlings of the rich (however temporary) also confirmed the possibility of upward social mobility under existing conditions, tending to drain off from the peasant movement many people who might have provided it with strong, charismatic leadership.

The blurring of the traditional center-periphery distinction also had an important effect upon those who had lived outside the peripheries, particularly those living close enough to have had to develop a rudimentary defensive posture for protection against raids. The crumbling of the peripheral boundaries meant that sporadic protection measures were no longer enough. When almost any area was liable to change from "center" to "periphery" according to the swaying political fortunes of those on top, only permanent, organized defensive measures offered any secure hope for survival. At the same time, the extension of periphery conditions also enforced periphery-type solutions. That is, communities had to be ready to undertake aggressive rather than purely defensive actions when necessary. Some, under the impact of increasingly deadly military activities, even developed into predominantly aggressive or predatory organizations; others simply remained in a state of permanent military preparedness.

Behind these surface developments was the extension of the circumstances responsible for the periphery conditions in the first place: resource scarcity, consequent insecurity, remoteness from reliable political centers, and so on. As the military struggle for power among warlords, government, and Communists (and later the Japanese Imperial Army) gathered momentum, more and more regions were reduced to the status once reserved for the peripheries, and predatory banditry became an increasingly common reaction to adverse circumstances, undertaken under a variety of superficial titles.

Banditry's relationship with Japanese military aggression was perhaps the logical conclusion to this process. At the start of the warlord period most bandits had still been obliged to operate at least nominally as "social bandits"—that is, they avoided attacking their own immediate neighbors to ensure their neutrality—but the constant fighting took many bandit gangs out of their native areas or else militarized them to such an extent as to remove the social ties that might have kept the gang to at least a modicum of responsible behavior. As the process of militarization went relentlessly forward, drawing the bandits further from their civilian origins, a whole new ethos grew up that identified respect and honor not with being able to lord it in front of one's close neighbors, but with achieving a position within the regular army.

Seen in this light, there seems to be a need to reassess the pro-Japanese alliances formed by many gang leaders (and by many ex-bandit militarists). While the charges of unpatriotic behavior constantly leveled at them were no doubt true, such charges fell on deaf ears, for they reflected the point of view of a community whose values were alien to everything those chiefs lived by. The arrival of a militarily superior force, regardless of its being a foreign invader, represented above all the potential for unrivaled patronage, outweighing the attraction not only of local power-holders but even of Chinese national figures such as warlords and Nanjing generals, now seen to be vulnerable. For ambitious chiefs, that is, alliance with the Japanese Imperial Army was not unscrupulous behavior but a perfectly rational decision in the context of the rules they adhered to, providing them, it must have seemed, with a chance to steal a march on all their rivals for power and influence.

In the same terms, it also becomes clear why the Communists achieved success with bandits not when they appealed merely to their social consciousness or to their patriotism, but when they presented themselves as the representatives of a new order that would supersede even the Japanese. What the Communists did, in other words, was to harness the bandits' essentially reactionary and self-aggrandizing traits to a forward-looking policy of social change that would ultimately transform the bandits themselves by eliminating the center-periphery contrast and with it the conditions that made banditry possible.

# Reference Matter

# APPENDIX A

# Character List

THIS LIST provides the characters for all Chinese and Japanese terms introduced in the text, with three exceptions: place names at the county level and above, personal names given in the Index of Boorman 1967, and bandit slang. Bandit slang terms are listed separately in Appendix B.

Bai Lang　白朗(白狼)
Bai Zhendong　白振東
Bailian jiao　白蓮教
bangke　棒客
bangpiao　綁票
Banzai Rihachirō　坂西利八郎
bao　包
baobiao　保標
Bao Dequan　鮑德全
Bao Fen　寶棻
baogu　包榖
baowei　包圍
bazoku　馬賊
beigui　北歸
benpaodui　笨炮隊
bi　筐
bishang Liangshan　逼上梁山
bingfei　兵匪
bingfei bufen　兵匪不分
bingfeiguo　兵匪國
Cha Tianhua　查天花
chiqing　吃青
Chūka　中華(中禍)
Chūka hikoku　中華匪國
Dadao hui　大刀會
Da Han jiangjun　大漢將軍

daye　打孽
Daliu　大劉
dao　盜
daofei　盜匪
daofeng　盜風
daoke　刀客
Dao Zhi　盜跖
Date Junnosuke　伊達順之助
Daying　大營
dipi　地痞
Dongbei Kang Ri yiyongjun　東北抗日義勇軍
Du Qibin　杜其彬
duo ru niumao　多如牛毛
Eyuwan　鄂豫皖
fafei　法匪
fan　飯(犯)
Fan Mingxin　范明新
fanzheng　反正
Fan Zhongxiu (Laoer)　樊鍾秀(老二)
fei　匪
feifen　匪氛
feiguo　匪國
feijiao　匪教
feitu　匪徒
fufei　幅匪

gan 杆
gan tou 杆頭
ganerzi 乾兒子
ganzi 杆(桿)子
Gao Yongcheng 郜永成
Gelao hui 哥老會
gongfei 共匪
Gong Fukui 弓富魁
guanbi minfan 官逼民反
guan dage 官大哥
Guan Di 關帝
guanfei 官匪
guan fei fenzhi 官匪分治
Guan Laojiu (Fuen) 關老九(福恩)
guantufei 官土匪
Guan Yu 關羽
guanggun 光棍
gui 鬼
gui hui beishan 歸回北山
guishun 歸順
Guo Jian 郭堅
Guomin jun 國民軍
haidao 海盜
Haihu hui 海湖會
Han Taitai 韓太太
Han Yukun 憨玉琨
haohan 好漢
heihua 黑話
heng 橫
hengsi 橫死
hizoku 匪賊
hongfei 紅匪
honghuzi 紅鬍子
Hongqiang hui 紅槍會
hu 虎
hufei 湖匪
Huguo jun 護國軍
hukou 虎口
Huaibei 淮北
huangbiao 黃表
Huang Chao 黃巢
Huangdao hui 黃道會
huangshulang 黃鼠狼

huifei 會匪
Ji Yulin 季雨霖
jianer 健兒
Jiangfei 蔣匪
jianghu 江湖
Jianghu hui 江湖會
jiaofei 教匪
jiaofei 剿匪
jiaofei anmin 剿匪安民
jiao fu jianshi 剿撫兼事
jiao paizi 叫牌子
jiefu jipin 刦富濟貧
Jinfei 金匪
Jin Hengzhao 金恒超
Jinggangshan 井崗山
Jingguo jun 靖國軍
junfa 軍閥
Kaoshan 靠山
Kawashima Yoshiko 川島芳子
Kayano Nagatomo 萱野長知
kefei 客匪
Kohinata Hakurō 小日向白朗
kou 寇
lang 狼
Lao Bai Lang 老白朗
laoer (duiwu) 老二(隊伍)
Lao Taiye 老太爺
Lao Yangren 老洋人
Lao Zi 老子
li 禮
Li Hongbin 李鴻賓
Li Kui 李逵
Li Laoda 李老大
Li Mingsheng (Baoguo) 李明盛
  (保國)
Li Shican 李時燦
Li Yongkui 李永奎(魁)
Li Zicheng 李自成
Liangshanpo 梁山泊
ling 靈
Ling Yue 凌鉞
Liu Bang 劉邦
Liu Baobao 劉保寶

Liu Guitang (Heiqi)　劉桂棠(黑七)
Liu Pei　劉備
Liu Qunren　劉春仁
Liu Yongfu　劉永福
Luguo duodao　魯國多盜
Lu Jingbo　魯景博
lülin (daxue)　綠林(大學)
Ma Enliang　馬恩亮
mazei　馬賊
Manshū gigun　滿洲義軍
Maofei　毛匪
Matsumoto Yōnosuke　松本要之助
meng　夢
minjun　民軍
mou　畝
nifei　逆匪
Nian　捻
Niu Shengwu　牛繩武
nongfei　農匪
nü guanggun　女光棍
o-mikoshi　お神輿
Qianshan　千山
Qin Jiaohong　秦椒紅
Qing Bang　青邦
qingxiang　清鄉
Qiu Er　邱二
Qiu Liang　仇亮
Renyi hui　仁義會
Ren Yingqi　任應岐
rōnin　浪人
Sa Mengwu　薩孟武
san buguan　三不管
*Sanguo zhi*　三國誌
shantang　山堂
Shang Xudong　尚旭東
Shen　瀋
shengguan facai　升官發才
shitou zier　石頭子儿
Shi Youjian (Yan)　石又簪(言)
Shouwang she　守望社
shu　梳
*Shuihu zhuan*　水滸傳
shuikou　水寇

Song Jiang　宋江
Song Laoda　宋老大
Song Laonian (Yiyan)　宋老年(一眼)
Songshan　嵩山
Su Sanniang　蘇三娘
Sun Guan　孫官
Sun Huating　孫花亭
Sun Kuiyuan　孫魁元
Sun Meisong　孫美松
Sun Meiyao　孫美瑤
Sun Yuzhang　孫玉章
ta　塔
Taiping jing　太平經
tairiku rōnin (goro)　大陸浪人(ごろ)
tangjiang (jiang)　蹚匠(將)
Taofan hui　討飯會
Tao Furong　陶芙蓉
Taozei jun　討賊軍
titian xingdao　替天行道
tian di jingshen　天的精神
ting er zouxian　挺而走險
Tōhi no uta　討匪の歌
Tōhikō　討匪行
Tongmeng hui　同盟會
tou　頭
tudi di jingshen　土地的精神
tufei　土匪
tuhao lieshen　土豪劣紳
Wang Chuanxin　王傳心
Wang Cong'er　王聰兒
Wang Jixiang　王繼香
Wang Laowu (Zhen)　王老五(王振)
Wang Shengqi　王生岐
Wang Tiancong (Tianzong)　王天從
　(天縱)
Wang Zuo　王佐
Wu Cangzhou　吳滄洲
wulai　無賴
wulun　五倫
wuxia　武俠
xixin gemian　洗心革面
xiabai　下拜
xiangjian　響箭

xiangma    響馬

Xiao Bai Lang    小白狼

Xiao Bailong    小白龍

Xiaodao hui    小刀會

xiaofei    梟匪

Xiao Qunzi    蕭春子

Xiao Tianlong    小天龍

Xie Baosheng    謝寶勝

Xie Bingkui    謝秉奎

xiexie    謝謝

Xiong Siyu    熊思羽

Xu Qunpu    徐春甫

ya    牙

Yamamoto Kikuko    山本菊子

yamen    衙門

yan(yan)fei    鹽(烟)匪

Yan Zigu    閻子固

yang    陽

Yangshan    羊山

yi    義

Yi jun    毅軍

Yi Laopo    伊老婆

yin    陰

Yizhi Hua    一枝華

yongwu    勇武

youyong    游勇

youxia    游俠

yuan    圓

Yuan Wencai    袁文才

Zaiyuan hui    在園會

zei    賊

Zhai Yunsheng    柴雲陞

Zhang Baima    張白馬

Zhang Damazi    張大痳子

Zhang Desheng (Guowei)    張得勝
  （國威）

Zhang Fang (Peiying)    張鈁(伯英)

Zhang Fei    張飛

Zhang Guafu (Juwa)    張寡婦(菊娃)

Zhang Guoxin    張國信

Zhang Ping    張平

Zhang Qing    張慶

Zhang Xianzhong    張獻忠

Zhang Xiyuan    張錫元

Zhang Zhigong    張治公

Zhang Zonghuan    張宗援

zhaoan    招安

zhaofei chengjun    招匪成軍

Zhao Jie    趙傑

Zhao Ti    趙倜

Zhao Yongling (Mama)    趙永齡
  （媽媽）

Zhen Songjun    鎮嵩軍

Zhong Xing    中興

zhu    猪

Zhuge Liang    諸葛亮

Zhuang Jiao    莊蹻

zhua    抓

zhuo    捉

zhuozei    捉賊

Zongshe dang    宗社黨

zongsiling    總司令

Zou Yongcheng    鄒永成

## Selected List of Bandit Slang

bafeng 把風    To spy, scout ("grasp the wind")

bashou 垻手    Bandits charged with warding off surprise attacks

bashou 把手    Trainee bandits

baimi 白米    Bullets ("white rice")

baishan 白扇    Gang secretary ("white fan")

ban heilao 搬黑老    Deal in opium

ban shitou 搬石頭    Deal in small children (Shanghai)

baohuo 抱火    Bandits who volunteered to lead a night attack carrying torches ("fire-carriers")

baomibao 包米包    Local militia

baoquan jugong 抱拳鞠躬    Bandit salute ("enclose the fist and bow")

bao tongzi 抱童子    Kidnap small children (Shanghai)

baotou    See paotou

baoxian 保險    A captive ("insurance")

baozha 包砟    Eliminate a rival gang ("wrap the tablet"; Manchuria)

benpiao 本票    Chinese captive ("local ticket")

beng 嘣    Shoot dead (Henan)

bengtou 崩頭    Subchief

biantiao 邊條    Boundary between rival gangs' territories (Manchuria)

caihua 探花    Kidnapping women or children ("plucking flowers")

caiming 探命    Single combat on horseback (Manchuria)

caipiao 彩票    Rich captive ("lucky ticket")

caoer 槽兒    Receivers ("stable-boys")

caojuan 草卷    Cigarettes

chaqian 插籤    Bandits charged with investigating rich houses ("tally-takers")

chiermodi 吃二饃的    Bandit confederates in the army who pick up what the gang leaves behind ("eat two dumplings"; south Hebei)

chihongqian 吃紅錢    Ransom money ("good fortune")

choutong 臭筒    Socks ("reeking tubes")

dadan 打單    Intimidation letter (Shanghai)

dadangpu 大當鋪    Receiver ("pawnbroker")

daershao 打二捎　Peasants who take advantage of a bandit attack to steal things

dafeng 大風　Soldiers ("typhoon")

dage 大哥　Elder brother

dagui 大匪　Bandit gang

dajiazi 大家子　Gang leader (complex gang)

dalanba 大覽把　Gang leader (Manchuria)

dashui 大水　Great riches ("big water")

datoumu 大頭目　Gang leader (complex gang)

datugaozi 大兔羔子　Soldiers

dayang 大洋　Bullets ("silver dollars." so called because of their high price)

daye 大爺　Gang leader (complex gang)

dazhanggui 大掌櫃　Gang leader ("the manager"; south Hebei)

daicai 帶彩　Be wounded ("wear colors")

daigan 帶桿　Become a bandit ("carry a stick")

daixian 帶線　Experienced bandit

danjiabaozi 單家堡子　Enemy forces (Manchuria)

danjin zhongsan 彈盡衆散　"When the bullets are exhausted, the gang scatters" (bandit proverb)

dangjiadi 當家的　Gang leader (simple gang; "family head")

dangpiao 當票　Poor captive ("pawn ticket")

defeng 得風　Win in battle ("get a good wind")

dibengzi 地蹦子　Small-time or local gang

dilong 地龍　Buried silver ("earth-worm"; literally "earth dragon")

dimazi 地碼子　Plains gang (Guangdong)

dipai piao 地牌票　Female captive ("earthly ticket")

diren 敵人　Magistrate ("the enemy")

dishe 地蛇　Buried copper cash ("snake")

dishu 地鼠　Buried gold ("shrew-mouse")

dixian 底線　Bandit spy

dixiong 弟兄　Younger brother

diaoyang 吊羊　Take a middle-rank captive ("hang up a sheep"; Hunan)

die 疊　Store stolen goods ("fold up"; Henan)

dingcao 頂草　Straw hat

dinglangzi 頂浪子　Fish ("braving the waves")

dingtian 頂天　Military cap ("head reaching to Heaven")

dingzi 釘子　Bullets ("nails"; Henan)

doufugan 豆腐乾　Wear a cangue ("dried bean curd")

dui 堆　Shoot

erdangjia 二當家　Deputy gang leader (complex gang)

erjiazi 二家子(二駕子)　Deputy gang leader ("deputy family head")

erwu 二五　Unmarried woman; virgin ("two-five")

erye 二爺　Deputy gang leader (complex gang)

erzhanggui 二掌櫃   Deputy gang leader ("deputy manager"; south Hebei)

fanshui 反水   (Soldiers who) return to banditry

fang 放   Kill ("release")

fangfeng 防風   Lookouts ("wind-barriers")

feipang 肥胖   Rich captive ("corpulence")

feiya 肥鴨   Rich captive ("fat duck")

fen 墳   Spot where treasure is buried; target for attack ("grave")

feng 風   Police or soldiers ("wind")

fengjin 風緊   Attack is imminent ("the wind is pressing")

fengtou 風頭   Be pursued ("fate")

gangerpaodi 扛二砲的   Gun borrowed from another bandit

gangshan 扛扇   Bandits charged with breaking down the gates and mud walls of villages under attack ("door-carriers")

gaomazi 高碼子   Mounted gang (Manchuria)

gebo 胳膊   Rifle ("arm")

gouzi 狗子   Soldiers ("dogs"; Henan)

guzi 古子   Magistrate ("the ancient")

guacai 挂彩   Be wounded ("gaily dressed")

guazhu 挂注   Join a gang ("stake one's all")

guantiaozi 官條子   Road ("official line")

guofang 過方   Die ("exceed the limit")

haizuizi 海嘴子   Tiger ("wide-opened mouth")

hanqianyan 喊錢眼   Extortion letter

hanyanguan 旱烟管   Stick ("tobacco-pipe")

heju 合局   Combine gangs (Manchuria)

hema 合碼   Combine gangs (Shandong)

hei 黑   Attack a friend ("dark, evil")

heijiniang gouzi 黑脊梁溝子   Unmarried women (Henan)

hengliangzi 橫梁子   Kill a person ("crossbeam")

hongshao 紅燒   Raze to the ground

houshuzi 後卡子   Rearguard unit

humazi 湖碼子   Gang operating mainly on water

husunxi 猿猻戲   Be displayed publicly in a cangue ("monkey play")

hua 化   Warn of danger (Manchuria)

huapiao 花票   Female captive ("flowery ticket")

huan guiju 還規矩   Conform to bandit rules ("return the compasses")

huangliang 黃粱   A dream ("yellow millet")

hui laojia 回老家   Be killed ("return home")

huo 火   Bullets ("fire")

huolong 活龍   Ready cash or silver ("live dragon")

jicha 稽查   Internal spies, reporting to the chief

jiama 家碼   Rank and file bandit

jiapiao 架票   Kidnap for ransom ("steal tickets")

jiaqiang 架槍   Go over to the enemy ("steal a gun")

jiazilou 架子樓   Receiver ("house of stolen goods")

jian chouyu 檢臭魚   Be arrested ("inspect rotten fish")

jianfu 翦拂   Kneel down ("trim and brush")

jianpiao 剪票   Cut off a captive's ear or finger ("clip the ticket")

jianzi 揀子   Local militia ("select men")

jiaoliangzi 叫亮子   Chicken ("dawn chorus")

jiaopiao 叫票   Haggle over the ransom price ("call the ticket")

jie caishen 接財神   Take a rich captive ("receive the God of Wealth")

jiedao zou 借道走   Request soldiers' permission to pass unmolested ("borrow the road")

jie Guan Yin 接觀音   Take a female captive ("receive the Goddess of Mercy")

jubu 拒捕   Bandits charged with warding off surprise attacks ("resist arrest")

juzi 局子   Bandit gang (Manchuria)

juanzi 圈子   County seat ("circle")

junshi 軍師   Gang tactician, usually using divination books to decide movements

junxu 軍需   See liangtai

kaicha 開差   Launch an expedition ("set up business")

kaihua 開花   Divide the loot ("flowers bloom")

kai tiaozi 開條子   Deal in women

kaiwei 開味   Engage troops in battle ("have fun")

kang sanqiangdi 抗散槍的   Bandits who take care of the gang's weapons; rank and file bandits (south Hebei)

ken haijiangzi 肯海江子   Smoke opium

koufengzi 口鋒子   Sword

kuaipiao 快票   Female captive ("quick ticket")

kuaiyao 快窰   Prison ("brothel of the magistrate's runners")

kunju 梱局   Cease activities ("tie up the guns and bury them")

kunlong 捆龍   Rope

la feizhu 拉肥豬   Take a rich captive ("pull a fat pig")

la ganzi 拉桿子   Become a bandit ("seize a stick")

lagou 拉鈎   Distribute the gang's income

lapiao 拉票   Kidnapping for ransom ("grabbing tickets")

laxian 拉線   Bandit guide (Manchuria)

laisum 拉心   Kidnap for ransom (Guangdong)

lanba 攬把   Gang leader (simple gang; Manchuria)

lao 撈   March ("pull")

laogedan 老疙疸   Youngest bandit in a gang ("pimple")

laopai tiaozi 老牌跳子   The army

laotang 老湯   Bandits (Henan)

lengzi 冷子   Soldiers ("sleet")

lianzi 簾子   Horse

liang bian 兩便　Amicable relations between bandits and the authorities ("double convenience")

liangtai 糧臺　Commissariat chief, responsible for the gang's everyday needs

liezuizi 裂嘴子　Wolf ("Gaping mouth")

lingmeng 蛉蜢　Soldiers ("mosquitoes")

liuzi 流子　Bandit gang (Manchuria)

long 龍　Valuables ("dragon")

loushui 漏水　Reveal secrets ("leak water")

lupiao 擄票　See chaqian

lunzi 輪子　Cart ("wheel")

luocao 落草　Become a bandit ("fall into the weeds")

luodi 落底　Dispose of stolen goods

luoshui 落水　Be killed or captured by the army ("fall into the water")

matou 碼頭　Gang territory

mazi 碼子　Bandit gang (mainly north China)

menshen 門神　Military tactician in a gang ("Door God")

mo shuitou 沒水頭　Embezzle the gang's wealth

naluo maofeng 拏落帽風　Wanted notice

nao geming 鬧革命　Make revolution

naozheng 鬧正　Be enrolled in the army ("settle things by causing a fuss")

niuyi 牛一　See baishan

pa 爬　Rob or steal

pafeng 爬風　Lie low for the winter (Manchuria)

pai doufu 拍豆腐　Beat on the buttocks ("slap bean-curd")

paiju 排局　Subchiefs who desert a gang with their followers

pai pianzi 排片子　Distribute the income ("arrange visiting cards")

paocheban 跑車板　Gangs operating on trains

paodizi 跑底子　Gangs operating on ships

paohuangche 跑荒車　Gangs operating on trains

paotou 炮頭　Military tactician in a gang

pentong 噴筒　Gun ("rocket")

peng 棚　Bandit gang (Sichuan)

peng 砰　Meet someone

pengsuo 篷索　Clothing and accessories ("playing cards")

piba 劈霸　Divide the gang's income

pitang 劈堂　Shoot someone; an execution ("torn asunder")

piyang 疲羊　Poor captive ("tired sheep")

pianzifang 片子房　Overseer of gang finances (Manchuria)

piao 票　Captive ("ticket")

piaobazi 瓢把子　Rearguard fighters (Manchuria)

piaofang 票房　Lockup for captives

piaofangzitou 票房子頭　Overseer of the gang's captives

pufeng 撲風　Resist soldiers' attack ("charge the wind")

puju 舖局　Reconnaissance activities (Manchuria)

qilun 騎輪　Take over a ship ("ride a boat"; Fujian and Guangdong)

qipiao 棄票　Unredeemed captive ("rejected ticket")

qizi 旗子　Gun ("flag")

qianshuzi 前卡子　Advance units (Manchuria)

qiangtouzi 槍頭子　Soldiers ("spearheads")

qiao 嶣　Shoot dead (Henan)

qiao sizi 撬死子　Rob family tombs and demand ransom for the remains ("prise open the ancestors")

qing zhutou 請豬頭　Kidnap for ransom ("invite a boar's head")

renjiaoqing 認交情　Bandits and soldiers on good terms

roupiao 肉票　Captive ("meat ticket")

shanmazi 山碼子　Mountain- or land-based gang

shanzu 山祖　Gang's "elder statesman"

shang 賞　"Return to allegiance" by giving up banditry and joining the army ("reward")

shangma 上馬　Become a bandit ("mount a horse")

shangxian 上線　Advance

shangyuntou 上雲頭　Move in disguise ("head above the clouds")

shaopiao 燒票　Roast a captive to death or as a form of torture ("burn the ticket")

shengkou 牲口　Pistol

shengyi 生意　Banditry ("business")

shi 拾　Be arrested or captured

shifeng 失風　Be defeated or captured ("lose the wind")

shou 瘦　Poor ("thin")

shouya 瘦鴨　Poor captive ("scraggy duck")

shujia 贖價　Ransom price

shupiao 贖票　Pay the ransom ("redeem the ticket")

shui 睡　Death ("sleeping")

shui 水　Gang property ("water")

shuitou 水頭　Gang property ("water level")

shuixiang 水箱　Gang accountant ("water box")

shuixiang 水餉　Overseer of gang security, usually non-combatant (Manchuria)

shunju 順局　Cease activities (Manchuria)

shuopiao 說票　Ransom negotiations ("discuss the ticket")

shuopiaofei 說票費　Middleman's fee in a ransom deal

shuoxiangfei 說項費　Middleman's fee in a ransom deal

sicha 私差　Independent operations (strictly forbidden)

sipiao 撕票　Kill an unredeemed captive and send the head back to the family ("tear up the ticket")

sum 心　Ransom victim ("heart"; Guangdong)

take 踏殼　Shoes ("treading husks")

taxian 踏線　Bandit specializing in spying on developments near military bases

taipiao 抬票　Take a captive for ransom ("take a ticket")

tang 堂　Person

tianpai piao 天牌票　Male captive ("heavenly ticket")

tiao 挑　Set out on a raid ("provoke trouble")

tiaoyao 跳窰　Brothel

tiaozi 條子　Letter; married woman

tiaozi 跳子　Police

tiejin 貼金　Be hit by a bullet ("receive a decoration")

toudan 頭彈　Bandit riding in the front line ("first bullet")

touming zhuang 投名狀　Application to join a gang

toumu 頭目　Gang leader (simple gang)

touqianren 頭前人　Subchief, similar to paotou

tupiao 土票　Peasant or local captive ("local ticket")

tuzi 兔子　Soldiers or police ("rabbits")

waiguo tanglianzi 外國糖蓮子　Bullets ("sugared lilies from abroad")

wanwanr 玩玩儿　Banditry ("playing")

wang chengjuan 望城圈　Be arrested and executed ("view the city wall")

weiwuyao 威武窰　Yamen or police station ("brothel of power")

wuchashi 武差使　Big raid ("military requisition")

xishou 洗手　Give up banditry ("wash the hands")

xianer 線兒　Guide

xianyuan 閑員　See paotou

xiaoshui 小水　Scant riches ("little water")

xiaotoumu 小頭目　Subchief

xin 尋　Rob or steal ("request")

xingshui 行水　Protection money (Guangdong)

xunfeng 巡風　Spy ("cruise the wind")

xunlengzi 巡冷子　Lookout ("watch out for sleet")

yabayao 啞吧窰　Deserted Daoist temple, often used as hiding-places ("brothel of the dumb")

yacheng 押城　Attack ("press the city wall")

yashui 壓水　Middleman; sentry (Manchuria)

yayao 押窰　Forcibly demand hospitality

yazi 鴨子　Ransom captive ("duck")

yangdizi 洋底子　Ship or boat

yang e shengdan 養鵝生蛋　Force captives to reveal their wealth ("coax the goose to lay its eggs")

yangpiao 洋票　Foreign, especially Western, captive

yangpiao 羊票　Ransom captive

yangzi 養子　Adopted son of a chief

yangzifang 秧子房　Youngest or least experienced bandit in a gang ("young sprout")

yangzifang 養子房　Bandits charged with guarding the captives

yaobizi 腰逼子　Pistol ("hip persuader")

yaotang 窰堂　House ("brothel")

yaozi 搖子　Fan ("shaker")

yezi 葉子　Captives (Henan); clothes and accessories ("playing cards")

yili jindan 一粒金丹　Bullets ("drops of the Elixir of Gold")

yinshui daixian 引水帶線　Lead soldiers to the gang's camp

zazhonghui 雜種會　Secret societies at loggerheads with the gang ("mongrel groups")

zaizi 崽子　Rank-and-file bandits (Manchuria)

zang 葬　Bury ("inter") money

zha 柵　Bandit gang ("palisade")

zhaguding 扎估丁　Captives requiring a quick sale

zhameng 蚱蜢　Police patrols ("locusts")

zhaying 扎營　Call a halt

zhanggui 掌櫃　Gang leader ("the manager")

zhangjia 賬架　Gang treasurer

zhangqilai 掌起夾　Form a gang (Manchuria)

zhedaozi 折刀子　Tooth ("broken sword")

zheguaner 澤管兒　Cease activities (Manchuria)

zhenshang shifeng 陣上失風　Be caught or killed on the spot

zhipiao 質票　Poor captive ("pawn ticket"; Guangdong)

zhongerlang 衆兒郎　Rank-and file-bandits

zhua yangzi 抓養子　Kidnap for ransom

zhuang 壯　Rich ("stout")

zhuo Lohan* 捉羅漢　Take a child captive ("seize a Lohan")

zonggui 總柜　Gang leader (large complex gang or bandit army; "general manager")

zonglanba 總攬把　See zonggui

zou shazi 走沙子　Deal in salt

zouxian 走線　See taxian

---

*The word *zhuo* was usually avoided by bandits. This must be either an exception to the rule or a mistake in the original text.

# APPENDIX C

# Bandits Who Became Militarists

THE TERM "militarist" is used here to refer to all those men who achieved some degree of military recognition, whether as warlords or as commanders in the Communist Red Armies. It excludes the soldier-bandits, however, whose military careers were usually too fleeting to warrant inclusion. Wade-Giles transliterations of their names have been added to aid recognition.

Bao Guiqing (WG Pao Kuei-ch'ing; Manchuria; 鮑貴卿)
Chen Shufan (WG Ch'en Shu-fan; Shaanxi; 陳樹藩)
Chu Yupu (WG Ch'u Yü-p'u; Shandong; 褚玉璞)
Du Lisan (WG Tu Li-san; Manchuria; 杜立三)
Fan Shaozeng (WG Fan Shao-tseng; Sichuan; 范紹增)
Fan Zhongxiu (WG Fan Chung-hsiu; Henan; 1888–1930; 樊鍾秀)
Feng Delin (Feng Linge) (WG Feng Te-lin/Feng Lin-ko; Manchuria;
　　1866–1926; 馮德麟/馮麟閣)
Guo Fangming (WG Kuo Fang-ming; Fujian)
Guo Jian (WG Kuo Chien; Shaanxi; d. 1921; 郭堅)
Guo Zhencai (WG Kuo Chen-ts'ai; Henan; 郭振才)
Han Yukun (WG Han Yü-k'un; Henan; ca. 1891–1925; 憨玉崐)
Han Yuzhen (WG Han Yü-chen; Henan; 憨玉珍)
He Long (WG Ho Lung; Hunan; 1896–1969; 賀龍)
Hong Zhaolin (WG Hung Chao-lin; Guangdong; 1871–1925; 洪兆麟)
Hu Jingyi (WG Hu Ching-i; Shaanxi; died 1925; 胡景翼)
Hu Lisheng (WG Hu Li-sheng; Shaanxi)
Li Jinchun (WG Chi Chin-ch'un; Manchuria; born 1877; 波金純)
Li Fulin (WG Li Fu-lin, Guangdong; 1877–1952; 李福林)
Li Haiqing (WG Li Hai-ch'ing; Manchuria)
Li Shaozong (WG Li Shao-tsung; Yunnan)
Li Wanlin (WG Li Wan-lin; Henan; 李萬林)
Lin Yinqing (WG Lin Yin-ch'ing; Manchuria)
Liu Guitang (Liu Heiqi) (WG Liu Kuei-t'ang/Liu Hei-ch'i; Shandong;
　　1892–1943; 劉桂堂/劉黑七)

Liu Zhidan (WG Liu Chih-tan; Shaanxi; 1902–1936; 劉志丹)

Long Jiguang (WG Lung Chi-kuang; Guangdong/Guangxi; 1860–1921; 龍濟光)

Long Jinguang (WG Lung Chin-kuang; Guangdong/Guangxi; died 1917; 龍覲光)

Lu Rongting (WG Lu Jung-t'ing; Guangxi; 1859–1928; 陸榮廷)

Lu Xingbang (WG Lu Hsing-pang; Fujian; 1880–1945; 盧興邦)

Lu Zhankui (WG Lu Chan-kuei; Shaanxi; died 1924; 盧占魁)

Ma Zhanshan (WG Ma Chan-shan; Manchuria; 1884–1950; 馬占山)

Mo Pu (WG Mo P'u; Yunnan)

Mo Rongxin (WG Mo Jung-hsin; Guangdong/Guangxi; 莫榮新)

Pang Bingxun (WG P'ang Ping-hsün; Henan; 1879–1963; 龐炳勳)

Ren Yingqi (WG Jen Ying-ch'i; Henan; died 1934; 任應岐)

Shi Wancheng (WG Shih Wan-ch'eng; Henan; 史萬成)

Sun Baiwan (WG Sun Pai-wan; Shandong; 孫百萬)

Sun Dianying (Sun Kuiyuan) (WG Sun Tien-ying/Sun K'uei-yuan; Henan; 1898–1947; 孫殿英/孫魁元)

Sun Liechen (WG Sun Lieh-ch'en; Manchuria; 1873–1924; 孫烈臣)

Tang Yulin (WG T'ang Yü-lin; Manchuria; 1871–1935; 湯玉麟)

Wang Laowu (Wang Zhen) (WG Wang Lao-wu/Wang Chen; Henan; died 1930; 王老五/王振)

Wang Tianzong (WG Wang T'ien-tsung; Henan; 1885–1918; 王天縱)

Wang Zuo (WG Wang Tso; Jiangxi; 王佐)

Wu Baofeng (WG Wu Pao-feng; Manchuria; 吳寶豐)

Wu Junsheng (WG Wu Chün-sheng; Manchuria; ca. 1866–1928; 吳俊陞)

Xu Baoshan (WG Hsü Pao-shan; Jiangsu; 1855–1913; 徐寶山)

Yang Chunfang (WG Yang Ch'un-fang; Sichuan; born 1885; 楊春芳)

Yang Hucheng (WG Yang Hu-ch'eng; Shaanxi; 1893–1949; 楊虎城)

Yang Yuting (WG Yang Yü-t'ing; Manchuria; 1885–1929; 楊宇霆)

Yuan Wencai (WG Yüan Wen-ts'ai; Jiangxi; 袁文才)

Yuan Ying (WG Yüan Ying; Henan; 袁英)

Zhai Yugui (WG Chai Yü-kuei; Henan; 柴玉貴)

Zhai Yunsheng (WG Chai Yün-sheng; Henan; 柴雲陞)

Zhang Chong (WG Chang Ch'ung; Yunnan; 1903–1941; 張沖)

Zhang Fang (Zhang Peiying) (WG Chang Fang/Chang P'ei-ying); Henan; 張鈁/張伯英)

Zhang Fenghui (WG Chang Feng-hui; Shaanxi; born 1871; 張鳳翽)

Zhang Haipeng (WG Chang Hai-p'eng; Manchuria; born ca. 1868; 張海鵬)

Zhang Jieba (WG Chang Chieh-pa; Yunnan; 張結疤)

Zhang Jinghui (WG Chang Ching-hui; Manchuria; 1872–1962; 張景惠)

Zhang Jingtang (WG Chang Ching-t'ang; Hunan; 張敬湯)

Zhang Jingyao (WG Chang Ching-yao; Hunan; 1880–1933; 張敬堯)

Zhang Ruji (WG Chang Ju-chi; Yunnan; 張汝驥)

Zhang Yingfang (WG Chang Ying-fang; Manchuria; 張應芳)

Zhang Yunshan (WG Chang Yün-shan; Shaanxi; born ca. 1863; 張雲山)

Zhang Zhigong (WG Chang Chih-kung; Henan; born ca. 1891; 張治公)

Zhang Zongchang (WG Chang Tsung-ch'ang; Shandong/Manchuria; 1881–1932; 張宗昌)

Zhang Zuolin (WG Chang Tso-lin; Manchuria; ca. 1872–1928; 張作霖)

Zhang Zuoxiang (WG Chang Tso-hsiang; Manchuria; born 1881; 張作相)

Zhao Tianyong (WG Chao T'ien-yung; Henan; 趙天永)

Zou Fen (WG Tsou Fen; Manchuria; 鄒芬)

# APPENDIX D

# Bai Lang's Proclamation

THE FOLLOWING proclamation was reproduced in the *North China Herald* on April 25, 1914 (p. 268). I have made some slight editorial emendations. Parenthetical additions are in the original.

Bai, Great Commander of the Army for the Support of Han in China, hereby proclaims:

For nearly three hundred years, our fathers and elders had been subject to the despotic rule of an alien race. They suffered horrible tortures and were denied redress and justice. By the law of nature, a change is bound to occur when any condition has reached the extreme point; so the extremity of their misery brought about the last revolution.

We were just feeling some felicitation at the downfall of the monarchy and the assertion of popular rights, and thinking that the godly offspring of China would henceforth enjoy liberty within the bounds of the law, and suffer no more injury and injustice at the hands of despotic tyrants. To our surprise, however, the traitor Yuan Shih-kai, with the cruel heart of a wolf, has dictated laws according to his own inclinations and is bent upon arrogating the role of an emperor, repelling and banishing the virtuous and the learned, welcoming and employing his own paws and jaws, putting the meritorious to the sword or killing them in cowardly fashion by hired assassins, encouraging his shameless satellites with official ranks and gold, paying no need to the alienation of Urga, caring less for the revolt by Tibet, and worrying not about the secret existence [and] growing strength of the Imperial Party.

His only daily occupation is to strengthen his own party, to seek self-interest, to expel and extirpate dissidents, to abandon his brothers, change the laws and systems, whitewash his faults, and ill-treat or sacrifice our people upon divers pretexts, in all of which actions he is much worse even than the Manchus. Thus, our country is splitting and our people care not to live. Nevertheless, his flatterers call him Washington, and even the critics compare him with Napoleon. But, in reality, he is not surpassed in despotism and barbarity even by Lü Cheng and Sing Mang (two very cruel statesmen flourishing during the Ch'in dynasty and the later Han regime, respectively).

I, Bai Lang, feeling my heart rent by pain and my head ache with indignation, have risen in revolt, and assembled heroes and patriots, with the determination to save the lives of the people, so I call my work the Support of Han. Confucius said: "If no support is given to a tottering country, what would be the use of having that minister?" Although Han is now restored, yet if the traitor Yuan were allowed to have everything his own way without our timely support being given, our country would soon tumble down, and what would be the use of having our people then?

As every citizen should be responsible for the welfare of his own country, can you, the people of Shaanxi, who have long been famous for bravery and patriotism, witness the arch scoundrel usurping the power of government, and the numerous murderers crowding about the Court, the sure ruin of our fine country and the ultimate extinction of our Han Race, with composure and indifference, and refuse to stretch out your hands to the rescue? I, Bai Lang, by the grace of the spirit of Huangdi in Heaven, have been victorious wherever I go since I raised my patriotic standard. At present, my army has penetrated Shaanxi, all large towns and strongholds having showed submission at my approach. Although this may be due to the bravery and prowess of my army, yet it cannot be gainsaid that the people's despair under tyrannical government and the troops' unwillingness to fight for such a government have also contributed to my successes.

Having now crossed Mount Ch'in, passed the valley Tagu, and made a military demonstration at Xianning and Changan, I hereby assure you that on the day on which the city (Xian) is taken, I shall promulgate Three Articles of Law as was done by the Duke of Pei (the founder of the Han dynasty, who gave protection to the people that acclaimed him as the emperor, and prohibited the usual slaughter and pillage), and I shall not imitate Prince Hang that permitted burning and looting (Prince Hang was a rival to the Duke of Pei but was soon defeated; and he committed suicide).

Therefore, our fathers and elders, be quiet and at ease. This is my notice.

A Seal of Bai Lang was affixed to every copy of his proclamation, containing twenty-four Chinese characters which mean in English: Act in everything as Heaven wills, and as law provides, to my seal denoting five blessings no disrespect shall be shown, I use it to mark my authority, let each and all make an effort. [This last paragraph was an *NCH* editorial explanation appended to the actual proclamation.]

# Notes

The following abbreviations of periodical titles and archives are used in the Notes. All other abbreviations refer to works whose full citations can be found in the Bibliography.

BSOAS    *Bulletin of the School of Oriental and African Studies* (London).
CWR    *China Weekly Review* (Shanghai). Known before 23 June 1923 variously as *Millard's Review, Weekly Review of the Far East,* and *Weekly Review.*
DFZZ    *Dongfang zazhi* (Shanghai). 東方雜誌
FO    *Foreign Office Archives, Great Britain.*
GWZB    *Guowen zhoubao* (Tianjin). 國聞週報
JAS    *Journal of Asian Studies* (Ann Arbor, Michigan).
JDSZL    *Jindaishi ziliao* (Beijing). 近代史資料
MLB    *Minli bao* (Shanghai). 民立報
NCH    *North China Herald* (Shanghai).
SD    *U.S. State Department Records Relating to the Internal Affairs of China, 1910–1929.*
STSB    *Shuntian shibao* (Beijing). 順天時報
SXYK    *Shixue yuekan* (Kaifeng). 史學月刊
XDZB    *Xiangdao zhoubao* (Shanghai). 嚮導週報
ZFGB    *Zhengfu gongbao* [Government Gazette] (Beijing). Known until April 1912 as *Linshi gongbao* or *Linshi zhengfu gongbao.* 政府公報, 臨時公報, 臨時政府公報
ZYWX    *Zhongyuan wenxian* (Taibei). 中原文獻

## Preface

1. See, for example, Angiolillo 1979; Arnold 1979; Blok 1974; Cheah 1981; Crummey ed. 1986; Lewin 1979; O'Malley 1979; Salazar 1977; Shears and Gidley 1984; Singelmann 1975; Tiedemann 1982.

2. Hobsbawm 1972a: 17.

3. *Ibid.:* 19–20.

4. *Ibid.:* 24.

5. Blok 1972: 498.

6. *Ibid.*

7. *Ibid.:* 499.

8. *Ibid.:* 499–500.

9. Blok 1974: 94–102.

10. Blok 1972: 500–501.

11. *Ibid.:* 499.

12. Hobsbawm 1959: 13.

## Chapter One

1. Representative examples of antibandit legislation may be found in *MLB*, 28 Oct. 1912: 6; *DFZZ* 12, no. 1 (1 Jan. 1915), "Fa-ling": 1–2, 6; *ZFGB* 775 (3 July 1914), 931 (7 Dec. 1914); *DFZZ* 20, no. 17 (10 Sept. 1923): 4; *NCH*, 29 Sept. 1923: 895–96; Nagano 1924: 261–66.

2. *ZGNC*: 299.

3. See Dai Xuanzhi 1973: 61.

4. *NCH*, 29 Jan. 1927: 172. See also *NCH*, 26 May 1923: 548–49; Swallow and Lu 1934; and Dailey 1923d: 358.

5. Gotō 1923: 58, 71–72; MacNair 1925: 258; Osame 1923. Note also the title of Inoue 1933 and the writings of Yano Jin'ichi, which were more scholarly but based on the same assumptions.

6. *CWR*, 16 June 1923: 76. See also *CWR*, 2 June 1923: 3; *NCH*, 12 May 1923: 357, 394.

7. He Xiya 1925a: 25; Perry 1980: 64; Kaltenmark 1979: 32–33.

8. Mao Tse-tung 1965: II, 308 (translation amended).

9. English versions of the book have been published under the titles *Water Margin* (translated by J. H. Jackson); *All Men Are Brothers* (translated by Pearl Buck; New York 1933); and *The Tale of the Marshes* (excerpts translated by Liu Wu-chi in his *An Introduction to Chinese Literature*; Indiana University Press, 1966). For a synopsis and discussion of the novel, see Irwin 1966.

10. Chesneaux 1971a: 2; Ruhlmann 1960: 145.

11. Muramatsu 1960: 262–64.

12. *STSB*, 15 May 1914: 3; Kōkaku Sanjin 1924: 160.

13. See, for example, Hobsbawm 1959, 1972a; Queiroz 1968; and Angiolillo 1979.

14. See, for example, Li Jianer 1938.

15. Powell 1945: 88; Washio 1928: 6; Li Xin et al. 1978: 240. On Zhang Zuolin's early career, see Chang Cheng ed. 1980: 1–10; Li Xin et al. 1978: 179–89. On Zhang Zongchang, see Li Xin et al. 1978: 236–42.

16. Cited in Lü Jiuyu 1980: 313; Lin Baohang 1961: 535. See also Guo Moro 1982: 113.

17. Davis 1977: 3; Perry 1976: 9.

18. Overmyer 1976: 11, 58. See also Lilius 1930: 229–33; and Wu Cangzhou 1961.

19. Overmyer 1976: 3.

20. He Xiya 1925a: 2–3; Huang Zhongye 1979: 43–44; Mantetsu chōsaka 1930: 23–24; Meng Ti 1931:1; Grafton 1923: 600.

21. Borst-Smith 1917: 185; Keyte 1913: 58.

22. Ch'ên 1961: 101; Watanabe 1964: 30; Jansen 1954: 63; Hsüeh Chün-tu 1961: 62; *XHGM*, VII, 361, 366, 382.

23. The quote is translated from Wen Yiduo 1948: 23. See also *MLB*, 1 July 1912: 2; *STSB*, 17 June 1914: 2.

24. Wou 1978: 87. See also Li Xin et al. 1978: 122.

25. Wou 1978: 133–36; Xu and Xu 1955: 38; Zhi Che 1926: 540, 543; Lary 1985: 59.

26. Hsieh 1969: 16n; *STSB*, 18 July 1914: 8; Li Xin et al. 1980: 158.

27. Bertram 1937: 309–10. See also *Bukan hōmen*: 1; "Shina kakushō ni okeru hika ni tsuite": 32–33.

28. Yung-fa Chen 1986; 471.

29. See, for example, Dai Xuanzhi 1973; C. K. Yang 1975.

30. "China's Booming Bandit Business": 44.

31. SD 893.00/4435 (Beijing to Washington, D.C., 26 Apr. 1922), 893.00/7963 (Hankou to Washington, D.C., 15 Nov. 1926); Martin 1938: 174–75; Yao Xueyin 1981: 67; Xing Bei 1924: 8; Arlington 1931: 239; Zhuo Ran 1935: 120.

32. Wu Rui 1970: 19.

33. *BLQY*: 98.

34. Kōkaku Sanjin 1924: 164–65: Arlington 1931: 239; Wu Shixun 1936: 48; Nagano 1938; Fang Hongchou 1974; Wu Rui 1970.

35. Gillin 1967: 103.

36. *NCH*, 12 May 1923: 380; *La Chine* 43 (1 June 1923): 696; Chen Wuwo 1923: III, 3–4, 6. For an English summary, see W. W. Chen 1923: 3–8.

37. Zhang Jungu 1967: 196–97; *NCH*, 30 June 1923: 869; W. W. Chen 1923: 26; Dailey 1923c: 245, 1923d: 358; SD 893.00/5345 (Jinan to Beijing, 28 Dec. 1923); Cai and Xu 1980: 1375–79.

38. *NCH*, 30 June 1923: 869, 18 Aug. 1923: 440–42; "Diplomatic Notes on the Lincheng Incident": 242–50; *China Yearbook*, 1924: 818–30; W. W. Chen 1923: 28–31; Nagano 1924: 258–66. Foreign reactions to the crisis are set out in *NCH*, 26 May 1923: 548–49. The bandits' demands are given in *La Chine* 43 (1 June 1923): 696, and in Hatano 1925: 61. For Japanese views, see Baba 1976, which emphasizes the restraint the Japanese government urged on the Western powers, and Hatano 1925.

## Chapter Two

1. Bianco 1975: 321; Kapp 1970: 300. Note also Lü Pingdeng 1936: 166; *Shaanxian zhi*: I/18b.

2. Shabad 1972: 104.

3. See Perry 1980.

4. Gain 1909: 413.

5. Wu Shixun 1936: 118. See also *NCDC*: 107, 113.

6. Gotō 1923: 53, 55–56; Gotō 1928: 62. See also Nagano 1938: 122, 202; Xi Min 1939: 202.

7. Selden 1971: 32; Li Xiaoting 1969.

8. See Chesneaux 1971b: 66–67.

9. Powell 1955: 111.

10. See, for example, Nagano 1938: 198; Parsons 1970. 123–24, 244 45.

11. Chesneaux 1971a: 18–19. For examples of antibandit legislation that foundered on the special problems of the border areas, see *STSB*, 16 Jan. 1913: 4, 7 Dec. 1913: 9; *MLB*, 26 May 1913: 8.

12. Lattimore 1932: 230–31; Shek 1980: 172–73; Lattimore 1941: 28; McCormack 1977: 119. For examples, see *Zhengxuan* 1, no. 1 (Jan. 1914), "Zhongguo dashiji": 7, 9, 13, 22–23; Xu Zhiyan 1922: 1916/41–42.

13. Mackay 1927: 253; Mancall and Jidkoff 1972: 126; Howard 1926: 20, 32, 41–42, 135–36; *Gendaishi shiryō* 31: 587.

14. Watanabe 1964: 32–40; McCormack 1977: 17–18; _Gendaishi shiryō_ 31: 583–84, 32: 580.

15. Laffey 1972, Laffey 1976; McAleavy 1968: 94–95, 105–12, 167–71.

16. Lattimore 1932: 67, 229.

17. Nozawa 1972: 47.

18. _STSB_, 29 Mar. 1911: 4.

19. _BLQY_: 75; Wang Zongyu 1964: 21.

20. _MLB_, 23 May 1912: 7, 28 May 1912: 8, 22 June 1912: 7, 11 July 1912: 8, 13 July 1912: 9, 28 July 1912: 8; FO 228/1841 (Hankou to Beijing, 10 July 1912), 228/1873 (Hankou to Beijing, 14 Jan. 1913); _STSB_, 20 Apr. 1912: 7, 18 Sept. 1912: 4, 20 Oct. 1912: 4, 24 Oct. 1912: 4; _ZFGB_ 175 (23 Oct. 1912), 179 (27 Oct. 1912), 231 (18 Dec. 1912); _BLQY_: 75; Nozawa 1972: 134–35.

21. _DFZZ_ 11, no. 3 (1 Sept. 1914), "Zhongguo dashiji"; Du Qunhe ed. 1980: i–ii; _BLQY_: 83–85; Lai Xinxia 1957b: 12–13; Wang Zongyu 1964: 21.

22. Lai Xinxia 1957b: 12; _Shina_ 4, no. 8 (15 Apr. 1913): 63, 4, no. 11 (1 June 1913): 57–58; _NCH_, 3 May 1913: 309–10; _STSB_, 20 Apr. 1913: 4; _MLB_, 20 Mar. 1913: 8, 8 Apr. 1913: 8, 9 Apr. 1913: 8, 12 Apr. 1913: 10, 1 May 1913: 8, 10 May 1913: 8, 17 May 1913: 8; FO 228/1873 (Hankou to Beijing, 11 Apr. 1913, 11 July 1913). See also Dong Kechang 1958: 34–35.

23. _Zhengyang xianzhi_, III/47b; Hutchison 1936: 181, 214; Banno 1970: 15; Xian Yun 1956: 151; _BLZX_: 3; _STSB_, 2 June 1913; Dong Kechang 1958: 35, 37; _BLQY_: 87; Wang Zongyu 1964: 21; _China's Millions_, Sept. 1913: 141.

24. Perry 1980: 23.

25. Gamble 1963: 109–11; _NCH_, 13 Nov. 1915: 525.

26. Pawley 1935: 140.

27. Kanamaru 1933: 103. See also _NCH_, 11 Aug. 1917: 317; Tanaka 1934: 154; Hedges 1923: 609.

28. Gotō 1923: 64–66; Yoneda 1941: 114; Gain 1909: 414.

29. Muramatsu 1966: 590; Fu-mei C. Chen 1975: 138; _NCH_, 13 Nov. 1915: 525. "Shanxiang nuhuo": 24, provides a vivid description.

30. Zhi Ning 1936: 113. See also Kuchiki 1966: 90.

31. Ch'ên 1968: 570. See also Chesneaux 1973: 78–79; Wen Gongzhi 1930: III; Zhang Youyi et al. 1957: II, 609, III, 2.

32. Ozaki 1949: 16.

33. Myers 1970: 276; Yang Zhongjian 1920: 117.

34. Tachibana 1923: 65; Lai Xinxia 1957a: 8–11; Sheridan 1966: 24. See also Jian Hu 1923; Mantetsu chōsaka 1930: 25, 60–72; McDonald 1978: 32–37, 56–58, 231; Zhang Youyi et al. 1957: II, 594–96.

35. See Zhang Youyi et al. 1957: vols. II, III; Sheridan 1966: 29. Isaacs 1974 and Jenner 1970a offer vivid fictional evidence.

36. Borst-Smith 1916. See also Jing An 1930.

37. Mantetsu chōsaka 1930: 1.

38. He Xiya 1925a: 77–101. He's figures are almost identical to those given in the 22 Mar. 1925 edition of the _Shehui ribao_, cited in "Chūgoku ni okeru dohi": 62.

39. Lattimore 1932: 225. On the origins of the "Red Beards" and the reasons for that nickname, see He Xiya 1925a: 14–15; Watanabe 1964: 3–12; Tanaka

1934: 153–55; Li Shiyue 1959: 60; Inoue 1923: 135–38; Chesneaux 1971b: 133–34.

40. Kurushima 1952: 229–30; Lattimore 1932: 228, 68; Mancall and Jidkoff 1972: 126.

41. Nagano 1938: 285–90; Lattimore 1932: 187–97; Zhang Youyi et al. 1957: II, 649; He Xiya 1925a: 78–81; *ZGNC*: 314–19. Compare also Des Forges 1973: 36.

42. O. J. Todd, quoted in Selden 1971: 1.

43. Keyte 1913: 227.

44. Nagano 1938: 241–44; Sheridan 1966: 102–4.

45. Nagano 1938: 244–47, *Bukan hōmen*: 18–19; *Shina meibutsu*: 6–7.

46. *ZGNC*: 312–19.

47. Nagano 1938: 247–50; Gillin 1967: 109.

48. *Minguo ribao*, 20 Oct. 1928, quoted in *ZGNC*: 299–300; Zhang Youyi et al. 1957: III, 902.

49. Nagano 1938: 250–56; He Xiya 1925a: 101; *ZGNC*: 299–301.

50. Parsons 1970: 45, 47, 87; Teng 1964: 183.

51. *STSB*, 16 Jan. 1913: 4, 9 Nov. 1913: 11, 9 Dec. 1913: 8, 14 Feb. 1914: 11; *DFZZ* 20, no. 17 (10 Sept. 1923): 4–6.

52. *NCH*, 29 Sept. 1923: 895–96; *DFZZ* 20, no. 22 (25 Nov. 1923): 5.

53. Nagano 1938: 190–93; *NCH*, 11 Aug. 1917: 317. See also Tiedemann 1982; Perry 1980: 58–80.

54. He Xiya 1925a: 83; *ZGNC*: 301–5; Uchiyama 1978: 212–19; Zhang Youyi et al. 1957: II, 613.

55. He Xiya 1925a: 83–88; Nagano 1938: 193–213; *ZGNC*: 301–5. See also Mantetsu chōsaka 1930; Meng Ti 1931.

56. He Xiya 1925a: 96–97; Nagano 1938: 225–31; *ZGNC*: 338–40. See also Bianco 1969.

57. He Xiya 1925a: 94–96; Nagano 1938: 231–36; *ZGNC*: 330–35.

58. Nagano 1938: 237–40, 300–303; He Xiya 1925a: 100; Tang Leang-li ed. 1934: 73.

59. Nagano 1938: 235–36, 268–71; He Xiya 1925a: 17, 97–98; McDonald 1978: 231; *Bukan hōmen*: 15–16; Nagano 1933: 272–73; Lary 1985: 16. See also Gotō 1928: 430–33; Gotō 1937: 65–105.

60. Nagano 1938: 271–74; *ZGNC*: 334–38.

61. Nagano 1938: 275–76; *ZGNC*: 337; Lamley 1977; Mackay 1927: 253–54. See also Xi Min 1939; Caldwell 1925.

62. Nagano 1938: 291–95; Lilius 1930; He Xiya 1925a: 17; *ZGNC*: 323, 328, 337–38. See also Murray 1982; Gotō 1928: 416–30; Miller 1970; Fox 1940. For two photographs of female pirate chiefs, see Lilius 1930. 39, 42.

63. Blue 1965: 79–82; *NCH*, 20 Jan. 1923: 143; Nagano 1938: 291; Inoue 1923: 156; "J.D." 1927: 166–68. See also Monsen 1931; Lilius 1930.

64. *NCH*, 20 Jan. 1923: 142–43; Nagano 1938: 236.

65. He Xiya 1925a: 99; Lü Pingdeng 1936: 159.

66. He Xiya 1925a: 99–100; Nagano 1938: 257–65; *ZGNC*: 320–22; Gotō 1928: 74–75, 414–16; *China's Millions*, Apr. 1918: 47.

67. See *China's Millions*, various issues, and especially Taylor 1922.

68. Fitzgerald 1941: 80–81; Nagano 1938: 266–68; He Xiya 1925a: 101. See also Benson 1925; Xie Bin 1928: 15–16, 20–22; Xue Shaoming 1937, especially pp. 40–41, 50–51, 132–35.

69. Shibuya 1928: 128, 131, 134–45; Nagano 1938: 276–84; ZGNC: 322–29; He Xiya 1925a: 98; Guang Xiaoan 1926: 18–21; Lin Baohang 1961.

## Chapter Three

1. *STSB*, 6 June 1911: 4, 9 Mar. 1912: 4, 12 June 1913: 4, 25 Feb. 1914: 4; He Xiya 1925a: 94; *HZB*: II, 13, 14; Wu Shixun 1936: 48; *NCDC*: 2, 90; He Xiya 1925a: 56. See also Belden 1950: 49.

2. Wu Shixun 1936: 48–52, 112, 117, 119, 121, 131–33, 158–59, 161, 163, 168, 170, 174, 199, 200, 202, 208; *NCDC*: 105–9, 114.

3. Des Forges 1979: 17–19, 24–26; Teng 1964: 51–64; Chiang Siang-tseh 1954: 2; Wang Tianjiang 1979; Wu Cangzhou 1961.

4. He Xiya 1925a: 88–94; Nagano 1938: 213–25; *ZGNC*: 306–11; *NCDC*: 2, 118–19; Zhang Xichang 1934: 48; Keyte 1913: 187; *STSB*, 12 June 1913: 4.

5. *NCDC*: 4–8; Zhang Xichang 1934: 47–49; Banno 1970: 18. See also Wu Bingro 1927: 51; Thaxton 1979: 2; Wou 1979: 17. I am grateful to Ralph Thaxton and Odoric Wou for their permission to cite their earlier unpublished work. Thaxton's thesis is comprehensively set out in his book *China Turned Rightside Up: Revolutionary Legitimacy in the Peasant World* (New Haven, Conn., 1983). The first half of Wou's paper has been published in *Asian Profile*, 12, no. 3 (June 1984), pp. 215–30, under the title "Development, Underdevelopment and Degeneration: The Introduction of Rail Transport into Honan."

6. *BLQY*: 71. See also Banno 1970: 14–15; Lai Xinxia 1957b: 12; Wang Zongyu 1964: 20; Shimamoto 1974: 3–7; Qi Cheng 1939: 53; Institute of Pacific Relations 1939: 3.

7. *BLQY*: 76–77; *ZGNM*: 284.

8. Shimamoto 1974: 63; Richthofen 1903: 34.

9. *BLQY*: 73–74. See also Shimamoto 1974: 5; Sun 1967.

10. Xi Chao 1934: 68; *NCDC*: 109; Shimamoto 1974: 4–5.

11. Xian Yun 1956: 153–54; *BLQY*: 77–78, 89; Yao Xueyin 1981: esp. p. 14.

12. Thaxton 1979: 7; *BLQY*: 74–75.

13. Thaxton 1979: 8–12; Friedman 1974: 120, 124. See also Wou 1979: 18; Zeng Jianquan 1927; Zhang Youyi et al. 1957: II, 95; Bianco 1971: 106; Shimamoto 1974: 4.

14. The following section is based chiefly upon Wou 1979: 3–20, supplemented by Wu Shixun 1936: esp. pp. 13–48.

15. Wu Shixun 1936: 132; *NCH*, 7 May 1927: 267.

16. *China Yearbook*, 1920–21: 821–22; *The Times* (London), 21 Sept. 1920, 2 Oct. 1920; Zhang Youyi et al. 1957: II, 618.

17. Yang Zhongjian 1920: 116; Lundeen 1925: 66.

18. Xi Chao 1934: 71; Ho 1931–32: 358–64; Zhang Youyi et al. 1957: III, 899.

19. Zhang Xichang 1934: 62–63; Zhang Youyi et al. 1957: III, 883, 885; Xi Chao 1934: 68, 71; "Shanxiang nuhuo": 23; *BLQY*: 77.

20. Prusek 1970: 181–82. See also *ZGNC*: 306, 146–52; *NCDC*: 12–19.

21. Wu Shixun 1936: 48–52, 137; Wou 1979: 22; *NCH*, 5 Mar. 1927: 383, 11 Aug. 1917: 317; *NCDC*: 90.

22. See Franck 1923: 362–63; Keyte 1913: 225; Gotō 1928: 103; Howard 1926: 9–10; Augustana Mission 1915: 114; White 1966: 30.

23. Alabaster 1899: 402–3.

24. He Xiya 1925a: 89–91; *NCDC*: 108–9; Wou 1979: 22–24.

25. *NCDC*: 105.

26. Wu Shixun 1936: 132–33; Gotō 1923: 59; Yoneda 1941: 26–27. See also Teng 1964: 48.

27. Xiao Xiang 1926: 1545; *Taikang xianzhi*, "Bingzai feihuo": 51b–54b. See *China's Millions*, Nov. 1926: 171, for a description of one attack.

28. He Xiya 1925a: 89.

29. Nagano 1938: 214; *NCH*, 5 Mar. 1927: 383; Arlington 1931: 236.

30. *ZFGB* 179 (27 Oct. 1912). See also Wu Shixun 1936: 49, 52.

31. Augustana Mission 1915: 13. See also Wu Shixun 1936: 121.

32. Wang Jianzhao 1928; 57b. See also Wu Cangzhou 1961: 372; Wang Zongyu 1964: 20; *BLZX*: 1; Cao Hongxu 1930: 6.

33. Wu Shixun 1936: 109–10.

34. Dong Kechang 1958: 35; Huang Guangkuo 1960a: 24.

35. *NCH*, 5 Mar. 1927: 383.

36. Nagano 1938: 179; Teichman 1921: 74–75.

37. Wu Shixun 1936: 25; Shimamoto 1974: 12; Lü Jiuyu 1980: 313.

38. *ZFGB* 59 (28 June 1912); Nagano 1938: 214; *NCH*, 5 Mar. 1927: 383.

39. Nagano 1938: 178; Dai Xuanzhi 1973: 61.

40. *NCH*, 5 Mar. 1927: 383; Lundeen 1925: 35, 37–38, 54.

41. Wu Shixun 1936: 110, 115, 119–20, 49; Richthofen 1903: 28; Cao Hongxu 1930: 29.

42. Keyte 1913: 66; Borst-Smith 1917: 118–19. See also Wang Jianzhao 1928: 17–18.

43. *XHGM* VII: 371. See also Keyte 1913: 285–93.

44. *ZHMG*: 146; Zhang Xiuzhai 1961: 373–74; Shimamoto 1974: 11, 18.

45. See *XHGMHYL*, vol. V; Mitani 1974.

46. Teng 1964: 61; Feng Zigang and Liu Ruisheng 1934: 139. See also Parsons 1970: 46–47; *NCDC*: 105–6, 108.

47. *STSB*, 13 Mar. 1914: 10; *MLB*, 26 Oct. 1912: 8; *Central China Post*, 12 Nov. 1913, enclosed in SD 893.00/2035 (Hankou to Beijing, 12 Nov. 1913). See also Shimamoto 1974: 11.

48. *MLB*, 6 May 1913: 8; *Shibao*, 29 Oct. 1913, quoted in *XHGM Hubei*: 723; *STSB*, 6 June 1911: 4, 9 Mar. 1912: 4; Wu Shixun 1936: 158.

49. Wu Shixun 1936. 168, Chiang Siang tseh 1954: 2; Du Qunhe ed 1980: 282; Nagano 1924: 4–5; Nagano 1938: 128; Perry 1980: 107. See also Nagano 1938: 224–25.

50. Friedman 1974: 122. See also *NCH*, 8 Aug. 1914: 417.

51. Franck 1923: 343; Dailey 1923a: 209; *CWR*, 18 Nov. 1922: 426.

52. C. K. Yang 1975: 179, 181–82; Zhang Kaiyuan et al. 1979: 932; Wang Tianjiang 1963: 92–95; Hsiao Kung-chuan 1960: 403, 691; *BLQY*: 78–79.

53. Liao Yizhong ct al. eds. 1981: 279–82; *CPM* 1913: 23; Nozawa 1972:

45–48; Banno 1970: 8–9. See also Yang Bingyan's articles on the popular struggle against the Peking Syndicate in *SXYK*, Aug. 1964: 13–17 and Mar. 1965: 10–13.

54. Wang Tianjiang 1979: 789.

55. Wang Tianjiang 1963: 95; Banno 1970: 10; *BLQY*: 80. For similar occurrences in other provinces, see Hsieh 1972: 160–64; Prazniak 1980; Esherick 1976a: Chap. 4.

56. Lust 1972: 168; Zhang Youyi et al. 1957: I, 959–60; Augustana Mission 1915: 10. On the riots, see Dong Kechang 1960: 22–27; Wang Zongyu 1964; Banno 1970: 5–11; Qiao Zhiqiang 1981: 542–44; Liao Yizhong et al. eds. 1981: 279–80; Des Forges 1973: 28–30; *XHGM 50 Years*: 218; Jurgensen 1965: Chap. 1.

57. Wang Tianjiang 1979: 789.

58. *ZHMGS*: 79–83; Du Qunhe ed. 1980: i. See also *ZFGB* 59 (28 June 1912); *STSB*, 20 Apr. 1913: 4, 8 Oct. 1913: 8, 25 Feb. 1914: 4.

59. *ZHMGS*: 80, 83; Wang Tianjiang 1979: 789.

60. *ZHMGS*: 82.

61. *BLQY*: 81–83; *ZGNM*: 285; Li Xin et al. 1980: 154. The principal biographical sources on Bai Lang, from which the following was prepared, are as follows: *BLQY*: 80–96; *BLSM*: 10–19; Li Xin et al. 1980: 153–60; *ZGNM*: 283–89; Du Qunhe ed. 1980: i–v.

62. Huang Guangkuo 1960b: 33; Xian Yun 1956: 147; Han Xuexu 1965: 37; Banno 1970: 11.

63. *STSB*, 31 Oct. 1912: 4 (citing only twelve chiefs). Shimamoto (1974: 48–49) describes the affair in detail, as does *BLQY* (84). Fifty years later, the notorious episode continued to inspire village plays and folk songs.

64. *NCH*, 21 June 1913: 907.

65. *BLSM*: 18; Du Qunhe ed. 1980: ii; *STSB*, 5 Dec. 1912: 4.

66. Yamazaki 1913: 12–15; Watanabe 1964: 51–52; Nozawa 1972: 114.

67. Yamazaki 1913: 20; *STSB*, 31 July 1912: 4.

68. *NCH*, 31 May 1913: 639; *Shina*, 4, no. 12 (15 June 1913): 75.

69. FO 228/1817 (Beijing to London, 28 Mar. 1912); Yamazaki 1913: 15. See also Ch'ên 1968: 575; Sheridan 1966: 318.

70. *MLB*, 6 May 1913: 8, 30 June 1913: 3; Yamazaki 1913: 16–18; Wang Canli 1979: 30.

71. *MLB*, 7 Aug. 1913: 8; *STSB*, 17 Aug. 1913: 8, 12 Oct. 1913: 8, 17 Oct. 1913: 8, 25 Oct. 1913: 8, 17 Feb. 1914: 8. See also Xu Yaoshan et al. 1961.

72. *NCH*, 7 Mar. 1914: 718; Tao Juyin 1957–58: II, 40; Tao Juyin 1947: 179.

73. Cai and Xu 1980: 332–33.

74. FO 228/1907 (Hankou to Beijing, 23 Mar. 1914); *NCH*, 25 July 1914: 271.

75. Li Xin et al. 1980: 154–55; *NCH*, 8 Nov. 1913: 411–12, 7 Feb. 1914: 380; Du Qunhe ed. 1980: 241–45; Tao Juyin 1979: 345. See also *Zhengxuan* 1, no. 3 (Mar. 1914), "Zhongguo dashiji": 6. On the sack of Zaoyang and the death of the French priest, see *DFZZ* 10, no. 9 (1 Mar. 1914), "Zhongguo dashiji": 10; *The Times* (London), 30 Jan. 1914. For vivid eyewitness accounts of the sack of Luan, see Lü Jiuyu 1980; *China's Millions*, Apr. 1914: 61.

76. *STSB*, 12 Mar. 1914: 2; *NCH*, 18 Apr. 1914: 914; FO 228/1907 (Hankou to Beijing, 20 Mar. 1914), FO 371/1942 (Beijing to London, 21 Feb. 1914, 9 Mar. 1914, 14 Mar. 1914, 30 Mar. 1914, 11 Apr. 1914, 13 Apr. 1914, 22 Apr. 1914), FO 371/1946 (London to Beijing, 27 May 1914), FO 405/214 (Beijing to London, 9 Feb. 1914); *The Times* (London), 12 Mar. 1914, 17 Mar. 1914, 5 May 1914; *NCH*, 7 Feb. 1914: 378; Li Xin et al. 1980: 156–57; *BLSM*: 27–30; *China's Millions*, May 1914: 76. For a Chinese summary of Robertson's reports, see Du Qunhe ed. 1980: 242–44. Unfortunately, neither the promised comprehensive British government report on the campaign, nor the *Woodlark*'s log for the period is to be found in the London Public Records Office. Both, presumably, went astray amid the confusion accompanying the outbreak of World War I soon after Bai Lang's death.

77. *STSB*, July 1914; all issues; *XHGMHYL* V: 183; *BLQY*: 93, 96–97.

78. *BLQY*: 98–99.

79. *China Yearbook*, 1923: 574–76; *NCH*, 27 May 1922: 594–96; *DFZZ* 19, no. 18 (25 Sept. 1922): 144; SD 893.00/4582 (Hankou to Washington D.C., 28 June 1922); Dailey 1923a: 210; Wen Gongzhi 1930: II, 13, 167. See also Sheridan 1966: 110–11; Tao Juyin 1957–58: VI, 117–18.

80. *NCH*, 22 Jan. 1927: 129; *Central China Post*, 28 June 1922, enclosed in SD 893.00/4582 (Hankou to Washington D.C., 28 June 1922); *NCH*, 30 Dec. 1922: 850; Dailey 1923a: 208, 210; Hedges 1923: 606; "Yanjiu tufei wenti zhi yanjiu": 10–11.

81. *DFZZ* 19, no. 23 (10 Dec. 1922): 129; *DFZZ* 19, no. 24 (25 Dec. 1922): 133, 142; *DFZZ* 20, no. 1 (10 Jan. 1923): 156–57; *NCH*, 22 Jan. 1927: 129; *Peking and Tientsin Times*, 3 Jan. 1924, in SD 893.00/5346 (Beijing to Washington D.C., 10 Jan. 1924); Dailey 1923a: 208–9; Hedges 1923: 609; Lundeen 1925; A.N. 1923.

82. *DFZZ* 20, no. 12 (25 June 1923): 5–6; *DFZZ* 20, no. 14 (25 July 1923): 8–9; *DFZZ* 21, no. 3 (10 Feb. 1924): 8–9; *NCH*, 22 Jan. 1927: 129; SD 893.00/5346 (Beijing to Washington D.C., 10 Jan. 1924); Cai and Xu 1980: 1379–83; Ban Su ed. 1928: 326–27, 330.

83. Zhang Youyi et al. 1957: II, 608.

84. Nagano 1924: 150–51.

85. *DFZZ* 21, no. 3 (10 Feb. 1924): 156; *China Yearbook*, 1925–26: 1132, 1163; Wen Gongzhi 1930: II, 36, 45, 100–101, 104–8, 171–77; *Shina jihō* 2, no. 4 (Apr. 1925): 50–51; no. 5 (May 1925): 35–36; no. 6 (June 1925): 36; *ZGNC*: 309–12; Nagano 1938: 221; He Xiya 1925b: 44; *Mianchi xianzhi*, XX/10a; *The Times* (London), 16 Mar. 1925; Sheridan 1966: 161–62; Ding Wenjiang 1926: 63–70. See Yao Xueyin 1981 for a semifictional account of one gang caught up in all this turmoil. For gazetteer observations, see *Fengqiu xianzhi*, "Tongji": I/8; *Changge xianzhi*, III/11.

86. Wen Gongzhi 1930: II, 175; Zhang Youyi et al. 1957: II, 608.

87. *Shina jihō* 2, no. 5 (May 1925): 36; *Changge xianzhi*, III/11; Sheridan 1966: 162; Jing An 1930: 6; SD 893.00/6192 (Hankou to Beijing, 4 Apr. 1925). See also 893.00/6190 (Hankou to Beijing, 19 Mar. 1925).

88. He Xiya 1925a: 89–94. More or less identical figures for the country as a whole may be found in Nagano 1924: 121–214; Nagano 1938: 190–290;

*ZGNC*: 297–345. "Chūgoku ni okeru dohi" (1928), Shibuya 1928, and Mantetsu chōsaka 1930 not only repeat many of He's findings and even his 1924 figures verbatim, but also translate without credit large chunks of his book. Thus they should not be relied upon as current assessments of banditry in China. All of these items, in fact, should be used only with the utmost care, for even He's own figures are no more than a guess, and in any case represent no more than the tip of the iceberg.

89. Yao Xueyin 1981: 13. See also *NCDC*: 106, 109; Jing An 1930: 8.

90. *China's Millions*, July 1926: 105–6. See also *Guangshan xianzhi*, quoted in Dai Xuanzhi 1973: 78; *Yanling xianzhi*, "Dashiji": 29–30.

91. *The Times* (London), 6 Mar. 1926; Mitani 1974: 247–48; Slawinski 1972: 202.

92. *NCH*, 31 Dec. 1926: 97.

93. Perry 1980: 168; He Xiya 1925a: 96; Gotō 1937: 239–48, 262; *Bukan hōmen*: 6. See also *HZB*: 4–15; *China's Millions*, July 1927: 108–9, Oct. 1927: 158; Cao Hongxu 1930: 28–29.

94. Huang Renzhi 1935: 6. See also *NCDC*: 2, 108–9.

95. *Shaanxian zhi*, I/18a; C. Y. Chang 1937: 498.

96. *Shaanxian zhi*, I/18a; *ZGNC*: 306–7; *Bukan hōmen*: 3, 6, 17; Xi Chao 1934: 71; *NCDC*: 12–19, 108; Cao Hongxu 1930: 28–29. See also Xi Chao 1934: 68; Xia Zhaorui 1974: 33.

97. *ZGNC*: 306; Jing An 1930: 9.

98. *NCDC*: 109.

99. Sheridan 1966: 252, 255, 248–49.

100. *Ibid.*: 234–35, 263–67; "Shina kakushō ni okeru hika ni tsuite": 42. See also Dai Xuanzhi 1973: 77; *HZB*: part II; *Bukan hōmen*: 2–3, 17.

101. Wong Yin-seng et al. 1939: 103, 105, 107; Hatano 1963: 25; Clubb 1968: 29. See also Zhang Youyi et al. 1957: II, 615; III, 69, 880.

102. Zhang Xichang 1934: 48; *NCDC*: 2, 5–8. See also *ZGNC*: 306–11.

103. C. Y. Chang 1937: 498; Nagano 1938: 215; Yung-fa Chen 1986: 447–50; Chen Hongjin 1939: 86.

## Chapter Four

1. Ueda 1924: 9.

2. Ly 1917–18: 370. See also Fei Hsiao-t'ung 1946: 10–11; Chow Yung-teh 1966: 218–19.

3. See Smith 1900: Chap. 20.

4. Eberhard 1965: 100–103. See also Tachibana 1923: 40–41.

5. *NCH*, 26 Feb. 1927: 344, 12 Mar. 1927: 431.

6. Yang 1945: 30; Fei Hsiao-t'ung and Chang Chih-i 1945: 293. See also Ly 1917–18: 367–68, 377, and the opening pages of Chao Shu-li 1953.

7. MacNair 1925: 219–20; "Bandit Rule in China": 8–9.

8. See Lee Solomon 1923; Aldrich 1923: 677, 680; Chen Wuwo 1923: I, 3.

9. Banno 1970: 15; Xian Yun 1956: 151; *BLZX*: 3; Dong Kechang 1958: 35, 37; *BLQY*: 87; Wang Zongyu 1964: 21; *China's Millions*, Sept. 1913: 141. See also Kuchiki 1966: 100.

10. Friedman 1974: 128–29.

11. Lattimore 1932: 230–31; Lattimore 1941: 28; Xue Shaoming 1937: 40–41, 51.

12. Lattimore 1932: 67–68, 187–97, 226–27; Lee 1970: 91–93; Mancall and Jidkoff 1972; Nagano 1938: 289–90. See also Zhang Youyi et al. 1957: II, 649; Takahashi 1967: 796–98; *Gendaishi shiryō* 32: 580.

13. Suleski 1981: 356–72; Shimamura 1973: 178; Nakajima 1973: 259. See also Okabe 1978.

14. Kuchiki 1966: 48–49; Tanaka 1934: 156; Lundeen 1925: 43, 53–54. See also Yao Xueyin 1981: 146–47; Naquin 1981: 40.

15. Lundeen 1925: 14, 25, 53; Aldrich 1923: 677; Strauss 1931: 5; *China's Millions*, May 1922: 70; *NCH*, 7 Feb. 1914: 345, 12 Mar. 1927: 431; Yao Xueyin 1981: 98; Takahashi 1967: 798; Cao Hongxu 1930: 24. See also Kurushima 1952: 177; Johnson 1934: 54, 85.

16. "*Li Zicheng*": 306–7; Yao Xueyin 1981: 76, 98.

17. Takahashi 1967: 798; Inoue 1923: 158–59; Kuchiki 1966: 461; He Xiya 1925a: 98.

18. See, respectively, Chen Wuwo 1923: I, 25; *NCH*, 26 Mar. 1927: 521; "La Fuite du Loup Blanc": 14 (also Xian Yun 1956: 153–54); Lü Jiuyu 1980: 312; *BLQY*: 80; Wu Cangzhou 1961: 365; Howard 1926: 165, 38; Takahashi 1967: 798.

19. Chen Wuwo 1923: I, 30–31.

20. Perry 1976: 12–13; Huey n.d.: 23; Croll 1978: 39–41; Shih 1967: 60–65, 310–14. See also Murray 1982: 7.

21. Davin 1979: 121–24; Wu Bingro 1927: 52.

22. Davis 1977: 96. See also Naquin 1981: 44.

23. For an example, see Laffey 1972: 87–89.

24. Naquin 1981: 40.

25. Perry 1980: 51–52.

26. See Mowll 1925.

27. Pawley 1935: 140; *CWR*, 26 May 1923: 448.

28. C. K. Yang 1965: I, 66.

29. *Ibid.*: I, 5–6.

30. Smedley 1956: 301; Davis 1977: 87. See also Murray 1982: 8.

31. Davis 1977: 90–92; Wang Tianjiang 1963: 83–85.

32. *NCH*, 28 Mar. 1914: 917; Tao Juyin 1947: 184; Xian Yun 1956: 147; Friedman 1974: 127.

33. Lattimore 1932: 186, 225. See also Lary 1985: 68–70.

34. Chesneaux 1971b: 72.

35. Tachibana 1923: 53, 67, Mantetsu chōsaka 1930: 34. See also Nagano 1924: 54–55.

36. *MLB*, 28 Oct. 1912: 6; *DFZZ* 19, no. 10 (25 May 1922): 122; Dailey 1923a: 207; *NCH*, 12 Mar. 1927: 432. See also Cao Hongxu 1930: 8.

37. *China Yearbook*, 1912: 286; He Xiya 1925b: 44.

38. *The Times* (London), 20 Nov. 1913. See also *NCH*, 12 Mar. 1927: 432; Lary 1985: 68.

39. *La Chine* 42 (15 May 1923): 635; *NCH*, 3 July 1920: 45–46, 15 Jan. 1921: 119, 2 June 1923: 620; Chen Wuwo 1923: I, 28–30; Tachibana 1923: 64; Lee Solomon 1923.

40. Tachibana 1923: 65–66; *NCH*, 12 Mar. 1927: 432; Lü Pingdeng 1936: 166; *La Chine* 43 (1 June 1923): 698; Lary 1985: 68.

41. Ueda 1924: 24, 53–59; "Lincheng Incident."

42. See Luo Yaojiu 1957: 64, and the critique in Dong Kechang 1958: 37.

43. Banno 1970: 16–17; Shimamoto 1974: 41–42.

44. *MLB*, 25 Apr. 1912: 7, 2 May 1912: 7, 19 May 1912: 3, 23 May 1912: 7, 22 June 1912: 7, 9 July 1912: 7, 10 July 1912: 5, 11 July 1912: 8, 13 July 1912: 8–9, 14 July 1912: 3, 15 July 1912: 3, 16 July 1912: 3, 17 July 1912: 3, 18 July 1912: 3, 25 July 1912: 7, 12 Oct. 1912: 8, 26 Oct. 1912: 8. See also *STSB*, 20 Apr. 1912: 7, 9 July 1912: 4, 18 Sept. 1912: 4, 10 Oct. 1912: 4.

45. *MLB*, 21 May 1913: 3. See also *ibid.*, 20 Dec. 1912: 3, 27 Apr. 1913: 8; *ZFGB* 231 (18 Dec. 1912).

46. *STSB*, 13 Nov. 1913: 2, 30 Dec. 1913: 8.

47. *DFZZ* 10, no. 10 (1 Apr. 1914), "Zhongguo dashiji."

48. *DFZZ* 10, no. 9 (1 Mar. 1914), "Zhongguo dashiji": 5; Qiao Xuwu 1956: 136; Wang Zongyu 1964: 21; Banno 1970: 16.

49. Swallow and Lu 1934; Du Qunhe ed. 1980: 382; *BLZX*: 8.

50. *STSB*, 19 Feb. 1914: 9, 22 May 1914: 4; Lai Xinxia 1957b: 15.

51. Buck 1928; Perry 1980: 171–72.

52. Lamley 1977: 4, 19, 24.

53. See Kurushima 1952: 17–22.

54. Caldwell 1925: 139–42; Andrews and Borup 1918: 207–9. See also *CWR*, 10 Oct. 1925: 137–38; Hsiao Kung-chuan 1960: 368–69.

55. Swallow and Lu 1934; Dong Kechang 1958: 35; Wu Shixun 1936: 48; C. Y. Chang 1937: 498. See also *NCH*, 5 Mar. 1927: 383; *NCDC*: 90.

56. See Dong Kechang 1960: 22–27; Wang Zongyu 1964; Qiao Zhiqiang 1981: 542–44; Liao Yizhong et al. eds. 1981: 279–80; Banno 1970: 5–11.

57. *NCH*, 5 Mar. 1927: 383; Kuchiki 1966: 48–49; *China's Millions*, May 1922: 70.

58. *NCH*, 16 May 1914: 527, 1 Aug. 1914: 383; Lü Jiuyu 1980: 316.

59. *BLZX*: 8–9.

60. *STSB*, 13 Mar. 1914: 10; *BLZX*: 7.

61. See Howard 1926: 180–81; *CWR*, 10 Oct. 1925: 137–38.

62. *STSB*, 3 Apr. 1914: 4; *BLZX*: 7; "La Fuite du Loup Blanc": 15; Xian Yun 1956: 153–54; *STSB*, 9 Aug. 1914: 8.

63. Lundeen 1925: 129. See also Strauss 1931: 25; *CWR*, 10 Oct. 1925: 137–38; *STSB*, 8 Oct. 1912: 4, 13 Nov. 1912: 4.

64. *NCH*, 2 Apr. 1927: 45. See also Howard 1926: 220.

65. *CWR*, 26 May 1923: 448. See also Gotō 1928: 101.

66. *BLQY*: 82; *MLB*, 27 Jan. 1913: 8. See also Laffey 1972: 88; McAleavy 1968: 100–101; Chao Shu-li 1953.

67. *BLQY*: 80; *MLB*, 23 May 1912: 7; *STSB*, 5 Oct. 1912: 4; Shimamoto 1974: 43–45.

68. Dailey 1923c: 245; *NCH*, 19 May 1923: 453–54. See also Nagano 1933: 269.

69. See Hsieh 1969: 84–90; Zhang Xiuzhai 1961: 373; Yang Yiping 1961: 380; Friedman 1974: 133.

70. Howard 1926: 116, 165–66, 219. See also Kurushima 1952: 40.

71. Ruhlmann 1960: 174; Yu Ming 1965: 11; Wu Cangzhou 1961: 364.

72. Klein and Clark 1971: I, 297. See also "China's Booming Bandit Business": 42.

73. Taylor 1922: 50, 59; *China's Millions*, Aug 1922: 116–18. See also Nagano 1938: 267–68.

74. *NCH*, 24 Sept. 1921: 927. See also Liu Ruming 1966: 85; Sheridan 1966: 102, 104; Hall 1976: 73–74.

75. Manshū rōnin 1938: 81–82; Kuchiki 1966: 132, 508.

76. Swallow and Lu 1934; Clubb 1968: 69; Nagano 1938: 137. See also Qiao Zhiqiang 1981: 540; Lin Baohang 1961: 542.

## Chapter Five

1. He Xiya 1925a: 42–43.

2. Ueda 1924: 27; Kuchiki 1966: 98–109, 154–63; Tanaka 1934: 154.

3. See Kuchiki 1966: 160–63, 296–301; Laffey 1972: 92–93; Ikeda n.d.: I. For captives' experiences, see Pawley 1935: 60, 192–95, 240; Johnson 1934: 48–53; Mackay 1927: 192.

4. He Xiya 1925a: 35; Hedges 1923: 610.

5. Tanaka 1934: 156; Howard 1926: 209, 232, 250–51, 255–57, 266–67.

6. See *Yanling xianzhi*, "Dashiji": 27a; *MLB*, 2 June 1913: 8.

7. Gotō 1923: 54; Tachibana 1923: 42; Nagano 1938: 176–77; W. W. Chen 1923: 8.

8. Kanamaru 1933: 109; Tachibana 1923: 43; *NCH*, 2 June 1923: 595; *CWR*, 26 May 1923: 448; Powell 1945: 108. See also Borst-Smith 1917: 220.

9. *NCH*, 6 Dec. 1913: 751, 764; *STSB*, 6 Apr. 1914: 9, 7 Apr. 1914: 4, 23 Apr. 1914: 4; Xian Yun 1956: 145; Cai and Xu 1980: 335–36.

10. *NCH*, 12 May 1923: 385, 19 May 1923: 453, 457, 26 May 1923: 521; W. W. Chen 1923: 7–9; Ueda 1924: 84. See also Gamble 1963: 301–3; Nagano 1933: 255.

11. Dardess 1972: 109.

12. Hobsbawm 1972a: 71.

13. *NCH*, 21 Mar. 1914: 867.

14. *The Times* (London), 17 Mar. 1914; *STSB*, 25 Nov. 1913: 4; *NCH*, 11 July 1914: 147; Xian Yun 1956: 144–45.

15. Qiao Xuwu 1956: 135; Huang Guangkuo 1960a: 27; *STSB*, 10 Dec. 1913: 8, 13 Jan. 1914: 3, 28 May 1914: 9, 1 Aug. 1914: 8; *NCH*, 7 March 1914: 718, 13 June 1914: 831.

16. Caldwell 1925: 194.

17. *The Times* (London), 7 Mar. 1914; *BLZX*: 7. See also Xian Yun 1956: 44–45.

18. *NCH*, 21 Feb. 1914: 561; *BLZX*: 9.

19. Huang Guangkuo 1960a: 26; Qiao Xuwu 1956: 139–40.
20. He Xiya 1925a: 32–33; Nagano 1932: 388; C. Y. Chang 1937: 498. See also *CWR*, 26 May 1923: 448; Murray 1982: 3–4.
21. Shih Nai-an 1963: 251–53. See also Huey n.d.: 16–17; Kuchiki 1966: 62; Murray 1982: 8, 15.
22. He Xiya 1925a: 33; Shibuya 1928: 129. See also Murray 1982: 9.
23. Chen Wuwo 1923: I, 14; W. W. Chen 1923: 8; *CWR*, 19 May 1923: 408, 26 May 1923: 448.
24. *La Chine* 42 (15 May 1923): 635; *NCH*, 2 June 1923: 620; Chen Wuwo 1923: I, 27–31; Powell 1945: 97.
25. *NCH*, 2 June 1923: 593; Dailey 1923c: 245; W. W. Chen 1923: 8.
26. *BLQY*: 85–86; Huang Guangkuo 1960a: 26; Xian Yun 1956: 146; *Xiping xianzhi*, "Feijie": 3b; *STSB*, 14 Dec. 1913: 8.
27. Wang Tiancong 1971: 9; *Xiping xianzhi*, "Feijie": 2b; Wang Jianzhao 1928: 17a.
28. *MLB*, 10 June 1913: 7; *STSB*, 3 Apr. 1914: 4.
29. Wu Rui 1970: 21; *BLQY*: 86; Huang Guangkuo 1960a: 26; Xian Yun 1956: 146. See also Yao Xueyin 1981: 21, 54; "*Li Zicheng*": 306; Murray 1982: 8, on the practice of adopting sons; and *STSB*, 14 Dec. 1913: 8; *BLQY*: 92.
30. Liu Ruming 1966: 12; Cai and Xu 1980: 336; Wu Rui 1970: 21.
31. Tao Juyin 1957–58: II, 44; *MLB*, 1 Sept. 1912: 3; *Xiping xianzhi*, "Feijie": 3b; Huang Guangkuo 1960a: 26.
32. *STSB*, 2 Apr. 1914: 4; *BLQY*: 86; Cai and Xu 1980: 335–36. Compare also Laffey 1972: 93; Kuchiki 1966: 155.
33. Han Xuexu 1965: 37; Qiao Xuwu 1956: 136; Tao Juyin 1957–58: II, 41; *BLQY*: 92; Du Qunhe ed. 1980: 222; *STSB*, 1 May 1914: 4, 10 May 1914: 4, 12 June 1914: 10; *ZFGB* 741 (30 May 1914). On Li Zicheng, see Parsons 1970: 36, 38–39. Compare also Kuchiki 1966: 576; Howard 1926: 186.
34. *BLQY*: 92; Cai and Xu 1980: 332–33; *DFZZ* 11, no. 2 (1 Aug. 1914), "Zhongguo dashiji": 18; Du Qunhe ed. 1980: 183–98. Compare also Lundeen 1925: 49.
35. *BLQY*: 93–94; Xian Yun 1956: 154; "La Fuite du Loup Blanc": 14; *STSB*, 3 Apr. 1914: 4.
36. See Ueda 1924: 83; *Mingmo nongmin qiyi shiliao* (Materials on Righteous Peasant Uprisings of the Late Ming Period), Beijing 1952: 326–27.
37. Harrison 1970: 76; Dardess 1972: 112; Gotō 1928: 101–2.
38. Howard 1926: 175. See also Ueda 1924: 76; Kuchiki 1966: 485; Parsons 1970: 119.
39. Hobsbawm 1959: 15; Hobsbawm 1972a: 50. On the mysterious circumstances surrounding Bai's death, see *DFZZ* 11, no. 3 (1 Sept. 1914), "Zhongguo dashiji": 25; *STSB*, 12 Aug. 1914: 4, 14 Aug. 1914: 2, 19 Aug. 1914: 4; *ZFGB* 813 (10 Aug. 1914), 816 (13 Aug. 1914); Du Qunhe ed. 1980: 211–16; Xian Yun 1956: 156–57; Tao Juyin 1947: 187; Feng Yuxiang 1944: I, 209; Cheng Yufeng 1978: 25–27.
40. *NCH*, 26 Mar, 1927: 521; *DFZZ* 20, no. 14 (25 July 1923): 9–10; SD 893.00/5345 (Jinan to Beijing, 29 Dec. 1923). Compare also Gotō 1928: 101

Howard 1926: 265. For a different version of Lao Yangren's death, see *BLQY*: 99.

41. *CWR*, 23 June 1923: 98; Washio 1928: 5; Swallow and Lu 1934; Kuchiki 1966: 48, 461; McCormack 1977: 17; *BLQY*: 93–95.

42. Wen Gongzhi 1930: II, 42, 184; Nagano 1938: 197; Nagano 1924: 77; Chang Kuo-t'ao 1972: 20. See also Murray 1982: 7–8.

43. Maxwell 1956: ix.

44. He Xiya 1925a: 55; Nagano 1932: 389.

45. *NCH*, 26 Mar. 1927: 521, 2 Apr. 1927: 45; *CWR*, 2 June 1923: 3; *DFZZ* 20, no. 14 (25 July 1923): 4; *NCH*, 21 Mar. 1914: 867, 8 Nov. 1913: 411. See also Washio 1928: 5; Ueda 1924: 21; *BLQY*: 98; Perry 1980: 134; Lust 1972: 271–72n.

46. *NCH*, 26 Mar. 1927: 521; Kuchiki 1981: 236; Wu Cangzhou 1961: 361.

47. Lü Jiuyu 1980: 316; *MLB*, 25 June 1913: 13; Xian Yun 1956: 142; Wu Rui 1970: 19; Wang Shucun 1964: 31; Cheng Ying 1962: 555; Lundeen 1925: 48. Compare also Eastman 1974: 288, 290.

48. *NCH*, 26 Mar. 1927: 521; *BLQY*: 98–99; *NCH*, 21 Mar. 1914: 867–68, 2 Apr. 1927: 45. See also Kuchiki 1966: 39, 140.

49. McCormack 1977: 1. Compare also Shimamura 1973: 75.

50. McCormack 1977: 18. See also Washio 1928: 5.

51. Tian Buyi et al. 1967: 61. Compare also the description of Li Zicheng in "*Li Zicheng*": 185.

52. Takahashi 1967: 800; Kuchiki 1966: 134–43. See also He Xiya 1925a: 35.

53. Kuchiki 1966: 58, 66–67: Ueda 1924: 54.

54. Shih 1967: 332; Laffey 1972: 89.

55. *NCH*, 16 May 1914: 519.

56. *Ibid.*, 2 June 1923: 597–98. See also Muramatsu 1960: 251–52; Ruhlmann 1960: 164–65.

57. Howard 1926: 166.

58. *DFZZ* 21, no. 3 (10 Feb. 1924): 8–9; *STSB*, 25 Nov. 1913; 9. See also Lü Jiuyu 1980: 315.

59. Schram 1966: 138; Smedley 1934: 140–41. See also Perry 1980: 113.

60. Kuchiki 1966: 540.

61. Xian Yun 1956: 154; "La Fuite du Loup Blanc": 14; Kuchiki 1966: Chaps. 1–13. See also *NCH*, 26 Mar. 1927: 521.

62. Kuchiki 1966: 128; *NCH*, 5 Mar. 1927: 383.

63. Howard 1926: 90–91. Compare also Mackay 1927: 251; Manshū rōnin 1938: 84–85; Lilius 1930: 229–33.

64. He Xiya 1925a: 33; Tanaka 1934: 156; Kuchiki 1966: 50. For a close description of the organization of southern Chinese pirate gangs, see also Murray 1982, esp. pp. 5–6.

65. Kuchiki 1966: 67, 110; Howard 1926: 36.

66. He Xiya 1925a: 33. See also Carpenter 1925: 271; Taylor 1922: 20.

67. *CWR*, 23 June 1923: 99. See also *CWR*, 1 June 1923: 208.

68. Howard 1926: 162–63; Kurushima 1952: 113, 198; Lundeen 1925: 27.

69. Borst-Smith 1917: 218; *China's Millions*, June 1922: 88; Lundeen 1925: 25; Yao Xueyin 1981: 56; "*Li Zicheng*": 306; Ueda 1924: 21–22, 40–42, 58.

70. *STSB*, 3 Apr. 1914: 4; *BLZX*: 7. See also Pawley 1935: 105; Dailey 1923a: 208.

71. He Xiya 1925a: 33; Inoue 1933: 63; Howard 1926: 168. See also Murray 1982: 6.

72. Kuchiki 1966: 56; Tanaka 1934: 156.

73. Kurushima 1952: 35–36; Howard 1926: 53; Ueda 1924: 36; Lundeen 1925: 65. See also the photographs accompanying Kuchiki 1966, Tsuzuki 1974, and Watanabe 1981.

74. He Xiya 1925a: 33.

75. Kurushima 1952: 197, 235; He Xiya 1925a: 33; Mantetsu chōsaka 1930: 31–32; Yao Xueyin 1981: 95–96. See also Takahashi 1967: 799.

76. Tsuzuki 1974: 34.

77. He Xiya 1925a: 33–34; Takahashi 1967: 799; Gain 1909: 414. See also Pawley 1935: 39.

78. He Xiya 1925a: 33. See also Howard 1926: 227.

79. Hedges 1923: 610. See also Gotō 1928: 19; Carpenter 1925: 271.

80. Lü Jiuyu 1980: 317; *NCH*, 21 Mar. 1914: 867; *BLQY*: 85. See also Gain 1909: 414.

81. He Xiya 1925a: 33, 47; Hsiao Kung-chuan 1960: 462–63; Mowll 1925.

82. He Xiya 1925a: 34; Kuchiki 1966: 148. See also Watanabe 1964: 85.

83. He Xiya 1925a: 34; Mowll 1925; Aldrich 1923: 674; Strauss 1931: 25; Kurushima 1952: 119; Howard 1926: 181; Ueda 1924: 13–14; *NCH*, 12 Feb. 1927: 257.

84. Chang Cheng ed. 1980: 6; Kuchiki 1966: 51–52, 55.

85. Howard 1926: 54; Johnson 1934: 56, 212; *CWR*, 2 June 1923: 3; Aldrich 1923: 675, 680; *NCH*, 12 Feb. 1927: 257.

86. Howard 1926: 53–54; *NCH*, 12 Feb. 1927: 257.

87. Howard 1926: 167; Johnson 1934: 99.

88. Chen Wuwo 1923: I, 31.

89. *ZGNC*: 335. See also Pawley 1935: 205–6.

90. Hedges 1923: 609; Mantetsu chōsaka 1930: 42–43.

91. Kuchiki 1966: 59; Johnson 1934: 57; Tanaka 1934: 164; Swallow and Lu 1934.

92. *Central China Post*, 4 June 1914, in SD 893.00/2156 (Hankou to Beijing, 8 June 1914); King 1927: 169–71.

93. Howard 1926: 98–101.

94. Hedges 1923: 610: Carpenter 1925: 271; Swallow and Lu 1934. See also Mantetsu chōsaka 1930: 42–43; *Shina meibutsu*: 14–15.

95. Nagano 1932: 389–90. See also He Xiya 1925a: 47; C. Y. Chang 1937: 498; Takahashi 1967: 802; Tanaka 1934: 160.

96. Strauss 1931: 7; Lundeen 1925: 114; *NCH*, 9 Apr. 1927: 98; Murray 1982: 9. See also Cai and Xu 1980: 1288.

97. Tao Juyin 1947: 180.

98. He Xiya 1925a: 67; Gain 1909: 413; Swallow and Lu 1934. See also Hal 1919: 1019; Howard 1926: 55; Tanaka 1934: 159–60.

99. Howard 1926: 183.

100. He Xiya 1925a: 33; Ikeda n.d.: I.

101. *China's Millions*, Aug. 1922: 117. See also Murray 1982: 8.

102. Qiao Xuwu 1956: 139; Caldwell 1925: 195; Kuchiki 1966: 145. See also Lü Jiuyu 1980: 316; *NCH*, 9 Apr. 1927: 98; *BLSM*: 47.

103. *STSB*, 2 Apr. 1914: 4; *BLSM*: 48–49; *Central China Post*, 12 Nov. 1913, in SD 893.00/2035 (Hankou to Beijing, 12 Nov. 1913).

104. See Lü Jiuyu 1980: 316.

105. Lundeen 1925: 129–30. See also *NCH*, 9 Apr. 1927: 98; Cable and French 1934: 222, 232–33.

106. He Xiya 1925a: 37–38. See also Takahashi 1967: 799; Murray 1982: 8.

107. Gu Hang 1927: 77. See also Chesneaux 1971b: 61–63; Mancall and Jidkoff 1972: 127–28, 261n. Compare also Ch'ên 1970: 819.

108. *STSB*, 13 Mar. 1914: 10; *BLQY*: 88.

109. Tsuzuki 1974: 30–31.

110. Huey n.d.: 19.

111. Wu Cangzhou 1961: 364–65.

112. Tao Juyin 1947: 181; Howard 1926: 180–81. See also Swallow and Lu 1934; Laffey 1972: 90.

113. Howard 1926: 182; Osame 1923: 12.

114. Johnson 1934: 124, 130, 226; Taylor 1922: 43–44.

115. Shih Nai-an 1963: 803; *BLSM*: 49; Du Qunhe ed. 1980: 364; Tsuzuki 1974: 62–67.

116. Howard 1926: 108–9; Guillon 1868: 362. For the information on the Taipings, I am indebted to Ms. E. J. Perry.

117. Howard 1926: 86.

118. *BLQY*: 88.

119. Kuchiki 1966: 60–67. See also Ueda 1924: 55; Tanaka 1934: 159.

120. Ch'ên 1970: 818.

121. *BLQY*: 88–89; Cai and Xu 1980: 207–9; Qiao Xuwu 1956: 139.

122. *BLQY*: 88; *NCH*, 2 Apr. 1927: 45.

123. *STSB*, 26 May 1914: 4, 7 Apr. 1914: 4.

124. Nagano 1938: 141; Franck 1923: 346. See also Hsiao Kung-chuan 1960: 305.

125. Lattimore 1941: 28–29.

126. Lundeen 1925: 60–62; Dailey 1923a: 208; *The Times* (London), 27 Nov. 1924; Pawley 1935: 85, 120; Strauss 1931: 22; *NCH*, 4 Dec. 1926: 443. See also Zhi Che 1926: 542.

127. Nagano 1938: 288; Miller 1970: 122–23, 125. See also Lafferty 1930: 56.

128. Swallow and Lu 1934.

129. Lundeen 1925: 95.

130. Inoue 1933: 58. See also Davis 1977: 181–86; Chesneaux ed. 1972: 306–14.

131. See Inoue 1933: 59; Ueda 1924: 9–10.

132. *NCH*, 4 Dec. 1926: 443, 30 Apr. 1927: 224; Lundeen 1925: 38. See also Mao Xueyin 1981; Lindt 1933: 195.

133. He Xiya 1925a: 65–76.

134. Lundeen 1925: 39; *NCH*, 30 Apr. 1927: 224.

135. C. Y. Chang 1937: 498; Swallow and Lu 1934. Compare also Chu Po 1962: 200–204.

136. He Xiya 1925a: 46; Ueda 1924: 65–66; Kurushima 1952: 140; Tanaka 1934: 157.
137. Howard 1926: 108. See also Pawley 1935: 190; Kuchiki 1966: 194; Inoue 1923: 74–75.
138. Kuchiki 1966: 194–95.
139. Kurushima 1952: 125.

## Chapter Six

1. Howard 1926: 210–12, 188.
2. Kuchiki 1966: 44–55, 152.
3. Howard 1926: 184; Ueda 1924: 54; Ruhlmann 1960: 164. See also *BLSM*: 40.
4. Howard 1926: 87. See also Johnson 1934: 152.
5. Howard 1926: 88–89, 150–51; Strauss 1931: 21; Johnson 1934: 112.
6. Howard 1926: 33, 196; Tsuzuki 1974: 33; Johnson 1934: 83–84, 105, 121–22, 182–83; Pawley 1935: 105.
7. King 1927: 175. See also *Shina*, 3, no. 17 (Oct. 1912): 52; Gu Hang 1927: 74; Rock 1956: 127; Caldwell 1925: 213; Howard 1926: 192, 257.
8. *NCH*, 12 Feb. 1927: 258; Price 1937: 830. See also Johnson 1934: 162; Mackay 1927: 194, 250; Böcher 1932: 116.
9. Nagano 1938: 158. See also Johnson 1934: 151–52.
10. *China's Millions*, Mar. 1922: 42; Johnson 1934: 199. See also Mackay 1927: 191; Gotō 1928: 87–95.
11. *STSB*, 31 July 1914: 4; *DFZZ* 21, no. 3 (10 Feb. 1924): 8–9.
12. Ly 1917–18: 370; Howard 1926: 161, 168; *Shina meibutsu*: 14–15.
13. J. Hugon, *Mes paysans chinois* (1930): 135, quoted in Tiedemann 1982: 406.
14. A.N. 1923: 162; *CWR*, 26 May 1923: 448; Powell 1945: 102; Howard 1926: 78, 114; Mackay 1927: 192. See also Taylor 1922: 35; Howard 1926: 230; *CWR*, 19 May 1923: 407; Johnson 1934: 31, 41–42, 65, 71, 176–77; Kurushima 1952: 108, 137.
15. Kuchiki 1966: 84; Kurushima 1952: 131.
16. Gotō 1928: 49–50; Howard 1926: 168; Johnson 1934: 238; Kuchiki 1966: 182–93.
17. Howard 1926: 162.
18. *CWR*, 19 May 1923: 407, 23 June 1923: 99. See also Kurushima 1952: 136, 138; Lundeen 1925: 27, 33, 106; Pawley 1935: 105; Johnson 1934: 105; *China's Millions*, Aug. 1922: 117; Ueda 1924: 16, 42; Hall 1919: 1017.
19. Howard 1926: 105–6; also note pp. 65–66.
20. Ueda 1924: 72; Pawley 1935: 113; Johnson 1934: 101. See also Perry 1980: 65.
21. *China Yearbook*, 1925–26: 575.
22. Howard 1926: 155–56.
23. Kurushima 1952: 121, 142; Howard 1926: 147, 171; Pawley 1935: 114–16.
24. Johnson 1934: 65–66, 69, 86. See also Ch'i Hsi-sheng 1976: 181–82; Scott 1980: Chaps. 4–6.

25. Howard 1926: 147.

26. *La Chine* 43 (1 June 1923): 697; Howard 1926: 171, 231; Johnson 1934: 34, 63–64, 70; Kuchiki 1966: 387; Ueda 1924: 50; Pawley 1935: 114–16; Mackay 1927: 193; *NCH*, 29 Jan. 1927: 172.

27. Mackay 1927: 193.

28. Takahashi 1967: 801; Kuchiki 1966: 86–87. See also Kurushima 1952: 136.

29. Howard 1926: 39, 69, 92–93; Johnson 1934: 61, 145; Kurushima 1952: 121; *La Chine* 43 (1 June 1923): 697; *CWR*, 2 June 1923: 3; Pawley 1935: 89; Watanabe 1964: 83–84. See also Ruhlmann 1960: 143–44.

30. Eastman 1974: 300.

31. Pawley 1935: 108–9, 261. See also Mackay 1927: 194; Kuchiki 1966: 52.

32. *NCH*, 7 Feb. 1914: 396; Lü Jiuyu 1980: 316. See also Dannic 1912: 521; *China's Millions*, Aug. 1915: 129; Lü Jiuyu 1980: 311–12, 314; Swallow and Lu 1934; Naquin 1981: 115.

33. Fischle 1930: 9; Aldrich 1923: 674–75, 682; *CWR*, 19 May 1923: 407; Guillon 1868: 362.

34. Johnson 1934: 66–67. See also Howard 1926: 34; Mackay 1927: 194; Aldrich 1923: 676; Taylor 1922: 14–15.

35. Lundeen 1925: 50; Pawley 1935: 109, 138. See also Howard 1926: 42.

36. Close 1924: 22.

37. *CWR*, 23 June 1923: 99.

38. Aldrich 1923: 676; *China's Millions*, Aug. 1922: 116. See also Johnson 1934: 61; Böcher 1932: 117.

39. Taylor 1922: 19; *China's Millions*, Aug. 1922: 116; *NCH*, 4 Dec. 1926: 443. See also Wu Cangzhou 1961: 363; Guillon 1868: 362; Xian Yun 1956: 146; Yao Xueyin 1981: 49, 55; Cheng Ying 1962: 555. For a photograph, see Hobsbawm 1972a: plate 41.

40. Howard 1926: 158. See also Dailey 1923a: 208; Aldrich 1923: 674, 676; *La Chine* 43 (1 June 1923): 697; Chen Wuwo 1923: I, 28; *CWR*, 19 May 1923: 407; *NCH*, 12 May 1923: 382.

41. Johnson 1934: 150. See also Aldrich 1923: 674.

42. Kuchiki 1966: 52; Howard 1926: 208; Johnson 1934: 69, 90.

43. Nagano 1932: 248–49. See also Kuchiki 1966: 196–200; Yu Ming 1965: 6; Wu Cangzhou 1961: 364–65; Ruhlmann 1960: 167, 170–71.

44. *NCH*, 23 Apr. 1927: 183, 21 Mar. 1914: 845; Mantetsu chōsaka 1930: 35; Laffey 1976: 76; Wu Cangzhou 1961: 364–65.

45. Franck 1923: 338. See also Cheng Ying 1962: 555; *BLQY*: 97–98, 101–2.

46. Perry 1980: 64; Friedman 1974: 158; Wang Canli 1979: 31; *Gendaishi shiryō* 32: 581.

47. Shih 1967: 368; Friedman 1974: 130, 160.

48. Lai Xinxia 1957b: 14; Cheng Ying 1962: 553. For slightly different versions, see Tao Juyin 1957–58: II, 39, and Wang Tiancong 1978: 37. The *NCH* (3 May 1914: 590) gave a very loose translation. On the song's continued popularity, see Yao Xueyin 1981: 208.

49. Kuchiki 1966; Lindt 1933: 190–91; McCormack 1977: 16; *BLQY*: 84, 1–2.

50. Zhang Nanxian 1946: 31; Nan Yan 1924: 4; Xing Bei 1924: 10; Chen Wuwo 1923: I, 32; Hatano 1925: 57. See also *Yanling xianzhi*, "Dashiji": 30.
51. He Xiya 1925a: 10; Ruhlmann 1960: 168.
52. Nagano 1932: 264–65; Nagano 1930: 163–64. See also Ueda 1924: 8–9; Nagano 1933: 270; Perry 1980: 73–74.
53. *NCH*, 23 Apr. 1927: 183.
54. Nagano 1938: 123; Nagano 1933: 270. See also Tachibana 1923: 44–46; Chesneaux 1972: 18; Chesneaux 1973: 19.
55. Howard 1926: 157. See also Lundeen 1925: 43; Kuchiki 1966: 91.
56. *China's Millions*, May 1922: 70; Howard 1926: 220; Pawley 1935: 209. See also *China's Millions*, Mar. 1922: 42; Lundeen 1925: 31, 129; Johnson 1934: 59; *NCH*, 23 Apr. 1927: 182.
57. He Xiya 1925a: 67; Ch'ên 1970: 820n.
58. Kuchiki 1966: 94–95. See also Johnson 1934: 59; McDonald 1978: 55–56.
59. *NCH*, 2 Apr. 1927: 45; Kuchiki 1966: 91.
60. Howard 1926: 170.
61. Lundeen 1925: 43.
62. Howard 1926: 191–92, also 178.
63. Aldrich 1923: 673–74; *NCH*, 31 Jan. 1914: 312. See also *"Li Zicheng"*: 307; Lü Jiuyu 1980: 315; *NCH*, 29 Jan. 1927: 172.
64. Johnson 1934: 106–8. See also *NCH*, 12 Mar. 1927: 431; Strauss 1931: 5.
65. Howard 1926: 188–89.
66. *NCH*, 7 July 1923: 3.
67. He Xiya 1925a: 39–41. See also C. Y. Chang 1937: 498; *China's Millions*, Apr. 1923: 57, Sept. 1926: 142; *NCH*, 2 June 1923: 592, 9 Apr. 1927: 98, 16 Apr. 1927: 136; Strauss 1931: 6; Caldwell 1925: 144; *The Times* (London), 23 Mar. 1925; Pawley 1935: 39; Rock 1947: I, 367; Howard 1926: 197; Ueda 1924: 42–48, 81–83; Lundeen 1925: 64; Gotō 1923: 63; Nagano 1938: 145–46.
68. Howard 1926: 121; Ueda 1924: 47.
69. Gotō 1923: 60.
70. Nagano 1938: 179; Lundeen 1925: 127.
71. *NCH*, 5 Feb. 1927: 212, 19 Feb. 1927: 300–301, 26 Feb. 1927: 344–45; *China's Millions*, May 1914: 76; *The Times* (London), 12 Mar. 1914.
72. *The Times* (London), 7 Apr. 1914, 7 Mar. 1914, 17 Mar. 1914. See also Lü Jiuyu 1980: 314; Xiong Bin 1980: 300–301.
73. *Hankow Herald*, 29 Oct. 1926, in SD 893.00/7963 (Hankou to Washington, D.C., 15 Nov. 1926); Hsieh 1969: 57; *BLQY*: 84–85; *BLSM*: 31.
74. Nagano 1938: 229. See also Cao Hongxu 1930: 28–29.
75. *ZFGB* 622 (30 Jan. 1914); *CWR*, 23 June 1923: 98; Taylor 1922: 27 Ueda 1924: 58.
76. Tsuzuki 1974: 83; Tao Juyin 1947: 184; *NCH*, 28 Mar. 1914: 917.
77. Xian Yun 1956: 147.
78. Rock 1956: 25. See also King 1927: 40; Gain 1909: 413; *STSB*, 24 Ma 1914: 4; Mantetsu chōsaka 1930: 59.
79. *The Times* (London), 17 Mar. 1914, 3 Apr. 1914; Tao Juyin 1947: 184; L Jiuyu 1980: 313. See also Smith 1918; *China's Millions*, Sept. 1926: 142.
80. *BLSM*: 21; Du Qunhe ed. 1980: 343; Han Xuexu 1965: 37; Xian Y

1956: 149; Tao Juyin 1957–58: II, 44; Borst-Smith 1917: 187; Cable and French 1934: 228, 232–33.

81. Lü Jiuyu 1980: 318–20.

82. *NCH*, 12 Feb. 1927: 267.

83. *DFZZ* 10, no. 9 (1 Mar. 1914), "Dashiji": 10; *The Times* (London), 30 Jan. 1914; *BLSM*: 26; Lü Jiuyu 1980: 312. See also *NCH*, 31 Jan. 1914: 312; Friedman 1974: 123.

84. *NCH*, 7 July 1928: 24.

85. Huey n.d.: 12, 9; Shih Nai-an 1963: 447–48; Ruhlmann 1960: 168.

86. For punishments reserved specifically for women, see Mantetsu chōsaka 1930: 40; He Xiya 1925a: 41; note also Pawley 1935: 122.

87. Shih Nai-an 1963: 253–54, 692–95, 739, 828, 863, 899.

88. Parsons 1970: 236; Curwen 1972: 69.

89. Huey n.d.: 11, 13.

90. Shimamoto 1974: 35–36.

91. Strauss 1931: 8, 12; Nagano 1938: 211; Washio 1928: 5; Osame 1923: 13–14; Nagano 1938: 157. See also Yao Xueyin 1981: 107, 111, 114, 137, 143, 168.

92. Wu Zhongdao 1933: 19; Shimamura 1973: 77.

93. Pawley 1935: 210.

94. Miller 1970: 125; Pawley 1935: 140. See also Murray 1982: 7.

95. Huey n.d.: 9–10; Pawley 1935: 210, 218; Johnson 1934: 185, 208.

96. Kuchiki 1966: 508, 182.

97. See, however, Yao Xueyin 1981: 34–35; Mancall and Jidkoff 1972: 131.

98. Howard 1926: 163; Kurushima 1952: 138–39; Tsuzuki 1974: 33; Tanaka 1934: 156; Murray 1982: 9. See also Mackay 1927: 193.

99. Kuchiki 1966: 232–51; Watanabe 1964: 78–79; Kurushima 1952: 134, 172; Howard 1926: 225–26; Mackay 1927: 192. See also Takahashi 1967: 800; Overmyer 1976: Chap. 8.

100. Gu Hang 1927: 75.

101. *NCH*, 30 Apr. 1927: 224; He Xiya 1925a: 49, 68–69, 72–75; Mantetsu chōsaka 1930: 45; Swallow and Lu 1934; Inoue 1933: 62–64.

102. Howard 1926: 171–72; Johnson 1934: 68–69.

103. Swallow and Lu 1934; C. Y. Chang 1937: 498; *NCH*, 30 Apr. 1927: 224; Mantetsu chōsaka 1930: 45; Yao Xueyin 1981: 24; Takahashi 1967: 800; Gotō 1928: 21; Strauss 1931: 24. See also Tanaka 1934: 162; Shih Nai-an 1963: 53.

## Chapter Seven

1. Cited in McIntosh 1969: 1.

2. Ch'u T'ung-tsü 1962: 14–15; Wright 1955: 527.

3. Solomon 1971: 141.

4. Xiong Bin 1980: 299; Gamble 1963: 109; Dai Xuanzhi 1973: 72; *NCH*, 19 Feb. 1927: 300–301.

5. Jing An 1930: 10.

6. Cited in Bianco 1972: 275.

7. *Peking Leader*, 16 Apr. 1925, in SD 893.00/6219 (Beijing to Washington,

D.C., 21 Apr. 1925). See also *MLB*, 6 May 1913: 8; Curwen 1977: 2; Jen Yu-wen 1973: 52–54.

8. Gotō 1923: 70–71. See also Yano 1936: 172–77; Yano 1924: 44–45; Hsiao Kung-chuan 1960: 465–66; *ZHMGS*: 82; Cable and French 1934: 213–86.

9. *NCH*, 9 June 1923: 658; *Shina meibutsu*: 18–20. See also Dong Kechang 1960: 26; *STSB*, 13 Nov. 1913: 2; Chiang Siang-tseh 1954: 5; Perry 1980: 115–16; Dong Kechang 1958: 34; Murray 1982: 12.

10. *ZFGB* 622 (30 Jan. 1914); Swallow and Lu 1934; Nagano 1938: 182. See also Kuchiki 1966: 69; *NCH*, 4 Dec. 1926: 443; Cao Hongxu 1930: 31.

11. Nagano 1932: 222, 259; Yano 1924: 42, 45; Yano 1936: 172–75; Gain 1904: 162–63, 166.

12. Wang Tianjiang 1963: 85.

13. *MLB*, 28 Oct. 1912: 6; *DFZZ* 12, no. 1 (1 Jan. 1915): "Fa-ling": 1–2; *ZFGB* 775 (3 July 1914), 931 (7 Dec. 1914).

14. Dai Xuanzhi 1973: 67, 77. See also Lary 1985: 62, 135–36.

15. Tachibana 1923: 53–55; Nagano 1924: 55, 94–96; Lary 1985: 62.

16. Howard 1926: 106. See also Howard 1926: 206; *China's Millions*, Mar. 1923: 40–41; *NCH*, 22 Nov. 1913: 553; *La Chine* 43 (1 June 1923): 697; Johnson 1934: 110–11; Pawley 1935: 96–97.

17. Dailey 1923a: 207; Grafton 1923: 669; Cao Hongxu 1930: 8; Gotō 1928: 77; Teichman 1921: 74. See also Charlton Lewis 1972: 99; Lary 1985: 63.

18. Tao Juyin 1947: 178.

19. *STSB*, 25 June 1913: 4, 13 Feb. 1914: 3, 23 June 1914: 8; *NCH*, 24 Jan. 1914: 268; Tao Juyin 1957–58: II, 42.

20. *NCH*, 28 Mar. 1914: 917; *The Times* (London), 20 Sept. 1913, 23 Feb. 1914; *NCH*, 19 Mar. 1927: 477. See also Howard 1926: 260.

21. Nagano 1932: 239; Nagano 1924: 95; Tanaka 1934: 156. See also Hedges 1923: 610; *North China Daily Mail*, 17–20 Oct. 1923, in SD 893.00/5280 (Tianjin to Washington, D.C., 23 Oct. 1923); Friedman 1974: 150.

22. He Xiya 1925a: 63–64; Nagano 1924: 53–54; Grafton 1923: 670; Lary 1985: 60–61; *NCH*, 14 July 1923: 94; Kuchiki 1966: 61–62; *China's Millions*, Feb. 1924: 23; Tanaka 1934: 159.

23. FO 371/1942 (Beijing to London, 30 Mar. 1914).

24. Franck 1923: 338; *China's Millions*, Feb. 1923: 21, Feb. 1924: 23; *NCH*, 4 Dec. 1926: 443, 12 Feb. 1927: 257–58, 19 Feb. 1927: 301; Dailey 1923b: 292; *Central China Post*, 28 June 1922, in SD 893.00/4582 (Beijing to Washington, D.C., 28 June 1922); *Hankow Herald*, 15 Nov. 1926, in SD 893.00/7963 (Hankou to Washington, D.C., 15 Nov. 1926). See also *NCH*, 8 Nov. 1913: 422; *BLSM*: 19–20; Mantetsu chōsaka 1930: 44; Tanaka 1934: 158–59; Kuchiki 1966: 61–62; Hsiao Kung-chuan 1960: 706–7.

25. *BLQY*: 88; Qiao Xuwu 1956: 133; Teng 1964: 180.

26. *STSB*, 17 Jan. 1914: 8, 2 Mar. 1914: 3; Tao Juyin 1957–58: II, 39; Lary 1985: 61. See also *NCH*, 7 Mar. 1914: 656–57; Lü Pingdeng 1936: 560.

27. Powell 1923b: 916.

28. Clubb 1968: 41–42; *Hankow Daily News*, 26 June 1914, in SD 893.00/2161 (Hankou to Beijing, 26 June 1914). See also *MLB*, 2 May 1912: 8.

29. Yano 1936: 178; Ikeda n.d.: I; Johnson 1934: 196; Howard 1926: 248–51.

30. Osame 1923: 13; Yano 1924: 44–45; Zhang Jiehou 1927: 73; Borst-Smith

1917: 195; *Reminiscences of a Chinese Official*: 87–90; Howard 1926: 241, 250–51; Chow Yung-teh 1966: 184; Xiong Bin 1980: 303–4.

31. Gotō 1923: 68–69; Gotō 1928: 39–43.

32. He Xiya 1925a: 33–34; Ueda 1924; Franck 1923: 345; Yao Xueyin 1981: 13.

33. Tachibana 1923: 72–73; Osame 1923: 13–14; Hedges 1923: 609; Nagano 1932: 222, 259. See also Gain 1904.

34. *BLQY*: 93, 96; *STSB*, 9 Mar. 1912: 4, 5 Dec. 1912: 4, 11 Dec. 1912: 4; *ZFGB* 236 (23 Oct. 1912); Shimamoto 1974: 53–55.

35. Nagano 1924: 42–44; Tachibana 1923: 73–74. See also *NCH*, 11 Aug. 1917: 317.

36. Gotō 1928: 65; "Yanjiu tufei wenti zhi ziliao": 4.

37. Gain 1904: 170; Ueda 1924: 1–4; Tian Ran 1926; *ZGNC*: 345; *ZHMGS*: 81; *NCDC*: 106–7, 109, 113; Yung-fa Chen 1986: 473.

38. Gotō 1928: 64–66; Chen Wuwo 1923: I, 29; *CWR*, 2 June 1923: 18. See also Hsiao Kung-chuan 1960: 424; Gain 1904: 170.

39. Howard 1926: 168, 173.

40. Ueda 1924: 25; Yung-fa Chen 1986: 473; Yao Xueyin 1981: 200–206, 237. See also Tanaka 1934: 158; "*Li Zicheng*": 306–7.

41. Nagano 1938: 128–29.

42. See *MLB*, 28 June 1913: 10, 2 May 1912: 8; also Gain 1904: 163.

43. McIntosh 1969: 1.

44. *ZGNC*: 320–22; Toller 1948: 23.

45. Edgar Snow 1972: 58.

46. Rock 1925: 333, 335–37; Xue Shaoming 1937: 132–35; Dannic 1912: 521; Gain 1909: 413. See also Benson 1925: 28–29; Cao Hongxu 1930: 30–31; Rock 1947: II, esp. pp. 17–18, 26; Edgar Snow 1972: 47–49.

47. Skinner 1964; "Travelling in Robber Country": 235–36. See also Smedley 1956: 135.

48. Smedley 1956: 227; Smedley 1934: 59–60; Nagano 1932: 386; Nagano 1938: 236. See also Swallow and Lu 1934; Tominaga 1952: 165; "Yanjiu tufei wenti zhi ziliao": 4.

49. Watanabe 1964: 114.

50. *BLQY*: 81–83. See also "Guanzhong daoke"; Mackay 1927: 253; Mancall and Jidkoff 1972: 234.

51. Howard 1926: 98–100.

52. Faure 1973: 224–32; Kikuchi 1978: 142. See also Hall 1919: 1020.

53. *The Times* (London), 28 Jan. 1913; *China's Millions*, May 1914: 69; Kikuchi 1978: 134; *China Yearbook*, 1924–25: 555.

54. Kikuchi 1978: 143.

55. Edgar Snow 1972: 54.

56. See *Wenxiang xianzhi*, I/15b; Mantetsu chōsaka 1930: 17; *NCDC*: 108.

57. Lilius 1930: 135. See also *NCH*, 26 May 1923: 525, 2 June 1923: 592.

58. *STSB*, 1 Oct. 1912: 4.

59. Nagano 1933: 273.

60. *NCH*, 9 June 1923: 658; Huang Renzhi 1935: 2, 5–6; *Shina meibutsu*: 0–11.

61. Grafton 1923: 669; Nagano 1938: 143; *NCH*, 4 Dec. 1926: 443; Mantetsu

chōsaka 1930: 37–38; Yung-fa Chen 1986: 471; Nagano 1933: 271, 273; *NCDC*: 108–9.

62. Takahashi 1967: 801.

63. Nagano 1938: 162; *NCH*, 25 May 1906: 467, 14 Sept. 1918: 627; Ueda 1924: 46.

64. Gain 1909: 415; Perry 1980: 108; Gotō 1923: 54; Kurushima 1952: 236; Ueda 1924: 6.

65. Tiedemann 1982: 410; Nagano 1938: 162, 199–200; Tanaka 1934: 157.

66. Gotō 1923: 55; Swallow and Lu 1934. For examples of extortion letters, see also He Xiya 1925a: 53.

67. *The Times* (London), 22 Apr. 1924; Lilius 1930: 235. See also Pawley 1935: 60.

68. Pawley 1935: 240; Caldwell 1925: 194.

69. *Shina meibutsu*: 11; Kōkaku Sanjin 1924: 172; Nagano 1938: 140–41; Grafton 1923: 600; Gain 1909: 414; Watanabe 1964: 27; Kingston 1977: 207.

70. Cai and Xu 1980: 270; "Yanjiu tufei wenti zhi ziliao": 7; *The Times* (London), 20 Nov. 1923; Pawley 1935: 210; Ueda 1924: 37–38.

71. "Yanjiu tufei wenti zhi ziliao": 2; He Xiya 1925a: 62; Nagano 1938: 269; Cao Hongxu 1930: 28–29; FO 228/1802 (Hankou to Beijing, 5 Oct. 1911); *ZFGB* 175 (23 Oct. 1912), 231 (18 Dec. 1912); Ueda 1924: 36, 45; Augustana Mission 1925: 197–99.

72. "Yanjiu tufei wenti zhi ziliao": 4; Nagano 1938: 205.

73. Nagano 1938: 141, 211; "Yanjiu tufei wenti zhi ziliao": 13. See also Nagano 1924: 223; Dannic 1912: 523.

74. Perry 1980: 108; Nagano 1938: 141.

75. Powell 1923b: 957. See also Yao Xueyin 1981; FO 228/1802 (Hankou to Beijing, 5 Oct. 1911); He Xiya 1925a: 62.

76. McAleavy 1968: 183; Inoue 1923: 173–75.

77. Ueda 1924: 38; Grafton 1923: 600; Gotō 1923: 55; Nagano 1938: 141–42; Takahashi 1967: 801–2; Kōkaku Sanjin 1924: 172.

78. Ueda 1924: Howard 1926: 215; Swallow and Lu 1934; Nagano 1938: 141–43; Takahashi 1967: 801; Kōkaku Sanjin 1924: 172; Gain 1909: 415; Kurushima 1952: 205; Gotō 1923: 55, 63; Watanabe 1964: 27; Yao Xueyin 1981: 19.

79. Mackay 1927: 189; *NCH*, 12 Feb. 1927: 257; Lilius 1930: 235; Ueda 1924: 37–38, 54.

80. Ueda 1924: 40; C. Y. Chang 1937: 498.

81. Inoue 1933: 63–64; He Xiya 1925a: 70; *NCH*, 4 Dec. 1926: 443, 9 Apr. 1927: 98. See also Aldrich 1923: 680; Lundeen 1925: 55–56; Wu Zhongdao 1933: 19.

82. Lundeen 1925: 21, 40, 67; *NCH*, 4 Dec. 1926: 443, 9 Apr. 1927: 98; C. Y. Chang 1937: 498.

83. C. Y. Chang 1937: 498; "Yanjiu tufei wenti zhi ziliao": 2; Johnson 1934: 95; Howard 1926: 11.

84. Swallow and Lu 1934; Kuchiki 1966: 45; Yao Xueyin 1981: 8, 16; "L Zicheng": 306; Howard 1926: 90–91. See also Powell 1945: 111; Johnson 1934: 57; *NCH*, 4 Dec. 1926: 443; Mackay 1927: 251; Ch'ên 1970: 821.

85. Lundeen 1925: 38–39; Ueda 1924: 9–10; Gu Hang 1927: 75.

86. Kurushima 1952: 187.

87. Johnson 1934: 217–20, 229; Lundeen 1925: 132–33; *Peking and Tientsin Times*, 22 Jan. 1924, in SD 893.00/5365 (Beijing to Washington, D.C., 30 Jan. 1924).

88. Kurushima 1952: 195–96; Johnson 1934: 231.

89. Chen Wuwo 1923: I, 11–14; Tachibana 1923: 64; Ueda 1924.

90. Johnson 1934: 229; Ueda 1924: 58.

91. Grafton 1923: 600; "Yanjiu tufei wenti zhi ziliao": 8; *China's Millions*, May 1922: 70, Mar. 1922: 38; Johnson 1934: 171, 125; *NCH*, 26 Feb. 1927: 344, 19 Mar. 1927: 477. See also Howard 1926: 260.

92. Nagano 1924: 46–47; Wakeman 1975: 207.

93. *STSB*, 7 Feb. 1914: 2.

94. Liao Yizhong et al. 1981: 279–80; Qiao Zhiqiang 1981: 528, 542–44; Banno 1970: 5–9; Des Forges 1973: 28–30; Lust 1972: 167–70; Wang Tianjiang 1979: 789; CPM 1913: 13. See also Jurgensen 1965: Chap. 1.

95. *The Times* (London), 9 Apr. 1914.

96. *DFZZ* 19, no. 24 (25 Dec. 1922): 133, 142; *DFZZ* 20, no. 1 (10 Jan. 1923): 156–57; *China's Millions*, Dec. 1922: 189; *Peking and Tientsin Times*, 3 Jan. 1924, in SD 893.00/5346 (Beijing to Washington, D.C., 10 Jan. 1924); Nagano 1924: 47–48; A.N. 1923: 161–62; Dailey 1923a: 209; Hedges 1923: 609; "Yanjiu tufei wenti zhi ziliao": 11.

97. Lundeen 1925: 132–35; *DFZZ* 20, no. 1 (10 Jan. 1923): 157; *NCH*, 22 Jan. 1927: 129; *Huaiyang xianzhi*, VIII/54b; A.N. 1923: 162.

98. Nagano 1924: 48; *Relations de Chine*, Jan. 1924: 250–52; Dailey 1923c: 244; Ozaki 1949: 74; *North China Daily Mail*, 15 Jan. 1924, in SD 893.00/5356 (Beijing to Washington, D.C., 19 Jan. 1924); Nagano 1932: 386.

99. Hedges 1923: 606–7; Gotō 1928: 77 86; W. W. Chen 1923: 12–13; Howard 1926: 170, 227–28; Johnson 1934: 41; *China's Millions*, Mar. 1923: 41.

100. W. W. Chen 1923: 10. See also Nagano 1924: 46–50; *New York Times*, 20 May 1923, quoted in Lafferty 1931: 34.

101. *NCH*, 12 Feb. 1927: 257, 19 May 1923: 453–54; Lundeen 1925: 41–42, 134.

102. Nagano 1938: 163–64; Gotō 1937: 324–26; *China's Millions*, July 1927: 110, Dec. 1928: 188. See also Bianco 1969: 303.

103. Mackay 1927: 251; Dailey 1923a: 208; Strauss 1931: 12.

104. *NCH*, 29 Jan. 1927: 173; *China's Millions*, May 1918: 60.

105. *NCH*, 7 Feb. 1914: 380; *The Times* (London), 7 Mar. 1914; FO 228/1873 (Hankou to Beijing, 1 Nov. 1913). See also Chen Wuwo 1923: I, 16; Mackay 1927: 188; Howard 1926: 64.

106. Lundeen 1925: 28; Fischle 1930: 34 35, 38 39 (also 111, 116, 151, 184). See also Johnson 1934: 68, 72–73, 94, 106–10, 119–20, 193, 208; *NCH*, 26 Feb. 1927: 345; Mowll 1925; Mackay 1927: 191; Pawley 1935: 122; Howard 1926: 120–21; Ueda 1924: 42–48; *The Times* (London), 15 June 1923.

107. Dailey 1923a: 208. See also Aldrich 1923: 676; Kurushima 1952: 140; Johnson 1934: 161; Howard 1926: 145; Mackay 1927: 192.

108. Martin 1938: 175; *The Times* (London), 30 Mar. 1914; *STSB*, 21 Apr. 1914: 2.

109. Aldrich 1923; *CWR*, 19 May 1923: 408, 14 July 1923: 209. See also Johnson 1934: 169, 232; Gotō 1928: 94.

110. *China's Millions*, May 1922: 70; Howard 1926: 194–95; Johnson 1934: 31, 58–59, 94.

111. *NCH*, 4 Dec. 1926: 443, 12 Feb. 1927: 258; *China's Millions*, July 1927: 110, Dec. 1928: 188; Gotō 1928: 88–94.

112. Dailey 1923c: 245. See also Johnson 1934: 229.

113. SD 893.00/1999 (Hankou to Beijing, 8 Oct. 1913).

114. *The Times* (London), 21 Sept. 1923; *NCH*, 29 Sept. 1923: 895–96; Kurushima 1952: 205–6, 228. See also Aldrich 1923: 680; Howard 1926: 235–37.

115. Howard 1926: 248–49, 258–59; Johnson 1934: 217, 229; Lundeen 1925: 133.

116. Johnson 1934: 175, 185. See also Pawley 1935: 83; Lundeen 1925: 136.

117. C. K. Yang 1965: II, 114. See also Kuhn 1975: 289; Nagano 1933: 278; Yung-fa Chen 1986: 473.

118. Yung-fa Chen 1986: 472.

119. Caldwell 1925: 192–94, also 175–76, 217–27.

120. *Ibid.*: 209. See also *CWR*, 9 June 1923: 35.

121. See Huey n.d.: 21–22; Lust 1972: 199.

122. Teichman 1921: 79.               123. Yung-fa Chen 1986: 472.

124. Bianco 1969: 304.                125. Tawney 1964: 73–74.

126. Price 1937: 829.

127. Perry 1980: 131–32; Kuchiki 1966, esp. p. 391. See also Murray 1982: 10.

128. Smedley 1933: 46–47; Gain 1909: 413. See also Cao Hongxu 1930: 15–16.

129. Feng Yuxiang 1944: I, 206; Rock 1947: II, 465.

130. Lattimore 1932: 233. See also Watanabe 1964: 24; Ly 1917–18: 367.

131. *XHGM*: VII, 362; Wu Cangzhou 1961: 365; Aldrich 1923: 675, 677; *La Chine* 43 (1 June 1923): 698; Nagano 1938: 135; Hedges 1923: 610; Tiedemann 1982: 411.

132. Nagano 1933: 254. See also pp. 249, 258; Tachibana 1923: 57; *MLB*, 22 June 1912: 7; Price 1937: 835–36; "China's Booming Bandit Business": 42; Gotō 1937: 239–48.

133. *BLZX*: 8–9; Liu Ruming 1966: 11–12; Tao Juyin 1947: 186. See also Feng Yuxiang 1944: I, 209.

134. *NCH*, 31 Mar. 1914: 845; See also Tachibana 1923: 5.

135. Grafton 1923: 669. See also Gain 1909: 413; Perry 1980: 73; Dai Xuanzhi 1973: 75.

136. *BLQY*: 81–84; Li Xin et al. 1980: 153–54; *BLSM*: 10–16; Banno 1970: 11. See also "Guanzhong daoke": 526–27.

137. *STSB*, 1 Mar. 1914: 11.

138. Dong Kechang 1958: 36; Feng Yuxiang 1944: I, 206; Friedman 1974: 128. See also *NCH*, 16 May 1914: 524, and compare McCormack 1977: 16.

139. Hutchison 1936: 181; Teichman 1921: 23.

140. Friedman 1974: 156; *STSB*, 2 Apr. 1914: 3; *ZGNM*: 289; *STSB*, 2 May 1914: 4.

141. Han Xuexu 1965: 38n; Cheng Ying 1962: 555. See also Dai Xuanzhi 1973: 75, 78.

142. Wu Rui 1970: 19; *STSB*, 27 July 1914: 2.

143. Liu Ruming 1966: 11; Friedman 1974: 162; *La Politique de Pekin* 2 (26 Apr. 1914): 13. See also Borst-Smith 1917: 186; *NCH*, 28 Mar. 1914: 906–7.

144. *The Times* (London), 2 May 1914; *STSB*, 23 May 1914: 9, 27 July 1914: 2, 15 June 1914: 8.

145. *NCH*, 16 May 1914: 520; *BLQY*: 93. Compare also Parsons 1970: 207–8.

146. Kemal 1961: 56.

147. Pawley 1935: 229.

148. Tian Ying 1960: 266.

149. "*Li Zicheng*": 127. See also Ueda 1924: 54; *NCH*, 9 June 1923: 658; 15 Apr. 1930: 89; Mackay 1927: 252; Tachibana 1923: 51–53; Nagano 1924: 56–57, 94–95; Dannic 1912: 519, 523; Dai Xuanzhi 1973: 67; Hsiao Kungchuan 1960: 305, 706–7.

150. Li Xin et al. 1980: 158; Du Qunhe 1980: 205.

151. Tao Juyin 1947: 181. See also He Xiya 1925a: 102; Nagano 1938: 265, 279; Cheng Ying 1962: 567–68; Yu Ming 1965: 6; Lü Pingdeng 1936: 551; Tian Ying 1960: 266; Hsiao Kung-chuan 1960: 305; Kataoka 1974: 273; Kuhn 1970: 41.

152. Hobsbawm 1972a: 58–69; *BLQY*: 98.

153. Fried 1956: 229. See also Kuchiki 1966: 284.

154. See *NCH*, 7 Nov. 1898, cited in Tiedemann 1982: 413; Oxenham 1870: 406; *New York Times*, 24 Nov. 1929, cited in Lafferty 1931: 42–43; Xia Zhaorui 1974: 32–35; Yao Xueyin 1981: 87–97; "China's Booming Bandit Business": 41–42.

155. Guillon 1868: 359; Perry 1980: 88–94, 122–27, 158; Yung-fa Chen 1986: 447–49; *NCH*, 5 Mar. 1927: 383. For a peasant song that sharply expresses such anger, see Zhi Che 1926: 543.

156. *Central China Post*, 12 Nov. 1913, in SD 893.00/2035 (Hankou to Beijing, 12 Nov. 1913).

157. Hobsbawm 1972a: 50–51.

158. *ZFGB* 866 (2 Oct. 1914).

159. *BLQY*: 96; Friedman 1974: 164. See also *STSB*, 20 Aug. 1914: 7, and compare Uchiyama 1978: 215.

160. *NCH*, 9 Jan. 1915: 111; *STSB*, 20 Aug. 1914: 7; Cai and Xu 1980: 335–36; *China Yearbook*, 1916: 556; Du Qunhe ed. 1980: 219–22; *XHGM Hubei*: 728; *Xiping xianzhi*, "Feijie": 3b–4a; *BLQY*: 97.

161. Tao Juyin 1957–58: II, 46; *BLQY*: 101.

162. Chang Kuo-t'ao 1972: 290. See also Yao Xueyin 1981: 235.

163. Caldwell 1925: 177. See also Smedley 1956: 291.

## Chapter Eight

1. He Xiya 1925a: 9; Parsons 1970: 60–64; Perry 1980: 129; Faure 1973: 74–76; Li Shiyue 1959: 58; McCormack 1977: 17; Shih Nai-an 1963: 914. See also Belden 1950: 222–26; Clubb 1968: 33; Lary 1985: 62–64.

2. Watanabe 1964; McCormack 1977: 16–19; *Emperor Kuang Hsü's Reform Decrees 1898*: 54.

3. For examples, see Mantetsu chōsaka 1930: 3–23; *STSB*, 20 Jan. 1913: 7; *NCH*, 27 Nov. 1915: 617; FO 371/1942 (Beijing to London, 30 Mar. 1914); Huang Guangkuo 1960a: 25. See also *STSB*, 19 Sept. 1912: 4, 13 Oct. 1912: 7, 16 Oct. 1912: 4, 17 Nov. 1912: 4, 19 Nov. 1912: 7, 8 Dec. 1912: 2, 9 Jan. 1913: 7, 9 Nov. 1913: 11, 27 Nov. 1913: 2, 7 Dec. 1913: 8, 9 Dec. 1913: 8, 13 Dec. 1913: 8, 16 Apr. 1914: 2, 24 Apr. 1914: 8; and *NCH*, 29 Nov. 1913: 684, 27 Dec. 1913: 986, all describing the Yuan Shikai government's enlistment of 1911 hero Wang Tianzong to fight Henan bandits.

4. Nagano 1932: 383.

5. Smedley 1956: 299–300; McCormack 1977: 70–74, 102–6; Lary 1985: 67.

6. *The Foreigner in China*; Watanabe 1964: 89–90; Tuchman 1970: 109–13; Sheridan 1966: 160–63; 188–89.

7. See Tsuzuki 1974: 116, 124–25; Tuchman 1970: 183; Wen Gongzhi 1930: II, 163.

8. Hedges 1923: 610. See also Caldwell 1925: Chap. 15 *passim*.

9. *NCH*, 19 May 1923: 454.

10. SD 893.00/5345 (Jinan to Beijing, 28 Dec. 1923); Cai and Xu 1980: 1375–79; *DFZZ* 20, no. 14 (25 July 1923): 9–10; Dailey 1923c: 245, 1923d: 358; He Xiya 1925a: 85. See also Bianco 1969: 307.

11. Howard 1926: 169, 265–66.

12. Mao and Che 1968: 55; Kataoka 1974: 299–300.

13. *CWR*, 7 July 1923: 196. See also Swallow and Lu 1934; Mantetsu chōsaka 1930: 6–10; Kataoka 1974: 203–4; Li Xin et al. 1981: 215–19.

14. Wang Tiancong 1971: 12–13; *STSB*, 23 Aug. 1912: 4; *MLB*, 15 Aug. 1912: 5; Wu Cangzhou 1961: 362; Ch'ên 1968: 597.

15. Shimamoto 1974: 48–55.

16. *STSB*, 15 Dec. 1912: 4; *MLB*, 27 Jan. 1913: 8.

17. *STSB*, 9 Aug. 1914: 4; *ZFGB* 866 (2 Oct. 1914); Cheng Yufeng 1978 (Sept.): 27.

18. Wen Gongzhi 1930: II, 42, 100–102, 167; Zhang Yunjia 1958: 82; Wang Yuting 1976: 15; Wang Tiancong 1971: 12; *China Yearbook*, 1925–26: 1163.

19. *China Yearbook*, 1926–27: 1030; *Shaanxian zhi*, I/17a–18a; Liu Ruming 1966: 72–78; Mitani 1974: 251–52; Sheridan 1966: 206–9; Wen Gongzhi 1930: II, 109–10, III, 304–6; Zhi Che 1926: 541–43; *China's Millions*, Jan. 1927: 11.

20. Mitani 1974: 252–54: Wen Gongzhi 1930: III, 317–23.

21. Jing An 1930: 2–3.

22. Ch'ên 1968: 596.

23. Sonoda 1927: 481–82.

24. *NCH*, 24 Sept. 1921: 927; Sheridan 1966: 102. See also Borst-Smith 1916: 5–11, 27–28.

25. "Yanjiu tufei wenti zhi ziliao": 10–11; Clubb 1968: 28; Mitarevsky 1926: 103–4; Wen Gongzhi 1930: II, 163; *Gendaishi shiryō* 32: 583–84; *Yanling xianzhi* "Dashiji": 33–34.

26. *BLQY*: 97; Mu Jiang 1978: 4–5; Swallow and Lu 1934.

27. Chang Kuo-t'ao 1972: 20. See also Curwen 1977: 37, 174n.

28. *New York Times*, 23 Feb. 1930, quoted in Lafferty 1931: 17; Guo Zibin 1973: 30; Swallow and Lu 1934; Clubb 1968: 69.

29. Zhang Yunjia 1958: 79–81; Li Xiaoting 1969; Wen Gongzhi 1930: II, 97. See also Borst-Smith 1916.

30. Wen Gongzhi 1930: II, 97–98, III, 51–53; *XHSY*: IV, 213. See also Sheridan 1966: 62, 103–7.

31. Mu Jiang 1978: 5–8.

32. Li Xiaoting 1969; *XHSY*: IV, 213–14; *Shina* 15, no. 10 (Oct. 1924): 65; *NCH*, 6 Sept. 1924: 376; Li Yaxian 1969. See also Wilbur 1976: 254–58.

33. Wen Gongzhi 1930: II, 36, 42, 174–77, 182, 361; *Shina jihō* 2, no. 4 (Apr. 1925): 51; *Shina jihō* 2, no. 6 (June 1925): 37; *NCH*, 26 Dec. 1925: 556, 559, 2 Jan. 1926: 14, 9 Jan. 1926: 53, 16 Jan. 1926: 97, 15 May 1926: 292; Gillin 1967: 103; Mitani 1974: 251.

34. Mitani 1974: 250–51; Wou 1978: 139–44, 235–36; Jordan 1976: 280; *XHSY*: IV, 214.

35. Wang Yuting 1976: 16; SD 893.00/7963 (Hankou to Washington, D.C., 15 Nov. 1926); Mitarevsky 1926: 98; Pak Hyobom 1971: 379.

36. Liu Ruming 1966: 91–92; Sheridan 1966: 238; Mitani 1974: 270; *NCH*, 7 July 1928: 24; *HZB*: II, 13.

37. Nagano 1938: 239–40; Weller 1931; *Yanling xianzhi*, "Dashiji": 33; *Zhengyang xianzhi*, III/50a–51a; *Central China Post*, 1 Jan. 1932, quoted in Clubb 1968: 59.

38. Li Xiaoting 1969; Swallow and Lu 1934; *BLQY*: 100; Clubb 1968: 28.

39. *BLQY*: 100.

40. *NCH*, 27 May 1922: 594–96; *DFZZ* 19, no. 18 (25 Sept. 1922): 144; *China Yearbook*, 1923: 574–76; SD 893.00/4582 (Hankou to Washington, D.C., 28 June 1922); Dailey 1923a: 210; Wen Gongzhi 1930: II, 13, 167; Sheridan 1966: 110–11.

41. *Zhengyang xianzhi*, III/48a. See also Yao Xueyin 1981: 107, 111, 114, 137, 143, 168.

42. Cited in *Central China Post*, 28 June 1922, in SD 893.00/4582 (Hankou to Washington, D.C., 28 June 1922).

43. "Yanjiu tufei wenti zhi ziliao": 10–12; *DFZZ* 19, no. 18 (25 Sept. 1922): 142–44; *Shaanxian zhi*, I/15b; *Wenxiang xianzhi*, I/15a; *Xiping xianzhi*, "Feijie": 4a; *Queshan xianzhi*, XX/"Dashiji": 9b; *Yanling xianzhi*, "Dashiji": 28; A.N. 1923; Dailey 1923a: 208; 210; Hedges 1923: 606.

44. *BLQY*: 99; Hedges 1923: 608.

45. Lundeen 1925: 53–58. See also *DFZZ* 19, no. 23 (10 Dec. 1922): 129.

46. *Xiping xianzhi*, "Feijie": 4a; *Zhengyang xianzhi*, III/48a–48b; *Taikang xianzhi*, III/"Zhengwuzhi": 52b; *Huaiyang xianzhi*, VIII/54b; *Queshan xianzhi*, XX/"Dashiji": 9b; *China's Millions*, Feb. 1923: 21–24, Mar. 1923: 40–42, Dec. 1922: 189; Lundeen 1925: 58 139; A.N. 1923: 161–62; Mu Jiang 1978: 4–5; Dailey 1923a: 208–9; *DFZZ* 20, no. 1 (10 Jan. 1923): 156–57; *NCH*, 22 Jan. 1927: 129.

47. Tachibana 1923: 61–62; Dailey 1923c: 244–45. See also Nagano 1924: 84–86.

48. *Huaiyang xianzhi*, VIII/54b; *Xihua xianzhi*, I/24b. See also *China's Millions*, Nov. 1923: 174, Dec. 1923: 181.

49. *DFZZ* 20, no. 12 (25 June 1923): 8–9; SD 893.00/5346 (Beijing to

Washington, D.C., 10 Jan. 1924); Cai and Xu 1980: 1379–84; *NCH*, 22 Jan. 1927: 129.

50. *Peking and Tientsin Times*, 22 Jan. 1924, in SD 893.00/5365 (Beijing to Washington, D.C., 30 Jan. 1924).

51. *Far Eastern Times*, 25 Oct. 1923, in SD 893.00/5298 (Tianjin to Washington, D.C., 8 Nov. 1923).

52. Wang Yuting 1976: 16; Wang Tiancong 1971: 9; He Xiya 1925a: 91; *NCH*, 22 Jan. 1927: 129, 27 Feb. 1926: 376; Kataoka 1974: 203; Zhuo Ran 1935: 138; Nagano 1938: 221.

53. *NCH*, 29 Jan. 1927: 172.

54. Dailey 1923a: 208; "Yanjiu tufei wenti zhi ziliao": 3, 6. See also *NCH*, 5 Feb. 1927: 212.

55. Dailey 1923a: 207.

56. Nagano 1924: 50–52; He Xiya 1925a: 34; *Hankow Herald*, 29 Oct. 1926, in SD 893.00/7963 (Hankou to Washington, D.C., 15 Nov. 1926); *Peking and Tientsin Times*, 22 Jan. 1924, in SD 893.00/5365 (Beijing to Washington, D.C., 30 Jan. 1924).

57. Lundeen 1925: 43–44; emphasis added. See also Murray 1982: 16–17.

58. *Peking and Tientsin Times*, 22 Jan. 1924, in SD 893.00/5365 (Beijing to Washington, D.C., 30 Jan. 1924).

59. "Yanjiu tufei wenti zhi ziliao": 11; *Huaiyang xianzhi*, VIII/55a; *CWR*, 26 May 1923: 447; Chen Wuwo 1923: I, 32.

60. Ueda 1924: 18–19; *NCH*, 5 Feb. 1927: 212; Feng Yuxiang 1944: I, 102–4. See also Kanamaru 1933: 99; Bradley 1945: 114–16; Howard 1926: 254; Chao Shu-li 1953: 41; McAleavy 1968: 103.

61. *China's Millions*, May 1922: 70; Lundeen 1925: 62. See also Strauss 1931: 11–12; A.N. 1923: 162; Zhi Che 1926: 541.

62. *Xiping xianzhi*, "Feijie": 4a; *Taikang xianzhi*, III/"Zhengwuzhi": 52b; *Yanling xianzhi*, "Dashiji": 28; *Huaiyang xianzhi*, VIII/54b. See also *Peking and Tientsin Times*, 3 Jan. 1924, in SD 893.00/5346 (Beijing to Washington, D.C., 10 Jan. 1924); Nagano 1924: 223.

63. *China's Millions*, Mar. 1923: 37.

64. Lundeen 1925: 14, 44–45, 53; *China's Millions*, Dec. 1922: 189, Mar. 1923: 41; *BLQY*: 98–99. See also Dailey 1923a: 207.

65. Kuchiki 1966: 37, 68, 90, 214, 251; Watanabe 1964: 22; Howard 1926: 113–14, 193; Tanaka 1934: 157.

66. Gotō 1928: 36; Kurushima 1952: 235, 138, 143, 149; Howard 1926: 77–78; Johnson 1934: 200; Pawley 1935: 94–95; Lattimore 1932: 235.

67. *CWR*, 18 Nov. 1922: 428; *NCH*, 19 Mar. 1927: 477; Nagano 1938: 163; Osame 1923: 6. See also Sheridan 1966: 115; *Gendaishi shiryō* 32: 583–84.

68. Dailey 1923a: 210; *NCH*, 11 Nov. 1922: 363; *China's Millions*, Feb. 1923: 27. See also *DFZZ* 21, no. 14 (25 July 1924): 3–6.

69. *NCH*, 19 May 1923: 525, 9 June 1923: 652, 672; *The Times* (London), 6 July 1923; Close 1924: 20; *DFZZ* 20, no. 14 (25 July 1923): 9–10; Cai and Xu 1980: 1375–76.

70. Jowe 1925: 196; He Xiya 1925a: 57–60; Hedges 1923: 609; *Gendaishi*

*shiryō* 31: 583; *Gendaishi shiryō* 32: 580; Valliant 1972: 5. See also Kuo Ting-yee comp. 1965.

71. He Xiya 1925a: 74.

72. McCormack 1977: 15–27; Li Xin et al. 1978: 179–81; Tian Buyi et al. 1967: 61–64; Chang Cheng ed. 1980: 1–34; Washio 1928. See also Watanabe 1964: 26–29, 32–41; Jansen 1954: 110; Kanamaru 1933: 97–98.

73. "Japan's Intrigues in China": 426; "Fostering Banditry in China": 491, 494–98; Watanabe 1964: 51–55, 71–74. See also Jansen 1954: Chaps. 6–8; Kuchiki 1981; Tsuzuki 1972: 91–168; Valliant 1972.

74. Valliant 1972; "Fostering Banditry in China": 491–95. See also Jansen 1954: 198.

75. Reinsch 1922: 125; Yang 1945: 222–23; Close 1924: 19; Xu Zhiyan 1922: 1915/9; *Peking Leader*, 6 Sept. 1918, in SD 893.00/2889 (Beijing to Washington, D.C., 10 Sept. 1918). See also Franck 1923: 326–27.

76. *The Times* (London), 3 May 1922; *DFZZ* 19, no. 9 (10 May 1922): 128; *The Times* (London), 8 Dec. 1922.

77. Chen Wuwo 1923: I, 28–29; SD 893.00/5122 (Tianjin to Washington, D.C., 5 July 1923); *NCH*, 9 June 1923: 672.

78. Powell 1945: 106; Gotō 1923: 50–53, 70–73. See also Baba 1976: 50.

79. *CWR*, 9 June 1923: 37. See also *NCH*, 19 May 1923: 453.

80. SD 893.00/5122 (Tianjin to Washington, D.C., 5 July 1923); *CWR*, 19 May 1923: 408.

81. Kuchiki 1981: 235. See also *Gendaishi shiryō* 31: 584; Watanabe 1964: 32–33.

82. Kuchiki 1966: 46–48. See also Andō 1963: 8; Watanabe 1964: 45; Shimamura 1973: 11–12.

83. "Fostering Banditry in China": 494–95; Watanabe 1964: 74–77, 81–86, 119–25, 171–75; Tsuzuki 1976: 303–10; Tsuzuki 1972.

84. Valliant 1972: 8–14; Watanabe 1964: 76, 85–86; Tsuzuki 1976: 305.

85. Watanabe 1964: 100–110; Iwasaki 1934: 56; Kanamaru 1933: 99–100; Taira 1933: 116. See also Lindt 1933. The Japanese case is set out in Dairen Chamber of Commerce and Industry 1931.

86. Watanabe 1964: 119–21, 125, 129–31; Kataoka 1974: 203–4. See also Böcher 1932: 111–32; Watanabe 1972.

87. Kuchiki 1966: 388–93; Watanabe 1964: 106–12, 165–66; "Fostering Banditry in China": 497–98; "Creation and Organisation of a Bandit Army". See also Dairen Chamber of Commerce and Industry 1931.

88. Pawley 1935: 130, 139, 168; Watanabe 1964: 133–36; Kuchiki 1966: 406–41, 469–71. On the gang's previous anti-Japanese activity, see Dairen Chamber of Commerce and Industry 1931: 21.

89. Johnson 1934: 19–20, 107, 224, 196.

90. Wu Zhongdao 1933; Kataoka 1974: 204, 288–91; Yung-fa Chen 1986: 474–75; Esherick 1974: 102; Hinton 1966: 79, also Part I *passim*. See also Chao Shu-li 1953.

91. Yung-fa Chen 1986: 475.

92. Watanabe 1964: 108; Kuchiki 1966: 393.

93. Watanabe 1964: 163–68, 171–89; Kuchiki 1966: 546–86, 646–67; Tsuzuki 1974: 10–14, 198–208; Kataoka 1974: 204.

94. Belden 1950: 93, 223.

95. See also Chu Po 1962.

## Chapter Nine

1. Quoted in Hobsbawm 1972a: 110.

2. Quoted in Venturi 1966: 368–69.

3. Payne 1961: 58–59; Schram 1966: 127.

4. Chesneaux 1971b: 70–71. See also Harrison 1970: 52.

5. Mao Tse-tung 1965: I, 324; Harrison 1970: 99; Schram 1974: 213.

6. Smedley 1956: 136, 300; Kataoka 1974: 299–300.

7. Hsia 1968: 93.

8. Hofheinz 1969: 62–63.

9. *ZGNC*: 344–45; Yao Xueyin 1981: 240.

10. See Hsieh 1969: 70–72; Shimamoto 1974: 13–14.

11. Chang Kuo-t'ao 1972: 19–20.

12. Curwen 1972: 248n; *STSB*, 27 Apr. 1913: 4; *Bukan hōmen*: 20.

13. Cai and Xu 1980: 203–4; Wang Tiancong 1971: 9.

14. Zhi Che 1926: 540; Close 1924: 193. See also Nagano 1938: 178.

15. See "Guanzhong daoke": 520–26.

16. Song's diary, quoted in Li Xin et al. 1978: 44; Price 1984: 67–73; Hsüeh Chün-tu 1961: 63–65; Nozawa 1972: 32; Li Shiyue 1959: 60; He Xiya 1925a: 11–13. See also Song Jiaoren 1981: 11–13; Boorman ed. 1967: III, 192–93.

17. Hsüeh Chün-tu 1961: 80–81; Zhang Nanxian 1946: 31.

18. Wang Tianjiang 1979: 788; *ZHMG*: 146, 149, 151–53; *ZHMGS*: 82; Zhang Kaiyuan et al. 1979: 947, 950.

19. *MLB*, 29 Dec. 1911, quoted in Shimamoto 1974: 17.

20. Wang Tianjiang 1979: 797–98; *ZHMG*: 146, 148–50. See also *XHGM*: VII, 352–88.

21. Lust 1972: 195; *XHGM*: VII, 356, 368, 386; *MLB*, 19 Dec. 1911: 2, 9 Feb. 1912: 2; Ren Zhiming 1961: 393.

22. Lust 1972: 195; Wang Tianjiang 1979: 797–99; Wu Cangzhou 1961: 365, 380. See also Shimamoto 1974: 18, 26, 40–41; Hsieh 1969: 36–39, 52.

23. See various issues of *MLB* for this period; also Shimamoto 1974: 40–41.

24. Lust 1972: 184–85; Wu Cangzhou 1961: 361–62; Shimamoto 1974: 19.

25. "Zou Yongcheng huiyilu": 121.

26. *MLB*, 6 May 1913: 8; Zhang Kaiyuan et al. 1979: 933; Esherick 1976a: 192–94; *STSB*, 6 Nov. 1913: 8.

27. "Zou Yongcheng huiyilu": 121; Dong Kechang 1960: 24–25; Li Xin et al. 1980: 155; Du Qunhe ed. 1980: 226–27.

28. Du Qunhe ed. 1980: 226; Wang Zongyu 1964: 22. See also *STSB*, 2( July 1913: 4; *NCH*, 9 Aug. 1913: 450; *The Times* (London), 7 Mar. 1914; Ca and Xu 1980: 269.

29. Young 1977: 142–45; Du Qunhe ed. 1980: 226–34; *STSB*, 9 June 1913 3, 19 July 1913: 4, 31 Oct. 1913: 8, 9 Nov. 1913: 10, 12 Nov. 1913: 8, '

Feb. 1914: 8; Cai and Xu 1980: 207–8; Qiao Xuwu 1956: 133; Nozawa 1972: 127–31; *XHGM Hubei*: 724–25.

30. *NCH*, 17 Jan. 1914: 195; *STSB*, 6 May 1914: 10; *ZFGB* 528 (23 Oct. 1913); FO 371/1942 (Beijing to London, 21 Feb. 1914); *Shanghai shibao*, 30 Mar. 1914, quoted in Dong Kechang 1960: 26; Nozawa 1972: 133–35.

31. *STSB*, 30 Jan. 1914: 10, 23 Mar. 1914: 3; *NCH*, 21 Mar. 1914: 846. See also Qiao Xuwu 1956: 140.

32. *BLQY*: 90–92; Tao Juyin 1947: 177; *STSB*, 3 Apr. 1914: 4; *XHGM Hubei*: 725, 729, 732.

33. Du Qunhe ed. 1980: 223; Lü Jiuyu 1980: 316; Li Xin et al. 1980: 155.

34. *NCH*, 8 Nov. 1913: 411–12; Tao Juyin 1957–58: II, 38. See also Xing-yuan zhuren 1973: 18.

35. *STSB*, 3 Oct. 1913: 9; *NCH*, 8 Nov. 1913: 411–12; *STSB*, 22 Oct. 1913: 9. See also *Hankow Daily News*, 20 Oct. 1913, in FO 228/1873 (Hankou to Beijing, 21 Oct. 1913); SD 893.00/1999 (Hankou to Beijing, 8 Oct. 1913).

36. Cai and Xu 1980: 270–71; Li Xin et al. 1980: 154–55; Qiao Xuwu 1956: 133; Xian Yun 1956: 143. See also Xu Yaoshan et al. 1961; *The Times* (London), 17 Mar. 1914.

37. *STSB*, 3 Apr. 1914: 4; *NCH*, 7 Feb. 1914: 378.

38. Franck 1923: 344.

39. *STSB*, 22 May 1914: 9, 24 Apr. 1914: 9; *BLSM*: 26; Li Xin et al. 1980: 158; Xian Yun 1956: 152. See also *NCH*, 16 May 1914: 519.

40. Lü Jiuyu 1980: 315; Friedman 1974: 149; *NCH*, 14 Feb. 1914: 458; Cai and Xu 1980: 271.

41. *BLQY*: 91; *NCH*, 7 Feb. 1914: 379, 21 Mar. 1914: 845; Friedman 1974: 151.

42. *BLQY*: 92. See also *La Politique de Pekin* 13 (12 July 1914): 13.

43. Harding 1914: 109.

44. *XHGMIIYL*: III, 474 75; Duan Jianmin 1969: 25; Lust 1972: 184, 270n.

45. Dailey 1923a: 210; Tachibana 1923: 62; *Relations de Chine*, Jan. 1924: 250.

46. Powell 1923b: 958. See also Ueda 1924: 75; Wilbur 1976: 153.

47. Mitarevsky 1926: 98.

48. Snow 1968: 79; Smedley 1956: 135.

49. Hofheinz 1977: 160, 167.      50. Payne 1961: 114–15.

51. Smedley 1956: 113, 232–33.      52. Mao Tse-tung 1965: II, 96.

53. Nagano 1933: 188; Hofheinz 1969: 74.

54. Nagano 1933: 186.

55. Smedley 1934: 77–86; Hofheinz 1969: 39; Schram 1974: 97; Clubb 1968: 69; Lötveit 1970: 165–66.

56. Yung-fa Chen 1986. 591, n. 13.

57. Wou 1979: 28–30.

58. Mao Tse-tung 1965: II, 95.

59. Snow 1968: 210–11; Klein and Clark 1971: 586–87.

60. Keyte 1913: 227.

61. Snow 1968: 211; Selden 1967: 79.

62. Selden 1971: 43–78; Selden 1967: 68–70, 79. See also Kikuchi 1978: 43–46.

63. Clubb 1968: 67. See also Chang Kuo-t'ao 1972: 174–294.

64. Wou 1979: 28–30; H. F. Snow 1972: 152; Hofheinz 1969: 48; Kataoka 1974: 13; McColl 1967: 50–57; Clubb 1968: 66–67. See also "Shanxiang nuhuo"; Liu Manrong 1978.

65. Clubb 1968: 29; McColl 1967: 50; Nagano 1938: 225, 230, 240; "Shanxiang nuhuo": 28; *HZB*: II, 7–8.

66. Pak Hyobom 1971: 400–401 (grammar and punctuation amended). See also McColl 1967: 50.

67. Clubb 1968: 71; Nagano 1933: 152. See also Chang Kuo-t'ao 1972: 234, 236, 241–42, 265; *HZB*: II.

68. Clubb 1968: 59, 28.

69. McColl 1967: 46–47; *Dagong bao*, 5 Feb. 1932, quoted in Clubb 1968: 60. See also *Peking and Tientsin Times*, 23 Apr. 1932, quoted in Clubb 1968: 105.

70. Kataoka 1974: 14; H. F. Snow 1972: 299–303; *Dagong bao*, 7 Nov. 1931, quoted in Clubb 1968: 49; McColl 1967: 58; Clubb 1968: 61. See also Chang Kuo-t'ao 1972: 294, 463–64; "Shanxiang nuhuo": 26–27; Liu Manrong 1978: 78.

71. McColl 1967: 55, 58; Wou 1979: 29–30.

72. "Shanxiang nuhuo": 24; Liu Manrong 1978: 77. See also Chesneaux 1971b: 184; Hofheinz 1969; *Bukan hōmen*: 8.

73. Hofheinz 1969: 26; Chang Kuo-t'ao 1972: 289.

74. Chang Kuo-t'ao 1972: 215; Payne 1961: 105; Smedley 1934: 66, 77; Rue 1966: 107; Nagano 1933: 155.

75. *Journal de Pekin*, 23 Apr. 1930, quoted in Clubb 1968: 12–13. See also Nagano 1933: 158, 191–92.

76. Schram 1966: 128; Mao Tse-tung 1965: II, 110, I, 114. See also Mao and Che 1968: 34.

77. Esherick ed. 1974: 197.

78. Tsuzuki 1974: 130–33; Jaegher and Kuhn 1952: 35.

79. Kataoka 1974: 106; Perry 1980: 225.

80. Kataoka 1974: 107.

81. Perry 1980: 227.

82. Gao Jing 1939: 101–5.

83. Yung-fa Chen 1986: 476. See also Nagano 1933: 142–43, 149–55.

84. Smedley 1933: 57–60; H. F. Snow 1972: 182; Kataoka 1974: 106; Nagano 1933: 141–43, 185, 209–12.

85. Yung-fa Chen 1986: 475–76. See also Tachibana 1923: 72.

86. Esherick ed. 1974: 189–91; Jaegher and Kuhn 1952: 36–37.

87. Johnson 1962: 88; Yung-fa Chen 1986: 476–78.

88. Selden 1971: 171; Kataoka 1974: 133, 204–5; Perry 1980: 228, 234.

89. Jaegher and Kuhn 1952: 203; Perry 1980: 227; Yung-fa Chen 1986: 478.

90. Esherick ed. 1974: 189.

91. Gittings 1967: 33.

92. Ibid.: 33–35; *Huiyi He Long*: 537–39, 551–52. See also Shih Ch'eng-chih 1956.

93. Shih Ch'eng-chih 1956: 99.

94. Lewis 1964: 76–77; "Report by Comrade Fu Ch'iu-tao": 118–20, 123

*Miscellany of Mao Tse-tung Thought*: II, 240 (emphasis added); Griffith 1968: 270–72.

95. Moody 1977: 83.
96. *Ibid.*: 104.

## Chapter Ten

1. *NCH*, 16 June 1923: 719.
2. Mao Tse-tung 1965: III, 76; *Zhengxuan* 1, no. 3 (Mar. 1914), "Zhongguo dashiji": 10.

3. *BLQY*: 88–89.
4. Smedley 1956: 136.
5. Friedman 1974: 160n.
6. Hobsbawm 1959.
7. Blok 1972: 499–501.

# Bibliography

A.N. 1923. "Quatre mois de captivité chez les brigands du Honan," *La Chine* (Beijing), 35 (1 Feb.), pp. 161–63.

*Ajia rekishi jiten* [Encyclopedia of Asian history]. 1959. Tokyo; 10 vols. アジア 歴史事典.

Akizawa Jirō. 1923. *Taiwan hishi* [Record of banditry in Taiwan]. Taibei. 秋沢 次郎, 臺灣匪誌.

Alabaster, Ernest. 1899. *Notes and Commentaries on Chinese Criminal Law.* London.

Aldrich, Lucy Truman. 1923. "A Week-end with Chinese Bandits," *Atlantic Monthly* (June), pp. 672–86.

Andō Hikotarō. 1963. "Nihonjin no Chūgokukan to 'Shina rōnin'" [The Japanese view of China and the "Shina rōnin"], *Chūgoku kenkyū geppō* (Tokyo), 181 (Apr.), pp. 1–15. 安藤彦太郎, 日本人の中国観と「支那浪人」. 中国 研究月報.

Andrews, Roy Chapman, and Yvette Borup. 1918. *Camps and Trails in China.* New York and London.

Angiolillo, Paul F. 1979. *A Criminal As Hero, Angelo Duca.* Lawrence, Kans.

Arlington, L. C. 1931. *Through the Dragon's Eyes.* London.

Arnold, David. 1979. "Dacoity and Rural Crime in Madras, 1860–1940," *Journal of Peasant Studies* (London), 6, no. 2 (Jan.), pp. 140–67.

Augustana Mission. 1915. Augustana Mission in the Province of Honan. *Our First Decade in China, 1905–15.* Rock Island, Ill.

———. 1925. Augustana Synod Mission in the Province of Honan. *Our Second Decade in China, 1915–25.* Rock Island, Ill.

Baba Akira. 1976. "Rinjō jiken to Nihon no tai-Chūgoku seisaku" [The Lin-cheng Incident and Japan's China policy], *Kokugakuin daigaku kiyō* (Tokyo), 14 (Mar.), pp. 35–66. 馬場明, 臨城事件と日本の対中国政策, 国学院大学紀要.

"Bai Lang qiyi diaocha jianji." 1960. [Brief note on the investigation into Bai Lang's righteous uprising], *SXYK*, 1 (Jan.), pp. 18–23. 白朗起義調査簡記.

Ban Su ed. 1928. *Zhongguo liushinian dashiji* [A chronicle of major events in China over the last sixty years]. Shanghai. 半粟, 中國六十年大事記.

"Bandit Rule in China." 1923. *Literary Digest* (New York), 77 (19 May), pp. 8–9.

Banno Ryōkichi. 1970. "Byakurō kigi no rekishiteki yigi o megutte" [On the historical significance of Bai Lang's righteous uprising], *Rekishi hyōron* (Tokyo), 243 (Oct.), pp. 4–24. 坂野良吉, 白朗起義の歴史的意義をめぐって. 歴史 評論.

Belden, Jack. 1950. *China Shakes the World*. London.

Benson, Stella. 1925. "A Secret City," *Asia* (New York), 25 (Jan.), pp. 28–29.

Bertram, James M. 1937. *Crisis in China: The Story of the Sian Mutiny*. London.

Bianco, Lucien. 1969. "Fonctionnaires, Percepteurs, Militaires et Brigands en Chine—Le Anhui dénonce la mauvaise administration provinciale (1931)," *Revue d'histoire moderne et contemporain* (Paris), 16 (Apr.–June), pp. 300–318.

———. 1971. *Origins of the Chinese Revolution, 1915–1949*. Stanford, Calif.

———. 1972. "Secret Societies and Peasant Self-Defense, 1921–1933," in Chesneaux, ed., 1972, pp. 213–24, 274–77.

———. 1975. "Peasants and Revolution: The Case of China," *Journal of Peasant Studies* (London), 2, no. 3 (Apr.), pp. 313–35.

Blok, Anton. 1972. "The Peasant and the Brigand: Social Banditry Reconsidered," *Comparative Studies in Society and History* (London), 14, no. 4 (Sept.), pp. 494–503.

———. 1974. *The Mafia of a Sicilian Village*. New York.

BLQY. 1980. *Bai Lang qiyi diaocha baogao* [Report on an investigation into Bai Lang's righteous uprising]. Kaifeng. Originally published in *Kaifeng shifan xueyuan xuebao*, 5 (1960), pp. 68–104. 白朗起義調查報告. 開封師範學院學報.

BLSM. 1980. Wang Liuxian et al. "Bai Lang qiyi shimo" [The complete story of Bai Lang's righteous uprising], *Henan wenshi ziliao* (Kaifeng), no. 1 (Jan.), pp. 10–55. 王留現, '白朗起義始末' 河南文史資料.

Blue, A. D. 1965. "Piracy on the China Coast," *Journal of the Royal Asiatic Society, Hong Kong Branch*, 5 (May), pp. 69–85.

"Blue Trains." 1923. "Blue Trains and Bandits," *The Living Age* (Concord, N.H.), 318 (July), pp. 450–53.

BLZX. 1914. "Bai Lang zhi zhenxiang" [The truth about the White Wolf] *Yongyan* (Shanghai), 2, no. 4 (Apr.), pp. 1–9. 白狼之眞相. 庸言.

Böcher, Herbert. 1932. *Chinois, Japonais, et Brigands: récit d'un familier du maréchal Tchang-tsue-liang*. Paris.

Boorman, Howard L., ed. 1967. *Biographical Dictionary of Republican China*. New York and London. 5 vols.

Borst-Smith, Ernest F. 1916. *Scenes in Shensi's Civil War. Some Consequences of the Monarchical Movement: The Apotheosis of Brigandage*. Tianjin.

———. 1917. *Mandarin and Missionary in Cathay*. London.

Bosshardt, Rudolf Alfred. 1936. *The Restraining Hand: Captivity for Christ in China*. London.

Bradley, Neville. 1945. *The Old Burma Road*. London.

Buck, J. Lossing. 1928. "The Big Swords and the Little Swords Clash," *CWR*, 46, no. 7 (13 Oct.), pp. 213–14.

*Bukan hōmen*. 1930. *Bukan hōmen shoshō no hika* [The bandit calamity in the provinces of the Wuhan district]. Hankou. 武漢方面諸省の匪禍.

Cable, Mildred, and Francesca French. 1934. *Something Happened*. London.

Cai Dongfan and Xu Jinfu. 1980. *Minguo tongsu yanyi* [A popular chronicle o the Republic]. Beijing; 4 vols. 蔡東藩, 許厪父, 民國通俗演義.

Caldwell, Harry R. 1925. *Blue Tiger*. London.

Cao Hongxu. 1930. *Genji Shina ni okeru dohi no gaikan to sono taisaku* [The band pestilence in modern-day China and the measures required to counter it Tokyo. Translated from the *Sanmin banyuekan* (Apr. 1930).

Carpenter, Frank G. 1925. *China*. New York.

Chang Cheng, ed. 1980. *Zhang Zuolin*. Shenyang. 常城, 張作霖.

Chang, C. Y. 1937. "An Inside Story Concerning the Daily Life of the Bandits in Honan," *CWR*, 80, no. 13 (29 May), pp. 498–99.

*Changge xianzhi*. 1930. *Changge xianzhi* [Gazetteer of Changge county]. 長葛縣志.

Chang Kuo-t'ao. 1972. *The Rise of the Chinese Communist Party 1928–1938: Volume Two of the Autobiography of Chang Kuo-t'ao*. Lawrence, Kans.

Chao Shu-li. 1953. *Changes in Li Village*. Beijing.

Cheah Boon Kheng. 1981. "Social Banditry and Rural Crime in North Kedah, 1909–22," *Journal of the Malaysian Branch of the Royal Asiatic Society*, 54, no. 2, pp. 98–130.

Chen, Fu-mei Chang. 1975. "Local Control of Convicted Thieves in Eighteenth-Century China," in Wakeman and Grant, eds., 1975, pp. 121–42.

Chen Hongjin. 1939. "Minzhong liliang zai Yudong" [The Power of the Masses in East Henan], in *KZND*, pp. 85–88. 陳洪進, 民眾力量在豫東.

Ch'ên, Jerome. 1960. "The Nature and Characteristics of the Boxer Movement," *BSOAS*, 23, no. 2 (Apr.), pp. 289–308.

———. 1961. *Yüan Shih-k'ai 1859–1916: Brutus Assumes the Purple*. London.

———. 1968. "Defining Chinese Warlords and Their Factions," *BSOAS*, 31, no. 3 (July), pp. 563–600.

———. 1970. "Rebels Between Rebellions: Secret Societies in the Novel *P'eng Kung An*," *JAS*, 29, no. 4 (Aug.), pp. 807–22.

Chen Wuwo. 1923. *Lincheng jieche-an jishi* [A memorandum of the Lincheng train-attack incident]. Shanghai. 陳無我, 臨城刼車案紀事.

Chen, W. W. 1923. *The Lincheng Incident*. Beijing.

Chen, Yung-fa. 1986. *Making Revolution: The Communist Movement in Eastern and Central China, 1937–1945*. Berkeley, Calif.

Cheng, J. Chester. 1966. *The Politics of the Chinese Red Army*. Stanford, Calif.

Cheng Ying. 1962. *Zhongguo jindai fandi fanfengjian lishi geyaoxuan* [A collection of songs from China's modern anti-imperialist and anti-feudal history]. Beijing. 程英, 中國近代反帝反封建歷史歌謠選.

Cheng Yufeng. 1978. "Bai Lang shihua" [Historical discussion about the White Wolf], *ZYWX*, 10, no. 4 (May), pp. 26–30; no. 5 (June), pp. 31–34; no. 6 (July), pp. 26–29; no. 7 (Aug.), pp. 29–33; no. 8 (Sept.), pp. 23–28; no. 9 (Oct.), pp. 32–33. (This item is a continuation of Wang Tiancong 1978.) 程玉鳳, 白狼史話.

Chesneaux, Jean. 1971a. "The Modern Relevance of Shui-hu Chuan: Its Influence on Rebel Movements in Nineteenth- and Twentieth-Century China," *Papers on Far Eastern History* (Canberra), 3 (Mar.), pp. 1–25.

———. 1971b. *Secret Societies in China in the Nineteenth and Twentieth Centuries*. London.

———. 1972. "Secret Societies in China's Historical Evolution," in Chesneaux, ed., 1972, pp. 1–21, 235–40.

———. 1973. *Peasant Revolts in China, 1840–1949*. London.

Chesneaux, Jean, ed. 1970. *Mouvements populaires et sociétés secrètes en Chine aux XIXᵉ et XXᵉ siècles*. Paris.

————, ed. 1972. *Popular Movements and Secret Societies in China, 1840–1950.* Stanford, Calif.

Ch'i Hsi-sheng. 1976. *Warlord Politics in China, 1916–28.* Stanford, Calif.

Chiang Siang-tseh. 1954. *The Nien Rebellion.* Seattle.

*China Yearbook.* London, Tianjin, and Shanghai.

"China's Booming Bandit Business." 1923. *Literary Digest* (New York), (2 June), pp. 41–46.

*China's Millions.* London.

*Chine, La.* Beijing.

*Chongxiu Xinyang xianzhi.* 1936, 1968. [Revised gazetteer of Xinyang county]. 重修信陽縣志.

Chou Tsun-shih. 1969. "Profile of a Warlord," in Dun J. Li, *The Road to Communism: China Since 1912* (New York), pp. 10–18.

Chow Yung-teh. 1966. *Social Mobility in China: Status Careers Among the Gentry in a Chinese Community.* New York.

Chu Po. 1962. *Tracks in the Snowy Forest.* Beijing.

Ch'u T'ung-tsü. 1962. *Local Government in China Under the Ch'ing.* Stanford, Calif.

"Chūgoku ni okeru dohi" [Bandits in China]. 1928. *Pekin mantetsu geppō,* 4, no. 6 (Feb.), pp. 1–82. 中国に於ける土匪. 北京満鉄月報.

Close, Upton. 1924. *In the Land of the Laughing Buddha.* New York and London.

Clubb, O. Edmund. 1968. *Communism in China, as Reported from Hankow in 1932.* New York and London.

CPM 1913. Canadian Presbyterian Mission. *A Quarter Century in North Honan, 1889–1913.* Shanghai.

"Creation and Organisation of a Bandit Army." 1933. *People's Tribune* (Shanghai), 4, no. 9 (June), pp. 500–508.

Croll, Elisabeth. 1978. *Feminism and Socialism in China.* London.

Crummey, Donald, ed. 1986. *Banditry, Rebellion, and Social Protest in Africa.* London.

Curwen, C. A. 1972. "Taiping Relations with Secret Societies and with Other Rebels," in Chesneaux, ed., 1972, pp. 65–84, 247–51.

————. 1977. *Taiping Rebel: The Deposition of Li Hsiu-ch'eng.* Cambridge, Eng.

Dai Xuanzhi. 1973. *Hongqianghui* [The Red Spear society]. Taibei. 戴玄之, 紅槍會.

Dailey, Charles A. 1923a. "The Real Significance of Banditry in China," *CWR,* 23, no. 6 (6 Jan.) pp. 207–11.

————. 1923b. "Banditry, Bankruptcy or Boxers?," *CWR,* 23, no. 8 (20 Jan.), pp. 291–94.

————. 1923c. "Bandit Soldiers Bandits Still," *CWR,* 25, no. 8 (21 July), pp. 244–45.

————. 1923d. "Banditry, Bunco and Boobery," *CWR,* 25, no. 11 (11 Aug.) pp. 358–60.

Dairen Chamber of Commerce & Industry. 1931. *What Chinese Fugitive Soldier and Hunghudze Are Capable Of.* Dairen.

Dannic, J., S.J. 1912. "A propos de la révolution," *Relations de Chine* (Paris), (Oct.), pp. 514–23.

Dardess, John W. 1972. "The Late Ming Rebellions: Peasants and Problems of Interpretation," *Journal of Interdisciplinary History*, 3, pp. 103–17.

Davin, Delia. 1979. *Woman-Work, Women and the Party in Revolutionary China.* Oxford, Eng.

Davis, Fei-Ling. 1977. *Primitive Revolutionaries of China.* London.

Des Forges, Roger V. 1973. *Hsi-liang and the Chinese National Revolution.* New Haven, Conn.

———. 1979. "The View from Honan, 1900–1912." Unpublished paper.

Ding Wenjiang. 1926. *Minguo junshi jinji* [A contemporary record of the Republican-period military]. Shanghai. 丁文江, 民國軍事近記.

"Diplomatic Notes on the Lincheng Incident." 1923. *Chinese Social and Political Science Review* (Beijing), 7, no. 4 (Oct.), pp. 242–57.

Dong Kechang. 1958. "Bai Lang qiyi xingzhi yu zuoyong di yanjiu" [A study of the nature and function of Bai Lang's righteous uprising]. *Xueshu luntan* (Amoy), 3 (Mar.), pp. 34–38. 董克昌, 白朗起義性質與作用的研究. 學術論壇.

———. 1960. "Guanyu Bai Lang qiyi di xingzhi" [On the nature of Bai Lang's righteous uprising], *SXYK* 5 (May), pp. 22–27. 關於白朗起義的性質.

Du Qunhe, ed. 1980. *Bai Lang qiyi* [Bai Lang's righteous uprising]. Beijing. 杜春和, 白朗起義.

Duxiu [Chen]. 1923. "Lincheng louanzhong zhi Zhongguo xianxiang" [China's image amid the Lincheng kidnaping affair]. *XDZB* (Beijing), 26 (May), p. 189. 獨秀[陳], 臨城虜案中之中國現象.

Duan Jianmin. 1969. "Xinhainian Kaifeng qiyi zhi jingguo" [An account of the 1911 insurrection in Kaifeng]. *ZYWX*, 1, no. 2 (May), pp. 24–29. 段劍岷, 辛亥年開封起義之經過.

Eastman, Lloyd E. 1974. *The Abortive Revolution: China Under Nationalist Rule, 1927–1937.* Cambridge, Mass.

Eberhard, Wolfram. 1965. *Conquerors and Rulers: Social Forces in Medieval China.* Leiden.

*Emperor Kuang Hsü's Reform Decrees 1898.* 1900. Shanghai.

Esherick, Joseph W. 1976a. *Reform and Revolution in China: The 1911 Revolution in Hunan and Hubei.* Berkeley, Calif.

———. 1976b. "1911: A Review," *Modern China*, 2, no. 2 (Apr.), pp. 141–84.

Esherick, Joseph W., ed. 1974. *Lost Chance in China: The World War II Despatches of John S. Service.* New York.

Eto Shinkichi and Harold Z. Schiffrin, eds. 1984. *The 1911 Revolution in China: Interpretive Essays.* Tokyo.

Etō Toshio. 1928–29. "Hoku-Man no bazoku ni torawareta hanashi—Beikoku ishi Howard hakushi no shuki" [A story of captivity among north Manchurian bandits—the memoirs of the American doctor Howard], *Tōa* (Tokyo), 1, no. 6 (Oct. 1928) to 2, no. 6 (June 1929). 衛藤利夫, 北満の馬賊に囚はれた話—米国医師ホワード博士の手記. 東亜.

Fang Hongchou. 1974. "Minchu Henan jufei Bai Lang, Lao Yangren shilu" [A veritable record of the early Republican bandit chiefs, White Wolf and Lao Yangren], *ZYWX*, 6, no. 6 (July), pp. 19–21, 30. 方洪疇, 民初河南巨匪白狼·老洋人實錄.

Faure, David William. 1973. "Peasant Disturbances in North China, 1800–1868." Unpublished M.A. thesis, Univ. of Hong Kong.

Fei Hsiao-t'ung. 1946. "Peasantry and Gentry: An Interpretation of Chinese Social Structure and Its Changes," *American Journal of Sociology*, 51, no. 3 (July), pp. 1–17.

Fei Hsiao-t'ung and Chang Chih-i. 1945. *Earthbound China: A Study of Rural Economy in Yunnan*. Chicago.

Feng Yuxiang. 1944. *Wodi shenghuo* [My life]. Shanghai. 馮玉祥, 我的生活.

Feng Zigang and Liu Ruisheng. 1934. "Nanyang nongcun shehui diaocha baogao" [Report of an investigation into village society in Nanyang], *Guoji maoyi daobao* (Beijing), 6, no. 4 (Apr.), pp. 69–141. 馮紫崗, 劉端生, 南陽農村社會調查報告. 國際貿易導報.

Feng Ziyou. 1969. "Henan zhishi yu geming yundong" [The Henan heroes and the revolutionary movement], *ZYWX*, 1, no. 9 (Dec.), pp. 21–24. 馮自由, 河南志士與革命運動.

*Fengqiu xianzhi*. 1937. [Gazetteer of Fengqiu county]. 封邱縣志.

Fischle, Ernst. 1930. *Kidnapped in China*. London.

Fitzgerald, C. P. 1941. *The Tower of Five Glories*. London.

*Foreigner in China, The*. 1927. Ed. *North China Daily News*. Shanghai.

"Fostering Banditry in China—Organized Arms Smuggling by the Japanese." 1933. *People's Tribune* (Beijing), 4, no. 9 (Sept.), pp. 489–99.

Fox, Grace. 1940. *British Admirals and Chinese Pirates, 1832–1869*. London.

Franck, Harry. 1923. *Wandering in Northern China*. New York.

Fried, Morton H. 1956. *Fabric of Chinese Society: A Study of the Social Life of a Chinese County Seat*. London.

Friedman, Edward. 1974. *Backward Toward Revolution: The Chinese Revolutionary Party*. Berkeley, Calif.

"Fuite du Loup Blanc, La." 1914. *La Politique de Pékin*, 17 (16 Aug.), pp. 14–15.

Gain, Leopold, 1904. "A propos d'un brigand," *Relations de Chine* (Paris), 1 (Jan.), pp. 160–76.

———. 1909. "Les brigands du Siu-tcheou-fou," *Relations de Chine* (Paris), 2 (Oct.), pp. 412–16.

Gamble, Sidney D. 1963. *North China Villages—Social, Political, and Economic Activities Before 1933*. Berkeley, Calif.

Gao Jing. 1939. "Women zenyang gaizao tufeidi?" [How should we reform bandits?], in *KZND*, pp. 100–106. 高境, 我們怎樣改造土匪的?

*Gendaishi shiryō* [Materials on contemporary history]. 1966. Vols. 31–33 (*Mantetsu*, vols. 1–3). Tokyo. 現代史資料. 滿鐵.

Gillin, Donald G. 1967. *Warlord: Yen Hsi-shan in Shansi Province, 1911–49*. Princeton, N.J.

Gittings, John. 1967. *The Role of the Chinese Army*. London.

Gotō Asatarō. 1923. "Shina dohi heishi ni taisuru kiso chishiki" [Basic facts about Chinese bandits and soldiers], *Gaikō jihō*, 448 (1 July), pp. 50–73. 後藤朝太郎, 支那土匪兵士に対する基礎智識. 外交時報.

———. 1928. *Seiryūtō* [Black dragon sword]. Tokyo. 青龍刀.

———. 1937. *Dohimura angya* [A walking tour of bandit villages]. Tokyo. 土匪村行脚.

Grafton, T. B. 1923. "The Growth of Banditry," *NCH* (1 Dec.), p. 600; (8 Dec.), pp. 669–71.

Griffith, Samuel B., II. 1968. *The Chinese People's Liberation Army*. London.

Gu Hang. 1927. "Honghuzi di shenghuoguan" [The view of life of the Red Beards], *DFZZ*, 24, no. 13 (10 July), pp. 73–77. 孤航, 紅鬍子的生活觀.

"Guanzhong daoke" [The Shaanxi sword-fighters]. 1961. *XHGMHYL*, vol. 6, pp. 518–28. 關中刀客.

Guang Xiaoan. 1926. "Guangdong feihuo zhi gaiguan" [An overall look at the bandit calamity in Guangdong], *GWZB*, 3, no. 18 (16 May), pp. 18–22. 鄺笑菴, 廣東匪禍之概觀.

Guillon, Jean. 1868. "Les brigands dans le Pe-Tche-Ly: les Tchang-mao," *Annales de la propagation de la foi* (Lyon), 40, pp. 348–62.

Guo Moro. 1982. *Guo Moro quanji* [Complete works of Guo Moro]. Vol. 1, pp. 113–17. Beijing. 郭沫若, 全集.

Guo Zibin. 1973. "Zhuiyi Liu Zhenhua jiangjun jiaofei zhengji" [A retrospect of General Liu Zhenhua's achievements in bandit suppression], *ZYWX*, 5, no. 5 (June), pp. 29–31. 郭子彬, 追憶劉鎮華將軍剿匪政績.

Hall, J. C. S. 1976. *The Yunnan Provincial Faction, 1927–1937*. Canberra, Australia.

Hall, William L. 1919. "The 'Tiger' and a Foreign Devil," *Asia*, 19 (Oct.), pp. 1017–20.

Han Xuexu. 1965. "Bai Lang qiyijun zai Shaanxi di douzheng" [The Bai Lang righteous army's campaign in Shaanxi], *SXYK*, 7 (July), pp. 37–38. 韓學儒, 白朗起義軍在陝西的斗爭.

Harding, G. L. 1914. "White Wolf," *International Socialist Review* (New York), 15, no. 2 (Aug.), pp. 109–12.

Harrison, James P. 1970. *The Communists and Chinese Peasant Rebellions: A Study in the Rewriting of Chinese History*. London.

Hatano Ken'ichi. 1925. "Yōyaku kaiketsu seru Rinjō jiken" [The Lincheng Incident finally settled], *Shina*, 16, no. 4 (Apr.), pp. 55–88. 波多野乾一, 漸く解決せる臨城事件. 支那.

———. 1963. "Gunbatsu konsen no soko ni aru mono: Chūgoku nōson shakai no haaku to kanren shite" [The roots of the confused warlord conflicts and an approach to Chinese village society], *Rekishi kyōiku*, 1 (Jan.), pp. 20–27. 軍閥混戦の底にあるもの:中国農村社会の把握と関連して. 歴史教育.

Hatano Yoshihiro. 1954. "Shingai kakumei chokuzen ni okeru nōmin ikki" [Peasant uprisings on the eve of the 1911 revolution], *Tōyōshi kenkyū*, 13, no. 1–2, pp. 77–106. 波多野善大, 辛亥革命直前に於ける農民一揆. 東洋史研究.

He Xiya. 1925a. *Zhongguo daofei wenti zhi yanjiu* [An investigation of China's bandit problem]. Shanghai. 何西亞, 中國盜匪問題之研究.

———. 1925b. "Jiazi dazhanhou quanguo jundui zhi diaocha" [An investigation of China's armies following the great war of 1924], *DFZZ*, 22, no. 1 (10 Jan.), pp. 103–12; 22, no. 2 (25 Jan.), pp. 34–37; 22, no. 3 (10 Feb.), pp. 69–83. 甲子大戰後全國軍隊之調查.

Hedges, Frank H. 1923. "Bandits a Growing Menace in China," *Current History*, 18 (July), pp. 606–10.

Hegel, Charlotte Beahan. 1969. "The White Wolf: The Career of a Chinese Bandit, 1912–14." Unpublished M.A. thesis, Columbia Univ., New York.

Hilton, R. H. 1958. "The Origins of Robin Hood," *Past and Present*, 14 (Nov.), pp. 30–44.

Hinton, William. 1966. *Fanshen: A Documentary of Revolution in a Chinese Village*. New York.

Ho, Franklin L. 1931–32. "Population Movement to the Northeastern Provinces in China," *Chinese Social & Political Science Review*, 15, pp. 346–401.

Hobsbawm, E. J. 1959. *Primitive Rebels: Studies in Archaic Forms of Social Movement in the Nineteenth and Twentieth Centuries*. Manchester, Eng.

––––––. 1972a. *Bandits*. Harmondsworth, Eng. Orig. ed. 1969.

––––––. 1972b. "Social Bandits: Reply," *Comparative Studies in Society and History*, 14, no. 4 (Sept.), pp. 503–5.

Hofheinz, Roy. 1969. "The Ecology of Chinese Communist Success: Rural Influence Patterns, 1923–1945," in A. Doak Barnett, *Chinese Communist Politics in Action* (Seattle), pp. 3–77.

––––––. 1977. *The Broken Wave: The Chinese Communist Peasant Movement, 1922–1928*. Cambridge, Mass.

Howard, Harvey James. 1926. *Ten Weeks with Chinese Bandits*. New York.

Hsia, C. T. 1968. *The Classic Chinese Novel*. New York.

Hsiao Kung-chuan. 1960. *Rural China: Imperial Control in the Nineteenth Century*. Seattle.

Hsieh, Winston. 1969. "Peasant-Bandits in Towns and Cities: The Phenomenon of People's Armies in Kwangtung, 1911–1924." Unpublished paper.

––––––. 1972. "Triads, Salt Smugglers, and Local Uprisings: Observations on the Social and Economic Background of the Waichow Revolution of 1911," in Chesneaux, ed., 1972, pp. 145–64, 264–67.

Hsüeh Chün-tu. 1961. *Huang Hsing and the Chinese Revolution*. Stanford, Calif.

*Huaiyang xianzhi* [Gazetteer of Huaiyang county]. 1934, 1968. 淮陽縣志.

Huang Guangkuo. 1960a. "Youguan Bai Lang qiyi di yixie ziliao" (Materials on Bai Lang's righteous uprising], *SXYK*, 2 (Feb.), pp. 24–27. 黃廣廓, 有關白朗起義的一些資料.

––––––. 1960b. "Youguan diguozhuyi dui Bai Lang qiyi ganshe di ziliao" [Materials on the imperialist intervention against Bai Lang's righteous uprising], *SXYK*, 4 (Apr.), pp. 33–34. 有關帝國主義對白朗起義干涉的資料.

Huang Renzhi. 1935. "Yu-Shaan liangsheng zhi guanchatan" [Talk concerning an observation of Henan and Shaanxi provinces], *Fuxing yuekan* (Shanghai), 3, no. 10 (June), pp. 1–7. 黃任之, 豫陝兩省之視察談. 復興月刊.

Huang Zhongye. 1979. "Lun daozei" [On brigands], *Lishixue*, 1, no. 4 (Dec.), pp. 43–51. 黃中業, 論盜賊, 歷史學.

Huey, T. W. N.d. "The Shui-hu Zhuan and the Political Culture of Chinese Banditry." Unpublished paper.

*Huiyi He Long* [Recollections of He Long]. 1979. Shanghai.

Hutchison, James Lafayette. 1936. *China Hand*. Boston.

*HZB*. 1931. *Henan zaiqing baogaoshu* [Report on the disaster situation in Henan province]. Kaifeng. 河南災情報告書.

Ide Kiwata. 1921. "Shina ahen mondai no shinsō" [The truth about the opium problem in China], *Chūō kōron*, 36, no. 5 (May), pp. 29–58. 井出季和太, 支那阿片問題の真相. 中央公論.

Ikeda Momokawa (Tōsen). N.d. "Shina no danmen, dohi to himitsu kessha" [A cross-section of China, bandits and secret societies]. Newspaper cuttings. 池田桃川, 支那の断面：土匪と秘密結社.

Inaba Iwakichi. 1936. "Manshūkoku no chian to hizoku no yūrai: shakaishi no ichi danmen" [The security of Manchuguo and the origins of bandits: a cross-section of social history], *Tōa keizai kenkyū*, 20, no. 3 (Aug.), pp. 5–29. 稲葉岩吉, 満洲国の治安と匪賊の由来. 社会史の一継面. 東亜経済研究.

Inoue Kōbai (Shin). 1923. *Hito* [Brigands]. Shanghai. 井上紅梅（進）, 匪徒.

———. 1933. "Dohi no ango ni arawareta Shinashoku" [The flavor of China as revealed in the secret language of bandits], *Tōa*, 6, no. 8 (Aug.), pp. 58–64. 土匪の闇語に現れた支那色. 東亜.

Institute of Pacific Relations. 1939. *Agrarian China, Selected Source Materials from Chinese Authors*. London.

Irwin, Richard Gregg. 1966. *The Evolution of a Chinese Novel: Shui-hu Chuan*. Cambridge, Mass.

Isaacs, Harold. 1974. *Straw Sandals: Chinese Short Stories, 1918–1933*. Cambridge, Mass.

Iwasaki Keisei. 1934. "Manshū shakai to hizoku" [Manchurian society and bandits], *Dorumen*, 3, no. 5 (May), pp. 54–56. 岩崎継生, 満洲社会と匪賊. ドルメン.

Jaegher, Raymond J. de, and Irene Corbally Kuhn. 1952. *The Enemy Within*. New York.

Jansen, Marius B. 1954. *The Japanese and Sun Yat-sen*. Cambridge, Mass.

"Japan's Intrigues in China." 1933. *People's Tribune*, 4, no. 8 (16 May), 425–34.

"J.D." 1927. "Bandits and Pirates," *New Statesman* (19 Nov.), pp. 166–68.

Jen Yu-wen. 1973. *The Taiping Revolutionary Movement*. New Haven, Conn.

Jenner, W. J. F. 1970a. *Modern Chinese Stories*. Oxford, Eng.

———. 1970b. "Les Nian et le Laoniuhui: Les rebelles et leurs adversaires dans la tradition populaire," in Chesneaux, ed., 1970, pp. 205–18.

Jian Hu. 1923. "Bing yu fei" [Soldiers and bandits], *DFZZ*, 20, no. 7 (10 Apr.), p. 1. 堅瓠, 兵與匪.

Jing An. 1930. "Henan mingezhong di feizai yu bingzai" [The bandit and soldier calamities as seen in Henanese folk songs], *Minsu*, 110 (30 Apr.), pp. 1–11. 經庵, 河南民歌中的匪災與兵災. 民俗.

Johnson, Chalmers A. 1962. *Peasant Nationalism and Communist Power: The Emergence of Revolutionary China, 1937–1945*. Stanford, Calif.

Johnson, Clifford. 1934. *Pirate Junk: Five Months' Captivity with Manchurian Bandits*. New York.

Jordan, Donald A. 1976. *The Northern Expedition, China's National Revolution of 1926–1928*. Honolulu.

Jowe, Peter S. 1925. "Who Sells the Guns to China's War Leaders?," *CWR*, 32, no. 7 (18 Apr.), pp. 192–98.

Jurgensen, Barbara. 1965. *All the Bandits of China: Adventures of a Missionary in a Land Ravaged by Bandits and War Lords*. Minneapolis.

Kaltenmark, Max. 1979. "The Ideology of the T'ai-p'ing ching," in Holmes Welch and Ann Seidel, eds., *Facets of Taoism* (New Haven, Conn.), pp. 19–45.

Kanamaru Seiya. 1933. "Manshū no bazoku to hizoku" [The mounted bandits and robber bandits of Manchuria], *Mammō*, 14, no. 1 (Jan.), pp. 96–110. 金丸精哉, 満洲の馬賊と匪賊. 滿蒙.

Kapp, Robert Alexander. 1970. "Szechwanese Provincial Militarism and Central Power in Republican China." Ph.D. diss., Yale Univ., New Haven, Conn.

Kataoka Tetsuya. 1974. *Resistance and Revolution in China*. Berkeley, Calif.

Kemal, Yashar. 1961. *Memed, My Hawk*. London.

Keyte, J. C. 1913. *The Passing of the Dragon: The Story of the Shensi Revolution and Relief Expedition*. London.

Kikuchi Kazutaka. 1978. "Shinseishō ni okeru gunbatsu shihai to ahen" [Warlord control and opium in Shaanxi province], *Kindai chūgoku*, 4 (Oct.), pp. 127–53. 菊池一隆, 陝西省における軍閥支配とアヘン. 近代中国.

King, Louis Magrath. 1927. *China in Turmoil: Studies in Personality*. London.

Kingston, Maxine Hong. 1977. *The Woman Warrior: Memoirs of a Girlhood Among Ghosts*. Baltimore, Md.

Klein, Donald, and Anne B. Clark. 1971. *Biographic Dictionary of Chinese Communism, 1921–1965*. Cambridge, Mass. 2 vols.

Kōkaku Sanjin. 1924. "Shina no dohi ni tsuite" [On China's bandits], *Taiwan jihō* (Taibei), 60 (Sept.), pp. 160–75. 黄鶴山人, 支那の土匪に就て. 台湾時報.

"Kōnan dohi no kako genzai" [The present and past of Hunan's bandits]. 1914. *Shina*, 5, no. 18 (15 Sept.), pp. 23–31. 湖南土匪の過去現在. 支那.

Kuchiki Kanzō. 1966. *Bazoku senki: Kohinata Hakurō to Manshū* [A record of mounted bandit wars: Kohinata Hakurō and Manchuria]. Tokyo. 朽木寒三, 馬賊戦記:小日向白朗と満洲.

———. 1981. *Bazoku: Tenki shōgun den* [Mounted bandit: The biography of General Tenki]. Tokyo. 馬賊:天鬼将軍伝.

Kuhn, Philip A. 1970. *Rebellion and Its Enemies in Late Imperial China: Militarization and Social Structure, 1796–1864*, Cambridge, Eng.

———. 1975. "Local Self-Government Under the Republic: Problems of Control, Autonomy, and Mobilization," in Wakeman and Grant, eds., 1975, pp. 257–98.

Kuo Ting-yee, comp., and James W. Morley, ed. 1965. *Sino-Japanese Relations, 1862–1927: A Checklist of the Chinese Foreign Ministry Archives*. New York.

Kurushima Hidesaburō. 1952. *Bazoku o kataru* [Talking about mounted bandits]. Tokyo. 久留島秀三郎, 馬賊を語る.

KZND. 1939. *Kanzhanzhong di Zhongguo nongcun dongtai* [The dynamics of China's villages during the resistance war]. Shanghai. 抗戰中的中國農村動態.

Lafferty, Oma Clare. 1931. *Banditry and Piracy in China in the Nineteenth and Twentieth Centuries*. Unpublished M.A. thesis, Univ. of Chicago.

Laffey, Ella S. 1972. "The Making of a Rebel: Liu Yung-fu and the Formation of the Black Flag Army," in Chesneaux, ed., 1972, pp. 85–96, 251–54.

———. 1976. "In the Wake of the Taipings: Some Patterns of Local Revolt in Kwangsi Province, 1850–1875," *Modern Asian Studies*, 10, no. 1 (Feb.), pp. 65–81.

Lai Xinxia. 1957a. "Beiyang junfa duinei sougua di jizhong fangshi" [Some of the methods used by the northern warlords in their domestic exactions], *SXYK*, 3 (Mar.), pp. 8–11. 夾新夏, 北洋軍閥對內搜刮的幾種方式.

———. 1957b. "Tan minguo chunian Bai Lang lingdao di nongmin qiyi" [A discussion of the righteous peasant uprising led by Bai Lang in the early years of the Republic], *SXYK*, 6 (June), pp. 11–17. 談民國初年白朗領導的農民起義.

Lamley, Harry J. 1977. "Hsieh-tou: The Pathology of Violence in Southeastern China," *Ch'ing-shih wen-t'i*, 3, no. 7 (Nov.), pp. 1–39.

Lary, Diana. 1985. *Warlord Soldiers: Chinese Common Soldiers, 1911–1937.* Cambridge, Eng.

Lattimore, Owen. 1932. *Manchuria: Cradle of Conflict.* New York.

———. 1941. *Mongol Journeys.* London.

Lee, Robert H. G. 1970. *The Manchurian Frontier in Ch'ing History.* Cambridge, Mass.

Lerberghe, M., and A. Monestier. 1915. *Notes, documents et considérations pour servir à l'histoire de la révolution chinoise, 1911–1913.* Beijing.

Lewin, Linda. 1979. "The Oligarchical Limitations of Social Banditry in Brazil: The Case of the 'Good' Thief Antonio Silvino," *Past and Present*, 82 (Feb.), pp. 116–46.

Lewis, Charlton. 1972. "Some Notes on the Ko-lao Hui in Late Ch'ing China," in Chesneaux, ed., 1972, pp. 97–112, 254–57.

Lewis, John Wilson. 1964. "China's Secret Military Papers: 'Continuities' and 'Revelations,'" *China Quarterly*, 18 (Apr.–June), pp. 68–78.

Lewis, Norman. 1967. *The Honoured Society.* Harmondsworth, Eng.

Li Jianer. 1938. *Lin Yongfu zhuan* [Biography of Liu Yongfu]. Reprint ed. 1966. Taibei. 李健兒, 劉永福傳.

Li Shican. 1926. *Jiaoban Yubei Tang-Qi jifei shimoji* [Complete record of suppressing endemic banditry in Tangyin and Qixian counties, north Henan]. Kaifeng. 李時燦, 剿辦豫北湯淇積匪始末記.

Li Shiyue. 1959. "Xinhai geming shiqi Dongsansheng geming yu hangeming di douzheng" [The revolutionary versus counterrevolutionary struggles in the Three Eastern Provinces during the 1911 revolution], *Lishi yanjiu*, 6 (June), pp. 56–70. 李時岳, 辛亥革命時期東三省革命與反革命的鬥爭. 歷史研究.

Li Xiaoting. 1969. "Fan Zhongxiu zhuanji" [Biographical note on Fan Zhongxiu], *ZYWX*, 1, no. 4 (July), p. 16. 李肖庭, 樊鍾秀傳記.

Li Xin et al. 1978, 1980, 1981. *Minguo renwuzhuan* [Biographies of Republican period personalities]. Beijing. 李新, 民國人物傳.

Li Yaxian. 1969. "Guofu dianmian Fan Zhongxiu" [Sun Zhongshan's cable to Fan Zhongxiu], *ZYWX*, 1, no. 10 (Dec.), p. 41. 李雅仙, 國父電勉樊鍾秀.

"Li Zicheng." 1979. *Guanyu changpian lishi xiaoshuo "Li Zicheng"* [On the long historical novel "Li Zicheng"]. Shanghai. 關于長篇歷史小說《李自成》.

Liao Yizhong et al., eds. 1981. *Yihetuan yundongshi* [The history of the righteous fists movement]. Beijing. 廖一中, 義和團運動史.

Lilius, Aleko E. 1930. *I Sailed with Chinese Pirates.* London.

Lin Baohang. 1961. "Guangxi youyong" [The braves of Guangxi], *XHGMHYL*, vol. 6, pp. 529–47. 林寶航, 廣西游勇.

"Lincheng Incident, The." 1923. *Trans-Pacific* (9 June), p. 10.

Lindt, August Rodolphe. 1933. *Special Correspondent: With Bandit and General in Manchuria.* London.

Liu, James J. Y. 1967. *The Chinese Knight-Errant.* Chicago.

Liu Manrong. 1978. "Xueshengjun Macheng jiaofei" [The student army and bandit-suppression in Macheng], *Wuhan daxue xuebao*, 25 (Mar.), pp. 77–80. 劉曼容, 學生軍麻城剿匪. 武漢大學學報.

Liu Ruming. 1966. *Liu Ruming huiyilu* [Memoirs of Liu Ruming]. Taibei. 劉汝明, 劉汝明回憶錄.

Lötveit, Trygve. 1970. *The Central Chinese Soviet Area: Some Aspects of Its Organisation and Administration, November 1931–October 1934*. Ph.D. diss., Univ. of Leeds.

Lü Jiuyu. 1980. "Bai Lang raoliao ji" [A record of the White Wolf's rampage], in Du Qunhe, ed., 1980, pp. 307–27. 呂咎予, 白狼擾蓼記.

Lü Pingdeng. 1936. *Sichuan nongcun jingji* [Sichuan village economy]. Shanghai. 呂平登, 四川農村經濟.

Lundeen, Anton. 1925. *In the Grip of Bandits And Yet in the Hands of God*. Rock Island, Ill.

Luo Yaojiu. 1957. "Lun Yuan Shikai tongzhi shiqi jieji maodun di yanhua" [On the evolution of class contradictions during the period of Yuan Shikai's regime], *Xueshu luntan* 4 (Apr.), pp. 56–67. 羅耀九, 論袁世凱統治時期階級矛盾的演化. 學術論壇.

Lust, John. 1972. "Secret Societies, Popular Movements, and the 1911 Revolution," in Chesneaux, ed, 1972, pp. 165–200, 267–72.

Ly, J. Usang. 1917–18. "An Economic Interpretation of the Increase of Bandits in China," *Journal of Race Development* (Worcester, Mass.), 8, no. 3, pp. 366–78.

Mackay, Alexander Clarke. 1927. "Held in a Chinese Bandit Lair: The Survivor's Story of What Befell Two Lone Foreign Lumbermen in Fukien," *Asia*, 27 (Mar.), pp. 188–94, 250–54.

MacNair, Harley F. 1925. *China's New Nationalism and Other Essays*. Shanghai.

Mancall, Mark, and Georges Jidkoff. 1972. "The Hung Hu-tze of Northeast China," in Chesneaux, ed., 1972, pp. 125–34, 260–61.

Manshū rōnin—Okuno Fukudō. 1938. *Shinajin no uramen* [Hidden aspects of the Chinese]. Tokyo. 満洲浪人—奧野復堂, 支那人の裏面.

Mantetsu chōsaka. 1930. *Shina no dōran to Santō nōson*. [The chaos in China and Shandong's villages]. Dairen. 満鉄調査課, 支那の動乱と山東農村.

Mao Tse-tung. 1965. *Selected Works*. Vols. 1–4. Beijing.

Mao Tse-tung and Che Guevara. 1968. *Guerilla Warfare*. London.

Martin, David J. 1938. "A Few Notes on the Chinese Guerilla of the Past," *China Journal*, 29, no. 4 (Oct.), pp. 174–77. Shanghai.

Maxwell, Gavin. 1956. *God Protect Me from My Friends*. London.

McAleavy, Henry. 1968. *Black Flags in Vietnam: The Story of a Chinese Intervention*. New York.

McColl, Robert W. 1967. "The Oyuwan Soviet Area, 1927–1932," *JAS*, 27, no. 1 (Nov.), pp. 41–60.

McCormack, Gavan. 1977. *Chang Tso-lin in Northeast China, 1911–1928*. Stanford, Calif.

McDonald, Angus W., Jr. 1978. *The Urban Origins of Rural Revolution*. Berkeley, Calif.

McIntosh, Mary. 1969. "Racketeering: From Banditry to Monopoly Capitalism." Privately circulated paper.

Meadows, Thomas Taylor. 1856. *The Chinese and Their Rebellions*. London.

Meng Ti. 1931. "Tufei zhi yanjiu" [A study of bandits], *Xin beifang*, 2, no. 1 (July), pp. 1–9. 孟惕, 土匪之研究. 新北方.

Metzger, Thomas. 1974. "Chinese Bandits: The Traditional Perception Reevaluated," *JAS*, 33, no. 3 (May), pp. 455–58.

Miller, Harry. 1970. *Pirates of the Far East*. London.

*Miscellany of Mao Tsetung Thought (1949–1968)*. 1974. Arlington, Va. 2 vols.

Mitani Takashi. 1974. "Kokumin kakumei jiki no hoppō nōmin bōdō" [Peasant risings in north China during the national revolution period], in Nozawa ed., 1974, pp. 227–83. 三谷孝, 国民革命時期の北方農民暴動.

Mitarevsky, N. 1926. *World-Wide Soviet Plots*. Tianjin.

Miyazaki Ichisada. 1965. "The Nature of the Taiping Rebellion," *Acta Asiatica* (Tokyo), 8 (Mar.), pp. 1–39.

Monsen, Miss Marie. 1931. "In Perils in the Sea," in F. Strauss et al. 1931, 105–33.

Moody, Peter R. 1977. *Opposition and Dissent in Contemporary China*. Stanford, Calif.

*Morocco/Shanghai Express: Two Films by Josef von Sternberg*. 1973. New York.

Mowll, Bishop. 1925. "In Brigands' Hands: Missionaries' Trials in China," *The Times* (London), 22 Oct., p. 11.

Mu Jiang. 1978. "Fan Zhongxiu di yingxiong gushi" [Heroic tales about Fan Zhongxiu], *ZYWX*, 10, no. 8 (Sept.), pp. 4–8. 穆姜, 樊鍾秀的英雄故事.

Muramatsu Yuji. 1960. "Some Themes in Chinese Rebel Ideologies," in A. F. Wright, ed., *The Confucian Persuasion* (Stanford, Calif.), pp. 241–67, 353–58.

———. 1966. "A Documentary Study of Chinese Landlordism in Late Ch'ing and Early Republican Kiangnan," *BSOAS*, 29, no. 3 (Oct.), pp. 566–99.

Murray, Dian. 1982. "Mid-Ch'ing Piracy: An Analysis of Organizational Attributes," *Ch'ing-shih wen-t'i*, 4, no. 8 (Dec.), 1–28.

Myers, Ramon H. 1970. *The Chinese Peasant Economy: Agricultural Development in Hopei and Shantung, 1890–1949*. Cambridge, Mass.

Nagano Akira. 1924. *Shina no dohi to guntai* [Chinese bandits and soldiers]. Tokyo. 長野朗, 支那の土匪と軍隊.

———. 1930. *Shina shakai soshiki* [Chinese social organization], in *Dai Shina taikei*, vol. 6, pp. 1–253. Tokyo. 支那社会組織. 大支那大系.

———. 1932. *Zhongguo shehui zuzhi* [Chinese social organization]. Tokyo. 中国社会組織.

———. 1933. *Shina nōmin undō kan* [A viewpoint on the Chinese peasant movement]. Tokyo. 支那農民運動観.

———. 1938. *Shina hei, dohi, kōsōkai* [Chinese soldiers, bandits, and Red Spears]. Tokyo. 支那兵, 土匪, 紅槍會.

Nakajima Tatsujirō. 1973, 1976. *Bazoku ichidai: 1. Tairiku rutenki; 2. Bōryaku rutenki*. [A lifetime of mounted banditry: 1. A record of roving on the mainland; 2. A record of roving and intriguing.] Tokyo. 中島辰次郎, 馬賊一代: 大陸流転記; 謀略流転記.

Nan Yan. 1924. "Xiaoshi huada di Anhui feiluan" [The Anhui bandit disturbances which have turned from a minor to a major affair], *DFZZ*, 21, no. 14 (25 July), pp. 3–6. 南雁, 小事化大的安徽匪乱.

Naquin, Susan. 1981. *Shantung Rebellion: The Wang Lun Uprising of 1774*. New Haven, Conn.

*NCDC*. 1934. *Henansheng nongcun diaocha* [An investigation of Henan villages]. Nanjing. 河南省農村調査.

Nozawa Yutaka. 1972. *Shingai kakumei* [The 1911 revolution]. Tokyo. 野沢豊, 辛亥革命.

Nozawa Yutaka, ed. 1974. *Chūgoku kokumin kakumeishi no kenkyū* [Research on the history of the Chinese national revolution]. Tokyo. 中国国民革命史の研究.

―――. 1978. Kōza Chūgoku kin-gendaishi [Lectures on modern and contemporary Chinese history]. Tokyo. 7 vols. 講座中国近現代史.

Okabe Makio. 1978. *Manshūkoku* [Manchukuo]. Tokyo. 岡部牧夫, 満洲国.

Okuno Tamio. 1928. *Shinagai no ichiya* [A night in the Chinese quarter]. Tokyo. 奥野他見男, 支那街の一夜.

O'Malley, Pat. 1979. "Social Bandits, Modern Capitalism, and the Traditional Peasantry. A Critique of Hobsbawm," *Journal of Peasant Studies*, 6, no. 4 (Oct.), pp. 489–501.

Osame Takeshi. 1923. *Shina dohi no kenkyū* [A study of China's bandits]. Tokyo. 納武津, 支那土匪の研究.

Overmyer, Daniel L. 1976. *Folk Buddhist Religion: Dissenting Sects in Late Traditional China*. Cambridge, Mass.

Oxenham, E. C. 1870. "A Report to Sir R. Alcock, on a Journey from Peking to Han-kow, through Central Chih-Li, Honan, and the Han River, November 2 to December 14, 1868," in Rev. Alexander Williamson, B.A., *Journeys in North China, Manchuria, and Eastern Mongolia* (London), vol. 2, pp. 393–428.

Ozaki Hotsumi. 1949. *Chūgoku shakai no kihon mondai* [Basic problems of Chinese society]. Tokyo. 尾崎秀実, 中国社会の基本問題.

Pak Hyobom. 1971. *Documents of the Chinese Communist Party, 1927–1930: 89 Documents Selected from "Chung-yang T'ung-hsun"*. Hong Kong.

Parsons, James Bunyan. 1970. *Peasant Rebellions of the Late Ming Dynasty*. Tucson, Ariz.

Pawley, Tinko. 1935. *My Bandit Hosts*. London.

Payne, Robert. 1961. *Portrait of a Revolutionary: Mao Tse-tung*. London.

Perry, Elizabeth J. 1976. "Worshippers and Warriors: White Lotus Influence on the Nian Rebellion," *Modern China*, 2, no. 1 (Jan.), pp. 4–22.

―――. 1980. *Rebels and Revolutionaries in North China, 1845–1945*. Stanford, Calif.

*Politique de Pékin, La*. Beijing.

Powell, J. B. 1923a. "Esteemed Guests of the Chinese Bandits," *Asia*, 23 (Nov.), pp. 844–48, 857–60.

―――. 1923b. "The Bandits' 'Golden Eggs' Depart," *Asia*, 23 (Dec.), pp. 914–16, 956–59.

―――. 1945. *My 25 Years in China*. New York.

Powell, Ralph L. 1955. *The Rise of Chinese Military Power, 1895–1912*. Princeton, N.J.

Prazniak, Roxann. 1980. "Tax Protest at Laiyang, Shandong, 1910: Commoner Organization Versus the County Political Elite," *Modern China*, 6, no. 1 (Jan.), pp. 41–71.

Price, Don C. 1984. "Anti-Imperialism and Popular Resistance in the Revolutionary Thought of Song Jiaoren," in Eto and Schiffrin, eds., 1984, pp. 61–80.

Price, Willard. 1937. "Bandits of the Grand Canal," *Blackwood's Magazine*, 241 (June), pp. 829–43.

Prusek, J. 1970. "Chui-tzu-shu: Folk Songs from Ho-nan," in *Chinese History and Literature: Collection of Studies* (Dordrecht), pp. 170–98.

Qi Cheng. 1939. "Yu-E bianqu kangri genjudi" [The anti-Japanese base area on the Henan-Hubei border], *KZND*, pp. 50–56. 企程, 豫鄂邊區抗日根據地.

Qiao Xuwu. 1956. "Ji Bai Lang shi" [A record of the White Wolf affair], *JDSZL*, 3 (July), pp. 132–40. 喬叙五, 記白狼事.

Qiao Zhiqiang. 1981. "Xinhai gemingqian shinianjian nongmin douzhong di jige wenti" [Some questions about the peasant struggles of the pre-1911 decade], *XHGMS*, pp. 527–49. 喬志强, 辛亥革命前十年間農民斗爭的幾個問題.

Qu Qiubai. 1953. *Wenji* [Collected literary studies]. Beijing. 瞿秋白, 瞿秋白文集.

Queiroz, Maria Isaura Pereira de. 1968. *Os Cangaceiros, Les bandits d' honneur brésiliens*. Paris.

*Queshan xianzhi*. 1933. [Gazetteer of Queshan county]. 確山縣志.

Reclus, Elie. 1891. *Primitive Folk*. London.

Reinsch, Paul Samuel. 1922. *An American Diplomat in China*. London.

*Reminiscences of a Chinese Official*. 1922. Tianjin.

Ren Zhiming. 1961. "Liu Cuixuan xunnan jianji" [A brief note on the death of Liu Qunren], *XHGMHYL*, vol. 5, pp. 392–4. 任芝銘, 劉粹軒殉難簡記.

"Report by Comrade Fu Ch'iu-tao on the Inspection of Work of the Honan Militia," in J. Chester Cheng 1966, pp. 116–23. (Translated from *Gongzuo tongxun*, 1961, no. 4, pp. 21–27. 工作通訊.

Richthofen, Baron von. 1903. *Letters, 1870–1872*. Shanghai.

Rock, J. F. 1925. "Experiences of a Lone Geographer: An American Agricultural Explorer Makes His Way Through Brigand-Infested Central China en Route to the Amne-Machin Range, Tibet," *National Geographic Magazine* 48, no. 3 (Sept.), pp. 331–47.

———. 1947. *The Ancient Na-khi Kingdom of South-west China*. Cambridge, Mass. 2 vols.

———. 1956. *The Amnye-Ma-chhen Range and Adjacent Regions*. Rome.

Rue, John E. 1966. *Mao Tse-tung in Opposition, 1927–1935*. Stanford, Calif.

Ruhlmann, Robert. 1960. "Traditional Heroes in Chinese Popular Fiction," in A. F. Wright, ed., *The Confucian Persuasion* (Stanford, Calif.), pp. 141–76, 338–46.

Salazar, Evelio Buitrago. 1977. *Zarpazo the Bandit: Memoirs of an Undercover Agent of the Colombian Army*. University, Ala.

Schram, Stuart. 1966. *Mao Tse-tung*. Harmondsworth, Eng.

———. 1974. *Mao Tse-tung Unrehearsed. Talks and Letters: 1956–71*. Harmondsworth, Eng.

Scott, Dorothea Hayward. 1980. *Chinese Popular Literature and the Child*. Chicago.

Selden, Mark. 1966. "The Guerrilla Movement in North-West China: The Origins of the Shensi-Kansu-Ninghsia Border Region," *China Quarterly*, 28 (Oct.–Dec.), pp. 63–81.

————. 1967. "The Guerrilla Movement in North-West China (Part 2)," *China Quarterly* 29 (Jan.–Mar.); pp. 61–81.

————. 1971. *The Yenan Way in Revolutionary China*. Cambridge, Mass.

*Shaanxian zhi*. 1936, 1968. [Gazetteer of Shaanxian county]. 陝縣志.

Shabad, Theodore. 1972. *China's Changing Map*. New York.

"Shanxiang nuhuo." 1965. [Raging flames in a mountain community]. *SXYK*, 10 (Oct.), pp. 22–32. 山鄉怒火.

Shears, Richard, and Isobelle Gidley. 1984. *Devi, The Bandit Queen*. London.

Shek, Richard. 1980. "The Revolt of the Zaili, Jindan Sects in Rehe (Jehol), 1891," *Modern China*, 6, no. 2 (Apr.), pp. 161–96.

Sheridan, James E. 1966. *Chinese Warlord: The Career of Feng Yü-hsiang*. Stanford, Calif.

Shi Li. 1975. "Balu bingma zongzhihui Wang Cong'er" [Wang Cong'er, commander-in-chief of the Eighth Route Cavalry), *Lishi yanjiu* (Beijing), 4 (Apr.), pp. 130–32. 石立, 八路兵馬總指揮王聰兒. 歷史研究.

Shi Naian. 1952. *Shuihu* [Water Margin]. Beijing. 施耐菴, 水滸.

Shibuya Tsuyoshi. 1928. "Minami Shina no kaizoku oyobi dohi ni kansuru chōsa" [An investigation of the pirates and bandits of south China], *Tōa keizai kenkyū*, 12, no. 1 (Jan.), pp. 124–45. 渋谷剛, 南支那の海賊及び土匪に関する調査. 東亜経済研究.

Shih Ch'eng-chih. 1956. *People's Resistance in Mainland China, 1950–1955*. Hong Kong.

Shih Nai-an. 1963. *Water Margin*. Hong Kong. 2 vols.

Shih, Vincent C. Y. 1967. *The Taiping Ideology: Its Sources, Interpretations, and Influences*. Seattle.

Shimamoto Nobuko. 1974. "Byakurō no ran ni miru Shingai kakumei to Kahoku minshū" [The 1911 Revolution and the north China masses as perceived through the rebellion of Bai Lang], in Council of Young China Scholars, ed., *Chūgoku minshū hanran no sekai* [The world of Chinese popular rebellions] (Tokyo), pp.1–76. 嶋本信子, 白朗の乱にみる辛亥革命と華北民衆. 中国民衆反乱の世界.

Shimamura Takashi. 1973. *Bazoku burai: Tokuhisa Takemitsu to Manshū* [Mounted bandits and villains: Tokuhisa Takemitsu and Manchuria]. Tokyo. 島村喬, 馬賊無頼. 徳久武光と満州.

*Shina*. Tokyo. 支那.

*Shina jihō*. Tokyo. 支那時報.

"Shina kakushō ni okeru hika ni tsuite" [The Chinese bandit calamity province by province]. 1930. *Shina jihō*, 13, no. 5 (Nov.), pp. 32–46. (A summary of *Bukan hōmen shoshō no hika*). 支那各省に於ける匪禍に就て.

*Shina meibutsu*. 1931. *Shina meibutsu hizoku monogatari* [The story of China's acclaimed bandits]. Tokyo. 支那名物匪賊物語.

Shou Kang. 1923. "Kepadi bingbian" [The fearful troop mutinies], *Gujun* (Shanghai), 1, no. 4–5 (Jan.), *Zhiping* (commentary) section, pp. 3–4. 壽康, 可怕的兵變. 孤軍. 知評.

Singelmann, Peter. 1975. "Political Structure and Social Banditry in Northeast Brazil," *Journal of Latin American Studies*, 7, no. 1 (May), pp. 59–83.

"Situation de l'armée chinoise au 1$^{er}$ juillet 1908." *Revue militaire des armées étrangères*, 73 (Jan. 1909), pp. 51–75.

Skinner, G. William. 1964. "Marketing and Social Structure in Rural China, Part 1," *JAS*, 24, no. 1 (Nov.), pp. 3–44.

Slawinski, Roman. 1972. "The Red Spears in the Late 1920's," in Chesneaux, ed., 1972, pp. 201–11, 272–74.

Smedley, Agnes. 1933. *Chinese Destinies: Sketches of Present-Day China.* London.

———. 1934. *China's Red Army Marches.* New York.

———. 1956. *The Great Road: The Life and Times of Chu Teh.* New York.

Smith, Arthur. 1900. *Village Life in China.* Edinburgh and London.

———. 1918. "The Making of Bandits," *North China Missions, 1910–1919*, vol. 36, p. 374. New York.

Snow, Edgar. 1968. *Red Star Over China.* New York.

———. 1972. *Journey to the Beginning.* New York.

Snow, Helen Foster. 1972. *The Chinese Communists, Sketches and Autobiographies of the Old Guard.* Westport, Conn.

Sokolsky, George. E. 1923. "Banditry in China Viewed as Step to Higher Honors," *Trans-Pacific* (Tokyo), (16 June), p. 1.

Solomon, Lee. 1923. "Prisoner of Chinese Bandits Describes Life in Captivity," *Trans-Pacific* (Toyko), (9 June), p. 14.

Solomon, Richard. 1971. *Mao's Revolution and the Chinese Political Culture.* Berkeley, Calif.

Song Jiaoren. 1981. *Song Jiaoren ji* [Works of Song Jiaoren]. Beijing. 宋教仁, 宋教仁集.

Sonoda Kazuki. 1927. *Shina shinjin kokki* [Annals of important personages of new China]. Tokyo. 園田一亀, 支那新人国記.

Stott, A. O. 1927. "Chinese Knights of the Open Palm," *Asia*, 27 (Oct.), pp. 830–33.

Strauss, F. 1931. "In Perils of Robbers," in F. Strauss et al. 1931, pp. 1–33.

Strauss, F., et al. 1931. *We Are Escaped.* London.

Suleski, Ronald. 1981. "Northeast China Under Japanese Control: The Role of the Manchurian Youth Corps, 1934–1945," *Modern China*, 7, no. 3 (July), pp. 351–77.

Sun, E-tu Zen. 1967. "Mining Labour in the Ch'ing Period," in Albert Feuerwerker et al., *Approaches to Modern Chinese History* (Berkeley, Calif.), pp. 45–67.

Swallow, R. W., and Mark M. Lu. 1934. "Chinese Lights and Shadows: Interesting Glimpses into the Manners and Methods of China's Bandits," *NCH*, 11 Apr., p. 47.

Tachibana Shiraki. 1923. *Dohi* [Bandits]. Tianjin. 橘樸, 土匪.

*Taikang xianzhi.* 1933. [Gazetteer of Taikang county]. 太康縣志.

Taira Teizō. 1933. "Manshū bazoku to hizoku" [Mounted bandits and robber bandits in Manchuria], *Tōa*, 6, no. 7 (July), pp. 110–19. 平貞蔵, 満洲馬賊と匪賊. 東亜.

358 *Bibliography*

Takahashi Sutejirō. 1967. "Manshū bazoku ni tsuite" [About the bandits in Manchuria], *Gendaishi shiryō*, vol. 32, pp. 795–805. 高橋捨次郎, 満洲馬賊に就て.

Tanaka Tadashi. 1934. "Manshū bazoku to sono soshiki". [The mounted bandits in Manchuria and their organization], *Mammō*, 15, no. 2 (Feb.), pp. 153–64. 田中正, 満洲馬賊とその組織. 満蒙.

Tang Leang-li, ed. 1934. *Suppressing Communist-Banditry in China*. Shanghai.

Tao Juyin. 1947. *Liu junzi zhuan* [Lives of the six gentlemen]. Beijing. 陶菊隱, 六君子傳.

———. 1957–58. *Beiyang junfa tongzhi shiqi shihua* [A historical narrative of the period of the northern warlord regime]. Beijing. 6 vols. 北洋軍閥統治時期史話.

———. 1979. *Yuan Shikai yanyi* [Expanded commentary on Yuan Shikai]. Beijing. 袁世凱演義.

Tawney, R. H. 1964. *Land and Labour in China*. London.

Taylor, Mrs. Howard. 1922. *With P'u and His Brigands*. London.

Teichman, Sir Eric. 1921. *Travels of a Consular Officer in North-West China*. Cambridge, Eng.

Teng, S. Y. 1964. *The Nien Army and Their Guerilla Warfare*. Paris.

Thaxton, Ralph. 1979. "The World Regained." Unpublished paper.

Thomas, James A. 1928. *A Pioneer Tobacco Merchant in the Orient*. Durham, N.C.

Tian Buyi et al. 1967. *Xianhua junfa* [Cozy chats about the warlords]. Taibei. 田布衣, 閒話軍閥.

Tian Ran. 1926. "Wuxi junfa tongzhixia zhi Zhangde" [Zhangde under the rule of the Wu Peifu warlord clique], *XDZB*, 168 (Aug.), p. 1699. 天然, 吳系軍閥統治下之彰德.

Tian Ying. 1960. *Yijiuwubanian Zhongguo minge yundong* [The 1958 Folk Song Movement in China]. Shanghai. 天鷹, 一九五八年中國民歌運動.

Tiedemann, R. G. 1982. "The Persistence of Banditry: Incidents in Border Districts of the North China Plain," *Modern China*, 8, no. 4 (Oct.), pp. 395–433.

*Times, The*. London.

Toller, W. Stark. 1948. "Chinese Brigands," *Eastern World* (London), 2, no. 3, pp. 23–24.

Tominaga Yoshio. 1952. "Bazoku no hanashi to minshushugi" [Stories of the mounted bandits and democracy], *Keizai ōrai*, 4, no. 10 (Nov.), 163–67. 富永能雄, 馬賊の話と民主主義. 経済往来.

"Travelling in Robber Country." 1923. *Living Age* (Concord, N.H.), 319 (Nov.), pp. 234–36.

Tsuzuki Shichirō. 1972. *Date Junnosuke: Yūhi to uma to kenjū* [Date Junnosuke: the setting sun, a horse, and a pistol]. Tokyo. 都築七郎, 伊達順之助: 夕日と馬と拳銃.

———. 1974. *Bazoku: Chūgoku jinkyō no jiei soshiki* [Mounted bandits: the chivalrous self-defense organizations of China]. Tokyo. 馬賊: 中国仁侠の自衛組織.

———. 1976. *Bazoku retsuden: jinkyō to yume to roman* [Mounted bandit biographies: chivalry, dreams, and romance] Tokyo. 馬賊列伝: 仁侠と夢とロマン.

Tuchman, Barbara. 1970. *Sand Against the Storm: Stilwell and the American Experience in China, 1911–45*. New York.

Uchiyama Masao. 1978. "Minkoku shoki no minshū undō—Santōshō no baai" [The mass movement in the early Republic—the case of Shandong province], in Nozawa Yutaka, ed., 1978, vol. 3, pp. 195–227. 内山雅生, 民国初期の民衆運動—山東省の場合.

Ueda Eiichi. 1924. "Rokurin monogatari: dohi seikatsu no ichi danmen" [Tales of the greenwood: a cross-section of bandits' lives]. Supplement to Nagano Akira 1924. 上田栄一, 緑林物話: 土匪生活の一断面.

Valliant, Robert B. 1972. "Japanese Involvement in the Mongol Independence Movements, 1912–1919," *Mongolia Society Bulletin* (Bloomington, Ind.), 11, no. 2 (Fall), pp. 1–32.

Varé, D. 1938. *Laughing Diplomat.* London.

Venturi, Franco. 1966. *Roots of Revolution: A History of the Populist and Socialist Movements in Nineteenth-Century Russia.* New York.

Wakeman, Frederic. 1975. *The Fall of Imperial China.* New York.

———. 1977. "Rebellion and Revolution: The Study of Popular Movements in Chinese History," *JAS*, 32, no. 3 (May), pp. 405–23.

Wakeman, Frederic, and Carolyn Grant, eds. 1975. *Conflict and Control in Late Imperial China.* Berkeley, Calif.

Wang Canli. 1979. "Bai Lang xian Yuxiancheng zhuiji" [A retrospect of the White Wolf's seizure of Yuxian city], *ZYWX*, 11, no. 10 (Nov.), pp. 27–31, 48. 王燦藜, 白狼陷禹縣城追記.

Wang Jianzhao. 1928. *Jiaofei biji* [Bandit suppression diary]. Luoyang. 王建昭, 勦匪筆記.

Wang Shucun. 1964. "Guanyu Bai Lang guo Qinchuan di yifu banhua" [A woodcut print of Bai Lang's passage of Qinchuan], *Wenwu* 10 (Oct.), pp. 31–32. 王樹村, 關于白朗過秦川的一副版畫. 文物.

Wang Tiancong. 1971. "Liu Zhenhua jiangjun yu Xinhai geming" [General Liu Zhenhua and the 1911 Revolution], *ZYWX*, 3, no. 9 (Oct.), pp. 6–15. 王天從, 劉鎮華將軍與辛亥革命.

———. 1978. "Minchu feihuohua: 'Bai Lang'" [Stories of the bandit calamity in the early Republic: "the White Wolf"], *ZYWX*, 10, no. 2 (Mar.), pp. 29–33; no. 3 (Apr.), pp. 36–39. See also Cheng Yufeng 1978. 民初匪禍話「白狼」.

Wang Tianjiang. 1963. "Shijiu shiji xiaban zhi Zhongguo di mimi huishe" [Secret societies in China in the second half of the nineteenth century], *Lishi yanjiu*, 2 (Feb.), pp. 83–100. 王天獎, 十九世紀下半之中國的秘密會社. 歷史研究.

———. 1979. "Luelun Xinhai shiqi Henan di geming yundong" [Brief essay on the Henan revolutionary movement of the 1911 period], in *Zhongguo jindaishi lunwenji* [Essays on modern Chinese history], vol. 2, pp. 788–802. Beijing. 略論辛亥時期河南的革命運動. 中國近代史論文集.

Wang Yuting. 1976. "Liu Zhenhua yu Zhen Song jun zhi shimo" [The full story of Liu Zhenhua and the Songxian Pacification Force], *ZYWX*, 8, no. 5 (June), pp. 14–15. 王禹廷, 劉鎮華與鎮嵩軍之始末.

Wang Zongyu. 1964. "Shilun Bai Lang qiyi di xingzhi" [A tentative discussion of the nature of Bai Lang's righteous uprising], *SXYK*, 12 (Dec.), pp. 20–24. 王宗虞, 試論白朗起義的性質.

Washio, S. 1928. "The Bandit Governor," *Trans-Pacific* (Tokyo), 17 (21 July), pp. 5–6.

Watanabe Ryūsaku. 1964. *Bazoku: Nitchū sensōshi no sokumen* [Mounted bandits: a sidelight on the history of Sino-Japanese conflicts]. Tokyo. 渡辺龍策, 馬賊: 日中戦争史の側面.

———. 1972. *Kawashima Yoshiko: sono shōgai no shinsō to nazo* [Kawashima Yoshiko: the reality and the riddle of her life]. Tokyo. 川島芳子: その生涯の真相と謎.

———. 1981. *Bazoku shakaishi* [Social documents of mounted bandits]. Tokyo. 馬賊社会誌.

Weller, Rev. E. 1931. "In Perils in the City," in F. Strauss et al. 1931, pp. 35–61.

Wen Gongzhi. 1930. *Zuijin sanshinian Zhongguo junshishi* [A military history of China during the past thirty years]. Shanghai. (Reprinted, Taibei, 1962.) 文公直, 最近三十年中國軍事史.

*Wenxiang xianzhi.* 1932. [Gazetteer of Wenxiang county]. 閿鄉縣志.

Wen Yiduo. 1948. "Guanyu ru, dao, tufei" [On Confucianism, Daoism, and bandits], *Wen Yiduo quanji* [Complete works of Wen Yiduo], vol. 3, pp. 19–23. Shanghai. 聞一多, 關於儒、道、土匪. 聞一多全集.

White, William Charles. 1966. *Chinese Jews.* New York.

Wilbur, C. Martin. 1976. *Sun Yat-sen, Frustrated Patriot.* New York.

Wong Yin-seng, et al. 1939. "Military Requisitions and the Peasantry," in Institute of Pacific Relations 1939, pp. 101–9.

Wou, Odoric Y. K. 1978. *Militarism in Modern China: The Career of Wu P'ei-fu, 1916–39.* Canberra, Australia.

———. 1979. "The Impact of Differential Economic Change on Society in Honan in the 1920's and 1930's." Unpublished paper.

Wright, Mary C. 1955. "From Revolution to Restoration: The Transformation of Kuomintang Ideology," *Far Eastern Quarterly*, 14, no. 4 (Aug.), pp. 515–32.

Wu Bingro. 1927. "Huaihe liuyu di nongmin zhuangkuang" [Peasant conditions in the Huai river valley], *DFZZ*, 24, no. 16 (25 Aug.), pp. 51–54. 吳炳若, 淮河流域的農民狀況.

Wu Cangzhou. 1961. "Henan di liangci junshi xingdong" [Two military actions in Henan], *XHGMHYL*, vol. 5, pp. 358–69. 吳滄洲, 河南的兩次軍事行動.

Wu Rui. 1970. "Tan liukou Bai Lang" [Talking about the roving bandit White Wolf], *Changliu* (Taibei), 41, no. 11 (16 July), pp. 19–22. 吳蕤, 談流寇白狼. 暢流.

Wu Shixun. 1936. *Henan.* Shanghai. 吳世勳, 河南.

Wu Zhongdao. 1933. "Huabei zhanqu feihuo zhi zongjiantao" [An overall examination of the bandit calamity in the war zones of north China], *Xin Zhonghua* (Shanghai), 1, no. 22 (25 Nov.), pp. 17–22. 伍忠道, 華北戰區匪禍之總檢討. 新中華.

*XHGM.* 1957. *Xinhai geming* [The 1911 Revolution]. Shanghai. 8 vols. 辛亥革命.

*XHGM 50 years.* 1962. *Xinhai geming wushi zhounian jinian lunwenji* [ A symposium to commemorate the 50th anniversary of the 1911 Revolution]. Beijing. 2 vols. 辛亥革命五十周年紀念論文集.

*XHGM Hubei.* 1981. *Xinhai geming zai Hubei shiliao xuanji* [A collection of documents on the 1911 Revolution in Hubei]. Wuhan. 辛亥革命在湖北史料選輯.

*XHGMHYL.* 1961. *Xinhai geming huiyilu* [Reminiscences of the 1911 Revolution]. Beijing. 6 vols. 新亥革命回憶錄.

*XHGMS.* 1981. *Xinhai gemingshi lunwenxuan* [Selected essays on the history of the 1911 Revolution]. Beijing. 辛亥革命史論文選.

*XHSY.* 1981. *Xinhai shouyi huiyilu* [Reminiscences of leaders of the 1911 Revolution]. Hubei. 辛亥首義回憶錄.

Xi Chao. 1934. "Henan nongcunzhong di guyong laodong" [Hired labor in Henan's villages], *DFZZ*, 31, no. 18 (16 Sept.), pp. 67–72. 西超, 河南農村中底僱傭勞動.

Xi Min. 1939. "Minnan di feixiang" [The bandit districts of south Fujian], in *KZND* 1939, pp. 199–203. 錫民, 閩南的匪鄉.

Xia Zhaorui. 1974. "Yi Zhongyuan Huachengzhai" [A memoir of Huacheng fort, Henan], *ZYWX*, 6, no. 9 (Sept.), 32–33, 35. 夏兆瑞, 憶中原話城寨.

Xian Yun. 1956. "Bai Lang shimoji" [A complete record of the White Wolf], *JDSZL*, 3 (July), pp. 141–57. 閑雲, 白狼始末記.

Xiao Xiang. 1926. "Henan Hongqianghui bei Wu Peifu jundui tusha zhi canzhuang" [The tragic massacre of the Henan Red Spears by the troops of Wu Peifu], *XDZB*, 158 (June), pp. 1545–46. 瀟湘, 河南紅槍會被吳佩孚軍隊屠殺之慘狀.

Xie Bin. 1928. *Yunnan yuji* [Yunnan travelogue]. Shanghai. 謝彬, 雲南遊記.

*Xihuaxian xuzhi.* 1938, 1968. [Supplementary gazetteer of Xihua county]. 西華縣續志.

Xing Bei. 1924. "Luan feihuan shimoji" [Complete record of the bandit calamity in Luan], *GWZB*, 1, no. 2 (Aug.), pp. 8–11. 星北, 六安匪患始末記.

Xingyuan zhuren. 1973. "Huang Keqiang xiansheng yu Henan geming" [Mr. Huang Xing and the Henan revolution], *ZYWX*, 5, no. 7 (Aug.), pp. 13–18. 醒園主人, 黃克强先生與河南革命.

Xiong Bin. 1980. "Shangcheng shixianji" [A record of the fall of Shangcheng], in Du Qunhe, ed., 1980, pp. 299–306. 熊賓, 商城失陷記.

*Xiping xianzhi.* 1934, 1968. [Gazetteer of Xiping county]. 西平縣志.

Xu Jincheng and Xu Zhaoji. 1955. *Minguo waishi* [Anecdotes on the history of the Republic]. Hong Kong. 許金成, 許肇基, 民國外史.

Xu Yaoshan et al. 1961. "Minchu Zhang Zhenfang tusha geming dangren he qingnian xuesheng di pianduan huiyi" [Fragmentary recollections of Zhang Zhenfang's slaughter of revolutionaries and young students in the early Republican years], *XHGMHYL*, vol. 5, pp. 418–23. 許樂山, 民初張鎮芳屠殺革命黨人和青年學生的片斷回憶.

Xu Zhiyan. 1922. *Minguo shizhou jishi benmo* [A complete record of the first 10 years of the Republic]. Shanghai. 許指嚴, 民國十週紀事本末.

Xue Shaoming. 1937. *Qiandianchuan luxingji* [A travelog of Guizhou, Yunnan, and Sichuan]. Shanghai. 薛紹銘, 黔滇川旅行記.

Yamazaki Seiken. 1913. "Shina no Sōshatō" [The Royalist Party in China], *Toa*, 4, no. 12 (Dec.), pp. 12–21. 山崎誠軒, 支那の宗社党. 東亜.

"Yanjiu tufei wenti zhi ziliao" [Some materials for the study of the bandit problem]. 1922. *Shehuixue zazhi*, 1, no. 3–4 (Dec.), pp. 1–17. 研究土匪問題之資料. 社會學雜誌.

*Yanling xianzhi.* 1936. [Gazetteer of Yanling county]. 焉陵縣志.

Yang, C. K. 1965. *Chinese Communist Society: The Family and the Village. 1. The Chinese Family in the Communist Revolution; 2. A Chinese Village in Early Communist Transition.* Cambridge, Mass.

————. 1975. "Some Preliminary Statistical Patterns of Mass Actions in Nineteenth-Century China," in Wakeman and Grant, eds., 1975, pp. 174–210.

Yang, Martin C. 1945. *A Chinese Village, Taitou, Shantung Province*. New York.

Yang Yiping. 1961. "Luetan 'Zaiyuan' huodong" [A brief discussion of the activities of the "Peach Garden Society"], *XHGMHYL*, vol. 5, pp. 375–81. 楊依平, 略談 '在園' 活動.

Yang Zhongjian. 1920. "Beisisheng zaiqu shichaji" [Record of an inspection of the disaster areas of the four northern provinces], *DFZZ*, 17, no. 10 (25 May), pp. 114–18. 楊鍾健, 北四省災區視察記.

Yano Jin'ichi. 1924. "Shina dohi ron" [On Chinese bandits], *Gaikō jihō*, 458 (1 Jan.), pp. 38–47. 矢野仁一, 支那土匪論. 外交時報.

————. 1936. "Shina no dohi" [The bandits of China], in *Gendai Shina gairon* [General introduction to contemporary China] (Tokyo, 2 vols.), vol. 1, pp. 164–85. 支那の土匪. 現代支那概論.

Yao Xueyin. 1981. *Changye* [Long night]. Beijing. 姚雪垠, 長夜.

Yoneda Yūtarō. 1941. *Seikatsu shūkan: hokushi hen* [Everyday customs: north China]. Tokyo. 米田祐太郎, 生活習慣: 北支篇.

*Yongyan*. Beijing. 庸言.

Young, Ernest P. 1977. *The Presidency of Yüan Shih-k'ai: Liberalism and Dictatorship in Early Republican China*. Ann Arbor, Mich.

Yu Ming. 1965, 1967. *Zhang Zuolin waizhuan* [An informal biography of Zhang Zuolin]. Hong Kong. 郁明, 張作霖外傳.

Zeng Jianquan. 1927. "Gedi nongmin zhuangkuang diaocha—Guangshan" [An investigation of the condition of the peasants in various places—Guangshan], *DFZZ*, 24, no. 16 (25 Aug.), pp. 136–37. 曾鑑泉, 各地農民狀況調查—光山.

ZGNC. 1931. Zhu Xinfan. *Zhongguo nongcun jingji guanxi ji qi tezhi* [Economic relationships in rural China and their special character]. Shanghai. 朱新繁, 中國農村經濟關係及其特質.

ZGNM. 1976. *Zhongguo nongmin qiyi lingxiu xiaozhuan* [Short biographies of Chinese peasant rebel leaders]. Kaifeng. 中國農民起義領袖小傳.

Zhang Jiehou. 1927. "Huaibei nongmin zhi shenghuo zhuangkuang" [The living conditions of the Huaibei peasants], *DFZZ*, 24, no. 16 (25 Aug.), pp. 71–76. 張介侯, 淮北農民之生活狀況.

Zhang Jungu. 1967. *Du Yuesheng zhuan* [Biography of Du Yuesheng]. Taibei. 章君榖, 杜月笙傳.

Zhang Kaiyuan et al. 1979. "Wuchang qiyi yu Hubei geming yundong" [The Wuchang uprising and the Hubei revolutionary movement], in *Zhongguo jindaishi lunwenji* [Essays on modern Chinese history] (Beijing), vol. 2, pp. 930–54. 章開沅, 武昌起義與湖北革命運動. 中國近代史論文集.

Zhang Nanxian. 1946. *Hubei geming zhizhilu* [The known record of the Hubei revolution]. Shanghai. 張難先, 湖北革命知之錄.

Zhang Xichang. 1934. "Henan nongcun jingji diaocha" [An investigation of Henan village economy], *Zhongguo nongcun* (Shanghai), 1, no. 2 (Nov.), pp. 47–63. 張錫昌, 河南農村經濟調查. 中國農村.

Zhang Xiuzhai. 1961. "Huiyi Xinhai geming qianhou Yuxi diandi qingkuang"

[Reminiscences of the steadily eroding conditions in west Henan before and after the 1911 Revolution], *XHGMHYL*, vol. 5, pp. 370–74. 張修齋, 回憶辛亥革命前后豫西點滴情況.

Zhang Youyi et al. 1957. *Zhongguo jindai nongyeshi ziliao* [Materials on modern Chinese agricultural history]. Beijing. 3 vols. 張有義, 中國近代農業史資料.

Zhang Yunjia. 1958. *Yu Youren zhuan* [Biography of Yu Youren]. Taibei. 張雲家, 于右仁傳.

Zhao Jiemin. 1977. "Zatan Henan Langhuo" [Miscellaneous gossip about the White Wolf calamity in Henan], *ZYWX*, 9, no. 10 (Nov.), pp. 24–25. 趙介民, 雜談河南狼禍.

*Zhengxuan*. Beijing. 正誼.

*Zhengyang xianzhi*. 1936, 1968. [Gazetteer of Zhengyang county]. 正陽縣志.

Zhi Che. 1926. "Tufei shijie zhi yijiao" [One corner of a bandits' world], *Zhongguo qingnian*, 120 (Apr.), pp. 540–44. 知澈, 土匪世界之一角. 中國青年.

Zhi Ning. 1936. "'Maiqiu' he 'daqiu': Huabei nongmin shenghuo sumiao zhi ni" ["Wheat-harvesting time" and "Late autumn": an unadorned description of peasant life in north China, part 2], *Wenhua jianshe*, 2, no. 9 (June), pp. 109–17. 蟄寧, '麥秋' 和 '大秋' : 華北農民生活素描之二. 文化建社.

ZHMG. 1961–66. *Zhonghua minguo kaiguo wushinian wenxian* [Documents of the first 50 years of the Republic of China]. Taibei. 22 vols. Part 2, vol. 2, chapter 20: "Henan qiyi" [The Henan uprising], pp. 145–77. 中華民國開國五十年文獻. 河南起義.

ZHMGS. 1979. *Zhonghua minguoshi dangan ziliao huibian* [Compendium of archive materials on Republican history]. Vol. 1: *Xinhai geming* [The 1911 Revolution]. Jiangsu. 中華民國史檔案資料滙編. 辛亥革命.

Zhu Xinfan. 1936. *Zhongguo nongcun jingji di toushi* [The future of China's village economy]. Shanghai. 朱新繁, 中國農村經濟的透視.

Zhuo Ran. 1935. "Ji-Yu huifeizhi" [Annals of secret society banditry in Shaanxi and Henan], *Zhengfeng banyuekan* (Shanghai), 13 (1 July), pp. 120–22; 14 (15 July), pp. 118–20; 15 (29 July), pp. 139–41; 16 (12 Aug.), pp. 138–42. 卓然, 冀豫會匪誌. 正風半月刊.

"Zou Yongcheng huiyilu" [Reminiscences of Zou Yongcheng], *JDSZL*, 3 (July), pp. 77–131. 鄒永成回憶錄.

# Index

In this index an "f" after a number indicates a separate reference on the next page, and an "ff" indicates separate references on the next two pages. A continuous discussion over two or more pages is indicated by a span of page numbers, e.g., "pp. 57–58." *Passim* is used for a cluster of references in close but not consecutive sequence.

Library of Congress Cataloging-in-Publication Data

Billingsley, Phil.
    Bandits in Republican China / Phil Billingsley.
        p.    cm.
    Bibliography: p.
    Includes index.
    ISBN 0-8047-1406-1 (alk. paper)
        1. Brigands and robbers—China—History—20th century.
2. China—Social conditions—1912–1949. I. Title.
HV6453.C6B55 1988
364.1'552'0951—dc19                                    87-30518
                                                           CIP